W9-CCW-023

Ref
BF 1411
C32
1974

NOV 3 1975.

190435

Encyclopedia of

The Unexplained

Magic, Occultism and Parapsychology

Edited by
Richard Cavendish

Special Consultant on Parapsychology
Professor J. B. Rhine

McGraw-Hill Book Company
New York   St. Louis   San Francisco

This book was designed and produced
in Great Britain by
George Rainbird Ltd
44 Edgware Road
London W2

for McGraw-Hill Book Company
1221 Avenue of the Americas
New York, N.Y. 10020

Copyright © Rainbird Reference Books Ltd 1974

All rights reserved. No part of this publication may be
reproduced, stored in a retrieval system, or transmitted, in
any form or by any means, electronic, mechanical, photo-
copying, recording, or otherwise, without prior written
permission of the publisher.

Library of Congress Cataloging in Publication Data
Cavendish, Richard. The encyclopedia of the unexplained.
1. Occult sciences.   2. Psychical research.
I. Title.
BF1411.C32 133 .03 73–7991

ISBN 0–07–010295–3

House editor: Yorke Crompton
Picture Research: Sue Unstead
Design: Jonathan Gill-Skelton
Indexing: Ellen Crampton

Filmset and printed in
Great Britain by
Jolly & Barber Ltd, Rugby

Frontispiece A vision of elemental spirits, by Steffi Grant (see page 228)

Contents

Color Plates

Editor's Preface

Encyclopedias are usually intended to acquaint their readers with what is known of the subjects covered, with what a concensus of informed opinion holds to be the probable truth about those subjects. This is certainly one of our principal objectives in this work, but to a greater extent than the standard encyclopedias we are necessarily concerned with speculation and the reporting of speculation. We are very much in the position of an early geographer, trying to draw a map of the world on the basis of a mass of information from different travellers and explorers, some of it probably accurate, much of it uncertain, some of it almost certainly wrong. Rough outlines of continents and islands begin to appear on the map, but there are many guesses and tentative markings and blank spaces hopefully if somewhat dubiously marked 'Here be dragons' or 'Here the men whose heads do grow beneath their shoulders'.

All the territory we cover is disputed. In some areas much useful exploration has been carried out, in some little or none, and our subject-matter generally is in need of further investigation before too many conclusions are drawn. The other thing which is broadly true of our subjects is that they are now attracting greater interest in the West than at any time since the 17th century. So the main point which needs to be made at the outset is that this encyclopedia is not intended to convince you of the truth or falsity of any of the speculations with which it deals. The contributors, naturally, have different points of view, which show clearly through their articles. The general editorial attitude which we have attempted is one of sympathetic neutrality. You are expected to add your own pinches of salt, where you think they are needed. You will find 'supposedly', 'allegedly', 'purportedly' and similar cautious expressions not infrequently in these pages. I hope they do not occur so often as to be tiresome: if anything, they should appear more frequently than they do.

The subjects covered can be roughly – very roughly – sorted into three main groups: parapsychology and psychical research, including such 'psychic' abilities as clairvoyance, precognition and telepathy, mediumship, faith healing and Spiritualism; magic and the occult, an even broader and vaguer category, ranging from the astral plane to Atlantis to ritual magic to reincarnation, or in terms of people and groups from the Theosophical Society to the Rosicrucians to the Flat Earthers to the Golden Dawn to Jung, or from Gurdjieff to Steiner to Aleister Crowley to Reich to the witches; and the main systems of divination – astrology, the I Ching, the Tarot and others – which overlap with the other two groups. In fact, all our subjects overlap each other's boundaries and attempts to draw clear lines of demarcation between them fail. They have an underlying unity in being, as Dr Rhine says in his valuable Introduction, 'largely to do with theories of the nature and destiny of man, with his place in the universe and what he can do about it'. It is this which has brought our subjects back into the forefront of interest.

We could not have produced anything useful in one volume if we had pursued these subjects all through history and all over the world. We have concentrated on the modern West – 'modern' meaning the 19th and 20th centuries. Where we have gone further back in time, as in articles on alchemy, the Cabala, Gnosticism, the

Hermetica, the mystery religions and other topics, we have done so because background historical information on these matters is essential to an understanding of the modern scene, and we have approached these subjects from the point of view of their influence on contemporary groups and ideas. Similarly, in dealing with Eastern beliefs and speculations, in articles on such topics as karma, mandalas, Tantrism and Yoga, we have included them because they have become influential in the modern West and we have approached them from this point of view.

The articles are arranged in alphabetical order. Words in SMALL CAPITALS indicate an article on that subject. Numbers in *italic* type in the text refer to the Bibliography at the end of the book. We have provided extensive suggestions for further reading, which we hope will be helpful, and the Bibliography includes well over five hundred books and articles. It is not, of course, suggested that all the items listed are of equal value, though it is suggested that in their different ways they are all of interest. The same thing can be said of our subjects themselves.

It only remains for me to hope that you will find the book useful, and to express my grateful thanks to Dr Rhine and to all who have contributed articles, advice and help.

RICHARD CAVENDISH

Contributors

A. G. Alan Gauld, Lecturer in Psychology, University of Nottingham; author of *The Founders of Psychical Research*, 1968; formerly editor of the *Journal* and *Proceedings* of the Society for Psychical Research.

B. I. Brian Inglis, editor of the *Spectator*, 1959–62; author of numerous books, including *Revolution in Medicine*, 1958, *Fringe Medicine*, 1964, *Drugs, Doctors and Disease*, 1965, and *A History of Medicine*, 1965.

B. W. Benjamin Walker, Indian author and diplomat; formerly joint editor of the quarterly *Asia*; author of a two-volume encyclopedia of Hinduism, *Hindu World*, 1968, and *Sex and the Supernatural*, 1970.

C. B. Charles Bowen, authority on UFOs; editor of *Flying Saucer Review* since 1964; editor of *The Humanoids*, 1969, a study of reported 'visitors' from outer space.

C. M. Christopher McIntosh, historian of ideas; author of *The Astrologers and Their Creed*, 1969, a study of the history and principles of astrology, *Astrology*, 1970, and *Eliphas Lévi and the French Occult Revival*, 1972.

D. H. Douglas Hill, journalist and editor; author of numerous books, including *Magic and Superstition*, 1968, *Return From the Dead*, 1970, *Fortune Telling*, 1972; co-author with Pat Williams of *The Supernatural*, 1965.

E. C. Erika Cheetham, author of *The Prophecies of Nostradamus*, 1972; she became interested in Nostradamus when specializing in Ancien Provençal at Oxford.

E. H. Ellic Howe, historian of underground groups and ideas; author of *Urania's Children: the Strange World of the Astrologers*, 1967, and *The Magicians of the Golden Dawn*, 1972, the first detailed account of this influential and fascinating group of occultists.

F. K. Francis King, authority on modern occult groups and practices; author of *Ritual Magic in England (1887 to the Present Day)*, 1970, and *Sexuality, Magic and Perversion*, 1971; editor of *Astral Projection, Magic and Alchemy*, 1971, a collection of Golden Dawn papers.

J. A. W. John Anthony West, novelist and playwright, author of *Osborne's Army*; co-author with J. G. Toonder of *The Case for Astrology*, 1970, which discusses modern evidence for astrology.

J. B. R. J. B. Rhine, pioneer of experimental research in parapsychology as Director of the Parapsychology Laboratory, Duke University, Durham, North Carolina, and subsequently as Executive Director of the Foundation for Research on the Nature of Man; author of *The Reach of the Mind*, 1947; co-author of *Parapsychology: Frontier Science of the Mind*, 1957, and *Extrasensory Perception After Sixty Years*, 1966.

J. van D. Jan van Duren, author of *Crooks and Croziers*, 1972; born in Germany, he was educated at Brussels, Prague and London, and has held academic posts in Holland, Germany and England.

J. W. James Webb, historian of ideas; author of *The Flight From Reason*, 1971, and *The Occult Liberation*, 1973, which together form a history and analysis of the modern occult revival, and of a forthcoming book on Gurdjieff, *The Harmonious Circus*.

K. G. Kenneth Grant, author of *The Magical Revival*, 1972, and *Aleister Crowley and the Hidden God*, 1973; co-editor with John Symonds of *The Confessions of Aleister Crowley*, 1969, *The Magical Record of the Beast 666*, 1972, and *Crowley's Magick*, 1973.

Contributors

L. E. R.   Louisa E. Rhine, pioneer of experimental research in parapsychology at Duke University, Durham, North Carolina; author of *Hidden Channels of the Mind*, 1962, *ESP in Life and Lab*, 1967, and *Mind Over Matter*, 1970; an editor of the *Journal of Parapsychology*.

O. T.   Odette Tchernine, author and poet, a Fellow of the Royal Geographical Society; author of *The Snowman and Company*, 1961, and *The Yeti*, 1970; editor of *Explorers' and Travellers' Tales*, 1958, and *Explorers Remember*, 1967.

R. B.   R. Brzustowicz Jr, who took his B.A. in Chinese Literature and is now doing graduate work in medical history at the University of Washington.

R. C.   Richard Cavendish; editor of *The Encyclopedia of the Unexplained*; author of *The Black Arts*, 1967, a study of the European tradition of magic; editor of *Man, Myth and Magic*, 1970–2.

W. G. R.   W. G. Roll, Director of the Psychical Research Foundation Inc., Durham, North Carolina; author of *The Poltergeist*, 1971; formerly a member of the Parapsychology Laboratory, Duke University.

Introduction

How To Cope With a Mystery
by J. B. Rhine

This is a most unusual volume. In it are listed scores of the strangest topics imaginable, fantastic claims about man and his nature and destiny that in the past have been banned by Churches, governments or schools, and hidden from the young at home and in the public library. They have been ignored and scorned by scientists. Now, however, they are assembled and conveniently listed with readable articles for the growing number of people who are curious. There are even recommended readings for further study added to most of these articles. One point illustrated here is that freedom of thought has made a remarkable advance. Readers of a wider and more unselected range can more easily make up their own minds about the topics listed here than ever before. In fact, they are invited to do so.

Does it even raise an eyebrow that, as in my case, a person who has spent fifty years in scientific teaching and research could willingly participate as the consultant on the section of this encyclopedia related to his field? I did, however, ask for space to give some pro and con explanations. On the pro side I am glad of this opening up for study and discussion of once forbidden beliefs, practices and issues. Freedom to explore even the most incredible ideas is vital to the advance of knowledge; the unknown has all too often seemed impossible at first, and it has frequently looked like nonsense to many. Moreover, I think such a bagful of mysteries as this is preferable to the isolated treatment of individual topics and claims. Readers can in this volume easily get the comparative point of view and this tends to be soberingly corrective to the reasoning mind. Some theories offer alternative arguments and explanations against others, and thus accent the demand for validating evidence to bear on the issues.

Perhaps the best lesson to be obtained from this round-up of mysterious claims is in seeing what has already been done (or not been done) about the different questions raised. While many have nothing of reliable proof to support them – and therefore it would be plain credulity to accept them – others have been carried quite far towards scientific acceptance. It is reasonable to hope that most of you will gain from these comparisons, no matter what your topic of special interest may be, since you have before you all these many appraisals as background; for example, you will see the way in which one claim has been elevated to a firm and reliable position while another has been exposed – that is, shown not to be what had originally been claimed for it.

Oddly enough, too, some of these articles will reveal that certain mysterious beliefs were misinterpreted in the past, and in the course of investigation have yielded to a later, more verifiable explanation. Science has followed that course in many of its fields, converting magic and miracles to lawful principles of nature, sometimes trading one mystery for another, and often actually multiplying, at least for a time, the number of puzzles to be dealt with.

What makes the volume important? Mainly, the fact that the ideas collected here, wild as some of them will appear, have largely to do with theories of the nature and destiny of man, with his place in the universe and what he can do about it. Whatever they may be worth as suggested answers, these articles mostly concern a set of great human *questions,* some of them new and others centuries old. Given such great questions about man's world as many of these topics involve, and given improved ways of making sure about the right answers, the issues they raise leap into the first line of challenge to the open exploratory mind, now that the ban on their discussion is lifted and they are no longer so far out-of-bounds for the research student.

The fact that these topics are generally not in good repute with science should deter no independent mind. The sciences have a poor record in history regarding the reception of early discoveries. None of us, either in science or elsewhere, have had training in the detection of revolutionary ideas on their first appearance and still blindly require new findings to square with the old. At the same time, the strange new claim *does* have special requirements. If it is far out of the conventional scientific picture, more care is needed in approaching and dealing with it, and more evidence is required to justify taking it seriously. A greater burden of proof rests on the explorer of the unorthodox.

Another warning note. Today in the Western world some readers will come to this book with a more or less vigorous bias against science as such. They have a minor point but are being somewhat miscued. They are rightly dissatisfied with what they see of the narrow limits of the sciences and the need for a broader understanding of man and life. The aims do need extension and the method must be adapted (no one knows how much) to fit the problems still untouched. Science is ideally a way of finding dependable answers to our questions about ourselves and our world. At its best it adapts its methods to its problems and keeps its answers fitted to the results and the conditions from which they came. In other words, if there is an answer to any question these topics raise, and if the right methods are used, one of you should be able to find it and make sure about it. By way of illustration, see what you think of the way in which science has helped on the problems of parapsychology, and borrow freely from the example for your own study, just as its workers borrowed from other branches of inquiry.

Two Main Steps

If you were going to investigate one of these mysteries – astrology, mediumship, palmistry, or what not – and you invited my counsel, I would ask you to think of the venture in two main steps. The first step would be to make plans and preparations for your special subject as well as you could in advance. Consider the choice of your project, your estimate of its value and its promise, its feasibility and difficulties, the prospect of suitable conditions, the likelihood of success, and the expected reaction. This would compare with the on-shore preparation for a voyage of discovery.

Second would come your actual investigation. The method of dealing with an unknown is the real kernel of original scholarship, in history, in science, and in other areas of technology and problem-solving. It shows the rational mind in its most developed use and is of unknown and probably unlimited applicability. It can be explained most easily as scientific method, but is not limited to science, and although I can most easily use parapsychology here to illustrate it, the method is in no way peculiar to that one branch. The advantage is that this topic has been studied more intensively than most of the others in this encyclopedia and more progress has been made in solving its problems. This seems to have been due to the interest parapsychology has aroused, and not to any lack of difficulty in its problems. I mention this because it is reassuring in considering its value as an illustration.

Readiness for the Unconventional

Whoever plans to explore one of these topics (whether just to study what is known or to add to it) should know his own mind unusually well – that is, how firmly he is set on doing it, and why. Many people, some of them his 'best friends', may think him foolish and may try to dissuade him from the venture. It should help both sides somewhat to be able to discuss all the differences in viewpoints over the issues and to profit by making and asking for all reasonable concessions.

When in 1927 I was pressed in a friendly way by a mature professor of psychology at Princeton not to go into parapsychology (he had even offered me a good college position if I would change my mind) he asked me, on seeing that I was persisting, to agree never to publish any of my reports. I was impressed by his concern and I agreed with him to follow certain extremely stringent precautions before I would publish (and I met them in my first major report in 1934). He himself had caught mediums in fraudulent practices and knew some of the dangers that awaited my inexperience. Even though I was not persuaded to give up my plans, I think I was the better guarded for having his advice. There is no need to win over those who oppose you. It is often impossible; the Princeton professor did not accept my later findings, even though he could not see the error he was so certain was there.

The story of the professor will also illustrate my own persistent interest. The pressures were all strongly against my course of giving up an established field of science and venturing into so disreputable an area as psychical research was in 1927. In such a case, whatever the field, you must in all decency and common sense consider the risks and the consequences to those who depend on you and those who have helped you to acquire your status. Fortunately, my wife was a scientist also, and we were in complete harmony in taking this radical step. We had to think also of the lack of job opportunities in the new territory, and in fact there were hardly any then. There was no sure future ahead, even with full success in the new and uncertain branch. We knew, too, that a return to the old position left behind was unthinkable. We would have become identified as 'adventurers'.

Intellectual Preparation

But we had studied the field into which we were stepping; the risk was at least an enlightened one. Also, the path we proposed to follow had been pioneered by many scholarly people we had come to respect. As we carefully surveyed the grounds for taking up the challenge of parapsychology, we were most heavily influenced by William McDougall's *Body and Mind*, a book which brilliantly portrayed the key role of parapsychology in the understanding of man's nature, as John Beloff's *The Existence of Mind* did at a later stage (33). Since this branch of research was so important, we felt quite willing to run the added risk; it was, in fact, inspiring to think that we ourselves might help a little to strengthen the case for the independence of the mind as McDougall had pictured it. There was thus a strong sense of mission about our decision as well as the stir of intellectual adventure.

Was that good or bad? I think it could be either; when a person attacks one of these mysteries with an overly fanatic fervour he is liable to risk too much, to be less than objective, and to make reckless decisions. On the other hand, if you entirely lack any such zeal you may not be able to sustain the long pull of patient effort that is usually needed. Some of these initial enthusiasms about an unknown are cases of sheer curiosity, occasioned perhaps by a local incident such as a report of a 'flying saucer', or an impressive horoscope, or a poltergeist case. Such natural curiosity is good. It is an important human gift, too often suppressed in most of us as we are made timid and conservative by the over-disciplining of the questioning mind. On the other hand, interest in one of these queer occurrences or a theory of it needs the support of some intelligent appreciation of what the question means. This is necessary before launching an ambitious investigation.

The best first move, of course, is the study of what is already known on the chosen topic. It is one good way to test the depth and stability of your own interest before you go too far. It is considered a necessary safeguard in all the sciences to cover the literature on the subject as thoroughly as possible before beginning a new research project.

Your interest in witchcraft, Kirlian photography, or astrology will, in many cases, I suspect, be a response to mere fad or recurrent craze. This is a fair presumption today when many factors conduce to this effect, not all of them healthy or instructive and yet, on the other hand, not entirely bad. Most of us go more bravely into the dark of 'researching' a mystery if we have company; and group support for a program of inquiry is wonderful to have when it is an understanding support. For example, parapsychology owes its start largely to the societies for psychical research which backed the investigations of a few capable leaders who could hardly have succeeded in isolation.

Considerations of Status

Most pioneer explorers who 'survive' do so by building a team around the project, and with enough success this group grows into a permanent research centre or institute. In time, and it may be a long time, this centre may become a part of a university, and even a permanent department, or it may be asked to join a hospital or other institution. At first, the explorer has to support himself while limiting his research to a part-time effort or avocation.

It may be surprising to learn that most of the more revolutionary developments of science have been made outside the universities, as well as without financial aid, and for a long time without recognition. In the United States the great cultural vogue of philanthropy has been the saviour of many an inquiry that would have been unsuccessful without such help. The practice, a bright jewel of capitalism, is slowly spreading to Western Europe. The societies for psychical research have relied mainly on membership dues, but the American society is now benefiting from personal philanthropy. Nonetheless, we see that if you go off into the outer zone of mysteries, venturing beyond the close-in problems of university science, you had better count on making your own way unless you luckily discover a supporting donor or philanthropic foundation. Eventually you may be successful enough to be 'invited into the academic compound'.

Understandably, some of the topics in this collection are more difficult than others, just as some are less suitable for scientific study. Of the subjects touched by parapsychology, that of mediumship is one that did not hold up well enough to survive long on the university campus. Several American universities (Harvard, Clark, Stanford, and Duke) grappled with it, partly under the stimulus of grants of money, but the problem was too slow in adapting to the requirements set by the more advanced sciences of easy and dependable demonstration. Psychology itself was having a hard time doing so. Later, however, at Duke the choice of a more easily tested claim, that of extrasensory perception (ESP), led to greater and more persistent success and gained a longer tenure on the university campus; again, too, there was the ever-essential financial aid from philanthropy.

Risks and Safeguards

If you have an independent mind and you plan to identify yourself with one of these unexplained subjects, you need not wait for the approval of anyone. The same is true even if you wish, as I have done with parapsychology, to devote your main energies to its exploration, to make a career of it. But I hope it is also clear that there are other aspects to the matter which should be considered carefully. You need to know that most of the topics are risky and that hasty, credulous acceptance of some of them could distort your outlook on life and seriously endanger a career.

No one, however, need swallow any of these ideas uncritically. There is absolutely no necessity to decide at all about any of them until you are ready in your own good time. That is your safeguard against all claims, here and elsewhere – a good strong 'fence on the edge of the cliff'. This is what makes the book as safe in your own hands as it would be hidden in a restricted closet of the library (for research scholars only); the well-informed mind is its own protection as it learns how to make independent judgments reliably.

Exposed as most of you are in these times of free circulation of sensational claims, and social pressures to join groups that follow various mysterious practices, you will want to be able to compare the claims and strange notions of one cult and another. Whether or not you ever join one of them, in rash impulsiveness or through the pull of social contagion, you will at least gather from this volume some of the things you can do to make your choice really your own and really intelligent.

One of the proselytizing cults is Spiritualism. This book explains how the weird fantasies of Spiritualism gave way in the light of research to the scholarly revelation of another natural (not supernatural) range of communication in man's own nature – his psi (psychic) ability. It is now clear that the Spiritualists had a basis that was valid up to a point; they were, as they claimed, actually at times communicating with a 'beyond', a 'hereafter', and even performing 'miracles' in the sense of superphysical occurrences that transcended the sensory here-and-now. The Spiritualist seances were not all as utterly ridiculous, deceptive or degrading as they have been called. (Although plenty of them were, as I can personally testify.) They have, in fact, conveyed to the world a great message, not from the Summerland, but from science. There really are powers of exchange beyond the senses and muscles, as was implied in Spiritualism. In fact, it was out of the crude exhibitions of mediumship that some of the earliest indications of the psi (psychic or parapsychical) function were sifted.

So while many of the topics in this volume, perhaps most of them, leave me cold, I would be afraid to scorn and reject anything completely that has not been seriously investigated. There may be other great mysteries remaining that will in time reveal new worlds to the explorer. What most of the others lack is the promise of the great reward that the claim of spirit survival offered. Along with that was also the apparent demonstration of actual spirit communication through mediums. Many of us could not resist trying to make it soundly scientific if it actually was true. We failed to confirm it, but found instead a great human truth hidden in the cloak of mediumship itself.

The groping branch of psychical research, which down into the 1930s had been largely the study of mediumship and spirit survival, changed almost abruptly to an emphasis on the abilities assumed in mediumship. These are now investigated as an important part of the nature, not just of the medium, but of all mankind. But had there not been the earlier powerful interest in survival, and the promotion of mediumship in serving that interest, the eventual emergence of the psi research era would probably have been indefinitely delayed.

I will assume now that one of the topics of this encyclopedia (or another like them) has been selected either for study or for an attempt at original research. Quite possibly, though, you may still be in the process of making up your mind about which special project to focus on, and may be seeking a frame of reference for comparative judgment. What follows in this section should be of help in that stage, too, allowing you to hold up your tentative problem against the outline of the method for solving it. Thus you can better decide how solvable it may be (or how well solved it has been if it is at that stage).

The Question Should Be Clear and Simple

Since each of these topics involves a sort of lump of questions, one needs to begin by peeling off the less definite ones. Suppose your topic is 'Twins'. That item was not chosen for this book as a biological topic, nor even as one primarily belonging to general psychology. As it is, you are probably interested mainly in the special mystery of dramatic twin-coincidences in behaviour, such as the two having the same illness when widely separated, or even mysteriously dying at the same moment. So the question you want to answer would likely reduce to this: is there any valid basis for the popular belief that identical (one-egg) twins have a special relation to each other, one that allows communication not possible to other twins and siblings? This is a simple question of fact which does not make unnecessary assumptions or ask for premature explanation; also it is one that many people actually do ask, some of them scientists, because there is a considerable amount of case-study evidence to justify taking the question seriously. So it qualifies as a clear and proper question for this stage.

But suppose now your topic is a broad one like parapsychology. This subject started (as psychical research) nearly a century ago to investigate a number of claims; but they all had a central question in common: is there not something non-physical in man? Mediumship raised the question emphatically. Telepathy was thought to have the same implication. Many other claims, such as clairvoyance and precognition, had a similar bearing. Clairvoyance allowed an even simpler question to start with. Can a person reliably find objects hidden from the senses? With precognition the question was: can an individual predict events ahead of time?

These are beautifully clear, basic and simple questions for science, as may be seen by the researches that followed.

It Should Be Logically Answerable

The next step is to see if there is any inherent impossibility in the question, any logical 'road block'. It is like finding out, once the destination is fixed, if there is a possible route or a choice. Some of the routes may look as though they are leading the right way but may be deceptive; or they may have impossible stretches. These are not just idle figures of speech; this is exactly what was found to be the trouble with both mediumship and telepathy. Other questions at this stage have to do with the simplicity of method, relative controllability of conditions. As already indicated, clairvoyance came out as the winning choice for an approach to parapsychology and proved its efficiency in years of research. It yielded readily to objective tests (e.g. to the card-guessing techniques that had been used as far back as the 1880s).

This step of testing the logic of the method at the outset is a most elusive one; more people lose their way here than anywhere else in research. It is a serious matter in parapsychology because so many of the traditional problems have turned out to be logically unsolvable at present, but some people have gone right on working blindly as if they were. The trouble has been that conclusive tests cannot be designed at this stage; the questions have arisen faster than the facts and the methods to answer them. This applies to the claims of spirit survival and reincarnation, to the problems of telepathy and retrocognition, to the belief in astral projection, and to a variety of mystical experiences that must be set aside for the present by the researcher who wants to be sure of an all-the-way route to his objective – who wants to know what he is doing.

One more point about this second step is the sheer inefficiency of overlooking it. Probably more than half the work in parapsychology has been wasted for lack of alertness at this point. Take the example of telepathy. During the fifty-year period from 1880 to 1930 the psychical researchers conducted a great many 'telepathy' experiments. Some of these took place in the best psychology departments of Europe and America. But no matter how well-conducted or successful those experiments were, not a single case for telepathy could have been made for the entire half century.

Why? In every case the conditions permitted clairvoyance quite as freely as telepathy. Of course the researchers all knew about clairvoyance but they just did not take it seriously. In the Duke work in the early 1930s, the testing of clairvoyance was actually the easiest approach, and ESP was demonstrated quite as easily without allowing the sender to see the target card as when he looked at it.

It is one of the amazing things about scientific research that such blindness affects so many with such serious consequences. Even after it was pointed out that clairvoyance was a possible alternative in every one of the older telepathy experiments, many investigators still continued to disregard the mistake, and they even called their results 'telepathy'.

It is not just in parapsychology, however, that this happens. If we turn the spotlight on psychology to see, for example, what effect the establishment of ESP has had on the psychologist in his experiments, there is the same disregard. How often ESP has 'contaminated' the results of a psychological test, no one knows. Occasionally a case comes to light in which a child is being tested for reading difficulty and is found able to perform much better when his mother is looking over his shoulder at the page. Recently, however, well-controlled experiments at Tel Aviv University by two psychologists, Dr Hans and Dr Shulamith Kreitler, have shown that in laboratory experiments under good controls this ESP contamination can occur effectively without any of those involved knowing at the time that it is taking place.

How Well Does the Test Work?

The pay-off for all the preparation and planning is naturally in the testing operation itself. But while careful preparation is the best assurance of a good outcome, there are always variable factors and circumstances that complicate test performance.

This is the point at which the advantage of the simplicity of the question under investigation can be appreciated. If any further simplification can be introduced to make the initial step easier, it is usually wise to take it. It can often be done by making the initial project a shorter one, perhaps by restricting the part of the question to be considered in this first step. Small preliminary or pilot projects can often be arranged for the advantageous selection of conditions that will improve the evidential value of the results.

It is most advantageous to have two steps in mind in exploring a new field. The first should be as free as possible in the search for favourable starting points. The precautionary side can well remain secondary at this stage until the sorting out of the easier and best approach has been made. Even then, the beginning experiment with controls should be a pilot effort, made to verify the earlier exploratory tests, with the precautions added; but such a pilot study should not be considered conclusive. It is enough for it to show where and how a conclusive experiment is worth undertaking and the conditions for it. No doubt this two-step method has been used in other exploratory fields, but it has been particularly useful in parapsychology.

The whole aim of the exploratory tests for any mystery is to gain assurance of the efficacy of the method. It is like establishing a beachhead on a new shore. From this beginning point the coverage should be extended by repetitive effort to the point where other investigators are confident enough to follow and confirm. This second step, or independent confirmation, is an extremely important step, too, and in a difficult field it may sometimes take years.

Often in a new field the pilot study is not confirmed in exactly the way it was done first. Exact repetition is not essential, however, if the experiment is otherwise reliably done, and the essential point is confirmed. Often, too, a number of experiments may be necessary to produce an adequate confirmation. To some extent the methods need some adaptation to the special problems involved. It helps to study the exploratory stages of other scientific endeavours, since much of what is learned is transferable from one field to another. Parapsychology, because of its long, slow development and its many stages and branches, offers much to be applied to other unknowns in the behavioural sciences. The histories of hypnosis, phrenology, and psycho-analysis make interesting comparisons and offer some lessons as well.

What is most peculiar to parapsychology is the need at every step to measure abilities that are unconscious and therefore especially difficult for the subject to control for experimental purposes (or for his own). This unconsciousness has not only made quantitative assessment complicated, but it has thwarted the experimenter's natural desire to make his experiments easily repeatable. This easy repeatability remains a likely possibility for a later stage and time, and much progress has been made towards it already. Meanwhile, it has compelled the use of statistical method to measure test performance and has made introspective information of limited value. However, it has been helpful to learn that this is the way it is, and to make some progress towards enabling science to enter into this hidden area of the mind, the importance of which one can hope to assess only when it is fully explored.

What Can Safely Be Concluded?

At this point we are assuming, first, that a clear problem was stated; second, that the way to its solution was logically sound; and third, that it lent itself to a test design that would rule out all possible alternative answers. If so, and if a significantly positive result was obtained from a carefully conducted experiment, it would be said at this point that the question has been answered. Thus the result would add a new fact of scientific knowledge – at least to the experimenter's knowledge. If he then proceeded, as he should, to try to get others to duplicate his experiment and this too was successful, the research finding would be well on its way to becoming a generalizable one for science.

It would be wise, however, for the researcher to wait for a number of confirmation experiments before 'rushing into print', and to get repetitions by other scientists, if possible. This may, of course, be hard to arrange if his problem is a very daringly unorthodox one, although that would make it all the more important to do so. It would be best also to keep the project under active investigation with further tightening of all the conditions that have possible safeguarding value. Probably every field of research has known the tragedy of discovering errors too late and having to withdraw once confidently announced achievements. Furthermore, your colleagues may often resent even a normal display of interest in sharing your discoveries with your profession at large. Rather, they prefer a display of caution, to see that there is ample independent confirmation prior to releases. (Everyone inclines to wait for that stage anyhow, before acceptance.) Above all these considerations, however, is the simple fact that the more a good result is shared before announcement is made, the more comfortably it will be accepted and appreciated. In a new or unconventional field, this consideration is most important. The story of Charles Darwin's preparation for the announcement of his hypothesis of natural selection is a salutory lesson on this point.

Naturally, every researcher is eager to go on as fast as possible into further stages of his program of discovery. But the further he goes, the more he will appreciate the importance of spreading the base of his research program through added confirmation and supporting researches, even while he builds the structure of accomplishment to still more advanced levels. The crowning achievement of solving a mystery of nature is the eventual discovery of the larger relationships the new findings have to the system of nature already developed by the sciences. But this should be accomplished by building with the principles extracted from the researches themselves, rather than with the feeble and tenuous arm of speculative theorization. Just as a good ESP test is one that elicits and measures the ESP process, so a good hypothesis of its nature is one that presents a question in the most effectively testable form. One could add, too, that a good research design is one that will efficiently deliver a clear answer that solves the mystery. 'Handsome is as handsome does.'

Opposite the demon Asomvel revealing the black art to a neophyte, by Aubrey Beardsley (see page 229)

A

A∴ A∴

The Order of the Silver Star (*Argenteum Astrum*), founded by Aleister CROWLEY; the triangles of dots can be interpreted as symbols of the reconciliation of opposites in a higher harmony, can also be given a sexual reference, and are intended to indicate that 'the Order is a secret society connected with the Ancient Mysteries'. (*189*)

Abominable Snowman (Yeti)

In 1921, Colonel C. K. Howard-Bury, leading an Everest expedition, reported finding large naked footprints in snow at 21,000 feet. The porters said that the tracks belonged to the Metch-Kangmi. Kang means 'snow' and Mi 'man'. Language variations caused confusion over Metch, which was finally translated roughly to imply 'disgusting'. The Abominable Snowman was born, figuratively. It has travelled from controversy to controversy ever since.

My own research found what must be one of the earliest references to the phenomenon. This was in an Indian epic poem, the *Ramayana*, possibly of the 3rd or 4th century B.C. Passages refer to the demon-like Raksha (singular) and Rakshasa (plural). Rakshi-Bompo is the name of a type of Abominable Snowman, or Yeti, in Nepal. Other Himalayan names for the creature have been quoted as Bang, Bangjakri, Ban Vanas and Van Manas, and there are other variations. In Bhutan the term Yeti is used, and in 1966 that country's new stamps immortalized the Yeti as its national animal.

Carl Linnaeus, the Swedish botanist and naturalist, once wrote on 'Creatures resembling man', and named the Snowman *Homo nocturnus*, 'Man of Night'. A plausible reason for encountering it rarely. Though no skeletal remains have ever been found, and alleged Yeti scalps are artifacts, some of the evidence of centuries cannot be dismissed. The phenomenon is heard of in several geographical regions possessing similar characteristics. Apart from Himalaya, relevant regions are the Russian Caucasus, Mongolia, Tibet, China, and the wildest parts of British Columbia and California.

Professor Boris Porshnev, a Russian historian, and Professor J. R. Rinchen of Mongolia have conducted Snowman research for nearly a lifetime. Professor Porshnev's disciple, Professor Jeanne Kofman, who engaged for several years in field work in the remote Caucasus Mountains, and was still investigating with her team from 1970 onwards, has collected masses of evidence and accounts by eye-witnesses. She and her team found food hoards hidden in tall grasses, stolen by the mysterious creatures from orchards and plantations. Natives of isolated farms and plantations come across them sporadically. They take flight into dense cover when glimpsed. Reports of similar sightings have come from timber workers and road builders in Canadian wildernesses. The Snowman becomes SASQUATCH in Canada, and Bigfoot in America.

In the 19th century the Russian Colonel Nikolai Prsvalsky reported the existence of Almas, primitive animal-like creatures which he came across fleetingly in his exploration deep into Mongolia and the Gobi Desert. Apparently, the Government and the Imperial Court considered this half-human connotation too embarrassing to allow the natural sciences to investigate further. Other names applied to Almas or Yeti in Russia are Snezhnyy Chelovek (meaning 'Snowman') and Almast. From the Soviet Union's non-Russian-speaking republics come Abanauyu ('Forest Man'), Bianbanguli in Azerbaijan, Dev in parts of the Pamir Mountains, and Kiik-Adam, the Kazakh term for 'Wild Man'.

The Himalayan theory, first known to the Western world, divides the Snowman into three types. The very large Yeti is vegetarian except when driven by hunger. The lesser-sized one is considered an aggressive, predatory carnivore, while, according to reports, the third, Rakshi-Bompo, is smaller, mischievous, raids crops, and flees at human approach.

The term Snowman was established because the species was invariably seen above the snowline. Probably it was merely crossing from col to col to find new food and habitat, moving from one lower altitude to another afforested gorge or cave below the snowline. The few sightings obtained suggest an ape-like bi-pedal shape, with shaggy brown, black, grey or reddish fur or hair, no tail, the face hairless, the scalp rather pointed. A roaring or mewing sound is heard occasionally, and proximity brings a musty smell. While checking on places where Yeti have been reported, I discovered that tracing such regions across the map revealed an undulating distribution shape like a giant letter S lying on its back, and was able to draw the *S-map* of its apparent distribution.

The clearest known footprint photograph was taken by Eric Shipton in 1951 on the Everest Reconnaissance expedition. This was on the Menlung Glacier at roughly 22,000 feet. The tracks were $12\frac{1}{2}$ by $6\frac{1}{2}$ inches, measured against an ice-axe.

In 1925, A. M. Tombazi saw what was possibly a Yeti in Sikkim. In 1970, Don Whillans, deputy leader of an expedition to Annapurna's south face in Nepal, took

The S-map showing the apparent distribution of the Yeti

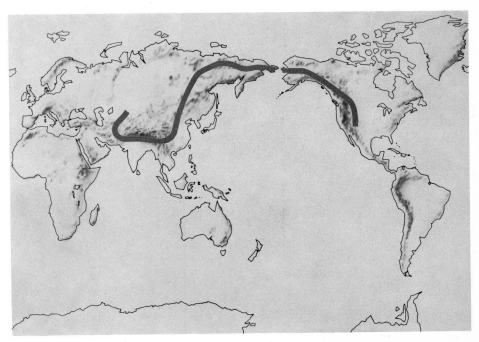

photographs of tracks in snow that was un-peopled until he and Dougal Haston set up camp at 14,000 feet (see plate, page 33). Later he watched through binoculars a dark two-legged creature scurrying about the mountain-side. After half an hour it disappeared among tree clumps. This sighting occurred in an area known in Nepal as 'the place of the great ape'. The altitude was not high enough to cause hallucinations, and as yet no whisky had arrived. And Whillans's previous lack of interest in Snowman stories suggests that he really did catch sight of 'something lost behind the ranges'.

Superstitions and hoaxes have been plenti-ful, but a considerable amount of puzzling Yeti data remains, sometimes repetitive, often conflicting, clues occasionally appear-ing in scattered legends. Is there a sub-human connotation to the mystery? Perhaps the elusive Snowman is a pre-hominid remnant of the ancient past, a creature left over from the time before man had become fully man.

A strange factor in the Yeti saga is that whenever a new incident like the Whillans sighting occurs, it is followed by a deathly hush, a conspiracy of silence. *Homo sapiens*, busy with his marvels of science and progress, repeatedly refuses to consider indications of a zone where anthropology and zoology appear to meet. O. T.

(Further reading: *212, 222, 244, 347a, 413, 450, 451*.)

Abramelin Magic

The system of magic contained in *The Book of the Sacred Magic of Abra-Melin the Mage* (*311*), allegedly of 15th-century origin but probably dating from the 18th, which was translated into English by MacGregor MATHERS and which strongly influenced both Mathers and Aleister CROWLEY. The 'sacred magic', which dispenses with much of the complicated paraphernalia and cere-monial of the European tradition of ritual magic, is based on the principle that the material world is the creation of evil spirits, which can be controlled by the magician, provided he has first acquired the 'know-ledge and conversation' of his Holy Guardian Angel, a being taken by practitioners of the system to be the magician's true self. Once he has achieved this, he can use the spirits (which can again be interpreted as factors within himself) as his servants. The book contains a large collection of magic squares – arrangements of letters which represent wishes in the magician's mind and which give effect to these wishes, though they are said to be extremely dangerous to use with-out the proper preparation: see RITUAL MAGIC; see also GOLDEN DAWN; SPIRITS AND FORCES.

Albert Abrams (1863-1924)

The American pioneer of radionics, inventor of the Oscilloclast, also known as the Black Box: see RADIESTHESIA.

Absent Healing

Spiritual or magical healing in the patient's absence, and sometimes without his know-ledge. In some cases healers pray for the patient; in some, according to Spiritualist belief, 'spirit doctors' from the world beyond death treat the patient. Magicians and witches also attempt to treat absent patients, and treatment in RADIESTHESIA often does not require the patient's presence: see FAITH HEALING.

Acupuncture

A Chinese system of healing which has been taken up in the West since the 1930s and has some impressive successes to its credit, though how it works is not understood: it involves the insertion of needles into the patient's skin at points which frequently have no apparent connection with the condition being treated: see FAITH HEALING. (See *304*)

Evangeline Adams (d.1932)

A celebrated American astrologer whose rich and influential clientele is said to have included J. P. Morgan and Mary Pickford: she had her own radio show in 1930, and is reported to have accurately predicted her own death: she prophesied, in 1931, that the United States would be at war in 1942 (*3*).

Aetherius Society

A society founded in 1956, by George King, which believes itself to be in touch with MASTERS, or spiritually advanced be-ings, who live on various planets. They include the Master Jesus, who lives on Venus, 'the great Cosmic Adept, Mars Sector 6', and Saint Goo-Ling, who resides on earth. In May 1954, in London, George King heard a voice saying: 'Prepare your-self, you are to become the voice of Inter-planetary Parliament.' According to the Society, this was 'no psychic apparition or vague voice in the head' but was 'completely physical and held a peculiar musical and deep penetrating quality, not possessed by any ordinary earthly voice'. Interplanetary Parliament is a body anxious to help our troubled world which keeps watch on the earth by means of flying saucers (see UFOS). The saucers are also used on occasion to radiate spiritual energy, and the Society reciprocates with a 'spiritual push'. The Masters have 'charged' various mountains, to which members go on pilgrimage, with spiritual force. Its first holy mountain was Holdstone Down in Devonshire, England,

where in 1958 the Master Jesus appeared to George King. The Master Jesus has also transmitted to the Society a new version of the Lord's Prayer. The slogan of the Society – 'Service is the Jewel in the Rock of Attain-ment' – was transmitted by Mars Sector 6. The Society has its English headquarters in London, and its American one in Los Angeles and branches elsewhere. (*303, 440*)

George King, founder of the Aetherius Society, on a mountain that it had 'charged with spiritual force'

Ahimsa

The Indian term for the principle of non-violence and respect for all living things: see YOGA.

Akashic Record

The enduring trace of all events that have ever occurred, including every thought, idea and emotion, said to be preserved in the astral light: numerous occult versions of history have been based on the 'observation' of this record by seers who claim to have penetrated the astral plane: 'akashic' is from the Sanskrit *akasha*, used in Hinduism for an all-pervading medium similar to the 'ether' of 19th-century physics: see ASTRAL PLANE; ATLANTIS; for William James's hypothetical 'cosmic reservoir' of memories, see MEDIUMS.

Alchemy

In modern industrial societies metallurgy is merely a branch of technology, with nothing 'supernormal' about it, but in its early days it was considered a mysterious and magical art, and the smith was a magician or priest as well as a craftsman (as he still is in some primitive communities). The European al-chemists, working in secret to produce marvels, cloaking their operations in deeply obscure symbols and incomprehensible form-ulae, concerned as much or more with spiritual progress as with chemistry, in-herited and preserved this tradition. Al-chemy, C. A. Burland says, 'became a necessary way of thought once man had mastered the strange process of applying heat to certain kinds of rock and thereby changing its nature into dross and shining metal. Then came the other wonder of mixing two metals in a fluid state and so producing a new metallic alloy which had different characteristics from its parents. Some metals tarnished and could be restored to health by washing with various vegetable juices. All could be purified by a renewed passage through the fire, by melting and burning away the dross, or by heating and beating until the impurities flaked away as swarf' (*67*).

Dross and shining metal, alloying, tarnishing, washing, purifying, the passage through the fire – these could be regarded, and by alchemists were regarded, as both physical and spiritual states and processes. They believed that through the secret operations of their art it was possible to turn base metals into the most valuable of metals, gold, and simultaneously to transform the alchemist himself into the 'gold' of spiritual perfection. It is true that some alchemists were charlatans and crooks, and some, the despised 'puffers', were only interested in making gold on the cheap. But in the true art of alchemy the chemical and spiritual processes seem to have been inextricably entwined. What was meant to happen was that chemical changes occurring in the alchemist's material were accompanied and paralleled by, and were part and parcel of, spiritual changes occurring in the alchemist himself. It was presumably because the medieval alchemists' knowledge of chemistry was defective, and their attempts to make gold always unsuccessful (or almost always, perhaps), that later adepts tended to turn away from metal-working altogether and concern themselves solely with the spiritual side of the art, or with the bodily and sexual alchemical techniques which some modern occultists have adopted.

The Paradoxical Stone

The supreme goal of alchemy was the mysterious Philosopher's Stone, which transmuted all other materials to gold at a touch and which was also the Elixir of Life, the universal medicine that cured all diseases and conferred immortality. Alchemical authors refer to it in highly paradoxical language. It is a stone and it is not a stone, it exists everywhere in nature but is ignored or despised, it is unknown and yet known to everyone, it is made of fire and water, it is a fluid without weight, it comes from God but does not come from God.

Not only the Stone itself but the processes through which to achieve it are concealed in alchemical texts behind enigmatic veils of symbols, allusions and hints, which frequently baffle modern interpreters and confused

A medieval alchemist attempting to transmute lower elements by fire

aspiring alchemists themselves. The king and queen, the serpent devouring its own tail, the phoenix, the dragon, the peacock's tail, the tree, the bath, the mountain, the rose, the green lion, the unicorn, the crucified snake, virgin's milk, the massacre of the innocents and innumerable other emblems make up the symbolic language of the art. A medieval Arab treatise, the *Book of Ostanes*, 'has 84 different names for the philosopher's stone and a fantastic dream concerning seven doors and three inscriptions in Egyptian, concerning the Persian Magi and a citation from an Indian sage concerning the healing virtues of the urine of a white elephant' (*454*). It is no accident that our word 'gibberish' is a corruption of Geber, the name by which the most famous of Arab alchemists, Jabir ibn Hayyan (*c.* 722–815), was known in Europe.

The *Golden Tractate of Hermes Trismegistus*, the bulk of which may date from the 4th or 5th centuries A.D., says: 'Take an ounce and a half of the humidity; and of the Midday Redness, the soul of gold, take a fourth part which is half an ounce. Of the citrine Seyre take similarly half an ounce. Of the Auripigment take half (which are eight) thus making a total of three ounces; and you must know that the Vine of the Wise is drawn forth in three, and the Wine of it is perfected in Thirty' (*67*). *Secrets of Nature*, attributed to Arnold of Villanova (1235–1311), draws a parallel between the making of the stone and Christ's crucifixion and resurrection. The world was lost through a woman, it says, and must be recovered

through a woman, so 'take the pure mother and put her in bed with the sons according to your intention and there let her do strictest penance until she is well cleansed from all sins'. She will then give birth to a son, 'who will preach to all, saying "Signs have appeared in sun and moon"'. He must be 'taken and beaten well and scourged lest by reason of pride he perish'. Then you must 'put him in bed to enjoy himself' and afterwards 'take him pure and extinguish in cold water'. After you have repeated this process, 'hand him over to the Jews to be crucified. And while he is crucified, sun and moon will be seen, and then the veil of the temple will be rent and there will be a great earthquake. So then the fire is to be increased and then he will give up the ghost' (*454*). What exactly these instructions meant is problematical, though there is little doubt about the light in which a modern sex magician would interpret them.

The first process in the *Twelve Keys*, a 17th-century work, is: 'Take a fierce grey Wolf. Cast to him the body of the King and when he has devoured it, burn him entirely to ashes in a great fire. By this process the King will be liberated; and when it has been performed thrice the Lion has overcome the Wolf, who will find nothing more to devour in him. Thus one body has been found fit for the first stage of our work.' In chemical terms, the wolf is probably antimony, so represented because it readily forms alloys with, or 'devours', other metals, and the process seems to be the purification of gold by repeated fusion with antimony sulphide (*386*).

The alchemists wrapped their art in mystery to preserve it from the unworthy. They also needed secrecy to protect themselves from kings, governments and powerful people greedy for gold, and because they were in an equivocal position vis-a-vis the Church, for they looked not to it but to their own efforts for salvation. But the mystification goes back beyond the Middle Ages to much earlier alchemical texts and it may be that the basic reason for it is that alchemy, like other branches of occultism, is an *art*, in the sense that it can be learned but cannot be taught. Though the apprentice alchemist may receive help from teachers, he must still essentially discover and realize the secret for himself.

Solve et Coagula

Alchemy is first discernible in Egypt in the late centuries B.C. and early centuries A.D. and combined the metal-working techniques of the ancient world with ideas drawn from the ferment of religious and philosophical theories current in the eastern Mediterranean area at that period – ideas drawn from Greek philosophy, Neoplatonism, the MYSTERY RELIGIONS, Christianity, GNOSTICISM and the HERMETICA. Alchemy was the 'hermetic' art because one of its reputed founders was the legendary Hermes Trismegistus, a form of the Egyptian god Thoth, and it was perhaps from Egyptian religion that alchemy drew one of its basic notions, the idea of 'first matter'. The theory was that the god or supernatural intelligence who created the world fashioned it out of a dark chaotic mass, the *prima materia* or *massa confusa*, which was not itself matter in any normal sense of the term but the possibility of matter, containing in potential all the forms and phenomena of life. This idea may have been drawn from much older Egyptian creation myths based on observation of swarming life springing up from the black silt deposited by the Nile in its annual flood.

It remained a cardinal principle of alchemy that you could reduce a metal or other material (and yourself psychologically and spiritually) to first matter by stripping all its characteristics from it. This was to 'kill' it. You could then restore it to 'life' and add desirable characteristics to it, or 'nurture' it like a growing child, until it became the Stone. The 'death' of the material is the mock death of initiation into the Mysteries, and of initiation rituals in many societies, which is followed by 'rebirth' to a new and better life. The whole secret of the art was said to be contained in the maxim *Solve et coagula*, 'Dissolve and combine'. To 'dissolve' means to strip away a substance's characteristics, to 'combine' is to build up a new substance. The same principle was expressed in calling alchemy the 'spagiric' art,

coined from Greek words meaning 'to tear' and 'to bring together'.

The theory of the four elements, drawn from Greek philosophy and accepted in Europe down to the 17th century, encouraged alchemists to think that transmutation was possible. All things were believed to be made of differing combinations of four basic elements – fire, air, earth and water – which were the first development from first matter. (In modern occultism they are taken to be four conditions in which energy can exist – respectively, electricity, the gaseous state, the solid state and the liquid state.) Gold was thought to be a mixture of the four elements in a certain proportion, and the other metals to be mixtures of the same elements in slightly different proportions, so that by changing the proportions in the mixture a base metal could be turned into gold.

The possibility of transmutation was confirmed for the alchemists by contemporary metal-working techniques, which involved the use of alloys and dyes to make imitation gold and silver. The emphasis was on changing the colour of a metal, yellowing or whitening it to make it look like natural gold or silver, and the alchemists took a change of colour to indicate a real change of substance. In the 5th century Aeneas of Gaza wrote: 'The changing of matter for the better has nothing incredible in it. Thus it is that those learned in the art of matter take silver and tin, make their externals disappear, colour and change the matter into excellent gold' (*291*). A legacy of the alchemical interest in colour was the term Tincture for the Stone.

The Living Male and Female

Like other magical thinkers, alchemists did not draw our customary distinction between animate and inanimate, and in dealing with metals they believed themselves to be dealing with life. The parallel between metallic life and human life runs all through alchemy and lies behind the belief that to penetrate and master the secrets of metals is to understand and master human nature. It also accounts for the belief that metals are propagated and grow in the belly of the earth in the same way that a human child is conceived and formed in the womb. A German handbook on metals and mining, printed in 1505, says: 'It is to be noted that for the growth or generation of a metal ore there must be a begetter and some subject capable of receiving the generative action.' These are sulphur and mercury, and 'in the union of mercury and sulphur in the ore, the sulphur behaves like the male seed and the mercury like the female seed in the conception and birth of a child' (*141*). This theory underlies the con-

stant use of erotic imagery in alchemical texts. 'Take the living male and the living female,' says *Novem Lumen Chemicum* (1604), 'and join them in order that they may project a sperm for the procreation of a fruit accord- to their kind' and, 'you must produce one thing out of two by natural generation' (*484*).

The 'life' of metals, the activating spiritual element encased in matter, corresponding to the 'divine spark' imprisoned in the body of a man, was sometimes identified as mercury, which plays a great variety of roles in alchemical theory and symbolism. It could be thought of as the activating principle, because it is mobile. It also contains opposites in a unity, since it is a metal but also a liquid, and it is liquid but does not wet a surface on which it rests, and so it could be identified with the undifferentiated first matter or with the Stone itself. Because it unites opposites it was frequently represented as a hermaphrodite and called 'the masculine-feminine'. Among other alchemical names for it were the divine water, the ever-fugitive, silvery water, the seed or bile of the dragon, divine dew, sea-water, moon-water, milk of a black cow.

This mercury, however, is not the metal found in nature but 'philosopher's mercury', an ideal substance to which ordinary mercury is only an imperfect approximation. Other materials of importance in alchemy were also of this 'philosophical' sort. In the 12th and 13th centuries it was generally accepted that metals were made of mercury and sulphur. Sulphur was the active, fiery, male principle and mercury the passive, watery, female principle, or frequently these were the two principles within the hermaphroditic mercury itself. The Stone was the product of philosophical sulphur and mercury (and so of 'fire and water') mingled in perfect balance, and the uniting of these two opposites was the supreme process in achieving the Stone. It was symbolized by the sacred marriage of king and queen, sun and moon, red and white, the red lion and the white eagle.

In later European alchemy, metals were thought to contain a third basic ingredient, salt. Paracelsus (*c.* 1490–1541) took this view, though without abandoning the four elements and the opposites. 'The world is as God created it. In the beginning He made it into a body, which consists of four elements. He founded this primordial body on the trinity of mercury, sulphur and salt, and these are the three substances of which the complete body consists. For they form everything that lies in the four elements, they bear in them all the forces and faculties of perishable things. In them there are day and night,

Paracelsus, by Peter Paul Rubens

warmth and coldness, stone and fruit, and everything else, still unformed' (*363*). In man this trinity is the physical body (salt); the soul (emotions, desires, natural drives; the ASTRAL BODY of modern occultism; sulphur); and the spirit (higher mental faculties; the divine spark; mercury).

The Processes

Alchemy was an extraordinarily difficult, laborious and perplexing pursuit. At the outset, the hopeful beginner was faced with the problem of discovering what raw material to work on. This was a profound secret and many texts would tell him only that the 'subject' of the work was the same as its end product, something found everywhere and universally despised as worthless. Similarly, Archibald Cockren, a modern alchemist who experimented for forty years before the secret of the art began to dawn on him, declined to reveal the nature of his raw material (*94*). When an alchemical text did specify a material, it frequently meant something else. For example, vitriol was recommended, but this really meant *Visita interiora terrae rectificando invenies occultum lapidem*, 'Visit the interior of the earth and by purifying you will find the secret stone', a sentence obtained from the word vitriol by notarikon (see CABALA).

From a spiritual point of view, it seems clear that the raw material of the work was the alchemist himself and that the 'interior of the earth' was his own interior. In practice would-be adepts experimented with all sorts of material, including blood, dung, urine, wax, wine, grass, herbs and roots, chalk,

antimony, arsenic, vinegar, mercury, and gold itself.

Having picked a raw material, the next problem was to decide what operations to perform on it and in what order. Some said there were twelve processes in the complete work, corresponding to the signs of the zodiac. Some said there were seven processes, corresponding to the seven days of creation in Genesis and to the seven planets. Each planet was believed to influence the development of its own metal in the ground, and the metals were arranged in a ladder or staircase leading from imperfection to perfection, with lead (Saturn) at the foot, then tin (Jupiter), iron (Mars), copper (Venus), mercury (Mercury), silver (the Moon), and finally gold (the Sun).

The first steps in the work, leading up to the process called 'putrefaction', culminated in the *nigredo*, or black stage, when the material in the alchemist's vessel had been reduced to first matter and its innate spark of life had been driven out of it in the form of vapour. This was called the Black Crow, Black Sun or Raven's Head, and might be represented by a dead and rotting corpse, a black bird, or a dead king eaten by a wolf. After this the 'dead' material was 'reborn' as its own vapour condensed into a liquid and saturated it, and this was soon followed by the *albedo*, or whitening, when the white tincture or white elixir formed in the vessel. The final processes led on to the *rubedo*, the appearance of the red tincture, red elixir or red powder, the miraculous Stone itself.

The alchemist laboured over his furnace and crucible, repeating the same operations over and over again, reading and re-reading his authorities and struggling to make sense of them, patiently wrestling with inefficient equipment and incompetent or dishonest assistants, surviving explosions, catastrophes and disappointments, devoutly praying for help from on high. And eventually, perhaps, the illumination would come, the great secret he had toiled and suffered for so long would dawn on his mind. Often, the alchemists said, the secret would be revealed by a figure in a dream, an angel or an old, wise man. It has been suggested, tentatively, that on rare occasions alchemists may have succeeded in making gold, if only in tiny quantities, through a type of PSYCHOKINESIS, the influence of the mind on matter. 'The long and intense concentration of an alchemist on his materials and operations, and the physically exhausting toil of the work, might induce an unusual condition of mind in which the alchemist was able to cause abnormal chemical reactions in his materials. . . . On this hypothesis, the "grace of God" for which alchemists devoutly prayed

and without which, they said, the work could not succeed, would be interpreted as the rare and fleeting psychic ability to cause parachemical change in the alchemist's materials – an ability which in a pious age seemed to be something coming from outside the alchemist himself, as a gift from God' (*303*).

The Sacred Marriage

That the work of alchemy was not mere muddle-headed chemistry but a psychological and spiritual quest has increasingly been recognized in this century, largely through the influence of C. G. JUNG. Jung noticed alchemical symbolism cropping up in the dreams of patients who knew nothing whatever of alchemy. He believed that these symbols came from the 'collective unconscious' and regarded the alchemical work as a process of 'individuation', the development of an integrated personality. The various stages, trials and difficulties of the work were a projection of the long, toilsome path towards unity of the self.

Before Jung's day, however, in 1850, Mary Anne Atwood published *A Suggestive Enquiry into the Hermetic Mystery*, in which she argued that the real goal of alchemy was spiritual perfection. After publication she came to feel that the inquiry was too suggestive and, fearing she had revealed too much, she bought up as many copies of the book as she could. Others occultly inclined pursued the same track. Franz HARTMANN, for example, said in *Magic White and Black* that alchemy taught how the base metals, which were really the animal driving energies deep in human nature, 'could be transformed into the pure gold of true spirituality, and how, by attaining spiritual knowledge and spiritual life, souls could have their youth and innocence restored and be rendered immortal'.

Aleister CROWLEY later drew the clear parallel between alchemy and magical initiation, in saying that alchemical texts 'all begin with a substance in nature which is described as existing almost everywhere, and as universally esteemed of no value. The alchemist is in all cases to take this substance, and subject it to a series of operations. By so doing, he obtains his product. This product, however named or described, is always a substance which represents the truth or perfection of the original "First Matter"; and its qualities are invariably such as pertain to a living being, not to an inanimate mass. In a word, the alchemist is to take a dead thing, impure, valueless, and powerless, and transform it into a live thing, active, invaluable and thaumaturgic. . . . The First Matter is a man, that is to say, a perishable parasite, bred of the earth's crust, crawling irritably upon it for a span, and at last returning to the dirt whence he sprang. The process of initiation consists in removing his impurities, and finding in his true self an immortal intelligence to whom matter is no more than the means of manifestation' (*102*).

Lying behind this is an interpretation of alchemy in terms of the human body as well as the human soul. The alchemists' belief that they were dealing with life in matter, their reticent secrecy, their erotic symbolism and their references to 'philosophical' substances whose true nature is concealed under cover names, have led some modern magicians to take the red and white elixirs and other alchemical terms as references to physical, bodily products and processes. We are told, for example, that: 'In certain forms of occult practice, concealed under the veils of alchemy, the assimilation of solar energy from food by the lacteals in the small intestine is tremendously increased. To this practice we may refer alchemical references to the First Matter as "virgin's milk", prepared under the regimen of Mercury; to the process of putrefaction symbolized by a black dragon (the convolutions of the intestines in the darkness of the abdominal cavity); and to the fact that, in its visible aspect, the First Matter is a thing accounted by all men to be the vilest thing on earth' (*82*).

The alchemical 'sacred marriage' of opposites provides the symbolic basis of the so-called 'Mass of the Holy Ghost' (the parallel between the alchemical work and the Eucharist is an old motif). This operation of sexual magic has been described by Israel REGARDIE, who quotes the 16th-century cabalist and alchemist Heinrich Khunrath to the effect that the two major instruments of alchemy are 'one circular, crystalline vessel, justly proportioned to the quality of its contents', called the Cucurbite, and 'one theosophic, cabalistically sealed furnace or Athanor'. The pure gold or Amrita, the dew of immortality, which is the object of the operation, is produced by mingling two substances, 'the Serpent or the Blood of the Red Lion', whose source is the Athanor, and 'the Tears or the Gluten of the White Eagle', which is housed in the Cucurbite. 'Through the stimulus of warmth and spiritual fire to the Athanor there should be a transfer, an ascent of the Serpent from that instrument into the Cucurbite, used as a retort. The alchemical marriage or the mingling of the two streams of force in the retort causes at once the chemical corruption of the Serpent in the menstruum of the Gluten, this being the *solve* part of the general alchemical formula of *solve et coagula*. Hard upon the corruption of the Serpent and his death,

Alchemists from a 15th-century woodcut

arises the resplendent Phoenix which, as a talisman, should be charged by means of a continuous invocation of the spiritual principle conforming to the work in hand. The conclusion of the Mass consists in either the consumption of the transubstantiated elements, which is the Amrita, or the anointing and consecreation of a special talisman. . . . The supreme power operating in this technique is love' (*391*).

To what extent, if at all, the earlier alchemists employed physical and sexual techniques is in doubt. Chinese alchemy, unsuspected by Jung, was closely connected with sex magic (see *263*), some of the European texts do make more sense if read in this light than in any other, and some of the later European alchemists regarded the presence of a woman, the *soror mystica* or 'mystic sister', as an essential element of the work.

On the other hand, the use of erotic imagery by mystically-minded authors frequently does not imply the use of any erotic technique. In the main, the alchemists of old have successfully preserved their secrets, but although there are a few laboratory workers to this day earnestly seeking to make gold by alchemical methods, the hermetic art's principal influence on modern magical practice has been as a psycho-physical 'chemistry', a set of techniques involving both body and soul. It is in this way that the moderns, rightly or wrongly, have understood the old alchemical maxim, *Ars totum requirit hominem*, 'The art requires the whole man.' R. C.

(Further reading: *67, 85, 94, 102, 141, 227, 232, 256c* and *d, 262, 263, 291, 303, 386, 391, 449, 454, 484.*)

Alpha Devices, Alpha Waves, Electronic Meditation

See MEDITATION.

AMORC

The Ancient and Mystic Order Rosae Crucis, a prominent American Rosicrucian society, founded by Harvey Spencer Lewis (d. 1939), who has been described as a 'metaphysical merchandising genius' (*163*). The Order, which is well known for its extensive advertising and its correspondence courses, claims a membership of over 100,000 in the U.S.A. and abroad. The principal subjects of study, listed in one of its brochures, include: 'the mysteries of time and space; the human consciousness; the nature of matter; perfecting the physical body . . . development of will; important discoveries in Rosicrucian chemistry and physics . . . ' The Order traces Rosicrucianism back to the 'mystery schools' of ancient Egypt, *c.* 1500 B.C., and the administration building at its headquarters in San Jose, California, is a copy of an Egyptian temple. The founder's son, Ralph Maxwell Lewis, succeeded as Imperator of the Order on his father's death: see ROSICRUCIANS. (*163, 287*)

Amulets See LUCK.

Analgesia

Insensibility to pain, reported of numerous holy men, yogis, wonder-workers, mediums and persons in the grip of religious enthusiasm: see PHYSICAL POWERS.

Animal Magnetism See FAITH HEALING; HYPNOSIS.

Ankh

The ancient Egyptian symbol of life, now a popular lucky charm: see LUCK; SPIRITS AND FORCES.

Anthroposophical Society See Rudolf STEINER.

Apparitions

The term 'apparition', like 'ghost', with which it is practically synonymous, is one that has been used popularly for centuries, but never with a closely defined specific meaning. Therefore, it is not one that can be defined neatly and precisely. A purely descriptive dictionary definition concentrates on phrases like 'immaterial ghostly appearance' and 'seems real and is generally sudden or startling', but gives no hint as to the cause or meaning of 'appearances' of this kind. The term, however, usually refers to the 'immaterial appearance' of a human figure, one which, if identifiable, is that of someone deceased.

A simple but typical example was recently reported by a woman in Albany, New York. She knew that her father-in-law was ill, and so she was startled one day to see him in her room, and even more so when the impression faded and she realized its nature. Within an hour her husband received a phone call telling him that his father had passed away.

Apparitions are not seen by everyone. Only an occasional individual reports such an experience. It usually occurs when he is alone, although instances when more than one person seem to have the same impression at the same time have been reported sufficiently often to call for explanation. In any event, however, an apparitional experience is transient and not likely to be repeated. Consequently, the occurrence is not easily verifiable and the report of it is likely to excite scepticism or disbelief in the majority of listeners.

Reports of apparitions, in spite of much scepticism about them, came to have a certain importance, both in folk belief (see plate, page 34) and in the history of religion. The ghosts of Banquo and of Hamlet's father, though literary creations, were based on a common and accepted idea of the time, the idea that apparitions were the spirits of deceased persons somehow manifesting in visible form. Sometimes an apparition appeared as if simply to bring a message to the living observer just by being seen (and thus assuring him of the survival of the spirit). Sometimes it brought a more specific message or warning, like those of the Shakespearean ghosts.

Apparitions have also played a part in religion, although experiences claimed more particularly in that field come more often under the heading 'vision' than 'apparition' or 'ghost'. The distinction will be clear later. But appearances (immaterial) of visible and audible divine beings and their angels as message-bearers make up much of the record of religious communication.

Today, however, the simple and direct interpretation of apparitions as manifestations of deceased persons is outmoded. Too much has been learned in experimental parapsychology to make it any longer tenable. Naturally, the advances of knowledge in the last few decades have affected the interpretations of this age-old phenomenon.

The effect of this increased knowledge, however, must be seen in context to be appreciated. The term 'apparition' cannot even now be intelligently appraised as an isolated item. Nor can its origin and meaning be considered without its background, any more than one part of an organism could be understood without its relationship to the rest of it.

The rest of it is the entire range of experiences reported by individuals in which unexplainable elements appeared of the kind that came to be known as 'psychic'. Psychic experiences were those personal ones that seemed real and meaningful, but which did not obey the ordinary rules of the physical world. Apparitions appearing to healthy persons were psychic in this sense. They were inexplicable by ordinary rules, but still real and meaningful. They therefore seemed mysterious, even supernatural. Today they, and the entire list of experiences of which they are a part, are referred to as spontaneous psi, or parapsychical, experiences (see PARAPSYCHOLOGY).

Apparitions as Spontaneous Psi Experiences

Spontaneous psi experiences, of which apparitions once seemed to make up a larger part than they do today, are as old as history. They have been reported in every age and culture. They came in so many different forms that for ages no common characteristic was seen in them, each one was a separate mystery. But then in time it was recognized that all of them appeared to bring a person information about the world, although not in any ordinary way.

By the late 19th and early 20th centuries, the experimental method in science was developing, and it was suggested that properly controlled experiments could show if it were true that the mind could obtain information in some still unrecognized manner, as implied in psi experiences. Experiments to test this idea were first made in the field now known as parapsychology.

By the end of the 1930s, the experiments had given the answer. They had established that the mind can, indeed, sometimes get information when the senses are quite shut out. It was *extra*-sensory perception (ESP). Then its subtypes, too, were each shown to occur: clairvoyance, the awareness of inanimate objects; precognition, the awareness of events still in the future; and telepathy, the awareness of another person's thought. In addition, psychokinesis (PK), the direct effect of the mind on objective matter, had also been demonstrated.

ESP and PK together came to be considered as innate abilities which are probably present in the human race in general, even though inhibited to a large extent, so that their existence was not easy to demonstrate. The two abilities, which may well be but different aspects of a basic one, came to be called the psi ability.

Once psi ability was demonstrated, its implications for the explanation of psychic experiences began to be recognized. It gave a new insight into most of them. Whereas before, even 'true' DREAMS had posed a problem of explanation, now with the recognition that ordinary people – not only

Biblical prophets – have an ability to foresee the future, even if only to a limited extent, the explanation was clear. Similarly, all of the simpler forms of psychic experiences fell into place as instances of psi ability in action. Apparitional experiences, too, of course, came up for re-examination. But in order to understand this, a historical glimpse of psi phenomena will first be necessary, and then the effect of parapsychological discoveries can be appreciated.

Early Studies of Apparitions

One could go far back in time, indeed, in an attempt to trace the history of apparitions. In folklore and religion they seemed to show a link between this world and the next. In this, of course, they were not alone. In those ages, natural phenomena did so too. The moon and tides, eclipses, even lightning and thunder, spoke of supernatural influences. But for all of them the progress of knowledge has meant the substitution of the natural for the supernatural. It should almost be expected, then, that the history of apparitions should show a similar shift of interpretation.

Psychic experiences, apparitional or other, were never collated and studied in any really comprehensive way before the discovery of the psi ability. In fact, such a study could not have been expected until after the inclusive concept of psi (clairvoyance, precognition, telepathy, and PK) had been established to serve as a guideline. But even so, they had not been completely neglected by any means. Earlier studies made of some of them, and of apparitional experiences in particular, helped to furnish the impetus towards experiment which could supply the key to their greater understanding. Landmarks among the earlier studies of spontaneous psi experiences were those made by the Society for Psychical Research (S.P.R.) in London, and the later study of apparitions by G. N. M. Tyrell in England.

One of the reasons for the S.P.R.'s foundation in London in 1882 was an interest in studying reports of apparitional experiences. A project by three of the founders, Edmund Gurney, F. W. H. Myers and Frank Podmore, to collect accounts of such experiences was among the initial ones undertaken. Their studies resulted, in 1886, in the volume *Phantasms of the Living*. The basic objective of their inquiry was to estimate the real meaning and bearing of such experiences on the question of life after death, the survival question. According to the reports, apparitions appeared to be instances in which the spirit of a dead person seemed to communicate with a living one. They therefore gave presumptive evidence of survival. If they were what they appeared to be, then they represented a kind of communication between the two, but of course without sensory means. Such communication would be telepathy.

Telepathy, however, was a disputed topic. It was not generally considered to exist; the concensus of educated persons was against it. Therefore, it was necessary to try to establish whether it was a fact. On that account, Gurney, Myers and Podmore decided to collect all the possible cases of presumptive telepathy, whether or not they were in the apparitional form.

Of course, the bearing of telepathy on survival, if indeed its existence could be established, was based on the way they thought that it must operate, which was on the analogy of message-sending, in which one person, whom they labelled the agent, sends his thought to another, the receiver. An example of an experience that would seem to show telepathy as operating in this way, would be a case like that of a woman in Indianapolis, Indiana, who had gone to visit her sister in St Louis. When she was returning home, she was unable to notify her husband of her time of arrival and realized that he would not be there to meet her train, which would arrive at 2 a.m. She decided to try to reach him by telepathy, and kept thinking over and over, 'Meet the 2 a.m. train.' He was there to meet her. He said he had been asleep, but awoke when something kept telling him to meet the 2 a.m. train from St Louis.

Obviously in such a telepathy case the transfer of thought seemed to depend on the active sending of the agent. He or she appeared to be the one who initiated the transfer. The receiver, usually called the percipient (the husband in this case), appeared to be more or less passive. In such a transfer, then, messages seeming to come from a dead or dying person would be especially meaningful, because if they really occurred it would follow that the dead person sent them, and hence his spirit must have survived even though his body had died.

It followed naturally, then, that all the telepathic experiences that could be authentically shown to occur were taken as bearing particularly both on the reality of telepathy and on the survival of the spirit. The researchers therefore made a collection of reports of spontaneous cases that appeared to offer evidence that telepathy had occurred.

These cases seemed to fall naturally into two main classes, depending on whether the percipient's impression was 'externalized' or not. The apparitions, of course, were externalized, but a few cases of apparent telepathy were not. Instead, they consisted only perhaps of an idea, a sensation, or an emotion that appeared to have been transferred from one person to another. Naturally, the major interest, both for proof of telepathy and for evidence bearing on the survival question was centred on the apparitions, the externalized impressions of a human being, and practically always of one dying or already dead.

The apparitional cases, which they classed as hallucinatory, varied somewhat in the sense modality involved. Auditory as well as visual impressions were involved, as in cases when a person heard his name called, often in a voice he recognized. A modern auditory hallucination occurred, for instance, to a man in New York. His father still lived in Wales, and the son was awakened from sleep one night by hearing, as he thought, his father calling him by the special name of his childhood that was used by no one else. The man was quite affected by the reality of the impression, and even more so when in due time he learned that his father had died in his sleep the night the call was heard.

Auditory experiences like this, however, were not as impressive as those in which the dying or dead individual was 'seen'. Visual experiences were thus given the greatest emphasis. The persons so recognized usually seemed to bring a message. It did not matter, however, if the person 'seen' was someone the observer knew. The effect could still be considered as bearing both on survival and telepathy, even if he was a stranger – for instance, a ghost observed in a haunted house. Even a modern case like the following could still be considered as bringing a message.

A woman who was watching her husband repairing his recently purchased second-hand motorcycle noticed a young man come into the yard and appear to be observing the repair job too. But when she asked to be introduced, he vanished. She found that her husband had not seen him. However, she had seen him clearly and could describe his appearance in detail. Upon inquiry they found out that the description exactly fitted that of the former owner of the motorcycle. They found that he had been killed on it two years before. The appearance could be taken as bringing information about him.

Thus, the general idea of apparitional experience, at this period, was that the spirit of the deceased person had survived and was able to become visible to the living. The significance of such manifestations, however, depended upon the fact that they could be

In Arundel church, an apparition said to be of a priest

considered as bringing information. In other words, they had a 'veridical' or truth-telling aspect. Simply seeing a figure that had no discernible connection or meaning would then, as now, have been ignored as probably a figment of imagination. The cases that brought a message, whether of a death, a warning, or information needed by a living person, made apparitional experiences meaningful to students of the survival question. The possible explanation of the way in which such a message could be communicated could seemingly only be as a telepathic impression from the deceased person.

Tyrell's Theory of Apparitions

After a number of years that produced only scattered references to the nature of apparitions by members of the S.P.R., one member, G. N. M. Tyrell, gave the subject concentrated attention. In 1943 he published a small volume, *Apparitions*, giving a rather complicated theory of their genesis. Although Tyrell's book appeared after the psi ability as a capacity of living persons had been demonstrated, and clairvoyance had been shown to be an ability just as likely to operate as telepathy, emphasis, particularly in England, continued to be centred on telepathy. The possibility of clairvoyant mental action where either one was possible was largely ignored.

Tyrell's position, however, was an improvement on that of the authors of *Phantasms of the Living*, in terms of the analysis of reports of apparitions in depth. It was his major objective, while to them it had only been an incidental aspect of their larger inquiry. He studied the cases they had reported and others that had accumulated in the interval of fifty years or more. Even so, however, they had at least noticed a few of the items that did not fit smoothly into the accepted idea that apparitions were externalized forms of telepathic messages from agents (dying or deceased) to percipients. Two major stumbling blocks, for instance, were the clothes and other appurtenances sometimes observed on apparitional figures, and the fact that sometimes more than one person in a group saw the same figure, each from his own angle of perspective.

Tyrell's careful analysis of these seeming anomalies led him to realize that the percipient was not a passive receiver of a message sent by the agent. Instead, he concluded that the figure as seen was actually the production of the percipient's mental processes (by a fairly complicated scheme, analogous, as he conceived it, to the normal process of perception), which had only been stimulated or activated by the mental processes of the agent. He thus retained the

The ghost of a victim depicted as appearing at his murderer's trial

telepathic motif, which of course meant that, in his view, the bearing of such experiences on the survival question was also retained.

Tyrell apparently did not realize that by clairvoyance the percipient could have received a stimulus from the crisis of the agent. This explanation, however, would have nullified the survival implication, which fact alone no doubt would have led it to be viewed with disfavour by the author as well as by the audience for whom he wrote; and the long history of the telepathic explanation had produced deeply ingrained bias for it, as against the clairvoyance one. However, Tyrell's theory, by recognizing that the percipient was not just a passive receiver of a message, but an active participant in it, was a long step ahead in the quest for a real understanding of the nature of apparitions.

Forms of Psi Experience

For a time after the experimental program in parapsychology had begun, and while its investigations were demonstrating the reality of the types of ESP, psychic experiences, including apparitions, were more or less ignored by researchers. Their attention was concentrated on the experimental research. The accounts of experiences were ostensibly much less reliable than experimental results. They were open to counter-explanations, such as chance coincidence between experience and event, over-interpretation, mal-observation, exaggeration, and mistakes of many kinds. They therefore did not appear to be of much value to experimenters.

The situation changed somewhat, however, after ESP and PK had been established. Presumably, experiences from life-situations might give suggestions to the experimenters as to the conditions under which the psi effects occurred when not restricted by the necessary laboratory conditions. Such suggestions might be helpful for guiding future research and might tend to broaden the general understanding of the psi ability. Even though the reliability of observations derived from case material was limited, their value was not negligible either.

In 1948, at the Parapsychology Laboratory of Duke University in Durham, North Carolina, a comprehensive collection of all reported kinds of spontaneous psi experiences was begun. The effort has continued ever since, now at the successor to the Parapsychology Laboratory, the Institute for Parapsychology. All the cases reported to these institutions by the general public over the years have been collected for study if they fall within a general definition. That definition is a simple one, the only requirement being that they be cases in which the person obtained an item of information which seemed not to have been obtained by sense impression and which could not reasonably be explained as a chance coincidence between the experience and the event to which it seemed to pertain.

The major objective in making this collection of experiences was not limited, like the earlier one in *Phantasms of the Living*, to evidence for any single type of ESP, but rather it was to make a completely inclusive list. With the psi ability established, it was desirable to find all of the ways in which it operates in nature.

As already mentioned, reports of such experiences, coming from individuals as they do, are vulnerable to all the usual weaknesses of human testimony. But at the same time, they include truthful elements that could give new insight into the operation of the mental processes of psi. It was recognized, therefore, that they could have considerable suggestive value, even without the high reliability of controlled experiments. Also, if large numbers of items showed a given characteristic, it would add to the probability that the characteristic was a real one.

Large numbers of cases with a given characteristic, at least fifty or more, and usually hundreds or even thousands, accumulated in the collection. The cases now number well over 15,000 in all. They are now probably numerous enough to give as much validity to observations made on them as could be expected from such material. The large numbers also give a degree of assurance that all of the ways in which psi occurs in nature are represented.

Both types of psi, ESP and PK, are represented in the collection, as well as all three subtypes of ESP: clairvoyance, precognition, and telepathy. In addition, all the cases fall into one or other of these categories, which appears to indicate that the types now known cover the entire range. The inclusion of precognition and clairvoyance, neither of which was recognized as possibly having a bearing on the nature of apparitions, is significant for their understanding.

More to the point on the topic of apparitions, however, is the classification of cases according to the forms in which they were expressed. When the entire group of apparent spontaneous psi experiences was divided according to the forms they took, it was found that they fell into one or another of only four kinds. These were sufficiently different to suggest that they must have been produced by basically different mental processes. In a few instances a combination of two forms occurred, but the majority of the cases were quite distinct in this aspect. This was a significant point for the apparitional experiences, for their form was distinct and generally not confused with those of any of the others.

Two of the four forms occurred when the person was awake, and two when he was sleeping. The two sleeping forms, realistic and unrealistic dreams, not of direct interest here, were characterized more by the fact that they carried their content or meaning by imagery than because they occurred in sleep. In fact, an occasional waking experience of the day-dreaming kind had to be classified with the dreams because the imagery was dream-like.

Of the experiences that occurred when the person was awake and are of more relevance here, the great majority were in the form of an intuition. The person suddenly 'just knew' something, without any discernible reason and without detail or imagery. An instance of an intuitive experience occurred to a family in a New York town during dinner one night. Suddenly the mother stood up and screamed, 'My mother! My mother! Something has happened to my mother!' The family was still in a state of consternation fifteen minutes later when a call came to tell them that the woman's mother had died fifteen minutes earlier. Although she died in the hospital, her daughter did not know that she was there, or even that she was ill.

The fourth form of experience and the second of those that occurred when the person was not sleeping was the hallucination. Hallucinatory experiences, which are, of course, well known outside parapsychology, have one common characteristic: they seem to be cases of sense experience without any objective stimulus. This apparently means that the sense organ is activated by an internal influence instead of the light or air waves in normal sense impressions. In the collection of spontaneous psi experiences, this form included apparitional experiences along with all the rest of those which fell within the general definition of bringing the observer information not secured by the senses; but in this case by means of sense experience without an objective stimulus.

The general similarity of the intuitive experience just quoted and the apparitional one of the woman in Albany is obvious. In both the person received a 'sign' of the death of a relative who was at a distance, and in both instances, when awake. The difference was only in the form of the experience; one 'saw' the individual involved, the other 'just knew' that something had befallen her. The suggestion thus is that the two forms are related, in spite of their surface difference.

Meaning of the Forms

In all the cases, by definition, information which did not come by the senses was received by the percipient. By contrasting the different forms, something was learned about the way they seem to originate. In all of them the information or message was apparently first acquired unconsciously. The person became aware of it only when it was expressed in one of these forms. Then at an unconscious level one of them obviously was selected and utilized.

If the person was asleep at the time, the meaning of the message was transformed into dream imagery that embodied the idea it involved. If the person was awake, in the intuitive kind of experience, the message crossed the threshold from the unconscious directly into consciousness. The person 'just knew' it.

However, if it appeared as a hallucinatory experience, the form of special interest here, apparently the direct transmission into consciousness was interrupted by what one can suppose from the evidence was a suggestion that took the form of a sense impression. The suggestion created by the ESP message usually seemed to have been a memory of the way the agent looked or the way his voice sounded. Then this, instead of the message itself, was transmitted to consciousness as an image of the agent. This, of course, only occurred in persons in whom the senses presumably could be triggered from internal causes, as well as from the ordinary external ones of light or air waves. Since only a few persons report hallucinatory experiences, it seems likely that the majority of people do not make this transformation. For those who do make it, the result is a seeming visual or auditory experience of the person involved in the ESP message, the agent who is apparently producing the effect.

The experiences of these two forms, and the dreams too, for that matter, all appear to begin in the same way in unconscious levels. However, the hallucination proceeds less directly than the intuition, and imagery of a kind is produced, though it is much more restricted than that of dreams. It seems likely that in sleep greater freedom pertains than when the person is awake. At any rate, instead of being wide-ranging, the imagery is almost entirely limited to that which would result from an influence like memory when the agent is a person known by the percipient, and who might possibly have been involved in the circumstances concerned.

In the cases in which the percipient did not know the agent, as in haunted houses, and so could not have constructed imagery about him from memory, it presumably would be supplied by ESP. In a case such as that of the young man in the motorcycle episode given above, and if the description of him was accurate, then that information was secured by ESP, presumably clairvoyantly, or by a combination of clairvoyance and telepathy. It was then reconstructed as necessary by the percipient. All this, of course, is done quite unconsciously and in presumably very much the same way as in dream imagery. Possibly the difference between dream imagery and that of hallucinatory experiences is the measure of the difference in the percipient's state of consciousness in the two situations. In dreaming he is asleep; in constructing the imagery of a hallucinatory experience, he is not asleep, but a good question can be raised as to whether he is fully awake. It could well be that most hallucinatory experiences occur in a 'twilight state' that is neither sleep nor full wakefulness.

Apparitions as Hallucinatory Psi Experiences

By 1956 some 8,000 reports of presumptive psi experiences were in the Duke collection. Of these, 825 were in the hallucinatory form, in which the person seemed to get information as a sense impression, but without an objective stimulus. The apparitional cases, of course, were included, by definition. They were simply the hallucinatory experiences in which the agent was dying or dead, and it was because of the significance of this kind of experience for the survival question that they were to be compared with the rest of the hallucinatory experiences. Since from the case study of psi experiences in general the origin of hallucinatory experiences appeared to be as suggested in the preceding section, the objective here was to see if the apparitional experiences seemed to originate in the same way as the rest, or whether they were different and the result of the influence of a deceased spirit.

The points to be considered were those involved in the traditional explanation for apparitional experiences. That explanation, as we have seen, was that the agent, when dying or deceased, was able, by telepathy from himself to the percipient to manifest himself, usually in the visual form. In the first step, therefore, the entire list of hallucinatory experiences was assessed as to the respective categories: sense modality, ESP type, and the condition of the agent, living, dead, or dying at the time of the percipient's experience.

The sense modalities involved in all of the hallucinatory experiences varied so much that four separate headings were necessary in order to classify them all. They included visual, with 231 cases; auditory, with 435 cases; olfactory, with 36 cases; and somatic, with 123 cases. In this last category, the percipient felt pain or illness without an objective reason, but when another person emotionally close to him was actually experiencing it. The olfactory and somatic types are not of special interest in regard to apparitions because they do not involve the human form.

As these figures show, the auditory modality predominated. It was about twice as frequent as the visual, but both together made up the large majority of hallucinatory experiences.

Although the telepathic type of experience had been the one recognized in the historical background of apparitions, this collection of hallucinatory experiences included 66 clairvoyant cases and 60 precognitive ones. A majority of 431, however, seemed to be telepathic in that the meaning could be considered as a message to the percipient. The remaining 268 cases were instances in which either clairvoyance or telepathy could have been involved.

To illustrate the kind of hallucinatory experience that can be taken to be of the telepathic type, a case can be cited that involved a woman who intended to visit her sick daughter. She missed the one bus that would get her there that day, but two people, her daughter's nurse and a friend of her daughter, both 'saw' her get off the bus near the daughter's house. They both saw her wave to them, and both noticed that she was carrying the peculiar shopping bag which she always used. But they waited in vain for her to come to the door. The impression of the two observers could have been based on the mother's intention to arrive on that bus.

An example of a non-telepathic case is that of a woman who, with her family, was returning home by car late one night in 1935. Her husband was driving at high speed over a deserted country road, and she, with a severe headache, was leaning her head back with her eyes closed. Suddenly she saw a vivid flash of red light and called a warning to her husband. He slammed on the brakes, and in seconds the car lights picked up a team-drawn wagon with a second team of horses fastened to the back. There were no lights of any kind on the wagon, and had it not been for the wife's hallucination of a red light, her husband could not have avoided hitting the wagon and teams.

The non-telepathic cases show that hallucinatory experiences are not necessarily telepathic. They may be, but the type cannot be taken for granted. However, in the days before the recognition of ESP in the living, the significance of presumed telepathic types of apparitions lay in the idea then current of the way in which the telepathic process works, that the agent is the active party and that he sends the message which the more or less passive percipient receives. This idea, however, can no longer be taken as reliable.

A study of all of the telepathic cases in the Duke collection, exclusive of the hallucinatory experiences, had been made earlier. It did not support the idea that the agent was necessarily an active participant in telepathy. The fact that such activity on the agent's part was not necessary was now clear because in many instances the agent was a living person, and so his part in the occurrence could be determined.

Some of the cases that showed this very clearly were cases of child telepathy. Such a case was reported by a woman who lived on

Possible Yeti footprints photographed by Don Whillans on Annapurna in Nepal (see page 22)

the fourteenth floor of a New York sky-scraper. She had just finished reading a magazine article about the problems of fire control in skyscrapers and was sitting pondering about it when her three-year-old daughter, who had been playing in her own room, ran out and said, 'Mommy, what would we do if a fire broke out on our floor?'

It is quite clear that the mother, who would have been the agent, had no intention whatever of sending the thought to the child, the percipient. In many such cases it seemed obvious that the percipient was the one who took the initiative in a telepathic transfer. He could grasp the agent's thought because of his own psi ability. The old idea of the way telepathy works was not a reliable one. Therefore, it cannot be assumed that the cases involving a deceased agent necessarily mean that the spirit of the agent must have sent them.

Living Agents

Of the 825 hallucinatory experiences reported, there were 297 instances in which the agent was dying and 88 in which he was already dead at the time of the percipient's experience. The apparitions thus made up somewhat less than half of the total. However, of the 440 remaining cases, 344 were similar to the apparitional cases, in that an agent and a message were involved. The only difference between them and those classed as apparitional was that, in them, the agent was living.

Before the establishment of ESP as an ability of living persons, the idea that discarnate spirits in apparitional form communicated with the living involved an unspoken assumption. This was that at the time of death and afterwards, the spirit attained a freedom or ability it had not possessed in life, one that enabled it to come to the living person, make itself visible or heard, and bring a message.

The message-bringing aspect suggested telepathy and gave such experiences a supernatural connotation, since telepathy in the living was not an accepted idea. In fact, the concensus among educated people was that it was impossible. One mind could not know the content of another when it was not expressed in any objective way. This was the general climate of opinion when the English psychical researchers began their study of telepathy cases, and this was why they put so much emphasis on telepathy. Today,

Top An apparition conceived by the Spanish painter Francisco Goya (see page 27), and *bottom* the astral plane of the ancient Egyptians, entered by ten gates and seven doors (see page 38)

however, the recognition of telepathy in the living affects the classification of experiences that can be called apparitions as far as they have a bearing on survival. In addition now, the recognition of apparition-like experiences with *living* agents throws new light on the situation.

In the past, cases of hallucinations with living agents apparently were seldom noticed. When they were, they excited some curiosity and raised questions, but apparently they generally went unrecognized or ignored, for the records do not show a majority of them, as the modern collection does. Experiences like this one, for example, were rarely reported then.

This experience, involving an agent who was still living, is from a woman who as a child had been brought by her father to Canada, after he had quarrelled with his mother and cut off all connection with his early home and relatives. His daughter, then an adult in Canada, awoke one morning feeling someone in the room and saw her grandmother sitting on the side of her bed. But when she reached out to touch her, the figure vanished. The daughter at once wrote to the old home and learned that her grandmother was dying of cancer, and was constantly thinking of her son and his family who had gone out of her life so long before. She lived to get a return letter from her granddaughter.

After all, hallucinatory experiences with living agents were not of great interest in connection with survival, except as instances of telepathy, and it was the survival question, not that of the nature of hallucinations, that was then the focus of interest. Today, however, any information received by a percipient that is not supplied by the senses is explainable as a case of ESP. In the above experience, the granddaughter apparently had an ESP message about her grandmother which she hallucinated into a visual impression and even dramatized as if her grandmother had come and sat on the side of her bed. The agent, in this instance the grandmother, was thinking strongly of her son and his family, though whether or not of the granddaughter especially is not specified. At any rate, the granddaughter's experience could not be considered the result of the grandmother's spirit, but of the granddaughter's hallucinatory ESP experience.

Dying Agents

ESP has been demonstrated in living persons, but whether it is also an ability of the deceased, if they do survive, is unknown. However, since experiences with living agents can be explained as ESP of the living percipient, those with dying agents cannot be con-

sidered as evidence of survival unless the agent was already dead at the time of the percipient's experience. Unfortunately, in very few such cases has the timing been ascertained or reported with sufficient accuracy to show what the actual condition of the agent was when the percipient had the experience. The evidential value, then, of cases with dying agents must be considered as too unreliable for consideration.

This leaves only the cases with deceased agents as tentatively giving evidence of spirit manifestation. Thus the study of cases with living agents in a practical way nullifies a large section of evidence, in cases with dying agents, formerly held to have value.

One other aspect of cases with living agents affects the interpretation of apparitions, for what helped to make apparitions seem meaningful as messages from the deceased was the fact that often the agent appeared to *come to* the percipient. For this reason, apparitions of the dying were quite generally taken by the percipient to mean that the agent came to tell the percipient of his death. It seemed to be a gesture of farewell. A study of experiences with living agents throws light on this seeming activity of the agent.

In some cases with living agents, the appearance is so realistic that the percipient does not know until later that the experience must have been hallucinatory. For example, a sailor on his way home with his crew had to pull ashore and camp for a while on an island. He lay down and dozed, dreaming that he had gone through his brother-in-law's field, and was sampling the wheat by pulling it through his fingers. Then the cook called him for lunch and he awoke, still remembering the dream. At home, however, his mother was preparing lunch when she looked out of the window and saw him returning through the wheat field. They put an extra plate on the table and did not know why the expected son did not arrive, or where he had disappeared to, or that the experience was hallucinatory, until later when he returned and related the dream.

In contrast to cases like that in which the agent appeared so realistically that the hallucinatory aspect was not recognized, are those like that of the grandmother in the case above who seemed to come to the percipient. It was found that in all the instances in which the hallucinatory nature of the experience was not immediately recognized, the agent was seen in an accustomed location or, as in the wheat field, one where presumably his appearance was not too unexpected. His locality and that of the percipient were about the same. But in a case like that of the grandmother, the locality of the percipient and that of the agent were so different that it was at once obvious to the percipient that the figure she saw could not be real. Also, when she hallucinated the figure, it had to be within her own visual range, and therefore it had to appear as if the agent, the grandmother, *came*, though actually there is no reason to suppose that she did.

The majority of apparitional experiences were of this same semi-realistic nature and gave this false impression that the agent came to the percipient. Obviously, the hallucination of a person known to be at a distance could not seem otherwise. The study of cases with living agents thus explained quite logically one of the items traditionally thought to be a significant feature of apparitional experiences, that they came to the percipient. The study showed that this impression at least in all the cases with a living agent (which included certainly many in which he was dying), was an artifact created by the relative locations of percipient and agent. Of course, cases in which the agent was deceased could be different, but nothing from this study suggested it.

Deceased Agents

After the study of hallucinatory experiences with living agents, only those whose agents were deceased remained as possibly reliable instances of spirit origin. The cases with dying agents could contribute nothing reliable on the point, since no way existed to determine if in them the agent was still living or already dead. But in 88 cases in the collection the agent was deceased. About half of them were auditory experiences and half were visual.

These 88 experiences seemed, in the main, much the same as those with living agents. They brought information to the percipient. A few of them seemed realistic, just as some of the cases with living agents did, as, for instance, the one involving the sailor in the wheat field. These, however, were all cases in which the percipient did not yet know that the agent was dead, and then saw him in a place where he might well have been seen when alive.

For instance, a young woman standing in line to deposit a cheque in a bank noticed a gentleman whom she knew very well, standing in another line. She noticed that he looked as if he had been ill. As she was about to speak to him, he turned and went out of the bank. She commented later to a friend about seeing the man, and that he looked ill. She learned then that he had died several days before she saw him.

One characteristic of these cases, and of the realistic ones with living agents, was that the agents appeared to be going about business of their own and were not oriented specially towards the percipient. In a number of haunting cases, too, the agents seemed to pay no attention to the percipient. For instance, a woman awoke repeatedly with a sense of being smothered, and once, when she thought she was awake, she saw towering over her a woman in a long black robe, with long black hair and a single curl down her back. It was the proximity of the figure, the percipient thought, that had given her the feeling of being smothered, although the figure made no move towards her. Her description of the figure led to the supposed identification of the agent as the former occupant of the house, who had died there some years before.

In practically all the cases in which the agent was a stranger, he appeared to have no interest in communicating. But in the rest, about half, the agent appeared oriented towards the percipient and seemed to bring a message. Most of these appeared to be no different from the cases with living agents, except for the fact that the agent was dead. A small number remained, however, that did seem different in degree, if not in kind. These were the cases in which the message brought was a warning, or at least information, concerning a third person. This addition of a third person made these cases more complex than those with living agents. About 35 of them were auditory experiences, and 9 were visual.

An example of an auditory experience of this kind was that of a grandmother whose granddaughter was staying with her and recovering from mumps and measles. The doctor had given a sedative and reported the child to be improving. In the night the grandmother was awakened by her own deceased mother's voice, saying, 'Do something for Sara, quick!' The child had developed pneumonia, and only by immediate action was her life saved.

An example of a visual case (with an auditory component) was that of an eighteen-year-old girl whose father, to whom she had been very close, had died three months before. She awoke one night and saw her father in the doorway. He said, 'Don't worry. Mama is going to the hospital, but she will be all right.' About two months later her mother had a very serious operation, but she survived and eventually came back to normal health.

The difference between these cases and the rest was one of the degree of complexity of the message. The imagery which the percipient would have to produce to cause them involved what one could call a higher level of dramatization than any of those with a living agent.

As already mentioned, in the production of psi hallucinations it appears that the incoming ESP information is diverted by a memory, or some comparable influence, so that the sense organs are stimulated and an auditory or visual sense experience involving the percipient's memory of the agent seems to result. It is as if the percipient were saying, as in the case of the woman whose ill grandmother in Wales came and sat on her bed, 'Grandmother is ill. I must see her here just as if she were present.' In these more complex cases, the percipient instead would have to say, for instance, 'Sara is worse and needs help at once; I must have my mother call and warn me as she used to warn me in crises.'

This added complexity of some of the cases with deceased agents was the only aspect noted that distinguished them from the rest. They could mean that the spirits of the deceased agents caused them, just as the simple direct interpretation would say. But this is not the only explanation. It also could be that only these few individual percipients were able to construct imagery so complex as to express their ESP messages. After all, these were exceptional cases, being only part of the entire 88, which in turn was only a small part of the entire list of 825 hallucinatory experiences.

The study of cases to determine the real meaning of the kind of experience that had been called apparitional could go no further than this with case material. It showed at least that the form of visual or auditory hallucination in itself does not imply, by any means, that spirit agency is involved or that apparitions represent the spirits of the deceased. Certainly most of them represent cases of ESP experiences expressed in pseudo-sensory terms. Whether or not in a few instances a discarnate influence is involved remains a possibility that could only be confirmed by a kind of experimental research not yet developed. In the meantime the likelihood is strong that this aspect of the naïve interpretation, like the rest of it, is wrong, and that all apparitional experiences have the same origin, and are ESP experiences couched in imagery that could not but be misinterpreted before the reality of the psi ability had been demonstrated.

If this is the conclusion almost certainly to be reached about the apparitional experiences that have puzzled human beings for so long, it, of course, removes them from any special bearing on the question of survival. And that in turn, no doubt, could seem to many to be the disproval of an inspiring myth, or worse still, it could shed an entirely negative light on one of the kinds of experience that has seemed to mean that man is more than a mechanical entity; that he has an indestructable spirit that survives the body's death.

Upon reflection, however, this attitude is a mistaken one. It could have been adopted (and perhaps was) just as logically when the earth was found to be a satellite of the sun, instead of a cozy little home made for man especially. It could have been adopted (and was) when the evolutionary origin of man was realized. If he was descended from animal ancestors, he was demoted from the 'grand origin of a special creation by God in the Garden of Eden. So, also, in other developments towards an understanding of man and his nature and place in the scheme of things. All of them could be decried for exploding myths that had sustained mankind.

Today, however, no one considers these now established advances of knowledge as negative or retrograde findings. Instead, each one has advanced humanity in many ways that could not have been foreseen. No intelligent person today would want to go back to the mental horizon of the cave men. More than that, no intelligent person would want to travel the wrong road to any goal. Everyone wants to travel the correct one, and most will no doubt agree that regardless of the outcome, the object of scientific inquiry is to separate the true and false, confident that the outcome will be the better for it.

In this case, the inquiry has shown man as able to exercise the psi ability to bring him information regardless of time or distance, and sometimes so to visualize it that his concept rivals that of nature herself. He still needs more knowledge, not less, to give him complete information about his own nature and capacities. L. E. R.

(See also CONSCIOUSNESS; MEDIUMS.) (Further reading: 200, 398, 464.)

Apportation, Apports

From French *apporter*, 'to bring', a phenomenon of mediumship, the apparent penetration of matter by objects, called apports, which seem to enter the seance room through walls, closed doors and windows; the objects are often reported to feel hot when they arrive. An asport is a reversed apport, an object which vanishes from the room and appears again outside. The Spiritualist explanation is that spirits dematerialize the objects outside the room and put them together again inside. A spirit named White Hawk said of his production of apported stones: 'I can only explain it by saying that I speed up the atomic vibrations until the stones are disintegrated. Then they are brought here and I slow down the vibrations until they become solid again' (16). The

movement of objects into and out of sealed rooms has also been a feature of some POLTERGEIST cases in which it is thought that PSYCHOKINESIS, the power of mind over matter, may be involved. An entertaining reported case of the apportation or TELEPORTATION of a human being was that of the engagingly named Mrs Samuel Guppy, a British apport medium of the 19th century who produced live lobsters and eels, and fresh flowers, fruit and vegetables apparently out of nowhere at her seances. She was sitting quietly doing her accounts in her home at Highbury in London when she was suddenly transported by spirits to 69 Lambs Conduit Street, where the spirits lowered her through the roof and ceilings, and deposited her with a bump on a table, her pen still in her hand and the ink on it still wet. Unfortunately, this occurred at a seance staged by a medium known to have been fraudulent (see 136).

Aquarian Age

The period expected by the astrologically-minded to begin somewhere about the year 2000 (estimates vary considerably and some say it has started already) in which the world will come under powerful influence from the beneficent zodiacal sign of Aquarius, the Water-Pourer, because as a result of the precession of the equinoxes the sun will be in that sign at the spring equinox (see ASTROLOGY): it is expected to be a golden age of peace, harmony, goodwill, international cooperation and general blessedness.

Aradia See LELAND.

Archetypes See JUNG.

José Arigó

The nickname of a Brazilian healer, José De Freitas, who is claimed to have performed hundreds of successful surgical operations, without anaesthetics and without causing pain, using unsterilized and homely instruments such as ordinary kitchen knives, nail scissors and tweezers. As a boy he experienced the presence of mysterious moving lights and heard a voice speaking to him in a strange language. His operations are performed under the direction of the spirit of 'Dr Fritz', a German surgeon killed in the First World War, and with assistance from other deceased medical men. (437, 510)

Armanen See Guido von LIST.

Asanas

Bodily postures in YOGA, many of which are believed to confer on the adept the powers

of the animals, plants or objects that they represent.

Asomatic Experiences See OUT-OF-THE-BODY EXPERIENCES.

Asport

A reversed 'apport': see APPORTATION.

Association of Invisible Aryans

A German occult society promoting the 'blood interests' of the 'Aryan Germanic race': led by Siegfried Adolf Kummer, author of *Heilige Runenmacht* (Holy Rune-Power), 1932, who believed that the RUNES, the old alphabet of northern Europe, contained magical power. He devised special runic Yoga exercises, recommended meditation on runes for the cure of disease, and in 1927 founded a Rune School to teach his theories.

Astral Body, Astral Plane

The physical world in which the natural experiences of sight and sound occur, does not constitute the sole area for the operation of the human being at all levels of his existence. Men in all countries and at all stages of culture have sought to penetrate into other regions of awareness that lie outside the scope of the ordinary faculties. There is believed to be another dimension, not so far amenable to explanation in scientific terms, of which it is possible to have first-hand experience. Saints and prophets have recorded their visits to places that have been as real to them as any location on the earthly map. St Paul speaks of a man he knew who, 'whether in the body or out of the body, God knoweth, was caught up into paradise and heard unspeakable words, which it is not lawful for a man to utter' (II Cor. xii, 3).

This is a universe beyond conception, which in its hidden planes holds all the heavens and all the hells. To this world the mystic ascends, to this world the shaman travels, here the ancestors of the tribal peoples live. It is a landscape of wondrous beauty, yet it can present a scene out of a nightmare. Popularly the existence of some such area beyond earthly geography is recognized in our assumption of a 'fourth dimension', and in talk about 'second sight' and a 'sixth sense' by which this dimension may be perceived.

Man functions at several levels, and at each level a different facet of his multiform being is brought into operation. There is his body, the tangible part of him that everyone accepts. The Greeks called the body *soma*, and equated it with a prison or tomb, because within it a non-physical element lay entrapped. There is something that animates this inert mass of bone and flesh, and gives it vitality, enabling man to function on the physical and physiological levels, an ability he shares with the animals. When he reasons, another aspect of his personality is revealed. But he also responds to higher impulses, and aspires to something that he recognizes, however dimly, as greater than himself. This has been expressed by saying, for what it is worth, that man has a soul.

After long centuries of speculation about the non-physical components of the human being, it is still difficult to define, or distinguish precisely between, such concepts as the soul, the spirit, and what the ancient Egyptians called the *ka* and *ba* (see plate, page 34), the Greeks called the *psyche* and *nous*, the Jews the *neshamah*, *ruah* and *nefesh*, the Muslims the *sirr*, *ruh* and *nafs*, the Hindus the *atman* and *jiva*, and medieval scholars the *anima divina* and *anima humana*, and the scores of other names by which these elusive elements have been christened by various peoples through the ages.

But cutting across the complex stratifications of all these notions is the simple theory of the astral body, the minimum concession sought by the occultist, which provides a workable hypothesis to account for a wide range of human phenomena, for which no acceptable explanation is forthcoming from any other source. With this theory occultists have tried to account for sleep and DREAMS, for various types of insanity, the epilepsies, multiple personality, visions and ecstatic states, and, for those who believe in such things, also POSSESSION, BILOCATION, THOUGHT-FORMS, ghosts (see APPARITIONS, MEDIUMS), vampires, and seance-room phenomena like ECTOPLASM, materialization and APPORTATION.

There is, besides, the ever-growing evidence of OUT-OF-THE-BODY EXPERIENCES among ordinary people in normal circumstances, who have suddenly become aware of themselves outside the physical frame. One man describes how, knocked down by a car, he felt himself rise from himself, a disembodied consciousness, and saw a crowd collecting around his prostrate form. Patients undergoing surgery have recorded the same experiences of shifting out of themselves and watching from a vantage point somewhere near the ceiling what was being done to their physical bodies. Ernest Hemingway, when hit by shrapnel in an Italian trench in the First World War, felt something emerging from his body, 'like you'd pull a silk handkerchief out of a pocket by one corner'.

The natural habitat of the astral body is the astral plane, and at times even the impulse of an accident is not required for it to detach itself and move away. People have described how, walking down a street or

Astral projection: the phantom body floating above its physical counterpart

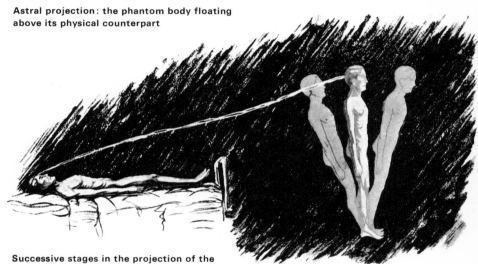

Successive stages in the projection of the phantom body

working in the garden, they have become briefly disembodied and sailed some distance off to observe themselves and others at their various occupations, before returning, after a few seconds, to reoccupy their physical bodies. Such ecsomatic (ex-somatic) experiences, where you find yourself outside your own body, incredible as they may seem to those who have never had them, are vouched for by people of integrity, and are today becoming increasingly accepted by many who were once sceptical, and are being earnestly studied by researchers.

Like the soul, the astral body has a vast nomenclature, each of its many names representing an attempt to describe one or other of its functions or attributes: the subtle body, the energy body, the nerve body, the vital body, the double, the mortal soul (as distinct from the immortal soul), the feeling or emotional body, the consciousness body, the dream body, the desire body, the thanatic body (the body that undergoes the experience of dying and the after-death state), the body of light, the luminous body. The astral body is visualized as an exact though non-material replica of the physical body, and in the waking state of the normal adult the two bodies are thought of as being exactly in alignment, when they are said to be 'in coincidence'.

Under certain circumstances the two bodies move out of alignment. Infants, for example, are normally in discoincidence. The very old, and the very weak and ill, tend to discoincide easily. Those who are under the influence of drink or DRUGS are to a greater or lesser degree also likely to get out of coincidence. At all such times, if in the waking state, the physical body operates in a kind of blur, and things are out of focus; there is a perceptible lack of coordination, a clumsiness of gait and gesture, a thickening of speech, and a loss of contact with the practicalities of everyday life.

During sleep, the body of the normal person discoincides naturally. The irresistible desire for sleep that overwhelms us all is explained by occultists as the natural urge on the part of the astral body to set itself free from the limitations of the flesh and take a breather 'out there'. While out there, its experiences may occasionally be projected to the mind as dreams, which however are usually distorted in transmission by the cerebral apparatus. According to some occultists, when the astral discoincides it remains attached to the physical body by a thin cord, and this cord, which some sensitives claim to be able to see, is the means by which contact and communication between the two bodies are maintained. At death the cord is severed and the astral freed permanently, much as the severed umbilical cord frees the infant from the mother's womb.

Astral Projection

Against the background of this belief, the astral plane may be defined as the area where the higher occult experiences take place. When for any reason the astral body moves out of coincidence it enters into the plane of another dimension. Many of the experiences that take place there during involuntary discoincidence may be only dimly remembered, and if remembered at all their significance may not be understood. Men have therefore sought for some means whereby the separated astral body can bring back to the waking consciousness a clear remembrance of its sojourn on the astral plane. In occult parlance, the occultist ascends the planes (there is more than one plane) by a special ritual procedure that can be taught to those who are fit to receive the teaching. The principle of training in this technique is deliberately to project the astral out of coincidence while retaining full consciousness of what occurs to it thereafter. One therefore ascends to the astral plane in full consciousness, since the link between normal consciousness and astral awareness remains unbroken.

There are several ways of achieving astral projection. In one, you lie down, shut the eyes and relax; then imagine yourself standing up at the foot of the bed and watching your recumbent form. Visualization is the key to this method; it must be intensified and sustained, and then the consciousness transferred until it actually moves out of the body and joins the watcher. Another, more difficult, method is to work out a prearranged dream before going to sleep, and then, just before actually falling asleep, 'step into the dream'. Still another is to lie still, concentrate on the toe of one foot until it begins to tingle, then draw the tingling sensation to

the other toes, then shift to the other foot until both feet are tingling. Slowly work your way up the ankles, knees, hips, stomach, chest, arms, neck and head so that you feel the whole body buzzing. Suddenly you will find yourself floating. With those who are constitutionally prone to discoincide the astral will project without much difficulty, but in most cases it might take months, indeed years, of practice.

The interiorization of the astral, that is, its return to the body, is easy and leisurely when you wake up in the morning after a good night's rest. If for some reason you are suddenly awakened, coincidence is instantaneous. It can return with 'lightning-like speed'. If the astral does return in a hurry, the physical body receives a jolt at the moment of coupling that can cause palpitations and a brief feeling of panic. In many parts of the world, therefore, it is thought that a sleeping man should never be awakened suddenly in case his 'soul' is unable to return in time, or returns too violently and kills the body.

The astral world is a place of many mansions, with topographical features of bewildering variety. A few small areas, however, have been painstakingly mapped out, and these constitute the field of operation for various occult schools. The secret work of most esoteric orders, both Eastern and Western, is based on the knowledge of these inner planes, and each school teaches the 'geography' of the particular planes of its specialization, together with a description of the inhabitants, their dwellings, the language they speak. One does not proceed haphazardly along the planes. A strict protocol must be observed and each plane has its own procedures.

When a student is first initiated, he is taught the rituals of his grade, along with the appropriate invocations, the names of the guardian angels, and the colours, scents and other symbols pertaining to the planes. He is forewarned about the vengeful demons who menace the thresholds of each plane, and is armed with protective formulas and banishing rituals in case of need. The type of initiation varies with the stage of the student's advancement, and with the type of occult training given in the school. Some esoteric orders use religious symbols, and the progress of the candidate is linked with his moral conduct so that there is no deviation from the accepted religious and social code. The black magical schools, on the other hand, resort to drugs and perverse sexual rites, and abjure religion.

An adept of a sorcerous school can enjoy what is called *congressus subtilis*, which is sexual intercourse, while in the astral body,

with the astral or physical body of another person. It is believed possible to attract the astral bodies of living persons while their physical bodies are asleep and to unite with them in sexual congress. Certain modern magicians, like the Abbé Louis Van Haecke (d. 1828) and the Abbé Joseph-Antoine BOULLAN (d. 1893), have claimed to be able to teach pupils how to use the astral bodies of persons both living and dead for sexual pleasure.

References to the astral body are found scattered in ancient writings. The procedures described in the Egyptian *Book of the Dead* are said to be methods for helping the soul of a deceased person to obviate the perils he may encounter in the next world. While ostensibly meant for the spirits of the dead, they are regarded by many occultists as rituals intended, not for dead souls, but for initiates proceeding on the planes. A death-and-resurrection rite forms part of many occult initiations. The *Book of the Dead* provides formulas for greeting the gods, and also gives the correct responses to the various demon entities who haunt and bar the way. One has to confront the crocodile and the serpent, and parley with and cajole the guardians of the underworld gates. There are spells to assist travel in the barque of the sun-god, spells to prevent a person from walking with his head downwards, and formulas to help the soul to return to earth.

The Hidden Centres

In all rituals the object of ascending the planes is to establish contact with and explore another dimension. Certain occultists have described this dimension as the region of the astral light, invisible to our sight but of exceeding brightness, and full of creative potency. Before the Fall, Adam was said to have 'heard the Light speak'. In physical terms, this dimension is described as a tingling web of vibrations which sends ceaseless pulsations interweaving through the cosmos. Because of this web, which forms the fabric of the universe, all things are interconnected. Because of this web, nothing is ever lost, and somewhere in its tapestry every single thought, word and act is permanently captured and enmeshed. Occultists speak of the etheric record or AKASHIC RECORD (from the Sanskrit word *akasha*, 'ether'), which contains the whole history of the world from its creation. Men of high degree are said to be able to penetrate into the past, journeying on these radiations and scanning the events of long-lost ages.

Man himself is part of this web. His body is a microcosm, a miniature universe or specialized segment of the general structure, and as such he is in contact with everything that exists around him. We are in the midst of a seething ocean of constantly interacting events, but are fortunately insulated against its full impact. A merciful Providence has given us ears to keep out the cacophony of this other world, eyes to blind us to much that is happening about us, and a brain to filter the tide of impressions which would otherwise flood and overwhelm us.

But at the same time the physical body contains certain built-in centres which provide entry for occult potencies. The theory that there occurs an actual intrusion of the astral world into these centres, which provide the point of contact and the medium of communication between two worlds, forms the basis of much occult teaching. Like the astral body itself, and the astral plane on which it operates, the hidden centres are invisible. Each centre consists of a plexus of vibrations, and in the Hindu system of occult physiology such plexuses are known as CHAK-RAS (Sanskrit, 'wheels'). The conscious activation of these chakras is the mode by which the astral plane is explored.

Rising on the Planes

Although a number of Western occultists employ the chakra system, many others favour ascending the planes by means of the sefirotic tree, derived from the Jewish CABALA. According to the cabalists the world was created through a series of ten emanations or outpourings from God, each stage of the series constituting a sefira. In their totality these ten sefiroth comprise the universe in its entirety. The ten sefiroth are arranged diagrammatically in the shape of a tree. When inscribed on paper the tree is shown as being on a single plane, but in reality the sefiroth are in different levels, representing different 'worlds'.

Rising on the planes consists in ascending from the lowest sefira upwards stage by stage towards the higher. Although ten in number, the sefiroth through their interconnections form twenty-two paths, and progression along these paths constitutes the experience of ascent or descent. The ten sefiroth and the twenty-two paths make up a series of thirty-two linked stages on the tree. Here again a vast and highly charged pattern of correspondence has evolved around the sefiroth. They are associated with deities, archangels, demons, bodily correspondences, virtues, vices, TAROT cards, colours, numbers, plants and animals, and many other categories of objects and qualities. The symbols for each sefira must be learned so that the grade of one's ascent can be recognized by the symbols appropriate to it.

The early stage of occult training is very complex, demanding great powers of concentration and a considerable degree of meditative competence. Once the association patterns have been mastered and the subconscious enriched by the symbolism of the path, the pupil has long sessions of 'brooding among the symbols', without any attempt at this stage to proceed in any direction, and during this period of free and relaxed musing the astral body is gradually loosed and advances to the point for which he has been initiated.

Once on the move the astral consciousness again requires careful direction. There are several ways of progressing along the planes, descriptively called by such names as the 'lightning flash', where the path zigzags; the 'flaming arrow', where the movement is straight along the trunk of the tree; or the 'fiery serpent', which winds upward. Whatever course is chosen the procedure is strictly laid down beforehand. It is futile and even dangerous to attempt to tread a path for which one has not been duly prepared.

Whether it is possible or not to reach the topmost plexus, if one follows the chakra system, or the topmost sefira in cabalism, is disputable. In any case it is extremely rare. Hindu texts describe in exuberant terms the wonderful feeling that pervades the spirit on reaching the last chakra situated just above the crown of the head: it is the Great Bliss, the Final Revelation, the Divine Union, the Infinite Light. Cabalists too have described a parallel experience, and speak of going into a profound trance and communicating with angelic beings on the higher planes. The ultimate stage is known as the *mors osculi*, the 'death of the kiss', whereby the soul, transported to a supra-mundane realm, experiences a bliss of so great an intensity that the body suffers a kind of death.

Sages of the Hasidic sect of Jews refer to a kind of death 'that is as difficult as putting a rope through a ring on a tall mast, and there is a death as easy as pulling a hair out of milk, and this is called the death in the kiss'. The Renaissance scholar Pico della Mirandola (d. 1494) wrote: 'The learned cabalists have written that many of the patriarchs of old, including Abraham, Isaac, Jacob, Moses, Aaron and Elijah, died in a state of spiritual rapture, that is they died beneath the death of the kiss'. The English writer and mystic Thomas Vaughan (d. 1666) mentions the *mors osculi* in passing but does not describe it because it is a matter 'of which', he says, 'I must not speak one syllable'.

The Feast of Demons

But besides the divine ecstasy that awaits the advanced adept on the astral planes, experiences of indescribable anguish are also possible on the lower levels. Some of these occur through unforeseen encounters, but some are deliberately sought by the student in order to strengthen the fibre of his spirit when faced with the denizens of the inner planes and to learn at first hand what they are capable of doing. The astral body may receive frightful injuries and may even be torn apart and disintegrated in the process, in which case the student may never have the courage to venture forth again. If on the other hand he emerges victorious he is promised power over these beings while on earth. In Western occultism the terror-forms who haunt the inner planes are given such titles as the Headless One, the Dread One, the Destroyer, the Tearer, the Consumer of Souls, or are named after Mesopotamian, Canaanite and other ancient demons.

In the Tibetan rite of *chod*, or 'cutting', the highly trained adept invites elemental beings to feast on his body. It is a terrifying rite and the whole operation is carried out on the astral plane, and with full awareness on the part of the practitioner. It is always performed at night and alone, in a cremation ground, cemetery or other solitude where he is not likely to be disturbed. He executes a bizarre hopping and whirling dance and intones a mantra (see MANDALAS) in wild gibberish, inviting the demons to come and partake of the feast that is being offered. Slowly spirit forms appear in answer to the invitation, and one of them, usually a hideous demoness, advances on the adept with a sword, and cleaves his body apart, rips out his heart and viscera and rends his limbs. With cries of ghoulish triumph the other demons pounce on the victim, tear off pieces of his flesh and drink his blood. Throughout the feast the adept himself undergoes the agony of his sacrifice, for he feels all that is happening to him. When the spirits depart his astral body slowly returns to wholeness.

A modern occultist, Victor NEUBURG, who was a friend and disciple of Aleister CROWLEY, has left a record of his adventures on the planes that are reminiscent of these terrible Tibetan rites. He describes himself being drawn into whirlpools and funnelled through vast swirling abysses, and having encounters with strange phantoms. Once he meditated on himself according to the ritual of the 'Bornless One' and met the archangel Gabriel, whom he describes as being dressed in white with green spots on his wings. He rose on the planes and was crucified by two angels. Then he was attacked by a Red Giant against whom all his weapons were powerless. He was hacked to pieces and driven back to his own body. 'I had great difficulty', he writes in his *Magical Diary*, 'in rearranging myself in my body.' In one confrontation with a virgin priestess his hands and feet were cut off and he was sacrificed upon an altar; the priestess then pronounced certain formulas and he rose again, glorified.

All such adventures take place in a world of their own, with long vistas like a surrealist landscape, peopled by Egyptian gods, denizens of the Hindu underworld, and the nightmarish beings one sees in fever or delirium. Voices are heard, or rather overheard, that seem to speak in the background; just outside the border of sound, threatening or cajoling. Such descriptions might be found duplicated almost word for word from the visions of people under the influence of LSD or mescaline.

Like other borderland experiences, astral experiences have in the past tended to be dismissed as hallucinatory, or explained away as recollections of some archaic memory from the collective unconscious, vivid dramatizations of deep-seated fears, or visualizations of secret wishes, all entirely subjective and not worth taking seriously. But increasingly today the challenge that the subject presents is being met by another line of approach: 'If it's all in the mind, let's know more about this mind.' The revelation might lead to a new mysticism. B. W.

(See also RITUAL MAGIC.) (Further reading: *64, 162, 195, 279, 340, 373, 501.*)

Astrology

Astrology may be loosely defined as 'the study of the real or pretended relationships between the heavens and the earth'. It is one of the oldest and most widespread of human activities and interests. A recognizable astrology played an integral part in every highly developed civilization of the past – Egyptian, Babylonian, Greek, Indian, Chinese, Muslim, Mayan. Though very much alive today, there has probably never been a time in which astrology has been so grossly misunderstood.

On the one hand, a vast audience follows the daily horoscope in the newspapers and believes astrology to be a more or less valid system of fortune-telling. On the other, a united body of sceptics comprising the 'educated public' believes astrology to be absolutely without foundation, a superstitious attempt by primitive man to read order into an essentially chaotic and meaningless universe, and to stave off the unknown through bogus divination.

But a study of astrology soon shows it to be more complex than either believers or sceptics allow. Like religion or art, astrology is multi-faceted and many-levelled. Just as it is pointless to discuss the religion of the Jesus Freaks alongside the religion of Meister Eckhardt, or to talk about a pop song in the same terms as a Beethoven quartet, so it is futile to try to deal with astrology as though

A magician, in his circle of astrological symbols, controlling a demon

it were all of a piece. The astrology that occupies space in the daily paper bears little relationship to the sophisticated symbolic astrology that attracted so many of the great minds of the past. Men such as Plato, Pythagoras, St Thomas Aquinas, and Johann Kepler accepted astrology not as a means of foretelling the future but as a symbolic master-plan of the structure and functioning of the universe that satisfied their inner experience. It is interesting that, in recent years, modern physical science has discovered many relationships and correlations between celestial and terrestrial events: relationships an earlier generation of authorities would have flatly declared impossible. Modern astrologers maintain that these discoveries are sufficiently numerous and sufficiently telling to acquit astrology of the charge of outright superstition and to make it again worthy of serious consideration, at least as far as its principles are concerned.

Underlying Principles

Fundamental to astrology is the assumption that the universe is unaccidental; a manifestation of Divine Will, ordered and coherent and therefore susceptible of interpretation. Astrology has always been considered a key toward such interpretation.

The reasoning behind the astrological method is analogical rather than logical, perhaps best and most commonly expressed in the saying 'As above, so below'. The universe is conceived of as an interrelated whole, an immense spiritual organism in which each part relates to every other part. The solar system, in astrology, is not a chance agglomeration of stellar matter, but a sentient, organized cosmos, whose operation is inextricably entwined with that of the earth, and of man and everything related to him on the earth.

Unmodern as this manner of hierarchical thinking may seem, it is the focus more than the manner that is responsible. The pathologist who, regarding evidence of an excessive flow of adrenalin, concludes that the absent patient is angry or disturbed, is operating in similar fashion to the astrologer who, studying the horoscope of an unseen child born with the planet Mars in the constellation of Scorpio, and badly 'aspected', concludes that this individual will tend to be violent, sensual and domineering, indeed, subject to excessive flows of adrenalin. Perhaps the chief difference lies in the ease with which the pathologist can test and control his conclusions and the extreme difficulty for the astrologer of doing the same.

In astrology, the constellations and planets are credited with differing 'characters' corresponding to the different functions or processes they are supposed to control or symbolize. Everyone is familiar with the qualities supposed to be visited upon the individual by his 'Sun sign', that is, the constellation against which the Sun appears to rise on any given birthday. The individual born under Aries is supposed to tend to hot-headedness, impulsiveness, assertiveness; the individual born under Taurus to conservativeness, patience, deliberation, and so on.

Critics of astrology believe that ancient priests and astrologers arrived at these characteristics through sham empiricism and fanciful imagination, and assume them to be without foundation. But in fact fancy and accident played no part whatever in their development. The characteristics of the constellations and planets are derived from numerical considerations and depend upon the meaning allegedly inherent in number – a type of thought usually associated with Pythagoras.

The Pythagorean approach makes it possible to investigate qualities, functions and processes systematically. If numbers are viewed as neutral abstractions this cannot be done at all, nor can logic or reason aid in the understanding of the processes that invest the physical world with 'life' – birth, growth, assimilation, fecundation, death, renewal.

The number one, in all developed philosophical and religious systems, represents unity or the Absolute. It is the conscious and deliberate scission or division of the Absolute that is held to account for the manifested universe. The first quality or function to result from this scission is polarity, represented by the number two, and familiar as man-woman, active-passive, positive-negative.

But polarity is fundamentally static, a tension of opposing forces. Before anything can 'happen', relationship or interaction must be possible. The number three represents this possibility. Man-woman is not a relationship, but man-woman-desire is. To take a chemical example, sodium-chlorine is not a relationship, but sodium-chlorine-affinity is. The artist and the canvas are insufficient to produce a picture, there must be a third term: inspiration.

Yet a relationship of three terms remains potential; three terms are insufficient to account for the fact of matter, of substance. Sodium-chlorine-affinity is not yet salt. To account for salt four terms are required, sodium-chlorine-affinity and then salt itself. Thus the meaning of the number four is substantiality or matter, and it is this that lies behind the old notion of the four elements. The four elements represent the constituent *principles* of matter, not their chemistry (see also NUMEROLOGY).

Through number, all the functions, processes and qualities that we experience in the

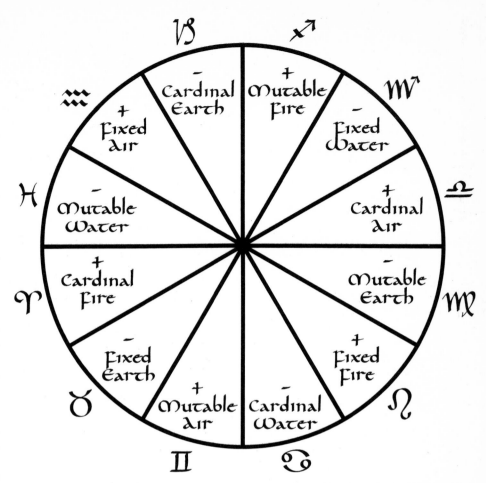

The zodiac divided into polarities, quadruplicities and triplicities

physical world can be accounted for. A system of twelve terms is required, and it is this twelve-term system that lies at the root of Western astrology with its zodiac of twelve signs. (Eastern astrology is based upon a related but somewhat different numerical system, with different emphases.)

Thus the meanings ascribed to the various signs of the zodiac and to the planets do not result from fancy but are dictated by number, and the choice of Ram, Bull, Twins, Crab and the rest occurs because the given symbol best represented the qualities, functions and processes inherent in the given numerical position.

In astrology, the signs are first distinguished by polarities; Aries is positive, Taurus is negative, and so on. Simultaneously, they are divided into quadruplicities, called 'modes of action': cardinal (instigator of action), fixed (that which is acted upon), mutable (that which facilitates the action). Finally, again simultaneously, they are divided into triplicities, corresponding to the four elements of fire, earth, air and water, represented by a set of three signs each.

Thus each sign has an inescapably different character, while in this twelve-term

system all combinations of two, three, and four are played out (see figure above). The zodiac may be seen therefore as the symbolic chart upon which all the world's forces interact. And it is this systematic symbolic method that lies behind the simple-minded generalizations in the daily papers. Aries is 'hot-headed and impulsive' because, as the first sign of the zodiac, it is positive, cardinal, fire. And Pisces is 'reclusive, mystical, receptive' because, as the last sign, it is negative, mutable, water.

The Horoscope

The horoscope or 'map of the hour' is the astrologer's chief operational aid. It is a symbolic representation of the zodiac of twelve constellations containing within it all possibilities. The Sun, Moon and planets act within or upon the zodiac, and their positions in the various signs as well as their positions relative to each other are said to determine or to represent the nature of any given moment. Thus a child born at any given moment is believed to partake of the nature of that moment – it is not so much that he is 'influenced' by the position of the planets as that he is, himself, of the nature that their positions represent (see also SYNCHRONICITY). With recent discoveries of the highly charged electromagnetic nature of what was thought to be mere empty space, it becomes legitimate to revive the ancient and medieval analogy of the 'music of the spheres'. The solar system maintains a constantly changing vibratory state analogous to music; a child born shares in the vibratory nature of that moment, and astrology claims to be able to ascertain more or less accurately, in human terms, its meaning.

No attempt is made here to show how to cast a horoscope. (See the bibliography for literature on this subject.) And because a detailed list of the meanings of signs and planets is useless without a horoscope to study them against, it will also be omitted. This article concerns itself with the principles of interpretation, rather than with interpretation *per se*.

Because the earth revolves about the Sun once a year, the Sun appears to make a circle of the zodiac. The constellation or sign against which the sun appears to rise on the day of birth is the familiar 'Sun sign', the 'I'm a Gemini, are you a Leo?' of cocktail conversations. The Sun sign is held to be the most important single factor in the horoscope – the Sun representing the activating or creative principle.

Because the earth turns on its own axis once a day, there is a second daily cycle of the zodiac. The sign against which the eastern horizon is found at the moment of birth is called the 'rising sign' and the sunrise point itself is called the 'ascendant'. This is held to be the second most important single factor in the interpretation of a horoscope. The ascendant determines a further twelve-fold division of the horoscope into 'houses', corresponding in significance to the twelve constellations. In a very general way it may be said that the Sun, Moon and planets in their signs represent a man's essential character, while the position of the ascendant and the planets within the houses represents what he will tend to do with that character. Thus a man born with Aries as his Sun sign and with his ascendant also in Aries would tend to behave significantly differently from a man born at nearly the same time, but with a Pisces ascendant. In the former case, Arian tendencies would be reinforced, while in the latter they would tend to manifest themselves through Piscean channels.

In judging a horoscope, the astrologer also takes into account the Moon, the second most important body, and all the planets. To each planet is ascribed a set 'character', but that character produces differing effects depending upon the sign in which it is found – just as an actor giving a set speech will produce an effect that differs considerably according to the lighting employed. So Mars in Scorpio is believed to convey or to stimu-late a tendency to violence and sensuality, while Mars in Libra provokes refinement and a capacity to cooperate.

Further, the relationships between the planets are taken into account. At certain specific angles, planets are said to be in 'aspect' to each other. For fundamentally numerological reasons, these aspects are held to be harmonious or inharmonious. Thus a man born with Mars at a 90° angle to the Sun – an inharmonious 'square' – will differ from a man born with Mars at a 120° angle, the harmonious 'trine'. And by the same token, the signs in which the aspects operate must be considered: an Aries–Cancer square will manifest itself differently from a Taurus–Leo square.

The above constitute the main areas of horoscope interpretation – though the working astrologer will take in many other subtler considerations simultaneously. Apart from the self-evident complexity of the task, it is further complicated by the inescapable individuality of the horoscope. For not until the earth has 'precessed' through the twelve signs of the zodiac will any given configuration of planets recur. This precession, caused by the wobble of the earth upon its axis, gives rise to the familiar 'Ages': the Age of Aquarius, Age of Pisces, and so on. A cycle of ages takes over 25,000 years and is called the Great, or Platonic Year.

Satisfying as it may be from a moral, aesthetic and philosophical point of view, the built-in individuality of the individual presents insoluble problems, particularly to those who would like to see astrology placed upon an acceptable scientific basis. If, for example, a scientist wants to put astrological claims to the test, and to find out what – if anything – Mars in Scorpio actually signifies, it would not do simply to take a test group of all people born with Mars in Scorpio, since the multitude of mitigating and contingent factors would make it impossible to isolate whatever Mars–Scorpio effects there might be. If, on the other hand, a test group was selected comprising sufficiently similar horoscopes to make effects detectable in theory, then that test group would tend to be too small to be acceptable to science.

For similar reasons, this makes astrology extraordinarily difficult to teach as other subjects are usually taught, or to explain. When the astrology textbook maintains that Mars in Scorpio brings forth a powerful, passionate character, determined, self-reliant, indomitable, authoritative, this does not mean that everyone with Mars in Scorpio (which would amount to one out of every twelve people) would conform to such a description, but rather that given support from other aspects in the horoscope, Mars in Scorpio would incline to these traits, and may appear the dominant force.

In the study of astrology, the multitude of meanings – Sun signs, rising sign, planets within the signs, aspects between the planets, polarities, modes, the four elements – can only be explained as though each existed in isolation, and yet can only be applied while simultaneously bearing the whole in mind. Thus, the rational mind cannot interpret a horoscope; this must be accomplished through the exercise of understanding – which alone is capable of such an act of synthesis. And it is this that makes astrology so inimical to that common modern cast of mind that would reduce the universe to rational explanation, all else being discounted as no more than superstition or pseudo-problem.

Types of Astrology

The astrology that concerns itself with analysing the character and predicting the future of the individual on the basis of the horoscope is called natal, or genethliacal astrology. But if the analogical and organic type of thinking peculiar to astrology has any validity, then other areas of inquiry ought to be susceptible to astrological interpretation as well. There are two main types commonly employed.

Mundane astrology concerns itself with large-scale phenomena – wars, natural cataclysms, the fat years and the lean, and long-term political and psychological trends. The theory is that, just as the various planets and signs are supposed to symbolize and 'influence' the various parts and organs of the body, so the whole of the earth is divided into areas of affinity and influence. Moreover, corporations, nations and races are held to represent more-or-less recognizable spiritual organisms or entities – which makes a kind of intuitive if not rational sense (even the most insensitive tourist knows that the Germans are different from the French who in turn are different from the Spanish). It sometimes seems that the typology of astrology can account for these differences more satisfactorily than anything in history or sociology. But, unfortunately, casting a horoscope for a nation, or a race, or even a corporation is a perilous enterprise, and conclusions drawn from such a horoscope are even less justifiable and demonstrable than those drawn from a birth horoscope.

Nevertheless, it appears that mundane astrology antedates the more familiar natal sort. The earliest known horoscope dates back only to the 5th century B.C., while it is known that astrologers in Babylon were making mundane predictions much earlier. The temples and monuments of ancient

Astrology under the Moghuls of India in the early 17th century

Egypt were erected and inaugurated according to astrological considerations as well. Unfortunately, nothing is known of the methods employed by these early mundane astrologers. But since the structure and coherence of astrology invalidates the premise that it was developed empirically and willy-nilly by imaginative priests, it is at least conceivable that in the past a valid mundane astrology existed, the letter or spirit of which has been lost.

The third type of astrology, horary astrology, is based upon the analogous theory that the horoscope of any given moment determines the meaning of that moment, not only insofar as it applies to a child born at that time but to anything whatsoever that is 'born'. Thus a question may be asked and a chart erected for the moment of inquiry, making horary astrology a sort of astrological I CHING.

Modern Evidence for Astrology

In practice, astrology today scarcely differs from that of Claudius Ptolemy (2nd century A.D.), whose astrological manual is the earliest extant. And though all serious modern astrologers agree that modern astrology is inadequate, and rife with assumptions that are difficult to verify, still all continue to believe that astrology is based upon truth.

In support of this conviction, they call attention to an accruing body of evidence from the physical sciences, evidence for the most part discovered inadvertently by scientists, not by astrologers.

In 1950, Michel Gauquelin, a Sorbonne-trained statistician, set out to disprove claims to have statistically proved astrology, made by certain French astrologers. Gauquelin showed that these claims rested upon naïve and faulty statistical method, but in the course of his disproof he encountered discrepancies within his own data that could not be explained away. Pressing his examination further, and working with large and acceptable test groups, Gauquelin discovered a correlation between the position of the planets at birth (roughly corresponding to the ascendant and the 'angles' of traditional astrology) and the profession later chosen by eminent men from a variety of distinct professions – including scientists, athletes, military men, clerics, and actors among others. Against odds often reaching millions to one against chance, Gauquelin found that scientists were likely to be born with Saturn on the ascendant or one of the angles, while soldiers and athletes tended to be born with Mars there.

Gauquelin's methods could not be faulted, but initially critics believed that, despite the prodigious odds, he had merely uncovered a national fluke, since his categories were all derived from French personnel. A repetition

of the initial experiment using data from four other European countries supported the original findings. In every case, though with varying but generally high degrees of significance, positions of the planets at birth corresponded to the professions later chosen by eminent men. The test groups now numbered many thousands, the patterns drawn from the data all supported each other, and the final conclusion was that by no stretch of the imagination could chance be held to account for Gauquelin's results.

In most, if not all, instances Gauquelin's work also bore out favourite astrological axioms. Thus, Saturn was important for scientists, Mars for soldiers and athletes, Jupiter for actors. Subsequent work by Gauquelin has shown planetary relationships between parents and children, and many other correlations that can only be explained in terms of astrology.

Recognizing the value of statistics as a tool for astrological research, a number of astrologers have studied statistical techniques, and there now exists a body of statistical evidence in a variety of fields attesting the existence of astrological relationships and correlations: between rainfall and the phases of the moon, in cases of longevity, and in susceptibility to specific diseases, among others.

Physical Evidence

Apart from statistical evidence, astrologers

also cite the many celestial-terrestrial correlations discovered by physical science. Oysters open and close their shells according to tidal rhythms. To test if this was caused by the action of the tide itself, or by the moon, Dr Frank O. Brown of Northwestern University took oysters from the Atlantic and moved them in darkened pans to Illinois. Within a fortnight, the oysters had adjusted their opening and closing rhythm to what the tide would have been had there been a tide in Illinois, proving that it was the moon, exercising an influence undetectable to the instruments of science, that caused the oysters to open and close their shells, and not the tidal action itself.

In a long series of careful experiments, Brown also showed lunar and solar rhythms to operate under a wide variety of circumstances with a wide variety of organisms. A rat in a darkened cage was twice as active when the invisible moon was above the horizon as when it was below it. The rate of growth of beans and potatoes varies according to extra-terrestrial rhythms. Similar findings have come from experiments in inorganic chemistry. Dr Giorgio Piccardi of Florence University has discovered that the speed at which chemical precipitates form varies according to extra-terrestrial conditions.

Working with emotionally disturbed patients, Dr Leonard J. Ravitz of Duke University showed that the electrical potential of their bodies changed according to the phases of the moon, and moreover, that the amount of change was greatest in those patients who were most disturbed – corroborating the ancient link between the moon and lunacy.

A considerable body of evidence also exists linking earthly phenomena with sunspots, the huge magnetic storms upon the surface of the sun. A Russian scientist, Dr A. K. Podshibyakin, has found that road accidents increase by as much as four-fold on the day after a solar flare. And this discovery has been supported by independent studies in a number of European cities showing an increase not only in accident rates but in other forms of violence, such as suicide and crime.

Most interesting from an astrological point of view is the related evidence of John H. Nelson, a radio engineer, who has discovered that magnetic disturbance in the earth's atmosphere (which corresponds to the incidence of solar flares) can be predicted according to the conjunctions and aspects formed by the major planets. When the planets line up in the traditionally 'inharmonious' angles, magnetic disturbance is strongest; when they line up in traditionally 'harmonious' angles, weakest.

Finally, there is the vast accumulation of cycles evidence. It has been found in thousands of instances that phenomena on earth follow cyclical patterns corresponding to the rise and fall of the number of sunspots. Salmon catches in Canada, the price of pig iron, the number of marriages in St Louis and the incidence of specific diseases, among many other phenomena, have been found to follow cyclical patterns. And though a planetary link to the incidence of sunspots has long been suspected, it has only recently been found. It can now be shown that the conjunctions and aspects of the planets correspond to the rise and fall of sunspots, and are therefore inescapably connected to the wealth of earthly phenomena that have been shown to be cyclical in nature.

Astrologers do not claim that these discoveries of science alleviate the inadequacies of present-day astrology, but they do claim that the evidence supporting the validity of the *fundamental premise* of astrology is now overwhelming, and that there can be no doubt today that events in the heavens correspond to events on earth. Astrologers believe that a revival of legitimate astrological research could help mankind toward a better understanding of the higher laws that govern the universe, but at present, in view of astrology's standing in scientific and academic circles, such a revival cannot be predicted with confidence. J. A. W.

(Further reading: *29, 35, 95, 179, 248, 317, 318, 498*: for the casting and interpretation of a horoscope, see *78, 79, 80, 315*.)

Atavisms
Factors deep in the unconscious mind which, according to occult theory, are survivals of man's pre-human ancestry, legacies from the time of creatures part man and part beast: Austin Osman SPARE believed that he had devised a method of conjuring up these energies and desires in visible form, usually intensely horrific: see SPIRITS AND FORCES.

Atlantis
Atlantis has been a name to conjure with since Plato wrote the *Critias* and the *Timaeus*. According to Plato the legend of the lost continent was discovered by the Athenian lawgiver Solon at Sais in Egypt. An old priest deciphered a papyrus which spoke of how there had once been a large continent 'beyond the Pillars of Hercules', which had been punished for its impiety with destruction. There had been a royal island, or Basileia, on which stood the castle of the Atlantean kings and a temple dedicated to the sea-god. Here the Atlanteans had mined an unknown metal called orichalc. From the

very first the idea of Atlantis has been associated with the legendary and the occult. Scarcely more than a legend itself – though the scientific arguments about it, based on geology and diffusion of cultures, are unending – Atlantis is associated even in its first recorded appearance with man's search for hidden wisdom. For Solon's seeking in Egypt represents the perennial search of the Greek world and its successors for the lost knowledge that the world possessed in the Golden Age – if one chooses to believe, as many Atlantologists have chosen – before the Flood.

Speculation about Atlantis has occupied every age since the Renaissance, but grew during the 18th century with the type of antiquarianism which delighted in discovering the religion of the DRUIDS from three or four classical references and an acquaintance with the Hermetic revival of the century before. In 1882 Ignatius DONNELLY published his *Atlantis, or the Antediluvian World*, which gave the fullest expression to the theory in terms of Victorian science. This work greatly influenced Madame BLAVATSKY and her disciple Walter Scott-Elliot, who incorporated Atlantis into their occult synthesis. In her book *The Secret Doctrine* (1888) the founder of the THEOSOPHICAL SOCIETY attempted to provide a counter to the theories of Darwin and the evolutionists. Atlantis happened to tally with her argument; for Madame Blavatsky's theory was that several races had lived on the earth before humanity as it is now known. Of these the fourth vanished race had its home in Atlantis. From this encirclement by the occult it has rarely been possible to extricate the Atlantis of Plato.

Rudolf STEINER used clairvoyant vision to elaborate on the arguments of earlier Theosophists. From the impression that events made on the permanent AKASHIC RECORD, Steiner claimed to be able to describe what had taken place in Atlantis. The Atlanteans had thought in pictures, possessed extraordinary memories and used the energy latent in plants to drive airships. The most evolved among them were gathered together in Central Asia by a great leader and subjected to a process of spiritual refinement with the object of making them understand the divine powers. From this group were descended the early priest-kings of the Aryans.

Atlantis and the Master Race
The involvement of the Aryan race betrays precisely where the idea of Atlantis had gravitated within the pull of the occult. For in their efforts to provide a convincing alternative to the threat of materialism,

Madame Blavatsky and her successors had incorporated into their occult synthesis the ideas of the school of thought known as the Diffusionists. These theorists were concerned with the wanderings of primitive peoples throughout the world, which they attempted to trace through the evidence of archaeology. A favourite theory in the early days had been that all culture had spread from one spot on the earth's surface – for which the religious naturally read the Garden of Eden. It was a short step from speculation of this sort to theories of racial superiority: the idea of cultural diffusion gave added sanction to claims that one race was the supreme bearer of civilization. It is within this context that the Nazi obsession with Atlantis can be understood.

Certain predecessors of the Nazi movement were known as the *Völkische* – the 'folkish' movement – and they contained a large sprinkling of occultists and near-occultists. In the chaos and distress of Germany after the First World War, there was an amazing boom in occultism of all sorts, sometimes coupled with politics in the fashion of the *Völkische*. Of the leaders of the Nazi party, Hitler, Himmler, Hess and Rosenberg were all to some degree affected by occultism, but after the party came to power, such preoccupations were mostly dropped as not helpful to the business of iron government. However, some of the *völkisch* thinkers did survive into the Third Reich, for it was quite easy to combine certain forms of occult speculation with the myth of the master race. And, of course, Atlantis appeared as the original home of the Aryan supermen.

In Alfred Rosenberg's *The Myth of the 20th Century*, which had sold over a million copies by 1944, this idea found its most famous exposition. 'These waves of Atlantean people travelled by water on their swan and dragon ships into the Mediterranean to Africa; by land over Central Asia to Kutschka, indeed perhaps even to China, across North America to the south of that continent.' It was crucial to Rosenberg's Atlantis that it lay in the far north, for he went on to explain various symbols of Middle Eastern religion as based on primitive memories of the Arctic sun.

The *Myth of the 20th Century* was published in 1930: in October of the following year an exhibition of trance paintings dealing with Atlantis was on view in Berlin. Rosenberg was merely part of a widespread current of opinion among the *völkisch* elements. For example, Albert Herrmann, Professor of Geography at Berlin University, became convinced that a part of the Tunisian desert had once been covered by the sea and was the former site of the capital city of Atlantis. Herrmann was perfectly clear about his aim

in writing on the Atlantis question: this was 'to abolish the dogma that our most ancient ancestors were primitive barbarians'. But even he was embarrassed by over-credulous supporters of the thesis, like Karl Georg ZSCHAETZSCH, whose book *The Aryans* was published as early as 1920 and who identified Atlantis both with Asia and with the home of the Norse gods, Asgard. He claimed a monopoly of blonde hair and blue eyes for the Atlantean race.

The most influential theorist of the Aryan Atlantis was Professor Hermann Wirth (see also COSMOLOGY), a German-Flemish specialist in prehistory who maintained that a pure monotheistic religion had originated in Atlantis and spread throughout the world, leaving behind it a trail of symbols. Wirth derived his evidence from the Norse Eddas, and also from a notorious late 19th-century forgery called the 'Ura-Linda Chronicle'. Even Alfred Rosenberg had his doubts about the Ura-Linda Chronicle; although these did not prevent him from using Wirth's theory of a northern Atlantis in his *Myth of the 20th Century*.

Hermann Wirth devoted much time to trying to legitimize his dubious specialities. Finally he did obtain a form of official framework for his researches with the aid of Heinrich Himmler. In 1935 Himmler established the *Deutsches Ahnenerbe* – literally, 'German ancestral heritage' – as a private institute of learning, devoted chiefly to the researches of Wirth, and with himself as Curator. By 1939 this institute had become part of Himmler's personal staff, and Wirth himself had been elbowed into the background. But *Völkische* eccentrics and pseudo-scholars of the calibre of Wirth continued to be absorbed by this organization to satisfy Himmler's whims. So it was that the *Ahnenerbe* became the custodian of another strange theory with which it proved convenient to incorporate the idea of Atlantis. This was the Glacial Cosmology of Hanns HÖRBIGER.

From the point of view of speculation about Atlantis, the important feature of the Glacial Cosmology was that it embodied the idea that the earth had possessed several moons before the satellite at present in the sky. These moons had crashed on the earth, each time destroying civilization. The fall of the last moon had been recorded in myths and legends; and in particular in legends of the Flood. Atlantis-theorists pounced on this idea, which provided the explanation of why the original home of the Aryan race had sunk beneath the waves. The most successful of these fantasists was the surveyor Edmund Kiss, who was known as the 'poet of Atlantis' and concocted a synthesis of Wirth and Hörbiger. The *Völkische* found evidence to

support this new world-picture in the Edda, and a handbook describing the Germanic cosmology was issued to the S.A.

It is quite well known that Hitler believed in the Glacial Cosmology of Hörbiger, and admitted to an interest in the more or less occult prehistory purveyed by Edgar Dacqué, a Munich palaeontologist who was also a member of the Theosophical Society. Himmler's agents in the *Ahnenerbe* tried to place the books of Kiss in the Führer's path, but it is not known whether their machinations were successful. It is a disturbing coincidence that the theories of Wirth and Hörbiger fit so neatly together, and interesting to speculate on what would have happened if the Nazi world-view had been victorious. Would Atlantis now be accepted as established historical fact?

Yet if it was possible for the supporters of the idea of the master race to discover material in the Atlantis legend, their opponents could use the theory against them. A Scottish occultist and Atlantis-student, Lewis Spence (see also DRUIDS), published in 1941 a book on *The Occult Causes of the Present War*, in which he argued that the war was the result of a Satanic conspiracy centred in Munich and the Baltic states. The next year Spence asked *Will Europe Follow Atlantis?* and did not conceal his aims. 'Plainly stated,' he wrote, 'the purpose of this book is to reveal that calamities brought about by floods and earthquakes and other natural upheavals descend upon nations as a result of their wickedness and profligacy. . . . That a similar fate awaits the Axis Powers in the near future appears to me as highly probable. . . . ' This obviously posed grave problems for a prospective army of occupation for defeated Germany. 'To dispatch Allied troops to a country a large part of which has been submerged, while its remaining territories are ravaged by conditions unparalleled in their savage confusion, is a policy which will scarcely commend itself to our statesmen. . . . Germany at first must be left to her doom.'

Countries of the Mind

Atlantis has continued to fascinate those interested in romantic and unprovable speculation. Egerton Sykes has brought up to date several editions of Ignatius Donnelly's *Atlantis*, and just after the Second World War applied to the Russians for permission to set up an expedition to Mount Ararat, where he expected to find, if not traces of Noah's Ark, at least some evidence of a great cataclysm. The Soviet authorities refused a permit, and occultists have ever since delighted in supposing them to be the custodians of some fearful cosmological secret,

The 'lost continent' Atlantis: a speculative map

rather than the over-cautious defenders of a strategic border. Hans Schindler Bellamy until recently kept the flag of Hörbiger flying in Britain with books based on the Glacial Cosmology and his own investigations in South America. Bellamy has interpreted various South American inscriptions as confirming the theory of the moon's spiralling down on to the earth and the exodus of a people of superior culture to found a new civilization in South America.

Occultists and mystics of all sorts still claim Atlantis as their special preserve. The occultist and 'psychic doctor' Edgar CAYCE made several statements about Atlantis. He described the continent as having been peopled with beings of advanced technological achievements, and predicted that Atlantis would rise again in 1968 or 1969. In a review of a book on magical orders published in 1970 (*262*), the British witch Alex Sanders claimed that its numerous appendices, designed to put into print previously unpublished material on which the author based his arguments, had been 'brought through by the Hidden Masters from Atlantis'. Atlantis is seen as a land of supermen; and it is possible to use it to support or attack a prophet of esoteric wisdom. Thus, if the writer approves of an occult doctrine he can trace it back to its 'source' in sacred Atlantis before the Flood; but if he is critical, the occult practices he condemns belong to the same tradition as 'Atlantean black magic', which brought divine retribution on the Atlanteans so long ago.

The continuing appeal of Atlantis needs little explanation. Countries of the mind can be a dreamer's personal possession, and allow an imaginative freedom which fantasies more anchored in the actual do not permit. Interference with a treasured fantasy may explain why the supporters of one or another theory of Atlantis have such strong feelings about it. For example, in 1929 the Congress of the Society for Atlantis Studies at the Sorbonne was interrupted when one delegate threw a pair of tear-gas bombs to demolish the suggestion made by a speaker that Corsica was the historical Atlantis. The drowned continent has also been a favourite setting for science-fiction novels. From Jules Verne to Jane Gaskell – who has an avowed allegiance to the theories of Hörbiger – countless supermen have discovered Atlantis, searched for Atlantis, or swashbuckled their way through Atlantis before the deluge. For both occultist and writer of science fiction the lost continent has provided an admirable setting for their dreams.

This tells us much about both occultism and fantasy. While it is never pretended that most science fiction dealing with Atlantis is anything but romance, the revelations of occultists claim the cachet of revealed truth. Yet it is often impossible to separate the visions of occultists gazing at the 'akashic record', or back into time, from the fantasies of romancers, except perhaps in point of inferior literary quality. The revelations of Rudolf Steiner or Edgar Cayce are tame compared with the Atlantis of Jane Gaskell. However, when the occultists turn their attention to the lost continent, they too cannot avoid writing science fiction. For example, Dr Otoman Zar-Adusht Ha'nish, alias Otto Hanisch, the founder of the once popular cult of MAZDAZNAN, attempted his own Atlantis revelation in an almost illiterate story called *Aetalonia or the Land of Lords*. But he was not content to describe a society of magicians, or derive sanction for his own esoteric system of dieting from the superior wisdom of Atlantis. Hanisch had to try to give the impression of mechanical marvels which is the stock-in-trade of the science-fiction writer. On the other hand, the Atlantis of many writers of fantasy contains magic often more intriguing than anything that occultists themselves recount.

The conclusion may be that fantasy which finds expression in the occult and fantasy expressed in reading or writing science fiction are products of the same impulse. The difference is that the occultist may well believe in the products of his imagination – the dividing line between the created world and the real world has broken down. It must be admitted that the pervasiveness of Atlantis

in occult thought has been less noticeable during the last twenty years, and this may be one indication that the possessors of prodigal imaginations are coming to draw a distinction between the real and the unreal. If this is so, it cannot but further enrich the colourful history of Atlantis in fiction.

And the reality at the bottom of the speculation? No amount of scientific argument will ever settle the question for the enthusiast. The sparse indications provided by literary references to Atlantis have kept aspiring archaeologists busy, and have provided some interesting results. For example, in 1956 Jürgen Spannuth published a book describing his quest for Atlantis. His starting point was obviously the speculation about the 'Nordic Atlantis' which was taken up by Rosenberg and Hermann Wirth. Spannuth worked out that Atlantis should be situated off Heligoland and became intrigued by legends of a 'castle under the sea' preserved by Heligolander fishermen. He sent divers down, and although the water was too cloudy to allow the taking of photographs, claims to have discovered the ruins of the Atlantean royal castle. Spannuth certainly seems to have found something, although it is doubtful if he located Atlantis.

More recently, it has been argued that the Atlantean civilization described by Plato closely resembles what we know of eastern Mediterranean civilizations in the period from about 2500 to 1500 B.C., and that Plato's Atlantis may have been based on the Minoan civilization of Crete. The cataclysm which destroyed Atlantis was, on this hypothesis, the explosion of the island volcano of Santorin, north of Crete, in about 1500 B.C., the greatest volcanic explosion ever recorded, which devastated the eastern Mediterranean and contributed to the collapse of the Minoan Empire (see *170, 296*).

While it is generally agreed that the contours of the earth and the position of the continents have altered appreciably over the millennia, it is less the scientific possibility of Atlantis than the hold it exercises over men's minds that is significant. The hypothesis would seem perfectly justifiable as long as it remains a hypothesis. It is doubtful whether a cataclysm sufficient to 'destroy' a continent would leave behind it relics which can be identified. Theorists will no doubt continue to titillate their readers with claims that the builders of the pyramids of Central America and Egypt came from the same archaic stock. It is by no means impossible, and a positive loss would be felt if Atlantis was one day conclusively shown to be a Platonic myth. There should be an organized conspiracy to prevent the disappearance of those barbaric heroes cleaving their paths

through the exotic and sorcerous world of Atlantis. But man the dreamer is so constituted that such an impoverishment is not really a possibility. J. W.

(Further reading: *31, 115, 125, 170, 296, 422, 431, 432, 433, 434, 439a, 494*.)

Aum (or Om)

The most famous of Eastern mystical syllables, believed to hold the key to the universe: see MANDALAS AND MANTRAS; see also CABALA.

Aura

The 'human rainbow', belonging to the same department of speculation as the ASTRAL BODY and the ETHERIC BODY, of which it is sometimes said to be the visible border. Auras are bands of coloured light allegedly radiating from and surrounding the bodies of human beings, animals and plants, and visible to clairvoyants and sensitives. The different colours and markings of an aura are supposed to indicate the physical and emotional, the mental and spiritual, condition of its possessor. One system of interpretation is: gold for spirituality, pale blue and purple for healing power, pink for pure love and affection, red for desire and anger, green for intellect, browns and dark muddy shades for disease (*48*). An aura which is shrivelling up is a sign of approaching death.

That beings of great spiritual force radiate light is an old and widespread belief, and in Christian and other religious art gods and holy men are represented with a surrounding aura of light called a halo (see also CHAKRAS).

Dr W. J. Kilner's illustration of a healthy aura seen through one of his screens

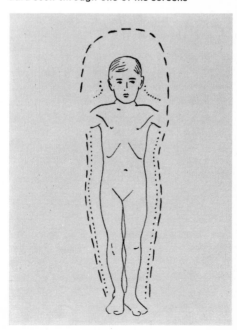

A nimbus is a halo which surrounds only the head, an aureole is one which surrounds the whole body.

In the 19th century Baron von REICHEN-BACH claimed that he had discovered radiations given off by human beings, animals, plants, magnets and crystals, which could be seen by sensitives. W. J. KILNER believed that illness caused changes in the human aura and tried to devise ways of making it visible to ordinary sight, as an aid to diagnosis. C. W. LEADBEATER illustrated his book *Man Visible and Invisible* with pictures of auras showing various colours and markings. Modern RADIESTHESIA is also concerned with radiations from the body. Kirlian photography is a process for taking photographs of the 'bio-luminescent' patterns of living things, invented by S. D. Kirlian, a Russian electrical technician. He is said to have produced photographs which show a complete aura even though the subject has had a limb amputated, and to have shown through experiments at a Russian agricultural station in the 1950s that diseases in animals and plants can be diagnosed from the aura before they produce physical symptoms.

(For Kirlian photography, see *2, 358*: see also *261, 309, 392*.)

Automatic Art, Speech, Writing See
AUTOMATISMS; SPIRITUALISM.

Automatisms
Automatic writing, automatic art, and other similar manifestations, are termed in psychology motor automatisms. An automatism is a type of behaviour in which there is limited consciousness. During automatic writing, for example, the writer does not consciously know what he is writing: this is described as 'dissociation', which means that there is some temporary separation of the part of the personality engaged in the writing process from the normal state of the individual. (For a general background on states of consciousness and automatisms, see CONSCIOUSNESS.)

Although the automatic practices, of which writing is the most familiar and important, belong to the general field of psychology and are of some interest to different branches of that subject, especially psychiatry, the discussion here is centred on parapsychology, the study of psi (psychic or parapsychical) abilities and experiences (see PARAPSYCHOLOGY). However, it is worth mentioning that during the first three decades of this century automatic writing was an approved method in psychiatry for exploring sources of mental disturbance in the unconscious mind. One of the leaders in the use of this method, Dr Anita Mühl (see *339*) used not

only automatic writing but other free artistic methods of allowing the patient to give spontaneous expression to hidden conflicts.

The importance of automatic writing in psychical research, however, goes back originally to the practices of the Spiritualist movement in the United States during the latter half of the 19th century (see SPIRITUALISM). In this movement the earliest and most primitive mode of communication with the alleged spirit world involved the use of a code for the answering of questions by the spirits. The first answers were given in the form of raps, but automatic table-tipping served the same purpose; answers of yes or no and the letters of the alphabet were indicated by the number of raps or table movements. Then followed the planchette, which consisted of a pencil attached to a small easily-moved board that was laid on a sheet of paper. Two persons would each rest a hand lightly on the board and, if they were capable of this type of motor automatism, the planchette would write answers to orally delivered questions. The questions were, as a rule, directed to a deceased person in whom one or both of the participants were interested.

From this method of seeking post-mortem communication there developed the technique of one individual holding the pencil in his hand to see if his hand would write automatically, without the teamwork required by other methods. This form of automatic writing thus gave free play to individuals who believed themselves to be in touch with discarnate agencies; it enabled them to write treatises on religious and philosophical topics, often of book length.

The musical automatist Mrs Rosemary Brown

Before the century was over, many large volumes of supposedly 'heavenly' communications were compiled from these automatic writings. One of these works became internationally famous, partly because of the interest taken in it by some of the leading psychologists of the day. This was *From India to the Planet Mars*, written by Professor Flournoy of Geneva (*155*). It was based on messages written automatically by a medium, Hélène SMITH, in a language represented as that of the people of Mars.

Cross-correspondence
The primary reason why automatic writing became a practice of interest to scientific parapsychology was that it provided a permanent record which the experimenter could examine. A number of the mediums who were important to the societies for psychical research around the turn of the century (and for a few decades thereafter) allowed themselves to be guided into the practice of automatic writing. Another advantage lay in the fact that individuals who were not practising mediumship professionally could in their own free way allow such messages to be delivered.

Some of these privately produced automatic writings, when collected and studied, especially in England, led to the discovery of inter-connecting patterns of apparent meaning between fragments of messages taken from different writers. These CROSS-CORRESPONDENCES, as they were called, were interpreted by some of the scholars devoted to psychical research as evidence of post-mortem communication. In fact, they found in these meaningful passages their most convincing evidence for the theory of personal survival. (See *341* for a convenient

Automatisms

review.) While this evidence lost much of its weight in the light of later developments of method, it played an important part in keeping the subject of psychical research supported and studied by competent people, and contributed to the steady progress of the societies for psychical research in Western Europe and the U.S.A.

Today, little attention is given by parapsychologists to the collections of automatic scripts, either for their content or for their value as evidence of post-mortem survival. This lack of attention has been caused primarily by the development of evidence of psi ability, which makes the possibility that the medium gets her information from discarnate entities less likely. It is now recognized that her information could just as well be acquired from the same sources against which the writings would have to be checked for accuracy. In its day, this method of supposed communication with personal agencies beyond the writer's own mind played an important part in the search for evidence of post-mortem survival, which in turn fostered the beginnings of parapsychology. However, no parapsychologist would want to say that the failure of this method, and the failure of the whole range of mediumistic methods, means that there is no further reason for considering the question of post-mortem survival, and probably no one would want to dismiss completely the question of whether automatic practices are any longer of significant use to parapsychology.

Rod and Pendulum

DOWSING is another familiar motor automatism, and along with the practice of dowsing with the 'divining rod' should be listed the related types of practices which depend on the pendulum and are widely associated with theories and practices known as RADIESTHESIA. These automatisms with rod and pendulum have been more concerned with practical aims – finding water or a lost object or a diseased organ of the body – than with the search for contact with another world.

The method of automatically locating hidden objects ranges well beyond the forked twig and the pendulum, which indicates that success is not dependent on the instrument, but is a question of the acceptance of the technique by the practitioner and his faith in it. Some muscular function that can be dissociated from conscious attention, as happens in automatic writing, is essential.

One of the prevailing practices that relies on automatic methods is the unorthodox diagnosis of disease. Most of this diagnostic effort is made with the use of an exploratory pendulum held over a chart of the human body. With a code of signals relating to movement of the pendulum when held over the chart, the nature and location of the disease are (according to the practitioner) revealed. Other techniques are used which similarly depend on unconscious muscular movement. For example, a finger or thumb, when rubbed against a smooth surface, produces automatic effects that can be coded. In all the many varieties of these techniques, the basic idea is that of an unconscious muscular movement; accordingly, if there is a psychic (or psi) factor involved, it would exert its influence in the same unconscious way as it is supposed to do in dowsing or table-tipping. The actual movement is muscular and in no case has it been shown to be psychokinetic; it is recognized as normal muscular action. The psi or psychic element, if any, would have to function as ESP and operate to direct the muscles in moving the rod or pendulum.

Automatic Responses in the Arts

Among the types of automatisms closer to the practice of automatic writing, in which the aim is to communicate verbal or artistic information (for example, to deliver a message), we find a fantastic variety of practices on record, of which a few can be reviewed. Some, like automatic writing, are passing out of the picture, but new ones are appearing. Next to writing (including spelling on the OUIJA BOARD), painting has probably been the most frequent type of automatic practice (see plate opposite), although it would be difficult to make any reliable estimate of such matters; there is no way of telling how many of the cases never come to the attention of serious students of this field.

An American psychical researcher, Professor James H. Hyslop, was much impressed by what he called the Thompson-Gifford case of landscape painting under what was interpreted as spirit influence. The story is that Frederic Thompson, who was not an artist, in 1905 suddenly felt the impulse to sketch and paint, and felt that he was under the influence of a deceased painter, Robert Swain Gifford. Hyslop reported the case in his book, *Contact with the Other World*; he was convinced that he had evidence that the spirit of Gifford was guiding Thompson in his attempt to imitate his style and quality.

Among the many cases that come to the attention of parapsychologists, there are some that look even more like true motor automatisms than the case just mentioned. Consider, for instance, the case of the Michigan woman, an undistinguished housewife with no training in art, who had the impulse to equip herself with materials for drawing. With no lessons whatever, she would begin at one end of a sheet of drawing paper and pencil the scene over the whole surface as she went across from left to right. She, too, thought that her hand was guided by a spirit painter and that she herself did not know in advance what the picture was going to be. The products were generally regarded as in moderately good proportion, taste, and artistic quality. Later, a similarly abrupt impulse led her to take up painting with oils. The result was comparable. She could only interpret the operation as due to spirit intervention, but she could not offer any proof.

Another oddity of the automatic type occurred to a Washington woman during a moment of boredom in which she found herself with a pencil and paper conveniently at hand. Placing the pencil on the square of paper she let it roam spontaneously *without stopping or lifting it* until the surface was completely covered with a maze of criss-crossings and scribbles. Then the pencil came to an abrupt stop. There was nothing consciously on her mind as she did this, and it was with only mild curiosity that she looked at the paper afterwards. To her surprise she found that a face stood out clearly through the many marks of the pencil on the page. It was, however, something out of another century and a different culture, a head unrecognized by anyone who saw it. If it was a message, she did not understand it, but anyone looking at the scribbles could not miss the portrait.

The woman, with renewed curiosity, tried the pencil on another sheet of paper. Again the pencil seemed to move itself, as the divining rod of the dowser seems to him to be pulling instead of being pushed. This time another face showed up through the 'aimless' scribbles, and each successive attempt produced another figure, another face, none of them recognizable and with no discernible message except that somehow the woman's unconscious mind was guiding her hand to make a picture for her in this unusual way.

The world of music has its cases of automatic responses to influences, at least of the unconscious mind, but giving the impression that some deceased musician is behind the product, either in composing the music as it was written, or in guiding the hands on the instruments playing it. Few cases have been publicized, but one is currently well known in England; Mrs Rosemary BROWN believes that her hands are sometimes controlled at the piano by Franz Liszt, although Bach and Beethoven also help her to write the music they wish to communicate to her.

An automatic painting by Madge Gill (see above)

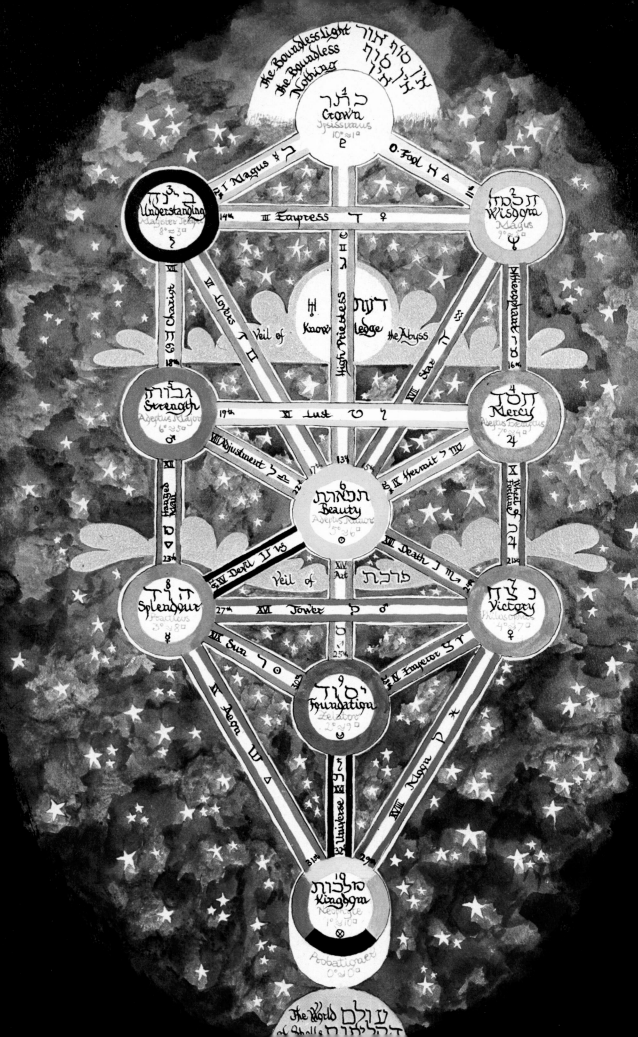

Automatic speaking or the use of a living person's vocal apparatus for communications purporting to come from a spirit personality has an old history in widely different cultures. Divine agencies have often been believed to speak through the vocal organs of men. In modern times, the Spiritualist medium has frequently been claimed to be used in this way by a discarnate communicator. Usually this vocal communication occurs in the TRANCE state, and sometimes the medium's voice is reported to converse in languages unknown to her.

This last performance would be a most interesting phenomenon if it ever really happened, with actual intelligent conversational exchange in a language which the medium could not have learned. It has been reported as having occurred, but there has never been adequate evidential support. This 'speaking in tongues' is claimed to have been produced in certain Christian sects and plays an important role in the faith of some Christian groups today. Automatic speaking in a familiar language would not be especially unusual in a suggestible person, but speaking intelligently in an unknown language would be much more impressive.

'Patience Worth'

It is in the literary field that the automatic arts flourish at their most interesting level so far as the product is concerned. The case of Patience WORTH comes first to mind in this connection. This is the story of Mrs Pearl Curran of St Louis, who as an automatist produced novels and poetry that won public attention; one of her novels won a Pulitzer prize. Her rise to moderate fame occurred in the first quarter of the century, but the story has recently been recalled in a readable book by Irving Litvag, *Singer in the Shadows, The Strange Story of Patience Worth.* Mrs Curran began receiving messages represented as coming from the spirit of an English girl, Patience Worth, who had lived hundreds of years before. For many years Mrs Curran's automatic production was all spelled out on a ouija board, but it later shifted to a sensory automatism of the hallucinatory type. She saw the pictures and words 'in her head' and called them out to be recorded.

This raises a good question of whether this is very unusual after all as to the *modus operandi*. One knows of a novelist, for example, who creates his characters as vividly as possible in his imagination and listens to them as they interact on the inner stage of his mind.

In the Cabala, the sefirotic Tree of Life, drawn by Steffi Grant (see page 57)

One of the more phenomenal aspects of Patience Worth's literature was her ability to begin producing impressively beautiful poetry immediately on the proposal of a topic. Dr Walter Franklin Prince, in his book *The Case of Patience Worth* (*377*), reported his repeated tests of this ability in his study of Mrs Curran.

Poetry has been reported as coming to the poet in various and unusual ways, often from sources beyond the individual himself. The ancient belief in the supernatural Muses must have owed something to this mysterious aspect of creative inspiration.

In this day of advancing knowledge of the frontiers of the mind it is just as well, perhaps, to keep open the possibility that there may be much more to the world of the mind and its background in the universe than is presently found in psychology textbooks. Whether or not any of the existing claims about transcendent sources of inspiration are ever validated, the continuing search for the ultimate explanation of creative genius may be served by the study of these automatic performances in all their mystery and complexity.

At the same time, there are reminders of how easy it is to be misled. Take, for instance, the case of a now deceased American poet who, already well known in his own right, began to acquire a local and restricted reputation as the medium through whom a deceased poet (his former friend) was communicating rather beautiful sonnets on the ouija board. Before fame and publication extended too far, a merciful slip in his operating technique showed unmistakable evidence in the public library of his advanced preparation of the gems of poetry that came so spontaneously through his hand on the fast-moving pointer of the ouija. It became clear that he had 'researched' there, and prepared in advance for the 'spontaneous' delivery via the board.

This strange case leaves only the mystery of why an able and recognized poet should conceal his own productions under the name of a spirit communicator. It would be hazardous to guess, and it is not necessary to do so. But it is obviously necessary to be cautious in reaching conclusions about who is behind automatic practices and the other 'hidden channels of the mind'. What is really there, and how it operates, are matters much too important to be decided prematurely.

Cases have come to our attention from time to time of the most bizarre complications in taking automatic writing too seriously at its face value. There have been reports that the family of a deceased novelist in Brazil sued a man who claimed that the novel he wrote and successfully published

had been communicated to him automatically by the dead writer. If, as the living author claimed, the dead man had produced it, then the family wanted the royalties. (British legal practice, in fact, has a rule on this point: the copyright belongs to the medium.)

Where do automatic writing and automatisms in general lead us? This capacity for extreme control of attention, limitation of consciousness, and dissociation of sections of the total mind may indeed extend the range of human ability and accomplishment. It is time, however, for a more systematic integration of what is known about this far-ranging and complicated control of the mind through its own self-regulation. The solution of many problems awaits the handling of this matter on a more comprehensive scale and a more general understanding of the many abuses that originate in misunderstanding of some aspect of automatism.

The most general difficulty with automatic behaviour is that it naturally tends to deceive the person who experiences it. As a rule, the individual thinks that some force or agency outside himself is making him do what he does; he does not understand that he is doing it himself or even how he could be; dowsing is a good illustration of this. Much of the real meaning of the religious experience of seeing a vision may be distorted by failure to understand these automatisms and to know that what is really happening is dependent on, even due to, one's own state of mind. It is not necessary for an individual to be misled about his own part in it for him to be convinced that behind the automatism (which was only the form in which a message came to him) there was the much more important fact that the parapsychical means by which the message was received can now be accepted as valid, in some cases at least. Parapsychology has now proved that a prophet might genuinely have transcended his own known powers in his transformed (automatic) state, even while he would have to accept the evidence today of his unknown psi abilities as the real medium for his message, however inspiring it might be.

It would appear, in summarizing, that for the most part in the past, men have been misled in their interpretation of automatisms such as automatic writing. But as understanding grows, it should be possible to turn these types of operation to the benefit of the individual and society to an extent too great to estimate. Fortunately, parapsychology is helping to re-examine these devices of the mind and to study their role and importance in human life. J. B. R.

(See also MEDIUMS.) (Further reading: *213, 341, 346, 396, 464.*)

B

Alice Bailey (1880-1949)

A prolific writer on mysticism and the founder of an international esoteric movement, Alice Bailey was born in Manchester, the daughter of an engineer. After a cloistered upbringing she entered on a period of evangelical work with the British army, which took her to India. In 1907 she married Walter Evans, whom she had met while he was serving in the army in India, and they emigrated to America, where he became an Episcopalian minister. The marriage was not a success, and after the birth of three daughters she obtained a separation and later a divorce.

In America she discovered the works of Madame BLAVATSKY and became active in the THEOSOPHICAL SOCIETY. The narrow, dogmatic Christianity which she had hitherto professed gave way to wider spiritual horizons, though the figure of Christ continued to play a central part in her beliefs. She later grew disillusioned with the petty intrigues of the Theosophical Society and ceased to play an active part in it, but she always recognized the valuable part that Theosophy had played in her life.

It was through Theosophy that she discovered the identity of a MASTER on the inner plane whose spirit had guided her from the age of fifteen. He was known as KOOT HOOMI. In 1919 she was contacted by the spirit of another individual whom she called 'the Tibetan', and she agreed to be his amanuensis. The result was a series of books devoted to a mystical teaching emanating from the Tibetan and carefully written down by her.

In 1920 she married another Theosophist, Foster Bailey, and in 1923 they started an 'Arcane School' to teach disciples how to further the Great Universal Plan under the guidance of the inner hierarchy of spiritual masters led by Christ. After her death in 1949 the school was carried on by her husband and still flourishes as a large international organization. C. M.

(See 9.)

Allan Bennett (1872-1923)

A member of the GOLDEN DAWN, in which his motto was *Iehi Aour* (from the Hebrew, 'Let there be light'), and of the Esoteric Section of the THEOSOPHICAL SOCIETY, who was for a time the friend and teacher of Aleister CROWLEY and presided over his early experiments with DRUGS. He wrote and performed a curious 'Ritual for the Evocation unto Visible Appearance of the Great Spirit Taphthartharath' (see RITUAL MAGIC). In 1900 he went to Ceylon to study Buddhism: he became a Buddhist monk under the name of Ananda Metteya. Crowley met him at a monastery in Burma in 1902 and said he saw him on one occasion hovering weightless in the air and being blown about like a leaf. Bennett had an important influence on the

Allan Bennett

British Buddhist Society, founded in 1908. (*100, 235, 446*)

Annie Besant (1847-1933)

A British social reformer and Theosophist, and one of the most active and remarkable personalities of her time. Born Annie Wood, in London, she married a Church of England clergyman named Besant in 1867, but the marriage failed. An ardent Anglo-Catholic as a girl, she moved towards atheism and became a leading figure in the National Secular Society. In 1877 she published *The Gospel of Atheism* and was unsuccessfully prosecuted for selling 'obscene literature' – a tract advocating birth control. She campaigned for feminist causes, led the London

match girls' strike of 1888, and became a member of the executive committee of the Fabian Society. In 1889 she announced that she had abandoned atheism and had joined the Theosophical Society. She swiftly rose to the highest ranks of the T.S. and after the death of Madame BLAVATSKY in 1891 she led the majority faction in the Society. With C. W. LEADBEATER, who had great influence with her, she sponsored Jiddu KRISHNAMURTI as the new world teacher. She also played an important part in Indian nationalist politics. She died convinced that she would swiftly be reborn again. Her numerous books include her *Autobiography*, 1893, a translation of the *Bhagavad Gita*, 1895, *The Ancient Wisdom*, 1897, *Man and His Bodies*, 1900, *Death and After*, 1901, *Esoteric Chris-*

Annie Besant

tianity, 1905, *Introduction to Yoga*, 1908; and, with Leadbeater, *Reincarnation*, 1898, *Thought Forms*, 1901, *Man: Whence, How and Whither*, 1913, and *Occult Chemistry*, 1919: see THEOSOPHICAL SOCIETY. (*38, 303, 351, 352*)

Bigfoot See ABOMINABLE SNOWMAN; SASQUATCH.

Bilocation

Being in two places at the same time, a phenomenon reported of various sages and holy men, and also in cases of APPARITIONS of the living: explained, according to one occult theory, as the separate appearance of the physical body and the astral or etheric body: see ASTRAL BODY; PHYSICAL POWERS.

H. P. Blavatsky

Black Box See RADIESTHESIA.

Black Mass See SATANISM.

Helena Petrovna Blavatsky (1831-91)

The Russian-born founder and head of the Theosophical Society, a 'flamboyant, outrageous and attractive personality', and the most influential single figure of the 19th-century occult revival. In her early days in the United States, which she reached at the age of forty-two after an ill-documented career of youthful adventure and at a time when SPIRITUALISM was all the rage, she claimed to have mediumistic powers. Her CONTROL was John KING and she referred to him as her guardian angel. However, she soon claimed to be in touch with far more elevated spiritual beings, the Brothers or MASTERS, godlike adepts concerned with guiding the progress of humanity, with their headquarters in the mountain fastnesses of Tibet. One of the Masters, she said, wrote large sections of her book *Isis Unveiled*, 1877, for her. The Masters also performed 'miracles' which impressed the members of the Theosophical Society, founded by Madame Blavatsky in 1875, though others attributed them to trickery and the Society for Psychical Research, which investigated her, described her as 'one of the most accomplished, ingenious and interesting impostors of history'. Her masterpiece was *The Secret Doctrine*, 1888, in which she attempted to reconcile and unite the Eastern and Western occult traditions and to bridge the gap which had opened between religion and science in the West. Both her occult synthesis itself and her claim to be guided by superhuman adepts have powerfully influenced 20th-century occultism: see THEOSOPHICAL SOCIETY. (*43, 44, 445*)

Body of Light

One of the many terms for the ASTRAL BODY.

Book of Shadows See WITCHCRAFT.

Book of Thoth

A modern term for the TAROT pack, reflecting the belief that it embodies the secret wisdom of ancient Egypt: Thoth was the Egyptian god of wisdom and magic.

Book Tests See MEDIUMS; SPIRITUALISM.

Joseph-Antoine Boullan (1824-93)

A French magician and defrocked Roman Catholic priest who in 1875 announced that he was a reincarnation of John the Baptist and appointed himself head of the Work of Mercy, which had been founded by the Norman wonder-worker Pierre VINTRAS. Boullan believed that the path to salvation lay through sexual intercourse with archangels and other celestial beings. He was attacked by a group of rival magicians who, it was claimed, eventually murdered him by magic. J.-K. Huysmans, who was a friend of his, portrayed him as 'Dr Johannes' in his novel *Là Bas*: see ROSICRUCIANS; SATANISM. (*12, 275, 493*)

Breath Control See YOGA.

Rosemary Brown

A British automatist, of Balham, London, who created intense interest in 1970 when it was discovered that she appeared to be in touch with famous and long dead musical composers who dictated works to her from the beyond: they included Liszt, Beethoven, Brahms, Debussy, Chopin, Schubert, and, more recently, Stravinsky. Selections of the music have been issued on records and, though experts disagree about its quality, there seems to be a general feeling that while it is accurately in the style of its reputed masters, it is not as good as might be hoped for from them. It has been suggested, by Rosalind Heywood, that Mrs Brown belongs to 'the type of sensitive whom frustration, often artistic, drives to the automatic production of material beyond their conscious capacity'. Mrs Brown wrote *Unfinished Symphonies*, 1971: see AUTOMATISMS. (*58, 216*)

C

Eva C

The pseudonym of Marthe Béraud, a medium famous for the production of ECTOPLASM. She was investigated by Professor Charles Richet, who met her in 1905 in Algiers, where she gave seances at which a bearded figure appeared, wearing white robes and a helmet, and describing itself as the departed spirit of a Hindu named Bien Boa; it drank lemonade and chatted with the sitters. She later went to Paris, where she was investigated with uncritical enthusiasm by Baron von Schrenck Notzing, who devoted most of his book *Phenomena of Materialisation*, 1920, to her: it included striking photographs of her 'ectoplasmic' creations, most of which were obviously pictures cut out of newspapers. She usually sat in a cabinet, behind a curtain which would be drawn back to show an ectoplasmic face or hand. Richet said he had observed 'a kind of liquid or pasty jelly' emerging from her mouth or breast and forming itself into the shape of a face or limb but, examined by the Society for Psychical Research in London in 1920, she produced ectoplasm apparently by regurgitating paper and fabric.

Cabala

This word is spelled in a variety of ways, of which Kabbalah is generally favoured by scholars and Qabalah by occultists. It means 'tradition', implying knowledge passed on by word of mouth, knowledge not openly revealed to all and sundry, and refers to a body of mystical speculation, originally Jewish, which was enthusiastically adopted by Christian humanists during the Renaissance, and which has made a powerful appeal to mystics and magicians of various schools of thought in the 19th and 20th centuries. It has also been persuasively argued that the Cabala influenced Freud (*11*). This article considers the Cabala primarily from the point of view of modern occultists, who have interpreted it and mingled it with other traditions in ways which tend to raise the hackles of scholars of Jewish mysticism.

Almost anything said briefly about the Cabala is bound to be over-simplified. It is not a single self-consistent structure but a grouping of speculations, centred round certain major themes and put forward by writers who have much in common, but who differ sharply from each other on occasion. There are particularly marked differences between the classic Cabala which took shape in the 12th and 13th centuries in the south of France and in Spain, and the Cabala of the 16th century and after, which was dominated by the teaching of Isaac Luria (1534–72), the 'holy lion' of Safed in Palestine. The Cabala is also highly complicated and abstruse, remote from our ordinary, accustomed ways of thinking. It consists of numerous writings by various and sometimes anonymous authors, the most important being the massive *Zohar* (*Sefer Ha-Zohar*, Book of Splendour, or Brightness), the bulk of which was written in Spain in the late 13th century, probably by Moses de León of Guadalajara. An important earlier work is the *Sefer Yetsirah* (Book of Formation), probably written between the 3rd and 6th centuries A.D.

The Cabala's obscurity, secrecy and enticing air of mystery have themselves attracted the occultly-inclined to it, but more importantly they have found in it some of the basic doctrines of Western occultism: that all the motley phenomena of the universe form an underlying unity, that all things are parts of an organized Whole; that there are secret laws which govern the universe and hidden connections between things which do not appear to be linked on the surface; that numbers and letters are significant keys to the pattern of the universe; that inspiration and imagination are better guides to ultimate truth than reason; that God is both immanent and transcendent, that all phenomena, including all human beings, contain something of the divine, though the divine transcends and is more than the total of phenomena; that man is both God and the universe in miniature; and, above all, that there is a path by which man can reach God, by which he can free himself of the limitations of being human and attain to the superhuman. Occultists have found these doctrines elsewhere as well, of course, and in particular the Cabala has many ideas in common with GNOSTICISM.

Cabalists, ancient and modern, have frequently led devoutly blameless lives, but there are thick strands of magic in the Cabala's web. Abraham Abulafia, the great 13th-century Cabalist and mystic, believed that the Cabala could be used effectively for magical purposes, and warned people against this perversion of it. Paul Ricci, a

Jew converted to Christianity who taught at Pavia University in the 16th century, said that the Cabala 'enumerates many sacred names to be invoked, and various bodily movements, by means of which we attain more easily and beyond the use of nature to the glories of the Eternal Father and our prerogatives in this world, which resemble them' (*42a*). The Cabala's ladder from earth to heaven can serve both the mystic who longs for the indescribable bliss of communion with God, and the magician who hungers to dominate all forces spiritual and material, and whose concept of God is himself raised to the highest power.

The Hidden Godhead

The Cabala attempts to answer questions which plague all religious thinkers. If God is good, how has evil entered the world which God made? What is the connection between God who is limitless, infinite and eternal, and a world which is finite, limited in space and time? How could variety arise from unity, or matter from pure spirit? And if God is so far beyond anything that man can conceive as to be unknowable, how can man know God? To these questions, the Cabalist answers that the world was not created by God in the sense of being manufactured, but emanated from God. It is not a question of evil or limit invading a world which exists separately from God. The world flows from the godhead, of which it is a manifestation. 'He fills everything and He *is* everything,' said Joseph Gikatila, a leading Spanish Cabalist of the 13th century (*420*). So God contains and transcends all things and all qualities, good and evil, limitless and limited, infinite and finite, unity and variety, spirit and matter, unknowable and knowable, all of which are reconciled and united in the great Whole which is the godhead; with the implication that the man who would reach the godhead must similarly reconcile and transcend all factors in himself.

The God of the Cabala is more 'It' than 'He'. It is 'the Infinite' (*En-Sof*, or *Ain Soph*: transliterations from the Hebrew again vary). It is a hidden godhead, unknown and unknowable. You cannot say that it is 'good' or 'merciful' or 'just', or even that it is 'real' or 'living', nor can you say that it is not these things. It can be called 'Nothing' (*Ayin* or *Ain*), because you cannot ascribe any qualities to it, but equally it is everything. It can also be called 'Infinite Light' (*Or En-Sof* or *Ain Soph Aur*), a boundless divine radiance. The process through which the unknown godhead makes itself known begins with the divine radiance emanating something from itself – often described as a light or a ray – and from this come a succession of further emanations, or lights, until there are ten of them in all. These emanations are called *sefiroth* and, in characteristically paradoxical language, the *Zohar* explains that: 'The Aged of the Aged, the Unknown of the Unknown, has a form and yet has no form. He has a form whereby the universe is preserved and yet has no form because he cannot be comprehended. When he first assumed the form [of the first emanation] he caused nine splendid lights to emanate from it, which, shining through it, diffused a bright light in all directions . . . So is the Holy Aged an absolute light but in himself concealed and incomprehensible. We can only comprehend him through those luminous emanations which again are partly visible and partly concealed. These constitute the sacred name of God' (*181*).

The Cabala: hands with astrological correspondences, set on a magic square

The Tree of Life

The splendid lights of the sefiroth constitute God's name because they are his manifest identity, and the process of emanation is the process through which he unfolds and reveals his identity. The sefiroth are facets or aspects of the divine personality, stages in God's revelation of himself and phases of the divine life, and they underlie the construction of the universe and the nature of man, both of which are made in the image of God. They are the driving forces of the universe and the impulses which move man. The relationship between them is shown in what Cabalists call the Tree of Life (see plate, page 52). The Tree's branches spread through the entire universe, reconciling all diversity in a unified pattern. It is a map of everything and a classification of everything. It shows both

the descent of the divine into manifestation and the ascent by which man can reverse the process of emanation and climb back up the Tree, as it were, to regain the godhead.

The picture of man ascending the Tree is based on the old belief that the soul came originally from God and descended to its incarnation in a physical body on the earth by way of the planetary spheres, picking up characteristics from each of the planets in turn – aggressiveness from Mars, sensuality from Venus, intelligence from Mercury, and so on (this theory being one of the bastions of traditional ASTROLOGY). After death, the soul rose again through the spheres, shedding characteristics in each of them in turn, until it returned to its original source. This ascent could be made not only after death but, by mystical and magical techniques, during earthly life. In either case, however, the ascent would not be easy. Legions of demons lurked in wait for the soul in the atmosphere between the earth and the moon, and if it escaped their clutches, the guardians of the planetary spheres would try to turn it back. The Jewish *Hekhaloth* texts, edited in the 5th and 6th centuries A.D., describe the experiences of mystics who during their earthly lives had risen to perceive the glory of God. The Hekhaloth were the celestial palaces through which they passed on their journey to the Throne of the Holy King in the seventh heaven, and the ascent was resisted by the 'gate-keepers' (corresponding to the Gnostic rulers of the planetary spheres). To pass these dread beings, the soul needed to know the correct passwords. Similarly, the sefiroth of the Cabala are guarded by orders of angels, and each sefira has a password, a divine name, knowledge of which indicates that the aspiring soul has grasped the wisdom or achieved the spiritual condition needed to progress to that sphere.

The Tree of Life has ten sefiroth or spheres, corresponding to the spheres of the earth, the seven planets known in antiquity, the fixed stars or zodiac and, at the summit, the sphere of the Prime Mover. They are also the numbers from one to ten, the basic building blocks from which all other numbers are constructed. They are arranged in three triangles with the tenth sefira, Malkhuth, left over at the bottom. In each triangle there are two opposing forces and a third force which reconciles them. The Tree reads from right to left, like written Hebrew. The sefiroth on the right-hand side or 'pillar' are positive and male, those on the left are negative and female. The Tree is also sometimes shown in the form of a man's body, the man being Adam Kadmon, the 'heavenly' or 'universal' man, the original spiritual and ideal form of humanity.

The first sefira, Kether, the crown, also called 'the Aged' or 'the primordial point' or 'the point within the circle', is the godhead as Prime Mover and First Cause. It is the unity in which all diversity is reconciled, and the first stage in the progression from infinite to finite. Its guardian angels are the 'living creatures' of Ezekiel, Chapter 1, which 'had the form of men' and which emerged from the 'great cloud, with brightness round about it, and fire flashing forth continually', a vision of the appalling glory and gigantic energy of the concealed godhead. It is in this sphere that man, achieving the most profound understanding of himself, communes with the Divine Presence.

From Kether emanate two great opposing principles or forces, Hokhmah and Binah, which are two aspects of the creative divine intellect. Hokhmah is male and active, the force behind everything which is positive, dynamic, thrusting. It is the impulse which originates action, which lies behind all growth, movement, change, evolution. Its angels are the wheels of Ezekiel's vision, which had 'the spirit of the living creatures' in them. Hokhmah is God's active, creative thought, the life-giving Spirit brooding over the waters in Genesis. Where Hokhmah is 'the Father' of all things, the opposite sefira, Binah, is 'the Mother'. Hokhmah is the wisdom of God, Binah the understanding or intelligence of God, passive where Hokhmah is active, responding where Hokhmah is thrusting, the dark waters of Genesis which were inert but contained in potential all the teeming life of the world, the lifeless waters from which, once fertilized, all things had their origin. Binah lies behind everything which is potential rather than actual, stable rather than changing. It is the sphere of Saturn, the planet of stability and inertia, and also of death, old age, time and fate. It is to Binah that the Cabala assigns the origin of the *neshamah*, the 'holy soul', the divine spark in each human personality, the true self in the inner depths of each man's being.

Between the first three sefiroth and the rest is the Abyss, the gulf which separates the ideal from the actual, the infinite from the finite, divine consciousness from ordinary human consciousness – though it is a gulf that can be crossed. The two opposing principles of the next triangle are those which impose form on what at this stage is still formless, which give substance to ideas. Hesed, or Gedulah, the love or mercy of God, is the force which moulds and organizes things, which constructs and builds up. In terms of a human family, it is the kindly, merciful authority of the father who protects and encourages the child, guiding him in the right way, gently moulding his character. In terms of the physical body, it is the force behind the building up of food into tissue. It looms in the background of all constructive energy, system, solidity, civilization, government, justice, law and order. It is the sphere of Jupiter, the active ruler and organizer, the father of gods and men, regarded in astrology as an essentially benevolent influence.

The opposite sefira, Geburah (or Din or Pachad), the power and stern judgment of God, balances the constructive activity of Hesed with destructive activity. It is the severe authority of the mother who disciplines and thwarts the child. In the body it governs the breaking down of tissue in the expenditure of energy. It is the sphere of Mars, the planet of war and violent force, and Geburah lies behind all destruction, havoc, cruelty, rage and hatred. The Cabala tends to stress the evil nature of the feminine, and all the female sefiroth on the left-hand pillar of the Tree, though necessary to the equilibrium of the universe, have threatening and ominous associations. This is especially true of Geburah, in which many Cabalists find the root of the world's evil. It is said that part of the fierce energy of this sefira overflowed, so to speak, and led to the formation of a hierarchy of evil emanations arranged in a Tree of their own: which is to say that the ultimate source of evil is the wrathful fury of God.

The Beauty of God

All phenomena are governed by the interplay of construction and destruction, Hesed and Geburah. They are united and reconciled in Tifereth (or Rahamin), the beauty of God, which is the sphere of the sun. The sun shines warmly on men and beasts and crops with the nurturing benevolence of Hesed, but also blasts and withers them with the destroying ferocity of Geburah. Tifereth is vital energy, the life force, the drive which impels life to continue. Its angels, the *shinanim*, ride in chariots, like the chariot of the sun. In Christian Cabala it is connected with Christ, the spiritual Sun, who brought to all men the possibility of eternal life, and Tifereth is the 'son' of Kether in the sense of being directly descended from it on the Tree. In the body Tifereth is the heart, pumping the life-blood round the system in a circular motion like the sun's apparent circling of the earth, and it is the 'heart', the centre, of the spheres on the Tree. Psychologically, Tifereth is the enlightened consciousness, the most elevated spiritual condition attainable in any normal mental state. The higher spheres can be attained only in supernormal states, and Tifereth on the threshold of the supernormal stands for death as the gateway to new life, as Christ died and rose again, or as the sun

'dies' in the evening to be reborn again at dawn.

In the third triangle, Netsah, the lasting endurance of God, is the sphere of Venus, goddess of nature and desire. It is the force of attraction and cohesion in the universe, the force which binds things together. It lies behind animal drives, the senses, the instincts and passions, immediate and unconsidered reactions, the natural as opposed to the contrived. It is balanced by the opposite sefira, Hod, the majesty of God. This is the sphere of Mercury, the god of intelligence, communication, mental activity, craft and trickery, and 'it represents essentially a mercurial quality of things – ever flowing, shifting, and in constant flux . . . ' (*391*). It stands for the higher mental faculties, intuition, insight, imagination, but like the other spheres on the left-hand pillar it has an evil side – reason and logic, which the Cabalists distrust, the whole apparatus of restrictive conventions imposed on the mind through education and social conditioning to restrain the impulses of the natural man, whose sphere is significantly placed on the good side of the Tree. Hod is the force behind schooled, considered, artificial reactions, and its angels are the *benei Elohim*, the 'sons of God' of Jewish legend, who marred the original natural innocence of humanity by teaching them the arts and crafts.

Cohesion and flux, the natural and the contrived, are reconciled in Yesod, the foundation of all active forces in God, which is connected with initiation into the mysteries and with the magical power which springs from the union of the mental faculties of Hod with the animal drives of Netsah. Yesod is the sphere of the moon, whose light shines in the darkness, and of the glimmering light of the true, inner self concealed in the depths of the personality. The moon flows through constant changes in the sky which yet form a cohesive cycle, and by long tradition it governs the increase and decrease, the growth and decay, of all things on earth. Moonlight is reflected sunlight and Yesod is the link between Tifereth (the sun or the life force) and Malkhuth (the earth or the body). It is 'the spout for the waters from on high', the channel between divine vital energy and the earth or earthly man, and when the Tree is shown in the form of a man's body, Yesod is the genitals.

The last sefira, Malkhuth, is the sphere of the earth, matter and the physical body. Malkhuth is the union of the sefiroth in the entire Tree, the whole manifest kingdom of God. It is frequently called the Shekhinah, the divine presence in the world, and especially the divine presence in God's people, Israel. In the Cabala the Shekhinah is a

feminine element in God, the divine Queen, Bride and Daughter. It is through Yesod, 'the spout', that the higher sefiroth flow into her. As the last of the sefiroth, she is in exile, fallen into matter, with the implication that 'a part of God Himself is exiled from God' (*421*). But equally as the last sefira she is the entrance to the divine, the sphere in which man begins his ascent of the Tree. The overriding purpose of the Jewish Cabala is to reunite the fallen Shekhinah with her 'husband', to restore the wholeness of God. 'He who worships God out of love', says the *Zohar*, 'lifts everything to the stage where all must be one.'

The Astral Plane

Modern occultists regard the ascent of the Tree, or 'rising through the spheres', as a journey into the ASTRAL PLANE, the world in which the products of thought and imagination have their reality. To achieve success, the magician needs to sharpen his powers of imagination and concentration to the highest pitch, and he may also employ breathing techniques and special bodily postures. Jewish mystics also used 'yoga' techniques and a writer of about A.D. 1000 said that he who wishes to ascend to the heavenly palaces to behold the divine Throne must 'fast a number of days and lay his head between his knees and whisper many hymns and songs whose texts are known from tradition. Then he perceives the interior and the palaces with his own eyes, and it is as though he entered one palace after the other and saw what is there.' Professor Scholem comments that the bodily posture involved is an 'attitude of deep self-oblivion' which appears to be 'favorable to the induction of prehypnotic autosuggestion'. Scholem also quotes two Jewish Cabalists who experienced what a modern occultist would describe as the separation of the astral body from the physical body. 'Know that the complete secret of prophecy', said one, 'consists for the prophet in that he suddenly sees the shape of his self standing before him and he forgets his self and it is disengaged from him and he sees the shape of his self before him talking to him and predicting the future . . . ' And the other wrote, 'I call heaven and earth to witness that one day I sat and wrote down a Kabbalistic secret; suddenly I saw the shape of myself standing before me and myself disengaged from me . . . ' (*420*).

Since the sefiroth are ten aspects of God, the universe and man, ten great principles or forces underlying all things, it is possible to classify all phenomena in terms of them, as if, to use Aleister CROWLEY's analogy, you had to sort all the papers on your desk into ten pigeonholes. An extensive system of correspondences was worked out by MacGregor MATHERS and Crowley (see *102, 104*), which classifies numerous phenomena in terms of the sefiroth and the Twenty-two Paths, which are lines drawn on the diagram of the Tree of Life, connecting the sefiroth (see also TAROT). The paths, along which the adept travels in the ascent of the Tree, are linked with the twenty-two major trumps of the Tarot pack and the twenty-two letters of the Hebrew alphabet.

The correspondences are employed in meditation, to gain understanding of the nature of a sefira or path by considering the phenomena and symbols associated with it. They are also guideposts and warning signs for the occultist who is attempting the ascent of the Tree. If he believes he is in the region of Netsah, the sphere of Venus, and he sees a horse or a jackal, he knows that something is wrong. The horse belongs to Mars and the jackal is a creature of the moon. He would expect to see doves or sparrows, or perhaps a leopard or a lynx, which belong to Venus. If he is working up the twenty-second path, leading from Malkhuth to Yesod, and he sees a figure in scarlet, then he has lost his way, for this path belongs to Saturn and the colour of Saturn is black (*160*). The ascent of the Tree is agreed by all authorities, ancient and modern, to be extremely dangerous, exposing the soul to numerous sinister agencies and situations.

The correspondences are also employed in magical operations, to arouse and concentrate force. For example, a magician performing a ceremony of hatred and destruction against an enemy will use objects and ideas related to the sefira Geburah – scarlet robes and hangings, a ruby set in an iron ring, an iron sword or wand. He may light five candles and have pentagrams (five-pointed stars) embroidered on his robes. He will also arouse, and fiercely concentrate on, all his own inner impulses of rage and malice, filling his mind with images of blood and torture, ruin and pain. Through these phenomena linked to Geburah he summons up the force of destructive energy within himself and in the universe outside him, to project it against his victim with what he believes will be crushing and devastating effect.

Gematria

The Hebrew alphabet has an important place in cabalistic mysticism and magic. Words, after all, are formidable weapons of ordinary life, through which we exercise power and influence over other people, and early systems of writing, including the hieroglyphics of ancient Egypt and the RUNES of northern Europe, were credited with divine and magical power. The story in Genesis of

God creating the world by expressing commands in words ('And God said, Let there be light: and there was light') gave Hebrew pride of place in the Judaeo-Christian tradition as the language of God, the supreme magical instrument through which God brought the universe into being. In the Cabala the process of emanation in which God revealed his identity was also described as the unfolding of the divine language, which was itself God's identity, each Hebrew letter being an aspect of God charged with divine energy.

God had also used the Hebrew language as the vehicle of his self-revelation in the Old Testament. But the Cabalists, observing that on the surface the scriptures were sometimes trivial, confusing, inconsistent, and not always entirely creditable to the Almighty, looked beneath the surface to mine the ore of divine truth concealed within. They treated the Old Testament, in effect, as a code which could be deciphered by mathematical and anagrammatic methods, of considerable antiquity, the most important of which was *gematria*.

Gematria is based on the fact that the Hebrew letters also stood for numbers (see also NUMEROLOGY). You could turn any Hebrew word or phrase into a number, and then translate that number into a different word or phrase, and feel that you had discovered the true, underlying meaning of the original. For example, when Abraham was on the plains of Mamre, Genesis says, 'and, lo, three men stood by him'. The letters of 'and, lo, three men' in Hebrew add to 701, and the words for 'these are Michael, Gabriel and Raphael' also add to 701, and so it was deduced that the three 'men' were really the three archangels. An example of a genuine use of this type of code in the Old Testament comes from the book of Daniel, in which the identity of the Seleucid king Antiochus IV Epiphanes is cloaked under the pseudonym Nebuchadnezzar, both names adding to 423 in Hebrew. Similarly, in the 13th century, Abulafia wrote some of his books under the pseudonyms Raziel and Zechariah, which had the same number value as his given name of Abraham.

Two other methods are *notarikon*, in which the first or last letters of the words of a phrase are joined together to make a new phrase, and *temurah*, which involves letter substitutions and anagrams. For instance, the first and last letters of the Hebrew words for 'who will go up for us to heaven?' (Deuteronomy xxx, 12) can be used to form the words for 'God' and 'circumcision', showing that God instituted circumcision as the passport to heaven. *Berashith*, 'in the beginning', the first word of the Bible, was subjected to many

ingenious elaborations of this sort, including one which helped to persuade a Jewish Cabalist of the 17th century to turn Christian: 'Ye shall worship my first-born, my first, whose name is Jesus.'

Christians adopted these methods early, the most famous example being the Great Beast of Revelation, whose identity is concealed under the number 666. Modern occultists also use them enthusiastically, to discover the true significance of the traditional 'names of power', formulae which are believed to contain esoteric knowledge and magical energy, and to devise new formulae. An example is Crowley's word of power Aumgn, an expansion of the Indian mystic syllable AUM. Transliterated into Hebrew, Aumgn adds to 100, which equals 20 + 80. The Hebrew letters standing for 20 and 80 are *kaph* and *pe* which, turned into Greek, are the initial letters of *kteis* and *phallos*, the female and male sex organs. In Aumgn, therefore, Crowley found what he regarded as the central formula of the Cabala itself, 'a synthetic glyph of the subtle energies employed in creating the Illusion, or Reflection of Reality, which we call manifested existence', which 'indicates the Magical formula of the Universe as a reverberatory engine for the extension of Nothingness through the device of equilibrated opposites' (*102*).

Methods like these seem extremely peculiar at first sight, but are a natural outgrowth of the belief that the outward variety and disconnected confusion of the universe conceals a unified pattern. Letters and numbers, linked respectively with the paths and the sefiroth, provide a key to the pattern because they give rise to innumerable different combinations and permutations – the innumerable phenomena of the universe – and yet are orderly and obey logical rules of behaviour. They are just such instruments as the divine might use to evolve complexity from an underlying simplicity, the many from the One. R. C.

(Further reading: for the Jewish and Christian Cabala, see *42a, 181, 420, 421, 460*; for modern occult Cabala, see *73, 85, 102, 160, 313, 389, 391, 482*.)

Candomblé

An Afro-Christian religion of Brazil, originating from the identification by imported Negro slaves of their own gods with the divine beings and saints of their Christian masters: the Virgin Mary being identified with the West African goddess Iemanja, Jesus with the god Oxala, John the Baptist with the god Xango, and so on. These composite beings are worshipped at *candomblés*, or meeting places, each presided over by a high priestess, the 'Mother of the

Saints'. During the services worshippers become possessed by the gods and spirits, and behave in their characteristic ways. (*437*)

Cards

Cartomancy, or card-reading, is a relatively modern art by comparison with ASTROLOGY or NUMEROLOGY, since cards are a relatively modern invention. Our packs of playing cards are probably descended from the TAROT packs and are, from an occult point of view, the Tarot's poor relations. The Tarot is believed to contain a set of symbols of cosmic significance, but no such claim is made for ordinary playing cards, which are used for fortune-telling in comparatively humble circumstances, at home or in the card-reader's parlour or the gypsy's tent at the fairground. Compared with modern astrology and numerology, cartomancy is more concerned with predicting the future and less with divining character and personality. It lacks the logical structure of its older rivals and because of its humble status is particularly preoccupied with matters of love and marriage, dark strangers, true and false friends, legacies and windfalls.

Most card-reading, amateur or professional, falls somewhere on a scale between light-hearted entertainment at one end and slick charlatanry at the other, but there may sometimes be more to it. Some people do appear to have a curious ability to divine salient facts about other people's characters and circumstances, and evidence from PARAPSYCHOLOGY suggests that some individuals can on occasion predict the future. A layout of cards may stimulate or act as a focus for psychic gifts of this sort, even though the cards by themselves are devoid of significance. Parapsychological evidence also suggests that some people can psychically affect the shuffling of cards, which opens up the possibility of a 'sensitive', well versed in the 'meanings' of the cards, being able unconsciously or half-consciously to produce a fall of cards which does reflect a reality of character or the future.

All this is speculative and before giving easy credence to the claims of card-readers it is necessary to remember that in cartomancy as in other forms of divination much of the impression of startling accuracy, if created at all, is created by the vagueness of the fortune-teller's language. It is all too easy in the light of subsequent events to interpret as an exact and accurate forecast of what has happened a prediction which was really so vague and all-embracing that it was unlikely not to come true in some form or other. It is also easy to remember forecasts which came true and forget those which did not.

Eighteenth-century cards made by Johann Matthias Backofen of Nuremberg

Court Cards

Card-reading is a complicated art because of the large number of units involved – the fifty-two cards of the pack – and their almost endless variety of possible combinations with each other, for each card's significance is affected by the cards close to it in the layout. You usually begin by selecting a court card to represent the consulter or questioner (or 'querent' or 'querist'). The simplest way of doing this is to base the choice on the colour of the consulter's hair: Diamonds for a blonde or red-haired person, Hearts for light-brown hair, Clubs for dark-brown hair, Spades for black hair. A man is represented by a king and a woman by a queen, so that the 'significator' or consulter's card for a black-haired man would be the King of Spades. A young man may be allotted a knave but more often nowadays the knave of a suit is taken to indicate the thoughts of the corresponding king. Any widow, regardless of colouring, should be represented by the Queen of Spades, and some say that a man in uniform should be assigned the King of Diamonds. If the consulter is a married woman, the king of her suit represents her husband, and vice versa. Lovers are also represented by the kings and queens of the appropriate suit.

Once the consulter's card has been chosen, the other court cards stand for people in the consulter's life – past, present or future. The knaves represent friends, or sometimes relatives, or else the thoughts of the kings. Interpretations of the court cards vary in detail from one cartomancer to another, but there is a rough general agreement amongst them, as follows:

Spades

King A man of ambitious, determined, forceful character, likely to be successful in life and love; a relentless enemy if opposed; possibly of military inclinations (Spades are Swords in the Tarot pack).

Queen A widow; also, or alternatively, a temptress, a seductive but cruel and dominating woman, with an appetite for power, money and luxury; treacherous and unscrupulous; she means trouble.

Knave A man who exploits his friends, or one who means well but makes trouble; dark, handsome and lazy; according to one authority, possibly a murderer – 'he has the nature of an assassin' (*383*) – or, according to another, 'a lawyer, to be avoided' (*448*).

Hearts

King A handsome, kindly, amiable man, probably of high social status or holding some important position; generous, indiscreet, irritable, fundamentally good-natured; of amorous disposition; possibly a naval officer.

Queen A good woman, lovable, faithful and affectionate; sensible, good-tempered, easy-going, fond of company.

Knave The consulter's best friend or closest relative, male or female, in which case the cards next to him reveal his inclinations at the moment: alternatively, a charming but unreliable and unscrupulous young man (it was the Knave of Hearts who stole the tarts); a practical joker; possibly a homosexual.

Diamonds

King A man primarily interested in money and wordly matters; a businessman; dominating, ruthless and obstinate, crafty, hot-tempered; an unfaithful husband or lover; not a friendly person, unless he wants something from you.

Queen A good-looking, flirtatious woman, very attractive to men, pleasure-loving, fashionable and sophisticated; empty-headed and extravagant, a lover of gossip and scandal.

Knave An able young man, likely to succeed; not a reliable friend, as he concentrates on his own interests; obstinate and easily angered.

Clubs

King A man of strong and honourable character, a good husband and father, a loyal ally; upright, humane, clever, helpful.

Queen An attractive, intelligent, highly-sexed woman, moody and changeable but affectionate; good at keeping secrets and likely to have a sardonic sense of humour.

Knave A good friend, reliable and helpful; sincere and open-hearted, a person of integrity; enterprising and intelligent, likely to be touchy and perhaps dashing and extravagant.

The suits have fairly marked characteristics. Broadly speaking, Diamonds are to do with money and finance (because they are the suit of Coins in the Tarot). Hearts is the suit of good luck, pleasure, happiness, friendship, love and passion (because it is the Tarot suit of Cups and the cup is a female sex symbol). Clubs is the suit of worthiness, loyalty, hard and honourable work, but also of debauchery and drink (because it is the Tarot suit of Wands, which are phallic and therefore 'upright' in more senses than one). Spades stand for bad luck, violence, disease, death, ruin (the Swords of the Tarot). A preponderance of any suit in the layout colours the whole interpretation in the direction of that suit. A mass of Hearts means good luck and success, a mass of Spades means the opposite. If the layout is more or less equally weighted between two or more suits, they are now generally thought to take precedence in the order Diamonds, Hearts, Clubs, Spades.

The Remaining Cards

The remaining cards of each suit have a considerable variety of meanings and some of the principal alternatives are shown in what follows. The most important single cards are traditionally the Ace of Hearts, which stands for your home; the Ten of Hearts for good luck; the Nine of Hearts, which is the 'wish-card'; the Five of Diamonds for money, health and happiness; the Ace of Spades, which means death; and the Ten and Nine of Spades, which are extremely ominous. In Britain the full pack of fifty-two cards is generally used, but in other countries it is quite common to use a smaller pack, removing all the cards from the two to the six, inclusive, of each suit.

Spades

Ace A death; illness, bad news, broken relationships, worries, misfortune; cruelty and malice.

Two A move; a change or separation, the break-up of a home or the loss of a friend; an operation or a long journey, possibly a death; the card of the wanderer.

Three Tears; quarrels; a broken love-affair; failure; a journey over water.

Four Illness, sadness; a will; sudden loss of money; poverty; envy and jealousy.

Five Anger, quarrels; try to keep your temper and your patience will be rewarded.

Six A child; 'to the unmarried, a card of caution' (*448*); a delay or a setback.

Seven Loss of money, or loss of a close friend; suffering and sorrow; danger of quarrels.

Eight Be very careful, danger threatens in connection with some current project; expect opposition and treachery; keep a sharp eye out for damaging errors; consider changing your plans.

Nine Said to be the most ominous card in the pack, signifying ruin, failure, poverty, sickness and death, hopes and plans frustrated, families broken up; particularly threatening if close to other black cards.

Ten Bad luck; trouble; disgrace; prison; it cancels the effects of fortunate cards near it; be cautious and trust no one.

Hearts

Ace Your home and what happens there; if near other Hearts, it means love and friendship; if near Diamonds, money on the way or news of distant friends; if near Clubs, happy domestic or social events; if near Spades, misunderstandings and quarrels at home: alternatively, a love-affair.

Two Success and good luck; a happy marriage or friendship.

Three Poverty, shame, imprudence; beware of rash decisions.

Four Sadness, anxiety, jealousy, domestic difficulties; a broken engagement or a marriage postponed, or a marriage delayed till late in life.

Five A gift or an inheritance; a change of scene; a new admirer; unsettledness, indecision; jealousy causes trouble.

Six A courtship or intrigue; do not be gullible or unwisely generous: alternatively, fond memories.

Seven Delusions; dreams that fail to come true; a disloyal or mischief-making friend; a betrayal, broken promises; doubts, puzzlement.

Eight Pleasant company, good food, active social life; a flirtation or affair.

Nine The wish-card; if favourably placed, the wish will come true: alternatively, good luck, hopes fulfilled.

Ten Good luck; the card cancels the effects of ominous cards close to it; health, happiness, success, numerous children.

Diamonds

Ace An engagement or wedding ring; wealth; a letter brings important news.

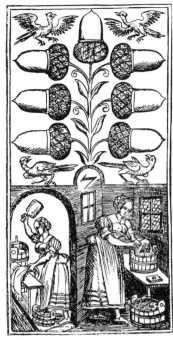
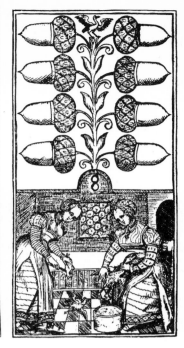

Playing cards showing domestic scenes, designed in the 16th century

Two An unhappy love-affair, or an affair opposed by family and friends; take care, something unexpected is in the offing.

Three Domestic disagreements and unhappiness; possible separation or divorce; legal entanglements.

Four A secret betrayed, or an unfaithful friend; interfering neighbours or relatives; a short journey; a legacy.

Five A very fortunate card; health and success; unexpected good news; your children will do well; happy family life.

Six An early marriage likely to fail or to be ended prematurely; not a favourable card for anyone contemplating marriage; a gift; caution needed.

Seven Minor loss of money, or unfriendly gossip; danger of scandal; lie low and keep quiet.

Eight A late and unhappy marriage; a favourable card in financial matters; travel and exploration; a busy social life.

Nine A surprise connected with money or, if next to a Heart, with a love-affair; restlessness, travel, adventure.

Ten Money; success in business; a rich husband or wife; a legacy; danger from thieves.

Clubs

Ace Prosperity, domestic concord, peace of mind; a letter; success in business; good news.

Two A major disappointment; expect opposition and rely only on yourself.

Three Discord; a long-lasting marriage or affair, or more than one marriage; or a period of time, three years, months, weeks or days.

Four Radical changes, inconsistency, misfortune as a result of some caprice; danger of accident; a land journey.

Five A prudent or wealthy marriage; or news from the country.

Six Hard work brings adequate rewards; a profitable partnership.

Seven Good luck through your own sex, but serious danger from the opposite sex; a prison.

Eight Greed; avoid speculation, do not borrow money; a journey.

Nine Drunkenness; bad luck; friction with friends.

Ten An unexpected inheritance; a successful journey; a reunion; speedy wealth.

Numerous combinations of cards have special meanings, though there is space to list only a few of them here (extensive lists will be found in *306*). The grimmest combination of all is to find the Ace, Nine, Seven and Four of Spades next to each other, which is a portent of total disaster, destruction, ruin and death. Others are:

Two queens facing each other: gossip, rumour
Two knaves back to back: treachery
Queen and knave close together: a clandestine relationship
Ace of Diamonds next to Ace of Spades: a railway journey

Four kings together: excellent luck, unexpected success
Four queens together: pleasure, amusement, lively company
Four tens together: happiness, profit, legacies
Two black nines together: bad news
Two red nines together: good news
Two black eights together: mourning
Two red eights together: wedding clothes
Four sevens together: intrigue, scandal
Two black fives together: danger by falling or water
Two red fives together: unexpected good news
Two black aces together: unexpected news by telephone or cable
Two red aces together: an agreeable invitation
Ace of Diamonds next to Ten of Hearts: an engagement to marry
Queen of Spades next to Ten of Spades: danger by fire
Ace, Ten, Nine and Seven of Spades together: divorce
Five of Hearts with any three tens: love returned, happiness

Laying Out the Cards

Before you can read the cards, of course, you must lay them out in a pattern. There are a great many possible patterns and the apprentice card-reader tries various methods until he hits on those which seem to give him the best results. Before laying out the cards, they must be shuffled by the consulter (*not* the reader), who must meanwhile concentrate on his, or her, plans and hopes, fears and worries, or on a particular question which the cards are to answer. The consulter must then cut the cards, with the left hand and cutting towards the left, and must pick them up with the left hand – the left being traditionally the side of evil and the uncanny or, in the modern occultist's terms, of the unconscious. The reader then deals out the cards and interprets them.

One fairly simple method is to place the consulter's card in the centre and deal six cards in a circle round it, repeating this twice more, so that you have six piles of three cards each. The first pile dealt refers to the consulter himself, the second to his home, the third to a close friend of his, the fourth to his job, the fifth to what is nearest his heart, and the sixth to his immediate future.

In another comparatively simple method, the consulter's card is placed on the table and the rest of the pack is shuffled and cut into three piles. The reader turns each pile face up and uses the three cards showing to give a rough general indication of the trends of fortune. Then the cards are again shuffled and cut, and the reader deals them out in threes, face downwards, round the consulter's card in the shape of a 'wheel of fortune'. If the consulter's card is imagined lying at the centre of a compass, the first set of three cards is placed at the north point, the second at the south, the third at the west, the fourth at the east, the fifth at the north-west, the sixth at the north-east, the seventh at the south-west, the eighth at the south-east, and the last is placed below the second set. While dealing, the reader says, 'Three above you, three below you, three behind you, three before you, three for your house and home, three for your hopes and fears, three for what you don't expect, three for what you do expect, and three for what is sure to come.' The cards 'above you' indicate factors in the atmosphere around you at the moment, those 'below you' indicate factors within your control, three 'behind you' refer to the past and three 'before you' to the future.

Incidentally, you should not read the cards for the same consulter more than once in twenty-four hours. To do so is said to be extremely unlucky.

Another way, after the inspection of the first three cards turned up by cutting, is to deal out seven heaps of three cards each, face downwards. The reader interprets each card separately, then each set of three in combination, and finally takes all of them together. Alternatively, the reader puts one card face down at each point of an eight-pointed star, surrounding the consulter's card, putting them down anti-clockwise from the north point of the star. The consulter then takes the pack and repeats the process twice more, so that there are finally three cards in each of the eight heaps. The reader interprets them singly, then in sets of three, then all together, taking them in anti-clockwise order (which again means movement to the left). Alternatively again, the cards can be set out in the form of the Tree of Life of the CABALA.

To find out if a wish will come true, the cards should be shuffled and cut into three piles. If the Nine of Hearts, the wish-card, is near the consulter's card and in the same pile, the wish will come true, unless the Nine of Spades or Two of Clubs or some other unlucky card is in the same pile.

A Sense of Doom

Yet another way of laying out the cards is to deal them face up in rows, with nine cards in each row until the last. Each ninth card is particularly significant, nine consecutive cards form a complete combination, and each card has a special bearing on the ninth card from it. The consulter's card is included in the deal and the card or cards next to it are particularly important.

Or again, the pack can be shuffled and cut into three piles. Then put the centre pile on top of the right-hand one, and the left-hand pile on top of the rest. Turn the pack face towards you and take the first three cards. Remove the highest card and retain it, putting the other two aside. Continue in this way all through the deck. Then the cards set aside are shuffled again and you look through them, taking out any sets of three of a kind and adding them to the retained cards. Then read the retained cards.

There are many far more complicated methods and various ways of getting the consulter or fate to indicate which cards are particularly significant. The consulter may cut the pack into two or more piles, face down, and pick the pile to be read. Every third or fifth or seventh card may be selected as specially meaningful. When the consulter's card is left in the pack and laid out in the deal, every fourth or seventh or ninth card from it, in any direction, may be taken as more than usually important.

The reader's skill, intuition, psychic gift, artfulness or whatever is at work, comes into play when the cards have been laid out and are to be interpreted. Two or more cards in combination can be interpreted in various ways and the reader's impression of the consulter's personality and circumstances is naturally likely to influence the interpretation. To take a brief example at random, suppose a set of three cards consists of the Ten of Diamonds, Seven of Hearts and Ten of Clubs. This could be interpreted as (a) 'you have good financial prospects, perhaps through business or an inheritance, but beware of betrayal by a disloyal friend or acquaintance', or (b) 'a legacy or a wealthy marriage may be in store for you, but do not rely on all your dreams coming true', or (c) 'you will make a successful journey and perhaps enjoy a reunion with an old friend or old flame, but there is a danger of burglary while you are away and your burglar alarm system may prove inadequate', and so on.

Anyone who attempts a little simple fortune-telling for fun is likely to find that he can frequently sense when he is on what seems to the consulter the right track. He will also discover that even sophisticated people take the game more seriously than he might expect, and if he is of kindly inclination or anxious to continue as a diviner, he will need to be careful about predictions of death and serious misfortune. It is best to state these cautiously and with an express or implied assurance that the consulter can find a way around threatened catastrophes. The chilling feeling of hopeless doom which strikes many people in the face of an unfavourable fortune-teller's prediction (which can sometimes contribute to causing the predicted disaster: see DIVINATION) is a reminder of the fact that we still share with the generations before us a sense of being caught in the iron grip of destiny, of man's helplessness amid the entanglements of fate. R. C.

(Further reading: *306, 382, 383, 448, 483*.)

Catholicate of the West See WANDERING BISHOPS.

Edgar Cayce (1877-1945)

A famous American healer, born in Kentucky, the son of a farmer. In TRANCE he appeared to have the ability to diagnose his own and other people's illnesses – even when

Edgar Cayce

a patient was far distant from him – and to prescribe what were often effective, if sometimes distinctly odd, treatments. He also described people's previous lives in trance (see REINCARNATION) and predicted the future. He was interested in ATLANTIS and believed that the Atlantean civilization was founded on the use of 'Terrible Crystals' which 'could draw force from stars when triggered by psychic concentration' (*163*), and that an excessive concentration of energy from this source caused the catastrophe in which Atlantis was destroyed. Cayce's sons now lead the Association for Research and Enlightenment, which was founded in 1931 to keep records of their father's cases. (For biographies, see *272, 330, 438*.)

Chakras

Also called 'plexuses', and *padmas* or 'lotuses': in Hindu theory, adopted by many Western occultists, they are points at which the physical body and the astral or subtle body are connected, and are centres of psychic

A symbol of the heart chakra

energy. Hindu occultism recognizes 88,000 of them, but only some thirty are considered sufficiently important to have been named. There are seven major chakras, six of which are within the body, including the *muladhara* or sacral plexus in the perineum, which is 'the seat of pleasurable and aesthetic sensations, and the source of desire on the physical plane'. The seventh is the *sahasrara*, the Lotus of the Thousand Petals, or in Buddhism the Head Lotus, which is 'located about four finger-breadths above the crown of the head, and thus lies outside the body and is said to be the halo or emanation of the cerebral cortex' (*485*): see ASTRAL BODY; TANTRISM; YOGA.

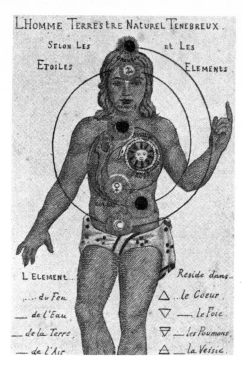

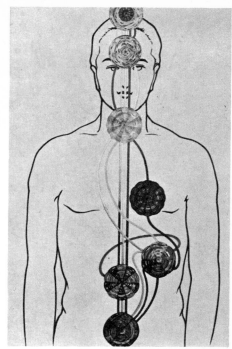

A 17th-century and a modern representation of the chakras

Cheiro

The pseudonym of Louis Hamon, author of numerous popular books on palmistry and other methods of fortune-telling: see PALMISTRY. (*89, 90*)

Paul Christian

The pseudonym of J.-B. Pitois (1811–77), the French author of a *History of Magic*, 1870, and other works, including a book on the 'Red Man', Napoleon's spirit guardian supposed to have guided his career: he devised a blend of ASTROLOGY and the CABALA, in which the planets and signs of the zodiac were connected with the TAROT cards and the 'spirits' of cabalistic magic.

Christian Community

A section of the Anthroposophical Society, formed in 1921 for those members who were Christians: see STEINER.

Christian Science

The Church founded by Mary Baker Eddy (1821–1910), which teaches that sin, disease and death, and even matter itself, are illusions, based on man's failure to understand his true, godlike nature. It is best known for its principle of healing without recourse to medicines and physical treatments, in the belief that what matters in healing is not the body but a true understanding of God. Mrs Eddy, a semi-invalid in her forties, was a patient of P. P. QUIMBY in the 1860s and appears to have been influenced by his

principle of healing mentally, by changing the patient's thought, though the extent of his influence on her has been heatedly disputed. Mrs Eddy published *Science and Health*, the basic textbook of Christian Science, in 1875. The movement grew rapidly, still has a large following and many churches, and publishes the *Christian Science Monitor*: see FAITH HEALING. (*26, 27, 54, 135, 249, 365, 509*).

Church of Light See ZAIN.

Church of Satan See SATANISM.

James Churchward See LEMURIA.

Clairaudience See CLAIRVOYANCE.

Clairvoyance

The psychic ability to see or sense what is not present to ordinary sight, including objects or events far away and ghosts, spirits or 'presences' (clairaudience refers to hearing rather than seeing); awareness of things or objective events that is acquired without sensory means; regarded in parapsychology as a subtype of extrasensory perception (ESP): see PARAPSYCHOLOGY, SPIRITUALISM; for the clairvoyant theory of apparitions, see APPARITIONS, and for the role of clairvoyance in healing, see FAITH HEALING.

Reuben Swinburne Clymer

The founder of the Rosicrucian Fraternity, which is still in existence, with its headquarters at Quakerstown, Pennsylvania; author of *The Rosicrucian Fraternity in America*, 1935: see ROSICRUCIANS. (*93*)

Consciousness (Special States of)

Consciousness, common as it is to all normal healthy human beings (and probably in some degree to a much wider range of living species) is still a perfect mystery to scientists. Familiar and easily manipulatable though it is, its real nature is still unexplained. Consciousness ranges widely in its degree of intensity, all the way down to complete unconsciousness. This gradation may be due to, for example, limited blood supply to the brain, which can result in fainting, or to narcotic DRUGS that affect the nervous system. Purely mental factors themselves also may alter the intensity, the scope, or the variety of conscious experience.

A familiar mental factor that affects consciousness is concentration. Intense preoccupation with one thing may make one insensitive to all others (for example, a man engaged in a fight may not even know of a wound he has received). Habits, too, can be formed that cut off attention to normal distracting stimuli. Hypnotic suggestion (see HYPNOSIS) can make the subject unconscious of normally painful treatment. And various methods of self-discipline are known which can build up intensification or restriction of attention to designated targets. In a word, the state of consciousness is extremely adaptable.

For our purposes here, the chief interest lies in the *unconscious* area of mental agency. This is not the complete absence of mental action, but rather the lowering of introspection to the vanishing point. Yet the mind is still active, in ways that are indirectly verifiable, whether through overt action that follows or through an effort at recall that pulls the hidden thought into the focus of attention by association. There are other phenomena which reveal the unconscious mind in action. Some of these are overt types of behaviour; that is, motor or muscular modes of response. These have been called *motor automatisms* because the person is acting unconsciously ('like an automaton'). The turning of the 'divining rod' in a demonstration of DOWSING, as in locating a suitable site to drill a well, is unconscious, even though the dowser sees and feels the rod turn. His muscles operate without his being aware that they are doing so. They are also guided by an unconscious judgment as to where or when to turn the rod.

This capacity of the mind to operate below the conscious (introspective) level accounts for a vast range of mental activity. Most, but not all, of it is closely connected with the internal functions of the body, and with the sensorimotor system in general. The science of PARAPSYCHOLOGY (which deals with functions beyond the sensorimotor range) studies this area of unconscious mental action at several known points. For example, if the dowser can actually locate underground water without any sensory cues, he must have extrasensory perception of the clairvoyant type. This psi, or 'psychic', ability operates unconsciously in the control of the dowser's muscular movements. This one example illustrates a wide range of motor automatisms in which it can be assumed that ESP takes place.

Another example is the use of the OUIJA BOARD. This is a game-like way of letting the unconscious mind express itself by spelling out messages by means of the letters of the alphabet, stamped on a board or table top. A movable indicator responds to the unconscious muscular actions of the participants (there are usually two), who each have one hand on it. It is popularly used as a 'medium' of communication with unseen agencies; the assumed nature of these agencies depends on the beliefs of the operators. The same opportunity for the use of ESP occurs in this as in all automatic procedures.

Automatic writing (or painting, drawing, sculpture, speaking, and so on) offers another outlet for the unconscious, and one that is more individual than the ouija board. The content of the writing provides for the development of a more personal style and philosophy than the other automatic modalities. It lends itself to experiences interpreted as the invasion or POSSESSION of an individual by an alien spirit, who may write a book or create painting, sculpture or poetry. There is, however, no way to prove the external source of these influences, because the ESP ability which the subject may have would enable him to acquire whatever unusual knowledge his performance may indicate (see AUTOMATISMS).

Thus far it has been found that ESP can and does occur in tests of these motor automatisms, though this is not a better or even a particularly efficient way of demonstrating it. However, the study of motor automatisms has not received intensive research attention as yet, either from parapsychology or general psychology. In fact, the nature of the 'dissociation', or limited state of consciousness, has still not been clarified, though present trends indicate that it will be. Exploration of how the mind can allow a part of the body to separate itself for a time, and to a degree that allows a selective mental control that is hidden from the normal 'self', should be a fascinating research venture.

The *sensory automatisms* are an equally important section of this realm of unconscious mental functions. These are mental activities of restricted unconsciousness which are tied up with a sensory limitation instead of a set of muscles, as in dowsing. Let us take the example of a subject in hypnosis who is temporarily made blind or deaf by suggestion. This is quite different from true blindness or deafness; in this case the subject is functionally insensitive through a limitation of his consciousness. In a deep TRANCE (hypnotic or self-induced), he may for a time be made completely unresponsive or even induced to fall into natural sleep. These are all varying degrees of consciousness which permit sections of mental action to be cut off for a time. In this state of altered consciousness the subject may be induced to experience positive hallucinations (to see a vision, for example) or negative effects such as anaesthesia or amnesia.

Such variations of the range of consciousness (and many more) are not limited to the hypnotic state, but can occur also in other situations in which ESP messages are received. In fact, certain states of limited consciousness are necessary to the operation of psi or psychic ability. This was discovered through the study of spontaneous cases of psi and is gradually being confirmed by experiments. For example, dreaming appears to be one of the states favourable to the experience of ESP, not only in everyday life (as indicated in Louisa E. Rhine's case studies), but also under experimental conditions (see *467*).

Apparitions are other familiar vehicles for ESP experiences. They are, of course, hallucinatory, since they are not physically real, and thus they occur in special states of consciousness. In the normal waking state the average person is not likely to see an apparition. Classifying apparitions as part of the general class of hallucinations, which itself belongs to the sensory type of automatism, helps but still leaves the essential question of the psi apparition untouched. How any vision of an absent person can be experienced as in life is in itself phenomenal, but how it can be conjured up by the mind at the moment of the person's unexpected death (or even some time before), perhaps in some far distant place, is one of the great mysteries of nature.

Even habit, seemingly the simplest sensory automatism, is really profoundly puzzling, for it somehow economically screens conscious attention away from all unnecessary introspection of life's ceaseless changing flow. Only through this protective efficiency can free and uncluttered attention be given to what is essential. Most of the daily trivia that need no introspective vigilance can then go on below the screen of a good habit system. The person with such a system, however, can be reached by his unconscious when the need arises. Such a person is said to be 'intuitive', one who knows what he needs to know without having to be aware of all the details. If the habit system is very protective, the person knows little of how he makes up his mind. He has hunches or intuitions without knowing or caring how they originate. They may have been memories, unnoticed sensory perceptions, rational judgment, or ESP.

These intuitions and something of the way in which they convey ESP messages (when they do) are further discussed, along with other forms of psi experiences, in the article on APPARITIONS. There, against the background of the complex phenomena of parapsychology, will be seen how the varying states of consciousness provide a wide range of manifestations, many still unexplained. J. B. R.

(See also MEDIUMS.) (Further reading: *346, 396a, 397, 447, 467.*)

Control

The term used in SPIRITUALISM and psychical research for an apparently alien personality which speaks through the mouth of a medium, in a voice and manner unlike those of her ordinary personality; generally explained as a secondary personality of the medium, split off from her normal CONSCIOUSNESS. However, Spiritualists regard the control or 'guide' as the spirit of a deceased person which takes POSSESSION of the medium and is in charge of the proceedings in the spirit-world, organizing other communicators, delivering messages from them through the medium, and sometimes allowing them to speak for themselves. Controls claiming to be small children or American Indians are common. A leading British Spiritualist, Maurice Barbanell, says of the latter: 'In the days of their prime, the North American Indians were masters of psychic laws, with a profound knowledge of supernormal forces and how they operated. This qualifies them after their passing, to act as tutors and guides to their mediums' (*16*): see MEDIUMS; TRANCE.

Florence Cook (1856-1904)

A British materialization medium who was investigated in the 1870s by the distinguished physicist Sir William Crookes. Crookes announced that her phenomena were genuine, that he had enjoyed long conversations with Katie KING, one of the materialized spirits, and had once embraced her, and that he had also seen and photographed other spirits. Trevor Hall, in his book *The Spiritualists*, which was received with mixed reactions by psychical researchers, maintained that Florence Cook was Crookes's mistress and that he knew very well that she was fraudulent. (See *136, 203, 204.*)

Correspondences see CABALA; DRUGS; HERMETICA; RITUAL MAGIC; TAROT; TRANCE.

Cosmic Consciousness

The term for a type of mystical experience, coined by R. M. Bucke, a Canadian doctor, author of *Cosmic Consciousness: a study in the evolution of the human Mind*, 1901. He was on his way home in a hansom cab one night when: 'All at once, without warning of any kind, I found myself wrapped in a flame-coloured cloud. For an instant I thought of fire, an immense conflagration somewhere close by . . . ; the next, I knew that the fire was within myself. Directly afterward there came upon me a sense of exultation, of immense joyousness accompanied or immediately followed by an intellectual illumination impossible to describe . . . I saw that the universe is not composed of dead matter, but is, on the contrary, a living Presence; I became conscious in myself of eternal life. . . . I saw that all men are immortal; that the cosmic order is such that without any peradventure all things work together for the good of each and all. . . . ' Bucke believed that his experience showed that 'the universe is God and that God is the universe'. This type of experience, which Freud described as 'the oceanic feeling', is sometimes called 'nature mysticism', a sense of being merged into the One, the sum total and underlying unity of all things, which brings with it, since nature does not die, a conviction of immortality. (*61, 247, 519*)

Cosmic Ice Theory See COSMOLOGY; see also ATLANTIS.

Florence Cook

An invitation to one of her seances

Cosmology (Occult)

Explanations of the universe and of man's place in it are no longer a matter of taste – or not for most people. Physicists, biologists and astronomers have long since constructed a 'scientific orthodoxy' in which various specialized approaches to life and its problems find a measure of agreement. Unfortunately there always comes a time when the conscientious scientist must say simply, 'I do not know'. At this point the occult cosmologist rises triumphantly from his underworld proclaiming that he does know, and that his explanation of the question which has baffled the orthodox scientist explains a great many other natural enigmas as well. The inquirer may be alarmed to learn that he lives not on a round earth, but a flat one, not on the outside of a sphere but inside it, or that his children's children are under sentence of death from the moon's falling out of the sky.

Why are such odd theories of the cosmos called 'occult'? The world 'occult' means 'hidden', and there are two main reasons for the association of strange cosmologies with the more religious and magical regions of the occult underworld. The first is that religious or magical groups often trace their origins back to a time before the emergence of 'modern science' and adopt indiscriminately the cosmologies of their ancestors. The second is that the 'occult' represents in one sense a society of rejects: both rejected people and rejected theories. The word 'rejected' is not necessarily used in an unfavourable sense; for the ideas and the people have been rejected by the Establishment of the day, and there is no reason to suppose that the Establishment is always right. The result is that aspects of human nature – such as the spiritual aspirations of many esoteric groups – with which the Establishment cannot cope, are lumped together in the category 'occult' with theories which the Establishment has in fact tried and found wanting.

Among these are the occult cosmologies. The Flat Earther, Hollow Earther or supporter of the Glacial Cosmology are on shaky ground, and their beliefs are nearer religious faith than seriously argued alternatives to the prevailing wisdom. But unless their jealously maintained theories can be shown to be conclusively false – and few bother to undertake this task – the occult cosmologists enjoy one great advantage. They could always *just possibly* be correct. As a character in a novel by Theodore Sturgeon is made to say, there is every possibility that up there between the orbits of Mars and Jupiter is an object about the size of a basketball made entirely of chocolate cake. Every possibility? Why, yes; its existence has not been shown to be impossible, and therefore it surely must exist.

The Flat Earth

Twentieth-century supporters of the idea that the earth is flat may simply derive their inspiration from a wish to reject both Galileo and Copernicus. However, one centre of the doctrine in modern times has been provided by the remnant of the Catholic Apostolic Church in Zion founded by a Scotsman, John Alexander Dowie, in 1895. His followers banned alcohol, tobacco and a host of other unclean products of nature or modern civilization. Oysters had no place in the Zion City, neither had modern medicine. In 1905 Dowie's most trusted lieutenant, Wilbur Glenn Voliva, led a coup which ousted Dowie from his office of General Overseer; and for the next thirty years Voliva trumpeted forth a fundamentalism more pronounced than that of Dowie.

Dowie's preoccupation had been with medicine – he held to ideas of faith-cure rather similar to those of CHRISTIAN SCIENCE. Voliva turned his attention to the cosmos. Because the Bible was regarded by both Dowie and his successor as true in every literal, ancient ideas of a flat earth became part of Voliva's doctrine. The North Pole lies in the centre of Voliva's world, and the South Pole is represented by the circular circumference, surrounded by a wall of snow and ice to keep ships from sailing off the edge. The stars revolve around the earth, the moon shines with its own light and the sun is 'only 32 miles across and not more than 3,000 miles from the earth'.

Koresh and the Hollow Earth

Voliva's ideas of a flat earth were only incidental to his interpretation of fundamentalist Christianity. In the cult founded by 'Koresh', alias Cyrus Reed Teed (1839–1908), an eccentric cosmology was made the basis of a new religion. Teed's theory was brilliantly perverse: we live *inside* a spherical or egg-shaped cosmos in the centre of which are the sun, moon and planets. In this conception he may have been indebted to the earlier

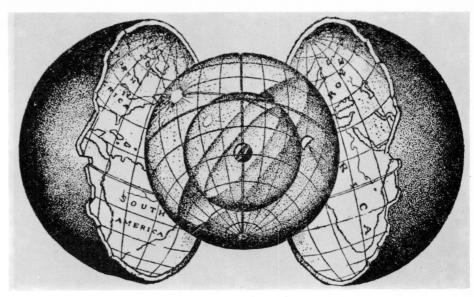

The Hollow Earth as visualized by Cyrus Reed Teed

theories of John Cleves Symmes, a retired infantry officer who devoted much time in the early part of the 19th century to petitioning Congress and stumping the country lecturing on his obsession: that there are openings at the North and South poles through which we can pass to a world inside the globe on which we live. Symmes thought that there were five concentric spheres capable of supporting life, and in 1820 was published a romance called *Symzonia* by Captain Adam Seaborn – who may have been Symmes himself – describing an expedition to an inner world by way of the South Polar opening. In the inner world the gallant Captain discovers a Utopian society, but returns to be defrauded of the profit from the voyage by a rascally entrepreneur.

Symzonia influenced Edgar Allan Poe in writing his uncompleted *Narrative of Arthur Gordon Pym*, and the diagram in the book of the Symmesian inner world looks remarkably like the anatomy of the universe according to Koresh. Koresh, however, claimed the hollow earth as a personal revelation. Early in his life he had been a devout Baptist, and progressed through fringe medicine to ALCHEMY and the occult. In 1869 Koresh was sitting in his alchemical laboratory in New York State, after carrying out laborious operations towards realizing the Philosopher's Stone. A beautiful woman appeared and revealed to Koresh his mission: he was the new Messiah who was to enlighten the world with the gospel of the hollow earth. In the account of this vision there are interesting hints of the affiliations of Koresh with other occult entrepreneurs of the day. The divine visitant spoke to the alchemist calling him by the name of 'Horos'. This name is never

explained, merely recorded; but it provides a link with a pair of notorious tricksters, Theo and Annie Horos, whose impersonation of members of the magical order of the GOLDEN DAWN created a great scandal in London towards the turn of the century. During the 'Horos Case', Annie Horos claimed that she had been a founder of the movement known as 'Koreshan Unity', the sect established by Koresh on the basis of his revelation. This claim has always been regarded as just another instance of Madame Horos's inventive powers, but it seems from the account of Koresh that the name 'Horos' meant something to him also, though what the connection was can only be guessed.

Once possessed of the knowledge that 'we live inside', Koresh set out to demonstrate it to the world. If we do live on the inside of a curving surface, a straight line projected for a sufficient distance must meet the upwards curve described by that surface. Accordingly Koresh organized a band of the faithful, with a device he called a 'rectilineator', to produce a straight line along the surface of the Illinois Drainage Canal. The experiment was repeated the next year on the Florida Coast. Unfortunately for Koresh, the straight line proved to go straight into the sea. However, this did not deter the prophet, who was now convinced that a denial of the earth's concavity was a denial of God.

Koresh abandoned his medical practice and established himself in Chicago, where he founded his Koreshan Unity movement, pledged to uphold the principles of Koreshan Universality and the Cellular Cosmology. In 1894 there were said to be 4,000 followers of Koreshanity; but it was in the expectation of 8,000,000 true believers that Koresh constructed the settlement of Estero in Florida, which he predicted would become the capital of the world. To the doctrine of the Hollow Earth the members – numbering in fact some 200 – of the colony coupled vague ideas of world federation and a doctrine of sexual abstention. Estero kept going until after the Second World War, although the founder, Koresh, Cyrus the Messenger, had expired in 1908. Koresh had predicted that after his death he would arise and bear his followers to Heaven. A vigil was kept over his body, which went the way of all flesh. Finally health regulations required that the unrisen prophet be buried.

Cosmic Ice

So far, the eccentric cosmologies described have all been American, but the occult theory of the universe which has attracted most support was the creation of an Austrian and found its public in Germany. This is the Glacial Cosmology or Cosmic Ice theory of Hanns HÖRBIGER.

Hanns Hörbiger (1860–1931) began life as a blacksmith's apprentice and graduated to becoming an engineer. His success in his profession made him sufficient money to enable him to devote his time to the propagation of his cosmology. The first hints of the Cosmic Ice theory had come to Hörbiger in 1882, when he wondered whether a comet which made its appearance in that year could be made of ice. Some ten years later Hörbiger had a vision which gave him the clue to the universe. By 1906 his theory was complete and he had contrived to convince Philipp Fauth, an amateur astronomer who specialized in observation of the moon. In 1912 Hörbiger and Fauth published their *Glazialcosmogonie* and set about making their views known to the world of learning. It is clear that Hörbiger became quite obsessed with his theory: he once had to take a rest-cure on the advice of doctors concerned for his health, and his letters and telegrams assailed the astronomers of Europe.

The basis of Hörbiger's theory was that the universe is filled with 'cosmic building stuff' which occurs in the form of hot metallic stars and light gases – chiefly hydrogen and oxygen existing as H_2O, 'in its cosmic form', ice. When a block of Cosmic Ice plunges into a hot star a great explosion takes place, and generates a stellar system. Such systems are governed by further Hörbigerian laws, chiefly that of spiral motion towards a central sun. This results in the capture of small fragments resulting from the original explosion by larger bodies in the system. In this way the earth has captured several of the dozen small planets originally existing between it and Mars; and these earlier moons spiralled down on to the earth with cataclysmic results. Our present moon was captured some 13,000 years ago, and the tragedy of its descent will inevitably repeat the great horror when an earlier moon crashed, of which memories are preserved in myths and legends. There is some resemblance between the theories of Hörbiger and those of Madame BLAVATSKY, and to his supposedly 'scientific' ideas Hörbiger coupled a metaphysics which included a Platonic World Soul, the influence of Nietzsche and a belief in a separate world where the laws of Cosmic Ice did not apply.

The theory was naturally pounced upon by European occultists. In particular it appealed to supporters of the existence of ATLANTIS, who found in the idea of a former moon crashing on the earth a marvellous explanation of why their beloved continent had vanished beneath the sea. The idea of Atlantis had in its turn become bound up with the mystical circles of German nationalism known as the *völkisch* movement, which were themselves riddled with occultism. A school of thought arose which followed the eccentric Professor Hermann Wirth and argued on the basis of the flimsiest evidence that the original Aryan master race had arisen in an Atlantis somewhere in the Northern hemisphere. This branch of the *völkisch* movement took Hörbiger to its heart.

Although most of the mystical nationalists who were involved in the early days of the Nazi movement rapidly found themselves in the cold, a number of men who can only be described as 'occultists' did find themselves highly placed in the Nazi hierarchy. Of these one of the most important was Heinrich Himmler. Himmler met Wirth and in 1935 founded an organization known for short as the *Deutsches Ahnenerbe* with the object of cultivating Wirth's ideas. It was only natural that the theories of Hörbiger, fitting so neatly with those of Wirth, would find a place among the pseudo-scientific interests cultivated by the *Ahnenerbe*, and as Wirth himself was gradually elbowed out of the organization, the Cosmic Ice Theory came to occupy a prominent position among the clutter of occultism and antiquarianism which the *Ahnenerbe* made its business.

Himmler's personal interest resulted in frenzied jockeying for position among the propagandists of Cosmic Ice. The Reichsführer-S.S. subsidized the researches of the playwright Edmund Kiss in Abyssinia, and appointed a Dr Hans Robert Scultetus as the head of a department of the *Ahnenerbe* specializing in weather forecasts made on the basis of Hörbiger's ideas. Himmler sent Cosmic Ice literature to high-ranking Party officials, ordered the German expedition to Nanga Parbat to make experiments in the service of Hörbiger and attempted to suppress attacks on his favourite interpreter of the universe. Accordingly, obscure theorists suddenly found themselves the possible recipients of powerful patronage.

On 19 July 1936 at Bad Pyrmont the leading representatives of the new cosmology signed a document known as the 'Pyrmont Protocol'. The burden of this agreement was that Cosmic Ice must be stripped of its fantastic accretions, which would damage the reputation of Himmler, that in this strictly 'scientific' form Cosmic Ice was a 'really Aryan intellectual treasure', and that Hörbiger's son, Hanns Robert Hörbiger, should be appointed intellectual director of Cosmic Ice. Three Cosmic Ice specialists were named as not adhering to the agreement. They represented the out-and-out occultists, the lunatic fringe of the lunatic fringe. One of the three was Hanns Fischer, a friend of Professor Hermann Wirth. He could on no account stomach the appointment of Hanns Robert Hörbiger as Cosmic Ice Führer and wrote angrily to Himmler denouncing the son of the Great Master as a Freemason and a Roman Catholic. The final outcome of the dispute is unknown, but Hanns Robert Hörbiger was still publishing after the war, which is more than can be said of most of the other Cosmic Ice specialists.

The theory of Hörbiger became ever more Nazified. In 1937 the culmination of the process was achieved with the publication by a Nazi propagandist who called himself Rudolf von Elmayer-Vestenbrugg of a pamphlet on Cosmic Ice as part of a series of handbooks for the S.A. The pamphlet concluded that here at last was a German scientific world-picture. 'The Theory of Relativity is to it (Cosmic Ice) as the Talmud is to the Edda.'

An Impulse of Fear

Himmler's own interest was paralleled by that of a personage even more august: Hitler himself. Hitler declared that when he created his ideal city in his birthplace, Linz, he would erect an observatory dedicated to Hörbiger as one of the three great cosmologists. It is probable that Hitler had absorbed the theory through the works of Edgar Dacqué, a Munich scholar who purveyed a sort of occult anthropology with the object of uniting science and religion, and it is fairly certain that the topic was discussed in early Nazi party circles in Munich. What this interest on the part of the Nazi leader shows is not, as some have tried to argue, that Hitler based his military decisions on Hörbigerian premises, but the sort of man he was. A fugitive from the occult underground, an adherent of theories most of the world rejected, Hitler is a terrifying example of what may happen when the conditions of ordinary life are disrupted.

For all the occult cosmologies – Flat Earth, Hollow Earth, Cosmic Ice – have at their root an impulse of fear. It was fear – of new things, of modern science, of criticism of Holy Writ – which drove Voliva to proclaim his flat earth. Martin Gardner has suggested that the Hollow Earth of Koresh represents a return to the womb. In the confused and desperate conditions of Germany between the wars unorthodox and unprovable theories like those of Hörbiger found a ready hearing. It was logical that the Hollow Earth should also find German supporters. The doctrine of Koresh was imported by the First World War pilot Peter Bender, who was in correspondence with the Koreshans. Bender eventually died in a prison camp, and the Hollow Earth Theory never received the official patronage accorded to Cosmic Ice. The department of Alfred Rosenberg did investigate the Koreshan doctrines, when in 1938 one Johannes Lang applied for permission to lecture on the subject. Rosenberg's department discovered that Lang had published a horoscope of Hitler and refused to sanction his plans, denouncing the Hollow Earth as 'a completely unscientific explanation of the cosmos'.

There may still exist Flat and Hollow Earthers. The supporters of Cosmic Ice survived in some numbers after the Second World War, and were particularly active in Britain, where Hörbiger's disciple Hans Schindler Bellamy wrote a series of books linking Cosmic Ice with Atlantis and South American archaeology. The Hörbigerian Egerton Sykes tried to organize an expedition to look for traces of the Ark on Mount Ararat, which would presumably provide ammunition for arguments in favour of a great deluge caused by the crash of Hörbiger's previous moon upon the earth. The Soviet authorities refused the expedition entrance to a strategic zone and were suspected of complicity in some occult conspiracy. The writer Jane Gaskell has issued a trilogy of Atlantis novels and avowed her allegiance to Hörbiger. Recently the supporters of Cosmic Ice have become quiescent, possibly under the impact of man's landing on the moon about which Hörbiger had so much to say.

There are other 'occult cosmologies' besides those discussed in this article, which should be briefly mentioned. These are more sophisticated interpretations of the universe which do not attempt to ape official science. Science, they say, is wanting: it can describe endlessly *how* things work without explaining *why*. In search of an explanation – and often of a First Cause – esoteric cosmologists frequently fasten upon the traditional analogy made by Plato and Pythagoras between the structure of the universe and the musical scale. This complex and intriguing comparison is found in many forms. Two modern examples are the Spiritualist Andrew Jackson DAVIS, who elaborated what he called 'the Harmonial Philosophy'; and the enigmatic figure of G. I. GURDJIEFF, whose detailed exposition of the musical analogy is so complicated that it cannot be summarized. Davis at one end of the scale of sophistication and Gurdjieff at the other might both be described as 'occult cosmologists', yet their cosmologies are of a different type from those of Hörbiger or Koresh. They are 'occult' because they deal with problems which official science neglects, and in the case of Gurdjieff comprehend a different approach to the universe and perhaps different categories of thought from those conventionally regarded as established. But they must be treated differently from the cosmology put forward by proponents of the Hollow Earth.

As for the defiant antagonists of scientific orthodoxy, it is possible to admire their courage in the face of ridicule, and to keep an open mind. You may wake up one morning to find yourself *inside*. And there is always that tiny chocolate-flavoured asteroid just awaiting discovery, whose existence is almost certain because it has not been disproved. There is unlimited scope for the occult cosmologist in the present state of our knowledge. J. W.

(Further reading: *30, 173, 494.*)

Coven

A group of witches: Margaret MURRAY argued that in the period of the witch trials, witches were organized in covens of thirteen, though in fact there is little convincing evidence of this: see WITCHCRAFT.

Crisis Apparition

The ghostly or immaterial appearance of a person who, at or close to the time, is undergoing a crisis, often the crisis of dying; apparitions of this type are quite frequently reported: see APPARITIONS.

Gerard Croiset

A Dutch sensitive, object reader and healer, famous for psychically tracing lost people and objects, who has been intensively investigated by Professor W. H. C. Tenhaeff at Utrecht University. With Croiset, Tenhaeff developed the 'chair test', in which the sensitive describes the characteristics and some experiences of a person who he predicts will occupy a certain chair in a lecture hall at a future date. (*303, 371.*)

Gerard Croiset

Cromlech Temple

A British occult group, apparently founded about 1900, teaching a GNOSTIC interpretation of Christianity: many of its members also belonged to the GOLDEN DAWN. 'The Cromlech Temple itself did not practise Ceremonial Magic – its rituals were largely confined to its initiations, an extremely Christianised version of the Qabalistic Cross, a ritual known as the consecration of the Golden Ark, and the Mystical Adoration of the Quipus, a cord of seven colours worn as part of the Lodge regalia (*262*).

Cross-correspondences

Automatic writings, numbering in all more than 2,000 scripts, produced early in this century by several mediums, including Mrs PIPER and Mrs WILLETT. They produced separately, and almost certainly without collusion, scripts which appeared to emanate from F. W. H. Myers, who had died in 1901 and in life had been prominent in the Society for Psychical Research, and deceased friends and associates of his. It appeared that the communicators had decided to send to the living through different mediums messages which would make sense only when put together, and would then leave no doubt that the communicators had survived death. The scripts, some of which have been published in the *Proceedings* of the S.P.R. from 1906 onwards, are extremely complicated and the correspondences between different

Aleister Crowley

scripts are teasingly ingenious and frequently involve obscure classical and literary allusions. Most investigators at first concluded that the scripts emanated from the dead, but unconscious TELEPATHY between the mediums has been suggested as an alternative explanation: it is doubtful whether any final judgment about the scripts can safely be made in the present state of knowledge: see MEDIUMS; see also AUTOMATISMS. (*213, 303, 341, 411*)

Aleister Crowley (1875-1947)

Aleister Crowley was born in Warwickshire, England, in the year in which Madame BLAVATSKY founded the THEOSOPHICAL SOCIETY. Crowley considered this fact to be highly significant because he and Blavatsky had, in certain respects, similar missions. Both believed themselves to be used as channels of communication by occult intelligences of superhuman knowledge and power, and both were set against what they considered to be the false and pernicious doctrines of historic Christianity.

Crowley was born into a family atmosphere of fanatical sectarian bigotry. His father was a prominent Plymouth Brother and a lay preacher. These circumstances spurred the younger Crowley to acts of rebellion so violent that his mother believed him to be the Beast 666 of the Apocalypse, Antichrist in person. The hell of Crowley's boyhood struggles against the stifling moral code of those days is vividly described by him in his *Confessions*. This, however, was nothing compared with what was to come once he had determined the nature of his life's work, the rehabilitation of 'Magick'. He adopted the old spelling in order to 'distinguish the science of the Magi from all its counterfeits'.

He spent his youth travelling, rock climbing, reading, love-making, and writing poetry, and during the course of his life persisted in these occupations and excelled in each. He climbed some of the highest mountain ranges in the world, attempting Chogo Ri in 1902, and Kanchenjunga in 1905, both in the Himalayas; wrote poetry of great power and beauty – *Aha!* (1909), *The City of God* (1913), *Happy Dust* (1920), to mention

a few of the finest; and he loved innumerable men and women. He also developed a penchant for DRUGS, to which he was introduced in 1898 by Allan BENNETT, the Englishman who became a Buddhist monk and played an important part in establishing Buddhism in the West.

Crowley supplemented his orthodox studies at Trinity College, Cambridge, with delvings into obscure and occult sciences. His mind yearned toward the infinite, his spirit was avid for experiences not to be encountered on earth. At Easter, 1898, at the age of twenty-two, his hunger for spiritual knowledge grew acute. He had been reading *The Cloud upon the Sanctuary* by Carl von Eckartshausen, a book that hints at the existence of a hidden brotherhood of adepts that has guided the evolution of mankind. *The Cloud* exerted such a profound influence on Crowley that he vowed to take his place among the adepts of this invisible hierarchy, the Great White Brotherhood of MASTERS mentioned in works on occultism.

Crowley's spiritual crisis led to his initiation into the Hermetic Order of the GOLDEN DAWN on 18 November 1898 in London. Its chief, MacGregor MATHERS, was not only a scholar of repute, having translated such abstruse treatises as Rosenroth's *Kabbalah Denudata*, he was also a practising magician of considerable attainment. Crowley looked upon him as a Master.

The Golden Dawn collapsed soon after Crowley joined it. Crowley regarded this as due to Mathers's inability to maintain contact on the inner planes with the Secret Chiefs of the Order who were – as Crowley described them – 'the directors of the spiritual destinies of this planet'. This disaster seriously affected Crowley, but he was more than ever determined to contact the real sources of knowledge and power behind such arcane orders as the Theosophical Society and the Golden Dawn. It was from the debris of the Golden Dawn that Crowley gradually developed his Order of the Silver Star (the *Argenteum Astrum*, or A∴ A∴).

Disappointed in Mathers, Crowley travelled in Mexico, Hawaii, Ceylon and India. He studied and practised YOGA, TANTRISM, Buddhism, and pioneered the adaptation of the sexual techniques of Tantric Yoga to the exigencies of the Western tradition of magic. Some years later, during travels in China, he was initiated into the inner working of the I CHING, the ancient Chinese system of magic, which he also brought into line with Western occultism.

The Book of the Law

By 1904 he was on the verge of a major initiation, through which he became convinced that he had re-established the contact with the Secret Chiefs that Mathers had failed to maintain. The event occurred in the most unlikely circumstances. He was honeymooning in Cairo with his wife, Rose, whom he had married in Scotland, in 1903. She was the sister of Gerald Kelly, the portrait painter and eventual President of the Royal Academy, who had been friendly with Crowley at Cambridge. Crowley described Rose as 'purely social and domestic'; she was the last person on earth through whom he would have expected any occult manifestation, so that when she began to receive communications from the ASTRAL PLANE, Crowley was understandably sceptical. She insisted, however, that a vitally important message was about to be transmitted to the world through him, and that he should prepare himself accordingly. She also mentioned names and numbers that tied up with certain cabalistic calculations and ciphers known only to Crowley.

The outcome of it all was *The Book of the Law*, a strangely compelling composition of three short chapters that was dictated to Crowley in Cairo by a discarnate intelligence named Aiwass. The dictation began at noon and ended at one o'clock precisely on three consecutive days in April 1904. Aiwass declared a new law for mankind and the beginning of a new aeon, or era, in the evolution of mundane consciousness.

In his book *Magick in Theory and Practice*, Crowley identifies Aiwass not only as his own genius, but also as that magical current of solar-phallic energy which had, Crowley believed, been worshipped in ancient days in the form of Shaitan, the 'devil-god' of Sumer. The Christians later misrepresented this primordial deity and called him Satan, the adversary of man. As the great god Set, Shai-was worshipped in the deserts of Egypt in pre-dynastic times. According to Crowley, this god was the true initiator of humanity, the Serpent of Wisdom that bade 'Know thyself', adored by the Gnostics, abhorred by the Christians.

The Book of the Law enunciates the Law of Thelema, or the magical will: 'Do what thou wilt shall be the whole of the Law!' The hippie generation of today takes this to mean 'Do as you please', but Crowley discovered to his great cost that it means almost the opposite: 'Do what you have to do, and nothing else.' It accords more with the Taoist idea of letting things take their course without interference by the conceptualizing mind.

Crowley repeatedly tried to shirk the mission with which he believed the Secret Chiefs had charged him, the work of expounding the Law of Thelema and infusing humanity with the dynamism of its magick. He tried to forget *The Book of the Law*; he deliberately went counter to its instructions, and even succeeded in 'losing' the manuscript for five whole years. But, slowly and surely, its influence asserted itself.

The Magus

In 1909, Crowley explored the further reaches of the astral plane, the 'aethyrs' that Edward Kelley and John Dee had investigated three centuries earlier (see ENOCHIAN MAGIC). Crowley claimed that he had been Edward Kelley in a previous incarnation, so in effect he was but continuing the work he had then commenced. The poet Victor NEUBURG accompanied Crowley on these astral excursions, and the traffic they had with the denizens of the aethyrs is described in detail in one of Crowley's most important works, *The Vision and the Voice*.

Between 1915 and 1919 Crowley lived in the United States. There he underwent a series of magical ordeals that resulted in his attaining to the grade of Magus, the penultimate grade in the magical hierarchy to which he had aspired in 1898, and which he had come to identify with the A∴ A∴. He was initiated into the mysteries of this grade, he says, by Egyptian gods who appeared to him in the form of various women. He likened their physical peculiarities to those of the beasts which these gods used as their totems or channels of power (see SPIRITS AND FORCES). The women acted as officers in a temple of initiation wherein the secrets of the new aeon were revealed to him.

By the time Crowley founded his Abbey of Thelema in Cefalu (Sicily), in 1920, he was prepared to spend – and did spend – the remainder of his life promulgating his Great Work, that of acting as the Grand Hierophant or revealer of mysteries to mankind during its transition from one aeon to another. Three such changes occurring within historic times Crowley described as the aeons of Paganism, Christianity, and Thelema, characterized respectively by the dominance of the Mother (represented by Isis), the Father (Osiris), and the Child (Horus). The aeon of Horus, announced by Aiwass in *The Book of the Law*, is that of the Crowned and Conquering Child, of whom Crowley writes: 'Everywhere his government is taking root. Observe for yourselves the decay of the sense of sin, the growth of innocence and irresponsibility, the strange modifications of the reproductive instinct . . . the childlike confidence in progress combined with nightmare fear of catastrophe.'

Scarlet Women

Crowley identified himself not only with the prophet of the new aeon but also with the Beast 666, and *The Book of the Law* does not fail to mention the 'Mother of Harlots and Abominations of the Earth', alluded to in Revelation, Chapter 17. She is the 'Scarlet Woman' who rides upon the Beast. This office was fulfilled by many women during Crowley's lifetime, by none so colourfully perhaps as Leah Hirsig, with whom he set up his Abbey of 'Do what thou wilt'. Together they practised sexual magick and took 'strange drugs', with the object of exploring unseen worlds. Enflamed by drink and drugs, dynamized by sex, Leah saw visions and sometimes apparently succeeded in contacting Aiwass in unknown dimensions of consciousness. Her accounts of these exploits were recorded by the Beast in his magical diaries.

In Crowley's system, one of the most important innovations caused by the change of aeon concerns the basic mechanics of practical occultism. For nearly two thousand years these have depended on elaborate ceremonial. Aiwass unequivocally condemns such methods: 'The rituals of the old time are black. Let the evil ones be cast away; let the good ones be purged by the prophet!'

A certificate presented to Aleister Crowley by the secret Order of Malta

In 1923, having been expelled from Italy, Crowley had to abandon his Abbey of Thelema in Cefalu. He retreated to Tunisia, then to France, where he suffered appallingly in a lonely and desperate fight against heroin addiction; then to Germany, before returning to England for the last fifteen years of his life.

Crowley never relinquished the idea of establishing a magical colony, a community where Thelemites could call forth the strange powers that once had manifested to him through his daemon, Aiwass. Until his death, in Hastings in 1947, he was ceaselessly at work, publishing books and pamphlets, writing poems and innumerable letters to people in all parts of the world. During these latter years, amid the upheaval of the Second World War, he produced his last great work, *The Book of Thoth*, a reinterpretation of the ancient symbolism of the TAROT in accordance with the magical formulae of the new aeon which he had helped to inaugurate. K. G.

(See also RITUAL MAGIC; SATANISM; TRANCE.) (Further reading: *99* to *104* inclusive, *189*, *189a*, *446*.)

Cubic Stone

The Order of the Cubic Stone, a British occult society founded in the 1960s; it publishes a magazine, *The Monolith*: see RITUAL MAGIC. (*262*)

Geraldine Cummins (d. 1968)

An Irish automatic writing medium, whose *Scripts of Cleophas*, 1928, purported to contain detailed information about incidents in the early history of Christianity, conveyed from the world beyond death; more historical information appeared in *When Nero Was Dictator*, 1939. She also wrote *The Road to Immortality*, 1932, *Beyond Human Personality*, 1935, *The Fate of Colonel Fawcett*, 1955, *Mind in Life and Death*, 1956. Her *Swan on a Black Sea*, 1965, is an extremely impressive series of scripts which appeared to be communicated by Mrs Charles Coombe Tennant, herself an automatist under the cover name of 'Mrs WILLETT', who had died in 1956 (see also MEDIUMS). C. D. Broad said of the book: 'These automatic scripts are a very important addition to the vast mass of such material which *prima facie* suggests rather strongly that certain human beings have survived the death of their physical bodies and have been able to communicate with certain others who are still in the flesh.' (*106*, *107*, *108*, *136*, *215*)

Cupido

A hypothetical planet: see HAMBURG SCHOOL.

Crowley set about 'purging' the rituals of the Golden Dawn. He published them in his monumental periodical, *The Equinox* (ten numbers, 1909–13). His former guru, Mathers, vainly took out an injunction against their publication in 1910. By his action, Crowley believed he had finally rendered obsolete not only the Golden Dawn, but in fact all similar orders operating on old-aeon lines.

In ceremonial magic in its traditional form the magician was 'armed' with his weapons, resplendent in robes of 'office' emblazoned with the insignia of his 'dignities', his 'rank'. He was, in effect, arrayed for battle against invisible hosts. But the magic of the new aeon is not of this militant order. Its formula is 'Love under Will', the complement of 'Do what thou wilt'. It requires 'the passionate union of opposites', and a total nakedness of spirit. This is possible only when man discards his rigid attitudes, his mask. He must strip himself even of his body, so that as spirit alone he may explore the interior reaches of consciousness. Without this total identity of matter and spirit he can neither fulfil his destiny nor enter the stream of the new aeon. Man is no longer to confine himself within the magic circle, isolating himself from the rest of the universe, he is one with it, his entire being aflame with the ecstasy of union. Characteristically, Crowley interpreted this cosmic union in sexual terms, and his teaching of sexual magic led to an offer, which he accepted, of high rank in the *Ordo Templi Orientis* (O.T.O.) of which he became the head in 1922 (see GERMAN OCCULT GROUPS).

Crowley believed that man is destined to engender gods. Some of the mysteries of this trans-human alchemy were woven into his novel *Moonchild* (1929), which tells the story of a magician and a woman specially chosen for the purpose. It is doubtful if Crowley ever actually performed the rite described in *Moonchild*, but his magical record shows that he several times attempted to beget a 'magical child' on various scarlet women.

D

Andrew Jackson Davis (1826-1910)

Andrew Jackson Davis was born in Poughkeepsie, New York State, and became the leading theorist of the Spiritualist movement. He was heavily influenced by the Swedenborgian New Church and the Mesmeric movement (see HYPNOSIS). In 1843 there appeared in Poughkeepsie a travelling Mesmerist, who inspired Davis to experiment with trance. The young man rapidly developed remarkable powers, although some of his feats were little better than simple conjuring. He was transported about the country and initiated into the secrets of medicine. Davis opened two 'clairvoyant clinics' which applied the remedies he claimed to have learned, while he himself made diagnoses in trance. He did not obtain a recognized medical degree until 1886, and his prescriptions savour of the rustic magic of several centuries earlier. For a poisoned finger, a frog's skin was to be applied; for deafness, rats' skins behind the ear.

In 1845 Davis began to dictate his chief work, *The Principles of Nature*, in which a poetic and impressive cosmology was coupled to a rabid socialism. The whole was an opaque but powerful mixture, which his English publisher was compelled to disclaim when he published it amid the agitation of 1847. However, while the next year saw the outbreak of revolution all over Europe, in America it witnessed the notorious 'Rochester Knockings' which signalled the beginnings of SPIRITUALISM. Davis and the group round his paper, *The Univercoelum*, established themselves as the leading popular commentators on supernatural matters. Davis rapidly developed the power of CLAIRVOYANCE without going into trance, and from his reports of the spirits living in the 'Summerland' countless mediums have constructed their material. The spiritual geography mapped out by Davis was extremely influential; but to a reader of *The Principles of Nature* it may seem a pity that the prophet departed from the histrionic but impressive mode in which he first began. J. W.

De la Warr Camera See RADIESTHESIA.

Demons See SPIRITS AND FORCES.

Dermatoglyphics

The study of correlations between illnesses and lines and patterns on the hand: see PALMISTRY.

Dermo-optical Perception See PAROPTIC VISION.

Peter Deunov (1864-1944)

'The Master': A Bulgarian prophet who claimed to have descended to the earth from 'Alfeola, the Star of Stars' to pave the way for the coming 'Age of the Slavs'; in 1914 he announced the advent of the AQUARIAN AGE. (*494*)

Devil-worship See SATANISM.

Dharana, Dhyana

Respectively, concentration and meditation in YOGA.

Dieppe Raid Case

In the summer of 1951 two English ladies were on holiday near Dieppe, France; in the early morning of 4 August they heard noises which they thought resembled the sounds they would have heard if they had been in the same place nine years before, during the wartime raid on Dieppe – gunfire, dive-bombing, shouts and screams; whether their experience was psychic in any way is disputed. (*243*)

Andrew Jackson Davis

Direct Voice

A phenomenon associated with some MEDIUMS, a 'spirit' voice speaking directly to the sitters at a seance, not speaking through the medium's vocal apparatus (see CONTROL). It was reported in the early days of Spiritualism in the United States: for example, at the house of Jonathan Koons in Dover, Ohio, spirits spoke through a speaking-trumpet and also sang and played musical instruments. In Spiritualist theory the voice comes from an artificial larynx, constructed by the communicating spirit out of ECTOPLASM – 'often the "voicebox" is attached to a megaphone or trumpet which moves around the room apparently unaided, but really activated by rods of the ectoplasm' (*48*). Direct-voice mediumship has always been particularly suspect because of the obvious possibilities for deception, but some impressive evidence has been obtained: see SPIRITUALISM.

Dissociated States, Dissociation

States of mind in which one part of the personality becomes separated from the rest and behaves as if it was an independent person: see AUTOMATISMS; CONSCIOUSNESS; CONTROL; FAITH HEALING; MEDIUMS; TRANCE.

Divination

To 'divine' something, in everyday speech, means to have knowledge without knowing how one has gained it, without having deduced it or been told it. The fact that the word comes from the Latin for 'a god' and is primarily used of deities is an indication of the old belief that knowledge which springs from an inspiration or intuition or hunch – knowledge which 'something tells me' or which 'I feel in my bones' – is not explainable in natural human terms. It must have a supernatural source, some god must have put it into my mind. There is a built-in implication that knowledge from such a source is generally more important and reliable than knowledge gained by ordinary methods (though with the reservation that the gods speak in crooked ways on occasion), which suits occultism's deep-rooted distrust of reason and preference for inspiration and revelation as wellsprings of truth. It remains psychologically true that people often feel surer of what they divine than of information they acquire by more conventional means, but the tendency now is to explain genuine cases of divination not in supernatural but in natural terms, as some variety of ESP – clairvoyance or precognition or telepathy – possibly with an element of psychokinesis in cases involving the fall of objects such as cards or dice (see PARAPSYCHOLOGY).

All societies have had their specialist

diviners, people thought to be divinely inspired, people possessing or credited with possessing unusual psychic gifts, from the priestess who delivered the riddling oracles of Apollo at Delphi to the gypsy palmist and the modern professional clairvoyant. And although the history of divination is riddled with unsuccessful prophecies, inaccurate diagnoses, false readings, delusion, charlatanry and fraud, confidence has continued to be placed in it, at least at popular levels, perhaps basically because 'sensing' and 'knowing' something without being able to explain how is such a common human experience. Modern parapsychology suggests that this confidence has been rather more justified than the sceptics have allowed, if less justified than the credulous prefer to think.

Though popularly associated with predicting the future, divination can just as well be concerned with the present or the past. Many diviners, including the medicine-men of tribal societies and the village 'cunning men' or 'wise women' of Europe, have concentrated primarily on the diagnosis and cure of disease. Some cases of automatic writing (see AUTOMATISMS) appear to involve divination of either the past or existing records of the past. Object-reading mainly involves divination of the past and present ownership and associations of an object, and diviners like Gerard CROISET and Peter HURKOS have achieved reputations for locating missing people and objects. Dowsing deals with the present – the location of water or oil or, nowadays, bombs. The *New York Times* reported in 1967 that U.S. Marine Corps personnel in Vietnam were using divining rods made out of wire coat-hangers to detect concealed mines, booby traps and tunnels, with some success. In an earlier war, a Pendulum Institute was established in Berlin, in 1942, directed by Captain Hans Roeder of the German navy, in the belief that the British Admiralty was successfully employing diviners to locate German submarines at sea by holding pendulums over maps of the Atlantic, the pendulums moving and swinging when held above the position of a U-boat. The purpose of the German institute was to investigate these supposed pendulum techniques so as to use them against British and American shipping, and the German operators spent hours solemnly and unrewardingly dangling pendulums over charts of the Atlantic (*234*).

Astrology, and to a lesser extent palmistry and numerology, have recently come to be taken more seriously in sophisticated circles than at any time since the 17th century, but as methods of character analysis rather than prediction (though obviously a person's character is bound to affect his future). At more popular levels, however, interest in the future remains paramount, as in newspaper horoscopes, and it is the successful prophecies which hit the headlines. An American seer, Jeane Dixon, for example, came to fame because she had predicted in 1956 that a blue-eyed Democratic President, who would be elected in 1960, would be assassinated: though when 1960 came she predicted that Nixon, not Kennedy, would be elected (*332*).

A Design Behind Chance

An important element in the general tendency to believe in divination, and to want to believe in it, is the human longing for order and design. Divination implies that behind the apparent chaotic confusion of the world and the menace of an unknown future there is system and regularity, and behind the outward randomness of events an orderly pattern. This comforting principle, which also underlies beliefs about LUCK, accounts for the fortune-teller's reliance on apparently coincidental or random factors – the planetary configurations at birth, the fall of playing cards, the lines on the hand, the patterns which tea leaves or coffee grounds happen to form at the bottom of a cup, the page at which a book happens to open, the way in which a few bones or pebbles or twigs chance to fall when dropped (which is the basic method of the I Ching). The principle is that these indicators are not random or coincidental at all. They form part of a hidden design and, if properly understood, are clues to other segments of the design and so to people and events of the past, present and future. The fortune-teller's universe is that of occultism in general – a great, ordered unity whose various phenomena are linked together in mysterious ways. A good many occultists, and others sensing some validity behind traditional systems of divination, have welcomed C. G. JUNG's concept of SYNCHRONICITY, a principle connecting events but not through any mechanism of cause and effect.

The major methods of divination take as their indicators planets and stars (see plate, page 101), lines on the hand, numbers, Tarot cards, or ordinary playing cards, or the hexagrams of the I Ching, which combine a principle of order with a great variety of possible permutations in a way thought to reflect the nature of the universe and the characters of men. Each planet or number or other indicator has one or more key words and ideas attached to it, which are combined with those of other indicators to produce a reading. For example, one of the key words of Venus in traditional astrology is love and one linked with the sign of Cancer is stomach. If Venus was in Cancer when you were born

(as in Napoleon's case), this could imply an undue affection for your stomach and hence a tendency to overeat. But as evasiveness is another key idea of Cancer, the same planetary position could be interpreted to mean fickleness in love and the avoidance of serious emotional involvements. This key word system makes it possible to programme a computer to turn out horoscopes, but as it also allows the individual diviner considerable latitude in his interpretations it may provide a platform and jumping-off point for divination based on genuine intuitive or psychic gifts.

The key words and ideas themselves depend on poetic logic, on parallels, resemblances, analogies and established chains of association. Cancer, for instance, is the sign of the Crab, and so we are told of its natives: 'Like the crab, when hurt or apprehensive they go off sideways, they take evasive action. Like the crab again, they suddenly snap unnecessarily.' This quotation comes from a textbook of the Faculty of Astrological Studies in London, which also says that people with a predominance of planets in Air signs at birth will tend to be 'airy-fairy' and inclined to 'talk hot air', while the natives of Water signs may be 'wet', 'sloppy', 'drips' or 'wet blankets' (*229*). These are simple and naïve examples but the same type of word-play runs all through popular divinatory lore. It is based on the old tradition of man as the microcosm, a miniature copy of the universe at large; so that associations of ideas in the human mind are evidence of real connections and correspondences between the phenomena of the universe.

Self-fulfilling Prophecy

The generally vague and woolly nature of fortune-tellers' language, which is readily observable in newspaper horoscopes and in books by popular astrologers, palmists and the rest, but extends to more academically respectable methods of personality analysis as well, makes it impossible to check the accuracy of most readings but also accounts for much of divination's popularity. Anyone who has tried a little amateur fortune-telling for fun will have noticed people's readiness to fit themselves and their lives into a vaguely worded piece of character description or prediction. This is responsible for the success of some predictions which turn out to be self-fulfilling prophecies. A drastic example, apparently based on an unusually specific prediction, is quoted by Gustav Jahoda in his book on the psychology of superstition (*246*). A woman of forty-three died in hospital in Canada, in 1965, for no discernible reason, soon after a minor operation which had gone perfectly well. It turned out that at the age of five she had been told by a fortune-teller that she would die when she was forty-three. Her birthday had been one week before the operation and she had told her sister and one of the nurses that she did not expect to survive it. The surgeons cautiously suggested that the emotional tensions caused by her expectation that the prophecy would come true may have had a bearing on her death.

A problem which continues to vex all forms of divination is the old one of fate versus free will. Very few modern astrologers, for example, believe that their clients cannot assert themselves against what is written in the sky. On the contrary, they maintain that 'the stars impel but do not compel' and that we need astrological advice to help us to take advantage of or to escape the trends and patterns of fate. But the same astrologers tend to claim a very high rate of accuracy for their predictions: as high as 80 per cent or more, which suggests either that they think that most of us rarely use our free will and seldom follow the astrological advice for which we have paid, or that they do not worry themselves unduly about the difficulty at all. But the problem, that on the face of it if the future can be foreseen it cannot be avoided, is still with us and the modern parapsychological discovery of genuine precognitive abilities in some subjects raises perplexing questions about the nature of time. R. C.

(See also ASTROLOGY; CARDS; DOWSING; DREAMS; I CHING; NOSTRADAMUS; NUMEROLOGY; OBJECT READING; PALMISTRY; RADIESTHESIA; SCRYING; TAROT.) (Further reading: *85, 163, 220, 229, 234, 246, 326*.)

Jeane Dixon

An American crystal-gazer and prophetess: see DIVINATION. (*332*)

Ignatius Donnelly (1831-1901)

An American lawyer and Congressman, best known for his book *Atlantis, the Antediluvian World*, 1882, which has been frequently reprinted. He also wrote *Ragnarok: the Age of Fire and Gravel*, 1883, to show that the Pleistocene Ice Age was caused by a collision between the earth and a comet, and *The Great Cryptogram*, 1888, to prove that Bacon wrote Shakespeare: see ATLANTIS. (*115, 125*)

Double (or Wraith)

An exact replica of oneself, common in folklore, where to see it is usually an omen of death; in modern occultism it is explained as the 'subtle body', which has become detached from the physical body with which it normally coincides: see ASTRAL BODY; ETHERIC BODY; PHYSICAL POWERS.

A pair of dowsers at work

Dowsing

Dowsing, which is often referred to in America as 'water-witching', is the supposed art of finding water, minerals, information or even hidden treasure by non-physical means. Some dowsers use no paraphernalia in their art, simply walking with arms extended over the area of their search and physically reacting, often by violent trembling, to the underground presence of the sought-after substance. More often, however, some simple device is held in the hand as an indicator. The traditional dowser's device is a forked stick, usually of hazel wood, rowan or ash – all woods with a reputation for magical power in European folklore – but most present-day dowsers have abandoned the forked stick in favour of some such implement as a curved piece of whalebone, a pendulum or even, as a more modern expedient, a pair of twisted wire coat-hangers.

A certain confusion exists between the terms dowsing, radiesthesia and radionics (see RADIESTHESIA). Some authorities use radiesthesia as an alternative and more up-to-date term for dowsing: others use it only in a medical sense, defining it as the application of dowsing to the diagnosis and treatment of disease. For our purposes here, however, the use of the term radiesthesia is confined to (a) the body of quasi-scientific and occult theory and practice which has grown up around dowsing, including the manufacture and use of radionic 'machines', and (b) map dowsing.

Dowsing is of comparatively modern origin. Indeed, it is the most junior of all the occult 'sciences', except for such recent and doubtful additions as phrenology. There is no evidence that dowsing was known in classical antiquity and it seems likely that it first came into use in the 14th century in Germany and Hungary, those centres of medieval mining technology, as an aid to the discovery of metallic ores. There are traces of a 15th-century Hungarian 'dowser saint' and at the same period the dowsing rod had already become a standard item in the equipment of those who prospected for ore in the Harz Mountains of Germany. At first the use of a divining rod does not seem to have been considered any more occult or mysterious than the use of a pig for discovering buried truffles. Even as late as the development of the Anglesey copper-mining industry in the late 18th century, at least some mining engineers regarded the dowsing rod as no more than a useful scientific instrument. Long before this, however, the theologians had begun to condemn dowsing – Martin Luther seems to have been the first in the field – and the occultists and magicians had begun to incorporate its practice into their own intellectual systems.

William Lilly, the famous 17th-century astrologer who supposedly predicted both the Great Plague of 1665 and the Great Fire of London of 1666, was particularly convinced of the efficacy of dowsing techniques in the discovery of buried treasure, and his well-authenticated use of what he called 'the Mosaicall rods' in an attempt to discover a treasure which horary astrology (see ASTROLOGY) had indicated to him lay buried in the churchyard of St Paul's Cathedral was the source of a particularly gruesome episode in one of the Gothic novels of the 19th-century writer Harrison Ainsworth.

The extent to which Lilly and other magicians had successfully assimilated dowsing into the body of their own tradition is indicated by the way in which the later grimoires (textbooks of ritual magic) give elaborate instructions for the preparation and use of the divining rod. For example, *Le Dragon Rouge*, a grimoire first printed in the 18th century but probably compiled a century earlier, instructs the magician to cut his hazel wand with one blow of a consecrated dagger at the moment of sunrise, saying: 'I pluck thee in the name of Eloim, Muthraton, Adonay and Semiphoras, that by their power thou mayest possess the virtues of the rod of Moses' (hence, one presumes, 'Mosaicall rods') 'for the discovery of all that I desire to know.' The operator is instructed to use a similar prayer each time the rod is to be used.

'This Wizard or Expert . . . '

Dowsing today is particularly associated with the discovery of water, and it was this aspect of the art that retained for it a semi-respectable status in industrial 19th-century Europe. However mysterious dowsing might be, however unsatisfactory and 'occult' some of its exponents, there seemed no doubt that it was able to produce fruitful results, in the shape of productive wells, when orthodox hydrology had failed to do so. Even the industrialists of Manchester, home of free trade and freethinking, had to recognize this.

The question as to the magical . . . value of the divining rod [wrote the *Manchester Examiner* in February 1886] has just been reopened by the success which has attended its use at the Felton Wagon Works of the Midland Railway Company. . . . The required diurnal volume of water was about five or six hundred gallons, and the well on the premises yielded only half that quantity. . . . Two new wells were sunk to no purpose. The services of a gentleman of the district . . . were then called in. This wizard or expert employed for his purpose a forked hazel twig . . . After walking about the premises for some time, the point of the fork began suddenly to bend down. . . . The wielder of the wand declared that in the spot indicated there would be found a plentiful supply of water. The same phenomenon was repeated at another spot . . . and the same confident assertions were made . . . assertions which the results obtained, by actually sinking wells, amply justified, the quantity of the water to be obtained being apparently inexhaustible. . . .

There have been no radical changes in

technique since the above description was written and, except for the fact that the hazel twig employed in 1886 would probably now be replaced by a pendulum or a 'fork' made of whalebone or metal, it could easily be an account of a dowser at work in the field today.

Does dowsing really work, or are its successes the result either of chance on the one hand or of the geological and hydrological knowledge (perhaps subconscious) of the dowser on the other? It is difficult to say with any certainty but it would be hard to reconcile either of these hypotheses with, for example, the results of a field test carried out in the 1890s on John Mullins, a noted British dowser of Colerne, near Chippenham in Wiltshire. This test, which took place in Sussex and is fully recorded in Sir William Barrett's *The Divining Rod*, 1926, resulted in the discovery of water by Mullins where professional hydrologists had signally failed to find it. Mullins's success was no mere flash in the pan, for only a few years earlier he had produced equally remarkable results in the course of a series of experiments in Yorkshire. Perhaps the most convincing evidence of Mullins's consistent success is provided by the fact that he undertook to sink and construct wells at the places where he claimed that water was to be found.

It is true that the experiments undertaken in the field with Mullins and other professional dowsers have not (and by their very nature could not have) conformed to the rigorous scientific standards of laboratory-based psychical research. It is equally true that in laboratory tests 'the level of success has always been inferior to the reports of outstandingly accurate performances in natural surroundings' (497). On the other hand, if dowsing or any other 'wild talent' does actually exist, the imposition of tightly controlled experimental conditions may well inhibit its appearance – the very existence of the experimenter invalidating the experiment.

Perhaps the position can best be summarized by saying that there is no absolute scientific proof of the existence of a 'dowsing faculty', but that if the possession of such a faculty had been a capital offence, Mullins and many other dowsers would indubitably have been hanged.

If the dowser *can* discover underground water or other substances where the scientist has failed to do so, how does he achieve his results? A possible answer was given in 1962 by Y. Rocard, Professor of Physics at the Sorbonne. He claimed to have established that the presence of substantial amounts of water in the soil is associated with very weak changes in terrestrial magnetism,

that a great many people are capable of biologically distinguishing weak magnetic gradients, and that magnetic currents cause a relaxation of dowsers' muscles and a consequent movement of the divining rod when subterranean water is present.

These claims are of great interest but, even if they are fully validated, they leave many questions unanswered. For example, some dowsers seem to be able to detect static water underground with considerable success. How? For only flowing water or water in contact with clay beds will produce changes in magnetic gradient. It is even harder to see how medical or map dowsing could be explained by theories involving terrestrial magnetism. Over 400 years after Luther denounced it as diabolical, dowsing remains almost as much a mystery as ever. F. K.

(See also AUTOMATISMS; CONSCIOUSNESS; DIVINATION.) (Further reading: *242, 324, 499, 503*; see also the *Journal* of the British Society of Dowsers.)

Dreams

Dreams are perhaps the most commonplace of all the mysteries experienced by mankind. They have been recorded in all ages, inspiring, counselling, delighting, and sometimes terrifying the dreamer. There has been universal speculation about them but as yet no one knows what a dream is, or why we dream. Dreams accompany sleep, another unexplained mystery. Here for the asking are two of the most fascinating problems that any person can encounter any night of the week.

Sigmund Freud, who wrote the classic work on dreams, never really finished his thesis. From its first publication in 1900, right up to the time of his last illness, he kept revising not only the text but the ideas it contained, and felt that research in the field should go on developing. Others have followed his clues but the skein of the mystery is still not unravelled.

Man sleeps for a period of almost eight hours every night, so that every healthy person is a kind of Rip van Winkle, sleeping away a huge fragment of his lifetime. A man living the Biblical span of threescore years and ten will have spent almost a quarter of a century of his life in sleep. In other words, at the age of seventy he has spent as many years in sleep as the full life-term of his grandson aged twenty-five. Of this time asleep, he has spent the equivalent of seven years, day and night, in dreaming.

A strange drama takes place in the theatre of sleep, with its division into acts, with the observance of its own dramatic unities and, like the denizens of another world, its phantasmagoria of actors. Some of the stages

Sigmund Freud

through which a man shifts from a condition of full consciousness to deep slumber have been noted from very early times, and others have been discovered as a result of recent experiments.

First there comes a preliminary stage of drowsiness, when the alert, practical senses seem to drift into a condition where the mind is no longer in control. There is a vague shimmering of consciousness, the awareness of things around us is slowly lost, while the real world, if real it is, recedes, and we find ourselves falling helter-skelter into the whirling abyss. The sable wings of sleep enfold us. When we return to normal consciousness some eight hours later we may have only a vague reminiscence of having dreamed. We have actually had about half a dozen dreams but if we have slept without waking, these dreams have faded beyond recall.

Certain curious features have been observed about this drift from drowsiness to slumber. Some people, just before falling asleep, have a prevision of the dream state in a series of spontaneous retinal images that flash past in the form of scenes and faces, such as are sometimes visualized when the eyes are shut. These hypnagogic hallucinations, as they are called, have been explained as elaborations of liver-spots that float before the vision, or as ocular spectra that stimulate the optic nerve and provide visual images to which the sleepy mind gives a local habitation and a form. Frequently accompanying the stage of hypnagogia is what is known as the myoclonic jerk, a sudden miniature burst

of activity in the brain like an epileptic seizure. This lasts for only a fraction of a second, but convulses the body and sometimes causes the sleeper to let out a muffled grunt. Precisely what causes the jerk is not known and must be added to the catalogue of enigmas that surround the dream process.

Physical Reactions

Dream research today is aimed at discovering something about the nature of dreams: what a dream is; why we dream; what part of the brain does the dreaming; how far internal and external stimuli condition dreams; how long a dream lasts; how often we dream during a normal period of sleep; whether we dream all the time we are asleep; whether everyone dreams, including those born blind; whether dreams vary with age and sex; whether dreams come to newborn infants, to the foetus in the womb, to animals. And most important of all, the meaning and purpose of dreams and their relevance to our everyday existence.

An important clue to guide us into this region is provided by the physical reactions of the sleeper, specifically the changes in his bodily position, the alteration in his pulse-rate, respiration and 'brain waves'. The brain is alert, excited and electrically active during sleep, but in a different manner from the waking state. Measured by the electro-encephalogram (EEG), it is found that faster waves, called alpha waves, characterize the conscious mind, while slower delta waves of high amplitude characterize the sleeper. During sleep EEG recordings show that we move from alpha to delta waves in irregular patterns that are still not clear and that may alter with the sleeper's health, mental state, conflicts and problems, the drinks and drugs he may have taken, and other factors.

In 1952 a young scientist noted that the eyes of babies sometimes moved under their closed lids while they slept, and an entirely new avenue was opened up for research. It was soon observed that such eye movements were natural in sleep, and that the eyes of children and adults, and also of cats, dogs and other animals, revealed the same curious agitation at certain times during sleep. At such times the movements of the eyeballs resemble the back and forth eye movement of a person watching actors on a stage. The discovery of these quick optical shifts, now known as Rapid Eye Movements (REMs), let a dim but distinct light into the darkness of the dream process. Interest in dreams moved from the couch of the psychiatrist to the laboratory of the scientist, and dream laboratories sprang up in America, Britain, France, Germany, Russia, South America and elsewhere.

Certain very significant conclusions have so far tentatively emerged from the analysis of REMs. Everyone dreams, including those who believe they never do. It is not true that we start dreaming as soon as we fall asleep and continue to dream till we wake up. We have periods of dreamless sleep. Dreams are accompanied by REMs; it is fairly well established that if a person manifests REMs, he is usually dreaming. REMs take place at recurrent intervals of about an hour apart and there may be between five to seven REM phases per night.

Certain physiological processes are also an invariable concomitant of dreams. The breathing becomes shallow, irregular and rapid; the pulse rate increases; blood pressure rises. The sleeper lies motionless and continues to lie still while the dream lasts. If a snorer, his snoring stops or is reduced. Sometimes the dreamer carries out miniaturized mimetic actions with his hands, legs or face, just as a sleeping dog's legs twitch as if it were chasing a rabbit. Infants may make sucking sounds, children grimace, and in adult males the penis may swell and erect. Most sleepers when awakened immediately after an REM phase can recall their last dream clearly, since it is still fresh in their minds. Each REM phase is followed by a phase where there is no REM, labelled NREM-sleep, which may last from 20 to 30 minutes. During NREM-sleep the sleeper stirs and changes his sleeping position. REM sleep is light sleep; NREM sleep is deep.

It has further been established that REMs vary with age. Dreams occupy somewhat less than a third of the sleeping time of adults, about half the sleeping time of children, and most of the sleeping time of infants. Researchers find some evidence to suggest that kittens 'dream' before their eyes are opened, and unhatched chickens 'dream' while still in the egg. But while the researcher can awaken a man during an REM phase and hear him relate his dream, he has no means of knowing, for instance, what makes up the dream of an unborn child in his mother's womb, if indeed he dreams at all. Not all REM phases coincide with dreams. Only when an electrode fixed to the abdomen of a pregnant woman can produce not lines on graph paper but pictures on a screen will we be sure that the foetus is dreaming and not merely doing a few 'cerebral jerks' to limber up his brain before entering the struggle for existence in the world outside.

Time and Illusion

How long does a dream last? Obviously not as long as the time covered by the dream experience, for the dreamer can live through a span of time much longer than the length of a night, even assuming that he dreams all the time he has been asleep. We can pack many weeks or months into a few minutes of dreaming. One early researcher, Alfred Maury (1817–92), recorded a lengthy dream in which a vast panorama of events of the French Revolution was witnessed by him in vivid and elaborate detail. He saw some of the horrors, spoke to the protagonists and was himself finally accused of crimes against the people, was tried, found guilty and led to the place of execution. He felt the drop of the guillotine at the same moment that the bed-tester slipped from its frame and fell on the nape of his neck. He concluded that between the time the post struck him and the time he awoke the whole preceding dream sequence of the French Revolution had flashed through his mind in a sudden burst, to rationalize and account for the falling bed-post.

Here we seem to enter into the nebulous world of illusive time. Hindu and Buddhist legends illustrate this concept, called Maya, the deceptive veil created by divine power by which men are made to believe in the reality of the phenomenal world, which is actually unreal. All things exist only in Brahma, who is the only reality. Among the great illusions is that of time. Time is instantaneity; all things are happening now, as the dream of Maury shows. The same point is made in Islamic legend, where the angel Gabriel once called on the prophet Muhammad to take him on a tour of heaven and hell. As they set out, Muhammad upset a vessel of water, but when he returned from the trip, which seemingly took many weeks, he was just in time to save the vessel from falling over. His whole journey through the two worlds had taken an infinitesimal fraction of a second.

We have also to consider how real dreams are, which is not as absurd as it sounds, for men in all levels of culture have given thought to the possibility that our dreams might have a reality of their own. For some decades now a new respect has been shown for the intuitive wisdom of 'savage' peoples, and it is interesting to reflect on the seriousness with which they regard their dreams. Anthropologists have found that a number of preliterate tribes do not distinguish between dreams and reality. Let a man dream he is bitten by a rattlesnake and he will take all the treatment necessary for snakebite when he wakes up. The sleeper who dreams that he has committed adultery will pay the rightful husband the fine due to him by custom. The man who dreams that he has fallen into a river will repair to a wizard to have his soul fished out.

Children often reveal the thought pro-

Transmitting an English lesson to students asleep in their beds

cesses of primitives, and frequently give as much credence to their dreams as they do to the world around them. Yet this credulity is not confined to children or to those who live in less advanced societies, for the idea of the possible basic reality of dreams has struck many sophisticated thinkers. 'During sleep,' said the Greek sage Heraclitus (d. 475 B.C.), 'each one returns to his true nature.' There is the oft-quoted story of the Taoist philosopher and mystic Chuang Tzu (369–286 B.C.), who on awaking from dreaming that he was a butterfly, asked: 'Am I Chuang Tzu who dreamed that he was a butterfly, or a butterfly now dreaming that I am Chuang Tzu?' The French thinker Blaise Pascal (1623–62) said, 'Apart from faith, no one has any assurance whether he is awake or asleep. Who knows that when we think we are awake, we may not be in slumber, from which slumber we awaken when we sleep?' The philosopher René Descartes (1596–1650) held the same view, and said he was 'clearly aware that there are no marks by which the waking state can be distinguished from sleep'. The German philosopher Schopenhauer (1778–1860) asked, 'Is there a sure criterion by which dream and reality may be distinguished?' and could not arrive at an answer. Some modern thinkers believe that our consciousness is a somnolent condition and that the mind is asleep. The Russian-born mystic G. I. GURDJIEFF said that most people are unawakened and for them life is a real dream. Only a handful of people of advanced degree are truly awake. Men, he declared, were sleep-walking, and his methods were evolved specially for waking them up.

The Meaning of Dreams

If Chuang Tzu had needless doubts and this world is indeed a reality, then we have to

ask, what is the relevance of dreams to our lives? And, do we dream true? Can one have precognitive dreams that reveal what the future holds in store? Many examples of such dreams have been quoted but few find scientific acceptance. The vast majority can be dismissed as coincidence, and some may be explained by TELEPATHY. Yet a certain residue remains of dreams which seem to be genuinely precognitive. In *An Experiment With Time* (*133*), J. W. Dunne put forward, with some scientific plausibility, the view that future events can be foreshadowed by dreams.

In any event, whether true or not, men have from early times sought for some meaning in their dreams. In one form or another every student of dreams has come up with a system of what was earlier known as *oneirocritica*, 'dream judging', or the interpretation of dreams. 'A dream not interpreted', said a 3rd-century Jewish writer, 'is like a letter not read', a statement reflected in the modern view that a dream is 'a letter to oneself'.

Occasionally a dream appears in a clear and undisguised form, and the interpretation is a straightforward one. Dream of failure in a forthcoming enterprise and it means that you will fail. The subconscious fear of failure may account for the projection of a failure-motif into the dream, but such considerations were not taken into account by the 'dream-judges' of earlier ages. In ancient times it was commonly believed that dreams were direct messages from the deities or the spirits. An Egyptian prince, later to become the Pharaoh Thothmes IV, dreamed that the sun-god appeared to him and commanded him to free his image, the Sphinx, from the sand that was piling up against it. As soon as he ascended the throne of Egypt, Thothmes obeyed the god's behest. In many parts of the ancient world the sick would go to a temple to sleep and dream that the gods healed them, and this practice of 'incubation', as it was called, continued in Europe till well into the Middle Ages.

There is also a punning interpretation of dreams, as in the dream of Alexander the Great. In the middle of his troublesome seven-month siege of Tyre, he dreamed that he saw a satyr dancing, and his dream-interpreter decided that this must mean *sa-tyros*, 'Tyre is thine', which spurred Alexander to victory. Similarly, some psychoanalysts today, looking for latent meaning in a dream, find in the eager girl's dream of violets her secret desire to be violated. Others interpret by contraries, so that if you dream of friends, enemies are meant, births signify deaths, and success failure.

The many popular chapbooks that interpret the apparitions which beset our sleep derive from a tradition going back to the Roman soothsayer Artemidorus of Daldis (fl. A.D. 150), who collected the current lore of his day. His manual became the source-book of dream-interpretation for over a thousand years. But the art was centuries old before Artemidorus made his compilation. Clay tablets of the royal library of King Assurbanipal of Assyria (c. 650 B.C.) bear inscriptions of dream-interpretations that were already old even at that time. An Egyptian papyrus dating back to 2000 B.C. is devoted to the same intriguing subject. Some of the interpretations in this document might be found in any modern popular dream-book which arranges dreams in alphabetical order and gives their meanings like a dictionary.

Today the psychologist has his own little glossary of dream-symbols which range from the alchemical to the zoological. To one school pointed things mean a phallus, round hollow things the vagina, rhythmic movements signify coition. Some give dreams a prehistory in ancestral fears and experiences. Some believe that we dream our desires. We are said to be responsible for our unconscious mistakes, slips and errors, for our forgetfulness, our daydreams, our inadvertencies. This is but one remove from the belief that we are responsible for our dreams.

Sleep and Death

One common feature has been noticed about the recollection of dreams. Most persons awakened more than about ten minutes after the REMs have ceased are unable to recall their dreams. The rapid loss of memory of a dream is among the most astonishing aspects of the whole subject. It is as if the state of wakefulness instantly sweeps away the delicate cobwebs that constitute the dream fabric. Since actual events that have occurred ten hours previously can be distinctly recalled by anyone, it is curious that a vivid dream only ten minutes old should vanish so utterly and without trace. In fact, a dreamer can wake up in the morning with the last dream still in his mind, yet between waking up and getting out of bed, his dream may be lost beyond recall.

It has been suggested that we have a dream memory which differs from the waking memory, and that some part of ourselves comes into operation during the dream-state that is only tenuously linked with the conscious mind. In OUT-OF-THE-BODY EXPERIENCES it has been found that our consciousness seems to shift out of coincidence with the physical body and becomes located somewhere outside the body, which it perceives as it might any other extraneous object unconnected with it (see ASTRAL BODY).

It has also been somewhat tenuously established that the source of REM activity, and hence presumably the seat of dreaming, is in the most primitive part of the brainstem. Hence it is conjectured that dreams are a dim instinctual groping back towards a primordial way of thought. If we proceed along this line we impinge on the landscape of death. It has become a cliché of poetry to link Sleep with his brother Death, and indeed the two have much in common.

Inertia being the natural state of things, consciousness is only a complication introduced into the slow drift of man's existence back towards inertia. The ritual of sleep is like a preparation for death. The nightly ablution of face, hands and mouth, the change of workaday clothes for shroud-like garments, the prone position we assume as we lie in bed, the gradual upturning of the eyes, the slowing heartbeat, the loss of awareness of the outside world, the sudden myoclonic jerk like the final convulsion, could be taken as the stages in a journey to our demise. The study of dying and the immediate post-mortem state has convinced some students that at death the brain-consciousness is extinguished and another consciousness supervenes which perhaps we carry with us into another sphere. If this conjecture has anything to recommend it, then the dream-mind too might belong to another dimension. Dreams are outside space and time, and 'happen' to us in their own illogical and surrealist manner.

The dream was once defined as 'sleep-consciousness', but this definition was soon abandoned as inadequate. Freud spoke of dreams as the royal road to the unconscious. But the unconscious is a rag-bag of no determinate dimensions and it is therefore impossible to say where the royal road will take us. The imagery of the dreamworld as a whole differs from that of creative thinking, imagination, daydreaming, hypnosis, or drug experience. All these are related to the conscious mind in some way. But not the dream. The Swiss psychologist C. G. JUNG regarded dreaming as a venture into a primordial archetypal world whose hinterland is the collective unconscious, with symbols common to all religions and mythologies.

Some theorists hold that conscious activity creates toxins in the brain which dreams help to dissolve. Others regard the dream process as a means for clearing the day's debris which has clogged the mind. Again, external and internal stimuli provide a background for a large proportion of dreams. A sleeper whose feet have slipped out from under the bedclothes and are exposed to the chill night air may dream of a march through Antarctica. A dinner of highly-seasoned food can

start a dream about a trek through a burning desert in a fruitless search for an oasis. A dream of stricture can follow a full bladder.

Freud believed that dreams protected sleep, and attempted partially to fulfil our inmost desires, unhampered by the puritanical superego that in our waking moments censored and repressed them. But dreams have other functions as well. For one thing, they assist creativity, and the history of literature, music, art and even science, provides ample illustration of how inspiration may come in the form of a dream, almost like the divine messages believed in by the ancients.

Are dreams necessary for our survival? It has seemed to some students of the subject that dreams are very important indeed and that there is an REM (i.e. a dream) cycle in every man which is necessary for his mental health and well-being. Alcohol, drugs, sleeping pills, reduced the amount of REM sleep and could in part account for the disturbed mental condition of the addict. If a sleeper is allowed to sleep undisturbed but is awakened each time his REMs begin, he then takes a shorter time to reach the REM phase when he goes to sleep again. The next time his dream phase is interrupted he will reach the dream stage still sooner, and repeated interruptions will quicken the tempo of his struggle to reach the REM objective in order that he may start dreaming again. It would appear that it is his dreaming and not his sleep that matters. There will come a time when he will have to be constantly awakened because he will be constantly snatching at a dream as soon as he falls asleep. Micro-sleeping will bring fleeting wisps of micro-dreams that come and go in flashes.

A person who is not allowed to dream while asleep will start dreaming when he is awake. The hypertense dream-psyche will burst through the waking consciousness and he will live in a dream world, the world of the psychotic and the disoriented. Continued dream deprivation will bring mental collapse and may eventually lead to death.

We must, it seems, work out our everyday tensions and lunacies in dreams. Wilhelm Wundt (1832–1920), the German experimental psychologist, called dreaming a state of 'normal temporary insanity'. St Thomas Aquinas, the great theologian of the 13th century, remarked that syllogisms go wrong in dreams, and Freud has said that the dreamer cannot do arithmetic. The dreamer lives in a ghost world and ghosts, they say, cannot count. Throw half a dozen pebbles at a pursuing spirit and he will feel a compulsion to count them, and will still be busy at it when cockcrow drives him to the nether regions again. A modern psychologist has perhaps summed up everything we can say for certain about dreams: that they allow all of us to 'go quietly and safely insane every night of our lives'. B. W.

(See also APPARITIONS; CONSCIOUSNESS; PARAPSYCHOLOGY.) (Further reading: *114, 117, 133, 164, 201, 289, 295, 300, 514.*)

Drop-in Communicators

Communicators at seances who are previously unknown to the medium and the sitters. If their statements about themselves can be verified, they are of particular interest as they militate against the view that information provided at a seance is obtained by TELEPATHY from those present. (*177*)

Drugs (in Modern Occultism)

With a few exceptions, modern occult writers have tended to condemn the use of psychoactive substances. 'Drug-taking', in fact, has often been portrayed as an attribute of either a villain or a victim or, at best, of some misled dabbler. Dion FORTUNE, for example, in her *Psychic Self-Defense* (*161*), calls the use of drugs in magic both dangerous and undesirable, as well as illegal (though she does leave open the possibility of experimentation by researchers under medical supervision). Another modern writer, William Gray (*193*), finds the results of psychedelic exploration empty of any real value, since it exposes people to perceptions which they cannot assimilate, due to lack of preparation.

At the same time, however, there are those who do think such drugs useful, and who even admit to having used them. For the most part these writers are connected (though perhaps at some distance) with the work of Aleister CROWLEY – for example, Israel REGARDIE and Louis T. Culling; though there are those whose connections with Crowley are so remote that they are probably inconsequential – for example, Andrija Puharich, some of whose experiments with *Amanita muscaria* (the fly agaric) were attended by Aldous Huxley, who had himself been introduced to mescaline in Berlin by Aleister Crowley. It is the general position of these people that psychotropic substances can be useful aids in some phases of occult work: all point out the need for caution and for an occultism that does more than merely rely on the drug to do all the work: see, for example, Regardie's *Roll Away the Stone* (*390*).

The notion that psychoactive drugs are not a legitimate part of occult practice does not seem to have developed until well into the 19th century. It is already noticeable in Eliphas LÉVI's *Transcendental Magic* (*284*, originally published 1855–6), but is strikingly absent from Francis Barrett's *The Magus*,

Aldous Huxley

1801 (*19*), in which experiments involving the use and preparation of naturally occurring psychotropic drugs are specifically described. Most of these are also found in much earlier writers; a recipe for extracting toad 'venom' somewhat like Barrett's (though the whole toad is used) can be found in 'The Vision of Sir George Ripley', in Elias Ashmole's *Theatrum Chemicum Britannicum*, 1652. Porta, in his 'Physical Experiments' (see *372*), describes how to use nightshade, poppy, datura and other drugs to cause sleep, dreams and madness; earlier, there was a time when distilled alcohol was thought to be the elixir of life, and the quintessence. Furthermore, such studies as Castaneda's accounts of his work with the Yaqui shaman Don Juan (*83, 84*) make it plain that the magical and religious use of psychotropes is not necessarily related to 'primitive' or 'degenerate' ways of life; and in Furst's *Flesh of the Gods* (*168*) there is ample evidence of the existence of a very sophisticated knowledge of the cultivation and processing of drug-bearing materials among certain groups of American Indians. It was the research of the Wassons (*489*) which first made plain the extent of magico-religious drug use, and it is appropriate that it was R. G. Wasson who explored the connection of *Amanita muscaria* with the beginnings of Vedic religion. More immediately, Puharich has investigated the effects of various drugs on psi phenomena, without reporting any dire results (*379, 380*).

The precise nature of this seeming difference of opinion about the legitimacy of drug use in occult work is somewhat obscure. Few occult writers deal with the subject in much detail (though the advocates are usually more specific and concrete, perhaps from feeling defensive): they seem to be, at best, no more sophisticated about particular substances and their effects than the exoteric pharmacology and pharmacognosy of their day. Many of the strictures of earlier writers (for example, Fortune's comments about the effects of psychotropes on the heart and about the problem of standardized dosages) have become outmoded through changes in the pharmaceutical industry (new drugs and better methods of preparation), through increased sophistication of the equipment and skills used in assaying, and through their increased general availability. Other warnings, about the effect of unprepared encounters with other forms of consciousness and so on, seem to derive more from the glamorized images of the effects of drugs, rather than from any concrete clinical experience with either psychedelic therapy or the management of upsetting reactions from personal experimentation with psychotropes.

The above comments are probably least true about Crowley's writing. In *777*, his essay in Cabalistic taxonomy (*104*), he makes a fairly detailed attempt to classify various drugs in terms of the Tree of Life (see CABALA), and in fact does one impressively unlikely thing: he assigns mace and nutmeg to the second TAROT trump, the Magician, which is attributed to the planet Mercury, and assigns peyote to the Sefira Hod, to which Mercury is also attributed. The attribution of peyote to Mercury fits in well with the native American use of peyote as a guide and teacher, sometimes personified as Mescalito, quite consonant with the role of Hermes as psychopomp. But it was not generally recognized until quite recently that the psychotropic substances in mace and nutmeg are very closely related chemically, though somewhat less so pharmacologically, to mescaline, one of the important constituents of peyote.

Also, Culling (*105a*) reproduces a painting attributed to Crowley about 1912, described as a glyph of initiation; in the foreground are what seem to be representations of both red and gold forms of *Amanita muscaria*. This would imply that Crowley had some knowledge of the psychotropic properties of the mushroom: yet it is not mentioned in *777* (first edition 1909). The suspicion that Crowley had some more effective insight into the pharmacology and pharmacognosy of drug plants is allayed, however, by some equally stunning lapses. One example of these is his treatment of mandrake, belladonna and datura, three solanaceous plants very similar in constituents and effects: they all have multiple attributions, and scarcely ever coincide. Even more peculiar is his use of heroin to treat his asthma, at the recommendation of a physician; the use of datura stramonium, while certainly no longer common, was known at the time, and would have been much more rational therapy.

Perhaps the clue to the division of opinion lies in the legal and social contexts of the drugs avoided: the more acceptable the drug, the more attention shifts from prohibition to moderate use; it is much easier, and more prudent, to avoid unnecessary trouble. Certainly the shift in occult opinion took place at about the same time as the shift in popular opinion; certainly, also, both excuse the use of substances which are not popularly regarded as 'drugs', but which have definite effects (for example, heavy incenses of dittany or camphor) on the nervous system.

Sanders's account (412) of the rather chilling use of psychedelics, by people in and near the circle of Charles Manson, as instruments of assault, and the probable use of

The addictive use of drugs: smoking opium in a den, Bangkok

these agents by all governments whenever they can get away with it, raises another motive for what seems to be a prudential silence on the part of many occult writers. Yet it is not by ignoring dangers that one copes with them, and occultists are scarcely the only persons with an interest in psychotropic agents. It seems reasonable that if, say, 'incapacitating agents' of a psychotropic sort were used, the only people left functioning would be those with prior experience, or with prior instruction in what to expect. Perhaps it is now more prudent to deal openly with these things by making more generally available the results of occult investigations into the links between consciousness and these agents. R.B.

(See also TRANCE.) (Further reading: *19, 75, 83, 84, 92, 104, 105a, 105b, 143a, 161, 168, 184, 193, 263, 284, 379, 380, 388, 390, 412, 421a, 489.*)

Druids (Modern)

Surprisingly little is known of the original Druids – the priesthood of the pre-Roman Celtic civilization of Gaul and Britain – but it is reasonably certain that they were the custodians of a complex oral tradition and

that they worshipped in forest shrines and honoured the mistletoe and the oak. It is also likely that they practised human sacrifice and that it was on this account that they were suppressed by the Romans, who were usually extremely tolerant of native cults.

As early as the 1st century A.D., some Alexandrian scholars began to romanticize the Druids and, in accordance with the tendency of civilized man to discover noble savagery and simple wisdom in the most unlikely places, to compare them as philosophers and sages with the Magi of Persia and the Gymnosophists (Yogis) of India. In the Middle Ages the Druids were almost forgotten, but with the Renaissance and the rediscovery of classical references to them, interest began to revive. In Elizabethan England they seem to have been regarded as the early defenders of a native British culture against Latin encroachments – almost as defenders of the Elizabethan settlement 1,500 years before it existed.

In the 17th century antiquarians became increasingly interested in the Druids and John Aubrey, remembered now for his enchanting *Brief Lives*, suggested that they had been the builders of Stonehenge, hitherto

Druids

almost universally thought to have been an elaborate memorial to the victims of the semi-mythical Saxon kings Hengist and Horsa. Aubrey's theory did not meet with easy acceptance and a rival theory, of the Danish origin of Stonehenge, was at first much more popular. But in the 18th century another antiquarian, William Stukeley (1687–1765), familiarly known as 'the Arch-Druid', championed and elaborated Aubrey's ideas. Stukeley, who must be regarded as the real creator of modern Druidism, saw the Druids not only as megalithic architects but as the custodians of the purest form of the patriarchal religion of the Old Testament. His ideas were taken up by several 18th- and 19th-century writers, who believed that the Druids had been the standard-bearers of what they called Helioarkite religion – the worship of the sun and of Noah's ark, in which the human race had been saved from watery extinction. This Helioarkite religion was entirely imaginary, of course, but belief in its former existence served to explain the similarities between religious beliefs of widely separated communities which so puzzled scholars in the period before the scientific study of comparative religion.

Gorsedd of Bards

Among the believers in Helioarkite religion and in Druidism as its purest form was Iolo Morganwg (Edward Williams, 1747–1826), a man of strange genius, a considerable Celtic scholar, trained in the authentic bardic tradition of Glamorgan. He was also a forger of supposedly ancient documents, on the basis of which he conducted on Primrose Hill in London, in 1792, an elaborate circle ritual, which he called the Gorsedd, and which was a typically 18th-century piece of mumbo-jumbo despite its supposed antiquity. By 1819 its inventor had managed to get this ritual attached to the Eisteddfod, a traditional Welsh festival of poetry and music, and there it has remained to this day. The Welsh Druids, under the leadership of the Archdruid who, amusingly enough, is usually a Nonconformist minister, provide the ceremonial that forms such a picturesque and photogenic part of each annual Eisteddfod. These Welsh Druids are in no sense practising occultists, but there are two bodies of English Druids with strong occult affiliations.

The exact origin of these English groups is uncertain. There is, of course, no question of their being of authentic Druid descent, but they may be descended from 18th-century mystical-cum-social groups which chose to call themselves Druids. Present-day Druids claim that in 1717 John Toland (1670–1722) organized some sort of Druid conference,

attended by delegates from ten parts of the country. The date coincides with that of the foundation of the masonic Grand Lodge of England, and it is possible that Toland's conference was an attempt to found a rival organization using a ritual based on a British tradition rather than on the legends of Solomon's Temple which were adopted by the Freemasons. Druids now claim both Toland and William Stukeley as 'Chosen Chiefs' of their order, perhaps with some truth, though there is no doubt that William Blake, also claimed as a Chosen Chief, loathed Druidism in all its forms.

The group which was the direct ancestor of the two contemporary English Druid fraternities probably came into existence in the 19th century, though it may have had some tenuous connection with the 'Rosi-crucian', 'Templar' and 'Druid' societies which hung on the fringes of 18th-century Freemasonry. Its most flamboyant chief was an Irish lawyer named Edward Vaughan Hyde Kenealy (1819–80) who won great notoriety with his defence of the Tichborne claimant, a grossly ignorant and even more grossly overweight Wapping butcher who convinced many people that he was Sir Roger Tichborne, the missing heir to a large estate. The claimant, whose real name was Arthur Orton, failed in his claim and was sent to prison for perjury, an event which seems to have convinced Kenealy, always somewhat unstable, that his client was the victim of a monstrous conspiracy involving the judge, the jury and all the witnesses against Orton and directed by the English hierarchy of the Roman Catholic Church. So intemperate were Kenealy's attacks on his professional colleagues who had taken the other side in the case and who he insisted were involved in the conspiracy that he was expelled from the Bar. Undaunted, he managed to get himself elected to the House of Commons, whose proceedings he enlivened with speeches which, though rarely even remotely connected with the subjects under debate, were remarkable for their frenzied attacks on the Catholic Church and their impassioned advocacy of both Orton and Druid cosmology.

A Schism

Kenealy can have made few converts to his Druid Order, but it managed to survive into this century and received a fresh infusion of life when the late Lewis Spence (see also ATLANTIS) became its Chosen Chief. Spence was a prolific author who exerted an important influence on the development of modern Scottish writing. He was also a self-proclaimed practising occultist and a member of at least one continental Rosicrucian organi-

zation. He seems to have been responsible for an influx of occultists into the Druid Order and for the introduction of a number of esoteric exercises of a THEOSOPHICAL or Western magical origin into Druid practice: though some of these may have been introduced by an earlier chief who was also an initiate of the GOLDEN DAWN – certainly the Druid exercise known as 'the illuminated spine' bears a close resemblance to a Golden Dawn technique called 'the exercise of the middle pillar'.

Until a few years ago the Druid Order enjoyed a placid existence, coming to the general public's attention only at each summer solstice when television cameras and newspaper photographers were usually on hand to record its ceremony at Stonehenge (see plate, page 102). This picturesque ceremony, involving a half-drawn sword, a gigantic drinking horn and the rhetorical question 'Is it Peace?', was and remains no more than a slightly modified version of the rite devised by Iolo Morganwg in 1792. In 1964, however, the Druid Order split into two groups. The first of these is led by Dr Thomas Maughan, a homoeopathic physician, and retains the original name of the Druid Order. The second and larger group is the Order of Bards, Ovates and Druids, which is led by Mr Ross Nichols.

The second of these groups is the more occultly inclined of the two. The rituals have been rewritten in a more 'mystical' way and new rituals have been devised to enable the Order to celebrate not only the solstices and equinoxes but the traditional witch festival of Walpurgis Night (30 April) and the following day, Beltane; All Saints Day (1 November), called Samhain; Lammas (1 August, Lugnasad); and Imbolc on 1 February. The festival on Samhain celebrates 'the links between the living and the dead'. This and the other three new Druid rituals fit in nicely with the Margaret MURRAY theory of witchcraft and have found favour with the more Celtically inclined covens of the modern WITCHCRAFT movement.

The major public activities of the rival Druids continue to be the midsummer ceremonies at Stonehenge and open lectures, often of excessive tedium, at Caxton Hall in London. In spite of the rivalry between the two factions – partly resulting from doctrinal disputes and partly, it seems, based on the type of personality clash which is the bane of all occult groups – both sets of Druids are extremely active and their membership is increasing. The name 'Druid' evidently still retains all the associations of wisdom and mystical insight which gave it such charm for the scholars of Alexandria almost 2,000 years ago.

Eckankar

A 'church of astral projection' in Las Vegas, Nevada, founded by Paul Twitchell, author of *Introduction to Eckankar, The Tiger's Fang, The Far Country*, etc., who believes that the experience of releasing the soul from the physical body (see ASTRAL BODY) leads man towards 'God realization'.

Escomatic Experiences See ASTRAL BODY; OUT-OF-THE-BODY EXPERIENCES.

Ectoplasm

In Spiritualist belief, the substance from which spirits make themselves visible forms. It is said to be extruded from some MEDIUMS, and is described as alive, sensitive to touch and light – if it is unexpectedly touched or a light is suddenly shone on it, it flies back into the medium's body, sometimes causing injury – cold to the touch, slightly luminous and having a characteristic smell. Whether such a substance exists and (if it does) what it is made of, has never been satisfactorily determined: see SPIRITUALISM; see also SPRITS AND FORCES.

Mary Baker Eddy See CHRISTIAN SCIENCE.

Harry Edwards (b. 1893)

A famous British healer and Spiritualist who has his headquarters at his 'sanctuary' at Shere, Surrey; author of *Spirit Healing*, etc. He began healing in the 1930s, practices both direct and absent healing, and claims success rates of over 30 per cent for complete cures and 80 per cent for improvements. 'He maintains that there are spiritual laws in the universe which even God would not upset and that hence cures cannot come directly from Him and miracles do not occur. He does, however, claim that at his hands the whole range of "incurable" diseases, including numerous forms of cancer, has been tamed. . . . And the power behind this, he suggests, is the superhuman but not limitless intelligence of the spirits of the dead. Harry

Edwards' own favourite controls were formerly Red Indians, but Pasteur and Lord Lister were later added to their number' (*407*; see also *138, 139, 331*).

Electronic Meditation See MEDITATION.

Elementals

Minor spirits of various types; originally, the spirits associated with the four elements of fire, air, earth and water: see SPIRITS AND FORCES; see also RITUAL MAGIC.

Eleusinian Mysteries See MYSTERY RELIGIONS.

Elongation

Lengthening of the body, reported of some mediums, notably D. D. HOME. In 1870 while Home was in trance, his body was observed elongated by as much as nine or twelve inches. The observer touched Home and reported, 'I could feel his flesh stretch and again shrink. It was most extraordinary to see him gradually lengthen' (*176*).

Enochian Language, Enochian Magic

The angels who communicated with Dr Dee, the famous 16th-century magician, and his partner and scryer, Edward Kelley, supplied Kelley with certain mysterious calls or keys in the 'Enochian' language, which Dee and Kelley recited as invocations to the angels before SCRYING. These calls have been used again in modern times to summon up spirits by the GOLDEN DAWN and by Aleister CROWLEY, who claimed to be a reincarnation of Kelley. Enochian is a genuine language, not gibberish. Its origin is unknown and there is no record of it before Dee. Richard Deacon, in his book on Dee, quotes a sample of it, with a translation: Madariatza das perifa Lil cabisa micaolazoda saanire caosago of fifia balzodizodarasa iada. Nonuca

Keys in the 'Enochian' language

gohulime: micama adoianu mada faods beliorebe, soba ooanoa cabisa luciftias yaripesol, das aberaasasa nonucafe jimicalazodoma larasada tofejilo marebe pereryo Idoigo od torezodulape. . . . The translation is: 'O you heavens which dwell in the first air, you are mighty in the parts of the earth, and execute the judgement of the highest. To you, it is said, Behold the face of your God, the beginning of Comfort, whose eyes are the brightness of the heavens, which provided for you the government of the earth and her unspeakable variety. . . .': see RITUAL MAGIC. (*113, 189*)

Episcopi Vagantes

The Latin term for WANDERING BISHOPS.

Eranos Conferences See JUNG.

Esbat

The term used by witches for a routine meeting of a coven, which may be held once or more each week, distinguished from the SABBATS or major festivities and rituals: this distinction was drawn by Margaret MURRAY in her books and has been adopted in modern WITCHCRAFT.

Esoteric Christianity See KINGSFORD.

ESP

The abbreviation for EXTRASENSORY PERCEPTION.

Etheric Body, Etheric Double

One of numerous varieties of 'subtle body' believed by different occult schools of thought to permeate but have a separate existence from the physical body. 'Etheric' refers to the all-pervading ether of 19th-century science and to the 'magnetic fluid' or 'aetheric continuum' of Mesmer and his followers (see FAITH HEALING; HYPNOSIS), which was thought to permeate the universe and to provide a medium through which spirit and matter could influence each other: see ASTRAL BODY; AURA; PARAPSYCHOLOGY; for the 'etheric record', see AKASHIC RECORD; for 'etherization of the blood', see STEINER; for 'etheric photography', see RADIESTHESIA.

Exorcism See POSSESSION.

Extrasensory Perception (ESP)

The reception of information through means other than the known senses; CLAIRVOYANCE, PRECOGNITION and TELEPATHY are regarded as subtypes of it: see PARAPSYCHOLOGY.

Eyeless Sight See PAROPTIC VISION.

F

Faculty X

A term coined by Colin Wilson for 'the ability to grasp the *reality* of other times and other places', the sense that sometimes momentarily comes to us of being present at past or distant scenes; 'that latent power that human beings possess *to reach beyond the present* . . . it is the power to grasp reality, and it unites the two halves of man's mind, conscious and subconscious' (*510*).

Faith Healing

'The greatest feature which distinguishes man from animals', Sir William Osler once claimed, is 'the desire to take medicine'. The quip enshrines a more important truth than Osler realized. Animals in their wild state rarely fall ill, except when deprived of essential nourishment – and even then, instinct will usually guide them to a salt lick, or whatever it is they need. But man, in acquiring his conscious mind, gradually lost this instinct. He began to rely on habit and memory in deciding, say, which berries were edible, and which were poisonous; and what to do if he was poisoned, or fell ill. And habit and memory were not always reliable guides. In the tribe, however, there was often somebody with the ability to shed consciousness, and to consult his animal instincts direct. This knowledge gave power; he would become the shaman – the medicineman, or witch-doctor.

The shaman was basically a 'seer', who gave a diagnosis, and a 'diviner', who gave a prognosis. In other words he was regarded as operating through what would now be called CLAIRVOYANCE and PRECOGNITION. Sometimes they came naturally to him; sometimes he had to induce a TRANCE state in himself, in which he could 'see' or 'hear' the answers to his questions. He would also seek to induce trance states in his patients, in an attempt to release their instincts, too. For this purpose, music, dancing or drugs were used to take the patients 'out of themselves'. The effects varied, in different individuals; but the general pattern was much the same –

they went into convulsions (losing control of their limbs); they 'dissociated', speaking with voices unlike their own (losing control of their minds); and then, they sank into comas, after which both mind and body appeared relaxed and refreshed.

Here lay the roots of faith healing – as distinct from nature healing, which was also used: diet, medicinal herbs, bone-setting, minor surgery. One method operated through the mind; the other, through the body. But of the two, shamanism was the dominant partner; particularly where a shaman found how his power over people could be enormously reinforced – to harm them as well as to heal them – by exploiting their suggestibility while they were in the trance state.

In time, the fact that the shaman was often prompted by some force or advice coming from outside himself (or so it appeared to him) led to the development of belief in external elemental powers; first in nature – a mountain, say, or thunder; then, in gods; and ultimately, in a God – and a Devil. And this in turn led to a new interpretation of how healing worked. In primitive communities, the convulsions and the dissociation were accepted as a natural part of the healing process. But to the priest, they were the Devil's doing – as, in the New Testament, Jesus clearly assumes. In dissociation, it was assumed to be the demons' voices which were heard; and the convulsions were the demons' struggles to avoid eviction (see POSSESSION).

It followed that for the priest himself to dissociate – to become what would now be called a MEDIUM – itself fell into disfavour, as it suggested a liaison with the demon. Jesus relied more on the use of suggestion, 'take up thy bed and walk'. His assumption was that God provided the healing force, and that the sick man could tap it through him (or his disciples); 'thy faith hath made thee whole'.

For centuries, in Christian countries, faith healing followed this pattern. Faith, it was assumed, was necessary to placate God; he would restore health in exchange for it. But in the Middle Ages, this belief began gradually to be eroded by the onset of the plagues. It became hard to believe that God was singling out the faithful for survival; and the fact that he would make those who did not survive welcome in heaven was inadequate consolation. At the same time, too, the Church was becoming institutionalized. Priests began again to see themselves more and more as preachers and exemplars – on the model of the Pharisees, rather than of the Apostles; less and less as members of a healing mission. The practice of medicine was increasingly allowed to fall into the

hands of physicians, surgeons and apothecaries, the descendants of the tribal naturecure-practitioner, or the bone-setter. The Church's role became limited to the provision of funds and of medical auxiliaries – nurses and lay brothers – for hospitals, and to the consolation of the sick by visits and prayer.

As a result, faith healing tended to be left to sorcerers, astrologers and assorted quacks. They did not necessarily repudiate the Church; but the Church tended to repudiate them. And with the Renaissance, and the development of more materialist attitudes about health and disease, belief in the effectiveness of faith healing began to go out of fashion altogether, except among the credulous poor.

The Magnetizers

It was kept alive by individuals who were (or were believed to be) endowed with the healing touch. In the 17th century, Valentine Greatrakes made a reputation for himself in Ireland, impressing even such men of the world as the diarist John Evelyn and the chemist Robert Boyle, through his technique of drawing illness from the body by stroking it. He attributed his powers to God – for which an ecclesiastical court, unimpressed, rebuked him; but he was widely imitated, and some of his disciples came to the conclusion that, just as an iron bar is magnetized by stroking with a magnet, the healing force involved must be not simply faith, but faith supplemented by magnetism.

There was also Johann Gassner, born in Austria a hundred years after Greatrakes. He became a priest; and in his personal wrestling matches with the Devil, he evolved a modified form of exorcism which, he found, he could use to cure diseases in others. The effects were very similar to those which the shamans produced: convulsions, dissociation, coma. He also found he could establish a remarkable degree of control over his patients in their trance state. They would follow his instructions even when he gave them in Latin, which they did not understand. But Gassner, too, fell foul of the Church authorities, and was ordered to stop his healing campaign.

These techniques – 'magnetizing' and shamanism – were to be fused by the Austrian Franz MESMER. The method Mesmer eventually adopted, when he practised in Paris, was to bring his patients together in a room where there was a tub filled with iron filings, into which rods were stuck. The patients held the rods, or held each others' hands; music played; they went into trances, dissociated, had convulsions, sank into comas – and felt better. Or so several of them told a committee of inquiry on which were some distinguished scientists of the period – Benjamin Franklin, Lavoisier, Pinel, and Dr Guillotin. The committee in its report could not deny that the method worked. But it only worked, they felt, in the imagination of the patients. In other words, it was faith healing.

Mesmer disagreed. The universe, he claimed, was held together by what he described as an 'aetheric continuum', of which the stars and planets were a constituent part: and from them flowed 'animal magnetism', which his apparatus was designed to transmit to people who were ill – illness being the result of failure to draw sufficiently on their aetheric continuum reserves. Had Mesmer talked of radiations, he might now be in the scientific Pantheon. Had he called his method faith healing, modified the apparatus, and attributed his results to God, he could eventually have become a candidate for canonization. As it was, the French Revolution interrupted his career. Wisely – as Marie Antoinette and others from the Court had been his patrons – he left France; he ended his days in obscurity in Switzerland; and from that day to this, his name has been synonymous with occultism and quackery. Yet Mesmer provides the essential link between the healing techniques of the shamans – and of Jesus – with faith healing in its various manifestations today.

His disciples continued to practice 'mesmerism', as it came to be called; but as they were in many different countries, and without any central organization, they tended to adopt whatever aspect of his method attracted them – sometimes reaching back to earlier methods. The American mesmerist Phineas QUIMBY, for example – unlike Mesmer himself – relied considerably on clairvoyance for his success in diagnosing and treating his patients' ills. And his disciple, Mary Baker Eddy, proceeded to strip mesmerism of what she considered its unnecessary accretions, transforming it into CHRISTIAN SCIENCE – the simplest form of faith healing yet evolved, dispensing as it did with techniques, apparatuses, and even with healers, in order to let the healing force come to the individual through his own direct link with his God. The patient did not even have to think what he was doing; as the Divine Mind was omnipresent, she argued, 'mortal mind is not a factor of the healing'. And in spite of the achievements of modern medicine, there is no evidence that Christian Scientists have been worse off for being deprived of its drugs and devices by their faith. On the contrary, a comparison of mortality statistics in one American State, Washington, has revealed them to be slightly longer-lived than the rest of the community.

Similarly, Dr John Elliotson (1791–1868),

one of the founders of University College Hospital, began to use mesmerism in treating patients, but soon became fascinated by one particular consequence of the treatment: dissociation. In some cases, he found, it did not merely help to relieve symptoms; it also gave the individuals concerned access to information, in their trance states, which they did not possess when fully conscious. They became clairvoyant. Elliotson's public demonstrations of these powers attracted many interested spectators, including Dickens and Thackeray; but they also attracted the disapproval of the hospital authorities, who banned them. And although Elliotson continued to investigate clairvoyance and allied phenomena, the link between them and their original purpose was eroded until by the time SPIRITUALISM emerged in the United States, later in the century, it was largely divorced from healing. Its mediums were employed chiefly to try to communicate with the spirits of the departed.

From time to time, however, individual mediums would find themselves credited with healing powers. Men such as Oral Roberts, in America, and Harry EDWARDS, in England, began to hold healing services, and eventually to found organizations and churches which the congregation attended not as a routine observance, but rather as people had flocked to see Jesus, seeking spiritual and physical health. Although the practitioners of spiritual healing (as they

The healer Harry Edwards

prefer to call it) are still often themselves mediums, working with spirit CONTROLS, the emphasis has shifted away from the attempt to establish contact with the dead, to treatment of the living; and the rapid growth of the movement, particularly in England, suggests that it is meeting a demand which the emptying orthodox Churches have failed to satisfy.

But the orthodox Churches have remained aloof. The Catholic Church, admittedly, has continued to recognize the possibility of miraculous cures, achieved by faith, or through the grace of God. Certain places, Lourdes being the best known, have been recognized as centres to which the devout can come in search of miracles. Saints' relics, too, are still in use for that purpose. But the Vatican authorities have for a long time been uneasy about the way in which the faithful are exploited commercially. They insist on a rigorous investigation of any cure supposed to be miraculous; so rigorous, that very few have been judged acceptable.

On the whole, there seems to be more enthusiasm among Anglican clergy for a revival of the Church's healing mission. So far, however, it has been curbed by the medical profession's determination not to allow medicine to be infiltrated. Two committees of inquiry, in the present century, have reported adversely on faith healing. Though full of genuflections to the clergy as part of the background – people suffering from disease, as one put it, 'are greatly comforted and relieved, and even physically

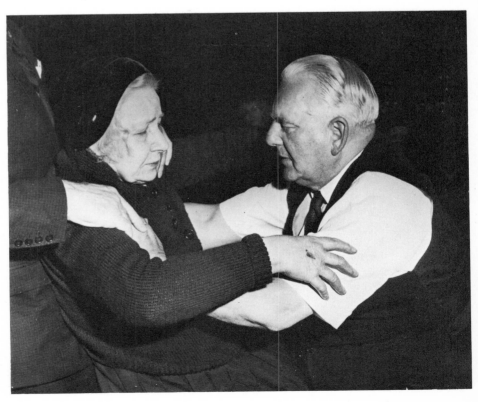

benefited, by spiritual ministrations' – both reports bluntly dismissed the proposition that there can be any real place for faith healing as a front-line treatment for organic disease.

The situation as it stands, then, is that although Christian Science appears to retain its adherents, and the Spiritualist Churches attract larger numbers every year, faith healing is still widely regarded, in civilized countries, as something odd; certainly distinct from, and antipathetic to, orthodox medicine. Its practitioners are accepted – if they are accepted at all – as individuals with some unexplained gift, worth taking a chance on when orthodoxy fails. They are also featured occasionally in the popular newspapers, with graphic accounts of their achievements, coupled with an editorial demand that the profession should sit up and take notice; but the demand is made with no expectation whatsoever that the profession will do anything of the kind. And the assumption remains that so it will always be: that a few men will continue to make national, or even international reputations, as healers, but the majority will continue to enjoy only local fame, for their inexplicable ability to relieve headaches, or charm away warts.

Healing and Suggestion

To charm away warts – here may lie a pointer to the future of faith healing. When the materialism which has dominated orthodox medicine for so long is finally overthrown, the unsightly and unwelcome wart will deserve some of the credit.

In his *Uses and Abuses of Psychology* (*147*), published in 1953, Professor H. J. Eysenck described a scientific experiment in which a group of children with warts were treated by faith healing; while another, the control group, were given the then orthodox medical treatment – which was shown to be far less effective. Yet warts are organic – they are virus-induced tumours. Describing the experiment, however, Eysenck – a hard-line Behaviourist – did not use the term faith healing. He preferred 'suggestion'.

Where does suggestion end, and faith healing begin? Or is faith healing no more than applied suggestion? Again, the history of mesmerism provides some clues. Mesmer himself, though he used suggestion to get people into the trance state, does not appear to have exploited it when they were actually in their trances. But many of his followers did, notably Dr A. A. Liébeault, a French family doctor, who worked largely among the poor and, as they could not afford drugs, treated their minor ailments by mesmerism. He put them into a trance, and then sug-

M. Coué visiting the blind

gested that their aches or other symptoms would disappear – not forgetting also to recommend measures to prevent recurrence, such as a change of diet.

This was old-style faith healing, but with a difference; the suggestion was reinforced by hypnosis (as the trance state came to be called). The medical profession, however, had set its face against hypnosis, as occultism. They refused to accept even that the hypnotic state existed, let alone that it could be used for treatment of the sick. And even when, largely owing to the experiments of J. M. Charcot (1825–93), the existence of hypnotism had to be accepted, its therapeutic potential was ignored – as indeed it still largely is, in spite of some spectacular achievements with its assistance, and in spite of the evidence, which Dr Stephen Black has summarized in his *Mind and Body* (*42*), that suggestion used on certain patients under hypnosis can produce striking alterations in their bodily behaviour; in other words, that it is possible to affect a wide range of organic changes by faith healing.

Nor is it necessary to employ hypnosis. Investigating the subject, Emile Coué (1857–1926) came to the conclusion that what was important in promoting health was not 'other suggestion' (as he described it) but auto-suggestion. In other words, the healing power lies in the patient's own imagination; the hypnotist is merely an agent, helping to stimulate it. And since Coué's death, his thesis has received ample confirmation from countless experiments with dummy pills – placebos – given to patients suffering from disorders ranging from sea-sickness to angina. The results of such experiments show a remarkable conformity. Around a third to a half of all patients are placebo reactors; a

dummy pill can remove their pain, or nausea, or whatever it may be, as effectively as most drugs.

Here then is a simple explanation of faith healing. The trouble is, it is too simple. For one thing, it does not account for such phenomena as clairvoyance and precognition, which constantly recur in the literature on the subject. Until very recently, they could not have been put forward as ingredients of healing, or of anything else, without encountering ridicule; but this climate has been changing, even within the medical profession, and it is reasonable to assume that they will soon become as acceptable (if not, for a while, entirely respectable) as hypnosis has done. And when this happens, some of the more mysterious accomplishments of faith healers in the past will seem almost commonplace.

The Healing Current

But there is another as yet unexplained phenomenon, constantly related to faith healing; the healing current – Mesmer's 'animal magnetism'. Again, the evidence that there is such a vital force has come from all times, and all places. In *The Secret Science behind Miracles* (*293*), for example, Max Freedom Long describes its use by the Kahunas in Hawaii, and their belief that it is some elemental current of very high voltage, capable of curing physical as well as mental disorders. The idea that this force can be used by a healer to draw the sickness out of a patient, as Greatrakes did, is also widespread. Some healers are disconcerted to find they can take headache from a patient into themselves, and will suffer agonies from it, if they do not take measures to throw it off (as the magnetizers who employ Greatrakes's method of stroking the patient, though without touching him, do; they go into a corner and flick their hands, as if they were getting rid of something dirty). Healers, too, often find that the temperature of their hands is raised, in such circumstances, much as the temperature of a wire is raised by an electric current passing through it. Patients may also feel warmth, or a sensation akin to pins and needles, in the part of the anatomy being 'stroked'.

The difficulty has been to find any way in which these manifestations can be satisfactorily demonstrated to convince materialists of their existence. As with other extrasensory phenomena, they tend to be resistant to testing under controlled conditions, which naturally gives sceptics the chance to say that they are bogus; and on the rare occasions when a trial has vindicated the healer, its results have been ignored.

Such a trial was given to Dr W. E. Boyd's radiesthetic apparatus in 1924, by an authoritative committee of the British Medical Association with Sir Thomas Horder (later Lord Horder) in the chair. RADIESTHESIA was a development from divination. Just as the water diviner searches for water with a divining rod, or a pendulum, so the radiesthetist uses the same adjuncts, or more elaborate ones, to diagnose and treat disease. In the test, Boyd was asked to use his machine to distinguish between various substances, none of which he was allowed to see, or feel, or smell, or taste – elaborate precautions being taken against fraud. He provided the right answer in every single test – the odds against his being right by chance being something in the region of 30,000,000 to one. The committee, baffled, recommended further research; but none has been undertaken by the Medical Research Council.

More recently a project was put forward for a scientific test of ABSENT HEALING, where individual healers, or groups of their followers, pray for the sick. The idea was to take a hospital ward, and divide its members into two groups: half of them would be prayed for and the other half left as controls. If such a test failed, it could of course be attributed to the inability of those praying to rouse the vital force under test conditions. But if it succeeded, it would be quite a convincing demonstration of the power of absent healing – so long as suitable precautions were taken to prevent either the patients, or their doctors and nurses, from knowing which patients were in which group. But the project had to be abandoned when the hospital authorities pointed out that if the experiment worked, it would mean that the patients who had responded were being treated by unqualified practitioners. This would be contrary to the regulations of the

General Medical Council; any doctor who had cooperated would find himself liable to be erased from the medical register.

It ought to be possible, in some instances, to demonstrate the existence of faith healing by its results in individual cases. Many attempts have been made to do so, notably with patients who have been told they have cancer, and who have biopsy results to prove it, but who then after going to a healer are found to have no trace of cancer. There are several such cases, well-attested. Confronted with them, however, the medical profession has resorted to defensive rationalizations. The biopsy (it is claimed) must have been taken from somebody else by mistake; or, in taking the fragment of the patient for the biopsy, all the cancer was luckily removed, too; or, it must have been a case of spontaneous regression, nothing to do with the healer.

Nevertheless research is now in progress, particularly in the United States, which has produced results to which recognition can hardly be indefinitely delayed into the effect of healing on enzyme activity, for example, and on metabolism; even into the effects of treatment of mice by healers. And once the phenomenon is accepted, much can be explained of what previously has been inexplicable; WITCHCRAFT, for example, so often linked with healing, as well as harming. On a more everyday level, too, it seems likely that much of what has passed for successful physical treatment will be shown to have an element of faith healing. This is well illustrated in the life and work of such men as Herbert Barker, the manipulative surgeon, who in spite of the fact that he had no medical qualifications, was so successful in treating his patients that he secured fame, fortune, and even a knighthood. Barker could demonstrate his technique, but he could not define or even describe it – any more than an artist can. More recently, too, there has been a well-known London physician whose results, measured in terms of satisfied patients, have been consistently and strikingly in advance of those achieved by colleagues using the same methods and the same drugs. The most probable explanation is that he is a faith healer.

Acupuncture

Assisting the breakdown of materialism is what might be described as a first cousin of faith healing: acupuncture. It has long been dismissed in the West *as* faith healing – a proposition which its devotees might accept, up to a point; certainly they share Mesmer's belief in a vital force which, they believe, flows through the human body, keeping us in health. Diseases occur, they claim, when

the flow is disturbed; but the flow can be restored by the use of needles, inserted into the flesh at specific points.

Early in the 1970s – following the publication of an article in the *New York Times* by its roving political correspondent, James Reston, who had fallen ill in China and had been treated by acupuncture – some senior and respected members of the American medical profession were invited to China to see acupuncture for themselves; and they came back impressed – particularly with its use as an anaesthetic; they watched elaborate and ordinarily agonizing operations taking place on patients who remained conscious and lucid throughout, but felt no pain. As the 'meridians' through which the vital force flows, according to acupuncturists, do not coincide with any channels known to physiology, the intriguing possibility is that the vital force is the same as, or related to, the force Jesus felt flowing into the woman who touched the hem of his garment; the force used by the Kahunas, and by medicine men in hundreds of primitive communities all over the world; the force used by diviners and radiesthetists, magnetizers and spiritual healers throughout the ages; the force used by scores of individuals, many of whom are unaware they are using it, to this day. B. I.

(See also HYPNOSIS.) (Further reading: the books on and around the subject are so many, and so varied, that a short bibliography can only indicate a few of the most useful of them, as the best starting-points for further exploration as well as on their own merits; see *7, 42, 112, 135, 138, 143, 147, 183, 196, 210, 271, 293, 304, 324, 342, 364, 365, 402, 407, 416, 453, 487, 496, 512.*)

Father Divine

'Father Divine' was the name adopted by an American Negro evangelist and self-styled Messiah whose real name was George Baker. He was born in Georgia and first came into the public eye when he began to establish religious communities which he called 'heavens'. These were made up of disciples called 'angels', who took vows of temperance and chastity, renounced all worldly goods and gave their labour free to the organization. Father Divine extended his interests to a wide variety of businesses including barber shops, laundries, restaurants and garages. He was fond of wearing silk suits and jewelled rings and driving in a white Rolls-Royce. He stood 4 feet 6 inches high. When he died in 1965 he was worth about ten million dollars. C. M.

(Further reading: *205.*)

Jules Ferrette (d. 1904) See WANDERING BISHOPS.

Father Divine

Flat Earth Theory See COSMOLOGY.

Flying Saucers See UNIDENTIFIED FLYING OBJECTS.

Francesco Forgione (1887-1968)
See PADRE PIO.

Dion Fortune

Dio non Fortuna was the motto of Violet Mary Firth (1891–1946), better known as Dion Fortune. Brought up in a CHRISTIAN SCIENCE household, she claimed that her life-long interest in paranormal powers was due to early contact with the teachings of Mary Baker Eddy. But it was more than a theoretical acquaintance with the occult that led her to become a practising magician with a following of her own.

About 1910 she had a frightening experience while working at an educational establishment. She believed herself to be the victim of a magical attack, launched against her by her employer, the principal, who had spent many years in India, absorbed some of its mystery-teachings and misapplied them for her own ends. As a result, Dion Fortune suffered a severe nervous breakdown. The attack led her to take up the study of psychology, and later of occultism. Her AURA, the shell-like envelope that protects the individual from the impact of external

influences, had been rent by the ferocity of the attack, and it had not healed. Vitality was constantly ebbing away from her and it was not until 1919 that the damage was finally repaired. At that time she was admitted to the Alpha and Omega Lodge of the STELLA MATUTINA, an offshoot of the GOLDEN DAWN, operated by a Scottish occultist, J. W. Brodie Innes, author of several highly informative novels on witchcraft and magic. It was from Brodie Innes that Dion Fortune learned how to energize and direct her innate powers to magical ends.

In 1924, Dion Fortune was in a position to found the Fraternity of the Inner Light which she operated until her premature death in 1946. She wrote several textbooks on the Western esoteric tradition, of which *Psychic Self-Defence* is, not surprisingly, the most successful, but she preferred to use fiction to convey the subtler aspects of the Mysteries. There are some very self-revealing observations in her early novel, *The Demon Lover*, and the book indicates a profound interest in the psychology of necrophilia, astral vampirism, and sexual commerce on the inner planes. She had begun writing about these themes a year earlier in *The Secrets of Dr Taverner*, 1926, a collection of macabre stories based on case-histories of occult pathology of which she had first-hand experience. Some of them approach the stories of Machen and Lovecraft for exquisite horror.

The ageless witch-woman, Vivian le Fay Morgan, who dominates *The Sea Priestess*, 1938, is a composite portrait of the author herself and a remarkable woman named 'Maia' Tranchell Hayes, who was her superior in the Stella Matutina.

Dion Fortune was among the first Western occultists to explain the interrelation of the endocrine system and the complex network of CHAKRAS which forms its subtle anatomy. Like Aleister CROWLEY, with whom she was in contact during the latter years of her life, she utilized the secret current based upon the magically directed energies of sexual polarity. Her novel *Moon Magic*, published posthumously, describes a priestess of Isis who comes to restore paganism to a world that has lost touch with the elemental forces that make life truly dynamic. Both *The Goat Foot God* and *The Winged Bull* deal with the influence of the Dionysiac current on the inhibited and the uninitiated, and show the interior mechanism whereby enlightenment arises through contact with elemental forces. During the course of a major initiation, Dion Fortune received direct teachings from the inner planes, part of which she published as *The Cosmic Doctrine*. It forms the basis of her work, which she once described as 'the

Dion Fortune

revival of the ancient Temple Mysteries'. K. G.

(Further reading: *156* to *161* inclusive.)

Fortune Telling See DIVINATION and related articles.

Fox Sisters See SPIRITUALISM.

Fraternitas Saturni

The Brotherhood of Saturn, or Saturn-Gnosis, the most important occult group in Germany in the late 1920s and early '30s; revived after the Second World War: see GERMAN OCCULT GROUPS.

Fraternity of the Inner Light

The occult society founded in 1924 by Dion FORTUNE.

John Frederick Charles Fuller (1878-1966)

A British soldier, strategist and military historian, who as a young man was a disciple of Aleister CROWLEY, attracted in part by the latter's right-wing political principles; he wrote a book in praise of Crowleyanity, *The Star in the West*, 1907, and an unfinished novel, *The Hidden Wisdom of the Illuminati*, 1926, in which Crowley is one of the main characters, but later fell out with the Beast. (*100, 165*)

G

Gerald Brosseau Gardner (1884-1964)

A British witchcraft revivalist and author of *High Magic's Aid*, a novel, *Witchcraft Today*, 1954, *The Meaning of Witchcraft*, 1959. He spent most of his early life in the Far East as a rubber planter and customs official. Returning to England in the late 1930s, he discovered, or said he discovered, a group of witches in the New Forest who convinced him that witchcraft was the old pagan religion of Europe, still surviving underground. Critics have accused Gardner of inventing the whole witchcraft revival, though this seems unlikely, but he was largely responsible for the rapid growth of the modern witchcraft movement: see WITCHCRAFT. (*171, 172*)

Eileen J. Garrett (1893-1970)

The famous Irish-born medium through whom, in 1930, the spirit of the dead captain of the airship R.101 apparently communicated a few days after the airship had crashed, killing most of her passengers and crew. Mrs Garrett began her career as a trance medium in Britain and later became an American citizen. She was less certain about the nature of her own mediumship than those who confidently assumed that the dead spoke through her, and came to suspect that her CONTROLS were really factors in her own mind. She founded the Parapsychology Foundation, New York, in 1951, to promote further research. She wrote *My Life as a Search for the Meaning of Mediumship*, 1938, *Many Voices*, 1968, and *Adventures in the Supernormal*, 1949, in the preface to which she said: 'I have a gift, a capacity – a delusion, if you will – which is called "psychic". I do not care what it may be called, for living with and utilizing this psychic capacity long ago inured me to a variety of epithets – ranging from expressions almost of reverence, through doubt and pity, to open vituperation. In short, I have been called many things: from a charlatan to a miracle worker. I am, at least, neither of these': see MEDIUMS. (*136, 174, 175*.) For a report of an impressive object-reading experiment with Mrs Garrett, see *283*.)

Gematria See CABALA; NUMEROLOGY.

Germanen Order

A German secret society, founded in 1912, much preoccupied with racial purity, the ideal of the Nordic master race and the threat of the supposed international conspiracy of Jews and Freemasons. Candidates for membership had to declare that they had no Jewish blood, and their skulls were measured with a device called a platometer to make sure that they were racially eligible. Much of the Order's teaching derived from Guido von LIST and several of its members were connected with the Nazi Party in its early days. The Order appears to have closed down in 1922: see GERMAN OCCULT GROUPS. (*303*)

German Occult Groups

Towards the end of the 18th century would-be alchemists and neo-Rosicrucians abounded in southern Germany and Austria in the 'Strict Observance' and its offshoot, the Order of the Gold and Rosy Cross (Gold-und-Rosenkreuzer Orden), both of which were pseudo-Masonic aberrations. By the end of the century, however, interest in occultism was beginning to go underground in German-speaking countries. Indeed, during the 19th century neither Germany nor the Hapsburg Empire produced the counterparts of Eliphas LÉVI in France, or of Masonic occultists such as K. R. H. MACKENZIE in England. Nor, during the 1890s, were there German or Austrian equivalents of the Parisian occult milieu in which PAPUS and Stanislas de GUAITA scintillated.

The German revival – in this article 'German' refers to all countries in which German is spoken – began in 1884 with the foundation of the German section of Madame Blavatsky's THEOSOPHICAL SOCIETY under the presidency of Dr Wilhelm Hübbe-Schleiden. However, it is difficult to identify occult groups which were either secret or in any sense exclusive before the mid-1900s. One important example emerged from Theosophical Society circles under the leadership of Dr Rudolf STEINER, before he and a loyal band of followers broke away from the T.S. and founded the Anthroposophical Society in 1912.

Steiner became Secretary-General of the German section of the T.S. in 1902. Never a Theosophist of the traditional 'Adyar' variety, meaning that he was never greatly interested in Hindu or Buddhist teachings, he was soon at loggerheads with Annie BESANT, who represented Theosophical orthodoxy, in London. Very few German Theosophists could have been aware that in 1906 he had acquired a warrant or charter for a Berlin Chapter of the Rite of Memphis and Misraim, which purported to be Masonic but was in fact irregular. With the foundation of his 'Mystica Aeterna' temple, which was open to members of both sexes, Steiner was in possession of rituals which could be 'worked' by members of his 'Inner Circle'. As far as Steiner was concerned, the connection with the Rite was simply a means to an end, meaning a link with so-called 'esoteric' Freemasonry, even if the Rite had no standing in orthodox Masonic circles.

The Rite of Memphis and Misraim had been imported from England in 1902 by Dr Karl Kellner, a wealthy industrialist who appears to have had at least a theoretical knowledge of Tantric sex magic techniques (see TANTRISM), and his friend Theodor Reuss. Kellner certainly ran an occult group in which sex magic must have been discussed although not necessarily practised. A year after Kellner's death in 1905, Reuss founded the Order of the Temple of the Orient, known in all parts of the world by its initials, O.T.O. In 1912 Reuss openly admitted in his periodical *Oriflamme* that the Order was in possession of *the* great Hermetic secret, meaning the nature and practice of sex magic. This claim may or may not have been true. In any event, it would probably be incorrect to describe the O.T.O. as a specifically occult group when Reuss founded the Order in 1906, although many of its original members appear to have been preoccupied with occultism. Furthermore, some of the more important post-1920 German occult orders were run by people who had some kind of connection with the O.T.O. milieu. Branches of the O.T.O. still exist in Germany, Austria and Switzerland today, also in England, each of them headed by a claimant to the title of the Order's Supreme Chief.

It is most unlikely that Rudolf Steiner, though he was obviously acquainted with Theodor Reuss, ever had any link with the O.T.O. and hence with sex magic. The average member of the German section of the Theosophical Society, and after 1912 of the Anthroposophical Society, was quite content to understand, to the best of his or her ability, the gist of Steiner's multifarious 'esoteric' teachings. However, Steiner ran a small and exclusive 'Esoteric Section' to which only chosen adepts were admitted, and in this he taught allegedly secret techniques for the development of CLAIRVOYANCE.

News of this group's existence reached England and an equally arcane 'Inner

Circle' in 1910. Its chief was Dr R. W. Felkin, the head of the Order of the STELLA MATUTINA, an offshoot of the original Hermetic Order of the GOLDEN DAWN, which had fragmented into at least three mutually hostile factions in 1903. Felkin was obsessed with the idea that the secret 'Rosicrucian' Order which was supposed to have been behind the G.D. when the latter was founded in the 1880s, must still exist in Germany. He made several efforts to contact it between 1906 and 1910 but without success. Then, in the latter year Dr Hübbe-Schleiden, who was not in Dr Felkin's confidence, advised him to try to see Steiner. Felkin visited Steiner in Berlin and was now convinced that he was on the right track. Unable to neglect his medical practice in London, Felkin sent a certain Neville Meakin, a member of the Stella Matutina, to study under Steiner. Meakin eventually returned to London with full particulars of what Felkin called the 'Continental Processes', meaning Steiner's methods for inducing clairvoyance. These were considered to be so secret that they were only taught to the Stella Matutina's 'Second Order' or inner group. Those in possession of them were forbidden to carry written notes or information on their persons. Steiner himself refused to take Felkin or the Stella Matutina very seriously.

The Germanen Order

In 1912, at about the time when Steiner founded the Anthroposophical Society, Theodor Fritsch, Hermann Pohl and a few others were busy launching an extraordinary secret society called the Germanen Order. This was not an occult group in the strict sense of the word, but many of its members were disciples of two Austrian occultists, Guido von List and Jörg Lanz von Liebenfels. Whereas the Theosophical and Anthroposophical Societies were international in outlook and membership, and freely admitted Jews, the Germanen Order represented German nationalism and anti-Semitism in its most extreme, even psychopathic form. While rabid forms of anti-Semitism had existed in both Austria and Germany since the 1880s, the Germanen Order had its own pet obsession. This related to the mystical purity of Germanic blood. Hence no Jew could possibly be a German; hence the necessity for combating Jewry in every shape and form. The G.O.'s racialist fanatics anticipated every feature of the National Socialists' anti-Semitic campaign, except the 'final solution' of genocide. This idea would probably have outraged them.

While the Germanen Order was violently opposed to Freemasonry, because it was an international institution and supposed to be run exclusively by Jews, it was itself organized on pseudo-Masonic lines and by 1914 there were G.O. lodges in about a dozen German towns. Pohl's theory was that the adoption of a Masonic format would ensure secrecy and, since the concept of brotherhood is one of regular Freemasonry's important tenets, prevent bickering and quarrels among the Order's members. This intention was frustrated by Pohl himself, who managed to quarrel with everybody.

The Germanen Order was, in fact, the 'Inner Group' behind the so-called Hammer League (*Hammerbund*), which was solely concerned with the dissemination of anti-Semitic propaganda. The G.O. found some of its 'mystical teachings' in the works of Guido von LIST (1848–1918), the Viennese eccentric who wrote extensively on such Germanic subjects as the magical significance of the old Nordic runic characters. At Vienna during the early 1900s there was even a Guido von List Society which financed the publication of the Master's writings. The voluminous writings of Jörg LANZ VON LIEBENFELS (1874–1954), yet another of Vienna's stranger citizens, were also diligently read and much admired by G.O. members with a taste for delusions about 'race' and the 'sanctity of the German blood'.

Lanz von Liebenfels had his own occult sect in his Order of New Templars, for which he wrote a series of 'ritualistic' readings. The Order's first temple (1907) was at Burg Werfenstein, an appropriately romantic ruin high up above the River Danube. Other temples were subsequently founded at Mari-

Anton Drexler

enkamp, near Ulm, and at Rügen on the Baltic coast.

It has been suggested that Hitler regularly read Lanz von Liebenfels's periodical *Ostara* when he lived from hand to mouth at Vienna before the First World War, also that he met the Master on at least one occasion. Whether or not this is true, von Liebenfels's works were banned in Germany about 1934.

With the majority of its members at the front, the Germanen Order was inactive between 1914 and 1918. Pohl seceded in 1916 and founded a rival Germanen Order 'Walvater', which had an inner group called the 'Holy Grail'. This suggests an unexpected mixture of 'Wotan worship' and Christianity. There were, in fact, a few minute contemporary sects which supposed that Christianity was an inferior, Judaized religion and preferred the ancient Germanic gods. Wagner did not compose his 'Ring' cycle in vain. During the First World War Pohl sold bronze rings inscribed with runic characters which, he claimed, possessed protective magical qualities.

The original Germanen Order was revived in 1918–19 and a new and elaborate constitution was drafted in 1921. The study of occultism was specifically mentioned in this document. The only known typescript copy is in the German Federal Archives at Coblenz.

The Thule Society

Most of the multifarious stories that Hitler was interested in or identified with occultism can be discounted. However, there was one curious link between the prehistory of National Socialism and Pohl's schismatic branch of the G.O. In January 1918 a very small group which called itself the Thule

Society was formed at Munich to study the alleged occult significance of the old runic characters and rune symbolism. One of its leading members was a fascinating adventurer who called himself Baron Rudolph von SEBOTTENDORFF (1875–1945). The Baron, who was steeped in all forms of occultism, was appointed chief of Pohl's new Bavarian Province in July 1918 and used the Thule Society's name as a cover for his G.O. activities. When Bavaria was in a state of revolutionary turmoil between November 1918 and April 1919, Sebottendorff used the Thule Society as a rallying point for the right-wing opposition and was in touch with Anton Drexler, the founder of the small and insignificant German Workers Party. Hitler joined this party in September 1919, quickly seized control and soon changed its name to the National Socialist German Workers Party. It has been widely supposed that in its heyday the Thule Society was essentially 'occult', but this was not the case.

It is doubtful whether either branch of the Germanen Order existed after the murder of Walter Rathenau, a famous Jewish industrialist, who was appointed the Weimar Republic's foreign minister in February 1922. It is probable that the chiefs of the original G.O. had links with right-wing terrorist circles and found it expedient to close down the Order. A number of small *völkisch* (nationalist and anti-Semitic) occult groups continued to exist until about 1933–4. None of them was particularly secret. They existed in all parts of Germany and produced a vast periodical and pamphlet literature.

The O.T.O. Revived

There does not appear to have been any very extensive interest in Germany in the traditional Western HERMETIC tradition until soon after the First World War. Very few of the new generation of German occultists could read either English or French, and they knew little or nothing about the lively occult scene that had existed in London and Paris since the 1890s. The first occult 'impresario' to appear was a certain Heinrich Tränker, about whom little is known, although he was still alive after 1945.

Tränker was an antiquarian bookseller who specialized in rare Rosicrucian and magical works. In about 1923 he founded a so-called Collegium Pansophicum, with a Grand Orient (Grand Lodge) in Berlin. The Collegium Pansophicum claimed to be the last repository of the old Rosicrucian wisdom, although as is usual in modern occultism the term 'Rosicrucian' has no precise meaning (see ROSICRUCIANS). The Collegium was certainly not an active magical society in the tradition of the Golden Dawn's Second Order, but then Tränker was a theorist rather than a magus in the MacGregor MATHERS style.

Tränker was acquainted with Theodor Reuss, who appointed him Head of the O.T.O. for Germany in about 1920. Reuss was then living in Switzerland and dispensed these regional titles, together with elaborate charters, because he himself was the Grand Master of what was supposed to be an international 'Masonic' order. Tränker later claimed that he never had any very great respect for Reuss or interest in the O.T.O. His link with Reuss is important in a historical context for two reasons: firstly because subsequent German occult groups, and the Fraternitas Saturni in particular, in which sexual magic was an important feature, derived from the Reuss-Tränker line; secondly because the present-day O.T.O. groups in German-speaking countries can trace their remote origins to this source.

When Reuss died in 1924, Tränker made energetic efforts to obtain possession of the O.T.O. archives, which were in the widow's possession. Tränker told her that they had no financial value but without them he could not continue her late husband's work. Frau Reuss smelled a rat and refused to part with the papers. While Tränker may not have wanted to reactivate the now more or less moribund O.T.O., he obviously supposed that the archive could be used to establish his own legitimacy as chief of a secret order. It should be mentioned that the heads of secret orders are always anxious to possess some kind of document that can be flourished when necessary to confirm their authority.

Aleister CROWLEY appeared upon the German scene during the summer of 1925. Twelve years after he had been summarily expelled from the Golden Dawn, he had encountered Reuss in London, in 1912. Since Crowley had divined the O.T.O.'s sex magic secret without even knowing that it or the Order existed, Reuss swore him to secrecy and thereupon appointed him as head of the O.T.O. for Great Britain. Nobody in Germany knew very much about Crowley or his books in 1925, but someone had suggested to Tränker that Baphomet-Crowley was the Master for whom he and others had been anxiously waiting. So Crowley was invited to spend a period at Tränker's country home at Hohenleuben, a remote Thüringian village.

When Tränker realized that he had landed a very large occult fish, he invited a number of German occultists to attend a secret conference at Hohenleuben. These eminent adepts included Albin Grau (the Master Pacitius) and Eugen Grosche (Frater Gregorius), both of whom were members of the Pansophic Collegium's Berlin lodge, and the Master Gebhardi from Danzig. Fräulein Martha Kuentzel, a Leipzig Theosophist, was probably also present.

There are two widely differing unpublished manuscript accounts of the secret conference: one by Crowley and the other by Eugen Grosche. Crowley ended his with the remark that 'every action of Tränker becomes intelligible only on the hypothesis that he is a perfectly unscrupulous and cunning peasant who is exploiting odds and ends of recondite knowledge with intent to defraud'.

According to Grosche's record, the discussions were fruitless because Crowley demanded recognition as the sole head of 'the collective [German] Rosicrucian movement and the Pansophia'. Tränker was of course unwilling to abdicate in favour of Crowley. There was the inevitable quarrel and, according to Grosche, a few weeks later the Berlin Pansophists learned that Tränker had applied to the legal authorities to have Crowley expelled from Germany. Tränker was probably bluffing, but the result was that the Berlin people ceremonially brought their lodge to an end and Tränker seems to have retired into obscurity.

Brotherhood of Saturn

The former Pansophists now formed the secret Fraternitas Saturni Lodge with Albin Grau as its prospective Grand Master. Although the brethren were not prepared to recognize Crowley as a 'Supreme Magus', to whom a faithful obedience was due, he had greatly impressed them and they had decided to accept him as an important teacher. Grau, however, disliked Crowley and refused the office of Grand Master in favour of Eugen Grosche. The Saturnian brethren remained in contact with Crowley and provided a modest market for translations of some of his minor works. These were published by the Thelema Verlag, which was run by his adoring disciple Fräulein Kuentzel. Owing to a perpetual shortage of working capital, she was not able to do very much with the business. However, between about 1928 and 1933 the Fraternitas Saturni was by far the most important occult group in Germany.

Grosche was at that time the proprietor of the Inveha occult bookshop in Berlin. A friend who met him there during the late 1920s told the author of this article that Grosche was a tall, autocratic and pompous individual who liked the sound of his own voice. This informant suggested, too, that Grosche was not a cultured person in the accepted sense of the term. However, he was clearly effective both as the head of an occult order and as a 'commercial' occultist.

The Fraternitas Saturni was never as secret as the Hermetic Order of the Golden Dawn and could be contacted without difficulty before 1933, when the Nazis closed it down, and after 1945 when Grosche revived it. The Order gained a good deal of unwelcome – or perhaps even not so very unwelcome – publicity during the late 1920s when there was a leakage of information about its sex magic practices. There were stories, which were very likely true, of parchment talismans being ritually consecrated with male sperm for insertion into a female initiate's vagina. During the late 1920s a duplicated typescript (marked 'Secret') outlined the theory that the respective male and female positions for sexual intercourse should be regulated by the angular position of the planets at the time. If Mars was in square (90°) aspect to Saturn, for example, the man would be on top, and so on. It must be emphasized that sex magic was never taught or practised in the Golden Dawn, and it is unlikely that Mathers or anyone else in the G.D. ever even thought of the possibility of such a novelty.

There is a detailed description of a Fraternitas Saturni ritual of sex magic in an extraordinary book published privately in a very small edition in 1971 by Dr Adolf Hemberger at Frankfurt-am-Main. Its somewhat misleading title is *Organisationsformen, Rituale, Lehren und Magische Thematik der Freimauerischen und Freimauerartigen Bünde in Deutschen Sprachraum Mitteleuropas*, which can be approximately translated as *The Organization, Rituals, Teachings and Magical Themes of Masonic and Pseudo-Masonic Societies in German-speaking Areas of Central Europe*. The title of Dr Hemberger's book is misleading because its contents have no connection whatever with regular Freemasonry. By comparison with the extensive Golden Dawn material published by Dr Israel REGARDIE in his *The Golden Dawn (389)*, the magical and occult pabulum offered by the Fraternitas Saturni was even more complex and in some respects more sophisticated. It is useless to try to compare MacGregor Mathers and Grosche as purveyors of magical lore. Of the two men Mathers was probably far more creative and imaginative because his range of source material was far smaller than the immense collection of post-1890 occult literature to which Grosche had access. In any case it cannot be established how much of the information in Dr Hemberger's book came directly from Grosche's writings and how much was derived from his pupils' literary output. One can only observe, with all due deference to Dr Hemberger, that the Fraternitas Saturni, which apparently still exists – Grosche died in about 1964 – incorporates a

positively fantastic medley of magical and occult information. The book itself was published with the aid of a grant from the Deutsche Forschungsgemeinschaft, the official German body which sponsors scientific and other research. In this case the grant was approved by the D.F.G.'s Social Sciences committee.

The Fraternitas Saturni is by no means the only occult group active in Germany at the present time. So-called 'illuminati' are active at Frankfurt-am-Main, with their own temple in a flat in the Adalbertstrasse. There are also a number of small 'Thelemite' (Crowley) groups. An anonymous person recently advertised in the periodical *Esotera* for prospective initiates for a revival of the Golden Dawn and then failed to reply to such applicants as are known to the writer of this article. At Stuttgart a mysterious new sect known only by the initials O.R.A. conducts initiations in a temple reeking with incense (information communicated by an initiate who was nearly asphyxiated and forthwith resigned). The O.T.O. still enjoys a lively existence in Switzerland, and gives weekly performances of Crowley's Gnostic Mass. These are often attended by people who hope that they will witness a demonstration of sex magic, but depart unsatisfied. E. H.

(See also ATLANTIS; COSMOLOGY; JUNG.)

Ghosts See APPARITIONS; MEDIUMS.

Kahlil Gibran (1883-1931)
Writer and painter, Gibran was the author of *The Prophet* and other inspirational books which continue to sell in large quantities. Born in the Lebanon, he emigrated to New York as a boy. For some years he was supported by Mary Haskell; their love letters and her private journal have recently been published (*223*).

Madge Gill (d. 1961)
A British automatic artist, an uneducated London housewife who produced hundreds of drawings and paintings which she said were 'undoubtedly guided by an unseen force': she attributed many of them to a spirit named Myrninerest.

Glacial Cosmology See COSMOLOGY.

Glastonbury Zodiac
Until recently it was generally accepted that prehistoric man was a comparatively simple creature. Stonehenge and other megalithic structures, for example, were regarded as cult centres, their form merely aesthetic in design and their dimensions the result of chance. In recent years this view has been increasingly challenged and it has been

suggested that our ancestors in the distant past had far more scientific and technological knowledge than had earlier been realized. It has been argued, for instance, that many megalithic constructions were sophisticated lunar observatories, capable of being used for forecasting such phenomena as eclipses and abnormally high or low tides. Theories of this sort have been viewed with considerable scepticism by most archaeologists. The megalithic yard, the unit of measurement on which most of the lunar observatories appear to have been built, was a subject for derision and was looked on as being quite as silly as the Pyramid inch – the imaginary unit which has been used for extracting prophecies from the Great Pyramid. Scepticism was increased by the fact that so many of the new hypotheses came from people who were not themselves archaeologists, but although there is still much disagreement about the new theories, they have made some headway.

This has greatly encouraged, and has given a new lease of life to, two associated sets of unorthodox and semi-occult archaeological activities which had their first airing in the 1920s, ley-hunting and the 'discovery' of giant earthworks outlining the signs of the zodiac. Neither leys – supposed lines of force connecting standing stones, hammer ponds and other natural features – nor the alleged zodiacs, notably those of Glastonbury and Kingston in England, are taken seriously by archaeologists. For one thing, the sheer size of them – the one at Glastonbury covers several square miles – seems to rule out their having been constructed, even over a long period of time, by the sparse labour force of prehistoric Britain.

Temple of the Stars
It is not clear whether the discoverer of the Glastonbury zodiac, Mrs K. E. Maltwood, was herself a practising occultist, but certainly her arguments have been uncritically accepted by many magicians and fringe scientists as a confirmation of their own belief that Glastonbury, so rich in history and legend, is the 'power centre' of what they call the Western Mystery Tradition (see *207*). Mrs Maltwood's theories, recorded in her book *Glastonbury's Temple of the Stars*, are quite impressive at first sight, as are the researches of her present-day disciples, whose discoveries include a supposed Glastonbury version of the Tree of Life of the CABALA worked into the design of the zodiac. Using an ordnance survey map, Mrs Maltwood found her zodiac – similar to but not quite identical with the zodiac of modern ASTROLOGY – outlined by roads and field tracks, by earthworks and natural banks, by rivers and pools. But her choice of tracks and other

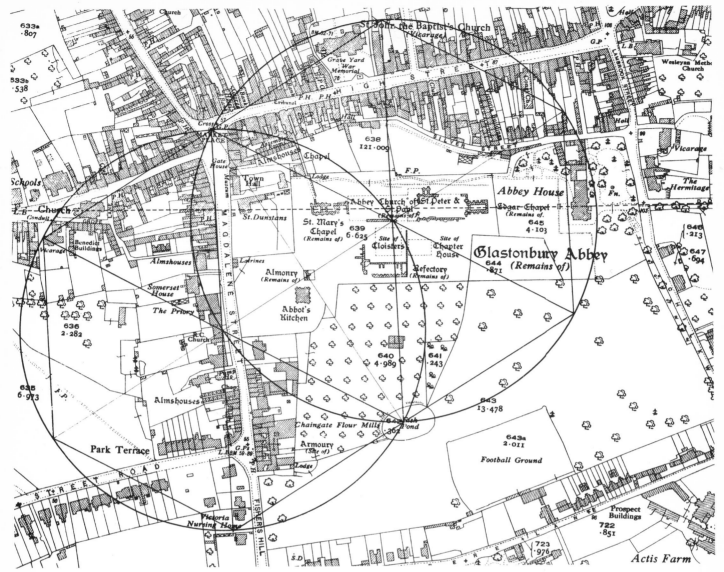

Glastonbury: the application of mystical theory to the layout of the town and Abbey

features was entirely arbitrary. She disregarded some which spoiled the outline of her zodiac as being of modern origin, but she included others, of still more modern origin, because they helped to complete the design. Besides the zodiac, Mrs Maltwood found other things recorded on her maps, among them the story of the Holy Grail. At Butleigh, near the centre of the zodiac, she saw a 'Grail table' on which were symbols of the sun, the moon, and the elements of fire and air, while at six points around Butleigh she saw the six mystic castles where the Arthurian knights experienced various tests. The 'Castle of the Giant', for example, is at the village of Compton.

The theories of Mrs Maltwood's successors have been even more remarkable. One group see the six castles as outlining a Seal of Solomon, or hexagram, indicative of the sphere Tifereth on the Tree of Life. The same group sees the lunar sphere, Yesod, and the

three aspects of the moon-goddess Diana – virgin, mistress and hag – indicated by three nine-pointed figures, all centred on South Cadbury hill (which some more orthodox archaeologists believe may have been the headquarters of the real 'King Arthur').

Other Zodiacs

Other individuals and groups have discovered more zodiacs. A series of articles in the English magazine *Prediction* announced the discovery of a zodiac at Kingston and a privately printed pamphlet has announced the finding of a Nuthampstead zodiac. Most surprising of all, a young magician living in the London suburb of Ealing has come upon a West London zodiac, its figures outlined by streets and parks. To the obvious objection that these features were laid out by the speculative builders of the later 19th century, the magician has a simple reply. The West London zodiac has existed for thousands of years on the ASTRAL PLANE, but without any physical reflection in the world of matter: for

reasons too complex to explain here, the 'Inner Plane Guardians' decided, about 1850, that the time had come for this zodiac to enjoy a physical existence, and they therefore inserted the design into the minds of the builders and architects of Victorian London.

It is this type of 'discovery' which gives the essential clue to the real nature of the Glastonbury zodiac. On a detailed map of any area, except perhaps a desert, it is perfectly possible to see zodiacs or Grail castles or anything else one wants to see. Just as a child may see exciting pictures of adventure in the glowing coals of a fire, or just as some 19th-century astronomers saw, and drew, complex patterns of 'irrigation canals' on the planet Mars, so the occultist sees meaningful symbols in the chance patterns recorded by the map-maker. But such an explanation is not likely to be acceptable to those who thirst to believe in wonders, and no doubt it will not be long before someone announces the discovery of an American zodiac. F. K.

Gnosticism

The gnostic position is the root of all occult philosophy. 'Gnosis' means 'knowledge' and 'occult' means 'hidden'. When the 'occult' has been stripped of its fantastic top-dressing, its seedy, psychopathic and deadening load of unwanted and rejected speculations, what remains is a collection of various gnostic positions, theories – like ASTROLOGY or the system of CORRESPONDENCES – which are incidental to those positions, or techniques of a magical or meditative nature which purport to help the aspirant to the practical realization of his goals. The gnostic is one who has attained or is seeking a secret knowledge. There are gnostics in all ages, but the collection of movements known generally as 'Gnostic' flourished in the Eastern Mediterranean area around the time of, and for several centuries after, the birth of Christ.

The knowledge which the Gnostic sought was knowledge of God and was achieved probably by revelation. It was a secret knowledge, not necessarily because the Gnostics hid their secrets in the fashion of later 'occultists', but because it could come only of itself as the product of certain realizations. The basic Gnostic realization was that the spirit of man represented the divine essence entrapped in matter: that the soul was a spark of God imprisoned in a world God had nothing to do with creating and which was the product of a Demiurge, sometimes evil, sometimes ignorant. Thus all Gnostic systems share a fundamental dualism: that is, they make a complete separation between man, the ensnared god, and the prison in which he lives. Whatever the kind of Gnostic, he can always be said to be world-rejecting; and there can be no more secret knowledge than a philosophical system which teaches that the world is sham and illusion, and that virtue lies in rejecting it. There can be no more secret knowledge than the knowledge – whatever this may be and however it is obtained – that the concerns of ordinary life are evil and irrelevant. In one form or another, this idea is common to Buddhist, Hindu, Western 'occult' and some Christian mystical thinking. It is useful to make distinctions for academic purposes, but all the differences vanish in the common characteristic of rejection of the world. It follows that if the world takes any notice of the Gnostic, it will be horrified.

In the centuries preceding and immediately following the birth of Christ, the Hellenistic world was in convulsion. The achievements of Greek rationalism were inundated in the 3rd century B.C. by a wave of magical and irrational thought from the Orient. The MYSTERY RELIGIONS attempted to reveal to the postulant the secrets of the

The fall of Simon Magus, in St Lazare Cathedral, Autun, France

cosmos, through inducing ecstasy or by a carefully planned series of initiations designed to induce an accelerated rate of 'spiritual progress'. It is easy to see that the mysteries can be regarded as one technique for achieving Gnostic 'knowledge', and in fact the theology of the Mithras cult is very definitely of a Gnostic character. At the other end of the scale, irrationalist currents of opinion influenced the school of philosophy known as Neo-Platonism, whose main advocates, like Plotinus and Porphyry, proclaimed a cosmology very like certain Gnostic systems, although they resolutely opposed the Gnostic doctrine that the world was evil. Both academic philosophy and religious ritual might go hand in hand with practical magic; and the irrationalist movement gathered strength in the latter days of the Roman Empire, achieving a peak in the 2nd and 3rd centuries A.D., which saw the compiling of the Gnostic treatises known as the *Corpus Hermeticum* (see HERMETICA). During the 4th century the Christian religion became the state religion of the Roman Empire, and by

the 7th century Western Europe had come to accept the monopolistic jurisdiction of the Pope at Rome on matters spiritual. Gnosticism may have continued to influence the Christianities of the East, but in Western Europe Gnostic sects were branded as heretical.

The Hymn of the Pearl

The earliest accounts of Gnosticism come from Christians concerned to refute their greatest rivals, like the famous *Adversus haereses* of Irenaeus, Bishop of Lyons at the end of the 2nd century. This fact has led to a possibly distorted view of what Gnosticism was. The Christian fathers regarded it as a heresy, the antagonist of the true faith. Irenaeus went so far as to derive all Gnostic systems – and hence all heresy – from Simon Magus, who is mentioned in the Gospel of St Luke. According to Irenaeus, Simon was the chief of John the Baptist's thirty disciples and thus his heresies infiltrated Christianity. This merely points the moral that in the melting-pot of religious ideas out of which Christianity was forged there was a substantial mixture of Gnosticism, present even before the birth of Christ, and it is fairly certain that there was an undercurrent of Gnostic-occultist speculation in Judaism, although as the rabbis ignored heresy rather than denounced it this has attracted little attention. The point is that Gnosticism was not the distortion of the Christian gospel that the early fathers would have had their flocks believe. It was a philosophical position which the Christian Church had abandoned, in particular when it reconciled itself to the world in becoming a state religion. There were Hellenistic Gnosticisms, deriving from Neo-Platonic roots; Judaic Gnosticisms springing from Jewish occultism; Christian Gnosticisms representing either distortions of the official party line or elements rejected by the Church in the purification of its doctrine. It is quite possible to find Gnostic elements in the New Testament, and indeed – as some occultists believe – the sayings of Jesus can themselves be read in a Gnostic fashion. When the Gnostic religions were supplanted by Christianity, their doctrines survived among certain groups of heretics in the West and in Islamic esotericism in the East.

It follows that there was great diversity among the various Gnostic prophets. As Irenaeus says, 'Every day some one of them invents something new.' It would scarcely be profitable to discuss the differences between various systems, and a short description of 'Gnosticism' should confine itself to showing the common ground.

The basic position is expressed in the beautiful 'Hymn of the Pearl' from the apocryphal Acts of the Apostle Thomas, where it is headed 'Song of the Apostle Judas Thomas in the Land of the Indians'. The opening is reproduced in the translation of Hans Jonas (250):

When I was a little child and dwelt in the kingdom of my father's house and delighted in the wealth and splendour of those who raised me, my parents sent me forth from the East, our homeland, with provisions for the journey. From the riches of our treasure-house they tied me a burden: great it was, yet light, so that I might carry it alone. . . . They took off from me the robe of glory which in their love they had made for me, and my purple mantle that was woven to conform exactly to my figure, and made a covenant with me, and wrote it in my heart that I might not forget it: 'When thou goest down to Egypt and bringest the One Pearl which lies in the middle of the sea which is encircled by the snorting serpent, thou shalt put on again thy robe of glory and thy mantle over it and with thy brother our next in rank be heir in our kingdom.'

Here the soul is shown setting off from the heavenly kingdom, donning the impure garment of the physical body and descending into the world of matter. The soul is given instructions for the journey: it is to go on a quest for the One Pearl which is in Egypt, protected by the sea and the serpent. The Pearl – as in the medieval allegory of the same name – is the style given to the soul to remind it of its divine origin. The instructions given to the incarnating soul are to enable it to escape from the prison of the material world – Egypt, the sea and the serpent – and recover its rightful place in creation. In the continuation of the 'Hymn of the Pearl' the soul receives a letter from its royal father, by a messenger who breaks the sleep into which the soul has fallen. It is reminded of its nature, of the instructions which were given it, and embarks on the quest for the Pearl. The serpent is overcome and the soul ascends to the heavenly kingdom where it resumes the garment of light in which it was originally clothed.

The fate of the soul in the world is expressed as 'numbness', 'sleep', 'drunkenness', and the divine summons is necessary to awaken the soul from its slumber. In the Gnostic Gospel according to St Thomas, Christ is represented as mourning for the intoxicated condition of man:

Jesus said: I took my stand in the midst of the world and in flesh I appeared to them; I found them all drunk, I found none among them athirst. And my soul was afflicted for the sons of men, because they are blind in their heart and do not see that empty they have come into the world (and that) empty they seek to go out of the world again. But now they are drunk. When they have shaken off their wine, then will they repent.

The soul has become trapped in its prison, which has been created by angels which are 'lower far than the unbegotten Father'. This idea is extended in some Gnostic systems into an elaborate scheme of successive emanations from the Godhead, each stage of creation giving birth to another and ruled over by an Archon. The world as man perceives it is created by a great Archon, who believes that he is self-created and does not owe his existence to the Absolute Power from whom all things have their source. Although this idea was sometimes elaborated into a complete dualism under Persian influence – the simple opposition of good and evil powers – the Gnostic position generally holds that the material world is indirectly a divine creation, although through the lower angels. This means that the situation of mankind is the result of a failure on the part of Deity, that something has gone wrong with the universe.

The System of Valentinus

The supreme exponent of this tragic view of the universe is Valentinus, who was born in Egypt and taught in Rome between A.D. 135 and 160. He sought to locate the source of matter and evil within the Godhead itself. His doctrine of the Creation begins with the original perfect Aeon, whose name is 'Fore-Beginning, Fore-Father and Abyss'. Fore-Father projected out of himself a seed into the womb of the Silence, from which came the Nous (Mind) and Truth. These are respectively male and female. They compose the first Triad and from this emanated other triads, groups of three forces. From the Nous – also called the 'Only-Begotten' – and his consort Truth, came the Word and Life who give birth to Man and the Church. These Aeons emanated further until there were thirty emanations, thirty qualities, attributes or principles, thirty Aeons which make up the fullness of creation which is called the Pleroma.

But of all the Aeons composing the Pleroma, only the Only Begotten, Nous, could know the Godhead, because he was the first emanation from it. The other Aeons strove to know their original Father, but could not; and in this striving the last emanation, the Aeon Sophia, who was the youngest created and hence the furthest from the Fore-Father, went out of her mind. Despite all her seeking to know the Father, she discovered that this was impossible, and narrowly avoided destruction. But the consequences of her attempt remained, inchoate but created, as the product of her mental state – Sophia had in fact emanated on her own account without deliberate intention. In order to take care of this formless emanation and to restore equilibrium in the Pleroma, Fore-Father emanated Christ and the Holy Spirit. By a series of further emanations and Aeonic activity, the by-products of Sophia's striving to know God become matter, soul and the divine essence or pneuma. The actual creator of the world is the Demiurge, whose cardinal characteristic is ignorance. He is composed of the same substance as the soul, and in order to communicate the Gnosis which will enable man to achieve salvation, the divine or pneumatic essence is incarnated in the historical Christ, whose message will appeal to the divine elements in man.

In the extraordinarily complicated system of Valentinus, the unfortunate position of man is attributed to a failure in the Pleroma, a lapse from perfection in the complete self-expression of the Deity. The creator of the world, the Demiurge, occupies a very lowly place indeed in an inadvertent creation. It is not suggested that he is deliberately evil. But the religion which the Christian Church had above all to overcome asserted that the Demiurge was equivalent to Satan. This was a question of complete opposition to all ideas that the world was good as the product of the direct or indirect activity of the Father.

The Manichees
Mani, the founder of the Manichee faith, was born about A.D. 216 in Babylonia and began his ministry in the late 230s. The attempts of Valentinus and his numerous disciples had been to create an elite of 'pneumatics' capable of understanding the esoteric meaning of Christian scripture within the Christian Church. Mani adopted similar Gnostic ideas, but founded a rival religion. He was crucified in 275.

Mani's starting point was the principle of dualism which had been developed in Persia: the absolute separation between good and evil powers which had existed from the beginning. These are the Darkness and the Light. The Darkness rose up against the Light, and because the Light is wholly good it could not resist Darkness with force. From the Light was emanated Primal Man, who sallied forth to do battle with the Arch-demon. Primal Man was overcome by his adversary, and gave himself and his five sons as food to the Darkness, 'as a man who has an enemy mixes a deadly poison in a cake and gives it to him'. The Darkness surrounded the five sons with matter, and they fell into the sleep of ignorance from which only the Gnosis could arouse them. Much of the Divine essence was saved by the intervention of a messenger from the Light, but that which did not escape was bound more firmly by the agents of Darkness, who created the forms of mankind in imitation of the forms taken by the divine messenger. From the Light yet another messenger was sent with the special mission of imparting the Gnosis to man – or more accurately, of collecting the divine pneuma still entrapped in matter from every part of creation where it still remains. This is the *Jesus patibilis* (suffering Jesus) whose work of salvation is an invisible, omnipresent and perpetual recovery of Light from Darkness.

Christian polemics against the Gnostic fifth column within their ranks gave way to a confrontation with Manicheism. In the West the doctrine of Mani was suppressed but in the East it survived. Other Gnosticisms endured among the Arabs and were soon given an Islamic colouring. Thus the Bektashi dervishes and other Sufi orders, as well as groups like the Ahl-i-Haqq of Western Persia, preserve Gnosticism in different forms to this day. There are other surviving communities of Gnostic origin, such as the

Yezidjes – the so-called 'Devil-worshippers' of Eastern Turkey and Persia – and the Mandaeans, of the areas in and bordering Iraq. In the Christian Middle Ages Gnostic cults appeared in the ranks of heresy. Apart from their theology, they can be recognized by the behaviour of their votaries, which always attracted the censure of the ecclesiastical authorities.

The Cathars and the Free Spirit
If one subscribes to a belief that the material world is evil or that it is a grievous error, a flaw in the universal design, there are two possible courses open with regard to personal morality. On the one hand there is the renunciation of all pleasures of the flesh and the development of an extreme asceticism. This was the attitude adopted by the Manichees: to deprive the Darkness of its power, by abstaining as much as was possible from dealings with its creation. On the other hand, the Gnostic is faced with the possibility that as his divine nature is imperishable in any case, the strictures of conventional morality do not apply to him. This moral freedom of the Gnostic may actually be adopted as a deliberate tactic, either as a defiance of the laws of matter or as an attempt to do everything and so exhaust the natural world of its power over the spirit. On the one hand the ascetic, on the other the seeker after excess: but in whatever form, the Gnostic always regards himself as one of the elect.

Perhaps the most famous of all medieval heresies, that of the Cathars, reveals itself as Gnostic of the ascetic type. The first time the name Cathar, meaning 'pure', was used was in 1030, of a community at Montefeltro in Italy; but the Cathar Church took deepest root in the south of France, where its doctrines had been introduced by the Lombard heretic Church called *de Concoresso*, which in turn derived its doctrines from the Manichee-influenced Bogomils of Bulgaria. The Cathars believed that there was a series of Aeons between God and the material world. The latter was the creation of Jehovah, the God of the Old Testament, who was equated with Satan. Because of man's position in this Satanic world, it was advisable to create no new life, for this would merely entrap another spark of the Divine. Marriage and procreation were anathema, although sexual contact was permitted as long as it did not result in children. The initiate or priestly class were known as 'Perfects' and were to all intents and purposes manifestations of God, filled as they were with the Holy Spirit. In 1207 Pope Innocent III solicited help from the magnates of northern France to crush the rival religion. The chief

Cathar fortress of Montségur fell in 1925, but for fifty years afterwards those skilful in detecting heresy were occupied in hunting down refugees from this once dangerous confession (see plate, page 119).

Precisely the opposite point of view was taken by the heretics of the Free Spirit, who practised a Gnosticism of the libertine variety. The Free Spirit seems to have had connections with a school of Neo-Platonic mysticism whose chief representative was Meister Eckhardt (c. 1260–1327), who at one time was supposed to have written *Schwester Katrei*, one of the texts of the Free Spirit. This treatise describes the struggles of Sister Katherine of the Free Spirit in her attempts to know God. Eventually she achieves the state of unity with the Godhead, and remains in an ecstatic coma for three days. On regaining consciousness she claims actually to *be* God. 'No soul can come to God unless he is God, as she was and as she had been created.' One of the chief charges against the Free Spirit was that of sexual licence: it was said that the adepts of the sect might eat and drink what they liked, need not necessarily work, might have sexual relations with either sex and procure bodily satisfaction by whatever means they chose. There is no doubt that the heresy was effectively Gnostic. Its sources are unclear: but it would be surprising if every Gnostic believer had been eradicated from Europe. There had been continual small eruptions of Gnostic protest in the early middle ages; for example, a group formed at St Malo about 1140 around one Eudes de l'Etoile who represented himself as an Aeon sent down from on high. From exactly whom the Free Spirit derived their doctrines is not known, although there seems to have been a link with the communities of wandering Béguines and Béghards who also practised an irregular sexuality.

The Gnosticism of the Renaissance
In the great disruption of states and consciences which took place during the Renaissance and Reformation the gnostic position once more came into prominence, as a learned and fashionable philosophy, known by the name of Hermetism, from the Gnostic treatises reputedly written by 'Hermes Mercurius Trismegistus', a fictitious personage of great reputation whose pronouncements were called in to strengthen the tottering Christian establishment. In the baggage of Hermes came the more practical appurtenances of Gnosticism, magic and meditational techniques for elevating the spirit on high. The Renaissance magus, the follower of Hermes and his kin, was a Gnostic in the fullest sense of the term, and like the Gnostics of the 2nd and 3rd centuries, he was always

inventing something new. Once more, conditions of ideological crisis saw the emergence of the Gnosis, and attempts to realize the divine knowledge it promised by means of techniques which had their origins in the same period as gave birth to the religious philosophy. Hermetists like Giordano Bruno, Pico della Mirandola or John Dee were Gnostic philosophers. They were therefore dangerous. Pico was at one time condemned for his doctrines, Dee was accused of heresy, and Bruno was finally burned. Apart from the traditional concern of the Church with purity of doctrine and the preservation of her spiritual monopoly, she found herself confronted with her perennial enemy, the world-rejecting Gnostic who took it upon himself to make himself as God.

There is a peculiar significance in this emergence of the learned Gnosticism of the

John Calvin

Renaissance. The Christian Church faced a negligible challenge from the Gnostic, but the attitude of some of her most pronounced adversaries among the Reformers resembled that of the Gnostic in no small degree. John Calvin, for example, with his belief in predestination and his doctrine of the elect, was in certain aspects preaching doctrine like that of the Hermetic philosophers. In a less esoteric fashion and without the magical appurtenances of the Renaissance magus, Calvinism proclaimed every man his own priest and organized a City of the Just in Geneva. Other Reforming denominations – particularly the Anabaptists – betray Gnostic characteristics in their denial of existing laws. But it is particularly in its denial of the priestly caste and the assertion that every man stood in a relationship to his Creator that the Reformation approaches Gnosticism. Not only might the Hermetists be seen as heretical, but they might appear as the

propagators of a message unpleasantly like that of the Reformers. Conversely, although there is little supporting evidence, it is possible that some of the Reformers did obtain fuel for their bonfires of vanities from a distantly apprehended Gnosticism. There is a constantly-maintained theory which links the mysterious Hermetic society of the ROSICRUCIANS with German Lutheranism. But after the furore of polemic, Inquisition and religious war, all concern with cities not of this world – whether the Gnostic or the modified Christian version – became less and less fashionable, until the Age of Reason chased such phantoms off the stage.

Modern Gnostic Churches

Towards the end of the 19th century there took place a revival of occult beliefs and practices in great profusion. Amongst the welter of Spiritualism, Oriental metaphysics, new cults and old credulity, the Gnostic position was naturally prominent, and formed as always the basis for investigation into magic, alchemy and religious philosophy. Those of a Gnostic temperament had now the derived Hermetism of the Renaissance to draw on, in addition to the products of the first few centuries after Christ, but some did investigate the original Gnosticism. Anna KINGSFORD and Edward Maitland were particularly concerned with Gnosticism as revealed by the Hermetica, for they discovered in Hermes confirmation for a philosophy revealed to Anna Kingsford under ether. The Theosophist G. R. S. MEAD also investigated Hermes but much earlier published his *Fragments of a Faith Forgotten* (1900), which collected and translated such reports of Gnosticism as were at that time available. In this book Mead denied any intention of 'refounding a Gnostic Church'. The denial was necessary to confute his critics, for across the Channel, in Paris, a Gnostic Church had actually come into being.

Paris at the end of the 19th century harboured more occultists and mystics than any other capital; and for the end of the 19th century that is a statement not to be made without caution. In Paris the poets and artists of the Symbolist movement drew most of their inspiration from the occult revival, and the society of artists and occultists overlapped. It is significant that this period saw the adoption by the artist – the name was coming also to be spelled with a capital 'A' – of a code of conduct which embraced both types of Gnostic morality. On the one hand was the ascetic genius, in touch with the source of inspiration through purity and the application of will; on the other the debauched Bohemian and lover of excess, whose muses lay in the gutter and whose

IOANNES CALVINVS THEOLOGVS Genevensis

Nasc: Novioduni Veromanduorum A: 1509. 10 Iulij Moritur A: 1564 27 Martÿ.

Gallia non alio tantum se Flamine jactat,
Nec se alio tollit Scotia Vate magis.

sufferings became Art. Nietzsche dubbed these two types Apollonian and Dionysian, but they are as accurately defined as Gnostic. In the poet Stanislas de GUAITA is found a magician who took the path of physical degradation; and in his colleague in magic Josephin PÉLADAN can be seen a novelist and aesthetician who tried to cultivate the ascetic will.

Amidst the explosion of the artistic occult it is quite natural to discover a Gnostic Church, whose leading spirit was the poet and Academician Fabre des Essarts. In 1888 a doubtful character called Jules Doinel discovered a manuscript written by a Cathar martyr who had been burned in Orleans in 1022. Doinel was an official in the Orleans library, and became involved in various enterprises of the irrationalist underground in late 19th-century France. The manuscript evidently turned his head and he became convinced that he had been consecrated by the Aeon Jesus to re-establish the Gnostic Church in France. By 1895 the erratic Doinel had fled back to the arms of Mother Church – although this did not prevent his wandering round Carcassone in episcopal trappings. Fabre des Essarts was left in charge of the Church under the style of the Patriarch Synésius. It seems that the Gnostic Church received its consecration at the hands of an Eastern bishop in the Paris house of a Theosophist, Lady Caithness. It included some quite distinguished members, amongst whom was the former director of one of the National Theatres. The Papacy noticed the Gnostics and issued an apostolic letter against the 'ancient Albigensian heresy'.

The creed advanced by Fabre des Essarts was an intelligent elaboration of Gnostic doctrine and appears to have been quite seriously supported. The world is the creation of Satan, and the solutions for the Gnostic are the familiar two: libertinism or asceticism. The Patriarch of the Gnosis did not declare himself definitely for either.

The Universal Gnostic Church of Doinel and Fabre des Essarts gave birth somewhat inadvertently to the Gnostic Catholic Church which is associated with the O.T.O. (Order of the Temple of the Orient). An occult entrepreneur, Theodor Reuss, who was at one point in control of the O.T.O., visited the Patriarchs of the Gnosis in Paris, and conferred on them some Masonic degrees for which he held authority. As a return of courtesy the Paris Gnostics made Reuss a Patriarch, and that shady character established the Gnostic Catholic Church which later became connected with Aleister CROWLEY. The headquarters of this organization is at present near Zurich, in which town lived a more serious prophet of a modern gnosis, Carl Gustav JUNG.

Jung and Gurdjieff

Jung often complained that his critics saw him as a religious mystic rather than as a scientific psychologist. He was both. He wore on his finger a Gnostic ring. He discovered parallels for the 'process of individuation', which he saw in his patients, in ALCHEMY and Oriental religion. In the extraordinary book *VII Sermones ad Mortuos* which he wrote at the beginning of his period of working independently of Freud, the psychologist proclaimed the destiny of the soul in terms which are purely Gnostic. The book was originally published under the pseudonym of Basilides, and sometimes it is hard to tell that it is *not* Basilides, the early Gnostic, who is speaking through the mouth of Jung. The principles which were to guide Jungian psychology were laid down by 'Basilides' in the terms of a religious revelation. It was the duty of man to differentiate himself from the Pleroma – the Gnostic term for the fullness of God – and to avoid the evils of the world of matter. The governing spirit of the material world Jung called by the old Gnostic name of 'Abraxas', who is 'force, duration, change'. The divine possibilities of man depend on his overcoming Abraxas:

Between man and his one god there standeth nothing, so long as man can turn away his eyes from the flaming spectacle of Abraxas.
Man here, god there.
Weakness and nothingness here, there eternally creative power.
Here nothing but darkness and chilling moisture.
There wholly sun.

There are obvious differences between Jungian Gnosticism and the classical systems; but there were many varieties of Gnosticism originally, and the system of the original Basilides is as different from that of Mani as Mani is from Jung. Parts of Jung's work represent a restatement of Gnosticism in terms suitable for 20th-century man. This can also be said of the most notable Gnostic of modern times, G. I. GURDJIEFF.

The cosmology elaborated by Gurdjieff, in the period when he taught in Moscow and St Petersburg, is set down by his disciple OUSPENSKY in his book *In Search of the Miraculous*. While it is evident that Gurdjieff derived his system from many different sources – perhaps like Mani he did so deliberately – there is little doubt that one substantial element in his explanation of the universe and of man's place in it is provided by a reinterpretation of the Valentinian Gnosis. The system of various Aeons, or spheres of being – called by Gurdjieff 'worlds' – is identical, and the Greek term 'Ogdoad' is applied to the initial progress of emanation in the same fashion by Gurdjieff and the early Gnostics. The imagery of man asleep or drunken is the same, and the originality of Gurdjieff's teaching consisted in the exercises he taught to overcome the state of sleep. It is an open question as to where Gurdjieff made the acquaintance of Gnostic sources. For 20th-century man, however, there could be no better introduction to the sort of speculation in which the early Gnostics indulged than to read Gurdjieff's version of the Gnosis. It is very difficult for Western man in the scientific age to approach the elaborate and concise terminology of the original Gnostics with any real idea of what it signifies. Gurdjieff's restatement of the Gnosis is couched in terms of 19th-century materialism, whilst that of Jung is in the less uncompromising vocabulary of psycho-analysis.

It is probably necessary for every age to have the basic philosophies restated in contemporary terms. The human being is a complex creature when viewed from one direction, but from another it appears that he is really surprisingly simple: unless he really can extend his constitutional capacities he is bound by the limits of the physical body and the material environment. There are consistent human problems and a limited and relatively consistent number of possible solutions. One of the possible solutions to the problem of being human is the Gnostic. At certain stages in the life of the individual, when imagination outruns possibility, when knowledge of what may be ultimately possible exceeds the means of present attainment; or during certain historical crises when the pressures on the individual become too acute, the Gnostic response becomes widespread. There seems to have been such a crisis around the time of the birth of Christ. There was undoubtedly one in the period of Renaissance and Reformation. The occult revival which began towards the end of the last century is one symptom of another such crisis, which is still going on.

The Gnostic response need not take the form of religion. It can even be found in politics. The incessant calls for 'liberation', coming from contemporary movements in the West, are based on a Gnostic response to a personal and historical situation. There are groups with very tangible material complaints whose liberation would seem to be an entirely material matter; but other movements, like 'Women's Liberation', have only a half-truth on the side of their seductive analysis. Women indeed are discriminated against, are materially repressed if they wish to stand as individuals; yet 'Women's Liberation' is often concerned with an impossible liberation from the biological destiny of being women. The same could be said of various recently popular groups of 'radical' revolutionaries. Those who follow Marcuse, or the International Situationists, who talk of 'false consciousness', are often unaware that they are voicing the perennial Gnostic appeal – wake up, and know your situation! The cry for 'liberation' is often a protest against the fact of being human – a lot miserable enough for some at all times and occasionally for a large number.

If the circumstances are sufficiently depressing, the call for liberation may begin once more to take a specifically religious form. It is a truism that the search for freedom is never successful. A freedom is won; there are other freedoms beyond, and what at first seemed a liberty to aim at becomes a condition of present slavery. There is left the ultimate freedom, the freedom from humanity, the metaphysical freedom of the Gnostic in search of knowledge. Thus arises the pneumatic of the 2nd century A.D., the star-demon philosopher of the Renaissance, the psychologist or occultist Gnostic of today. They are all in search of the same good, their Pearl, their robe of light. Let us hope that they attain their kingdom. J. W.

(Further reading: 126, 190, 191, 250, 281, 322, 359, 409, 493, 494, 515.)

God-forms, Gods See SPIRITS AND FORCES.

Golden Dawn

The Hermetic Order of the Golden Dawn, the magical society whose heyday was during the 1890s, has achieved a legendary reputation for several reasons. While those concerned with occultism regard it as a singularly authoritative repository of magical lore and instruction, the fact that W. B. YEATS was a member has intrigued the many academics, particularly in America, who are now preoccupied with his life and work. Next, since until recently the Order's origins have been surrounded with mystery, an apparently insoluble puzzle has provided its own peculiar fascination. Finally, the G.D.'s teachings have greatly influenced the theories and work, and to a lesser extent the internal organization, of many occult groups in English-speaking countries during the past fifty or more years. It was in fact a prototype magical order. Nothing with its strange vitality existed before its foundation in 1887–8, while later imitations have never matched its success.

The G.D. was to some extent a by-product of several related factors in the social history of 19th-century England. The Spiritualist movement attracted a widespread public interest and following between about 1850 and 1890 (see SPIRITUALISM). Dissatisfied with Spiritualism, with its many fraudulent MEDIUMS and unproven hypotheses, some men and women turned to the study of 'rejected knowledge', meaning knowledge which is rejected by the Establishment because it is held to be superstitious, lacking a rational foundation, and so on. All varieties of occultism may be regarded as 'rejected knowledge'. This new and more widespread preoccupation with occultism coincided with a notable increase of interest in Freemasonry which became evident after 1860, when many new lodges were formed. A fair number of men who were identified with 'rejected knowledge' joined the Craft at this time. One cannot speak of a mass invasion of Freemasonry by occultists. One can merely identify a small coterie of Master Masons, most of whom were acquainted with one another, who were particularly concerned with occultism. Their meeting place was the Rosicrucian Society of England, membership of which was restricted to Master Masons. It was not a Masonic lodge but, rather, the equivalent of a literary society. The Golden Dawn emerged from this milieu. Its founder, his two principal collaborators and many of the Order's original male members were Masonic 'Rosicrucians' (see ROSICRUCIANS and plate, page 120).

The Order was founded by Dr William Wynn WESTCOTT (1848–1925), a London coroner, with the assistance of Samuel Liddell MacGregor MATHERS (1854–1918), an eccentric pseudo-Highlander, of no easily identifiable occupation, and Dr William Robert Woodman (1828–91), a retired physician.

In relation to the G.D.'s early annals it is important to remember that Westcott conceived his plan for a secret and highly exclusive occult order only a few months after Helena Petrovna BLAVATSKY settled permanently in London in May 1887. Her presence provided a magnificent advertisement for the THEOSOPHICAL SOCIETY, which had hitherto been a small-scale affair. Its membership now rapidly increased, and many now became more or less familiar with her curious medley of the Eastern and Western occult traditions. Westcott clearly intended that his Golden Dawn project should provide a far more exclusive alternative, and furthermore one based firmly on the Western hermetic tradition. Anyone could join the Theosophical Society but admittance to the G.D. was not to be made easy. Whereas Freemasonry was (and still is)

MacGregor Mathers

a society with secrets rather than a secret society, the G.D. was essentially the latter from the very beginning.

The Cypher Manuscript

It is necessary to describe the G.D.'s conception and early history at some length because these matters show how Westcott in 1887–8 and Mathers in 1891–2 contrived an almost perfect formula for an occult order. In August 1887 the Reverend A. F. A. Woodford, an elderly parson who was well known in Masonic circles but not a member of the Rosicrucian Society, gave Westcott about sixty leaves of a manuscript written in a cypher, or more accurately an artificial alphabet. It was written on old paper, some of the sheets bearing an 1809 watermark date. The faded brown ink gave the manuscript an appearance of antiquity. The MS. was, however, a recent production, certainly not earlier than about 1870. Its provenance will probably never be known. Whoever wrote it was familiar with the structure of Masonic rituals and at the same time had a detailed knowledge of the Western occult tradition, including the CABALA, the symbolism of ALCHEMY, and ASTROLOGY, not to mention the works of the French Magus Eliphas LÉVI, who had died as recently as 1875.

Westcott, who knew his hermetic literature well, would no doubt have quickly found the key to the artificial alphabet in the *Polygraphiae* of Abbot Johann Trithemius (1462–1516). Again, when he began to transcribe the material he would have immediately realized that here were the very fragmentary outlines of a series of five rituals for something that called itself the 'Golden Dawn'. Again, since there were references to both *Fratres* and *Sorores*, the G.D., if it existed at all, had no connection with regular Freemasonry, to which women are not admitted.

On 4 October 1887 he wrote to Mathers and invited him to compose full-scale rituals, which could be actually 'worked', based upon the rather vague hints which were available in the Cypher MS. At the same time he suggested that Mathers should join him as Co-Chief of a new occult order to be called the Golden Dawn. 'We must then choose a 3rd [Chief],' he continued, 'and endeavour to spread a complete scheme of initiation as soon as possible.' Dr Woodman, the Rosicrucian Society's Supreme Magus or President, was invited to accept office as the third Chief and did so.

At this stage there was no question of providing instruction in the theory and practice of ritual magic. Westcott envisaged nothing more than a cosy little secret society of occultists, open to both sexes. They would work the rituals which Mathers was now busy expanding from the Cypher MS. and study for the simple examinations, to be devised by the three Chiefs, which would have to be passed before a member could be advanced from one grade to the next highest. Nothing could have been more innocuous.

A Freemason since 1871, Westcott was accustomed to the concept of hierarchy, which is an important feature in regular Freemasonry's 'organization'. In England, for example, no new lodge can be founded without the authority of the United Grand Lodge of England. Westcott obviously felt that he could not simply produce the G.D. as if from a conjurer's hat. What was lacking was evidence to show that the Order itself derived its being from a hierarchical succession reaching back into the distant past, hence an 'authority' in the background which would be the source of his own authority. Since it did not exist, it was necessary to invent it. This subterfuge of Westcott's, of which Mathers was probably aware at the time, bedevilled the G.D. 'story' until very recently when the present writer discovered a cache of original G.D. documents, which had remained hidden for more than fifty years, and was able to deduce what actually happened in 1887 and after. The strange feature is that those who had access to the documents during the early 1900s never realized their significance, or were perhaps unwilling to draw the logical conclusions, namely that the Order was founded upon a series of ingenious fabrications.

Someone – probably Westcott rather than Mathers – inserted an additional leaf of old paper into the Cypher MS. and, using the Trithemius artificial alphabet, wrote the following: 'Sapiens dom[inabitur] ast[ris] is a Chief among the members of die Goldene Dammerung [the Golden Dawn]. She is a famous Soror. Her name is Fräulein Sprengel. Letters reach her at Herr J. Enger, Hotel Marquardt, Stuttgart. She is 7=4

[figures in Hebrew characters] or a Chief Adept.'

By locating Fräulein Sprengel in Germany Westcott made her inaccessible, and by investing her with an exalted rank in a suitably mysterious German occult order he made her a credible source of authority, at least to the gullible. He even went so far as to produce a Hotel Marquardt billhead with details of refreshments consumed on 1 December 1887, on which he wrote 'SD Ast was here.' It is unlikely that Westcott himself went to Stuttgart at this or perhaps any other time.

The hoax was now elaborated by the production of a series of letters which purported to have been written to Westcott by the eminent Soror's secretary, Frater In Utroque Fidelis. He signed them with her Latin motto on her behalf. There are six 'S.D.A.' letters, all alleged to have been written between November 1887 and December 1889. All of them are brief and express no more than whatever Westcott currently required as evidence to support his claim that the G.D. was the English branch of a long-established Continental occult order. One further letter, dated 23 August 1890 and in a different handwriting – it was signed by Frater Ex Uno Disce Omnes – announced Fräulein Sprengel's very recent death at 'a village near B'. The Frater mentioned, too, that Westcott would not receive any further communications from Germany. By this time Fräulein Sprengel had served her purpose, although a decade later her 'ghost' was to haunt him.

It is possible to deduce how the correspondence was manufactured. Westcott wrote the drafts of the letters in English and gave them to an unidentified person to translate into German. Whoever did the translations had little knowledge of the German language and Anglicisms abound, hence he must have been an Englishman. Someone else produced the letter which purported to come from Frater Ex Uno Disce Omnes and he also perpetrated jargon. Once in possession of these 'German' texts, Westcott handed them to a certain Mr Albert Essinger, who never had any connection with the G.D., to translate back into English. Years later a few early members of the Order recalled that Westcott occasionally produced the letters, but only briefly. No one ever had the opportunity to subject them to any detailed inspection.

By March 1888 Westcott had written his so-called 'Historical Lecture for Neophytes', a curious document which was made available to newly-joined members of the Order. Once again there is the suggestion that the G.D. in England was directly descended

from a long-established foundation which existed in both Germany and France. He was even able to name well-known persons – all of them deceased, some of them very recently – who had been members: for example, in France J. B. Ragon (d. 1862) and Eliphas Lévi (d. 1875) and in England Frederick Hockley (d. 1885) and K. R. H. MACKENZIE (d. 1886).

Yet another fabrication belongs to this period. In or about March 1888 with the assistance of Miss Mina Bergson – the sister of Henri Bergson (later renowned as a philosopher) – who married his colleague Mathers in June 1890, Westcott produced a Charter of Warrant for the Isis-Urania Temple No. 3 of the Hermetic Order of the Golden Dawn. Westcott signed Fräulein Sprengel's Latin motto on her behalf and ineffectually tried to disguise his own handwriting.

The Grades and Chiefs

An apparently complicated system of grades was also devised.

Outer Order

$0°=0°$ Neophyte
$1°=10°$ Zelator
$2°=9°$ Theoricus
$3°=8°$ Practicus
$4°=7°$ Philosophus

Second Order

$5°=6°$ Adeptus Minor
$6°=5°$ Adeptus Major
$7°=4°$ Adeptus Exemptus

Third Order

$8°=3°$ Magister
$9°=2°$ Magus
$10°=1°$ Ipsissimus

The grades numbered from $10°$ to $1°$ in descending order referred to the ten sefiroth (emanations of the Deity) in the cabalistic Tree of Life, with the addition of the $0°=0°$ Neophyte degree. Initially the rank-and-file members of the G.D. could only belong to the Outer Order. After passing a simple examination they could be advanced to the next highest grade, with a $4°=7°$ Philosophus as the most senior. Mathers composed rituals for all these grades on the basis of the clues found in the Cypher MS. At first Westcott, Mathers and Woodman were the only members of the Second Order and assumed its lowest grade ($5°=6°$). They claimed to be subject to the authority of three Secret Chiefs who were $7°=4°$ and were only known by their Latin mottoes. These Secret Chiefs were none other than Mathers, the non-existent Fräulein Sprengel

Divination by the stars and writings in the sand (see page 74)

and Dr Woodman. They, the Secret Chiefs of the Second Order, were said to be ruled by the even more Secret Chiefs of the Third Order who, it was alleged, only existed upon the ASTRAL PLANE and hence were discarnate spirits. Regular Freemasonry had certainly never devised a grade system so likely to appeal to mortals who relished an aura of mystery.

In one of her letters Fräulein Sprengel informed Westcott that as soon as he had advanced three Outer Order members to the 5°=6° Second Order grade, the Isis-Urania Temple would be granted an independent existence. By October 1889 he was able to claim a fictitious independence, i.e. on the authority of a faked letter from Soror Sapiens Dominabitur Astris, and then proceeded to 'liquidate' her, because she was no longer necessary, during the summer of 1890. Between the autumn of 1889 and the end of 1891 about twenty Outer Order initiates were given the honorary status of 5°=6°.

By March 1888 Mathers had already written the 0°=0° Neophyte ritual, and completed the other four by the autumn. Thus Westcott's initial recruiting campaign began in the spring of 1888. By the end of the year the London Isis-Urania Temple had thirty-two members, of whom nine were women. The first dozen male initiates came from the Rosicrucian Society. During the same year he established branch temples at Weston-Super-Mare (Osiris No. 4) and Bradford (Horus No. 5). Amen-Ra No. 6 at Edinburgh was not founded until 1893. The Osiris Temple had a brief existence but Horus at Bradford flourished until about 1900.

The G.D.'s members were all respectable middle-class people with a penchant for occultism. There were, however, a few who could claim an aristocratic background. A surprising number of medical men – no fewer than eight – joined the Order before 1892. Literature was represented by the youthful W. B. Yeats, who joined the Isis-Urania Temple in March 1890 when he was twenty-five. At that time there was also a handful of minor writers, whose books have long since been forgotten. Arthur Machen and Algernon Blackwood did not arrive until much later, in 1899–1900, and neither of them was then well known.

During its first period (1888–91) the G.D. was nothing more than a kindergarten for would-be occultists. With Mathers, Westcott and Woodman as their teachers they followed an elementary curriculum which included the study of such subjects as the cabalistic

Modern Druids performing a ceremony at Stonehenge (see page 82)

Tree of Life, with its ten sefiroth and twenty-two paths, alchemical symbolism, astrology, geomancy and the symbolism of the twenty-two TAROT trumps. They also worked the Outer Order rituals, of which the one for the Neophyte grade was by far the most impressive.

The Rose of Ruby and Cross of Gold
By the end of 1891 more than eighty people had been initiated in the London Isis-Urania Temple, including forty-two women. There was also a flourishing G.D. group at Bradford with about thirty members. The G.D., which was essentially Westcott's creation, flourished mildly and pursued an almost humdrum existence. The situation altered radically early in 1892 when Mathers carried out a far-reaching reorganization and largely succeeded in supplanting Westcott, of whom he was undoubtedly jealous. Dr Woodman had died in December 1891 and no one was appointed in his place.

At this time Mathers produced a most impressive 5°=6° ritual for the first of the Second Order grades, and gave the Second Order an entirely new status. It now became the Order of the Rose of Ruby and Cross of Gold (Ordo Rosae Rubeae et Aureae Crucis, abbreviated R.R. et A.C.), with himself as its sole Chief. He settled permanently in Paris in the spring of 1892 and Westcott was content to act as Chief Adept in Anglia, in London. Henceforth admission to the new Second Order was to be by examination and invitation only. The R.R. et A.C. was a highly secret affair. Outer Order members were not allowed to know of its existence, who belonged to it or the address of its rooms. Next, whereas the old Outer Order curriculum was purely theoretical, members of the Second Order received instruction in the theory and practice of ceremonial or ritual magic.

The new 5°=6° ritual was based upon the legend of the mythical Christian Rosenkreuz and the chance discovery of his tomb or vault many years after his death. According to the story told in the *Fama Fraternitatis*, published at Cassel by an anonymous author (probably J. V. Andreae) in 1614, the tomb was hidden by masonry. When his successors, who were members of the esoteric order which Christian Rosenkreuz was supposed to have founded more than a century previously, displaced the mortar they found a seven-sided chamber, each wall being 8 feet high by 5 feet wide and decorated with symbols and inscriptions. They also beheld a circular altar and beneath it a coffin, in which they saw the body of Father Christian Rosenkreuz in a perfect state of preservation.

The 'theatrical properties' for Mathers's

5°=6° ritual required the physical reconstruction of the vault, complete with altar and coffin. However, since the descriptive information in the *Fama* was vague he used his own lively imagination, and with the help of his wife Mina, who had been trained as an artist at the Slade School, produced a full-scale 'replica' of the vault, in which fantastically complicated symbolical decorations were painted according to so-called occult colour scales, which were the vault's predominating feature. Psychologically this was a major achievement because no candidate for initiation who was in a sufficiently receptive state of mind could fail to be impressed. In effect, Mathers created a veritable 'storehouse' for psychic energies and at the same time provided the opportunity for an initiatory experience which served as an effective prelude to a preliminary acquaintance with the elements of ritual magic.

Soon after his or her initiation every member of the Second Order was required to make his own magical instruments: the Rose Croix lamen which was worn suspended from a ribbon at all Second Order ceremonies, the lotus wand, the magical sword, and four elemental weapons, namely the wand for fire, the cup for water, the dagger for air and the pentacle for earth. Furthermore, every one of these objects had to be decorated according to the occult colour scales, and where necessary with the appropriate astrological or alchemical symbols. All these objects had to be ritually consecrated and for this purpose Mathers composed seven short rituals which the initiate could perform in the privacy of his or her own home or at the R.R. et A.C.'s rooms.

It was not long before Mathers devised a formidable curriculum for a series of eight examinations which led to the newly-created senior 5°=6° grade of Theoricus Adeptus Minor, the junior one being that of Zelator Adeptus Minor. Anyone who passed this test – it was not compulsory, and probably only a minority of Second Order members had either the time or the staying power to complete the course – could claim to have received a thorough grounding in almost every feature of the Western occult tradition. In this respect the Second Order represented the equivalent of a hermetic university and was unique.

In many respects everything depended upon Mathers's ability to provide the necessary material for study purposes. His manuscripts were sent from Paris to Westcott, who made them available on loan for copying purposes. Absolutely nothing was printed and all these MSS. were regarded as most secret documents. In London Westcott's tasks were multifarious. He was still running the Outer Order, with its frequent admittance ceremonies for its five grades, private lectures, and so on. At the same time there was an immense amount of work connected with the Second Order, such as presiding at initiations (the so-called 'Vault Ceremony'); the supervision of the examination system and correcting or assessing papers; and deciding whether or not a member's magical instruments had been correctly manufactured and consecrated. However, by 1892 he had enthusiastic helpers who assisted him in various capacities with both the Outer and Second Order work and administration.

Clash of Temperaments

The Order's really great period was between the spring of 1892 and the end of 1896, a matter of five years. At this point, however, there were the first signs of decay. There was the inevitable clash of temperaments. The fault was not Westcott's. While his manoeuvres in 1887–8 show that he was capable of devious actions, he was a kindly man who enjoyed the affection and respect of all or most of the London members. The cause of all the trouble which came to a head late in 1896 was Annie Horniman's anomalous relationship with Mathers.

Mathers was an imperious eccentric, always more than a little mad, but obviously gifted, even if his accomplishments would hardly meet with the unqualified approval of the Establishment. Basically unemployable – he was unsuited for any conventional profession or occupation – he was the ideal person to be head of a magical order. He claimed to 'rule' the Order, and rule it he did, demanding absolute obedience. Once the rebellious Annie Horniman disputed his authority the fat was in the fire, because she was his financial benefactor. Without her generous subsidies he would have been penniless.

Annie Horniman (b. 1860) was the daughter of a rich tea importer. She was a comparatively early member of the G.D. (initiated January 1890) and had become a close friend of Mina Bergson when both were studying painting at the Slade School. After some hesitation she joined the Order in January 1890. Yeats, who had previously met Mathers at the British Museum Reading Room, arrived on the scene two months later and was initiated on 7 March 1890. It was undoubtedly Yeats who introduced the actress Florence Emery to the G.D. As Florence Farr she had recently created Ibsen roles in the West End. At one time G. B. Shaw greatly admired her, and she was his mistress for a while during the 1890s, at the

A passage from the Cypher Manuscript

time when she was deeply involved in the affairs of the Golden Dawn. It is unlikely that Shaw knew much about her preoccupation with ritual magic. By comparison with either Annie Horniman or Florence Farr, W. B. Yeats was never an outstandingly active member of the Order, although he achieved a brief prominence in 1900–1 during a particular period of crisis. During the years 1892–6 Annie Horniman and Florence Farr were the leading women members in London. Mina Mathers had already left for Paris in the spring of 1892.

Annie Horniman was partly responsible for the departure of the Chief and his wife. In 1891 she had come to their rescue when they were penniless and early in 1892 she provided Mina with money for a holiday in Venice, to be followed by an unspecified period in Paris so that she could study paint-

ing. There is at least the inference that both women may have had subconscious lesbian tendencies, also that Annie had a vague plan to separate Mathers and his wife. However, her respect for Mathers as a teacher of 'rejected knowledge' cannot be disputed.

Her plans, whatever they were, went awry, because Mathers refused to be parted from Mina and in May 1892 accompanied her to Paris. Except for occasional brief visits, Mathers never returned to England between 1892 and his death twenty-six years later in 1918. In 1892, then, Annie Horniman represented Mathers's sole source of income. Between 5 March 1891 and July 1896 she supplied no less than £1,334, a yearly average of £266. This subsidy made it possible for the Mathers couple to live in fair comfort, although his extravagance and demands for more money were to worry the generous Miss Horniman.

All went tolerably well during Mathers's

ניחון   פישון

In the Name
of the
Lord of the Universe!
We the undersigned Chiefs of the Second
Order hereby depute our V. H. Fratres:
① "Ri Rioghail Mo Dhream," ⑤°⑥
① "Quod Scis Nescis," ⑤°⑥ as Cancellarius;
① "Magna Est Veritas & Prævalebit," ⑨°⑥
as Imperator;
to constitute and to rule the Isis-Urania ~
Temple, No. 3, of the Order of the G. D.,
in the Outer, and to Initiate and Perfect therein
any person Male or Female who has been duly
approved of and certified by us. For which purpose
this shall be sufficient Warrant.
① Deo Duce Comite Ferro ————— 7°4
Ⅱ Sapiens Dom. Astris ...... 7°4
① .. Vincit omnia Veritas ....7°4

חדקל   פרת

The charter of Isis-Urania Temple No. 3

first four years in Paris. The R.R. et A.C. flourished quietly in London with a small but regular flow of newcomers from the Outer Order. W. B. Yeats, for example, was initiated in the Second Order on 20 January 1893. Almost a year later Mathers paid Annie Horniman the compliment of inviting her to consecrate his new Ahathoor Temple No. 7 at 1 Avenue Duquesne, Paris, in January 1894. Ahathoor was small by comparison with Isis-Urania in London; most of its members were American expatriates.

Annie Horniman's relationship with Mathers slowly began to deteriorate in 1895. She expected him to devote all his time to the Order, but he was now allowing himself to be diverted by Jacobite fantasies for the restoration of the House of Stuart and lunatic martial ambitions. Mathers was an army commander *manqué*, always dreaming

of great military exploits and leading his troops into battle. Their differences came to a head in the spring of 1896 when she rebuked him for neglecting his work for the Order and squandering his time on 'politics'. There must have been some gossip in London because he accused her of trying to undermine his authority. She thereupon resigned her office as Sub Praemonstratrix (Teacher of Ritual) in the Outer Order's London Temple. Finally, weary of his eccentricities and hectoring letters, she informed him in June 1896 that the remittance due in July would be her last.

By now the senior members of the Second Order in London were also becoming restive. On 29 October 1896 Mathers sent each of them a copy of an extraordinary manifesto with the demand that they must forthwith individually send him 'a written statement of voluntary submission in all points regarding the G.D. in the Outer and the R.R. et A.C.'

The word 'voluntary' was a misnomer, since the voluntary element was non-existent. In this megalomaniac document he revealed that he was in touch with and receiving instruction from the 'Secret Chiefs of the Order'. He wrote: 'I do not even know their earthly names. I know them only by certain secret mottoes . . . For my part I believe them to be human and living upon this earth; but possessing terrible super-human powers.'

It appears that all who received the manifesto complied, with the exception of Annie Horniman. Her reply did not satisfy the exigent Chief and in a fit of pique he expelled her from the Order on 3 December 1896, claiming privately that he was acting upon instructions received from the Secret Chiefs. The news of her expulsion caused a sensation in Order circles. It was only then that she told a few confidants that she had been Mathers's sole financial support since at least 1891. For the time being she remained discreetly in the background but kept in touch with many old friends in the Order.

The next blow to the G.D.'s stability came in March 1897 when the legal authorities got to know about Westcott's connection with an occult order. There is at least the possibility that Mathers, who was pathologically jealous of Westcott, leaked the information to them. With his coroner's post at risk, Westcott resigned all his offices in the G.D. and R.R. et A.C. and henceforth avoided almost all his former colleagues.

Florence Farr now succeeded Westcott as Chief Adept in Anglia and Mathers's personal representative in England. Westcott was an able, even enthusiastic administrator. Florence Farr, indolent by nature, was never willing to bother herself with the multifarious detail work which Westcott had obviously enjoyed. It was not long before the Second Order's ambitious examination system began to lapse. Mathers does not seem to have objected, because he was at least relieved of the chore of reading the candidates' papers. Since there was no longer very much serious study in London a fair number of members began to experiment with 'scrying on the astral plane'. These 'trips', which were sometimes made by small groups in the vault, were contrived without the assistance of hallucinogenic drugs. Those who experienced them simply used the techniques which they had learned from Westcott and Mathers.

In the meantime Mathers and his wife were leading a hand-to-mouth existence with recurring financial crises in Paris. Desperately short of money, Mathers decided to try to publish a translation of a 17th-century

French magical manuscript which he had found at the Bibliothèque de l'Arsénal. After brief negotiations he found a backer in the person of Frederick Leigh Gardner, a member of the R.R. et A.C. and a stockbroker by profession. Gardner, who had lent Mathers £50, hoped to make a substantial profit from his investment in the production and publication of the book that at long last appeared in 1898 entitled *The Book of the Sacred Magic of Abra-Melin the Mage* (see ABRAMELIN MAGIC).

Crisis followed crisis. Mathers managed to lose most of the manuscript of his translation in a Parisian suburban railway train, and repeatedly fell off his bicycle when riding to the Arsénal Library. Mathers supposed that the book was somehow bewitched. In due course he was to warn Gardner that even the physical possession of the manuscript was dangerous because certain line illustrations of so-called magical squares were 'endowed with a species of automatic intelligent vitality'. He even suggested that Mina's artwork for the title-page had been altered overnight 'by no mortal hand'. Gardner had issued a prospectus announcing that the edition would be limited to 300 copies but nevertheless printed 1,000. Only 120 copies were sold during the twelve months after the book was published in February 1898.

By then Gardner had already resigned from the Order. He was hardly on speaking terms with Mathers. As Frater De Profundis ad Luceum he was required to treat the Greatly Honoured Frater Deo Duce Comite Ferro (Mathers) with the appropriate deference. However, as Mr F. L. Gardner, who had lent Mathers money and made an investment in the Abra-Melin book, he felt entitled to write hectoring letters to Mathers, who could scarcely control his irritation. Then, to make matters worse, he had had a tremendous row with Florence Farr, who was unwilling to suffer any nonsense from Gardner, who was in any case a touchy individual. Nobody appears to have greatly regretted his departure.

The Expulsion of Mathers

The Order experienced a period of comparative peace throughout 1898-9. A bomb exploded in its midst in February 1900. Florence Farr had become increasingly weary of Mathers's eccentricities and dictatorial behaviour. She wrote to him and suggested that perhaps the time had come when the Order should be quietly allowed to end. Mathers, always suspicious, supposed that this was part of a plot to bring Westcott back and make him the Order's ruling Chief. He now injudiciously revealed that Westcott had forged the Fräulein Sprengel letters in 1887-9. Furthermore he indicated that he

had known what had been done at that time but had been sworn to secrecy before Westcott told him anything.

The fat was now in the fire because, if all this were true, then the G.D., which had attracted so much loyalty from its members, was based upon a whole series of lies and deceptions. There was an immediate crisis of confidence in London. To make matters worse Westcott refused to offer any explanation or even any defence. All this was closely linked with yet another troublesome complication. An obviously strange young man called Aleister CROWLEY had been initiated in the Outer Order in November 1898. By December 1899 he was nominally eligible to proceed to the Second Order (R.R. et A.C.) by invitation. He already knew of its existence. Florence Farr and her colleagues insisted among themselves that he could not be admitted. They realized that he was an unreliable person, even a potentially dangerous one.

Now aware that the London people had rejected him, Crowley went to see Mathers, who duly initiated him into the Second Order at his home in Paris. This initiation was not recognized in London and for the first time Mathers had a full-scale revolt on his hands. The dispute came to a head early in April 1900 when Crowley, after a lengthy conference with Mathers, returned to London with full powers to act as his Envoy Extraordinary. There was a richly comic episode when Crowley, wearing full Highland dress and a black mask, attempted to take possession of the Second Order's private rooms at 36 Blythe Road, Hammersmith. In this context the physical capture of the vault was intended to be the most significant symbolical gesture.

The Mathers-Crowley plan was frustrated largely through the vigilance of W. B. Yeats and a few others. The comedy came to an end with the London members expelling Mathers and Crowley, also a few others whose loyalty was doubtful. The R.R. et A.C. was now without a Chief. With the senior members tending to behave like frightened rabbits, Yeats quickly took command. He became Imperator of the Outer Order's Isis-Urania Temple and was also prominent in the committee which was now trying to reorganize the Order as a whole. Since there were no precedents for any form of democratic control there was a continuing state of confusion. In the meantime Annie Horniman had returned to the fold and was busy lifting metaphorical stones and being appalled at what she found beneath them.

She discovered to her horror that the old examination system had completely broken down, that there had been attempts to

tamper with the rituals and, even more horrifying, that there was now a secret group called the 'Sphere' which specialized in astral journeys. To make matters worse, Florence Farr and other leading members of the R.R. et A.C. were all involved. Nobody had invited Yeats to join, presumably because his cooperation was not desired. Annie managed to quarrel with almost all her old associates. Yeats did his best to keep the peace for about a year and finally resigned from any very active connection with the Order in February 1901. However, he was to remain a member of one of the original G.D.'s successor Orders – the STELLA MATUTINA – until as late as about 1923.

The original Order now began to fragment. A handful remained loyal to Mathers and formed the Alpha et Omega Temple. The original Isis-Urania Temple and, most important, the vault came into the possession of A. E. WAITE and a fairly large group of G.D. people early in 1903. Waite and his followers immediately abandoned ritual magic in favour of what he called the 'mystical path'. The Order's magical tradition was perpetuated, although in a new form, by Dr R. W. Felkin and his disciples, who formed the Order of the Stella Matutina. They were mainly interested in astral travel. Mathers, furious at having lost so much of his authority, fulminated in Paris against all and sundry.

The seeds of the great rumpus of 1900-3 had been sown as long ago as 1896-7 when Annie Horniman was expelled and Westcott was forced to retire. It was perhaps surprising that anything at all survived after 1903. The G.D.'s corpse, activated by the curious vitality which Mathers had given it, refused to be buried. Although the time came when all but a few had had their fill of Mathers, his genius as a source of magical instruction was never disputed except by Waite and his group. But they had hitherto gratefully accepted what he had to offer.

The Golden Dawn 'tradition' survives. Today there are still two temples in England and the full $5°=6°$ Second Order initiation ritual is apparently still worked, complete with vault, at Bristol.

The Golden Dawn was essentially a *fin de siècle* phenomenon. One can dispute the intellectual validity of almost everything that Mathers produced for his disciples, and one can dismiss the whole G.D. saga as a story of continuing lunacy. However, in relation to recent social history and the history of ideas in general, this story, with all its psychological implications, provides a unique case history. E. H.

(See also RITUAL MAGIC.) (Further reading: *235, 389.*)

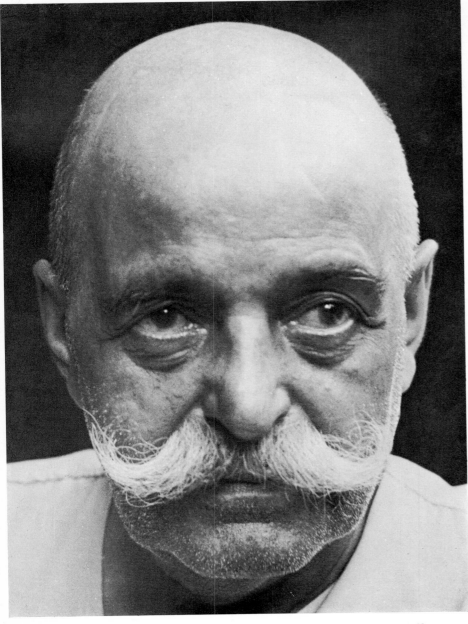

G. I. Gurdjieff

Gorsedd of Bards See DRUIDS.

Joan Grant See REINCARNATION.

Great White Brotherhood

One of several honorific terms for the MASTERS of occult theory, a group of super-human beings who guide the evolution of mankind.

Stanislaus de Guaita (1860-98)

A leading French 'Rosicrucian', associated with the Symbolist movement in literature: see ROSICRUCIANS; SATANISM.

Guide, Spirit Guide See CONTROL.

Mrs Samuel Guppy See APPORTATION.

Georgei Ivanovitch Gurdjieff (c.1877-1949)

Gurdjieff was born at Alexandropol (now Leninakan), near the Russo-Persian border. Even the date of birth of this extraordinary man is in doubt, for on several occasions he appeared to sanction different birth-dates. His family were Greeks who had lived for a period in Turkey before settling in Armenia: according to Gurdjieff, misfortune had deprived his father of a substantial fortune. Gurdjieff's father, who was the first important influence on the boy, was a celebrated *ashokh* or traditional bard. In the area where Gurdjieff was born, life remained organized on the patriarchal pattern, and the stories of the *ashokh* linked life at the turn of the century with the legend of Gilgamesh in an unbroken continuity. Gurdjieff frequently referred to the unusual circum-

stances of his upbringing, which had created conditions more favourable than most for the study of his special interests.

Soon after Gurdjieff's birth, the family moved to Kars, where Gurdjieff was tutored by his father's friend, Dean Borsh of the Military Cathedral. While still quite young, Gurdjieff left home and disappeared from view for some twenty years. During this period he seems to have wandered far and wide throughout Asia, Europe and Africa in search of the truth. The story he told in his book *Meetings with Remarkable Men*, 1963, is misleading if considered simply as autobiography; for while there is undoubtedly a strong element of autobiography in the narrative, the book was intended to serve other purposes and requires careful decoding. It is compounded of precept, parable, allegory and travellogue, with the vestiges of Gurdjieff's historical travels tantalizing the reader from time to time. Ostensibly, the book is a record of Gurdjieff's travels with the band of 'Seekers for Truth' about which he had told his earliest pupils. Without going into detail, it is possible to gather that Gurdjieff had been in Tibet and Central Asia; in India, Arabia – including Mecca – and all the near East; in Egypt and possibly elsewhere in Africa.

We hear of meetings with fakirs and dervishes; of how Gurdjieff devoted himself to the study of HYPNOSIS and YOGA; of monasteries concealed from casual access. Whatever the truth about Gurdjieff's journeyings may be, he returned to Russia with the material for the system he was to teach for forty years. It was a system which claimed to explain the nature of man and the universe, and while Gurdjieff's sources are probably diverse, the language in which he taught was that of materialist science. To understand this, it should be noted that although the area in which Gurdjieff was born was filled with archaic sects – Doukhobors, Nestorians, Jacobites and others – and although the young man was soon convinced that the solution to his 'psychopathic' quest to 'jump over his own knees' lay amongst the inheritors of ancient wisdom, he was at an early age a convinced Westernizer, read books on medicine and neuropathology, and was fascinated by mechanics. It followed that the truth which Gurdjieff found in his mysterious travels would have to complement the findings of Western science rather than flatly contradict them.

Gurdjieff arrived in Moscow in 1912, and set about collecting disciples. A Finnish specialist in mental illness, Dr de Stjoernval, was instrumental in forming the first group in St Petersburg. The composer Thomas de Hartmann joined the circle with his wife.

And through a sculptor called Vladimir Pohl there came within Gurdjieff's ambit his most distinguished disciple, Peter Demianovitch Ouspensky.

Ouspensky was a well-established journalist and lecturer on mystical subjects. He had been heavily influenced by Theosophical works, and had written one successful book, *Tertium Organum*, an argument for time as the fourth dimension. On the outbreak of war in 1914 he had been in Ceylon, during the course of a voyage round the world in an attempt to discover a teaching which would satisfy his questionings. He had been on the point of meeting some yogis whom he thought might help him, when he was forced to return home. What he was searching for he found in Moscow. Ouspensky's mystical interests were by no means exceptional in pre-Revolutionary Russia, which was a hothouse of occultism and exotic religion. At first Ouspensky considered Gurdjieff and his disciples to belong to categories all too familiar and from which little could be expected. Everything in Gurdjieff's manner conspired to put off the would-be disciple. He seemed sly and underhand, went out of his way to put himself in a bad light, made appointments only in seedy cafés, refused to set times for meetings. Nevertheless, Ouspensky soon realized with excitement that the system expounded by Gurdjieff was far more comprehensive and consistent than anything he had hitherto encountered.

The Fourth Way

The basis of the system is that man is asleep, and must wake up. He is a creature of habit; and more than this, he is a machine. Man is subject to a multiplicity of laws which determine his functioning. It is his job to become master of himself and alter certain of these laws as they affect him personally. This is done by a process of self-observation, and what Gurdjieff called 'self-remembering'. This approach to life entails a huge cosmology incorporating two fundamental laws – the octave and the triad – and an all-encompassing symbol called the enneagram, which stands in the Gurdjieff system as the hieroglyphic of the universe. Man the machine did not possess an immortal soul, Gurdjieff warned his pupils, but by 'work on himself' he might create something like one. Gurdjieff called his system 'the Fourth Way', meaning the way of the man engaged in ordinary life as opposed to the other three 'ways' of the fakir, the monk and the yogi. The system had another name: it was called 'the way of the sly man'.

In 1917 the Revolution interrupted the work of Gurdjieff and his groups. Gurdjieff returned to his family home in the Caucasus,

P. D. Ouspensky

and was joined by Ouspensky, the de Stjoernvals, the de Hartmanns and other members of his following. In Tiflis was established the 'Institute for the Harmonious Development of Man', where Gurdjieff continued his teaching, now less by means of exposition than by a method of creating difficult psychological situations for his disciples and a system of complex 'movements' designed to increase knowledge and self-control. The turmoil caused by the civil war was itself brought into use, and Gurdjieff led expeditions through dangerous country to try the endurance of his pupils. Fastidious ladies and Moscow intellectuals were set to selling goods in the market: all in the interests of creating conditions in which the pupils would be able to confront themselves and make the 'super-effort' which in the Gurdjieff system is said to give man the power

to draw on sources of higher energy.

Eventually life became so difficult that Gurdjieff and his followers were forced to leave Russia for Constantinople, where work was resumed. Ouspensky had begun to be suspicious of his master, and was able to leave for London through the financial help of an admirer of the American edition of *Tertium Organum*. Gurdjieff also left Constantinople and, after two abortive attempts to establish himself in Germany, arrived in Paris late in 1922. His supporters – who now included the painter Alexandre de Salzmann and his wife, who had joined the group in Tiflis – bought the Prieuré des Basses Loges at Fontainebleau, a château which had once belonged to Dreyfus. Here Gurdjieff re-established his Institute, issued an elaborate prospectus of its activities – which bore little relation to the work which actually went on – and held displays of his movements and sacred dances in Paris. Ouspensky paid visits from London, but though impressed with the work which was being done at the Prieuré decided that he could no longer work with Gurdjieff. On the other hand, many of the circle who had originally listened to Ouspensky's lectures in London came to Fontainebleau to study under the master whom Ouspensky always acknowledged as the source of the teaching he expounded.

To the Prieuré came A. R. Orage, the editor of the *New Age*, Clifford Sharp, the editor of the *New Statesman*, Rowland Kenney, who had been the first editor of the *Daily Herald*. The group around Middleton Murry and D. H. Lawrence was attracted, but both Murry and Lawrence disliked the thought of going to Fontainebleau. The only one of their circle who arrived in France was Murry's wife Katherine Mansfield, who died at the Prieuré in 1923. At the Institute work proceeded on the lines which Gurdjieff had initiated in Tiflis. The movements were taught to the accompaniment of music which Gurdjieff and Thomas de Hartmann composed; there was ceaseless manual work in the grounds of the château; and the inmates lived on short commons in a Spartan environment with the minimum of sleep. In 1923 Gurdjieff sent Orage as his ambassador to America, and the next year followed himself with a band of disciples who gave demonstrations of the movements in New York. There was already a body of support for Ouspensky's *Tertium Organum* which included writers grouped around Hart Crane, and on this basis Gurdjieff and Orage were able to build. Americans gathered round Orage in New York, or arrived in Fontainebleau, like Jane Heap and Margaret Anderson of the Chicago *Little Review*.

Beelzebub's Tales

In 1924 the direction of events was seriously altered when Gurdjieff was badly injured in a car accident, and the tempo of work at the Prieuré slowed down. Gradually Gurdjieff forced himself to recover, but although he continued to work at Fontainebleau till the end of the 1920s, his main efforts were concentrated elsewhere: in the preparation of his writings. He had decided that if he could not put his ideas into practice he must at least see that a theoretical knowledge of them was available. To the small groups of pupils whom he began teaching in his Paris flat were read chapter after chapter of Gurdjieff's *All and Everything*, in its first series, *Beelzebub's Tales to his Grandson*, and its second, *Meetings with Remarkable Men*.

The tales of Beelzebub to his grandson Hussein are written in a tortuous prose which although it seems obscure is always direct. Many readers have retired baffled from the encounter, thus duplicating the response of many who were put off by their first meeting with Gurdjieff. Under the ponderousness of the diction, Gurdjieff hid – and when his disciples showed signs of 'understanding' too readily, buried still deeper – the system which he had expounded to Ouspensky and others in Russia. The disturbing effect of *All and Everything* was designed 'to destroy mercilessly, without any compromises whatsoever, in the mentation and feelings of the reader, the beliefs and views, by centuries rooted in him, about everything existing in the world'. The object of *Meetings with Remarkable Men* was 'to acquaint the reader with the material required for a new creation and to prove the soundness and good quality of it'. In a third series, which seems never to have been completed, Gurdjieff proposed to help the reader towards an understanding of 'the world existing in reality'. It was only just before his death that Gurdjieff took the decision to publish, and for a long time his enigmatic writings were the property of the groups alone.

However, in England, Ouspensky continued to teach the system he had absorbed from Gurdjieff. Orage returned to England from America and died in 1934; but in 1931 Ouspensky had commissioned Dr Maurice Nicoll, a distinguished pupil of JUNG who had been to the Prieuré, to teach his version of the system. Nicoll and Ouspensky were therefore teaching what they themselves had drawn from Gurdjieff in fashions more direct than Gurdjieff himself employed; and the understanding of the aims of Gurdjieff is to some extent filtered through the perceptions of his two disciples.

During the 1930s Gurdjieff taught in a new way. Gathered round his table at lunch or dinner, his pupils hung on the words of the master. Gurdjieff's tongue-lashings and the accidents of personal encounter helped them in their efforts at self-observation. Gurdjieff made great play with a ritual he had introduced in the latter days of the Prieuré, of toasting the various categories of 'idiot' to which the pupils belonged. A pupil was, for example, a 'round' idiot or a 'square' idiot, an idiot in the Greek meaning of 'private person' – in short, someone trying to break down the illusory personality and come face to face with 'big I'. Each pupil had individual exercises and tasks to perform. Then 1939 drew a curtain between Gurdjieff and the English-speaking world.

Just before the outbreak of war the French had at last become interested in the master in their midst. The writer René Daumal joined a group run by Alexandre de Salzmann, and during the war, while the energies of the intellectuals were prevented from running in other channels, Gurdjieff continued to teach some individuals and small groups. During this time he is said to have supported himself by spreading the rumour that he was the heir to a Texan oil-well which would gush after the war. When pupils from England and America flocked back to him after 1945, this story proved to have at least an essential grounding of truth, in that Gurdjieff's debts vanished in a storm of dollars.

Until just before his death in October 1949, Gurdjieff continued to teach. Once more his flat in the Rue des Colonels Renard was filled with pupils, once more his table groaned with good things, once more the abstemious found themselves forced to drink quantities of Armagnac, the shy to overcome their shyness, the overbearing to be overborne. Gurdjieff in these last years has been compared to Father Christmas, presiding over a genial banquet in the hope that his ideas would spread from the cornucopia. He said little that was not paradoxical or designed to step on the most painful 'corns' of a man's personality. After the death of Ouspensky in 1947, pupils from both England and America, where Ouspensky had gone during the war, added to the crowd around the master, though there was a perceptible slowing up in Gurdjieff's activities before he died.

The pupils of Gurdjieff, Ouspensky, Orage and Maurice Nicoll carry on the work according to their own understanding of it in various parts of the world. Some have gone in strange directions, seeking new masters. Others have made their own adaptations. Still others have tried to keep the system 'pure'. Apart from the various groups who study Gurdjieff's teachings as an organized discipline, the influence of Gurdjieff's system has reached widely separated fields. Theatre, religion and psycho-analysis have found applications for the 'work'. The most potent residue of Gurdjieff is probably to be found wherever his ideas are least organized, in hippie groups and the 'underground'. How many people realize that the fashion for calling people 'negative' derives from a Gurdjieff–Ouspensky doctrine of negative emotions? There are many who have criticized Gurdjieff, the man, from the standpoint of conventional morality – several of his illegitimate children are alive – and others have wondered whether his car accident did not ruin his mind. But as for his ideas, a system of self-discipline geared to an age of relativity seems a gift not lightly to be passed over. J. W.

(See also GNOSTICISM.) (Further reading: *199, 359, 495*.)

H

Manly Palmer Hall

The founder, in 1936, of the Philosophical Research Society, Los Angeles; author of numerous books, published by the Society, including *Secret Teachings of All Ages, Man: the Grand Symbol of the Mysteries, Codex Rosae Crucis, Twelve World Teachers, The Philosophy of Astrology, The Most Holy Trinosophia of the Comte de St.-Germain*. (*202*)

Hallucinations

Pseudo-perceptual impressions occurring when no external objective stimulus is present to cause them: for hallucinations involving psychic ability, see APPARITIONS; CONSCIOUSNESS.

Hamburg School

A school of thought in German astrology, stemming from the theories of Alfred Witte (1878–1941), discoverer of Cupido, a hypothetical planet beyond Neptune, and seven other trans-Neptunian planets which remain unknown to astronomy; the supposed movements and influences of these planets are used in drawing up and interpreting a horoscope. (*234*).

Emma Hardinge-Britten (1823-99)

A medium and early member of the THEOSOPHICAL SOCIETY who was instrumental in establishing SPIRITUALISM as a religious movement in Britain. She set down the Seven Principles of Spiritualism, which were allegedly dictated to her by the spirit of Robert Owen, the pioneer Socialist; author of *Modern American Spiritualism*, 1870, *Nineteenth Century Miracles*, 1884.

Hare Krishna Movement

The International Society for Krishna Consciousness, which teaches that God is realized by chanting his names in the correct order for hours on end: 'Hare Krishna, Hare Krishna, Krishna Krishna, Hare Hare, Hare Rama, Hare Rama, Rama Rama.' Members, who are familiar sights on the streets of British and American cities, shave their heads and abandon sex except for the purpose of procreation in marriage. (*163*)

Thomas Lake Harris (1823-1906)

An American mystic and poet who, in the 1840s, met Andrew Jackson DAVIS and became interested in MEDIUMS, SPIRITUALISM and the doctrines of SWEDENBORG. From about 1850 he began to go into TRANCE and write long mystical poems. He vainly awaited the Second Coming of Christ at Mountain Cove, Virginia, and then, in the late '50s, founded the Brotherhood of the New Life, which settled in a community at Salem-on-Erie, New York. The *Dictionary of American Biography*, in its tongue-in-cheek but not unkindly article on Harris, explains that, 'This community was known as "The Use". All its members denied Self completely and surrendered themselves to the Divine Use or purpose. Their distinctive practices were "open breathing", a kind of respiration by which the Divine Breath (or Holy Spirit) entered directly into the body; and a system of celibate marriage whereby each person was left free to live in spiritual union with his or her heavenly "counterpart".' In 1875 the community split as a result of disagreement between Harris and his leading disciple, an English author named Laurence Oliphant. Harris founded a new community, Fountain Grove, in Santa Rosa, California. In 1894 he finally achieved union with his heavenly counterpart, the Lily Queen, and became immortal, after which he expected the world to come to an end almost immediately. It failed to do so and he spent the last years of his life in retirement in New York City. He wrote *The New Republic*, 1891, and numerous other books.

Franz Hartmann (1838-1912)

A German-born doctor, occultist, Theosophist and Spiritualist, who spent many years in the United States. His books include *Magic White and Black, Life of Paracelsus, Life of Jehoshua, Occult Science and Medicine*. Madame BLAVATSKY described him as 'a bad lot' and the British Theosophists nicknamed him 'dirty Franz' (*234*): see ROSICRUCIANS.

Hatha Yoga See YOGA.

Hauntings, Haunts See APPARITIONS; MEDIUMS; POLTERGEISTS.

Max Heindel or Max Grashof (d. 1919)

The founder of the Rosicrucian Fellowship of California; author of numerous books, including *The Rosicrucian Cosmo-Conception, The Message of the Stars, Simplified Scientific Astrology*. After emigrating to the U.S.A., he joined Kathleen Tingley's faction of the THEOSOPHICAL SOCIETY. His 'Rosicrucian' writings are largely based on lectures by Rudolf STEINER. After his death, the Fellowship was torn by quarrels and feuds which lasted until after the death of his widow, Augusta F. Heindel, in 1938: see ROSICRUCIANS.

Hermetica

The very word 'Hermetic' speaks of secrecy and magic, the hidden knowledge of the universe which so many occultists try to obtain. The classical figure of Hermes or Mercury, the messenger of the gods, with his serpent-entwined staff symbolizing wisdom, gave way in the 2nd century of the Christian era to a figure no less imposing: Hermes Mercurius Trismegistus, Hermes the Thrice-great, a prophet of salvation from the evils of the material world. The writings which pass under the name of Hermes Trismegistus or his Egyptian equivalent, Thoth, are no different in kind from many other papyri on philosophy or magic which circulated in Egypt in the centuries after the birth of Christ, and the doctrines attributed to Hermes differ little from gospels of salvation put in the mouth of other prophets. But for the history of European occultism the Hermetica are of extraordinary importance, because of the place accorded them in the Renaissance revival of the magical arts and Gnostic philosophy. Hermes Trismegistus has ever since remained a symbol of occult tradition in the West, and despite the explosion of cherished illusions about the great prophet as early as the 17th century it is true that the Hermetic writings provide a fair conspectus of the philosophical position which is the root of all occult systems.

The modern editor of the Hermetica divides the writings into two categories. The first is that of 'popular Hermetism'. The writings which make up this group are the earliest in point of composition, and some may date back to the 3rd century B.C. They comprise tracts on ASTROLOGY and astrological medicine, ALCHEMY, magic, and the system of occult sympathies or CORRESPONDENCES which underlies much magical tradition and purports to reveal secret links between various apparently unconnected parts of the universe. The second category is that of 'learned Hermetism' and dates from about the 2nd and 3rd centuries A.D. This consists of a body of religious philosophy, which has some ties with the more popular writings on magic and alchemy. The chief treatises are those known as the *Corpus Hermeticum*, the *Asclepius*, and a collection of

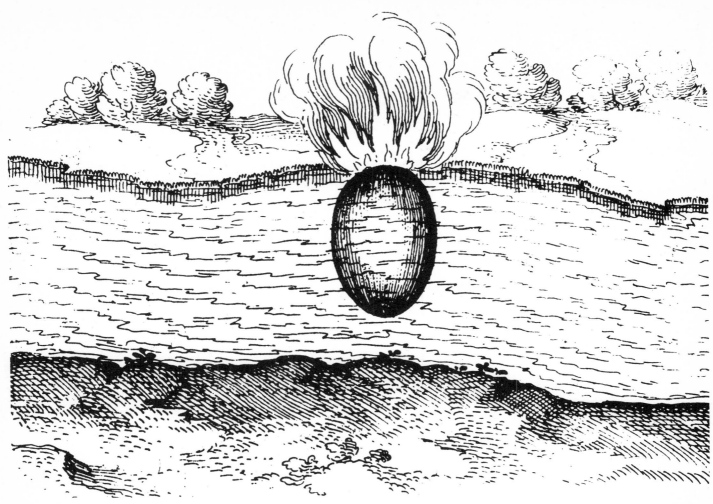

The Hermetic conception of the philosopher's egg burning on water

shorter fragments which appear in an anthology made by Stobaeus about the year 500.

The period in which the Hermetic writings were composed was one of civil disruption and ideological chaos. The intellectual achievement of Greek rationalism was challenged in the 3rd century B.C. by an influx of Oriental religious thought entirely alien to the spirit of Greece. The MYSTERY RELIGIONS, whose aim was to induce ecstasy, and magical or astrological ideas which seemed to give man a measure of control over a terrifying environment, became popular, and their popularity gradually increased. It seemed that the spectacle of individual responsibility revealed by the rationalists was too terrifying for the majority of mankind and, after the interlude provided by the *pax Romana*, Oriental religions – of which Christianity was one – began to gain the upper hand over the official pantheon of Rome and the relics of Greek rationalism. Mysteries like those of Mithras penetrated the highest reaches of society; the traditions of official philosophy veered towards the magical in

the speculations of Neo-Platonism. The various religious thinkers whom the Christians called 'Gnostic' preached that the world was evil and must be escaped (see GNOSTICISM). Veneration for a secret wisdom whose seat was Egypt became permanent.

Trapped in the Dark

It was in Egypt that the majority of writings which make up the Hermetica had their origin. Under the guise of a revelation proceeding from a single source – Thricegreat Hermes – the popular and the learned Hermetism came together. This in itself is an example of the chief tendency of the age of religious crisis: syncretism. In their need to discover some explanation of man and the universe, thinkers of the first few centuries A.D. adapted the elements which came to hand from the collection of anti-rational doctrines that had swept the Eastern Mediterranean. In this they were not alone, and it is difficult to separate Gnostics, Neo-Platonists and Hermetists, except on specific points of doctrine. They all shared the flavour of the age, and the division into 'popular' and 'learned' Hermetism made by Festugière is to some extent one of convenience; for the popular and learned forms

were united in their philosophical basis. The real difference is that the popular writings consist of instructions for practical magic, alchemy or astrology, while the so-called learned Hermetism confines itself to rendering a philosophical position in accordance with the forms expected by those whose educational traditions had been moulded by Greece.

From the magical, astrological and alchemical parts of the Hermetic corpus are derived most of the later speculations of Western Europe on practical magic. Descriptions of the sympathies which unite a particular star or sign of the zodiac to a part of the human body, or connect the part of the body with a certain precious stone, can be found in most of the later magical texts and had their greatest diffusion in the Hermetica. Rituals for the summoning of SPIRITS are similarly pervasive. With the question of alchemy it becomes more difficult to decide whether a text belongs to the 'debased' or popular Hermetism or to the more theoretical, 'learned' category. How speculative alchemy originated is not certain, but it is possible to imagine a philosopher taking as an allegorical illustration of the process of spiritual refinement which the soul must undergo in its ascent to God, the practical instance of how the Egyptian goldsmith refined, moulded and polished his gold to obtain the required quality.

For the greatest practical magic consisted of the perfecting of man, the making of man as God. The learned Hermetic texts give the essence of this philosophy, and provide the rationale for experiments in practical magic. This Hermetic philosophy can be seen as merely one form of Gnosticism. *Gnosis* means 'knowledge', and the Hermetic Gnosis comes as a revelation, perhaps produced by deliberate procedures of meditation. The most celebrated Hermetic treatise of all, the *Poimandres*, describes the visionary experience (*250*):

> Once, when I had engaged in meditation upon the things that are and my mind was mightily lifted up, while my bodily senses were curbed . . . I thought I beheld a presence of immeasurable greatness that called my name and said to me: 'What dost thou wish to hear and see and in thought learn and understand?' I said, 'Who art thou?' 'I am', he said, 'Poimandres, the Nous of the Absolute Power. I know what thou wishest, and I am with thee everywhere.' I said, 'I desire to be taught about the things that are and understand their nature and know God. . . .' And he replied, 'Hold fast in thy mind what thou wishest to learn, and I shall teach thee.'

There follows an account by Poimandres, the Nous (Mind) of the supreme God, of the genesis of the cosmos and of man. Man is born of God, and has descended into a sphere of creation fashioned by his equal, the Demiurge – also sprung from God, or rather the Divine Intellect. But he has become trapped in this world of darkness and has forgotten the light from which he sprang. After death those who have attained the Gnosis ascend through various spheres towards the godhead and enter it. This is the object of the Hermetic revelation – to become God, as man was originally created.

The complex cosmology described by the Hermetica, involving various degrees of creation, principalities and powers of the universe, gives a philosophical sanction to the more explicitly magical productions of 'Hermes'. How far any believer in Trismegistus actually carried practical magic was no doubt a matter of taste, and there is no evidence that even the *Corpus Hermeticum* ever formed 'the Bible of a Hermetic religion'. It does seem that particular methods of inducing the Hermetic revelation and thus attaining Gnosis were advocated. In a text known as 'The Secret Sermon on the Mount',

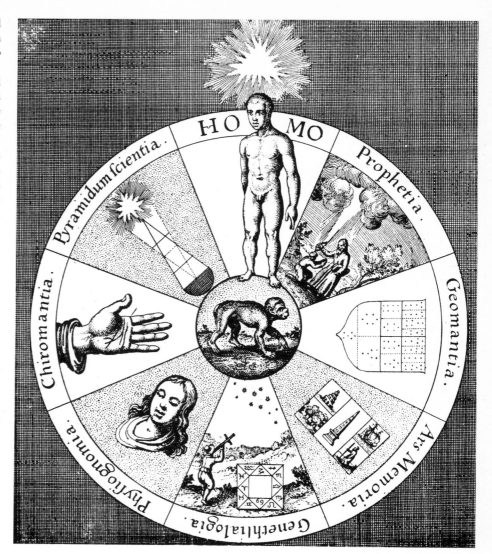

A Hermetic diagram from a work on cosmology by Robert Fludd

Hermes is represented as teaching his son Tat, who complains that he cannot achieve the necessary state to obtain the knowledge he seeks. Hermes advises: 'Withdraw into thyself, and it will come; *will* and it comes to pass; throw out of work the body's senses, and thy Divinity shall come to birth; purge for thyself the brutish torments – things of matter.' Hermes then describes the various 'torments' or sins which Tat must expel from his being. Tat cries that he now sees 'no longer with the sight of my eyes . . . but with the energy the Nous doth give me through the Powers'. He is in the transports of ecstasy. 'In heaven am I, in earth, in water, air; I am in animals, in plants, I'm in the womb, before the womb, after the womb, I'm everywhere!'

'Hermes' in the Renaissance
After the victory of Christianity in the 4th century A.D., rival speculations as to the nature of man and the universe were gradual-

ly suppressed. During the early Middle Ages the growing power of the Papacy contrived that the Christian interpretation of life was by and large the only interpretation. Sporadically heretics would resurrect different forms of Gnosticism, but the Hermetica remained to a certain extent approved by the Church. Early fathers like Tertullian and Lactantius, even St Augustine himself, gave sanction to the inspiration manifest by Hermes. Thus in the next great ideological crisis, which took place when the fabric of medieval society was destroyed by the Renaissance and the Reformation, the Hermetica occupied a privileged position. To some extent patristic theology approved the Hermetic writings. In the enthusiasm for new learning and the rediscovery of antiquity which was an integral part of the Renaissance upheaval, the figure of Hermes Mercurius Trismegistus once more took the stage. He was a real person, or so thought the philosopher-magus of the Renaissance, anxious to profit by the store of intellectual treasures revealed by the Renaissance, but not anxious to disrupt the theological world-picture.

Hermes was, with Moses and Zoroaster, one of the noble pagans, the *prisci theologici* who had – as it were under licence – prefigured in their writings the gospel of the Christ who was to come.

In 1460 a monk brought to Cosimo de' Medici a manuscript of the *Corpus Hermeticum*, minus the last treatise, and three years later Marsilio Ficino was ordered to translate the Hermetic writings – although he had the entire works of Plato awaiting translation. The reputation of Hermes, the *priscus theologicus*, had weathered the centuries, and was to rise steeply in the Renaissance. Ficino's translation was first printed in 1471 and had achieved sixteen editions by the end of the next century. In 1488 the pavement of Sienna cathedral was adorned with the figure of Hermes bearing a text in his hand, with words adapted from the *Asclepius* to give the Hermetic account of the supreme powers a Christian sense. Thus it came about that a form of Gnosticism re-entered Europe, and apparently with the sanction of the Church.

For two centuries the reputation of Hermes as a real person and a *priscus theologicus* stood high. Then in 1614 the scholar Isaac Casaubon demonstrated that Hermes could not have lived in the remotest antiquity but was probably post-Christian. As this revelation was buried within a lengthy work of ecclesiastical polemic, it was easy to overlook or ignore it; and during the 17th century transcendentalists like Robert Fludd, Athanasius Kircher and mystics who actually were or believed themselves to be ROSICRUCIANS continued to pay reverence to Hermes. And as it became less and less important to pay even lip-service to Christianity, there was correspondingly little need for those of a Gnostic temperament to regard Casaubon's dating of 'Hermes' as at all significant. The Hermetic writings continued to circulate in esoteric circles.

'Hermes' Revived

During the late 19th-century occult revival the Hermetica naturally increased in popularity. The 'pagan philosopher' Louis Ménard translated the texts in the 1860s and among groups attached to the THEOSOPHICAL SOCIETY the revelation of Hermes assumed its old importance. The most important of such groups was the Hermetic Society (1884–6) of Anna KINGSFORD and Edward Maitland – although the poet AE (George Russell) conducted another Hermetic Society in Dublin. The Theosophist G. R. S. MEAD, who was at one time Madame Blavatsky's secretary and in 1909 broke away from the Theosophists to found his own Quest Society, also devoted much time to interpreting the Hermetica in

the light of contemporary occultism; and his massive *Thrice-Greatest Hermes* may in fact come closer to the spirit of the original Hermetica than many less 'occult' renderings. In the Hermetic Order of the GOLDEN DAWN, the name of Hermes was again used to dignify a system of syncretist occultism. It is not true to say, with Anna Kingsford, that the Hermetic doctrine was the basis of the occult revival; but the prestige of Hermes was still such in esoteric circles that the long-available texts once more came fairly into the light of day.

Anna Kingsford wrote in 1885 that in the current upheaval of religious thought Hermetism had been given a prominence which it had not known for many centuries. She continued: 'The revival of that philosophy has been at once the condition and the result of every great religious *renaissance* the world has seen.' Without completely agreeing with that remarkable lady, it must certainly be admitted that during three periods of religious crisis – around the birth of Christ, during the Renaissance and the Reformation, and from the close of the last century – the figure of Hermes has been prominent. But in the *fin de siècle* period Hermes was no longer semi-divine or an anticipator of Christianity. The Hermetic approach stood for a broad Gnosticism, as it had done originally, although the name of the Thrice-great was again one to conjure with.

It is ironical that one of the results of the revival of Hermes in the Renaissance was to produce yet more of that commitment to matter which the true Hermetist – both of the Graeco–Roman world and of the late Victorian – was intent on circumventing. For with the Hermetic writings there had entered Europe the so-called 'Hermetic sciences' – astrology, alchemy and magic, the despised popular Hermetism. Partly because of the prestige of Hermes Trismegistus, the Renaissance discovered sanctions for the practice of the Hermetic sciences as it had for the study of Hermetic Gnosticism. One aspect of these sciences was their reliance on experiment – for magical or alchemical experiment is perfectly practical. Gradually the experimenters discarded their religious basis, the dross of conglomerate superstition, absurd theory and pagan gods. By so doing they also lost the spirit of Hermes. But from the sort of experiment encouraged by the Hermetic sciences sprang the developments of rationalist science. It would be interesting to speculate on whether a similar application to the spiritual precepts of the Thrice-great might achieve a parallel revolution of the soul. J.W.

(Further reading: *149, 150, 321, 515.*)

Hermetic Order of the Golden Dawn
See GOLDEN DAWN.

Hermetic Society See HERMETICA; KINGSFORD.

Jósef Maria Hoene-Wroński (1776-1853)

Hoene-Wroński was born at Wolsztyn in Poland, the son of the court architect Antoine Hoene. During the Polish rebellion of 1794 Wroński was captured by the Russians, with whom he then enlisted. After leaving the Russian army, he studied Kant in Germany and afterwards obtained a subsidy from the French Academy to study at the Observatory of Marseilles. This subsidy was withdrawn soon after the publication of Wroński's first work, and the hapless man of science was forced to look for funds. He inveigled a gullible businessman called Pierre Arson into signing a contract with him on the condition of revealing philosophical secrets; when this money ran out he proceeded to London in pursuit of a reward offered by the British Board of Longitude for a correction he had made to their theory of refractions. Despite petitions to Parliament and appeals to the Lord Mayor, Wroński remained penniless until 1833. In that year he signed a contract with a French company for the manufacture of a system of steam engines which he had invented. Wroński himself insisted on publishing the results of his experiments, and the company withdrew their offer. Only towards the end of his life did he find another patron, and he died complaining of his bitter lot.

Wroński was a mathematician of some eminence and a fertile inventor – he projected a tank. His philosophy of 'Messianism' owes something to his native tradition of POLISH MESSIANISM. But although his supporters try to derive his theories from Kant and mathematics, the real roots lie in the CABALA, GNOSTICISM and Jacob Boehme. Wroński's hoped-for 'Messianism' might consist, he thought, in an 'Absolute Reform of Human Knowledge' and he himself claimed in 1800 to have discovered through his rational intelligence the 'Absolute', or Truth. His long-awaited synthesis was never achieved, nor was he called to Russia by the Tsar, as he daily expected. His chief legacy was a small band of readers and disciples, which included Baudelaire and the Emperor Pedro of Brazil. Chief among these was Wroński's personal pupil Alphonse Louis Constant, or Eliphas LÉVI, who always looked on his Polish master as one who had 'defined the essence of God'. J.W.

Hollow Earth Theory See COSMOLOGY.

D. D. Home

Daniel Dunglas Home (1833-86)

The most famous of all mediums. Born in Scotland (the name is pronounced 'Hume'), he spent most of his life in the United States, and later travelled widely, producing astonishing phenomena which included CLAIRVOYANCE, ELONGATION, LEVITATION and mysterious movements of tables and other objects, knocks and rappings apparently conveying messages from the dead, mysterious voices, 'phantom' figures and, much more frequently, mysterious hands. On one occasion in 1853, for instance, in reasonably good light, while the sitters were resting their hands on the table, an extra hand and arm, 'gleaming and apparently self-luminous', appeared on the table at the side opposite Home and slowly moved towards the centre of the table. It also picked up a bell and rang it. One of the sitters grasped the hand, which felt warm and soft, and melted away in his grip (176). Home was also seen on various occasions to put his face and hands into the flames of a fire without being burned. Musical instruments played themselves in his presence, one of them being an accordion which sometimes appropriately included 'Home, Sweet Home' in its repertoire. He also produced an 'earthquake effect', when the seance room and the furniture in it trembled and moved up and down. Home wrote *Incidents in My Life* (first series, 1863; second series, 1872) and *Lights and Shadows of Spiritualism*, 1877: see MEDIUMS; SPIRITUALISM. (*118, 176, 368, 521*)

William Hope (1863-1933)

A British carpenter who became a celebrated 'spirit photographer'; his photographs were examined and discredited in several investigations.

Hanns Hörbiger (1860-1931)

The Austrian engineer who invented the Glacial Cosmology, the theory that the universe is filled with 'cosmic ice'. When a block of this plunges into a hot star, a vast explosion is set off and generates a stellar system. He also believed that the moon will inevitably crash into the earth at some future date, with catastrophic effect, and that previous moons crashed into the earth long ago, causing cataclysms recorded in the legends of the Flood, the destruction of Atlantis and the Twilight of the Gods, and in the apocalyptic imagery of the book of Revelation. His theories were enthusiastically taken up by Heinrich Himmler: see ATLANTIS; COSMOLOGY.

Harry Houdini (1874-1926)

The most famous of all escape artists; some considered his feats so astonishing that they could only be explained on the theory that he possessed psychic powers: see PHYSICAL POWERS.

Peter Hurkos (b. 1911)

A Dutch merchant seaman and housepainter who became a celebrated psychic. In 1941, after a serious fall, he sensed correctly that another patient in the hospital was a British agent who would be arrested and killed by the Gestapo later that day. After the war he began to give psychic readings and gained a reputation for divining the whereabouts of missing people and objects, and for detecting criminals. He was called in to help in the famous Boston Strangler murder case and other criminal cases. He wrote *Psychic*, 1961. (*237*)

Hypnagogic State

The borderland between waking and sleep; hypnagogic hallucinations are visions seen in a state of drowsiness just before falling asleep: see DREAMS; see also APPARITIONS.

Hypnosis

The state and status of hypnotism have been questions of hot debate for two centuries. Considering the immense possibilities for understanding the human mind and alleviating human suffering which the study of hypnosis might make possible, it has attracted far too little scientific attention. This is partly because of its chequered history, and partly because of the association which the word 'hypnotism' is apt to evoke with the shadier aspects of occult charlatanry. Hypnotism undoubtedly exists and the practice can be used to provoke useful effects, but even the hypnotic state is difficult to define. The most eminent 20th-century authority on the scientific study of hypnosis wrote in 1933: 'The only thing which seems to characterise hypnosis as such, and which gives any justification for the practice of calling it a "state" is the generalised hypersuggestibility . . . no phenomenon whatever can be produced in hypnosis that cannot be produced to lesser degrees by suggestion in the normal waking condition' (*236*). We shall see that it is possible to argue with this conclusion; but the main point is clear – to be hypnotized does not mean to be asleep, in a TRANCE or necessarily in any condition other than that of *readiness to accept suggestions*.

The history of hypnotism starts with Franz Anton Mesmer (*c.* 1734–1815), who began his career as a healer by studying medicine at Vienna University. In 1765 Mesmer passed his examinations with honours, but the title of his thesis harked back to the medicine of an earlier age. It was called *De influxu planetarum in corpus humanum*, 'Of the influence of the planets on the human body', and even Mesmer realized that this would draw accusations of reviving the dying art of ASTROLOGY. But his concern was with physical forces in the universe, real if intangible currents which he imagined might pervade space and exercise an unperceived influence on the human frame. For some years his ideas lay fallow, until in 1774 he heard of the experiments made by a Jesuit priest, Maximilian Hell, one of the Empress Maria Theresa's court astrologers, who was having astonishing success in curing his patients with magnets applied to their bodies. This was a prescription derived from the 17th-century magus and purveyor of mystic medicine, Paracelsus. Paracelsus held to a theory which was common among the magi and scholars of the late Renaissance who veered uneasily between the demands made by the contemporary revival of magic and the simultaneous reaching for a science of observation and experiment. It is known as the theory of CORRESPONDENCE or 'sympathies' and postulates a connection between parts of the universe which to us today would seem to have nothing to do with each other: one common form of 'sympathetic medicine' was the application to parts of the body of precious stones which were believed to have a beneficial link with the organ afflicted. Robert Fludd, a contemporary who shared many of the assumptions of

An operator projecting magnetism to induce a healing crisis

Paracelsus, discussed this sort of medicine and marvelled 'how, by relation of naturall things unto one another, they do, after a corporall contact or touch is made between them, operate wonderfully, and that by a Magnetical concert and Spiritual continuity . . . by mutuall operation at an unknown distance.'

Animal Magnetism

This was the doctrine revived by Father Hell, who followed Paracelsus in literally using magnets to induce the 'Spiritual continuity' or 'Magnetical concert'. Mesmer's earlier thoughts on the influence of the planets were obviously similar, and he began to improve on the theories of his master. After a period of experiment he became convinced that the successes he obtained were caused not by his magnets but by the effect of his own body. His ideas became more elaborate and he moved to Paris, where he drew up a *Memorandum* describing the new force he believed he had discovered and which he called 'animal magnetism'. His 'propositions' were that:

1. A responsive influence exists between the heavenly bodies, the earth and all animated bodies.
2. A fluid universally diffused, so continuous as to admit no vacuum, incomparably subtle, and naturally susceptible of receiving, spreading, and communicating all motor disturbances, is the means of this influence.
3. This reciprocal action is subject to mechanical laws with which we are not yet familiar.

Animal magnetism soon became the rage in Paris and Mesmer managed to cure several prominent people of various disorders. His methods were theatrical. The treatment took place in a large, darkened hall and centred round an oak tub filled with water and known as the *baquet*. The *baquet* was about a foot high, and into the water was placed a strange mixture of objects: ground glass, iron filings and empty bottles. Over this was a wooden cover, with holes through which projected jointed iron rods which the patients themselves held or applied to their afflicted parts. All the while 'plaintive' music played to heighten the atmosphere; and suddenly Mesmer would appear dressed in a bright-coloured robe. He went round the hapless crew at the *baquet*, gazing fixedly at some, passing his hands over others and touching still others with an iron rod. If Mesmer's operations were successful, there then set in the 'magnetic crisis' whose effects were so violent that a special padded room known as the 'Salle des Crises' was established next door to the room with the *baquet*. In 1782 a Commission was appointed to examine Mesmer's claims; one of its members was the new United States ambassador, Benjamin Franklin. The Commission described the magnetic crises:

The Commission has seen them last for more than three hours; they are accompanied by expectorations of a viscous matter, torn from the chest by the violence of the attack. Sometimes there are traces of blood in the expectoration. The convulsions are characterised by involuntary spasmodic movements of the limbs and of the whole body, by contraction of the throat, by spasms of the hypochondriac and epigastric regions; their eyes are wandering and distracted; there are piercing cries, tears, hiccoughs and extravagant laughter. The convulsions are preceded and followed by a state of languor and reverie, by exhaustion and drowsiness.

It is not surprising that Mesmer's patients often collapsed; but frequently they also pronounced themselves cured after two or three visits. The Commission found against Mesmer, principally because they could discover no trace of the 'magnetic fluid', which Mesmer's patients nonetheless persisted in seeing – although they could never agree on the colour – and which was often bottled and sent to places far away from Paris. How far Mesmer was a charlatan is open to question. He charged large sums for teaching people his secrets; these pupils often went away unenlightened. On the other hand he did produce cures; and it is probable that he was influenced in his methods by the Swabian priest J. J. Gassner, who was performing remarkable cures through exorcism in Bavaria when Mesmer was in the area. Whereas Gassner had chased the evil spirits he thought caused illness from part to part of the body and eventually expelled them, Mesmer pursued the illness with his animal magnetism.

Mesmer's disciples soon discovered that the elaborate apparatus of the *baquet* and the magnetic crisis was not necessary to effect cures. The most famous of these followers was the Marquis de PUYSÉGUR, who retired to his country estates having failed to learn the secrets for which he had paid so heavily. He discovered that he could throw his patients into a quiet sleep-like state from which they emerged bettered. At one point he magnetized a tree instead of the *baquet* and connected his patients to the trunk with ropes. The results were dramatic; unfortunately, so were those obtained by Benjamin Franklin when he told people to stand under unmagnetized trees. From de Puységur's experiments developed the notion of the 'magnetic sleep', a state soon known as 'somnambulism', on which investigators like the German experimenter Jung-Stilling began to concentrate their attention. Most people still believed in Mesmer's magnetic fluid and the study of mesmerism rapidly split into two different directions: a scientific and a popular. A third sort of interest in mesmerism often formed part of the popular mesmeric movement: this was specifically occult in tone.

Mesmerism, Occultism and Religion

The popular mesmeric movement was an American phenomenon and was fostered by travelling confidence tricksters who found it easy to don the title of 'Professor' or 'Doctor' and captivate backwoods audiences with a mixture of astrology, fortune-telling, phrenology and animal magnetism. Phrenology – the practice of reading character from protrusions on the head – arrived in America in the 1830s at the same time as mesmerism, and a strange hybrid grew up called 'phreno-magnetism' which worked with the mesmerist placing his hands on the phrenological organ he wanted to influence. From this popular mesmerism sprang several theorists who have largely been forgotten, although some of their ideas were by no means foolish.

About 1830 John Bovee Dods became convinced that electricity was the 'connecting link between mind and inert matter' and the 'grand agent employed by the Creator to move and govern the universe'. Thus was born the science of 'electrical psychology', on which Dods lectured nine times to the United States Senate by invitation. 'Electricity' was to Dods what 'animal magnetism' had been to Mesmer: he also used the terms 'galvanism' and 'nervous fluid'. Unlike Mesmer, but like most of the sincere popular mesmerists, Dods was very concerned with the religious implications of his speciality: body and mind were both manifestations of God, and every organ in the body had its spiritual counterpart, including the phrenological organs in the brain. In contrast to Dods, who used his AURA to gain contact with his patients, were Laroy Sunderland and William Fahnstock, who both deserve more attention than they have been paid.

Sunderland was an Episcopal Methodist clergyman and a successful revivalist preacher who left his ministry because he found that he could produce the same effects as medical mesmerists. He decided that the remarkable phenomena of ecstasy and conversion which accompanied the revival movement were of human origin and not divine. The 'spirit of God' might seize anyone

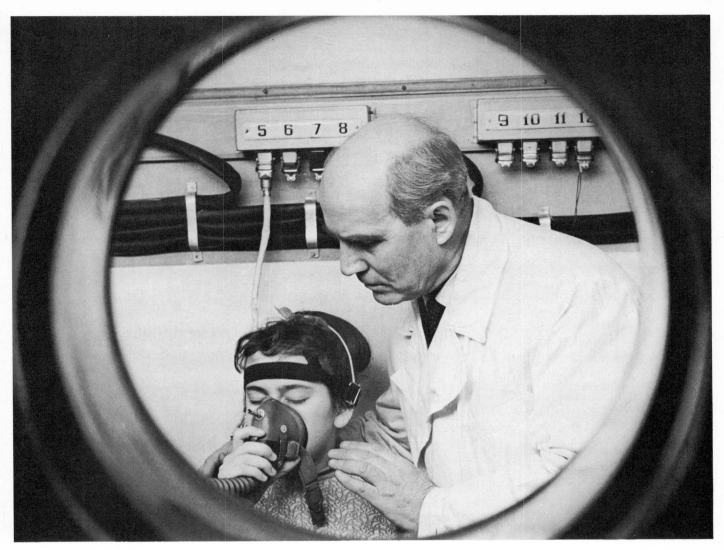

Under hypnosis, a patient being prepared for treatment of a lung complaint

at any time: thus Sunderland described how two cobblers had been suddenly struck motionless in their shop. 'There were those two young men on their benches; one had a shoe on his knee and a hammer in his hand, and the other his awl and waxed thread with which he was about to commence sewing when "the power came upon him".' Sunderland had a simple method of inducing the mesmeric sleep: he merely gave a lecture. Some of his audience went to sleep in their seats, while others came up to his platform and sat down. Two elements alone were necessary for success, thought Sunderland: the 'practitioner' must 'assume the authority' and the patient a 'corresponding faith'. 'Indeed, the more ignorant a "Dr", "Professor" or "Lecturer" happens to be, the more he will assume in regard to himself and his powers; and the more that is assumed, the greater his success. . . .' Sunderland called his doctrine 'pathetism' and published its cardinal text, *The Trance*, in

1860. Dr William Fahnstock was a pathetist before he broke away and founded his own discipline of 'statuvolism'; and he went even further than Sunderland in deciding that the patient himself was really responsible for entering the mesmeric sleep. Fahnstock talked of a 'statuvolic state' into which he persuaded his patients to cast themselves at will. At first he guided them – they were able, apparently, to throw their minds somewhere else completely; but then the patient would gradually assume powers of his own. Whilst someone was statuvolic, he could persuade himself that he had any disease he liked, and the symptoms associated with it would infallibly appear.

From the popular mesmerists arose both SPIRITUALISM and CHRISTIAN SCIENCE. One of the chief propagandists of Spiritualism was Andrew Jackson DAVIS, whose career as a prophet began when a travelling mesmerist called J. Stanley Grimes called at the village of Poughkeepsie in 1843. Grimes peddled phrenology and mesmerism under the title of 'electro-biology'; he had stolen his title and most of his ideas from the electrical psy-

chology of John Bovee Dods. Grimes failed to mesmerize Davis, but later the village tailor succeeded where the Professor had not. This was the beginning of Davis's career as a seer and miracle-worker. He was transported bodily around the country, he had vast and impressive visions and he acquired a fund of medical knowledge of an obscure and poetical sort. 'In the higher portions of the larger or superior brain I saw flames which looked like the breath of diamonds.' At first Davis practised mesmeric medicine; but then began to utter philosophy while in trance. His revelations were published in 1847, and the next year saw the epidemic of spirit rappings started by the Fox sisters in Rochester. Speaking from trance was by now familiar, and the travelling mesmerists, who practised clairvoyance while in the mesmeric sleep and foretold the future for profit, were replaced by 'spirit mediums' who did exactly the same thing. The reliance on the 'subtle fluids' had vanished, and the mediums wielded a more potent weapon than the magnetizers who had concentrated on curing illness. But they could not operate without the state of trance which had become so widely known through the practice of mesmeric medicine.

In Belfast, Maine, Phineas Parkhurst QUIMBY first heard of mesmerism at a lecture given by a Frenchman, Charles Poyan. Quimby was the son of a blacksmith with little formal education; but he soon became an adept of mesmeric medicine. He discovered a young man called Lucius Burkmar who could diagnose illness when in trance, and from 1838 to 1842 the pair travelled around the country giving 'exhibitions' and curing disease. One day Quimby decided to turn his own kidney trouble over to the clairvoyant powers of Lucius; but the absurdity of the cure prescribed made Quimby doubt whether his kidneys had anything wrong with them at all, and he became convinced that 'my troubles were of my own make'. From this disillusionment he deduced the principle by which he ever afterwards stood, that 'the doctor makes the disease'. Quimby was never able to see much difference between Spiritualism and mesmerism; and the method of faith-healing which he continued to practise entailed his own 'spirit' travelling with that of his patient to the place where the illness he was treating had first begun. The cure consisted in bringing the patient away from the place with which the illness was associated. He had been practising this method for some twenty years before Mary Baker EDDY came to him with spinal trouble. Mrs Eddy was cured temporarily; and took from Quimby's system the basis of her Christian Science, adding to the principle 'the doctor makes the disease' elements from all philosophies which supported the idea of 'mind over matter', and the belief that she had discovered the method of healing used by Christ.

If the idea of trance and the activities of the popular mesmerists gave birth in America to two modern religions, in Europe the study of somnambulism was joined to more occult theories. A second French Commission had published a report on mesmerism in 1831 which endorsed the idea that clairvoyance could result from the mesmeric sleep. Dr J. H. D. Petetin (1744–1808), in a book on 'animal electricity' published just after his death, gave an account of how he had observed that the senses of somnambules could be transposed to different parts of the body; for example the sense of taste to the stomach. On one occasion he examined a girl whose sight was transferred to her abdomen, against which he held a box. The girl told him that inside the box was a letter addressed to herself bearing a Swiss stamp: Petetin did not know himself what was inside. As early as 1787 'spirits' had been questioned in Sweden through the mouth of

a somnambule, and in 1848 the furniture-restorer Alphonse Cahagnet published his account of observations of the somnambule Adele Maginot who produced visions of dead people while in trance. As in America, the idea of the trance and the activities of the mesmerists had prepared those who were seeking a new faith, to replace the Christianity in which they no longer had any confidence, to accept all sorts of miracles proceeding from the mesmeric sleep. Occultists of all types pounced on the mysterious phenomena of trance, which they used to support their own chosen revelation. Thus during the high occult revival of the 1890s Colonel de Rochas carried out experiments in what he called the 'exteriorization of sensibility', which were not unlike those of Dr Petetin. He claimed that the magnetic fluid emanated from the mesmerized subject outwards; and that his experiments proved that somnambules could distinguish colours in blacked-out rooms.

Colonel de Rochas was continuing the tradition of the most famous of all students of occult mesmerism, Karl von REICHENBACH, a chemist of considerable standing; among his discoveries were creosote and paraffin. He ruined his reputation in the eyes of his contemporaries by the attention he paid to 'sensitives' – people supposedly psychic. Reichenbach claimed that there existed an 'odic force' by which such persons could perceive properly magnetized objects: this was not electricity, magnetism or heat, but an all-pervading something else. Thus Reichenbach left a pot-plant in a darkened room with Professor Stephan Endlicher, the Director of the Imperial Botanic Garden and a 'medium-power sensitive'. Soon Endlicher cried out, 'It is a blue flower, a gloxinia!' It was, wrote Reichenbach, a '*gloxinia speciosa var. coerulea*, which he had seen in absolute darkness and recognised both as to shape and colour'. But in 1862 seven Berlin professors of physics denounced Reichenbach's inconclusive experiments, and despite his claims that the odic force explained clairvoyance and innumerable other psychic phenomena, science abandoned the Od to the occultists.

Charcot, Bernheim, Freud

The scientific study of mesmerism in its medical applications was thoroughly handicapped by the association of the subject with the 'occult' underworld. In 1837 Baron du Potet, who had taken part in the investigations of the second French Commission, arrived in London, and John Elliotson, who was a professor at University College, allowed the Baron to practise on out-patients at University College Hospital. Next year Elliotson publicly mesmerized two hysterics

called Jane and Elizabeth Okey, and demonstrated that while they were mesmerized they behaved in a manner completely different from what was usual to them: for example, Jane tried to tell bawdy stories which Elliotson had to stop because of the clergymen present. Such goings-on irrevocably damaged Elliotson's standing and he was forced to resign his chair. In 1843 he started the *Zoist* to publicize the cause, and operations began to be carried out under mesmeric influence. The first of these was conducted in 1845 at Hooghly in India by the young Scottish surgeon James Esdaile, whose success so impressed the Governor of Bengal that he had a mesmeric hospital set up at Calcutta. Meanwhile, in 1843 a Manchester surgeon, James Braid, had published a book which for the first time used the word 'hypnotism' and marked a turning-point in the study of the subject: *Neurypnology, or the Rationale of Nervous Sleep*.

Braid numbered himself among those who were inclined to think 'animal magnetism' a fraud or a delusion. Then in 1841 he attended a demonstration of mesmerism and saw for himself how the patient was unable to open his eyes at will. Here was a real phenomenon, and Braid set about experimenting on his own account. He proved to his own satisfaction that this was caused by paralysis of the eyelid muscles brought about by a fixed stare:

> With the view of proving this, I requested Mr Walker, a young gentleman present, to sit down, and maintain a fixed stare at the top of a wine bottle placed so much above him as to produce a considerable strain on the eyes and eyelids, to enable him to maintain a steady view of the object. In three minutes his eyelids closed, a gush of tears ran down his cheeks, his head drooped, his face was slightly convulsed, he gave a groan, and instantly fell into a profound sleep, the respiration becoming slow, deep and sibilant. . . .

Braid made a complete separation between his discovery of hypnotism and the old animal magnetism. Of hypnosis, he wrote: 'I consider it to be merely a simple, speedy and certain mode of throwing the nervous system into a new condition, which may be rendered eminently available in the cure of certain disorders.' At first he thought the explanation was a simple physical one; he had induced an unusual state in his subject by compelling an unusual physical action. But gradually Braid was forced to modify this view, and in 1846 he published an attack on Baron von

Books of the Gnostic Cathars cast into the fire as heretical (see page 96)

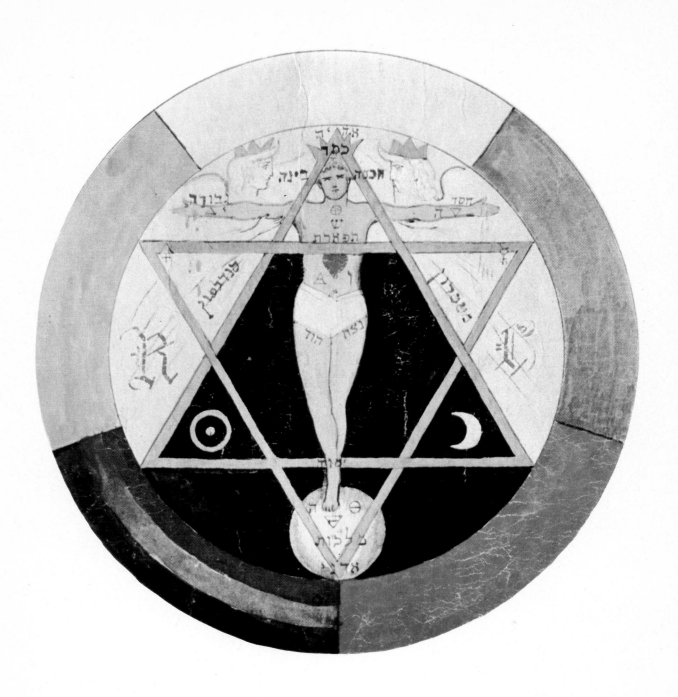

Reichenbach, who had begun to use magnets very much as Father Hell had done three-quarters of a century before. Reichenbach, he wrote, had left out of consideration the 'important influence of the mental part of the process'. Next year Braid issued a revised version of his theory, abandoning the term 'hypnosis' – which has nevertheless stuck – and proposing a new explanation of the trance. He called his new system 'mono-deism', which he defined as the 'condition resulting from the mind being possessed by dominant ideas', and thus abandoned his attempts to provide an explanation for hypnotic phenomena on the lines of a doctor examining his patient for a physical disease.

The conflict between those who still looked for a physical explanation of hypnosis and those who believed it was a purely psychological condition was to dominate the investigation of hypnosis during the next half-century. The year before Mesmer's death, the Portuguese Abbé Jose Custodio de Faria, who had enjoyed considerable success as a mesmerist in Paris, had proposed that the effects of mesmerism were brought on by *suggestion*; but despite this idea, despite Braid's revised theory, despite the observations of Sunderland and Fahnstock, the dominant figure in the study of hypnotism was for a long time Jean-Martin Charcot (1825–93), who was not only convinced that there was a physical explanation for hypnosis but regarded the state itself as symptomatic of an illness. Charcot arrived at the Paris hospital, the Salpêtrière, in 1862, and concentrated his efforts on the hysterics whom the hospital housed. Somnambulism, he thought, was connected with hysteria, and he distinguished three distinct stages of hypnosis: a lethargic state of relaxation; a cataleptic, in which the subject held any position in which he was fixed; and the deep somnambulic state of complete hypnosis.

However, in 1884 the theories of Charcot were decisively challenged by the President of the Nancy Medical Society, Hippolyte Bernheim (1840–1919), who had become interested in the successful practice of Dr Ambrose Liébault. Neither Bernheim nor Liébault – who had hypnotized over 6,000 people – was able to duplicate the stages described by Charcot; and Bernheim claimed to have seen the three sorts of hypnosis displayed only once. This was by a girl who had lived for years in the Salpêtrière and had obviously become conditioned to what the doctors expected. The cause of hypnosis, and of all actions performed hypnotically, Bernheim declared to be *suggestion*: and he

The Golden Dawn: its Rosicrucian symbol (see page 99, and compare plate, page 237)

proved his point in a series of experiments. For example, without even inducing trance, he persuaded a young man that a certain medical worker had attacked him in the street and robbed him. The young man believed implicitly that this had occurred and continued to believe it even when he was told that his supposed assailant was the editor of a magazine which the young man himself regularly set up in type. The theories of the Nancy school gained ground over the Salpêtrière, and even Charcot himself appeared to admit defeat in an essay on faith-healing published the year before his death.

In 1884–5 Sigmund Freud travelled to Paris to study under Charcot. He was overwhelmed by the great French master, and on his return to Vienna had to face severe criticism from opponents of hypnotism who began to refer to Freud as if he were a hypnotist purely and simply. In 1889 the founder of psycho-analysis was converted to the Nancy school's ideas on suggestion, and hypnosis played a leading part in the development of psycho-analysis, for Freud found that under hypnosis his patients were able to remember the repressed memories which he diagnosed as causing their neuroses. Eventually he gave up the practice because of the alarming results of the hypnotic 'transference' – a process which occurs under more conventional analysis and results in the patient's substituting the analyst for the person of someone close to himself. Freud discovered that this on occasion provoked amorous advances, and he replaced the hypnotic procedure – at which he was not very good – with laying his hand on the patient's forehead, an action designed to initiate the correct relationship of dominator and dominated. Jung, who also used hypnosis, followed Freud in discarding it, as he found that patients were quite liable to fall straight into a hypnotic sleep without any action on his part – a phenomenon already partly observed by Sunderland and Fahnstock. The process of 'auto-suggestion' which this implies was made the basis of the clinic set up in 1910 by Emil Coué, whose cures depended entirely on waking suggestion administered by the patient himself.

The present medical status of hypnotism is one of qualified acceptance. In the 1920s and 1930s the American psychologist Clark Hull did much to set the knowledge of hypnosis on a proper experimental basis, and the hypnotic procedure is used for ailments like migraine and anorexia (inability to eat), for allergies, and in gynaecology and obstetrics. Hypnosis is theoretically the safest anaesthetic in cases of minor surgery; and in November 1953 a committee of the British Medical Association decided that hypnosis

might well be the treatment of choice in certain neuroses, and recommended that the practice be taught to trainees in certain medical specialities. At the same time 'hypnotherapists' have revived the use of hypnosis in psychology and psychotherapy, both as an aid to discovering the causes of ailments and as a potential cure.

The possibility of hypnotically induced crime has always excited comment; and the standard answer is the assurance that no one can be made to do something he would not do in normal existence. This is simply not true. It has been proved by experiment that a man can be made under hypnosis to perform a criminal act: in one case to steal a dollar bill and to become convinced it was his own, and in another to attack a superior officer with murderous intent. However, both these experiments proved only that the hypnotized subjects could be *hallucinated* into such activities – the soldier was told that the colonel was an enemy – and not necessarily that a man's own conscience could be overridden under hypnosis. It has also been proved that a man could be hypnotically killed: test subjects were told to pick up a coiled rubber rope lying in a box. They were stopped only by an invisible sheet of glass from picking up a rattlesnake. Hypnosis might be used to produce abortion, murder or suicide; to have the subject harm someone else or himself; to procure false testimony or signatures on documents. All these are theoretical possibilities; and from the military point of view it has been proved that hypnotism can be used to extract secrets which torture might not acquire.

Neither has hypnotism escaped from the occultists. Those interested in different states of consciousness will always be fascinated by hypnosis, and several sets of occult exercises are based on auto-hypnotic procedure. On another level entirely are those who are regressed by hypnotists back through the womb and into a 'previous life'. Of these the most famous is the Colorado housewife who was supposed in a previous existence to have been an Irish girl called Bridey MURPHY (see REINCARNATION). It seems certain that under hypnosis what emerged was a different stratum of the subject's personality – something which has also been noticed in connection with spirit MEDIUMS. A London hypnotist has claimed that he has found patients whose hypnotized selves recount lives in 18th-century Paris or medieval England and speak languages or dialects unknown to their waking personalities. Much more work needs to be done on such problems if we are to achieve a deeper understanding of man. J. W.

(Further reading: *4, 236, 368, 369, 417*.)

I

I Ching

The I Ching (sometimes spelt Yi King) is an ancient Chinese text which is both a philosophical system and a method of divination. It is greatly revered in the Far East and is now widely used in the West as well. China's two principal religions, Taoism and Confucianism, were both influenced by the I Ching, and Confucius once said that if some extra years were added to his life he would devote fifty of them to the study of the I Ching.

The basis of the system consists of sixty-four 'hexagrams', each of which is made up of eight lines which can be either broken or

Throwing the 'sticks of fate' to foretell events by the I Ching

unbroken. The broken line signifies the female, negative and passive principle of Yin; the unbroken line signifies the male, positive and active one of Yang. According to ancient Chinese belief, every event and thing in the universe arises from the interaction of these two principles. Differences between things result from the varying proportions in them of Yin and Yang.

Yin and Yang are complementary aspects of what the Chinese call the T'ai Chi, that is the 'ultimate Cause', the principle behind everything. John Blofeld in his book on the I Ching (*46*) describes the T'ai Chi as 'the Never-Changing, the Ever-Changing, the One, the All. Nothing lies outside it; there is nothing which does not contain all of it. All things come from it; nothing comes from it. All things return to it; nothing goes into or returns to it. It IS all things; it is no thing.'

As the main observable characteristic of the T'ai Chi is change (though paradoxically on another level it does not change), so the combinations of Yin and Yang are constantly shifting. Each hexagram is therefore rather like a point on the curve of a graph. It is at once a picture of what is, what has been and what is to come.

Closely connected with the T'ai Chi is the idea of the Tao, usually loosely translated as the 'Way'. This concept embodies the tendencies of the great cosmic forces and also

of the appropriate courses of action for an individual if he is to accord with those forces. The functioning of the Tao within an individual is also referred to as Tê.

Another important concept, and one that is often alluded to in the I Ching, is that of the Chüntzû, or Superior Man. References to him are usually framed in such statements as: 'The Superior Man stands firm and does not change his direction.' It is a way of saying to the inquirer: 'If you wish to make the best and wisest use of the forces prevailing in this situation, then you will stand firm.'

Development of the I Ching

The origins of the I Ching are obscure, but it is at least 4,000 years old. It is thought to have evolved in roughly the following way. Originally the Yin and Yang lines were used simply to answer Yes–No questions. A Yang line would indicate Yes, and a Yin line No. When a simple Yes or No was found to be inadequate, two more possible combinations were added by the pairing of the lines, thus:

Greater Yang ══════
Lesser Yang ────══
Greater Yin ══────
Lesser Yin ──────

Then a third line was added, making eight possible 'trigrams'.

It has been suggested that the use of lines, rather than circles or any other device, came about because one of the favourite methods of divination in prehistoric times in China was the burning of a cow's shoulder-blade, producing cracks in the bone whose position and shape formed the basis of interpretation. A similar method used the shell of a tortoise and, interestingly, the eight trigrams are said to have been discovered on the back of a sacred tortoise.

The discovery of the trigrams is attributed to Pao Hsi, a mythical figure said to have been the first Emperor of China and to have lived about 4,500 years ago. The devising of the trigrams is described as follows in one of the commentaries on the I Ching:

> In ancient times, when Pao Hsi ruled all things under heaven, he looked up and contemplated the bright patterns of the sky, then looked down and considered the shapes of the earth.
>
> He noted the decorative markings on birds and beasts, and the appropriate qualities of their territories.
>
> Close at hand, he studied his own body, and also observed distant things.
>
> From all this he devised the eight trigrams, in order to unveil the Heavenly processes in nature and to understand the character of everything.

The names of the trigrams and their basic attributes, as set out by Richard Wilhelm in his translation of the book (*504*), are:

Name	Attribute	Image	Family Relationship
Ch'ien, the Creative	strong	heaven	father
K'un, the Receptive	devoted, yielding	earth	mother
Chên, the Arousing	inciting movement	thunder	first son
K'an, the Abysmal	dangerous	water	second son
Kên, Keeping Still	resting	mountain	third son
Sun, the Gentle	penetrating	wind, wood	first daughter
Li, the Clinging	light-giving	fire	second daughter
Tui, the Joyous	joyful	lake	third daughter

These eight trigrams range in a spectrum from the purely masculine character of Ch'ien to the purely feminine character of K'un. In between are varying combinations of the two.

The trigrams were further developed by Wên, who lived in the 2nd century B.C. He was a powerful feudal lord who incurred the jealousy of the last Shang Emperor, Chou Hsin, and was thrown into prison and sentenced to death. After a year, however, he was released through the influence of his friends. Following the overthrow of the Emperor, Wên's son, the Duke of Chou, became ruler and founder of the Chou dynasty and gave his father the posthumous title of King Wên.

While in prison, Wên meditated on the trigrams and combined them to form the sixty-four hexagrams, each of which he named and provided with an explanatory text. After Wên's death, the hexagrams were studied by his son, who added his own commentaries. During the Chou empire the book became known as the Chou I. In the 5th century B.C. Confucius studied the book and may have added a further commentary. Later commentaries were written by his followers.

The I Ching fortunately survived the great burning of the books under the Emperor Ch'in Shih Huang Ti in 213 B.C. For the next half millennium the I Ching was used mainly as an occult and divinatory device, but in the 3rd century A.D. the scholar Wang Pi wrote about the book as a mystical and philosophical system, designed to bring wisdom to the conduct of statecraft and everyday life. It is this view of the I Ching that prevails today.

In China and the countries much influenced by Chinese civilization, Japan, Korea and Vietnam, the book has continued to play an influential role to the present day. In Japan until very recently, military tactics were based on the oracle, and the book was required reading for the higher ranks of Japanese officers. Many Japanese believe that this accounts for the early naval victories won by Japan during the last war. Many ordinary people consult the oracle for advice on their problems. In 1963, for example, it was reported in the Hong Kong newspapers that a couple had successfully used the I Ching to find their lost child, who had wandered from home on a mountainous island near Hong Kong.

The I Ching in the West

The I Ching remained almost unknown in the West until the appearance in 1882 of James Legge's English translation. This is a scholarly piece of work, but marred by Legge's rather pompous attitude towards the subject. He disapproved of the divinatory aspect of the book and did not appreciate the beauty of the hexagrams. 'According to our notions,' he says, 'a framer of emblems should be a good deal of a poet, but those of the Yi only make us think of a dryasdust. Out of more than three hundred and fifty the greater number are grotesque.' This shows that Legge completely missed the point. The aesthetic appeal of the hexagrams lies in the marvellously simple and elegant way in which they fulfil their purpose.

A more sympathetic translator and interpreter of the I Ching was Richard Wilhelm, a German who lived in Peking for many years. His translation into German was first published in the 1920s and has since been translated into English. Wilhelm went to China as a missionary, but his Christian background did not prevent him from developing a strong attachment to Chinese thought, and he once remarked that it was a great source of satisfaction to him that he had never baptized a single Chinese. He was introduced to the I Ching by an old sage, Lau Nai Süan, who helped him to produce his version of the book.

Wilhelm was a friend of C. G. JUNG, and Jung describes this friendship and his own thoughts about the I Ching in his *Memories, Dreams, Reflections* (*257*):

> Even before meeting him [Wilhelm] I had been interested in oriental philosophy, and around 1920 had begun experimenting with the *I Ching*. One summer in Bollingen I resolved to make an all-out attack on the riddle of this book. Instead of traditional stalks of yarrow required by the classical method, I cut myself a bunch of reeds. I would sit for hours on the ground beneath the hundred-year-old pear tree, the *I Ching* beside me, practising the technique by referring the resultant oracles to one another in an interplay of questions and answers. All sorts of undeniably remarkable results emerged – meaningful connections with my own thought processes which I could not explain to myself. . . .
>
> Later . . . when I often used to carry out the experiment with my patients, it became quite clear that a significant number of answers did indeed hit the mark. I remember, for example, the case of a young man with a strong mother complex. He wanted to marry and had made the acquaintance of a seemingly suitable girl. However, he felt uncertain, fearing that under the influence of his complex he might once more find himself in the power of an overwhelming mother. I conducted the experiment with him. The text of his hexagram read: 'The maiden is powerful. One should not marry such a maiden.'

In his foreword to Wilhelm's translation,

The eight trigrams, with the symbol of Yin and Yang at the centre

Jung suggests an explanation of how the I Ching works:

Whoever invented the *I Ching* was convinced that the hexagram worked out in a certain moment coincided with the latter in quality no less than in time. To him the hexagram was the exponent of the moment in which it was cast – even more so than the hours of the clock or the divisions of the calendar could be – inasmuch as the hexagram was understood to be an indicator of the essential situation prevailing in the moment of its origin.

This assumption involves a certain curious principle that I have termed synchronicity, a concept that formulates a point of view diametrically opposed to that of causality. Since the latter is a merely statistical truth and not absolute, it is a sort of working hypothesis of how events evolve out of one another, whereas synchronicity takes the coincidence of events in space and time as meaning something more than mere chance, namely a peculiar interdependence of objective events among themselves as well as with the subjective (psychic) states of the observer or observers (see also SYNCHRONICITY).

John Blofeld, in the introduction to his translation of the I Ching, disagrees with Jung, on the ground that a question asked about a future event will receive a valid answer at whatever time it is asked. Blofeld himself is unable to explain how the I Ching works, but he shares Jung's feeling that in consulting the book one is consulting a living being. He gives a number of examples of consultations, including one remarkable prediction of future events. It was at the time of Chinese hostilities against India in the Tibetan border region. Blofeld cast up a

hexagram and interpreted from the text, against all current opinion, that the Chinese would call a halt and not advance beyond the Himalayan region. Soon afterwards this is exactly what happened. However, Blofeld also makes the point that on occasion, especially if it is used for frivolous purposes, the oracle's answers may be disappointingly banal.

Thanks to Wilhelm, Jung, Blofeld and other enthusiasts for the I Ching, the text is now enjoying a considerable vogue in the West. One occultist to use it was Aleister CROWLEY, whose comments on the oracle are illuminating (*102*):

It is in some ways the most perfect hieroglyph ever constructed. It is austere and sublime, yet withal so adaptable to every possible emergency that its figures may be interpreted to suit all classes of questions. One may resolve the most obscure spiritual difficulties no less than the most mundane dilemmas; and the symbol which opens the gates of the most exalted palaces of initiation is equally effective when employed to advise one in the ordinary business of life. . . . The intelligences which direct it show no inclination to evade the question or to mislead the querent. A further advantage is that the actual apparatus is simple. Also the system is easy to manipulate, and five minutes is sufficient to obtain a fairly detailed answer to any but the most obscure questions.

He adds that other systems of divination are often manipulated by demons who delight in misleading the inquirer, but that such malicious or pranksome elementals avoid the austere sincerity of the I Ching figures.

The Lines and Hexagrams

The meaning of each hexagram is derived from the meanings of the constituent trigrams. For example, Hexagram 12, P'i, combines Ch'ien, the purely masculine trigram, and K'un, the purely feminine one. As the stronger rests on the weaker, this signifies 'stagnation caused by evil doers'. The commentary adds that 'the celestial and terrestrial forces are without intercourse and everything is out of communion with everything else.' When, however, the positions of the two trigrams are reversed we get the hexagram T'ai, in which the feminine rests on the masculine. Here the portents are good, and the text says: 'Peace. The mean decline; the great and good approach – good fortune and success.' Between these two extremes the trigrams are joined in varying degrees of accord and discord.

The compilers of the I Ching also took

into account what are called the 'nuclear' trigrams. These are two interlocking trigrams, the first comprising lines 2, 3 and 4; the second, lines 3, 4 and 5 – that is, beginning at the bottom, which is the correct way to read a hexagram. Thus, for example,

Hexagram 30, Li, Flaming Beauty

has, for its nuclear trigrams ▬▬ Sun, meaning 'growth' and also 'sighing', and

▬▬ Tui, meaning 'autumn' and 'joyousness'.

As the trigrams represent a family, so the relationship between any two is indicative of the meaning of the hexagram formed thereby. The interpretations also use the analogy of a ruler and his various subordinates. Each hexagram has one or more 'ruling lines', one of which usually occupies the fifth place. Here the relationship of yielding (Yin) to firm (Yang) lines has an obvious bearing on the analogy. In general it is better for a yielding line to rest on a firm one than vice versa.

Now we come to one of the most important elements in the system: the so-called 'moving' or 'changing' lines, sometimes referred to as 'old lines', as opposed to the fixed or 'young' lines. The result of any throw of coins or division of yarrow stalks, as will be explained shortly, can result in four different types of combination. These signify respectively: a young Yin line, a young Yang line, an old Yin line (—x—) and an old Yang line (—o—). Where one or more lines appear in a hexagram it is necessary for the inquirer to read the text not only for that hexagram, but also for the one into which it changes by virtue of each moving line becoming its opposite. An old Yin line turns into a Yang line, and vice versa. There is also a separate text for each moving line in the first of the two hexagrams. The existence of the moving lines enormously increases the number of permutations. There are, in all, 4,096 possible answers to any question. Frequently the interpretation of a particular moving line will contradict that of the hexagram itself. In such cases it is the meaning of the moving line that takes precedence.

There are two methods of casting a hexagram: the first involves the use of fifty yarrow stalks between one and two feet long; the second is based on the tossing of coins. Most *cognoscenti* regard the second method as being a lazy alternative and prefer the former, which is more complicated. Ideally, any consultation of the I Ching should be attended by certain ritual formulae which help to sanctify the procedure and induce the right mood of reverence and detachment in the inquirer. When not in use, the book should be wrapped in a clean silk or cloth kept at a level not lower than shoulder-height.

The inquirer begins by washing his hands, unwrapping the book and placing it on the outspread wrapper. The book should rest on a table so that the inquirer is to the south of it – this accords with the custom of Chinese potentates who faced south when granting audience. In front of the book should be an incense burner and the receptacle containing the divining sticks. The inquirer bows to the ground three times and then, from a kneeling position, lights the incense and passes the bundle of sticks three times through the incense smoke by moving them in a circle clockwise. One of the sticks is then returned to the receptacle and plays no further part in the inquiry.

Now comes the more complex part of the operation, which is carried out in the following stages:

1. The sticks are divided at random into two heaps with the right hand.

2. With his right hand the inquirer takes a stick from the right-hand heap and places it between the last two fingers of his left hand.

3. Turning to the left-hand heap, he takes away sticks, four at a time, placing them in a pile to the left until there remain four or fewer in the heap.

4. This remainder he places between the third and fourth fingers of his left hand.

5. He then carries out the same procedure as in Step 3, but on the right-hand heap, adding the discarded sticks to the same pile as the other discarded sticks.

6. He places the remainder between the middle and index finger of his left hand.

He will now find that he is holding in his left hand a total of either five or nine sticks (1+1+3, 1+3+1, 1+2+2, or 1+4+4). Because of the way the sticks have been divided, these are the only possible combinations. He puts these sticks carefully aside.

His next step is to take the pile of discarded sticks and repeat the whole process again. This time, however, he will end up with a total of four or eight (1+1+2, 1+2+1, 1+4+3, or 1+3+4). These he places carefully aside and begins the operation yet again with the remaining discarded sticks. This time he will again finish with a total of four or eight.

The inquirer has now repeated the operation three times, and each time has ended up with a certain number of sticks in his left

hand. The three selected piles have eight possible combinations of numbers, and the one that is arrived at determines the bottom line of the hexagram. Each of the other lines is arrived at by going through the whole process again.

The coin-throwing method is very much simpler and quicker. All the inquirer needs is three coins, traditionally the old type of Chinese coin inscribed on one side and blank on the other. The inscribed side is given the value of 2 and the blank side the value of 3. If he is using modern coins he can choose to give the higher value to whichever side he wishes. Let us say, for example, that heads are 3 and tails are 2. Each time he throws he will get a total of 6, 7, 8 or 9. These are the so-called 'ritual numbers' of the different types of line and correspond respectively to the old Yin line, the young Yang line, the young Yin line, and the old Yang line.

The inquirer takes the coins loosely in his hands, which are held together to form a closed cup, and shakes them, concentrating meanwhile on the question. He then lets them fall to the table and records the bottom line of the hexagram according to the result. He does this five more times to arrive at the complete hexagram.

To give an indication of how the process of interpretation works, let us imagine a hypothetical situation in which the I Ching is consulted. Let us take the familiar case of a dispute between a large union and the government which has resulted in a serious confrontation, and suppose that the Prime Minister has been wise enough to ask the I Ching what will be the likely outcome if he takes a firm line with the union leaders and refuses to accede to their demands. Having been through the appropriate procedure, he ends up with Hexagram 10, Lü, with changing lines at 2, 3 and 5.

The moving lines, when they have changed into their opposites, give Hexagram 30, Li,

The main text of Hexagram 10 says: 'Though he treads upon the tiger's tail, it does not bite him. Success!'

But the moving line in third place contradicts this: 'Though a man have but one eye, he can still see; though he be lame, he can still walk; but he who treads upon the tiger's tail will get bitten – disaster!' Where there is a contradiction like this, it is the meaning of the moving line that takes precedence.

He then turns to Hexagram 30, where the main text tells him: 'Flaming beauty. Right-

eous persistence brings reward. Success! Rearing cows – good fortune!'

It is a characteristic of the I Ching that it rarely gives a cut-and-dried answer, and the inquirer must usually think hard to apply the interpretation to his own situation. In this case the Prime Minister must decide who is the tiger, the government or the union. If the government is the tiger then he can take a firm line and allow the union to bring disaster on itself by defying the government; but if the union is the tiger then he must avoid 'treading upon its tail' and take a more conciliatory line. If he makes the right decision then success will be the result. Here it seems clear that the tiger must be the government, since the phrase 'treading on the tiger's tail' suggests mischevous disrespect for a higher authority.

A country ruled by a leader who heeded the advice of the I Ching might indeed be fortunate, for such a leader would conform to the concept of the Superior Man, the great ideal that the I Ching holds out to all who use it. The Superior Man is a person who lives in harmony with the universal laws. He does not struggle against them, but accepts and uses them, and thus he lives a life of serenity and contentment. C. M.

(Further reading: *46, 128, 504*.)

An incubus draining his victim

Incubus and Succubus
Demons, male and female respectively, believed to prey on human beings sexually: see ASTRAL BODY; SPIRITS AND FORCES.

Inedia
The mysterious ability to survive without food, reported of various saints, mystics and wonder-workers: see PHYSICAL POWERS.

Intuitions
For cases involving psychic ability, see APPARITIONS; CONSCIOUSNESS; PARAPSYCHOLOGY.

J

Hargrave Jennings (1817?-90)

The British author of two highly eccentric books, *The Rosicrucians, Their Rites and Mysteries*, 1870, which took him twenty years to write, and *Phallicism, Celestial and Terrestrial*, 1884. For many years secretary to the manager of the Italian Opera in London, Jennings is thought to have been the original of the character of Ezra Jennings in *The Moonstone* by Wilkie Collins. Deeply preoccupied with phallicism and phallic symbols, he thought that the Order of the Garter was originally a phallic cult and that the Garter itself was a sanitary napkin (see *263*): see ROSICRUCIANS; WITCHCRAFT.

Charles Stansfeld Jones (1886-1950)

'Frater Achad' (Brother Unity), a British accountant and occultist who spent most of his life in Canada, where he founded the Fellowship of Ma-Ion. He met Aleister CROWLEY in New York in 1915 and became one of the Beast's principal disciples. He was particularly interested in the CABALA and published *Q.B.L., or The Bride's Reception*, 1923, and *The Anatomy of the Body of God*, 1925. He was convinced that Wagner's opera *Parsifal* contained important cabalistic secrets, which he expounded in *Chalice of Ecstasy*, 1923. His interpretation of Crowley's *Book of the Law* caused Crowley to acclaim him as his 'magical son', but Jones's later revisions of cabalistic doctrine did not meet with Crowley's approval. (*100, 189, 251, 252*)

William Quan Judge (1851-96)

An influential American Theosophist: born in Ireland, he was taken to the United States in his early teens, having already immersed himself in a precocious study of magic, mesmerism and Rosicrucianism. He became a lawyer and a partner of H. S. OLCOTT in the law firm of Olcott, Gonzalez and Judge. He was one of the founders of the Theosophical Society with Madame BLAVATSKY and Olcott in 1875. In 1883 Judge turned the New York branch into the Aryan Theosophical Society, with himself as president and, not infrequently, the only member present at meetings. In the late '80s, however, he founded branches of the T.S. all over the country and in 1893 gave up his legal practice to work full-time for the Society. He became president of the American T.S. after the break with Annie BESANT. He also, apparently, decided that he himself was KOOT HOOMI, one of the Society's principal MASTERS. He wrote an interpretation of the Yoga aphorisms of Patanjali, and other books: see THEOSOPHICAL SOCIETY.

Carl Gustav Jung (1875-1961)

Jung was the son of a Swiss country pastor. His early religious faith collapsed, and he began to seek a substitute while reading medicine at the University of Basel. Like Freud, Jung had opted for medicine as a compromise, as he had nourished both scientific and philosophical interests. During his second term at the University, he discovered a book on SPIRITUALISM, and read all the literature available on the subject, soon passing from Spiritualism to broader occult concerns. Besides the German idealists and mystics he read seven volumes of SWEDENBORG. Some three years later his interests were turned once more to the paranormal when two apparently meaningless explosions took place in his home, one splitting a solid table-top and the other shattering the blade of a carving-knife. A few weeks later Jung heard of some relatives who had formed a circle around a fifteen-year-old girl medium. For two years Jung atten-

C. S. Jones

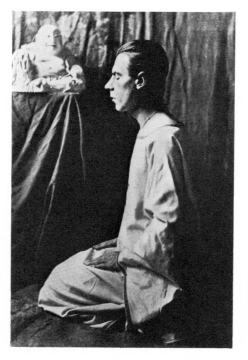

ded their weekly seances and the material he gathered became his doctoral thesis.

Meanwhile Jung discovered psychology through the works of Krafft-Ebbing, and became assistant to Eugen Bleuler at the Burghölzli Mental Hospital in Zurich. Bleuler had been interested in experimental HYPNOSIS, and for a time Jung was in charge of the hypnotism clinic. From 1907 until 1913 both Jung and Bleuler were devoted disciples of Freud. The defection of Jung, the 'Crown Prince', Freud's favourite son, was a great blow to the founder of psycho-analysis, but one of the strangest aspects of the relationship between Jung and Freud is that it occurred at all. Although Freud himself moved towards a consideration of the supernatural in the years 1921–2, it was with great reluctance and little skill, at least in taking the basic precautions against fraud. Jung, on the other hand, began his investigations of the human mind by examining a supposed spirit medium. The different backgrounds of the two men dictated the course their interpretations of the psyche would follow. At least up till the 1920s Freud maintained his distance from the occult, and on one occasion tried to make Jung promise to elevate his sexual theory of the neuroses into an unshakable bulwark 'against the black mud of occultism'. Jung in his turn thought that for Freud sex had become what he called a 'numenosum' – a sacred and absolute category. It has been said that Freud was afraid of religion and the occult; and that Jung was afraid of sex. Whatever the truth of this, Jung can be seen as the culminating point of the late 19th-century occult revival. He put into a terminology to which those brought up on the new and exciting language of Freud could respond, the insights into the psyche which the occultists and mystics of all ages had once expressed intelligibly – but which had been veiled and to all intents and purposes lost by the development of a vocabulary of modern science that excluded the areas of experience of which they spoke.

His experience with the spirit medium 'Miss S.W.' provided Jung with his first insights into the formation of subsidiary personalities and encouraged his reading in the philosophical aspects of occultism. Jung was not interested in the 'obvious autonomy' of the spirit-rapping which surrounded the medium, but rather in the content of the communications. These he divided into two categories: what Jung called the 'romances', involving tales of REINCARNATION in which the medium had been the Seeress of Prevorst and a mistress of Goethe; and the elaboration of a complex cosmology of a Gnostic type (see GNOSTICISM). The romances are very like the fantasies recorded through Hélène SMITH in Theodore Flournoy's *From India to the Planet Mars*, and the cosmology was derived from hearsay, Kant, and a fascination with the Seeress of Prevorst. In order to check parallel systems in occult literature, Jung waded through quantities of occult philosophy, and by the time he caught the medium cheating and broke off the seances he was as well grounded in such theories as any of his contemporaries.

The paranormal played a substantial part in Jung's own life, and from the visions of his childhood to those of later life, the supernatural remained an object of preoccupation. A spectacular incident occurred in the presence of Freud himself. Jung visited his master in Vienna in 1909, and discussed PARAPSYCHOLOGY with him. Freud denounced the whole area of inquiry in terms which annoyed Jung considerably, so much so that the Swiss psychologist felt his diaphragm becoming 'red-hot'. At that moment a loud explosion took place in a bookcase beside the two men. Jung told Freud that this was an 'example of so-called catalytic exteriorisation phenomena' and predicted a second explosion, which duly occurred. Freud was horrified, and initially tried to explain the incident away. In 1911 he had moved to a grudging acceptance of the paranormal under pressure from his friend Sandor Ferenczi, but at this time Jung informed him that he could no longer accept the exclusively sexual theory, and published a paper on 'Symbols of the Libido' which departed from Freudian orthodoxy and led to a complete break in 1913.

A Sacred Way

The psychology which emerged – very gradually, and with much feeling for the way – was described by Jung as a *Heilsweg*. The German word embodies two ideas : a method of healing, and a 'sacred way'. The map of the psyche drawn by Jung was based on a division between conscious and unconscious : the personal unconscious was, as it were, a branch on the tree of the collective unconscious. The journey of the self represented the bringing into consciousness of unconscious contents. The *Heilsweg* was a way of *individuation* – of differentiating the self from the communal unconscious which was the matrix of being. There were various defined stages on the way of individuation. The first was the encounter with the 'shadow', which was Jung's term for bringing into consciousness those aspects of the self which one's type had made one ignore. This involved the dissolution of the persona, or the illusory self with which one began the journey. Next the journeyer met the 'soul-image', the anima

or animus: these terms signify the feminine aspects of every male person and the masculine aspects of every female. Later various archetypes appear; for the man the image of the 'old wise man' and for the woman the 'great mother'. The archetype is a concept which corresponds to the Platonic idea, but unlike the idea embodies both good and evil sides of the phenomena for which it stands. The appearance of the appropriate archetypes – in dreams, or imagined worlds – indicates the birth of the self and the resolution of the polarities of conscious and unconscious.

To the description of the individuation process are of course added many more details of what might be called 'surface psychology'; like Jung's division into introverted and extroverted personalities and his classification of types according to their combination of the faculties of thinking, feeling, sensing and intuition. But the most significant aspect of Jungian psychology is the charting of the spiritual journey, and it was entirely appropriate that Jung should first express his ideas in the religious or occult form in which they had previously been clothed.

The Seven Sermons

The break with Freud precipitated Jung into a period of inner turmoil during which he published little. In 1917 came his *Psychology of the Unconscious*, which he himself described as an 'intuitive leap in the dark' containing 'no end of inadequate formulations and unfinished thoughts', and the first statement of the individuation process is contained in a strange work, *VII Sermones ad Mortuos*, which Jung published anonymously. The psychologist has described how he carried out a journey of exploration into his unconscious mind. Finally there came a period in 1916 when the Jung household seemed to be oppressed by 'ghostly entities'. Then occurred another of the paranormal experiences with which Jung's life was punctuated. One summer day the front-door bell began to ring violently. There was no one there. The house seemed to be 'crammed full of spirits'. Jung felt that something had to happen, but what was going on? He framed the question. 'Then they cried out in chorus, "We have come back from Jerusalem where we found not what we sought".'

With these words Jung begins his *VII Sermones*: 'The dead came back from Jerusalem, where they found not what they sought. They prayed me let them in and thus I began my teaching.' In three evenings Jung wrote his book in a semi-automatic fashion, and the subtitle of the sermons indicates their contents and the plan of the

rest of Jung's work: 'The Seven Sermons to the Dead, written by Basilides in Alexandria, the City where the East touches the West.' Basilides was a Gnostic writer, Alexandria the city of Neo-Platonism and alchemy, and the synthesis of Eastern and Western traditions was to occupy much of Jung's time. The message of the Seven Sermons is that of the way of individuation. Jung begins with the Pleroma – in which 'there is nothing and everything', and about which it is 'quite fruitless to think' – from which ground of being man must at all costs *distinguish* himself, following the principle of individuation; or run the risk of falling back into the Pleroma and losing all individual being. Man must free himself from the domination of 'Abraxas', the name of the supreme principle of Basilides, here used to designate the 'illusory reality' of 'force, duration, change'. Even a slight acquaintance with Gnostic or Eastern thought is enough to see that Jung was indebted to such sources, although he introduced significant changes, notably the idea of 'individuation' as the necessary way of 'spiritual progress'.

Jung himself wore an Egyptian 'Gnostic' ring, whose symbols he had changed so as to Christianize them. He certainly knew of contemporary cults which were explicitly Gnostic, and considered the occult revival of the latter years of the 19th century to be comparable to the 'flowering of Gnostic thought in the first and second centuries after Christ'. He later stated that he had studied the Gnostics 'between 1918 and 1926'; but this is misleading, for we know that he had made quite an extensive search through Gnostic literature while observing his spirit medium, and by the time he wrote the *Seven Sermons* part of him had already been strongly influenced by Gnostic theology. There was a 'Universal Gnostic Church', which has its headquarters not far from where Jung lived; and during the 1930s it was possible to buy 'Abraxas' armlets in Berlin. Jung must be seen in the context of the occult revival and particularly against the background of the disturbed condition of Germany between the wars.

The Wings of Hermes

The psychologist found in various occult ideas and Eastern philosophies material to reinforce his interpretation of the spiritual journey of man. There is little point in trying to summarize the material he derived from ASTROLOGY, his association with the Orientalist Richard Wilhelm (see I CHING) or the prefaces he wrote to Evans-Wentz's editions of Tibetan texts. The important thing is to notice that Jung's use of his sources was exactly that – a *use* or a reinterpretation.

To historians of astrology it is important what Jung thought of astrology, but to those interested in what Jung himself felt to be important, it is necessary to concentrate on the *Heilsweg*, the journey of the soul. The best illustration of how the psychologist made use

C. G. Jung

of traditional sources lies in the parallel he drew with ALCHEMY.

According to Jung's own account, written at the end of his life, he first investigated alchemy in response to the prompting of a dream in which he was 'trapped in the 17th century', and the insight that the alchemical process was itself a *Heilsweg* came after reading

The Secret of the Golden Flower, supposedly a text of Chinese alchemy sent him by his friend Richard Wilhelm. But in an earlier essay, 'A Study of the Process of Individuation', Jung told another story. Here he interpreted a series of paintings executed by one of his patients as representing various stages in the individuation process. The third of these

paintings, he wrote, 'brings in a motif that points unmistakably to alchemy and actually gave me the definite incentive to make a thorough study of the world of the old adepts'. The picture in question consists of a sphere, and in the corner a snake: the sphere is surrounded by a 'vibrating' silver band with the figure twelve inscribed on it. His patient told Jung that the band represented the wings of Mercury or Hermes (classically the messenger of the gods but in alchemy the world soul), and that they were composed of quicksilver.

Now the fact that the patient and not Jung suggested the symbolism is important. It is possible to identify her as Kristine Mann (1873–1945), one of the pioneer Jungian analysts in New York and the daughter of Charles Holbrook Mann (1839–1918), in his day the chief intellectual of the Swedenborgian New Church in America.

The significance of Kristine Mann's connection with the Swedenborgian New Church is twofold. First, Swedenborg and alchemy have always been associated in the minds of those who concern themselves with traditional thought, and particularly in the American New Church. Second, Charles Holbrook Mann, the patient's father, had himself played a leading role in the efforts of the Swedenborgians in the 19th century to develop for themselves a systematic 'mind-cure'. He had formed part of a movement which, over half a century before Jung, advocated the method which Jung himself was to employ in treating his daughter: that drawings be used to indicate the mental progress of those on whom the Swedenborgian 'spirit-cure' was to be tried.

We know that Jung himself had read a great deal of Swedenborg, and it is clear that even if the influence of the New Church mind-cure extended no further than Kristine Mann's suggestion of the alchemical symbolism, Jung's mind and that of his patient were running along similar tracks. Kristine Mann later wrote a paper on 'The Self-Analysis of Emanuel Swedenborg' for the Jungians of New York, and Jung turned his attention to alchemy itself.

By the time Jung came to make his completer pronouncements on alchemy in the 1940s and 1950s there could be no doubt where he stood. *Psychology and Alchemy* is reinforced by wide reading on the alchemical side of the occult revival. Mrs Attwood, A. E. WAITE, Arthur Avalon and G. R. S. MEAD jostle in the bibliography with less reputable esotericists. In his idea that medieval alchemy was 'rather like an undercurrent to the Christianity that ruled on the surface' Jung is certainly indebted to A. E. Waite, and in the notion that 'the central ideas of Christianity

are rooted in Gnostic philosophy' he is repeating the argument of Anna KINGSFORD and Edward Maitland, whose 'esoteric Christianity' had been so influential in the days of the high occult revival. Jung was careful to claim originality only in perceiving the psychological meaning of alchemy and in using the process mapped out by the alchemists as a model for the completed process of individuation, which he maintained did not under analysis display itself in any single case.

Jung and the Nazis

Because Jung's psychology could be recognized for what it was by the esoterically-minded, a host of kindred spirits began to collect around him. Kristine Mann is a single instance, and to take others from the period before the Second World War: Maurice Nicoll, who was Jung's choice as heir apparent in Britain, left the Zurich master for Gurdjieff's Institute at Fontainebleau (see GURDJIEFF), William MacDougall had become interested even before the First World War, and when Jung held seminars in England in 1923 and 1925 they were reported by the Theosophist and writer on magic W. B. Crow.

After 1933 the intellectuals of a Jungian cast of mind had a forum in the Eranos Conferences held at Ascona, in Switzerland. These were the creation of Olga Froebe-Kapteyn (1881–1962), who constructed a special auditorium in her villa by Lake Maggiore to house a project which was first described as a 'summer school for the study of Theosophy, Mysticism, the esoteric sciences and Philosophies and all forms of Spiritual research'. Frau Froebe was the friend and protectress of the Munich mystic Ludwig Derleth, and Ascona itself had been since the turn of the century a centre of attraction for esotericists of all sorts. It was probably the influence of Jung which turned the idea of an occult forum into a series of lectures on the subjects in which the psychologist himself was interested, and which the lecturers expounded in the sort of language that he had done his best to substitute for the one used in conveying the unduly vague and highly speculative theories of many occultists.

Yet the lecturers at Eranos cannot be removed too far from the more obviously 'occult' groups. One visitor to Ascona was Jacob Wilhelm Hauer, whom Jung had met through his leading Munich disciple, and who gave a seminar on YOGA at the Jungian club in Zurich in 1932. In 1934 he gave a lecture at Eranos on number-symbolism which was to influence Jung profoundly, and in the same talk used the concept of the collective unconscious to argue that there

existed a *racial* unconscious with a racial symbolism.

The significance of this is that Hauer was the founder of the Nordic Faith movement – it had been created the year before his lecture at Eranos. The members of this movement were pledged to admit no Freemasons, Jews or persons of coloured descent, and in 1935 at the Berlin Sportpalast Hauer gave vent to a speech of the most violent sort, acclaiming the heroic S.S. man and praising Adolf Hitler as the 'genius of our people'. Jung watched this development with mixed feelings. His essay 'Wotan', which has been used by those who wish to brand Jung as Nazi, can by no stretch of the imagination be interpreted in this sense, but it is not an unqualified condemnation of his friend Hauer. Jung proclaimed that the archetype of Wotan, the Teutonic god of strife and magic, was moving in the German unconscious. Jung disapproved of the so-called 'German Christians' and advised them to join Hauer's movement, led by a 'god-possessed' man. Hauer's activities were the 'tragic and really heroic efforts of a conscientious scholar' directed by the force of Wotan.

What Jung's association with Hauer shows is that he cannot be placed apart from the outburst of mystical and symbolic thought which was such a feature of the German-speaking lands between the wars and whose adherents furnished him with so many disciples. Some of the mystics were swept up in Nazi or neo-Nazi mysticism. Others managed to escape. Those who classify Jung as Nazi pick out elements in his psychology – such as the idea of a racial unconscious – which might be bent into a Nazi form. It is also true that during the late 1930s Jung made some unfortunate statements about the difference between German and Jewish psychology; and that he could do this without departing one whit from his system. But what his attackers have discerned is not questionable conduct but a similarity of approach between Jung and the mystical fringe of Nazism. Out of a widely-diffused body of ideas Jung plucked what he saw as essentials, and may have taken diseased fruit as well as that ripe for the plucking.

In the last resort only those who practise or undergo Jungian analysis are qualified to judge the validity of Jung's interpretation of the way of the soul. But to the layman, the wise man of Zurich has performed one general service, as well as providing countless specific insights. He has shown a method of investigation, provided an acceptable language, and indicated clearly a path to follow. J. W.

(See also SYNCHRONICITY.) (Further reading: *245, 256, 257, 504, 505.*)

K

Kabbalah See CABALA.

Kali Yuga

The 'Black Age', the Hindu term for the age in which we live, a period of violence and moral degeneracy which will end in a cataclysm: see TANTRISM.

Allan Kardek (or Kardec)

The pseudonym of Hippolyte Léon Denizard Rivail (1804–69), French doctor and Spiritualist, author of *The Book of Mediums, The Book of the Spirits, The Gospels According to Spiritism*. He was informed by a spirit message that in a previous incarnation he had been a DRUID named Allan Kardek. His books have been largely disregarded in Europe but have had great influence in Brazil, where numerous Kardek spirit temples communicate with spirits and attempt to help souls which are confused after death and wander about vainly trying to find their physical bodies. They also practise healing, the healers directing healthful radiations at a patient's AURA by moving their hands close to his body: see SPIRITUALISM; UMBANDA. (*437*)

Karma

The term *karma* comes from a Sanskrit word meaning 'action' or 'deed'. In Hindu and Buddhist philosophy it is the principle of universal causality, which states that all action is caused by antecedent action, and in its turn causes subsequent action. Things happen now because something else was done earlier, and the resultant succession of creative deeds is karma. Concepts like chance and luck are incompatible with karma, for all things are determined by the inflexible law of cause and effect.

In more general usage, karma specifically concerns individual action, and the way in which reactions arise from such action and determine a person's destiny, if not in this life then in the next incarnation. The good and evil that befall a man are what he has merited by earlier deeds; his actions constitute the links in the chain that fetter him to the wheel of *samsara*, the ever-recurrent cycle of birth–death–rebirth.

Karma is sometimes spoken of as a taint, which the soul acquires on earth, a taint that has to be eradicated by countervailing deeds in the earthly region. The earth, or the material environment in which we live, is therefore known as the *karma-bhumi*, the karma-sphere. We act out our destiny on earth, and must return to earth to square our accounts. If we have been good, we are allotted a high station in life and many physical, intellectual and social advantages, and if we have been wicked we are born in low estate, and in Hindu belief, sometimes even in animal form. Our karma, the sum total of our activities, therefore directly determines how and in what circumstances we are reborn each time.

Hindu mythology describes in picturesque terms what happens to the individual after death. His soul travels to the kingdom of Yama, Lord of the Underworld, and awaits its trial in the great judgment hall. The chief record-keeper, Chitragupta, prepares the balance-sheet of the soul's good deeds and misdeeds, and reads out the final account. Judgment is passed by Yama and according to the degree of the soul's spiritual evolution, it is allotted its new destiny on earth. Then follows a respite which may extend from a few hours to several years, when the good enjoy the delights of paradise and the evil are purged of their dross in hell. This non-earthly period provides an interlude for the soul, to enable it to reflect on its past. Then, just before it occupies the body of a newly-conceived embryo to start another round of life on earth, all knowledge of its previous life is obliterated, so that when it is born it has no remembrance of the past, and will be unable to recall it except in brief flashes.

The cycle of our being born, dying, and

Allan Kardek

being born again, continues from age to age, and each time, from the moment of birth, we start accumulating karma. Very few are exempt from this ceaseless round of transmigration from one incarnation to another, for karma is inseparable from action, and so long as karma exists, samsara will prevail.

The doctrine of karma has been subject to considerable interpretation in an attempt to define the precise nature of action. The rigid view that all bodily and mental activity generates karma has had to be mitigated and qualified to some extent, otherwise it would be virtually impossible for anyone to break the relentless circle that brings one again and again into the earth sphere. On analysis all action may be resolved into three parts: the motive of the action, the action itself, and the consequences of the action. Those who stress the motive of the action as carrying the karma-taint suggest that once the motive is conceived in the mind the action is as good as accomplished, whether it be actually carried out or not. Karma, according to this view, is determined by motives. Others stress the actual performance of the action, whatever its motives or consequences. The third and final view is that the consequences determine the action, and all action must be judged by its fruits.

Certain actions, however, might be considered neutral, bearing no fruit. Sitting still, for example, and doing nothing that might interfere with the lives of others, might be thought to be free from the danger of an adverse karma. But even this carries the contagion, for mere existence has its range of repercussions, and even when inactive one leaves the impression of one's presence on the environment.

One of the Upanishads says that a man should not try to avoid the performance of actions, but should spend all his time in activity. The activity meant in this context has been interpreted as ritual activity. The performance of rites, in this view, is a form of pure action, free from the taint of karma, and many disciplines are evolved both in the orthodox and the popular framework of Hinduism so to order one's daily life that everything takes on a ritual significance. The Mimamsa system of philosophy is largely devoted to rationalizing the ritual system of the Vedas.

Flowing from this doctrine is one of the basic beliefs of Hinduism, that there are certain actions appropriate to the status of life in which one has been born. Birth into a particular caste circumscribes the limits of one's actions, and within this cadre a man should perform the duties appropriate to his caste. In the context of Hinduism and the belief in karma, the idea of caste takes on a special significance. In the Bhagavad Gita the hero Arjuna asks his charioteer, Krishna, what he should do in a certain fateful situation: he is soon to be involved in a battle against his own people and he is stricken with doubt as to the propriety of winning a victory by killing his kinsmen. Krishna's reply is that as he is born into the warrior caste his duty is to kill, and there is no need for doubt or cause for remorse. All creatures are in any case destined to die, and the warrior's pity will not save them from death.

Thus a life of action lived within the framework of caste can be free from the contagion inherent in action. From this point of view caste provides the means of escaping from the bondage of eternal return. B. W.

(Further reading: *23, 52, 381, 424, 518*.)

Walter J. Kilner (1847-1920)

A British doctor, who was for some years in charge of electro-therapy at St Thomas's Hospital in London. He invented the dicyanin screen, a device intended to make the human AURA visible to ordinary sight as an aid to diagnosis of disease. Kilner found that when he looked at people through the screen – a glass cell filled with a solution of dicyanin – he saw a faint greyish mist round the head and hands, which he eventually became able to see without using the screen at all. Attempts to duplicate his findings have been unsuccessful, though 'Kilner goggles', through which, theoretically, to see auras, are still sold. Kilner wrote *The Human Atmosphere*, 1911. (*261*) (See also A. J. Ellison's review in the S.P.R. *Journal*, March 1967.)

John King

A 'spirit', claiming to have been in life the famous pirate, Henry Morgan, who was allegedly materialized by or communicated through numerous mediums, including Madame BLAVATSKY and Eusapia PALLADINO. 'Katie King' (see COOK) was supposedly his daughter. Robert Dale Owen, the American senator and reformer, son of Robert Owen, the Socialist, fell in love with Katie King and gave her jewelry which, perhaps influenced by her buccaneering ancestry, she took away with her when she returned to the world of spirits. John King claimed that Eusapia Palladino was his daughter, reincarnated.

Anna Bonus Kingsford (1846-88)

Anna Kingsford was in some respects the reviver of the idea of 'esoteric Christianity'. Early in her life she became the wife of a Shropshire clergyman and found an outlet for her frustrated talents in the campaign against vivisection. Through her writing, which included descriptions of dreams, she

met the barrister Edward Maitland, who was himself absorbed in mystical speculations. When Anna went to Paris to study medicine, in order better to further the anti-vivisectionist cause, Maitland accompanied her, as her husband could not leave his parish. Anna's ill-health made the constant use of chloroform necessary, and in Paris her dreaming took another turn. Under the influence of the drug spirits began speaking through her, preaching a new revelation which both the prophetess and Maitland thought corresponded to the doctrines of the Neo-Platonists, alchemists, Gnostics and Sufis.

This esoteric Christianity was extremely influential. In France it was spread by Baron Spedalieri, the disciple of Eliphas LÉVI, and by the Countess of Caithness, who was President of one of the Paris Theosophical societies. In London, Anna Kingsford and Maitland established their Hermetic Society, to which came MATHERS and WESTCOTT of the GOLDEN DAWN, and maintained cordial relations with Madame BLAVATSKY. Edward Maitland's life of his Pythia, published in 1896, is one of the most absorbing studies of abnormal psychology ever written, and it reveals that two years before her death, Anna Kingsford studied magic – probably with MacGregor Mathers – in an attempt to kill vivisectors from afar. She failed with Pasteur, but believed herself to have caused the deaths of two other vivisecting professors. Whatever the truth of the matter, Anna Kingsford enjoys the distinction of being the only woman whose character could fairly be said to have given pause to Madame Blavatsky. J. W.

(See also GNOSTICISM; HERMETICA; JUNG.)

Kingston Zodiac See GLASTONBURY ZODIAC.

Kirlian Photography See AURA.

Koan

A paradoxical riddle in Zen: see MEDITATION.

Koot Hoomi (or Kut Humi)

One of the Theosophical MASTERS, semi-divine beings who watch over the world's spiritual progress. He made himself particularly helpful to Madame BLAVATSKY and Colonel OLCOTT in the early days of the THEOSOPHICAL SOCIETY, and William Quan JUDGE seems to have thought that he was Koot Hoomi himself. The Master later inspired Alice BAILEY, who says in her *Unfinished Autobiography* that she was first visited by him, a tall man dressed in European

clothes but with a turban on his head, when she was fifteen. She later received indications that he was supervising her work, and described him as 'a Master who is very close to the Christ, Who is in the teaching line and Who is an outstanding exponent of the love-wisdom of which the Christ is the full expression'. More recently, Koot Hoomi has been one of the Masters inspiring Robert and Earlyne Chaney, who set up the Astara Foundation in 1951. The Chaneys have met him and other Masters in a cathedral concealed inside Mount Shasta, California, where they also saw a mirror-reflection of Jesus, whose home is in the higher spheres. (*9, 163*)

Koresh

The pseudonym of Cyrus Reed Teed (1839–1908), American proponent of the Hollow Earth theory and founder of the Koreshan Unity sect: see COSMOLOGY.

Karl Ernst Krafft (1900-45)

A Swiss astrologer; he moved to Germany in 1937 and published a book on 'astro-biology' in 1939. His attempts to find statistical evidence to vindicate astrology were examined and demolished by Michel Gauquelin after Krafft's death, though Gauquelin's own findings are of interest (see ASTROLOGY). Krafft invented Typocosmy, a mystical and astrological cosmology which he called the 'General Alphabet of the World of Phenomena'. He was employed to interpret the prophecies of NOSTRADAMUS for Nazi propaganda purposes. In 1941 he was arrested by the Gestapo and imprisoned, but was released a year later and put to work by the Propaganda Ministry, assessing the horoscopes of Allied statesmen and generals: he incautiously decided that General Montgomery's chart was stronger than Rommel's. It is not clear whether his superiors took his work seriously or merely intended to use it for propaganda. He was again arrested in 1943 and sent to the Oranienburg concentration camp, dying in transit to Buchenwald. (*234*)

Jiddu Krishnamurti

The 'World Teacher' of the THEOSOPHICAL SOCIETY. He declined to accept the role and in 1929 repudiated the Society and all religious sects and organizations: since then he has continued to teach and lecture, and is the author of numerous books. (*349*)

Nina Kulagina

A noted Russian medium: see MEDIUMS.

Kundalini See YOGA.

Kut Humi See KOOT HOOMI.

L

Jörg Lanz von Liebenfels (1874-1954)

Born Adolf Lanz, in Vienna, von Liebenfels founded the Order of New Templars, which he later claimed to have been the first manifestation of the Nazi movement, though in fact his books were banned in Germany in the mid-1930s and when the Germans invaded Austria in 1938 he was forbidden to write for publication. He was preoccupied with the purity of the Aryan master race and candidates for his Order had to meet Nordic racial specifications. He advocated the establishment of special breeding colonies for the production of more Aryans. The Order conducted elaborate Grail ceremonies at its temples, the rituals written by Lanz: see GERMAN OCCULT GROUPS. (303)

Latihan

A spiritual exercise in SUBUD. 'Thrice a week, people gather together in a large room or hall, where they remain for half an hour. During that time their effort, as individuals, is to receive and submit to the Power of God. They may stand or sit, walk around, jump, dance, sing or shout – there are no rules or requirements except the suggestion that they patiently seek a state of receptivity and freely follow whatever they may receive. There may be hundreds of people in the room or only a handful, but it is not a meeting in any ordinary sense. There is no discussion, no leader, no instruction. After this half-hour they go their separate ways and return to their lives' (349).

Charles Webster Leadbeater

An Anglican clergyman who became a leading figure in the THEOSOPHICAL SOCIETY and the right-hand man of Mrs Besant: he was primarily responsible for the KRISHNAMURTI episode. Later, in Australia, he became a Bishop of the Liberal Catholic Church and devoted himself to its affairs. He wrote numerous books, including *The Science of the Sacraments, The Masters and the Path, The Astral Plane, Clairvoyance, Dreams, Life After Death, Man Visible and Invisible*, and books with Mrs Besant. (38, 263, 279)

Charles Godfrey Leland (1824-1903)

A British folklorist who published in 1899 *Aradia, or the Gospel of the Witches*, a text which he had received from a Tuscan witch. The book has had considerable influence on the modern WITCHCRAFT revival and Aradia is one of the names of the witches' goddess. Leland had earlier published *Gypsy Sorcery and Fortune-Telling*, 1891. (282)

Lemuria and Mu

Lost continents, vanished empires, powers and panoply submerged in some enormous cataclysm: such is the stuff of which most dreams of Lemuria and Mu are made. It comes as something of a surprise to find that beneath the gorgeous trappings of successive romancers lies an argument which was in its day perfectly tenable and attracted support from prominent members of the scientific Establishment. In the middle of the 19th century, when scientists were busily engaged in classifying everything classifiable on the planet, some strange discoveries were made which resulted in a renewed wave of speculation about the lost continent of ATLANTIS and another lost continent to the east of Africa. It was discovered that the animal and plant life and even the geology of landmasses separated by thousands of miles of sea showed remarkable similarities.

A Fellow of the Royal Society, the zoologist P. L. Sclater, first put the case for Lemuria. He maintained: 'So certain, indeed, has the law been found to be of adjoining countries producing similar or nearly similar animals and plants, that the

C. W. Leadbeater

converse of this proposition is now generally accepted by naturalists . . . that if the animals and plants of two countries are alike, they must either now be or recently have been in geographical connection.' On this principle it was possible to devise a theory to explain the areas inhabited by the lemur. Although in the Eocene Age this animal possibly occupied the whole of the northern hemisphere, its home has become restricted to Africa, southern India and Malaya. It follows that if a continent once existed which stretched from the Malay Archipelago across the south coast of Asia to Madagascar, this might be thought of as the ancient home of the lemur, which now exists only on what were once the borders of this vanished land. Sclater's zoological arguments for his 'Lemuria' were supported by geological and botanical evidence: for example, out of thirty-five species of fossil found in Natal, twenty-two were identical with forms discovered across the sea in southern India.

Distinguished scientists supported the case for Lemuria. The evolutionist T. H. Huxley believed in a continent which had existed in the Indian Ocean in Miocene times. The naturalist Alfred Russell Wallace thought Sclater's Lemuria 'undoubtedly a legitimate and highly probable supposition', and Ernst Haeckel, who popularized Darwin's theories in Germany, agreed. It was Haeckel who suggested that Lemuria had held life more distinguished than the lemurs which gave it its name. He thought it the 'probable cradle of the human race, which in all likelihood here first developed out of anthropoid apes'. This was an idea which was immediately attractive to several bodies of opinion. The scientists searching for the 'missing link', the anthropologists who argued that humanity had spread across the globe from one central point, religious people distressed by Darwin's notion that they had evolved from apes and in quest of the physical location of the Garden of Eden, could all find in Lemuria – if the longer-established Atlantis failed to satisfy them – the solution to their problems.

Most importantly, the idea of Lemuria attracted the occultists, who were trying to reconcile a fundamentally religious view of life with the findings of contemporary science. Madame BLAVATSKY and her THEOSOPHICAL SOCIETY were responsible for making a perfectly legitimate hypothesis part of the occult world-view. In 1888 that stormy petrel of the occult world published her weighty work *The Secret Doctrine*, in which she declared that the findings of her 'esoteric ethnology' tallied with the speculations of Sclater and the scientists. Before present humanity there had been five races living on the earth. The first had lived on a mysterious continent called 'The Imperishable Sacred Land', the second in a 'Hyperborean Continent' off the north of Asia, while the third, fourth and fifth races had lived in Lemuria, Atlantis and America respectively. Present humanity was the sixth race, fast evolving towards a breed of super-beings. Madame Blavatsky believed that Lemuria had extended across the Pacific Ocean, and declared that the South Sea Islands were all that remained of that once immense continent. Later Theosophical writers were to elaborate the tale of the civilization which Lemuria had possessed.

Churchward and Mu
It was also in the Pacific that Colonel James Churchward located his own lost continent of Mu. He claimed that during a famine in India in the 19th century he became friendly with a Hindu priest, with whom he was supervising relief work. The priest taught Churchward the remains of an ancient language, called *Naacal* and believed to be the original tongue of mankind. Churchward used his new-found knowledge to decipher a series of ancient stone tablets of which his friend was the custodian. The inscriptions revealed the existence of Mu, a large continent in the Pacific Ocean, which had stretched 6,000 miles from east to west and 3,000 from north to south. Of course, it was the historical Garden of Eden in which man had first arisen some 200,000 years ago. Mu had possessed a highly sophisticated civilization and when the continent was destroyed in an outburst of volcanic action its population totalled 64,000,000.

From Mu all human races had developed and the differences between human beings resulted from the degeneration of colonists sent out originally from the Mu motherland. The most powerful of Mu's colonies had been the Uighur Empire, whose capital city is now buried beneath the Gobi Desert; the remnants of the Uighurs became the Aryans. This association of fantasy with the idea of racial differences can also be seen in some of the eccentric ancestors of Nazism, and it is interesting that for Churchward an essential feature of the society of Mu was the subservience of the coloured to the white races.

Needless to say, Churchward's sources are highly suspect. He never published transcriptions of his Naacal tablets and delighted in using almost every enigmatic carving in the repertoire of pseudo-archaeology to prove the existence of Mu. It is not surprising to find that the old priest was his guru, that they communicated by 'cosmic telegraphy' and once travelled back in time to see themselves as they had been in a previous incarnation. The Great Pyramid was held by Churchward

to be an expression of the 'original religion of mankind' which had emanated outwards from his lost continent. The Colonel's affiliations are made very clear by the fact that although his book *Cosmic Forces of Mu* was not published until 1934, it was begun in 1870, at the beginning of the late 19th-century occult revival.

It is from the romancing of such occultists that Lemuria and Mu draw their fascination. Writers of fantasy find such countries of the mind an excellent backdrop for tales of swords and sorcery. Thus Lin Carter's hero Thongor of Lemuria follows a venerable tradition in which stand other supermen, like Robert E. Howard's Conan, a dweller in a 'Hyborian Age' which derives from Madame Blavatsky's 'Hyperborian' continent. And despite the fact that Lemuria in particular may have existed, it is as refuges for romantics that we should salute that land and Mu. J. W.

(Further reading: *44, 91a to d, 115, 422, 439a.*)

Alan Leo
The pseudonym of William Frederick Allen (1860–1917), British astrologer and Theosophist, 'this century's major astrological publicist and, furthermore, the first astrologer of all time to practise his art on a large and well-organized professional scale' (*234*). He started life as a sewing-machine salesman, then managed grocery shops, joined the THEOSOPHICAL SOCIETY in 1890, and became a professional astrologer, doing extensive business by mail. He was proprietor of the magazine *Modern Astrology* and the author of numerous textbooks under the general title of *Astrology for All*.

Gladys Osborne Leonard (1882-1968)
A notable British trance medium and Spiritualist who was extensively investigated by the Society for Psychical Research, her cooperativeness, transparent honesty and remarkable gifts making her an excellent subject. Her CONTROL, named Feda, was purportedly the spirit of a young Indian girl who had died in childbirth. Rosalind Heywood describes Feda as 'a cheerful, childlike creature, with a squeaky voice, odd pronunciation and a marked sense of humour, which she occasionally indulged in at Mrs Leonard's expense. She once, for instance, gave away her jewellery.' Early in 1914 Feda predicted an approaching catastrophe and gave Mrs Leonard 'repeated instructions' to become a professional medium because her gifts were going to be needed. Apparent communications to Sir Oliver Lodge, the famous physicist, from his son Raymond, killed in 1915,

were transmitted through her. Most of Mrs Leonard's communications were spoken, but she also produced some automatic writing. She took part in numerous book tests and proxy sittings. That she possessed genuine psychic gifts is scarcely in question, though their precise nature is still a subject of argument. She wrote *My Life in Two Worlds*, 1931, *The Last Crossing*, 1938, *Brief Darkness*, 1942; see MEDIUMS, and for an example of the communications received by her, see SPIRITUALISM. (*56, 57, 213*)
(See also the S.P.R. *Journal*, September 1969.)

Eliphas Lévi
The pseudonym of Alphonse Louis Constant (1810–75), one of the leaders of the French occult revival of the 19th century and a prolific author, whose books on magic continue to exert a wide influence, both in France and abroad. He was born in Paris, the son of a poor shoemaker, and, showing a precocious intelligence, was educated at a free school run by the clergy. Later he entered the theological college of Saint-Sulpice to train for the priesthood, but abandoned the intention before taking his final vows. He toyed with the idea of re-entering holy orders, but finally renounced them in 1844, though he remained outwardly a loyal Catholic for the rest of his life.

After leaving Saint-Sulpice he entered on a period of radical political activity and writing, for which he was three times imprisoned. In 1846 he married an eighteen-year-old girl, Noémi Cadot. Their daughter died while still young, but an illegitimate son by a previous affair survived, and lived until the First World War. The marriage broke up in 1853 and was declared null and void in 1865. Soon after the separation Constant began to write works on magic and occultism, adopting the name of Eliphas Lévi, the Hebrew equivalent of his two Christian names. His first magical treatise was the *Dogme de la Magie*. His occult mentor was the Polish mathematician and occultist HOENE-WROŃSKI. Lévi twice visited England and was a friend of the novelist Edward Bulwer-Lytton, later Lord Lytton, who had a deep interest in the occult. On his first visit to England, Lévi carried out, in a house in London, an invocation of the ancient Greek wonder-worker Apollonius of Tyana.

He gathered about him a small nucleus of personal pupils, but it was through his writings that he exercised the greatest influence. After his death, his works became the inspiration of a new generation of occultists who included the leaders of the French Cabalistic Order of the Rosy Cross (see ROSICRUCIANS). His main works are the *Dogme et Rituel de la haute magie*, first published as one volume in 1856, *Histoire de la magie*, 1860, and *La Clé des Grandes Mystères*, 1897. C. M.

(See also RITUAL MAGIC.) (Further reading: *284, 285, 286, 319.*)

Levitation

The mysterious rising and floating in the air of people and objects, reported of holy persons and wonder-workers in the past. St Teresa of Avila, in her autobiography, reports having levitated in states of spiritual rapture, sometimes even when the nuns, at her request, were trying to hold her down on the floor. Levitation has also been reported of modern mediums, sometimes with irresistibly comic effect. In 1852, for example, at a seance in Barr, Massachusetts, the right hand of a Mrs S. F. Cheney was seen to rise in the air, higher and higher, until it pulled her body up after it and she swung in the air between the floor and the ceiling (*176*). D. D. HOME apparently had the power to levitate himself and objects. On a famous occasion in London in 1868 he floated out through a third-floor window and appeared in mid-air outside another: coming inside again, he returned to the first window, which was open, and was seen to shoot out through it, head-first and horizontal, returning feet-first (see *204*): see PHYSICAL POWERS; see also TELEKINESIS.

Harvey Spencer Lewis (d.1939) See
AMORC; ROSICRUCIANS.

Leys See GLASTONBURY ZODIAC.

Liberal Catholic Church

The Church founded by dissident members of Archbishop MATHEW's Old Catholic Church when the Archbishop pronounced that membership of it was incompatible with membership of the THEOSOPHICAL SOCIETY: C. W. LEADBEATER became the effective leader of the organization.

Liebenfels See LANZ VON LIEBENFELS.

Life after Death See APPARITIONS; MEDIUMS; PARAPSYCHOLOGY; SPIRITUALISM.

Guido von List (1848-1918)

The Austrian occultist who became a pioneer of the revival of interest in Teutonic mythology and folklore in a nationalist and mystical spirit. He is said to have dedicated himself to building a 'temple of Wotan' at the age of fourteen. He regarded himself as the heir and successor of the Armanen, a supposed ancient race of Germanic priests and sages, the swastika being one of their holiest emblems: see GERMAN OCCULT GROUPS. (*303*)

Eliphas Lévi on his deathbed

Lobsang Rampa

The author of *The Third Eye*, 1956, and other widely read books, purportedly the work of a Tibetan lama of high rank. After publication of *The Third Eye* it was discovered that the author was an Englishman named Cyril Henry Hoskin, then living in Dublin, and the book's authenticity was challenged. In reply the author maintained that he was a genuine lama, inhabiting the body of Hoskin, who had agreed to vacate it for him. His books continue to attract a large and enthusiastic readership. (*292*)

Levitation demonstrated by D. D. Home

Loch Ness Monster

The existence of aquatic monsters has been asserted since antiquity, at times with truth, as in the case of the fabled *kraken*, which proved to be the giant squid. Literate interest in sea-serpents was extended in the mid-16th century, when Olaus Magnus, a Swedish Roman Catholic archbishop exiled in Italy, published his drawings and descriptions of examples said to have been observed in northern waters, including Lake Mjøsa, Norway.

In 1933 attention became centred on a possible counterpart in Loch Ness, Scotland. By contrast with the many attempted hoaxes, systematic efforts were made to solve the problem, and in 1961 a body was formed called the Loch Ness Phenomenon Investigation Bureau, which kept five powerful cameras operating continuously during the five-month season. Teams of inquirers from various countries, notably the United States, arrived with ingenious and sometimes highly expensive equipment. Activity was further stimulated when a manufacturer of Scotch whisky offered a reward of £1m. for the capture of the monster. Evidence suggesting the existence of at least one unidentified large animal in the Loch has continued to accumulate.

A letter from the Executive Director of the L.N.P.I.B. published in *The Times* of London, 28 Sept. 1970, stated that the organization had acquired several sequences of film that 'defy any ordinary explanation'; one roll, it added, had been independently analysed by a Royal Air Force research unit with encouraging results. Moreover Professor Tucker of Birmingham University, England, had sonar-recorded 'large objects behaving in an animate manner' at a depth of several hundred feet.

Related literature has reached a bulk beyond the scope of the general reader. An excellent digest is *In the Wake of the Sea-Serpents* by Bernard Heuvelmans (*212a*). To supplement the historical account, it has a formidable bibliography, a list of nearly 600 sightings from before 1639 to 1964 of large unexplained aquatic animals, and a further list of more than fifty strandings and captures. *The Elusive Monster* by Maurice Burton (*68a*) surveys the first three decades of investigation at Loch Ness. Both books are fully illustrated.

Lucid Dreams

Dreams in which the dreamer knows that he is dreaming; they raise interesting questions about states of CONSCIOUSNESS and about the distinction between being awake and being asleep. (*194*)

Loch Ness: a disputed object

Luck

In surveys carried out in Germany in the 1950s by the German Institute of Public Opinion, 50 per cent of those questioned said that they had observed runs of good and bad luck. In Glasgow, Scotland, 45 per cent of a sample believed in luck (half of whom thought that they themselves had been born lucky) and 52 per cent did not. In England 24 per cent of a sample had their own lucky or unlucky numbers, and 15 per cent admitted to owning a lucky mascot (*246*).

We are all familiar with the persistent feeling that some people and things and periods of time are luckier than others. There are days when everything mysteriously goes right and days when everything equally mysteriously goes wrong. Some people consistently win at gambling and others consistently lose. Some people are always in the right place at the right time and others invariably

miss the boat. Or so it seems, at least. These patterns appear too consistent to be attributed to chance and so are put down to 'luck', with the implication that some unexplained but ordered and purposeful factor is involved.

Beliefs about luck are part of the long human struggle to discern principles of order in a mysterious universe. To think of yourself as the plaything of blind chance is for many people intolerable, and to believe that what happens to you is your own fault may be too self-destructive: better to feel 'unlucky' or 'accident-prone' than inadequate. Fate and providence are two of the purposeful mechanisms which have been seen at work designing the fabric of events. Luck is another, but is usually a more popular, less philosophical and high-flown concept. Fate is involved in the ruin of empires and the deaths of kings. Poorer and humbler people, who are not

sufficiently important to be the darlings or victims of fate, merely have good or bad luck. The ancient Egyptian god of luck, the dwarfish, bandy-legged, cheery Bes, was a poor man's god and numerous luck-charms representing him have survived to show his popularity, though he had no great temple or cult centre.

Black Friday

Luck consequently belongs in the realms of popular folklore, fortune-telling and superstition. The very old belief in lucky and unlucky days, for instance, which was taken seriously by kings and priests in ancient Mesopotamia, now survives at folk level, most noticeably in the superstition that it is unlucky to begin anything on a Friday. You should not get married, move house, start a new job or a long journey, or wean a child on a Friday. Nor should you cut your nails or turn a mattress. The reason seems to be that Christ was crucified on a Friday, and so it is

a day for endings not beginnings, and it was for centuries in Christian countries a day of restriction, fasting and resentful fish-eating.

Sunday is a fortunate day to be born on, but naturally not lucky for anything much else because it is supposed to be set aside for churchgoing and rest. It is appallingly unlucky, and consequently very rare, to bury anyone on a Sunday. It is also dangerous to leave a grave open over a Sunday: 'it yawns for another corpse and a second death in the parish will follow shortly' (*226*). Saturday, which is the correct day for digging up and disposing of vampires, is traditionally unlucky for weddings, though this is now largely ignored because so many people find Saturday convenient. The tradition that the whole month of May is unlucky for weddings, however, has retained its grip more successfully, and apparently derives from the Roman custom of making offerings to the dead in May.

Numbers are much involved with luck because they suggest a principle of order behind infinite variety. Some people find a particular number lucky or unlucky for them personally. Generally, odd numbers are lucky and three is the luckiest of all. Thirteen, of course, is so unlucky that hotels avoid numbering a floor thirteen and thirteen people at a table or in a room may cause marked uneasiness. This seems to be partly because Christ and his disciples made a group of thirteen, and the thirteenth was the traitor, and partly because twelve is a number of completeness and thirteen, exceeding it by one, is felt to go dangerously beyond proper limits (see NUMEROLOGY).

All sorts of common superstitions are concerned with avoiding actions which bring bad luck – walking under a ladder, for instance – or with cancelling out the effects of such an action, for example, by touching wood or crossing your fingers. Explanations of them are necessarily tentative but they seem to depend on a poetic and magical type of logic. Breaking a mirror brings bad luck because it damages your reflection, your other self, and so will damage you. Spilling salt is unlucky because it wastes a substance which is a preservative and therefore hostile to the forces of evil, which decay and corrupt.

Superstitions are reactions to uncertainty and anxiety, and it has often been observed that people in risky occupations – including miners, fighting men, sailors, gamblers and actors – are especially prone to superstition, and that even the most rigidly rational of men, placed in a situation beyond his control, may automatically react superstitiously, in a way of which he might not have thought himself capable. The view that superstitions are relics of outmoded beliefs of the past and therefore declining seems wide of the mark, for new superstitions appear and old ones are brought up to date. The introduction of the umbrella into England in the 17th century created the belief that it is unlucky to open one indoors. In this century superstitions about horses and carriages have been transferred to cars, and the old belief that it is dangerous to put a pair of new shoes on the table, originating from the custom of laying out a corpse on a table and fitting it with new shoes, has turned into the superstition that putting a new pair of shoes on a workbench in a factory is an omen of redundancy.

Amulets and Talismans

Charms, amulets and talismans are objects intended to attract good luck and ward off bad (see plate, page 161). Many people hang mascots in their cars or wear charm bracelets, and a horseshoe is a familiar countryside luck-bringer. A rabbit's foot carried in the pocket is still sometimes used by schoolchildren to bring them successfully through examinations (*356*), for the rabbit has inherited in European and American folklore the magical powers which used to be attributted to the hare. A nail, which contains the anti-demonic force of iron, is another luck-bringer and so is a lump of coal, which carries the warming protecting potential of fire.

A distinction is sometimes drawn between amulets and talismans: an amulet is basically protective and wards off bad luck, while a talisman is meant to attract favourable influences and bring good fortune. An alternative distinction is that a talisman is specially made for a specific purpose, while an amulet is a general shield against evil. Whether either of these distinctions is as clear in practice as in theory seems doubtful, but certainly lucky charms have been relied on all over the world. The ancient Egyptians were particularly addicted to them and two of their amulets – the scarab and the ankh – are still in use in the West. The scarab was a symbol of the sun as the source of life and the ankh or looped cross was a symbol of life itself. The Polynesian tiki, a small carving of a human figure, associated with birth, has also become a popular Western luck-charm. Jewels and semi-precious stones have been widely used as amulets and red coral is still attached to babies' rattles, the original purpose being to ward off the evil eye.

The usual occult explanation of the action of amulets and talismans is that the maker or wearer concentrates his thoughts and will-power on the object and so creates an effective psychic barrier or a focus of psychic influence. A good many talismans are astrological, intended to capture in an object, and so bring into the psychic atmosphere of those in contact with it, the influence associated with a planet. Botticelli's famous *Primavera* has been described as a talisman of Venus in this sense (*515*). An astrological talisman is usually made of the metal associated with a planet and is manufactured at a time when the planet is in a dominating position in the sky or in an appropriate sign of the zodiac. For example, Francis Barrett's *The Magus, or Celestial Intelligencer*, published in 1801 (*19*), says that if you carry a talisman of silver, the metal of the moon, engraved when the moon was favourably aspected by other planets, you will enjoy good health and the respect of others: if you make a talisman of lead, the metal of the ominous planet Saturn, when the moon is adversely aspected, and bury it near a house, it will bring evil to those in the house. Birth stones, associated with the signs of the zodiac, are astrological talismans of a pale, diluted sort, and are sufficiently popular for official lists of the stones appropriate to the signs to have been drawn up by jewellers' organizations.

A 17th-century amulet of silver

Luck in the Mind

Many people adopt as a luck-bringer and protector an object which has a personal, individual significance for them because they associate it with a fortunate event in the past. This illustrates an element of luck beliefs which has frequently been remarked on, that an action or object quite fortuitously linked with some success or piece of good fortune may be used again ever afterwards to ensure renewed success and continued good fortune. This is the root of much superstitious behaviour and the feeling of confidence provided by a superstition or a luck-charm may in fact help to assure success and so reinforce the belief in it. Equally, if you always superstitiously put your right shoe on first and your left shoe on second, but one morning accidentally reverse the order, your consequent uneasiness and pessimism may cause real trouble for you all day.

But the element of reality behind beliefs about luck may go further than this. Experiments in PARAPSYCHOLOGY suggest that in some of its aspects at least 'luck' is real and is an ability of the mind: for example, the ability to predict the fall of cards successfully, or to will dice to fall with pre-selected faces showing. There is no reason, quite the contrary, to suppose that this 'lucky' ability is confined to gambling situations. R. C.

(See also DIVINATION; for talismans, see also RITUAL MAGIC.) (Further reading: *63, 65, 98, 218, 226, 246, 269, 303, 305, 356*.)

Wincenty Lutoslawski (1863-1954)

A Polish occultist; born in Warsaw, he obtained degrees in chemistry and philosophy, and lectured at the Russian university of Kazan and also at London, Lausanne and Geneva. He was greatly influenced by his native tradition of POLISH MESSIANISM as well as by Western occultism, and claimed to have converted his students at Kazan to a belief in TELEPATHY by some conclusive demonstrations. In London he was thought to be wholly mad, yet published a highly-regarded study of Plato. In 1896 he issued an appeal for 'other true beings'. Lutoslawski wrote that he considered himself a 'true being' outside time and space, and despaired of the greater part of humanity as mere appendages of the godhead. His occult quest led him back into the fold of Polish Catholicism, but did not exclude a preoccupation with the occult side of sex. In 1911 he established his 'Polish Forge', an institute for attaining an 'integral psychophysics', at Tlemcen in Algeria, which was abandoned the next year.

Lutoslawski kept up a lengthy correspondence with William James, the psychologist, whom he twice met. James was deeply impressed by the Polish prophet, considering that through his yogic studies he had 'plumbed his deeper levels'. He tried to dissuade Lutoslawski from putting his ideas into political form, but with no success, for the Pole formed a political party called the Philaretes, intent on resurrecting his country by a display of superior virtue. Between the First and Second World Wars Lutoslawski occupied a respected if eccentric place in Polish society. He disappeared in Poland during the Second World War. Several of his books were translated into English and it is at least inviting to read the thoughts of a man who claimed to have found the truth in pursuit of which he had set out. He wrote *The World of Souls*, 1924, *Pre-existence and Reincarnation*, 1928, *The Knowledge of Reality*, 1930. J. W.

Kenneth R. H. Mackenzie (1833-86)

A British antiquarian 'and Rosicrucian, author of *The Royal Masonic Cyclopaedia*, 1877, and a leading member of the SOC. ROS. He was one of the first English occultists to concern himself with TAROT symbolism, though he never finished his book on the subject. His projected occult Order, the Society of Eight, was also 'probably stillborn' (*235*).

Macumba

A Brazilian religious cult: see UMBANDA.

Magnetism   See HYPNOSIS and related articles.

Magus

Generally, a master magician or adept; specifically, the next-to-highest grade in the system of ranks or degrees adopted by the GOLDEN DAWN and Aleister CROWLEY.

Maithuna

The Tantric term for sexual intercourse: see TANTRISM.

Edward Maitland

The author of the *Life of Anna Kingsford*, 1896: see KINGSFORD.

Mandalas and Mantras

The word *mandala* means a circle and in Hindu and Buddhist rites is applied to a diagram traced on the ground or painted on a board or piece of fabric, symbolizing the cosmic and heavenly regions. Properly drawn and duly consecrated it becomes a focus of occult energy, drawing down hidden powers and itself sending forth magical emanations like a talisman. In its simplest form it is circular in outline but any symmetrical figure such as a square, pentagon, star or floral shape can be used. The outer perimeter is meant to delineate the mandala's borders, to act as a protective barrier against outside intrusion and to confine the power engendered inside the enclosure.

Within the boundaries of the mandala various other geometrical shapes are drawn, lesser squares, circles and triangles, dividing the whole into a series of zones which are treated as sacred areas, each reserved for the spirit entities who will be called down to occupy the places allotted to them. Some mandalas are rich and complex works of art, whose pictures, colours, patterns and orientation all have a correspondence with the occult planes.

Although normally depicted on paper, cloth, wood or other flat surface, mandalas are believed to have more than two dimensions, and to project into the other world. Bon magicians of Tibet dance out the mandala, hopping this way and that in a prescribed manner to create out of their movements the pattern they desire. Adepts of high degree are able to sit in meditation and visually create and hold a mandala in the mind. The designs of these mandalas, however, are not known, for they are never depicted objectively. Masters transmit the details to pupils by secret means or telepathic transference.

The mandala is regarded as a cosmogram, a map of the universe, with the regions marked out for the spiritual guardians of the cosmos. The patterns are traditional and many are said to have been captured in the past by adepts meditating on the planes. Special rites go into the drawing of a mandala, special invocations call the deities down, and in the sacred area a high-powered operation is believed to take place in a confrontation with the self. Meditation on a mandala calls forth not only the beneficent deities, but also the terrifying apparitions, bloodthirsty demons and images of putrefaction and death which, according to a Hindu text, 'are images of thy own mind'. Modern psychologists have therefore called the mandala not only a cosmogram but a psychocosmogram, a plan or picture of the human psyche against a cosmic backdrop which reveals the deeper structure of the human mind.

In one form or another the mandala is found in almost every culture in the world. It is an archetype of holy ground, a round and hence 'perfect' zone, set aside as sacrosanct. In varying contexts it symbolizes the sun, the wheel, the dome and all rotundas, the disk, the ring, the ouroboros (the serpent with its tail in its mouth), the female breast, the yoni, the clock face, the ball, the round table, the eye.

In Western occultism its analogue is the magic circle whose exact demarcations are given in medieval grimoires. The difference between the two is that after the magic circle is drawn the Western magician steps inside its protective boundary so that the spirits he summons cannot invade his territory to molest him, whereas the Eastern practitioner remains outside the mandala while the spirit powers remain within.

Mantras and Seed-sounds

Closely associated with Hindu and Buddhist meditative practice on the mandala is the recitation of the *mantra*, which is a magical formula expressed in words or in non-verbal sounds. It is usually very brief, a short verse no more than a few lines in length, and its meaning may be quite clear, like other spells of the same kind. Conversely, it may be an arrangement of syllables which do not have any apparent meaning, because they have been put together like an anagram or other mnemonic device, whose significance has to be deciphered. Still more cryptic mantras are the 'seed-sounds', consisting of single syllables which often end on a humming note, like *m* or *n*. The best known mantra of this class is AUM (or Om), a magical tri-sonant believed to hold the key to the universe. A great deal of esoteric lore has become attached to it, and many miraculous claims have been made for it. Its echoes comprehend the three worlds, heaven, earth and hell, the three chief deities, Brahma, Vishnu and Shiva, and other cosmic trinities.

Mantras are formed in several ways. They can come as a result of inspiration, sent direct by the deity to the devotee. They may arise as a result of meditation, worked out, so to speak, by the unconscious mind of a yogi. Some are recovered from the *akasha* (ether) by adepts (see AKASHIC RECORD). A few are composed by poets and mystics. Many of the most potent mantras have been formed by one of the special methods used for reducing a large work to a hermetic formula. This process is sometimes carried to incredible length. Thus, a holy scripture consisting of several thousand verses may be summarized in a single chapter. This chapter may be further reduced to a paragraph, then to a line, and finally to a single syllable. So powerful is this final syllable that, like a microdot, it contains the essence of the full treatise and mastery of the mantra will give a man an intuitive understanding of the entire text.

Other seed-sounds, besides aum, are *krim*, *hrim*, *vam*, *gam*, *ram*, *shrim*, and so on, whose vibrations are first concentrated and then projected, either inward into oneself, or outward in the form of invocations, commands, blessings or curses, to function as protective instruments, healing potencies, defensive or destructive missiles.

The mantras directed internally are aimed at a particular part of the body such as the head, between the eyebrows, the solar plexus or the sex organs, and at these points they set up vibrations that create specific energies. Thus those directed to the cranium set up resonances in the chambers of the head, resulting in a kind of mystic illumination. Sometimes a mantra is sent on a journey in a

Elaboration in a mandala from Japan

circuit round the body and its reverberations cause the old bodily tissues to fall off and make place for new. They may be directed to a part of the body that needs strengthening or healing.

It is believed that there exists a mantra for every condition and every illness. More than that, every problem, no matter what it is, can be resolved by intoning its appropriate

charm, for every mantra is a sound, and sound-vibrations underlie the universe. Great importance is attached to the mantra, and the science relating to it is expounded in a special branch of study known as mantra-yoga or mantra-shastra.

The folklore of the mantra is replete with instances of its magical efficacy. It is commonly believed that the effects of a mantra

are enhanced if it is repeated. Intoning the formula over and over again brings a greater number of benefits. It acts on the mind and causes its deeper significance to be understood. Its constant iteration, especially in combination with pranayama or breathing techniques (see YOGA), helps to induce a state of TRANCE and bring on mystical illumination. Finally, it penetrates the supernatural realms and in a way coerces the gods into granting one's requests.

Many extraordinary promises are held out to those who successfully carry out this repetition a prescribed number of times in the proper manner. If a person repeats a given mantra 100,000 times, men and women will obey him implicitly; if he repeats it 200,000 times, he will be able to control all natural phenomena; if a million and a half times, he will be able to travel over the universe. Special rosaries are used to keep a tally of the number of repetitions made. They usually consist of dried seeds on a string, but when sinister powers are sought the smaller bones of men and animals take the place of seeds.

Another miraculous element that keeps cropping up in the legendry of the mantra is that of its intrinsic power. Certain mantras, if correctly uttered, need be chanted aloud only once or twice, for them to carry on repeating themselves internally day and night, whether the person himself is awake or asleep. A true mantra has its own life.

Many mantras are communicated by the guru whispering into the pupil's ear, as they contain the secret doctrines of the sect. A story goes that a certain illiterate workman employed in repairing the outer walls of a house, overheard the guru as he was standing near the window whispering the mantra to his pupil. In a flash the man received enlightenment as though the doctrine had been taught to him for many years.

The mantra functions as a magical incantation, conjuration, invocation, evocation, and all the varieties of spells that comprise the armoury of words of power. It is said before, during and after all important ceremonies. It is used as a curse, a blessing, a prayer, a way of remembrance. There is hardly an activity for which there is not a mantra. In the absence of every other aid the adept, by means of a mantra alone, whether uttered aloud, whispered, or repeated mentally, can do anything he desires, for all things are manifestations of the mantra. Brahma himself is the Sound that sustains the universe. B. W.

(See also MEDITATION.) (Further reading: 256a, 427, 463.)

Manicheans, Manicheism See GNOSTI-CISM.

Mantras See MANDALAS AND MANTRAS.

Margery

The pseudonym of Mrs L. R. Crandon, American medium: see MEDIUMS.

Luis Martinez

A Mexican physical medium: see MEDIUMS.

Martinism

The name loosely applied to a group of mystical and occult teachings originating in 18th-century France. It is used to refer sometimes to the doctrines of Martinès de Pasqually (1710–74) and sometimes to those of Louis Claude de Saint-Martin, who was for a time a disciple of Pasqually. The fact that the name could derive from either of these men has led to some confusion in its use.

Pasqually was the founder of an occult Masonic group called the Order of the Elect Cohens which operated at Bordeaux. The order practised a form of ceremonial magic which involved the use of complicated floor tracings and an elaborate ritual designed to invoke benevolent spirits, to banish evil ones and to communicate with what Pasqually called the 'Active and Intelligent Cause'. The most important rituals were carried out at the equinoxes. After Pasqually's death the order broke up, but his ideas continued to influence occult Masonry through his disciples.

Louis Claude de Saint-Martin, who was initiated into the Elect Cohens in 1768, later became known for his writings under the name of the Unknown Philosopher. These taught a kind of mystical utopianism.

A so-called 'Martinist Order' was revived in the late 19th century by the French occultist PAPUS and a number of orders calling themselves Martinist are still operating today. C. M.

(Further reading: 319.)

Mass of St Secaire See SATANISM.

Masters

The relationship of master and pupil is one basic to mankind. Learning of any sort depends to some extent upon it. In the traditions of Eastern religion and Western occultism this relationship takes on a peculiar significance. The pupil must place himself in absolute obedience to the master and obey his most eccentric commands. This is not only because the master is the guardian of the secret wisdom which the pupil is trying to acquire, but because it is his business to create conditions in which the pupil may undergo the psychological changes which it is the object of his disciple to induce. The master's methods vary from the deliberate confounding of rational thought used by the Zen teachers, through the astute engineering of psychological crises achieved by GURDJIEFF, to the harsh discipline dispensed by some Indian teachers who on occasion savagely assault their pupils. The master may teach by instruction or example: he may give elaborate spiritual exercises, or he may simply *be*. Very often what he and his pupil set out to achieve is quite incomprehensible to outsiders. The point is that master and pupil are operating within a defined and very powerful set of conventions towards a mutually desirable end.

This traditional pattern is represented in the East by the *guru* and the *chela* (disciple) and caricatured in the Western image of the sorcerer's apprentice. The pattern outlined is the ideal, and frequently the reality is very different. Because the powers assumed by the master are great, the chances of damage to his pupil are equally great. If the master is inept or a fraud, his experiments in psychic engineering may finish in madness and suicide. And if the pupil needs the master in order to learn, the master needs the pupil in order to teach. So the process of teaching is as necessary to the master as the pupil. It sometimes happens that a master is particularly voracious, and seems to forget his obligations to the pupil and concentrate on the benefit he himself derives from the relationship. In addition to the dangers of simple fraud, the seeker for a master has therefore a further pitfall to avoid: he may escape being plundered by charlatans only to fall victim to a domination which leaves nothing behind in the personalities it touches.

The idea of Masters with a capital M first gained currency in the West during the 18th century, when occultists began to seek for hidden knowledge among the Freemasons. The Freemasonic lodges were arranged in a system of grades. As a candidate advanced through the grades, he advanced in knowledge; always before him was the lure of the higher grade in which more secrets would be revealed. On the more occult fringes of Masonry there grew up the legend – perhaps in default of more visible secrets – that above the highest grade to which members were normally admitted were beings incredibly exalted – the *Superieurs Inconnus*. These Unknown Chiefs might be men who had become semi-divine or creatures of another order altogether. The source of this idea was probably the Spanish–French occultist Martinès de Pasqually, who died in 1774 (see MARTINISM). Although the order he founded did not outlast him, the belief in Secret Chiefs who were actually divine was preserved among his disciples and reappears in the traditions of the GOLDEN DAWN.

In 1875 H. P. BLAVATSKY and Colonel H. S. OLCOTT founded the THEOSOPHICAL SOCIETY in New York, and from the mixture they concocted of Hinduism, Buddhism, Spiritualism and Western occultism the idea of Masters received a great impetus. Through Madame Blavatsky, Olcott was soon receiving messages from one Tuitit Bey of the 'Brotherhood of Luxor'. Later instructions came from the 'Master Serapis'. When the Theosophical Society moved to India, its headquarters at Adyar near Madras became the scene of visitations from the Masters, who were now said to be watching over the work of the society from their home in a ravine in Tibet.

Morya and Koot Hoomi

The Masters who were chiefly concerned with the Theosophists were called Morya and KOOT HOOMI. Their chief means of communication with their devotees was by 'precipitated' letters; communications which would flutter out of the air or be found in the pocket of the person for whom they were intended. The Masters also appeared visibly to those who were sufficiently susceptible. The Russian novelist Vsevolod Soloviev recorded how, when he went to visit H. P. Blavatsky in Germany in 1886, he was kept sitting for hours in front of a brilliantly-lit portrait of the Master Morya which the Theosophists accepted as a faithful likeness of the Himalayan Adept. That night Morya appeared to him exactly as he had been in the picture.

Madame Blavatsky and her successors had to fight many battles over their Masters. In 1884 a representative from the Society for Psychical Research carried out an investigation at Adyar and reported unfavourably on the Masters. After the death of Madame Blavatsky in 1892 there was a struggle for control of the society between William Quan JUDGE in America and Annie BESANT, during the course of which both contenders claimed to have received letters endorsing their candidature. The Masters were seen less and less in the flesh – although they appeared at the death-bed of Colonel Olcott – and while the Theosophical Society was under the leadership of Mrs Besant aspirants for spiritual honours visited the Himalayas in their astral bodies. This development was partly a consequence of the tragic death of Damodar K. Mavalankar, a young and ardent Theosophist, who had set out for the Himalayas shortly after the disturbing verdict of the Society for Physical Research. It seems likely that he was frozen to death on his journey.

Among their hierarchy of 'Perfected Men', the Theosophists ranged many of the heroes of religious and occult tradition. Jesus and the Buddha were Masters, as were the Comte de Saint-Germain, Plotinus and the alchemist Thomas Vaughan. Through a series of reincarnations, the Theosophist might hope to rise on the evolutionary level towards the status of these supermen. This doctrine was to a large extent a reaction against the proclamations of the Darwinians that man was descended from the ape. Whereas others might throw up their hands in horror and abandon Christianity for materialism, the Theosophists could argue that the self-evident truth of evolution merely presaged higher things. The Masters themselves, as well as providing examples for those on the upward path of evolution, fulfilled the excellent function of father-figures in an age of chaos. If God had been displaced, the religious impulse would make man divine.

Through the Theosophical Society the idea of an occult Master first became popular in the West. It was a glamorous simplification of the traditions common to both East and West from time immemorial, of the searching spirit who asked, 'Master, what shall I do to inherit eternal life?' J. W.

(See also AETHERIUS SOCIETY; CROWLEY.) (Further reading: 260.)

Samuel Liddell MacGregor Mathers (1854-1918)

The British magician who took a leading part in the founding of the Order of the Golden Dawn, wrote its rituals and eventually became its head; 'an imperious eccentric, always more than a little mad, but obviously gifted . . . the ideal person to be head of a magical order' (see GOLDEN DAWN). His magical names were Deo Duce Comite Ferro (With God as My Leader and the Sword as My Companion) and 'S Rioghail Mo Dhream (Gaelic for Royal is My Race), which reflect his authoritarian, military and Jacobite inclinations. He married Mina, or Moina, Bergson, sister of Henri Bergson, the philosopher, whom Mathers attempted, unsuccessfully, to convert to a belief in magic. From 1894 on, the couple lived in Paris, where they founded an Ahathoor Temple and celebrated 'Egyptian Masses' with much stately ceremonial in honour of the goddess Isis. Mathers added 'MacGregor' to his name in the belief that he was descended from the Scots clan, styled himself Comte de Glenstrae, and was imbued with Jacobite ardour for the restoration of the House of Stuart to the British throne. He was the magical patron of Aleister CROWLEY until the two men quarrelled and conducted a ferocious occult battle against each other. Mathers's high pretensions were too much for the members of the Golden Dawn and he was expelled in 1900. He produced an English translation of the Key of Solomon, the most famous of the grimoires or textbooks of European ritual magic. He also translated part of Knorr von Rosenroth's Kabbalah Denudata as The Kabbalah Unveiled, The Book of the Sacred Magic of Abra-Melin the Mage and the Grimoire of Armadel: see RITUAL MAGIC; TRANCE. (100, 235, 262, 264, 311 to 314 inclusive, 446)

Arnold Harris Mathew (1852-1919)

An English clergyman and wandering bishop of eccentric habits – he once terrified his congregation at St Mary's, Bath, by taking a live tiger into the pulpit with him – who claimed to be Earl of Llandaff, and became an Archbishop of the Dutch Old Catholic Church. He also believed in the Baconian authorship of Shakespeare. Numerous churches and wandering bishops trace their line of descent from him: see WANDERING BISHOPS; see also THEOSOPHICAL SOCIETY.

Mazdaznan

An occult society with headquarters at Chicago and Leipzig, Germany, claiming Zoroastrian origin and founded by 'Dr Otoman Zar-Adusht Ha'nish', whose real name was Otto Hanisch (1854–1936; see also ATLANTIS). The Order's object was self-mastery, based on correct breathing techniques, strict vegetarian diet, abstinence from alcohol and tobacco, and colonic irrigation. Membership was restricted to fair-skinned 'Aryans'. The society is still in existence. (494)

G. R. S. Mead

A British Theosophist who was at one time secretary to Madame BLAVATSKY. In 1909 he founded the Quest Society. He translated and edited Gnostic and Hermetic texts in Fragments of a Faith Forgotten, 1900, and Thrice-Greatest Hermes, 1906: see GNOSTICISM; HERMETICA; THEOSOPHICAL SOCIETY.

Meditation

The word 'meditation' has many meanings. Here we restrict ourselves to meditation as a method of self-development. In general the purpose is to help the meditator become aware of a union which he believes exists between himself and all things. The practice of meditation does not presuppose any religious faith though it is found in most religions. Christian meditators may describe their goal as one of unifying with Christ, Muslims (the Sufis) with Allah, Hindus with the Atman (the Self), Jews (the Hasids) with God, and so forth. The experience sought by meditators is also called self-transcendence, expansion of consciousness, SAMADHI, satori and enlightenment. Lama Govinda, an exponent of Tibetan Buddhism (see plate, page 164), says that during this experience, human consciousness 'is not bound to one direction (of time), like the body and its senses' (*185*). Also, 'while in meditation space seems to expand. . . . In the higher stages of absorption the experience of the infinity of space immediately leads to the experience of the infinity of consciousness. After the elimination of all thing- and form-ideas or representations, space is the direct and intuitive object of consciousness' (*186*).

Meditation is not a kind of TRANCE or HYPNOSIS, since the meditator does not lose consciousness but on the contrary seeks to expand it. Nor is meditation like most kinds of prayer, since it does not involve a petition. It is also not like ordinary thinking; on the contrary, it is the aim of meditation to bring an end to those thinking and mental processes that conceal the basic unity which the meditator seeks to experience.

In meditation, the mind is usually occupied with some simple continuous task such as repeating a word mentally or visualizing (or looking at) an object. A word used for meditation is called a MANTRA. In Indian systems, the word AUM, which symbolizes all sounds in the universe, is often used.

Meditation may be done in a group or alone, preferably in a quiet room set aside for this purpose. Some meditation systems recommend that the meditator sits on the floor with legs crossed, others allow any comfortable position. In some systems the eyes are closed, in others open. Chanting and dancing are often part of meditation. Usually two or more periods a day are set aside for sitting meditation. In addition, it is often suggested that one should meditate whenever possible during daily activities.

It is sometimes reported that psychical abilities result from meditation. Usually it is not important to the meditator to develop such abilities since they may divert him from his goal. When they are treated seriously, it is often because they are seen as an objective indication that the meditator is not living in a private dream world but that his consciousness has expanded into the real one.

Richard Alpert, who was a psychology professor at Harvard University before he went to India and was initiated by a *guru* (teacher), gives several illustrations of the ESP abilities of this person. The day before they met, Alpert was staying in a monastery. During the night he went outside and suddenly he had a strong sense of presence from his deceased mother. She had died of a spleen illness the year before (the spleen swelled up and had to be removed). The day after this experience, Alpert unexpectedly and unannounced was taken to a small

temple at the foothills of the Himalayas where he met the guru. Some time after eating,

> . . . we were back with the Maharaji and he said to me, 'Come here. Sit.' So I sat down and he looked at me and he said,
> 'You were out under the stars last night.'
> 'Um-hum.'
> 'You were thinking about your mother.'
> 'Yes' ('Wow,' I thought, 'that's pretty good. I never mentioned that to anybody').
> 'She died last year.'
> 'Um-hum.'
> 'She got very big in the stomach before she died.'
> . . . Pause . . . 'Yes.'
> He leaned back and closed his eyes and said 'Spleen. She died of spleen' (*8*).

Another time, 'I was going through my address book and I came to Lama Govinda's name . . . and I thought, "Gee, I might go to visit him. I'm here in the Himalayas and it wouldn't be a long trip . . . I must do that some time before I leave." And the next day there is a message from the Maharaji. "You are to immediately see Lama Govinda" ' (*8*).

Hasidism and Sufism
Cultures and religions differ but the meditation systems developed by them are surprisingly similar – not only the goals but the means as well. SUFISM, which can be traced back to the time of Muhammad, emphasizes the importance of repetitive chanting and dancing (the 'whirling dervishes' are a Sufi sect) and so do the Hasids, a Jewish sect.

In both chanting and silent meditation the meaning of the words is often regarded as less important than the intention of the meditator and the intensity and energy he puts into them. Thus there is a story that Baal Shem Tov (1700–60), the founder of Hasidism, was once lost on a journey with his scribe. They were miraculously shown the way when the scribe recited the letters of the alphabet 'with the great fervor he always put into his prayers' (*60*). Similarly when the Sufis repeat the name of Allah they accompany 'the mechanical intonation with an intense concentration' (*353*). Many reports, usually of ESP but also sometimes of psychokinesis, or PK, are told of the Hasids and Sufis. 'A hasid who was traveling to Mezbizh in order to spend the Day of Atonement near the Baal Shem, was forced to interrupt his journey for something or other. When the stars rose, he was still a good way from the town and, to his great grief, had to pray alone in the open field. When he arrived in Mezbizh after the holiday, the Baal Shem

received him with particular happiness and cordiality. "Your praying," he said, "lifted up all the prayers which were lying stored in that field" ' (*60*).

There are stories of both ESP and PK from the lives of the Sufi saints. 'Avicenna paid a visit to Abu'l-Hasan Khurqani and immediately plunged into a long and abstruse discussion. After a time the saint, who was an illiterate person, felt tired, so he got up and said, "Excuse me; I must go and mend the garden wall"; and off he went, taking a hatchet with him. As soon as he had climbed on to the top of the wall, the hatchet dropped from his hand. Avicenna ran to pick it up, but before he reached it the hatchet rose of itself and came back into the saint's hand. Avicenna lost all his self-command, and the enthusiastic belief in Sufism which then took possession of him continued until, at a later period of his life, he abandoned mysticism for philosophy' (*353*).

Zen
Zen is a form of Buddhism which emphasizes an intense and concentrated form of meditation ('Zen' is derived from the Chinese 'Ch'an', which in turn comes from the Sanskrit word *dhyana*, which means meditation). Zen as practised in contemporary Japan and in the West was formulated in China by Hui-Neng (d. A.D. 713). During Zen meditation, or *zazen*, the meditator may focus his mind on one of the Zen paradoxes, called a *koan* ('What is the sound of one hand clapping?'), on a word from a koan (the word *mu*, nothing, is often used), on his breathing or on nothing at all. In any case he applies himself to the task with great concentration and energy. In Zen, there is much emphasis on right posture during meditation. The meditator sits on a pillow on the floor with legs crossed, preferably in the lotus position (right foot on left thigh, left foot on right thigh), the back straight, the hands folded in the lap (usually tips of thumbs touching), the eyes open and lowered.

Zen does not emphasize the development of psychical powers but these are believed to arise naturally as the meditator reaches enlightenment. A story from the life of the late Chinese Zen (Ch'an) teacher Hsu Yun is an illustration. After many years of meditation the master 'succeeded in realizing singleness of mind, and in his fifty-sixth year, one evening, in Kao Ming monastery at Yangchow, after a long meditation, he opened his eyes and saw everything inside and outside the monastery. Through the wall, he saw a monk urinating outside, a guest monk in the latrine and far away, boats plying on the river and trees on both its banks' (*517*).

Teaching meditation by Zen

Transcendental Meditation

Transcendental Meditation (TM) first came into prominence when the Beatles singing group and other stage personalities visited Maharishi Mahesh Yogi in India to learn meditation. TM is easy to learn and easy to teach. As a result there are already several thousand teachers and several hundred thousand TM meditators in the world.

The popularity of TM can be attributed to several factors. TM is adapted to the needs of the meditators. Many students begin meditating not because of some distant aim of enlightenment but because TM may help them become better students, more adequate in their social life, and so on. Also many people who meditate report almost immediate beneficial effects. They are less tense, feel more energetic, and are better able to concentrate. To become a teacher of TM only takes a few months' instruction as compared to the years of training and the high spiritual attainment of the teachers of other meditation systems. However, the ordinary TM teacher does not take the students beyond their initial training. Advanced training is done by the Maharishi himself or by a few persons he has specially trained.

The main meditation device in TM is a mantra chosen by the TM teacher as propitious for the student in question. In TM the mantra is a meaningless word with special sound qualities which are supposed to help the meditator to reach the source of the thinking process and thereby to gain self-transcendence. The mantra is repeated mentally during two periods of about twenty minutes each, one in the morning and one in the afternoon, while the meditator sits in a comfortable position with eyes closed.

Scientific Studies of Meditation

Psychologists are becoming increasingly interested in meditation. To a large extent this is because of the discovery that meditation may result not only in altered states of consciousness but also in physiological changes. In work with the electro-encephalograph (EEG) it has been found that there is often an increase of the alpha brain wave during meditation. This is a rather slow wave which is likely to occur when a person closes his eyes and is relaxed but still attentive and alert.

Lester Fehni, Professor of Psychology at the State University of New York, says that 'Alpha makes it possible to have something to point to that is correlated to mind and attention. This gives psychology an enormous boost that has been impossible till now' (231). Some of this work has been done by R. Keith Wallace and Herbert Benson at Harvard University with TM meditators. They found that meditation results in deeper relaxation than sleep, as indicated by greater reductions in metabolic rate. There are sharp drops in the body's use of oxygen, and in heart rate and respiration. There is an increase of the electrical resistance of the skin and a decrease of lactic acid in the blood, both showing reduced arousal and anxiety (488).

The alpha work has led to a new method of meditation. Joseph Kamiya of the Langly Porter Neuropsychiatric Institute in San Francisco, California, who first discovered the connection between alpha and meditation, found that people can actually control their brain waves and thereby their mental states (447). The method involves an EEG machine connected to a signal, such as a buzzer, which comes on when alpha is present. The person being tested is asked to keep the buzzer on for as long as he can. In this way it has been possible for people to prolong their alpha periods and thereby to develop altered states of consciousness similar to those reported by people using more conventional meditation methods. This procedure is called bio-feedback (it is now also used for health purposes to enable people to reduce their blood pressure and other functions which are generally outside voluntary control). It has resulted in several commercial ventures which sell alpha devices and teach 'electronic meditation'. Eleanor Links Hoover in *Alpha the First Step to a New Level of Reality* writes that ' . . . we seem to be on the brink of a new Consciousness Revolution that some social historians say will surpass in importance the Agricultural, Industrial and technological eras and usher us into a new age of man' (231).

Scientists have also become interested in meditation as an alternative to DRUGS. People who have used marijuana, LSD and other drugs often decrease their consumption, apparently because the meditation experiences are similar to drug experiences but safer and with no undesirable side effects.

Parapsychologists are interested in meditation as a possible means to develop psychical abilities. Because of the relationship between meditation and alpha waves, ESP and alpha may possibly be related.

Rhea White of the American Society for Psychical Research has shown that the methods used by some of the best ESP percipients to bring their impressions into consciousness are similar to meditation procedures (500). In a study with a group of meditators by Karlis Osis and Edwin Bokert, the people who were best at ESP had 'a feeling of merging with the others . . . and a feeling of oneness as if the boundaries of "what is me and what is not me" were disolving' (357). At the Foundation for Research on the Nature of Man in Durham, North Carolina, Francine Matas and Lee Pantas found that subjects who had practised meditation or similar forms of self-development were better in PK tests than those who had not (310). At the City University of New York, Gertrude Schmeidler found that the ESP scores of a small group of students increased after an Indian swami had given a brief instruction on breathing and meditation (419). At the Psychical Research Foundation in Durham, Robert Morris and others found that the ESP scores of the psychic Lalsingh Harribance were best when his brain showed most alpha (335). Charles Honorton and others at Maimonides Hospital in Brooklyn, New York, have explored alpha bio-feedback as a means to develop ESP, with promising results (230). W. G. R.

(Further reading: see references in the text.)

Mediums

The word 'medium' is used for people who are believed to possess psychical abilities which they use to communicate with the personalities of deceased individuals. Sometimes the words 'psychic' and 'sensitive' are used instead of medium but as a rule these terms refer to persons who do not claim that they communicate with the dead. Mediums are generally classified into two types, 'mental mediums' and 'physical mediums'. This distinction reflects the two basic types of psychical or psi phenomena, ESP and PK (see PARAPSYCHOLOGY). A mental medium is a person whose apparent interaction with deceased persons takes the form of mental impressions apparently obtained by means of ESP from the minds of the deceased. A physical medium, on the other hand, apparently acts as a channel for PK actions initiated by the deceased. The term incorporeal personal agent (IPA) is sometimes used for a supposed surviving personality.

Since ESP and PK abilities have been found in persons who do not claim to be mediums, it is possible that mediumistic phenomena are entirely due to the psychical abilities of the medium and do not involve any IPAs. Though it is uncertain whether or not mediums interact with deceased individuals, most parapsychologists agree that some mediums possess striking psi abilities. Mental mediums are less rare than physical mediums, perhaps because it may be easier to produce observable ESP than PK effects.

Mental mediums use different methods to bring on communications with IPAs. Whatever method is used, its main purpose is to by-pass the contents of ordinary waking CONSCIOUSNESS and establish a channel to mental processes which are usually unconscious and which may be more open to ESP than ordinary consciousness.

Some mediums work in what is very close to their normal waking state. To obtain their ESP impressions they may use unconscious muscular movements such as automatic writing (see AUTOMATISMS) or working the OUIJA BOARD. Others stimulate the creation of mental images by gazing at some object, such as a glass of water or a crystal ball (see SCRYING). Some mediums have 'development circles', in which they try to teach people to develop psychical abilities. These methods are sometimes similar to MEDITATION procedures.

TRANCE mediums work in a dissociated state, usually induced by themselves but sometimes by a hypnotist. Such mediums often give the impression that they have been taken over or 'possessed' by a spirit (see also POSSESSION). They may show startling changes in voice, facial expression and gestures, which resemble those of the supposed spirit. Most trance mediums have a 'spirit guide' or CONTROL. This is a supposed spirit entity which has attached itself to the medium and aids in seeking out the IPA whom the medium or his client wishes to contact. Sometimes spirit guides claim to be deceased individuals themselves.

Not all the entities who appear to communicate through mediums are IPAs. Depending on the religious belief of the medium, gods, angels and other non-human entities may seem to communicate through the medium, giving guidance for the affairs of the living or accounts of the spirit-world.

People consult mediums for many reasons. Some hope to communicate with their loved ones, to be reassured that they still exist; others wish to learn about the future through the supposed precognitive abilities of the medium or the spirit; others seek help in business matters and practical affairs. Occasionally, mediums are asked to perform 'exorcisms'. People sometimes believe that a person who seems to be mentally ill is in fact possessed by an evil spirit. Some mediums claim to be able to detect such spirits as well as the spirits who supposedly infest 'haunted' houses (see also POLTERGEISTS). These mediums may also claim that they can exorcise such spirits, that is, cause the spirit to leave the possessed person or the haunted house.

The Delphic Oracle

An example of a person consulting a medium about the future is found in the Old Testament. In the face of an impending battle between the Philistines and the Israelites, King Saul went to the 'witch at Endor' so that he might communicate with Samuel and learn the outcome of the battle. The woman had a 'familiar spirit' who apparently fulfilled the same function as the spirit guides of today. Samuel, we are told, accurately predicted Saul's defeat (I Samuel xxviii, 7–25).

Perhaps the most famous medium, or rather succession of mediums, in recorded history was the oracle of Delphi. For more than a thousand years a succession of entranced women were the centre of this highly influential religious institution. People from all walks of life would travel to Delphi in Greece to seek advice from the god Apollo, who was believed to speak through the medium. This woman, known as the Pythia, would enter a trance by a series of rituals and, on being addressed, would reply in an altered voice. At one time it was believed that underground gases produced the trance, but geological investigations have shown that there were probably no such gases. As with many present-day mediums, during her normal state the Pythia behaved like an ordinary person with no particular abilities or knowledge. When she became possessed by the god, she usually spoke in symbols and riddles which the priests then had to explain. But she was not the only such oracle; there were several others in classical antiquity who performed similar functions. Among them were the 'belly-talkers' who were thought to have a demon in their bellies which spoke through them and predicted the future (124).

Some of the physical phenomena of mediumship are also encountered in the classical world. In the 4th century A.D., Iamblichus mentions lights and spirit forms around the medium and LEVITATION of the medium's body. He also describes DIRECT VOICE phenomena where spirit entities appear to speak at a distance from the medium and without using the medium's vocal organs. The Jewish exorcist Eleazar, during his public demonstrations, kept a container of water close to the possessed person. When the exorcism was successful, the departing demon would overturn the container at the request of Eleazar as proof that the demon had left his victim. Similarly, it is told of Apollonius of Tyana that the demon would prove its withdrawal by overturning a statue. After this the possessed 'awoke as if from sleep, rubbed his eyes', and returned to normal (124).

Mediumistic practices are found in most periods and places. Siberian tribes and Eskimo settlements have their shamans and African tribes have witch-doctors who perform similar functions to those of, say, a London medium.

The first recorded test of mediums was conducted by Croesus, King of Lydia, in the 6th century B.C. Croesus sent messengers to seven of the best-known oracles, and these were to put the question to each oracle on a specified day: 'What is the King of Lydia doing today?' The messengers themselves did not know the answer so there seemed to be no possibility of sensory leakage and the King saw to it that a correct statement could not be the result of chance coincidence: on the day in question he was boiling a lamb and a tortoise in a copper pot. Five of the oracles failed the test and a sixth came up with a near hit. Only the Pythia of Delphi gave the correct answer (124).

The question of evidence is also a main concern of present-day parapsychologists. We can only know if a medium has ESP or PK capacities if these have been observed under controlled conditions. Most of the serious work with mediums was done in the early days of the Society for Psychical Research (S.P.R.) in England and by its American counterpart (A.S.P.R.), founded in the years 1882 and 1885 respectively. The

Mediums

scientific interest in mediumship then waned, partly because some mediums turned out to be fraudulent and partly because it could not be determined whether the genuine phenomena produced by mediums could be explained in terms of their own psi abilities without the aid of IPAs. In recent years interest in research with mediums has revived. This is because reliable methods have been developed to test their abilities and because these abilities may throw light on the nature of ESP and PK whether or not IPAs are involved.

Mental Mediums

Mrs Leonora PIPER (1857–1950) was the most thoroughly investigated medium in the early years of psychical research. Most of the work with her was done between 1885 and 1915 and gave a great boost to psychical research both in her native America and in England. Because she often produced strikingly accurate details about deceased persons, detectives were employed to follow her in order to discover whether she obtained her

Mrs Piper

knowledge fraudulently. No evidence of fraud was ever found. Sometimes she gave her statements orally and sometimes in automatic writing.

Mrs Piper found that she had mediumistic abilities in her mid-twenties when she went to a psychic healer to have a tumour treated. During one of the visits she went into trance and from then on began to hold mediumistic sittings at home with relatives and friends. Shortly afterwards, the American psychologist William James (1842–1910) came to see her, expecting that he would be able to explain the phenomena away. Soon, however, he became convinced that she was 'in possession of a power as yet unexplained' (247b).

Richard Hodgson

James was one of the most influential psychologists of his day and he also played an important role in parapsychology. He helped to found the American Society for Psychical Research and in 1894–5 he was President of the English S.P.R. He introduced Mrs Piper to Richard Hodgson (1855–1905), secretary of the American Society for Psychical Research. Hodgson had exposed several fraudulent mediums and expected Mrs Piper to do no better. However, Mrs Piper gave detailed and private information about Hodgson's deceased relatives and friends. As a result, he arranged for many persons who were unknown to Mrs Piper to have sittings with her, with similar results.

When Hodgson died, he became one of the principal IPAs who seemed to communicate through Mrs Piper. On one occasion, when Mrs Piper was using automatic writing, 'Hodgson' wrote, addressing James, ' "You seem to think I have lost my equilibrium . . ." James replied, "You've lost your handwriting, gone from bad to worse . . ." Another sitter remarked ironically "It was a perfectly beautiful handwriting." Hodgson responded, "Ahem! Ahem! William, do you remember my writing you a long letter once when you were ill? You had to get Margaret [James's daughter] to help you read it and you wrote me it was detestable writing and you hoped I would try and write plainer to a friend who was ill, next time. How I laughed over that, but I was really sorry to make you wade through it." ' This incident was as stated. It was verified by William and Margaret James.

Among the correct items, James found many inaccuracies and irrelevancies as well as 'obvious groping and fishing and plausible covering up of false tracks . . . and obedience to suggestion'. This is characteristic of medi-

umistic data in general. In James's words it suggests a 'will to personate', to imitate or create a personality. This 'will' may be able to tap the memories of the sitters and perhaps of people not present at the session and 'possibly some cosmic reservoir in which the memories of earth are stored, whether in the shape of "spirits" or not'. In addition to noting a 'will to personate', James said that, 'I myself feel as if an external will to communicate were probably there, that is, I find myself doubting, in consequence of my whole acquaintance with that sphere of phenomena, that Mrs. Piper's dream-life, even equipped with "telepathic" powers, accounts for all the results found. But if asked whether the will to communicate be Hodgson's, or be some mere spirit-counterfeit of Hodgson, I remain uncertain and await more facts, facts which may not point clearly to a conclusion for fifty or a hundred years' (247b).

Hope, Star and Browning

For the early members of the Society for Psychical Research the most burning question was the question of survival after death and how to obtain conclusive evidence for (or against) survival. It seemed natural that when these psychical researchers died they would try to supply evidence for their own continuation, if they did survive.

In the opinion of many of their living colleagues they succeeded in doing so by means of the CROSS-CORRESPONDENCES. A cross-correspondence is produced by two or more mediums and consists of disjointed and meaningless statements, sometimes drawings, which together make up a meaningful whole. The S.P.R. cross-correspondences were interesting not only because it seemed unlikely that the relationships between the

F. W. H. Myers

statements could be due to chance coincidence but also because the themes, for instance, references to a story or poem from classical Greece, were beyond the interests and education of some of the mediums who produced them but reflected the memories, interests and professional skills of the purporting communicators, several of whom were classical scholars. The cross-correspondences seemed to point to a complex plan conceived by the deceased S.P.R. investigators which could not easily be explained as telepathy between the living.

Mrs Piper was one of the cross-correspondence mediums. Another was Mrs Alice Fleming (1868–1948), known as 'Mrs Holland', a sister of Rudyard Kipling. Mrs Fleming had produced poetry in automatic writing and then, in 1903, after she had communicated with the Society for Psychical Research and had read *Human Personality and Its Survival of Bodily Death (346)* by F. W. H. Myers (1843–1901), Myers apparently began writing through her. There were also automatic writings which purported to come

Edmund Gurney

from Edmund Gurney (1847–88) and Henry Sidgwick (1838–1900), who with Myers were among the founders of the S.P.R. Mrs Fleming was living in India, which made it all the more unlikely that she could have obtained by ordinary means the information that she gave.

Another in this group of mediums was Mrs A. W. Verrall (1859–1916), a teacher of classics at Cambridge University. In 1901 she began to do automatic writing, in the course of which messages seemed to come from recently deceased members of the S.P.R. Mrs Verrall's daughter, Helen (later Mrs W. H. Salter, 1883–1959), also became a cross-correspondence medium. Miss Ver-

Henry Sidgwick

rall was active in the research and editorial work of the S.P.R., and for a period was one of its vice-presidents.

One of the cross-correspondences was the 'Hope, Star and Browning' case. In January 1907 the idea of an anagram was suggested by an unidentified source in an automatic script by Mrs Verrall and the words 'rats star tars' were written. Five days later 'Aster', the Greek word for star came and later the line, 'And all a wonder and a wild desire . . . A *winged desire* . . . the hope that leaves the earth for the sky – Abt Vogler for earth . . .' Mrs Verrall gave these scripts to J. G. Piddington (1869–1952), an S.P.R. investigator who was working on the cross-correspondences. (Piddington became President of the S.P.R. in 1924–5.)

Mrs Verrall and Piddington noted that much of the material consisted of near quotes from two poems by Robert Browning, including *Abt Vogler*. In February of the same year, Piddington had a sitting with Mrs Piper when Myers appeared to come through and said he had previously communicated something to Mrs Verrall: 'I referred to Hope and Browning. I also said Star.' Piddington noted that in the earlier scripts from Mrs Verrall there were references to stars, and to hope and Browning. Not only was the word 'hope' mentioned but it was specially emphasized because it came as a misquote from a poem. This poem was by Robert Browning. The quote should not have been 'the hope that leaves . . .', but 'the passion that left the ground to lose itself in the sky'. After the session, when Mrs Verrall read over her script she was surprised at the mistake: 'I knew perfectly when I read the script that it should have been "passion" . . . I wondered why the silly thing said "Hope".'

Mrs Verrall also noted that there were

references to birds in her script, both in 'A winged desire' and in the name Vogler which is close to the German word for bird, *Vogel*. Unknown to Mrs Verrall, this theme had already been woven into the pattern of the cross-correspondences, not by Mrs Piper but by Miss Verrall. About a week before her mother had produced the script on the Hope, Star and Browning theme, Miss Verrall wrote an automatic script with drawings of a bird and a star and a reference to song birds. She was then told by Mrs Verrall that there had been a cross-correspondence incident and was encouraged to contribute to it. The actual words which had been communicated were not mentioned except that a five-letter anagram had been part of the message. Two days later she drew a picture of a star with these words next to it: 'that was the sign she will understand . . . and a star above it all', and on the next line '*rats* everywhere in Hamelin town . . .' There was also reference in this script to a 'rhythm through all the heavenly harmony' and the 'mystic three(?)'. This seemed to reflect

Mrs Leonard

some lines in the earlier script by her mother of which Miss Verrall had no knowledge:

On the earth the broken sounds . . .
In the sky the perfect arc,
The C major of this life.

The material is all the more interesting because Myers was known to be an admirer of Browning's poetry and of the idealistic themes which run through the scripts.

Mrs Gladys Osborne LEONARD (1882–1968) already as a child experienced another world in her visions of a 'Happy Valley' inhabited by graceful and radiant people. But when her parents told her not to have such visions, they disappeared. When she

Sir Oliver Lodge

was grown up, an acquaintance invited her to a seance. Others followed and she gradually developed into a trance medium. She first came to public notice as a result of her sittings with the physicist Sir Oliver Lodge (1851–1940). Lodge, who was knighted for his work in physics, began experiments in TELEPATHY in the early years of the S.P.R. He also had a strong interest in the question of survival. In 1915, following the death of his son in the First World War, he began sittings with Mrs Leonard. In his book *Raymond* he described the material which convinced him beyond doubt of the continued existence of his son.

Mrs Leonard was also the subject in the 'book tests' conducted by the Reverend C. Drayton Thomas (d. 1953), an S.P.R. researcher and Council member. These experiments were designed to rule out the possibility of telepathy from living persons in mediumistic sessions. Usually the evidential information conveyed by ostensible IPAs through a medium is known to some living person, either the person consulting the medium or his friends and relatives. It therefore seems possible that the medium may use his telepathic abilities to obtain the information from the minds of these living persons rather than from any IPA. Drayton Thomas thought that if the medium could obtain information which was not known to anybody living, this would be evidence for survival.

In October 1921, Sir William F. Barrett (1844–1925) had a 'book test' sitting with Mrs Leonard. Barrett was one of the founders of the Society for Psychical Research. He was a distinguished physicist, whose researches led, among other things, to the development of the telephone. In the course of the sitting, Myers appeared to address Barrett through Mrs Leonard's control. Barrett reports:

He said that there were some books on the right-hand side of a room upstairs in our house in Devonshire Place, which . . . Mrs. Leonard has never visited. This statement was quite correct, a bookcase filled with books is on the right-hand side of the drawing-room upstairs. The control continued that, on the second shelf, four feet from the ground, in the fourth book counting from the left, at the top of page 78, are some words which he (Mr. Fred Myers) wishes you to take as a direct answer from himself to so much of the work you have been doing since he passed over. Asked if the name of the book could be given, the reply was 'No,' but that whilst feeling on the cover of the book he got a sense of 'progression.' The control continued: 'Two or three books from this test book are one or two books on matters in which Sir William used to be very interested, but of late years has not been so interested. It is connected with studies of his youth; and he will have particular memories of it, as it will remind him of his younger days.' I had no idea what books were referred to, but on returning home found that, in the exact position indicated, the 'test book' was George Eliot's *Middlemarch*. The cover of the book showed the name conspicuously, the latter half, 'march,' indicating as the control said, 'progression.' On the first line at the top of page 78 are the words, 'Ay, ay, I remember – you'll see I've remembered 'em all,' which quotation is singularly appropriate, as much of my work since Mr. Myers passed over has been concerned with the question of survival after death and whether the memories of friends on earth continued with the discarnate.

But the most remarkable part of this book test is contained in the sentence, 'two or three books from the test book,' etc. In dusting these bookshelves the maid-servant, unknown to us, had replaced two of George Eliot's novels by two volumes of Dr. Tyndall's books, viz., his *Heat* and *Sound*, which, to my surprise, were found exactly in the position indicated. In my youth I was for some years assistant to Professor Tyndall, and those books were written whilst I was with him, and the investigations and experiments they describe formed 'the studies of my youth.' A careful investigation of all the other shelves and books yielded nothing even remotely applicable to the test given. Chance coincidence, therefore, cannot account for this, nor can travelling clairvoyance explain the matter, as Mrs. Leonard knows nothing of our house, nor of my early life, with which Mr. Myers was familiar (*451a*).

The Rev. Drayton Thomas

Mrs Winifred Coombe Tennant (1874–1956), known as 'Mrs WILLETT', was another member of the S.P.R. group of cross-correspondence mediums. Mrs Coombe Tennant led an active professional life – she was a Justice of the Peace and also a British delegate to the League of Nations – and became actively interested in parapsychology after the death of her daughter in 1908. She began to produce automatic writing after corresponding with Mrs A. W. Verrall. Sir Oliver Lodge frequently had sittings with her but most of the work was done with Gerald W. Balfour (1853–1945). Gerald Balfour, later the second Earl of Balfour, was a Member of Parliament and held other government offices. He was President of the S.P.R. in 1906–7. His brother, Arthur Balfour, the first Earl of Balfour, was Prime Minister in

Sir William Barrett

1902–5. He, too, was interested in psychical research, and had been President of the S.P.R. in 1893.

While Mrs Piper and Mrs Leonard received their material in trance, through 'controls', Mrs Willett as a rule was fully conscious when she did her automatic writing.

One series of communications, referred to as the 'Palm Sunday Case', apparently originated from a Mary Lyttelton who had died on a Palm Sunday, shortly before it was expected that her engagement to Arthur Balfour would be announced. References to her and Balfour in Mrs Willett's scripts were always concealed and were not understood by the medium. On one occasion Mrs Willett wrote: 'The *May Flower* – the ship that sailed to the New World. But it is not of a ship but of a person I want it said . . . A slender girl with quantities of hair worn in heavy plaits . . . What has she to do with Coma Berenice?'

Mary Lyttelton was born in May and was called May by her family. During her terminal illness her hair was cut off and a large piece was given to Balfour, who had a silver box made for it. There is a reference to hair in the script, for *De Coma Berenices* is a poem by Catullus giving the story of Berenice's hair, which she cut off and dedicated in a temple to the safe return of her husband (*14*).

Arthur Balfour never married. He died at the age of eighty-one, fifty-five years after the death of Mary Lyttelton. Six months before he died he was staying at the home of his brother, Gerald Balfour, where Mrs Willett was also a guest. One evening Gerald Balfour brought Mrs Willett to see his brother for

Arthur Balfour

Geraldine Cummins

what was to be a brief visit. Arthur Balfour (A.J.B.) was lying on a couch and a gramophone was playing Beethoven's Trio in B flat. To the surprise of Gerald Balfour, Mrs Willett stayed on:

> Presently she shut her eyes, and whispered to me, 'This room is full of Presences.' . . . A.J.B. remained lying back, listening to the music. . . . Mrs Willett proceeded to describe to me in whispers what she was seeing, or rather, mentally *sensing* – for though she spoke as if she was *seeing a phantasm*, she explained that it was with the mind's eye only that she saw. Her whole attention was concentrated on a single figure, that of a lady in an old-fashioned dress, young, and with thick and beautiful hair. A brilliant light streamed from her whole figure; she was standing by the side of A.J.B.'s pillow, resting her hand on his arm and gazing down on him with a look of infinite tenderness. I said, 'I know who she is', but Mrs Willett took no notice. I think that it was about this time that she said, 'This room is like a Cathedral.' She complained of feeling cold; declared that there was an icy wind blowing between her and me; and seemed astonished and incredulous when I told her that I felt nothing. She also asked if it was possible that A.J.B. could be unaware of the lady's presence. I replied that I believed he was, and that he was as impervious and unpsychic as myself. Towards the end of the second movement of the Trio Mrs Willett remarked that she had been almost in trance, and only with much effort had succeeded in retaining consciousness (*14*).

The story of these communications and of Balfour's love for Mary Lyttelton only became known when his sister, Jean Balfour, published an article on the 'Palm Sunday

Case' in 1960 (*14*). Preceding the publication by three years, a chapter of the same story had been written by a different hand. The initiative came from W. H. Salter (1880–1970), a member of the S.P.R. and President of the Society in 1947–8. In 1957, a year after the death of Mrs Willett, Salter wrote to the medium and author Geraldine CUMMINS asking if she would try for a message from the deceased mother of a Major Coombe Tennant. Miss Cummins was unaware that this was Mrs Willett. In the course of the next three years Mrs Cummins wrote a series of scripts, apparently originating from Mrs Willett and referring to events in the life of Mrs Willett known only to Mrs Willett's immediate family and intimate friends. Among these memories were several concerning the Balfour communications. One concerned Mrs Willett's vision in the Balfour home:

> Many years ago I spent a strange hour in a room being one of a trio. We were listening to great music. All was peaceful. But music did not carry me away. It peopled the room with the invisible dead. But at first I felt rather than perceived their presences. As I know now I became linked with the third in the trio, the deeper mind of a living man, who was resting and relaxed and appeared to be half asleep. And suddenly the presences of the dead I sensed became one visible presence from another life. I saw nothing ghostly. It was as real to me as my hand – simply a woman wearing an old-fashioned costume. She was of another period . . . so attractive, the embodiment of youth, who literally shone down upon him as she stood beside him – rays of a hidden sun, as it were, emanating from her body, as she stood looking down at him. To me the effect was utterly strange, non-human, yet in appearance she was wholly human, with hair thick and beautiful. . . . I later learnt that I had seen and described to my companion, the second in the trio, one dead many years. That this vision of mine meant much to this old man who was lying down resting, oblivious of the visitor. She was of his early manhood, and there had been no other in his long life! . . . As she you will call the ghost appeared beside the aged man, I felt myself slipping, fading, passing into the sleep of trance. Oh! I was always afraid of losing control, of being banished. It meant I might unfit myself for my work in life, which was dear to me. So I struggled frantically to keep my hold on my self. I got back, but that meant the ghost disappeared (*108*).

Eileen J. GARRETT (1893–1970) was both

a remarkable medium and a gifted author and, through the Parapsychology Foundation which she founded and of which she was President, greatly influenced the research and educational growth of parapsychology. Mrs Garrett had psychical abilities since she was a child. They were developed under the direction of J. H. McKenzie (1869–1929) at the British College of Psychic Science. Mrs Garrett was a trance medium, though she also worked ·in the waking state. She convinced many people that she was communicating with the deceased, but was herself never certain about the identity of either her controls or the alleged IPAs. She spent the first part of her life in Ireland and England, and went to the United States in 1931 at the invitation of the American Society for Psychical Research. She participated in experiments at Duke University at the invitation of J. B. Rhine and William McDougall (1871–1938). McDougall was the first Chairman of the Department of Psychology and, with Rhine, founded the Duke Parapsychology Laboratory. Mrs Garrett was the subject in a series of experiments at Duke with J. G. Pratt which provided a major step in the methodology of testing mediums and in the statistical assessment of their responses.

Before coming to America, Mrs Garrett had produced an interesting series of messages connected with the crash of the R.101 airship. On several occasions Captain Hinchliffe, who had lost his life on a transatlantic flight, seemed to speak through Mrs Garrett predicting that the R.101 would crash. The warnings continued during the final flight of the airship. A few hours before the disaster Hinchliffe said at a seance: 'Storms rising. Nothing but a miracle can save them.'

Three days after the crash, deceased members of the R.101 crew seemingly began to communicate through Mrs Garrett, stating the circumstances leading up to the accident. The messages included technical information about the airship which Mrs Garrett apparently could not have known (25).

Like other mediums Mrs Garrett often used object association ('psychometry') as an aid in homing in on a distant person, be he living or dead (see OBJECT READING). In one such experiment conducted by Dr Lawrence LeShan, an American psychologist and parapsychologist, a piece cut from a shirt belonging to a missing person, a Dr B., was used. Dr B. had disappeared after attending a medical conference. At the beginning of the test Mrs Garrett was only told that it concerned a missing man and that his wife was upset and eager to discover his whereabouts.

After the first experiment (on 18 March 1966), which was done while Mrs Garrett was in trance, another object was used since her control had stated that the cloth '. . . does not have very much – only his anxiety,' and asked for an article such as a pipe or something else he usually carried around with him. In the next experiment (on 28 March) his pen, enclosed in packet, was used. The following is an excerpt from these experiments (283a).

Investigations of Haunted Houses with Mediums

Sometimes mediums help to investigate haunted houses. In 1965 Gertrude R. Schmeidler, Professor of Psychology at the City College of the City University of New York, conducted an investigation of a haunted

Selected Statements from the Transcripts

1966	Statements by Mrs Garrett	Comments by L. L. LeShan
No. 13 18 March	I think (that before he left) he has spoken much that he wanted to go to Mexico – is this so?	On this date, this information was not known to Mrs. B, the police, or me. However, after he returned (on April 8, 1966) Mrs. B found in his suitcase a fairly extensive correspondence discussing and planning his trip to Mexico. . . .
No. 16 18 March	I am sure he thought of going to California and then on to Mexico.	Correspondence described in No. 13 above shows he planned to go to California first and then to Mexico. (On this date, not known to Mrs. B, the police, or me. . . .)
No. 25 18 March	Going away was not without premeditation on his part.	As shown by correspondence described in No. 13, he had been planning this for at least 6 months. Also, 6 months before he had opened a special bank account (unknown to his wife) and withdrew all the money, turning it into traveler's checks, shortly before his disappearance. (Known to me on this date. Mrs. B had been notified by the bank on March 1 that the account had existed and on March 3 she told my wife about it.)
No. 55 28 March	I get the impression of someone who is in the middle 40's.	Dr. B's age was 42. (Not known to me at this date. However, I would probably have estimated his age to be in the 40's if I had thought about it.)
No. 57 28 March	A man who, as a youngster, was considered to be a prodigy.	On March 3 Mrs. B told my wife that he had been considered a prodigy as a child. (The fact was known to me on this date.)
No. 59 28 March and No. 60 28 March	Somewhere between the ages of 13 and 15, there was a loss in the family. I believe it was his father.	When he was 14 years old, his father deserted the family and was not heard of again for 25 years. (This was not known to me. . . .)
No. 67 28 March	(He is) about 5 feet 10.	He is 5 feet 9. (This was not known to me . . .)
No. 85 28 March	He has a good psychologist friend.	During Mrs. LeShan's visit to the B's home on March 3, she was introduced to a man, a psychologist, and his wife, by Mrs. B, who said, 'These are our closest friends.'
No. 92 28 March	I see him at La Jolla.	He spent nearly all the time of his disappearance, except when he was in Mexico, in La Jolla. His first letter home was mailed from there. (This 'hit' is a most unusual one. At the time this statement was made neither the police, Mrs. B, nor I had any idea where he was.)

Mrs Garrett

house in New York. She made a floor plan of the house, divided it into squares of 4 by 4 feet, and asked the family to mark the haunted places. She then obtained the co-operation of nine mediums. While the family was away, each medium was taken through the house by an assistant who did not know which areas were supposed to be haunted. The mediums were given an unmarked copy of the plan and asked to indicate the haunted parts. Their responses were compared with the family's by means of a standard statistical test. Two mediums gave statistically significant results. In addition, the family was asked to describe the personality of the 'ghost' by filling in a psychological checklist which the mediums also filled in. Four mediums had impressions of the ghost which corresponded with the family's.

Professor Schmeidler emphasized that it is not yet possible to choose decisively between three hypotheses: the family and mediums were influenced by common preconceptions about ghostly habitat or personality; the mediums responded by ESP to the family's impressions of their alleged ghost; they responded to a ghost.

The English medium, Douglas Johnson, who has often taken part in scientific experiments, has also helped in the study of haunted houses. One of them was located near Jacksonville, Florida, and was investigated in 1968–9 by two professors of engineering at Duke University, William T. Joines and John L. Artley, and by Miss Donna Cohen on behalf of the Psychical Research Foundation. The house belonged to a retired seaman aged seventy-three, Mr Cole (an assumed name). Mr Johnson was brought into the house without meeting Mr Cole or anyone else who had witnessed the phenomena or knew about them. Joines and Artley state in their report:

In the course of the two days we spent at the house, Mr. Johnson made three tours through it, always with a tape recorder. On the first, he was accompanied by Miss Cohen; during the second, she stayed in one room while Mr. Johnson examined the others. At both times they were alone in the house. On the third tour, he was accompanied by the three of us and Mr. Cole. Many of Mr. Johnson's statements could not be confirmed but none were in conflict with previous testimonies.

According to Mr. Johnson, a man named William, a blood relative of Mr. Cole, once lived in the house. He was described as a short man with a stubby beard, and Mr. Johnson felt he had some contact with the sea and something to do with music. Associated with this man, Mr. Johnson sensed heavy footsteps coming down the stairs. This description agreed with an earlier account by Mr. Cole of his father. Several [previous] witnesses had mentioned hearing footsteps on the stairs.

Mr. Johnson also had the impression of a crying teen-age girl whom he judged to be unhappy and afraid. A number of persons [had earlier] claimed they saw such a figure. In an upstairs bedroom, Mr. Johnson said he saw a grey-haired lady wearing old-fashioned clothes and a shawl. He received the impression of a pleasant personality and of the initial 'M.' This description matched Mr. Cole's account of an old lady he had known as a child, whose name was Agatha Murphy.

While alone in one of the rooms, Mr. Johnson said he heard voices and heavy breathing. He also felt a sensation of cold and saw a mass of light form in one corner. W.T.J. slept in this room on his first visit to the house. He woke up during the night and saw a light in a corner of the room, which he could not account for. In another room, also while alone, Mr. Johnson said he saw two oval patches of brownish light. J. L. A. saw an oval patch of light in the same room during his previous visit.

Mr. Johnson said that the house was built on the same site as another one. Mr. Cole also mentioned this during a previous visit.

While Miss Cohen was downstairs and Mr. Johnson upstairs, she heard the sound of moving furniture in an empty part of the house. Mr. Cole had said that such sounds often came from that area.

The unusual sounds heard by Mr. Johnson were picked up by the tape recorder and were therefore physical. None of the apparitional experiences were shared by us during this visit. The study reinforces the need for sensitive instruments to determine whether physical energies are responsible for the effects (249a).

Physical Mediums

D. D. Home (1833–86) was born in Scotland and went to America with an uncle and aunt when he was nine years old. Shortly after his mother died, poltergeist phenomena, including raps and movements of furniture, took place when he was near. When attempts to exorcize the supposed spirit failed, Home's aunt asked him to leave. He was then seventeen. Apparently Home was soon able to control the incidents, for already in 1851 he was known as a physical medium, a reputation he preserved until his death. In 1855 he left for England and from then on spent much of his life travelling in Europe displaying his abilities.

As a rule the room where Home performed was well illuminated. The manifestations usually began with raps and movements of the table. This, reportedly, would reach the state of LEVITATION with all four legs off the floor; musical instruments would play, light objects would move about and unseen hands would clasp the sitters and pull their clothes. Sometimes materialized hands were apparently seen. Occasionally the medium was levitated.

Perhaps the most striking incident was when Home allegedly floated out of an open window, perhaps forty feet above the ground, and entered the window of an adjoining room, 7 feet 6 inches from the first. Among those present were Lord Adare (who later became the Earl of Dunraven), the Master of Lindsay (later the Earl of Crawford), and Captain Wynne.

Sometimes Home gave messages purporting to come from the dead relatives and friends of those present and often showed acquaintance with facts that he should not normally have known. No evidence was ever found of trickery in his seances.

From the scientific point of view the most

Douglas Johnson

interesting observations were made by Sir William Crookes (1832–1919), the famous physicist who is best known as the discoverer of thallium. In psychical research his main interest was mediumship. He was President of the S.P.R. in 1896–9.

In an article published in the *Quarterly Journal of Science* in July 1871, Crookes described a simple apparatus he had built to test Home's supposed ability to cause changes in the weights of objects:

It consisted of a mahogany board 36 inches long by 9½ inches wide and 1 inch thick. At each end a strip of mahogany 1½ inches wide was screwed on, forming feet. One end of the board rested on a firm table, whilst the other end was supported by a spring balance hanging from a substantial tripod stand. The balance was fitted with a self-registering index, in such a manner that it would record the maximum weight indicated by the pointer. The apparatus was adjusted so that the mahogany board was horizontal, its foot resting flat on the support. In this position its weight was 3 lbs., as marked by the pointer of the balance.

Before Mr. Home entered the room the apparatus had been arranged in position, and he had not even the object of some parts of it explained before sitting down.... Mr. Home placed his finger lightly upon the extreme end of the mahogany board furthest from the balance, Dr. Huggins and Mr. Crookes sitting one on each side and watching; under these conditions the index of the balance moved several times, the greatest downward pull registered being 6 lbs. [i.e. the index showed a total weight of 9 lbs.]. It was particularly noticed, Mr. Crookes tells us, that Home's fingers were not at any time advanced more than 1½ inches from the extreme end of the board – that is, not outside the point of support – so that it was physically impossible for any pressure of his fingers to have produced the downward movements of the board shown by the index. Moreover, 'his feet as well as his hands were closely guarded by all in the room' (*368*).

Eusapia PALLADINO (1854–1918) was born in a small farming village in Italy. She was early left an orphan and she went to work as a laundress in Naples. The family she lived with conducted seances and these seemed to stimulate Eusapia's psychical abilities. The phenomena included raps, the appearance of lights, the twang of a guitar, movements of objects and levitations of a table. She was investigated by the **Italian physician and criminologist, Cesare Lombroso** (1836–1909), and by the French

Eusapia Palladino

physiologist, Charles Richet (1850–1935), a Nobel prize winner. Both became convinced that the phenomena were genuine. Experiments in England with F. W. H. Myers and others were less convincing to those present. In fact, there seemed no doubt that when the conditions were lax, Palladino took advantage of them to produce phenomena by simple trickery. However, when she was constrained so that she apparently could not interfere with the target objects, physical phenomena were again reported. To settle the matter regarding the genuineness of the phenomena, in 1908 the Society for Psychical Research appointed a committee to test her. It consisted of Everard Feilding, Hereward Carrington and W. W. Baggally.

Everard Feilding (1867–1936), the second son of the Earl of Denbigh, had investigated a number of physical mediums and exposed several as fraudulent. Hereward Carrington (1880–1958), who was born in Jersey but did most of his work in parapsychology in the United States, had similar experiences with physical mediums. He was an amateur magician as was also the third member of the group, W. W. Baggally. He too had a wide experience of physical mediums, as a result of which he had come to doubt whether genuine physical phenomena existed. Feilding similarly was sceptical of ever finding anything but trickery.

The three men conducted eleven experimental sessions in November and December 1908 in Naples (Baggally was absent for the first four). The experimental room was part of the living quarters of the investigators. It had a rectangular table set close to one of the corners of the room. This corner was partitioned off by a curtain to form a small cabinet. The medium sat at the end of the table

with her back to the cabinet. Usually two of the investigators would sit on either side of her, the third often facing her from the other side of the table. Inside the cabinet usually was a small table with several objects on it. The floor of the cabinet was made of tiles closely cemented together. One of the walls was of thick masonry and faced the street, the other was the wall to Baggally's bedroom. There were no doors or openings to the cabinet other than through the curtain. Occasionally, others took part in the tests, usually Italian investigators. The lights were dimmed but there was enough illumination to see the medium during the major occurrences.

During the eleven sessions, a total of 470 ostensibly paranormal phenomena were recorded, 305 of these when the arms and legs of the medium were observed or held by two of the members of the S.P.R. committee and 144 when she was controlled in this way by

Charles Richet

an S.P.R. member and another investigator. Among the incidents in the former group, on thirty-four occasions the table around which the investigators and the medium were sitting levitated completely from the floor. For instance, on one occasion, the table lifted off the ground, with all four legs off in full light, while Baggally and Carrington were watching the hands and legs (or rather long dress) of the medium and while Baggally had his right hand across her two knees. Fifty-nine times there were bulgings and movements of the curtains behind the medium, twenty-eight times objects within the cabinet moved, and forty-one times there were movements of objects – other than the table – outside the cabinet. Forty-two times the S.P.R. investigators were grasped or touched by a hand or some other tangible object either through the curtain or outside the curtain. Thus when Baggally was watching the medium's hands and was holding them separately in his hands, another hand, apparently a materialized one, grasped his arm and touched him in other places. Baggally ruled out the possibility that it might be the medium's foot that had grasped him in this way or that anyone else in the seance room had done it. He was 'driven to the conclusion (preposterous though it appears to me) that the supernormal force, which had given me conclusive evidence of its existence through the phenomena previously described, was able to produce the effects of tangible matter and assume the form of a hand' (148a).

Three times they actually saw a hand coming out from and then moving back into the cabinet. Five times they saw objects which looked like heads, again coming out and returning to the cabinet. At the end of the investigation, Feilding joined Carrington and Baggally in voicing the opinion that 'a large proportion of the manifestations of which we were the witnesses in Naples were clearly beyond the possibilities of any conceivable form of conjuring' (148a). However, when the conditions were lax, Eusapia Palladino would sometimes simulate the phenomena.

In 1909 Carrington took her to the United States and early the next year a series of experiments were held at Columbia University with members of the faculty attending as well as some experts in stage magic. Palladino produced phenomena under informal conditions but when controls were introduced the incidents fell off. Most of those attending did not think they had witnessed any genuine phenomena.

Fraudulent Mediums

It is not uncommon for physical mediums who on occasion produce seemingly genuine phenomena at other times to resort to trickery. The same is true of poltergeist agents (who can be regarded as temporary physical mediums; see POLTERGEISTS). Some physical mediums probably never use anything except conjuring and stage magic to create the ghostly shows which will attract the bereaved and credulous. Perhaps the most controversial of the physical mediums of the 20th century was the American medium known as Margery, whose real name was Mrs Mina Crandon. Apparently as a result of attending a seance, table-tilting phenomenon and raps began to occur in her presence. Later, her dead brother, Walter, seemed to communicate by direct voice. Moving lights and materialized forms were also reported including hands which rang

bells and even made thumb-prints on wax for all to see. The magazine *Scientific American* appointed a committee of five investigators, most of them well known in psychical research. In general they were dubious of the phenomena. One of the members of the *Scientific American* committee was the magician Harry Houdini, who declared Margery to be a fraud. But it was only in 1932 that clear evidence of this was found when Walter's thumb-prints turned out to belong to a Boston dentist who admitted making the impression for Mrs Grandon. He had not suspected the use to which they would be put.

In Mexico a physical medium, Luis Martinez, has been practising since 1933 and has attracted a wide following. W. G. Roll made an investigation of Martinez in 1964 and spoke to people who had witnessed the phenomena. One of these was General José Alvarez y Alvarez, a former Chief of Staff of the Mexican Army, who said he had once seen Martinez levitate in a heavy armchair and float about the room. Martinez is mainly known for the fully materialized forms which appear during his seances. Roll attended three of these conducted in an apartment in Mexico City. About fourteen persons crowded into a small room and seated themselves along three of the walls. In front of the fourth was Martinez's chair. During the sitting the room was in darkness and the sitters were instructed to hold hands to create psychic force. The medium was hypnotized by Mr Lopez, the owner of the apartment. Shortly afterwards faint lights appeared and moved around the room. One of the lights became a face and later a fully materialized form. There were about six of these at each sitting, appearing one at a time. Sometimes the forms were recognized by the sitters as their deceased relatives. Some of the apparitions administered psychic healing by passing their hands over the affected parts of the body of the sitter. The apparitions were covered in a sheetlike material. Some wore beards but otherwise looked similar and all were about 5 feet 3 inches tall. This was also the height of Mrs Lopez. Mrs Lopez was one of the sitters and occupied a chair at the end of a row, next to her sister-in-law. Roll speculated that she let go of her sister-in-law's hand and then dressed herself up as the apparitions. But he wanted to make certain that this was the explanation.

Roll had come equipped with camera and infra-red equipment for taking pictures in darkness but he could not obtain permission to use them. He was not able to take pictures unobserved because his hands were held. Roll did not want to cause a public exposure by interrupting the seance because this would have alienated him from the person who had

introduced him to Martinez and who was helping him to establish contact with other mediums in Mexico.

To discover the guilty person without disrupting the proceedings, Roll obtained a small jar-top, which he filled with toothpaste. Before the third session he placed this in his left shoe, where it fitted below the arch of the foot. At one time during the seance, a materialized form approached the person sitting next to Roll in order to administer psychic healing. Roll slipped his shoes off and dipped his right toe in the toothpaste. When the form was near enough Roll reached out with his foot attempting to mark the apparition's foot with the toothpaste. His foot hit something hard. After the sitting, Roll found a white smudge on one of the shoes of Mrs Lopez.

Rudi Schneider

Rudi SCHNEIDER (1908–57) and his older brother, Willi, are among the handful of physical mediums who have been seriously investigated. The Schneider brothers were born in Austria. The phenomena which surrounded them, first Willi and, when his powers waned, Rudi, were studied in the early 1920s by a German physician and psychical researcher, Baron Albert von Schrenck-Notzing (1862–1929). The experiments later involved the French physician and parapsychologist, Dr Eugène Osty (1874–1938), as well as British investigators. These experiments were generally conducted in darkness but Rudi was apparently under full control by the investigators when objects on a table moved and small materializations were observed, including a hand. Like other physical mediums, Rudi worked in trance. His 'control' called itself Olga.

Mrs Anita Gregory states in a survey of this work, in which her late husband C. C. L. Gregory, a British astronomer, participated:

Perhaps the most important and striking evidence produced during Rudi's career is that during three special investigations instrumental recordings were obtained of interference with infrared radiation by an 'invisible substance.' These observations were first made by Dr. Eugene Osty in Paris, who installed an infrared network surrounding the objects to be moved paranormally as an anti-fraud precaution: if anything such as a reaching device or a human arm approached the experimental table, it had first to cross the infrared beams, and as soon as this happened the system of alarm bells and/or photographic apparatus would come into action. It was found that at times during Rudi's trance the alarm system was indeed set in motion, but by no visible agency; the photographs taken at the time revealed that the infrared rays had been interrupted by, ostensibly, nothing. This interference was noted even in some sittings which were completely negative in all other respects. These interruptions of the network coincided with 'Olga's' announcements to the effect that 'she was going into the ray.' And such occultations of the rays preceded actual paranormal movements. These results were repeated in London by [Lords Charles] Hope and Rayleigh (*195a*).

Nina Kulagina is a housewife in Leningrad who can apparently cause small objects on a table in front of her to move. The experiments with her were begun by L. L. Vasiliev (1891–1966), a physiologist at Leningrad University who had also been doing research in ESP. In one of the recent studies the experimenters were Dr Genady A. Sergeiev of the Uktomskii Physiological Institute in Leningrad; Dr Zdenek Rejdak, a Czech philosopher and psychical researcher; and two Russians, B. Blazek and J. S. Zvierev, a psychologist and physician respectively.

In Rejdak's account of the experiment he said that he first examined the medium's body for concealed magnets, using a sensitive compass. The table and chair to be used were also examined. One of the tests was to cause a compass needle to spin. While Mrs Kulagina held her hand 2 to 4 inches over the compass, she succeeded in making the needle spin five to ten times on five different occasions during the tests. 'Then she moved the entire compass box on the table. Thereafter she moved a match box and some individual matches (both the box and the matches were the property of B. Blazek). She moved even a whole pile of about 20 matches at once. I

Meher Baba

put my gold ring on the table afterwards; its movements were the quickest of all the objects used. . . . I then selected some glass and china objects weighing up to 200 grams (seven ounces) from a sideboard. Without touching them, Kulagina made them move as well. On request, she carried out a whole series of tests with objects placed on a chair as well as on the floor. All this was performed in full light. According to the wishes of the experimenters, she was able to impart motion to objects both towards herself and in the opposite direction. I laid out matches in a circle, with a gap one or two cm. (less than an inch) between them and then pointed out one. She pushed it out of the circle without moving the other ones in the slightest.'

Dr Rejdak said that the tests seemed to exhaust Mrs Kulagina to the extent that her pulse became almost imperceptible and her muscular coordination deteriorated.

In another experiment supervised by Dr Sergeiev at his laboratory, studies were made of the medium's brain waves using an EEG (electro-encephalograph). Electro-cardiograph recordings were also made and the weight of the medium was measured. Zvierev noted that after thirty minutes of experimentation, Mrs Kulagina lost more than two pounds in weight. The EEG record indicated a strong emotional state and the electro-cardiograph showed arrhythmical heart beat. There was an unusually large amount of blood sugar in her blood. Her muscular co-ordination was again impaired. Rejdak noted that the measurements were similar to a stress alarm reaction (*392a*). Two American parapsychologists, Dr J. G. Pratt and Dr Montague Ullman have also observed the phenomena but only under informal conditions. W. G. R.

(See also SPIRITUALISM.) (Further reading: see references in the text.)

Meher Baba (1894-1969)

Meher Baba was born in Poona, India, of Persian parents belonging to the Zoroastrian faith. His name originally was Merwan

Sheriar Irani, but he adopted that of Meher Baba ('Compassionate Father') after having a revelation as a young man that he was destined to carry out a holy mission. In 1922 he began to train disciples and in 1924 established a headquarters near Bombay. His purpose was not, he said, to start a new religion but to 'revitalise all religions and cults and to bring them together like beads on a string'. In 1925 he took a vow of silence and, until shortly before his death, communicated by pointing at an alphabet board. He still has many followers throughout the world. C. M. (Further reading: *349*.)

Franz Anton Mesmer (c.1734-1815)

The founder of mesmerism and coiner of the term 'animal magnetism': see FAITH HEALING; HYPNOSIS.

Mind over Matter See PARAPSYCHOLOGY; PSYCHOKINESIS.

Morya

One of the principal MASTERS of the THEOSOPHICAL SOCIETY.

William Stainton Moses (1839-92)

A Church of England clergyman who received numerous communications by automatic writing from a group of spirits headed by 'Imperator', many of which were published in his book *Spirit Teachings*, 1883, a work known as the 'Spiritualists' Bible'. Other phenomena attributed to him include APPORTS, LEVITATION, TELEKINESIS, and mysterious lights, sounds and scents. He founded the journal *Light* and from 1884 till his death was President of the London Spiritualist Alliance. After his death, he and the 'Imperator' group purportedly communicated through Mrs PIPER. (*176*)

Motor Automatisms See AUTOMATISMS; CONSCIOUSNESS.

Winifred Moyes (d.1957)

A British trance medium who received communications purportedly from 'Zodiac', a spirit who claimed to be the scribe referred to in Mark xii, 28–34. The dissemination of Zodiac's teachings was one of the objects of the Greater World Christian Spiritualist League, founded in 1951.

Mu

A supposedly lost continent in the Pacific: see LEMURIA.

Muladhara See CHAKRAS.

Sylvan Muldoon

An American 'astral traveller', co-author

with Hereward Carrington of *The Projection of the Astral Body*, 1929, which describes his experiences and techniques. (*340*)

Bridey Murphy Case

The case reported by Morey Bernstein in *The Search for Bridey Murphy*, 1956, of a woman who, under hypnosis, was apparently able to remember her previous life as 'Bridey Murphy' in Ireland in the 19th century. In this previous existence she was supposed to have been born at Cork in 1798 and to have died in Belfast at the age of sixty-six: see HYPNOSIS; REINCARNATION. (*37*)

Margaret A. Murray (d. 1963)

The British Egyptologist and anthropologist who advanced the theory that witchcraft in Europe in the period of the great persecutions was an organized religion, the old pagan and pre-Christian religion of Europe, preserving the worship of the great mother goddess and the divine king, the incarnate god who at certain intervals was sacrificed for the good of his land and people. This brilliant and ingenious theory has been rejected by most scholars, but has made a powerful appeal to numerous readers and, in particular, has had a vital influence on the modern WITCHCRAFT movement. (*343, 344, 345, 508*)

Mysteria Mystica Aeterna

An irregular Masonic lodge, founded by Rudolf STEINER; see GERMAN OCCULT GROUPS; ROSICRUCIANS.

Mysteria Mystica Maxima

A magical Order, a subsidiary of the O.T.O. in England, founded in 1912 with Aleister CROWLEY at its head.

Mystery Religions

A number of ancient religious cults reserved a part of their teachings for disclosure to a select few, who were taught certain secret doctrines and initiated after prescribed ritual observances. These teachings and observances constituted the 'mysteries', a term derived from the Greek word *mysterion*, meaning private or secret rites. The mysteries arose from the belief that certain higher doctrines and spiritual experiences were not within the intellectual capacity or spiritual competence of everyone, and that only those endowed by nature and prepared by discipline to receive such knowledge could benefit by what was revealed. The mysteries formed, as it were, a private sanctum adjacent to the traditional religious structure. Side by side with popular worship of the deities, there was carried out a secret exercise in which the privileged few participated.

The ancient Greeks used to distinguish three kinds of knowledge: *mathesis*, or learnable knowledge; *gnosis*, meditative or intuitive perception; and *pathesis*, felt or suffered knowledge. The mysteries aimed at enlightenment through all three kinds, but particularly through the last named, by providing the candidate with the opportunity for personal experience of the higher teachings. Some of the mysteries had two broad grades: the exoteric or outer grade, in which the populace could participate, and the esoteric or inner grade, for the select few.

Prospective initiates were committed to the strictest secrecy. What was disclosed could never be revealed, for this would dissipate its power, vulgarize its content, and expose its sublime truths to contempt. Secrecy put a mystic circle around the rite, and within this magic enclosure the tensions of power were built up. The mysteries were taken very seriously. Alcibiades (*c.* 415 B.C.), a popular Greek hero and the idol of Athens, lost his popularity because once in a drunken moment he had spoken disrespectfully of the mysteries. No one has ever betrayed the mysteries. The oath of secrecy was most rigidly respected, even by Christians who had been initiated before their conversion, so much so that although the major mysteries were practised for nearly two thousand years, we know nothing about any of the crucial phases of the ceremonies. What we do know has been arrived at piecemeal, and the parts do not always fit, much being based on conjecture. There is a story told of a certain man who happened to dream part of the mysteries and his dream was found to be so close to the truth that he had to be promptly initiated in order that he might remain silent about it.

Among the earliest of the mystery religions was that associated with the death and dismemberment of the Egyptian god Osiris, and the search for his scattered remains by his sorrowing sister-wife Isis. His resurrection formed the nucleus of a cult that had an almost universal following in ancient Egypt. The public ceremonies included a phallic element, for the virile member of the god, symbolizing the life-giving principle, was accorded special veneration, when the image of the god was taken out in procession and his large phallus mechanically raised and lowered at intervals. The worship of Isis and Osiris was already well established by 2400 B.C., and when the Greeks first began to be acquainted with it in the 6th century B.C. it was regarded as being of immemorial antiquity. The cult was still a source of inspiration in the 2nd century A.D., for the Latin writer Apuleius wrote about his initiation into the rites in rapturous terms, in his book *The Golden Ass*.

The Mysteries of Eleusis

Probably the most famous of these cults were the Eleusinian mysteries. Eleusis was a place about 14 miles west of Athens which had been in use for ritual purposes since the 15th century B.C. by the predecessors of the Hellenic Greeks in the peninsula. The mysteries' origins have been traced back to Egypt, which provided the pattern for most of the mystery religions of the ancient Mediterranean world. During the historical period the Eleusinian mysteries absorbed a number of local cults and combined them into two main cycles, centred around the legend of the rape of Kore (Persephone) by Pluto, god of the underworld, and the search for her by her mother Demeter.

The lesser Eleusinian rites were celebrated in early spring when the crops were ripening. Few facts are available about this first stage of initiation, except that it was held in Agrai, a suburb of Athens. The greater mysteries, which were a matter of national importance, began six months later at the end of September and lasted for fourteen days, during which time all interstate hostilities ceased. For long only those Greeks who could speak Greek and had not been deprived of their civil rights were admitted to the mysteries. Candidates were given instruction by sponsors called mystagogues, and prepared themselves by abstaining from flesh, fowl, fish, eggs, garlic, beans, and pomegranates. They refrained from sexual intercourse, and largely from speech.

Two days before the autumn full moon they took part in a procession of people who went to Eleusis, and returned carrying objects concealed in a basket or chest, which they ceremoniously laid in a sanctuary in Athens. This rite was called *arretophoria*, 'carrying things not to be spoken of'. Since mention of these things was strictly tabooed, it is not known what they were. Various authorities have speculated that they were live snakes, pine or fir cones, ears of corn, small figures of the goddesses Demeter and Kore, or a replica of the male member or the female vulva or the two in union. They were regarded as symbolizing one of the keys to the mysteries and believed to have a profound mystical significance.

Two days later the candidates proceeded to the sea, each person taking with him a piglet which he washed on the beach, and he then bathed in the sea himself. The pigs were sacrificed and the blood was sprinkled on the candidate. The next important episode was a march from Athens back to Eleusis, when the sacred objects were reverently restored to the mother temple, and the last phase took place in the Hall of Initiation at Eleusis. This initiation was known as the

Mystery Religions

telete, 'completing', and was performed in the interior of the temple of Demeter and conducted by a high priestly official known as the hierophant, or 'revealer of sacred things'. Here again, little is known of what actually transpired and speculation is rife. It would appear, however, that the full paraphernalia of secret societies was brought into operation. There were passwords, secret tokens, a dramatic representation illustrating the highlights of the Demeter myth, a night-long vigil and a final revelation, in some of which the candidate himself took part. It was said that the initiate had not to learn but to experience, and the mysteries were not only explained to him, but acted out by him. They were connected with a sacred marriage, with the secrets of generation, or with the growth of corn. A sacramental meal of bread and wine brought the ceremonies to a close.

Dionysus and Serapis

Somewhat different in character were the mysteries of Dionysus, which were amongst the wildest in the Greek world. There was an earlier Dionysia, of which only reminiscences were preserved in the later, more tempered versions, but details of some of the ancient rites can be seen on Greek vases. It was originally a female cult, whose votaries were known variously as *maenads*, 'raving' women; *bassarides*, 'fox-bitches'; *potniades*, 'inebriates'; *thyiades*, 'excited' women; and *bacchantes*, followers of Bacchus, a revelling, drunken version of Dionysus popularized in Rome. The male followers were the *sileni* or satyrs, personifications of male lust, shown with erect phalluses and armed with whips, with which they flagellated the bare buttocks of the frenzied fleeing maenads whom they overtook and ravished. The celebrations included orgiastic revels to the accompaniment of wild Phrygian music, and the rite of *sparagmos*, in which a living animal, usually a goat or sheep, was rent with the bare hands and teeth by the participants, and the raw flesh devoured. There were also representations in dramatic form of the terrors of life in the underworld, and a strange, unexplained 'masque of phantoms'.

In the 3rd century B.C. Ptolemy I, the Hellene Pharaoh of Egypt, created his own mystery religion. In pursuit of his ambition to weld the Egyptian inhabitants and the Greek settlers in Egypt into a single nation, he conceived the idea of a common unifying cult. To this end he called to his assistance Manetho, an Egyptian priest and historian, and Timotheus, a Greek from the family of hierophants at Eleusis, and founded the cult of Serapis, the 'only god successfully

Isis, goddess of the Egyptian mysteries

made by modern man', complete with its mysteries for the appointed few. The origin of the god's name is uncertain, but it is generally thought to be derived from the composite name Usire-Hapi, Egyptian for Osiris, the saviour-god, and Apis the god of the Nile. A huge temple was built for Serapis in Alexandria and initiations involved oaths, cult-meals, and ceremonies connected with growth, fertility and the afterlife. It remained the established cult of the Ptolemies and flourished till the 4th century of the Christian era. In A.D. 385 the emperor Theodosius, in an attempt to stamp out paganism, banned the worship of Serapis, and six years later a fanatical patriarch, Theophilus, instigated a mob to break into the temple and destroy the god's shrine. The magnificent statue of Serapis was decapitated, dragged through the streets of Alexandria and hacked to pieces.

Mithras and the Bull

Perhaps the most widespread of the mystery religions, extending from the Crimea to Britain, was Mithraism. Mithras (see plate, pages 162–3) was a Persian deity of light, and an ally of Ahura Mazda, the principle of good in the universe, in his struggle against Ahriman, the principle of evil. The high point of Mithras's earthly career was the slaying of a great bull, and around this event the mystery of Mithraism revolved. The candidate underwent a long period of preparation, when his courage and fitness to participate in the mysteries were put to the test in various ways. A strict undertaking of secrecy was imposed and the candidate swore to guard with his life the rites that were to be revealed to him.

There followed a few days abstinence from food and sexual relations, then a ceremonial ablution, after which the candidate's hands were bound behind his back and he was laid on the ground as if dead. After certain solemn rites his right hand was grasped by the hierophant and he was raised up. Then followed the baptism of blood. He was made to stand naked in a pit covered with a grating, and over this an animal was sacrificed, so that its blood flowed over him. Whatever the animal was, it was regarded as a surrogate of the bull of Mithras. Prudentius (d. A.D. 390), a Christian poet writing in Latin, gives a vivid description of this rite, of which he may have had a personal recollection. 'Through the open grating the bloody dew flows into the pit; the neophyte receives the falling drops on his head and body, he leans back so that his cheeks, lips and nostrils are wetted; he pours the liquid over his eyes and does not even spare his mouth, for he moistens his tongue with blood and sips it eagerly.'

Symbolically the initiate has been raised from the dead and washed in the vitalizing blood of the bull, and is regarded as 'born again unto eternity'. He is received into the community of initiates as a brother, and is allowed to participate in the sacramental meal of bread and wine which establishes his status as one of the elect. The complete doctrine of mystic redemption and service was revealed to him in seven successive grades of initiation, from that of Raven to that of Father, but from the beginning he was one of the Brotherhood.

The Enigma of Death

All mysteries are an overflow of the religious instinct. They promise a transcendent experience of the numinous, the feeling of awe and reverence in the presence of the unknown. In a sense, therefore, mysteries are universal. In the Mediterranean region they grew up in association with most of the major, and several minor, deities. In the early post-Christian period the Gnostics took over the pagan tradition and created a prolific brood of minor mysteries which combined old pagan cults with Christianity (see GNOSTICISM). Modern scholars, not always with much supporting testimony, find evidence of mysteries among the Celts (the Druidic mysteries), the Norse peoples (as of Odin), in Asia Minor (the Cabiri), in Persia (Manicheism), and even in Pre-Columban America (the Xibalba mysteries of Guatemala). Most pre-literate peoples have a naturally built-in system of mysteries that forms part of the spiritual transit, by means of magical ceremonies, to a new status for the candidate in the community. Even the witches' sabbat has overtones of a mystery religion of sorts (see WITCHCRAFT).

Every secret society is a confraternity elaborated around a mystery, which, when accompanied by quasi-religious rites, assumes the dignity of a mystery religion. Freemasonry invokes the Grand Architect of the Universe, has passwords, grips, steps, oaths, and a kind of communal meal, the 'festive board'. There is also a solemn ceremony of 'raising', in which the candidate is symbolically slain in commemoration of an ancient prototype, 'our Master, Hiram Abiff', the principal architect of King Solomon's temple, and then by a special grip raised from the grave in which he has been interred.

The significance of the mysteries has been variously expounded. In the Eleusinian mysteries the agricultural motif predominates; in the Orphic the notion of immortality. Others are reminiscent of the annual 'return' of the sun after the long winter, the seasonal breeding of animals, and the psychic changes that seem to come over man and nature at the solstices and equinoxes. But while all these may have contributed their quota to the development of the mysteries, they were not basic to them. There was hardly any need to perpetuate the secrets of sex and agriculture when knowledge of them was already commonplace in the civilized world. The hierophant made no extraordinary disclosure when he held up for the candidate's inspection a stone phallus in union with a vulva, or a sheaf of freshly-harvested corn. What was fundamental to all the mysteries, without exception, was the revelation of the enigma of death, and its triumphal overcoming.

Thus, while on the surface the lowering and raising of the phallus of Osiris might suggest a fertility festival, the mysteries connected with that deity and his spouse Isis were essentially a triumph over death through the rising to life eternal. Even the riotous Bacchanalia included a presentation in dramatic form of the terrors of the afterlife, a *memento mori*, a reminder of death, like the mummy presiding at an Egyptian feast. The vessels of wine from which the participants in the Dionysia filled their cups were originally jars which contained the ashes of the dead, and the ceremonial opening of these jars was meant to release the spirits so that they might join in the festivities. On the last day of the rites, seeds were cooked and laid out for the god Hermes, the *psychopomp*, as he was termed, who conducted the dead back to the underworld. The mysteries that still exist in primitive societies are concerned with initiation into the tribal myth, and the duties of girls and boys as adult members of their community, but they all have one common feature, a ritual death and resurrection.

Death is never commonplace. It is the one unrepeatable experience, the final encounter that faces every man, and the mystery religion was a dramatic experience designed as a rehearsal for death. The *ars moriendi*, the art of dying, was embodied in religious traditions the world over. Death, the most awesome of the mysteries of existence, started man on the road to all the mystery religions.

There are several references to the mysteries in the New Testament, and some of them suggest a parallel with Greek usage. This is confirmed by St Paul's ecstatic declaration, in which he underlines the true purpose of all mysteries, beneath the tangle of rites connected with seedtime and harvest, with the cycle of the seasons, with the ecstasy of sex, with fertility and the phallus – that of death and resurrection. 'Behold,' he exclaims, 'I show you a mystery . . . For this corruptible must put on incorruption, and this mortal must put on immortality' (I Cor. xv, 51, 53). B. W.

(Further reading: *5, 77, 109, 191, 347, 354, 476*.)

N

Victor Neuberg (1883-1940)

A British poet and critic who was an ardent disciple of Aleister CROWLEY and his partner in various magical operations, including the homosexual 'Paris Working' (see RITUAL MAGIC). Crowley said of him, in his *Confessions*, 'He was an agnostic, a vegetarian, a mystic, a Tolstoyan, and several other things all at once. He endeavoured to express his spiritual state by wearing the green star of Esperanto, though he could not speak the language; by refusing to wear a hat, even in London, to wash, and to wear trousers. Whenever addressed, he wriggled convulsively, and his lips, which were three times too large for him, and had been put on hastily as an afterthought, emitted the most extraordinary laugh that has ever come my way; to these advantages he united those of being extraordinarily well read, overflowing with exquisitely subtle humour, and being one of the best-natured people that ever trod this planet.' He also had 'an altogether extraordinary capacity for Magick', though suffering from a leaking AURA which rendered him liable at any moment to 'become possessed of the devil': for his adventures on the astral plane, see ASTRAL BODY; for his 'possession' by the god Mars, see TRANCE. (*100, 167, 446*)

Teresa Neumann (1898-1962)

The celebrated stigmatic born at Konnersreuth in Germany, where she lived all her life. She became bedridden after an accident to her back in 1918, recovering in 1925 after praying to St Teresa of Lisieux. In the following year, in Lent, she saw visions of Christ's Passion and received the STIGMATA, the wounds suffered by Christ on the cross. For several years she appeared to have a vision of the Passion each week. She went into TRANCE, the wounds in her hands, feet and side bled, and she also bled from the forehead, as if she wore the Crown of Thorns. She appeared to exist on little or nothing to eat. Crowds of people flocked to see her in the 1920s and '30s, though the Roman Catholic Church treated her phenomena with cautious reserve. (*81, 187, 428*)

Hugh George de Willmott Newman

Mar Georgius I, Patriarch of Glastonbury, Prince of Saxe-Noricum, founder of the Catholicate of the West: see WANDERING BISHOPS.

New Templars See GERMAN OCCULT GROUPS; LANZ VON LIEBENFELS.

New Thought

The general term for a modern movement which has spread from the United States to other parts of the world and which is centrally concerned with the power of thought, the principle that 'as a man thinks, so he is', and with the 'power of constructive thinking', especially in healing disease. The movement derives from mesmerism (see FAITH HEALING; HYPNOSIS) and has been influenced by the ideas of the New England TRANSCENDENTAL MOVEMENT and, in particular, by the theories of P. P. QUIMBY. The International New Thought Alliance has summarized its goals as: 'To teach the Infinitude of the Supreme One; the Divinity of man and his infinite possibilities through the creative power of constructive thinking and obedience to the voice of the indwelling Presence, which is our source of Inspiration, Power, Health and Prosperity.'

Harold Percival Nicholson (d. 1968)

The founder of the British Ancient Catholic Church: see WANDERING BISHOPS.

Nostradamus (1503-66)

Michel de Nostredame, more commonly known under his latinized name of Nostradamus, was born in St Rémy de Provence. Although most commentators claim for him an illustrious descent from doctors at the court of Anjou, in fact his family came from the Avignon district. His Jewish grandfather, Pierre, was a grain dealer who married a Gentile girl. Their son Jacques, Nostradamus's father, married Reynière de St Rémy, the daughter of an ex-doctor turned tax-collector. By the time Nostradamus was nine years old, the family are listed as being converted to the Christian faith. The child's ability became apparent early on and he was educated by his maternal grandfather. The influence of their Jewish traditions upon Nostradamus should not be underestimated. He was taught Hebrew, Latin, Greek, mathematics, astrology and medicine. Then he was sent away to study at Avignon, where his interest in astrology caused comment. This worried his parents who, as ex-Jews, were still sensitive to the Court of Inquisition at Toulouse, and in 1522 he was sent to Montpellier University to take up the study of medicine.

Nostradamus obtained his degree with ease and, once he had his licence to practice, travelled widely, working among the victims of the plague then endemic in southern France. He seems to have had great curative powers; his solicitude towards the sick and his generosity to the poor were never questioned, even by the most vehement of his detractors. Some of the remedies he used are to be found in the definitive version of his book *Excellent et Tres-utile Opuscule* published in 1572, after his death: see also his *Traité Des Fardemens*, 1552.

In 1529 Nostradamus returned to Montpellier to complete his doctorate. He became unpopular among the faculty for his unorthodox methods, but his ability could not be denied and his doctorate was granted. Then he travelled again across France and at Agen chanced to meet Julius César Scaliger (1484–1558), a philosopher ranked by many in Europe second only to Erasmus (1446–1536). Scaliger held Nostradamus in high regard as both a philosopher and a physician and this should be remembered when one is faced with the problem of evaluating *Les Prophéties*. Almost certainly Scaliger introduced Nostradamus to the rewards of prophecy; he himself had been a pupil of the famous Italian astrologer Luca Gaurico (1476–1558). Having settled down, Nostradamus married a 'beautiful and admirable girl of high estate', but the idyll was short lived. The plague struck Agen and all Nostradamus's family. Their deaths had a disastrous effect upon his practice. At the same time he and Scaliger quarrelled and Nostradamus took to the road again, probably after he learned that the Inquisition at Toulouse wanted to interview him about his relations with a Huguenot teacher, Philibert Sarazin, a friend of Scaliger.

This next period of his life is badly documented. He apparently travelled around Europe and stayed in Venice and Sicily. About this time, in the 1540s, verbal references to Nostradamus's prophetic powers began to circulate. Between 1551 and 1555 he translated into French a book which indicates that his thoughts were veering towards the occult, *Orus Apollo, roi d'Aegipte*. Then followed the first part of the *Excellent et Tres-utile Opuscule*, which appeared as the *Traité des Fardemens* at Lyons in 1552. The book consisted mainly of beauty recipes gathered on his travels. In 1547 Nostradamus finally settled at Salon en Craux de Provence, and remained there until his death. In that year he married a rich widow, Anne Ponsart Gemelle, who bore him six children.

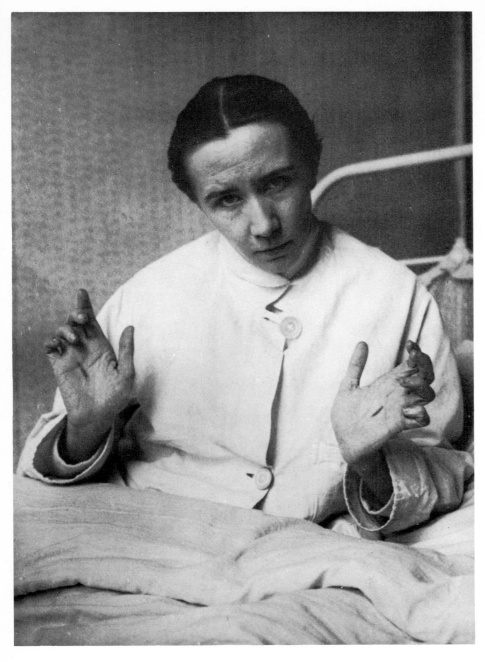

Teresa Neumann

place in 1559. Fortunately, Nostradamus managed to explain the quatrain satisfactorily, and the Queen then ordered him to draw up the horoscopes of all the Valois children, on whose tragic fates he had also touched. Another similar quatrain seems to have been recognized by courtiers during this period (X. 39) which referred to the fates of Francis II and Mary Queen of Scots.

Nostradamus returned as soon as possible to the quiet life of Salon, having found court life rather precarious and worried by the interest the Justices de Paris had taken in his activities. He continued working as a doctor and in 1557 his only medical and philosophical work was printed at Lyons, a translation into French, the *Paraphrase de C. Galen.* Nostradamus remained in Salon until 1564, when he was visited by the Queen and her second son, Charles IX, and was created Médecin du Roi. This was the final accolade. By 1566, already ill with gout, Nostradamus developed dropsy. He recognized his approaching death and predicted where his friends would find his body. He died on the night of 1 July and was buried in the walls of the Church of Cordeliers at Salon. During the French Revolution his bones were disturbed and then reburied in the Church of St Laurent, also at Salon, where the plaque donated by his wife Anne can still be seen.

The popularity of Nostradamus's *Prophéties* is perhaps difficult to understand when one considers their obscure style, but this same quality does allow for varied interpretations. Nostradamus wrote that he composed the quatrains in a trance-like state (see I. 1 and 2), gazing into a bowl of water on a tripod, an old method of prediction probably taken from the 4th-century *De Mysteriis Egyptorum* of Iamblichus. He appeared to both see and hear the 'Divine Presence' who inspired him as he wrote the quatrains at night in his study.

The most famous of the predictions are those which are easily recognized either through events (*Le Senat à Londres mettront à mort leur roy*, 'The London Parliament will put their king to death') or linked names of people and places, sometimes even a date. In these 'easier' quatrains one can read of Louis XVI's flight to Varennes (IX. 20), of Nostradamus's amazing comprehension of the French Revolution, of the accession of an Emperor called Napoloron (VII. 1, 57) linked with his crest of bees (IV. 26); and to these may be added the Hister or Hitler quatrains. This hard core of prediction is difficult for even the most rational person to ignore completely. Nostradamus probably owes his bad reputation to the complexity of the more obscure quatrains.

The Prophecies

From 1551 onwards Nostradamus published yearly *Almanacs* and *Prognostications*, some of which have survived. They predict local happenings, agricultural and weather lore, and similar topics. But a large number of similar almanacs forged in his name soon flooded the market. His reputation suffered greatly from these spurious publications.

In May 1555 his major work went to press, *Les Prophéties de M. Michel Nostradamus.* This edition was incomplete, containing only three and a half 'centuries'. The complete work did not appear until 1568, published at Lyons by Benoist Rigaud. The *Prophéties* were divided into ten *Centaines*, not chrono-

logical centuries, but so called because each contained one hundred individual prophecies, known as quatrains, collected together in no apparent sequence. The style is crabbed and obscure, archaic even for its period. The vocabulary is a polyglot mixture of French, Provençal, Romance, Greek and Latin words and their derivatives. The obscurity was deliberate. Nostradamus intended it to camouflage his secrets so that they could be understood only by the initiated.

Nostradamus's fame had by now spread across Europe. The year after his publication of the *Prophéties* he was sent for by the Queen at Paris. Catherine de' Medici had read a quatrain (I. 35) which many believed applied to the death of her husband Henri II in a forthcoming duel, which actually did take

Nostradamus

Nostradamus was frequently used for propaganda purposes; as early as 1649 by the anti-Mazarin faction in France, and as late as the Second World War. Selected quatrains were interpreted for the Nazis by the Swiss astrologer Karl Ernst KRAFFT, who was employed in the Propaganda Department at Berlin. Nazi Germany needed prophecy to order, not the inspirational kind. In 1940 Krafft's researches were used by the Germans who wanted to clear the Paris roads as they crossed into France from Sédan. Pamphlets of altered quatrains were circulated indicating that south-eastern France would not be troubled by the war, causing civilians and refugees to flee south and thus emptying the roads to the Channel Ports. In retaliation, British Intelligence arranged for the R.A.F. to drop booklets of Nostra-

damus's quatrains, purportedly published in Germany, over the occupied countries: they indicated that Germany would lose the war, and were not ineffective as propaganda.

The *Prophéties* appears to be one of the few books which have been continually in print since 1555. Whether Nostradamus was a genuine prophet may be in some doubt, but the interest he has aroused through the centuries is beyond question. E. C.

(Further reading: *88, 234, 274.*)

Numerology

At its popular level numerology is an entertaining and comparatively simple method of analysing character and predicting the future, in broad and vague terms at least. At a deeper level it is claimed to be one of the major keys to an understanding of the true nature of the universe and it plays an important part in magic and occultism. Like other systems of

DIVINATION, it finds order and regularity behind the bewildering multiplicity of phenomena and the confusing muddle of events and influences that confront us in the world outside us and in ourselves. Numbers make a good basis for such a system because they themselves are infinitely numerous and varied – corresponding to the phenomena of the universe – and yet are also logical and obey orderly rules, so that a pattern can be discerned behind apparent chaos. Western numerology, in fact, is based on the Pythagorean principle that reality is mathematical, that ultimately all things *are* numbers.

This means that each person's character and destiny can be expressed in numbers, which is one of the two main principles on which popular numerology is based. The other is the old magical principle that the name of a person (or of anything else) contains his essential reality. Your name, on this theory, is not a mere label hung on you as if you were a piece of luggage. Your name is your identity, it shows who you really are. The numerologist turns your name into a number, or several numbers, and analyses your personality by interpreting the numbers in the light of traditional rules.

Each letter of the alphabet is allotted a number. There are two systems of doing this. In one the numbers from 1 to 9 are written down and the letters of the alphabet are written underneath in their normal order, so that A is 1, B is 2, C is 3, I is 9, J is 1 again, and so on. The other system, which is employed here, uses the numbers from 1 to 8 and does not list the letters in the usual order:

1	2	3	4	5	6	7	8
A	B	C	D	E	U	O	F
I	K	G	M	H	V	Z	P
Q	R	L	T	N	W		
J		S					X
Y							

This system is based on the Hebrew alphabet, in which the letters also stood for numbers. A is 1 because the Hebrew letter *aleph* stood for 1, B is 2 because *beth* stood for 2, G is 3 because *gimel* stood for 3, and so on. Zeros are disregarded so that M (*mem* – 40) is 4, and so is T (*tau* – 400). Number equivalents for letters which are not in the Hebrew alphabet are taken from the Greek alphabet, in which the letters also did double duty as numbers. There is no 9 in the table because the Hebrew letters standing for 9, 90 and 900 have no equivalents in our alphabet.

To find the number of your name, write it down and turn each letter into a number. Then add the numbers. If the total has two or more figures, add them together and continue until you reach a single figure. For example:

WILLIAM F. MEREDITH

$6+1+3+3+1+1+4$ $+8$ $+4+5+2+5+4+1+4+5$ $= 57$

$$5+7 = 12$$
$$1+2 = 3$$

At this point complications begin. The number of the name William F. Meredith is 3, but the number of William Francis Meredith, spelled out in full, is 9. The number of Billy Meredith is 4. Numerologists say that you should begin by writing down the name by which you normally think of yourself, which is likely to come closest to the real you, but other variants of your name can be considered. The full name, given at birth, is especially likely to indicate the influence of fate or the mysterious governing forces of the universe. Nicknames and other names reveal the impression which you make on those who use them. A woman's maiden name shows her character before she married; her married name shows how marriage has affected her.

Other numbers can also be extracted from your name in confusing profusion. If you take the total of the vowels alone, this is called the Heart Number and is said to reveal your inner self, the person you are at heart. The total of the consonants alone is the Personality Number and reveals your outer self, the shell of outward characteristics and mannerisms in which your inward self lies hidden. (Y is treated as a vowel if there are no other vowels in the word, otherwise it is a consonant.) This distinction again goes back to written Hebrew, in which no vowels were written down, only consonants. Because the vowels were concealed in written Hebrew, their total shows your hidden, inner self. The total of the consonants, which were written down for all to see, relates to your outer, revealed personality.

Another number of importance to numerologists, the Birth Number, is found by adding up your date of birth. For example, if you were born on 19 September 1935, your birth number is 1, as follows: $1+9+9+1+9+3+5 = 37 = 10 = 1$.

This number is said to indicate the stamp which the guiding forces of the universe impressed on your character and fortune at birth, which will affect you for good or ill all your life and which may or may not harmonize with the number of your name: if it does not, you are likely to be torn by inner conflicts and to be always struggling against fate. By adding your day and month of birth to any given year of your life you can find your Personal Year Number. For instance, if your birthday is 12 August, then 1974 will be a 5-year for you, a time of change, experiment and, probably, a hectic love-life. But 1975 will be a 6-year, which should be a more settled, domestic, peaceable period.

For thorough analysis, numerologists recommend going through the name letter by letter, to see how many times each number appears and whether any number is missing. If a number is missing from your name, you will lack the qualities of that number and this is a disadvantage which you must try to overcome if you are to have a happy and fruitful life. On the other hand, if one number appears too many times, your personality will contain an excessive concentration of the qualities of that number.

The Numbers and Personality

People whose names add to *one* are said to be powerful and dominating personalities, unbending, unyielding, of fixed purpose and unswerving drive. Highly individualistic and self-centred, assertive and self-reliant, they make inspiring leaders and commanders but difficult subordinates. They create, originate and pioneer, and make effective organizers, inventors, designers, planners, engineers and technicians. Aggressive and ambitious, they are people who make things happen. They rarely experience close relationships with others and, though generous to those who support them, they are ruthless opponents. They can be tyrannical, vengeful and cruel, and are likely to be opinionated and quick-tempered, but their constructive potential is massive. Similarly, a year which adds to 1 is said to be a time of constructive activity, new beginnings and discoveries.

By contrast, those whose names add to *two* are followers rather than leaders, passive rather than active. They have a set of characteristics traditionally regarded as feminine, being charming, docile, attractive, intuitive, conciliatory, sweet and gentle, ministering angels and soothers of fevered brows. They get their way by persuasion, cooperation, tact and diplomacy, and a 2-year is a time of peace and quiet, reconciliation, harmony and gentle process. Two-people make useful subordinates as they are conscientious, sympathetic, modest, tidy and good at routine. They tend to be shy, indecisive, insecure and uncertain of themselves. There may also be a dark, deceitful, malicious and sinister side to them, for 2 is not only the number of woman but also of evil and the Devil.

Three is an extremely fortunate number, implying creative energy, brilliance, liveliness, versatility, glamour, and a natural attraction for both money and the opposite sex. People whose number this is are likely to

be highly talented and to have a gift for self-expression. Talkative, witty, charming, they succeed with ease and apparently almost without trying. They love pleasure, like to be the centre of attention and are anxious for constant applause and approval. Loving to show off, they can be superficial and conceited. They tend to expend their abounding energies in too many directions. Proud and independent, they may be overbearing and bossy, but are also cheerful and optimistic.

Four, on the other hand, is traditionally the number of failure, poverty and general gloom, though most modern numerologists do their best to disguise the fact. People in this category are solid, steady, reliable, practical, humdrum, uninspired and uninspiring. Capable organizers and administrators, industrious and fond of detail and routine, they lack the liveliness and sparkle of the threes. They make heavy weather of things. Success does not come easily to them and may well elude them altogether. They are plain, respectable, conventional and conservative personages, tending to be plodding and slow, regarding themselves as the salt of the earth and suspicious of anyone unlike themselves or of any change in established patterns. They also have a peculiar streak which comes out in fits of intense depression or sudden explosions of rage.

Five implies a very different type of character – nervous and highly strung, adventurous, impatient, restless and jumpy. Those whose names add to 5 are said to love change and variety for their own sake, and delight in travel, gambling and taking risks. They hate to be in a rut or tied down and they loathe responsibility and avoid it. Resilient, resourceful and versatile, they can turn their hands to anything but are supremely good at nothing. Although quick-tempered, self-indulgent and erratic, they are lively and attractive people, who probably have varied and highly unstable love-lives. Sensual and fickle, their interests constantly change and their attachments never last long.

Six is the number of balance, equanimity, adjustment, quiet domesticity and happiness. People whose number this is are well-balanced, loyal, affectionate and wholesome. Faithful and dependable, they have a talent for friendship and family life and are happiest by their own firesides. Capable and hard-working, they lack the glittering brilliance of the threes but may be more enduringly successful in the long run. Kindly and gossipy, they are inclined to be smug and self-satisfied, conceited and obstinate.

Seven is the number of people who are at one remove from the busy bustle of the every-day world. They are natural recluses, introspective and reserved, serious, dignified and self-controlled. This is the number of the scholar, philosopher or mystic. Sevens like to be alone, are not much interested in money or physical comfort, and have a strong bent for quiet reflection and meditation on deep truths and mysteries. People of penetrating intellect, they may find it extremely difficult to communicate their ideas, and they are sometimes profoundly unhappy and disappointed, pessimistic, superior and aloof.

Where 7 is withdrawn from the world, *eight* is caught up in it. This is the number of worldly involvement, material success or failure, money, power and status. Eight-people are tough, practical, strong-minded, efficient, probably involved in politics or business, but success does not come to them easily and the possibility of catastrophic failure is always present. They build their careers on dogged effort, hard work, persistence, tenacity and caution. They tend to be ruthless, selfish, unscrupulous, narrowly materialistic, but they may conceal under an unattractive surface a kindly heart and a streak of wayward eccentricity and wildness.

Finally, *nine* is the number of great mental and spiritual achievement. Nines are visionary idealists, romantic, passionate and impulsive people, of wide human sympathies and great charm, easily imposed on, with a powerful impulse to help others and to serve humanity at large. They make brilliant scientists, artists and teachers. They are sources of inspiration for others but are likely to be condemned by those of duller fibre as impractical and unorthodox. Rebellious, determined and strong-willed, always true to themselves, they are intolerant of opposition and despite their genuine humanitarianism, are highly egocentric. They love the limelight and hate obscurity, and they need beyond everything the admiration and affection of others.

The Vibrating Universe

One of the many obvious objections to numerology is that people acquire their names largely by chance and in ways which have nothing to do with their personalities. But numerologists, like magical thinkers in general, do not believe in chance. They argue that a person's name and character are part of the evolving pattern of the universe and that about the time of birth this pattern is so impressed on the subconscious minds of parents that they are bound to choose a name which accurately expresses the child's character and destiny. Others say that the soul which is to enter the child's body, and which has lived in many incarnations before, chooses a suitable name.

Numerologists also tend to explain their art in terms of the currently popular notion of 'vibrations'. 'We live in a universe of vibrations and every person coming into this world has a vibration peculiar to the individual that is distinct from others' (*333*). 'Numerology is simply an extended study of vibration' and the numbers from 1 to 9 'make a complete cycle of vibration' (*87*). The theory of the vibrating universe became fashionable in occultism in the later 19th century, based on 19th-century physics and particularly on the wave theory of light, but it essentially depends on an analogy with sound. It is as if the universe was a gigantic musical instrument – a colossal harp or grand piano – whose innumerable strings, vibrating and sounding different notes, are the innumerable phenomena of the universe. The numbers from 1 to 9 are the basic notes or rates of vibration, and each person or place or thing has a characteristic reverberation, which is part of the immense symphonic harmony of the universe as a whole at any given moment.

This picture of the universe goes back ultimately to the Pythagoreans, the discovery of the ratios of musical intervals, and the notion of the music of the spheres, the harmony of sound created by the heavenly bodies as they wheel in their courses through the sky. Pythagoras himself is a semi-legendary figure, a sage and teacher of the 6th century B.C., about whom very little is known for certain. It has been remarked of the ancient sources for his life and thought that 'it is only as they grow more distant in time from Pythagoras that the accounts grow more precise and more detailed; after a millennium they tell us the composition of the cakes that were his principal sustenance' (*366*). Various subsequent thinkers adopted and modified the views of Pythagoras, or what they thought were the views of Pythagoras, and there has descended to modern occultists a 'Pythagorean tradition' which, together with a belief in reincarnation and the kinship of all living things, is largely concerned with number as the basic principle of reality.

It may have been Pythagoras himself who discovered that the principal musical intervals known in his time – the octave, the fifth and the fourth – can be expressed in terms of simple ratios between the numbers 1, 2, 3 and 4. Aristotle suggested in his *Metaphysics* that it was this discovery that inspired the Pythagorean belief that the principle of order in the entire universe was numerical, 'such and such a modification of numbers being justice, another being soul and reason, another being opportunity – and similarly almost all other things being numerically expressible.' In fact, he went on, they said that 'the whole universe is number'.

The most startling thing about numerology remains its assumption that people, traits of character, periods of time and everything else can be expressed as numbers. The idea is hard to grasp but it has been pointed out that to understand how opportunity could be thought of as a number it is helpful to remember that we simultaneously think of a table as being a solid object but also as being 'really' a conglomeration of molecules (*69*). The Pythagorean principle has been strongly reinforced in numerology by the CABALA and the Jewish tradition that numbers and letters – the working tools of the numerologist's trade – were the building blocks with which God created the universe.

The numbers determining the musical intervals are 1, 2, 3 and 4, and these added together yield 10. The numbers up to 10 are the essential numbers, for once you count beyond 10 you are using the same basic numbers over again. The fact that 10 is produced by $1+2+3+4$ suggests that these four numbers are the source and basis of all numbers, and so the source and basis of all phenomena. The Pythagoreans confirmed this by finding the principle of the construction of all solid objects in the first four numbers: 1 is assigned to the point, which theoretically has no dimensions; 2 to the line, connecting two points, which has length but not breadth; 3 to the triangle, connecting three points, which has length and breadth but not thickness. When a fourth point is added above the triangle and four points are connected, the simplest solid body has been constructed.

The same line of thinking is applied to the coming into being and existence of all things and all forms. To begin with there is 1, alone by itself. This original unity emanates from itself a second term, making 2, a duality, a pair of opposites. The next step is 3, which reconciles the antagonistic opposites, and the next is 4, which creates solidity, form, the manifest appearance of things (see also ASTROLOGY). On this basis, and again strongly influenced by the Cabala, whose ten spheres which are the basis of all reality are, among other things, numbers, there has grown up the occult principle that the succession of numbers from 1 to 10 symbolizes, or is actually identical with, the coming into existence of the universe. 'Primarily considered, numbers are symbols of the beginning and development of the universe, of a solar system, or a series of such, or, indeed, of any rhythmic movement . . . Thus the 1 is in the All, the 0 or Circle Potential,

A Roman magic hand to ward off bad luck (see page 136)
Overleaf **Mithras slaying the bull: a marble relief from Sidon, *c.*A.D. 400 (see page 155)**

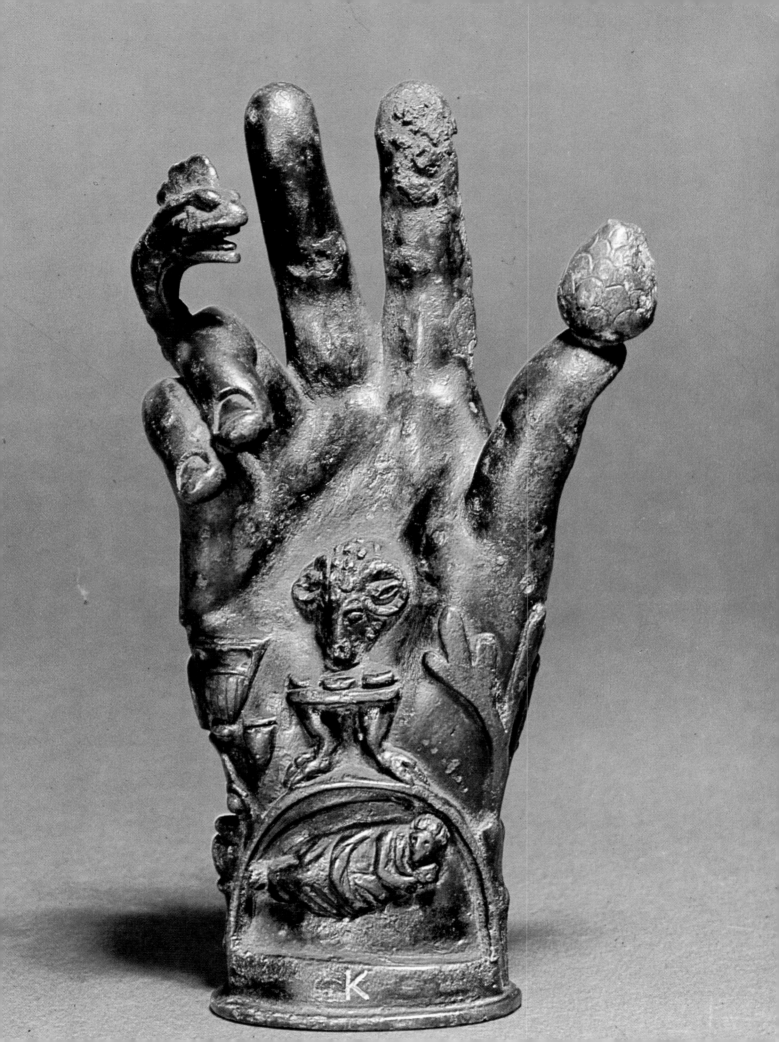

and acts with it to produce the Universe. The one in the nought polarizes it, as the human cell is polarized, and thus arise all numbers, the simple numbers, 1–9, emanating from the 1 in the 0 through this polarization. Hence in the beginning, the 1 and the 0 are *potentially* 10, i.e. complete and perfect, but have to become unfolded, as symbolized by the figures 1–10, before the Perfection innate within them can be manifested' (*51*).

The Opposites and the Sexes

Like other early thinkers in Greece and elsewhere, the Pythagoreans were impressed by the existence of pairs of opposites in the universe and believed that they were an important factor in the universe's construction. From the One, the original and underlying unity, came all the opposites which we experience – day and night, light and dark, hot and cold, wet and dry, summer and winter, life and death, youth and age, good and evil, male and female, and innumerable others. As a result, the chief characteristics which modern numerologists assign to the numbers fit neatly into a table of opposites:

1	Active, powerful, innovating, leading.	2	Passive, weak, receptive, subordinate.
3	Brilliant, creative, lucky; easy success.	4	Dull, uncreative, unlucky; hard work and failure.
5	Adventurous, nervous, versatile, insecure; sexuality.	6	Settled, placid, domestic, maternal love.
7	Withdrawal from the world; mysteries.	8	Involvement in the world; materialism.
	9 Mental and spiritual achievement.		

The odd numbers clearly have the more dominant, vigorous and exciting characteristics, and this is another inheritance from the Pythagoreans, who listed ten fundamental pairs of opposites in the universe, including odd and even, good and evil, male and female. Good and male were linked with odd numbers, evil and female with even numbers. The identification of good with male and evil with female is an old and characteristic product of man-dominated societies. And when numbers are represented by pebbles or dots, as they were in the ancient world and still are on dice, the odd numbers can be seen to be male in the sense

Meditation in Tibetan Buddhism, expressed on a wall-hanging (see page 141)

that they have a central, phallic dot, while the even numbers lack this dot and have an empty space or receptive feminine opening at the centre. An even number represented in this way can readily be reduced to nothing by splitting it in two, leaving only an empty space. An odd number cannot be reduced to nothing so easily – a dot is left in the middle. It follows, numerologically, that odd numbers are male, thrusting, positive, dominating and strong, while even numbers are female, receptive, passive and weak. Since the principles of numerology were worked out in ancient and medieval societies in which man was dominant and woman subordinate, the male odd numbers have almost a monopoly of vigorous, creative and admirable characteristics.

The Meanings of Numbers

Though based on Pythagorean principles, with support from the Cabala, modern numerology also bears the impress of medieval Christian number symbolism and of the Renaissance attempt to bridge the gap between the pagan world and the Christian one, between classical philosophy and religion and Christian doctrine. That all things form a unity, that underlying all the phenomena of existence there is a One which is the Whole, is a belief common to many religious and mystical traditions, and the number *one* has been reverenced by numerologists from the Pythagoreans onwards as God, the First Cause, the originator of all things, as 1 is the first of the numbers and the one from which all other numbers are made. The characteristics allotted to 1-people in numerology follow principally from the identification of 1 with God the Father in Christian number symbolism. The creativity, initiative and bent for organization and technology of 1 reflect the Creator of the world, and many of the other traits – including power, dominance, leadership, loneliness, self-reliance, ill temper, impatience of opposition, generosity to supporters – are drawn from the God of the Old Testament. The fact that the figure 1 resembles an erect phallus contributes to the number's characteristics of solitariness, egotism, unbending purpose and creative potential, though for this potential to be realized, the female, 2, is required.

Two is the number of woman and the Devil because it is the first of the even numbers, which are female and evil. It is evil because it is the first number to break away from the wholeness of 1, and so it creates a pair of opposites, a state of division and antagonism. Its characteristics largely follow from the fact that it is the number of femininity as the opposite and subordinate of masculinity. The reconciliation of the oppo-

sites, the healing of the breach represented by 2, comes with the number 3.

Three has probably the greatest richness of symbolism and significance of any of the numbers. It is 3 which fruitfully reconciles the opposites and which is linked with the triangle, the first plane figure, the first which has surface. Numerologically, 1 is the number of God as alone and unmanifested. In 2 an emanation from within God's wholeness creates the opposite forces which run all through the universe. In 3 the opposites are harmoniously reconciled and God is for the first time manifest, for the first time observable in having, as it were, a surface. So 3 is the number of creativity and self-expression on both the divine and the human planes. As the third term of the Trinity, it is the Spirit of God which brooded on the waters of chaos in Genesis and created the world. The connection with 'surface' also accounts for 3's brilliance and glitter, superficiality and love of showing off.

All this is reinforced by the sexual symbolism of 3. It is the first number to have a phallic central dot, the male genitals are threefold, and the opposites of male and female are reconciled and united in sex. And so 3 is potent and creative, and also energetic, pleasure-loving, attractive to the opposite sex and in constant need of admiration and affection. Three's easy and harmonious progress through life again springs from its function of harmonizing opposites.

Three is also the luckiest of numbers and it stands for completeness and perfection. As the number of the Christian Trinity it is naturally linked with the best, the most perfect, the superlative. But this link is older than Christianity and the notion of the superlative itself involves the third term in a series of three – good, better, best. And 3 is 'all' as well as 'best'. Everything has a beginning, a middle and an end. Time is made of three components – past, present and future – and so is space – length, breadth and thickness. Three crops up frequently as a number of completeness in folk tales and nursery rhymes: three wishes or suitors or attempts at a task, three bears, three blind mice. It is also the most important number of completeness in magic, where the instruction to do something three times occurs constantly, for to repeat an action or chant an incantation three times is magically to repeat it 'all possible' times.

Behind all this there may lie early methods of counting which used specific words for 1 and 2 but for 3 or more simply said 'many', and in this way 3 may have come to connote completeness, abundance, the best and the luckiest. Medieval Christian numerologists noticed various uses of 3 as a number of completeness in the New Testament, including the three gifts of the magi and the three days between Christ's crucifixion and resurrection, which they regarded as reflections of the Trinity. Groups of three deities can be observed in pagan pre-Christian religions, Osiris, Isis and Horus in Egypt, for example, or Serapis, Isis and Harpocrates at Alexandria. Three was a sacred number to the Celts, whose deities were sometimes threefold or portrayed with three heads or three faces. There were also numerous groups of 3 in Greek mythology, including the Fates, the Furies and the Graces.

These classical triads attracted the attention of humanists during the Renaissance, who connected them with the Trinity, so that even the three heads of Cerberus, the watchdog of the underworld, became a symbol of the Christian doctrine. The humanists interpreted the triads in terms of a unity manifesting itself by displaying its component parts – the opposites and the factor which reconciles them in a higher unity, both Three and One. The three Graces provided a favourite example of the theme for artists, as did the Judgment of Paris. Similarly, the classical myth that Mars, the god of war, and Venus, goddess of love, had a daughter named Harmony was taken as a demonstration of the truth that a higher unity is created by the mingling of opposites: Botticelli's *Mars and Venus* and Veronese's *Mars and Venus United by Love* are exercises on this theme.

Four, as we have seen, is connected with the simplest solid figure and is therefore the number of solidity and matter, of the construction of things, and especially of the earth itself, a solid body bounded by the four cardinal points. According to the old theory, which held sway in Europe down to the 17th century and in modified form still commands the allegiance of occultists, all things are made of four ingredients – the elements of fire, air, earth and water (see also ALCHEMY). The year is made of four seasons, the month of four weeks. It is the connection with solidity that in terms of personality analysis gives 4 its connotations of stability, dullness, stodginess, and the link with matter and the earth gives 4 its atmosphere of gloom and defeat, because so many classical and medieval authors despised matter and the body as the prison of the soul and regarded life on earth as hopelessly sin-ridden, toilsome and unrewarding. Many of the characteristics of 4 in numerology derive from a stereotype of the slow and plodding rustic and from a picture of agricultural labour on the earth's surface as back-breaking toil for uncertain and often minimal returns. Four's violent outbursts of anger are the earthquakes and eruptions that shake the earth and the fits of

Pythagoras

melancholy are the fog and mist and rain that shroud it.

The restless, many-sided, unreliable character of *five* follows from its position halfway through the numbers from 1 to 9, so that it 'faces both ways'. But the main key to 5 is that it is the number of the five senses, and so of liveliness, nervousness, sensuality and sex. Some of its characteristics – a dislike of being tied down, for instance, and resilience – have a directly phallic reference. Five is made of 1 (God) plus 4 (matter) and so it is the number of divine life infused into the inanimate, of the world of nature and of the living flesh, a connection strengthened by the five wounds suffered by Christ on the cross in his body of flesh. It is especially the number of man, because the human body has five extremities and, shown with arms and legs stretched out, can be fitted into a pentagram, or five-pointed star, which is an emblem of man as the microcosm, a miniature replica of the entire universe, the macrocosm.

Six is balanced, harmonious and free of inner conflicts because it equals the sum of its divisors, other than itself ($6 = 1 + 2 + 3$), and is the only number in the first 10 to do so. It is an even, female number but where 2 is the number of woman as man's opposite and subordinate, 6 is woman as mother and housewife – warm, domestic, companionable, a good worker, conventional, respectable, fussy and gossipy, smug and limited in outlook. The balanced, harmonious quality of 6 is reinforced by the two harmoniously interlaced triangles of the hexagram, or six-pointed star, which stands for the equilibrium of opposites. God made man 'in his image' on the sixth day of creation and where 5 is the number of man as microcosm, 6 is the number of man as macrocosm, the

Universal Man, man carried to the highest power. The number is taken to indicate that 'man's spiritual path lies in the balance of the spiritual and the physical, the eternal and the transitory. It represents harmony, proportion, co-operation, and implies order and harmony brought to manifestation' (*1*).

Seven is the most mysterious and uncanny of numbers, hence its association with people who delve into mysteries and remain aloof from ordinary everyday affairs. The story of the fall of Jericho in the Old Testament (Joshua, Chapter 6) illustrates the number's reputation for magical power and it occurs frequently in the Bible as a number of completeness, especially in the book of Revelation, which abounds in sets of 7, but the supreme example, of course, is God's creation of the world in seven days. The sabbath, the seventh day of rest, has contributed to the 7-characteristics of quiet reflection and withdrawal from the workaday world. The Jews also regarded every seventh year as a sabbatical 'of solemn rest for the land' and celebrated every fiftieth year, marking the end of 7 times 7 years, as a jubilee.

The key to 7 is this connection with significant periods of time, which arises from its link with the moon. It is an old and deep-rooted belief that the cycles of life and death, growth and decay, on earth are governed by the cycle of the moon and its waxing and waning in the sky. The moon's cycle consists of 4 phases of approximately 7 days each, which is the origin of the month of 4 weeks of 7 days each. Seven is consequently the number thought to govern the major rhythms of life on earth, including the menstrual cycle in women, on which all human life depends.

It is also an important number of completeness. Seven of anything makes a complete set. The planets known in antiquity, whose movements in the sky were thought to influence all events on earth, numbered 7 and could be linked with 7 metals, 7 colours, the 7 weekdays, the 7 notes of the musical scale and the 7 vowels of the Greek alphabet. Numerous other groups of 7 include the Wonders of the World, the Champions of Christendom, the Christian sacraments, the deadly sins, the sorrows of the Virgin and, more recently, the ROOT RACES of Theosophical theory. As a number of completeness, holding the key to the essential rhythms of the universe, 7 is powerful in magic and a seventh son, or especially the seventh son of a seventh son, is credited with magical and clairvoyant powers in folklore.

The loneliness and introspection of the 7-character follow from the fact that 7 is numerologically solitary, in the sense that it is not constructed by multiplication of any of the other numbers in the first 10, nor does it, multiplied, produce any of them. And 7 is also the number of reflection because of its connection with the moon – moonlight being reflected sunlight.

Eight is 4 doubled, and since 4 means matter and the earth, 8 means a double helping of interest in material and worldly concerns, power and money. The unluckiness of 4 brings in the ominous, ever-present possibility of failure, and this is also influenced by the shape of the figure 8, which suggests a dualism of success and failure. From a different point of view, 8 means a 'new beginning' and 'new life', perhaps because a man's body has seven orifices but a woman's has eight, and it is through the eighth that a baby comes into the world. This intensifies the numerologist's picture of 8 as meaning inescapable involvement in the world and material matters. The octave is the eighth note which restates the first note at a higher level and in Christian number symbolism 8 is the number of life after death, a new beginning in the next world: and so 8 means eternity and infinity and the mathematical symbol for infinity is an 8 lying on its side. The alternatives of an eternity in heaven or hell have contributed to the numerologist's alternatives of great success or great failure with 8. Numerologists also point out that 8 is the first cube number and so marks a new beginning in the sense of introducing a new dimension. They connect this with the Eightfold Path of Buddhism, which is the way of liberation from earthly existence, and again the shape of the figure 8 suggests crossing over from earthly life to the spiritual plane.

Nine is a number of completeness and high achievement because it is the last and highest of the series from 1 to 9, and because a human child is normally born nine months after conception. Some of 9's characteristics – dislike of obscurity, need for love, rebelliousness, hasty temper – are drawn from small babies, and others – service to humanity, compassion, affection – from fond mothers. Nine also marks the transition from one series of numbers to a higher series and is therefore the number of initiation, and initiation rituals frequently take the form of a mock 'death' followed by a 'rebirth'. Nine is creative and brilliant because it is made of three times three and so has the force of three tripled. Its completeness and self-sufficiency is reinforced by the fact that a circle has 360 degrees and $3+6+0 = 9$, and by the fact that if multiplied by any other number 9 always reproduces itself: $3 \times 9 = 27$, and $2+7 = 9$, and so on. This accounts for the egotism and obstinacy associated with the number.

Numbers above Ten

Though popular numerology generally concentrates on the numbers from 1 to 9, several higher numbers have symbolic importance. *Eleven* is the number of the faithful disciples of Jesus and the number of revelation and martyrdom, partly because of the disciples and partly because it is the first number above 10 and therefore stands for the entry to a higher plane. Revelation opens the way to a higher world of the spirit and the death of the martyr opens the gates of the kingdom of heaven.

Twelve is a major number of completeness. There are the 12 months and signs of the zodiac, 12 hours of the day and night, 12 gods of Olympus, 12 labours of Hercules, 12 tribes of Israel, 12 apostles of Jesus, 12 days of Christmas. The description of the celestial city, New Jerusalem, in the closing chapters of Revelation makes extensive use of 12 as a number of completeness and perfection. The 12 months of the year, making a complete cycle, appear to be the key factor, and 12 is numerologically related to 7, the other number of the universe's essential rhythms, since both are made of the 3 of spirit and the 4 of matter, added or multiplied. The fact that Jesus chose 12 apostles naturally set the seal on the number's completeness and perfection in Christian eyes, and it was said that he chose 12 to make known the Trinity to the four corners of the world, or to show that he was the perfect year or spiritual day, with the apostles as the months or hours.

Thirteen is persistently regarded as unlucky (see also LUCK), probably partly because Jesus and his disciples made a group of 13 and the thirteenth was the traitor, and partly because 13 is one more than 12 and so dangerously exceeds completeness and goes beyond proper limits. It is the number of necromancy, which transgresses proper limits in bringing the dead back to temporary life, and also the number of a coven of witches.

Twenty-two is another number of completeness and perfection because of the 22 letters of the Hebrew alphabet and the 22 major trumps of the TAROT pack. Finally, *forty* appears frequently in the Bible as a number of completeness: when God sent the Flood to destroy the world it rained for 40 days and nights, Moses communed with God for 40 days and nights on Mount Sinai, and Jesus was 40 days and nights in the wilderness. One of the factors involved here is the old belief that a human pregnancy normally lasts 280 days, which is 7×40, from which there developed a connection between 40 and health: hence the word quarantine, which originally meant a 40-day period. R. C.

(Further reading: *1, 29, 51, 68, 69, 76, 85, 87, 233, 265, 294, 333, 366, 511*.)

Oahspe

Oahspe, the Kosmon Bible in the words of Jehovah and his angel ambassadors is a work of automatic typewriting produced in 1881 by John Ballou Newbrough (1828–91) of New York.

Object Reading

Object reading or psychometry or, as it is perhaps better called, object association is a form of ESP in which a person seems to receive impressions about events, as a rule in the past, by means of objects which were associated with the events. Such objects are also sometimes used for psychic healing if the person being treated is absent and for other practices where attempts are made to influence people at a distance, presumably by PK (for ESP and PK, see PARAPSYCHOLOGY).

Psychometry means literally 'soul measurement'. Since the word also refers to psychological measurements and tests, it is not much used by contemporary parapsychologists. J. B. Rhine describes it as 'clairvoyant "free association" in connection with a token object' (*393a*). These kinds of experiments are usually now called object association tests. Other words for them are object reading and token-object tests.

It is not yet known why it is that an object seems to focus the ESP abilities of a person on events connected with it. Some parapsychologists believe that the object is helpful only because the person believes that it is, others are of the opinion that the object in a real sense is connected with the events in which it was once part.

Object association has not received much attention from present-day parapsychologists. Some exploratory testing has been done but most of the material consists of informal observations or older studies with sensitives.

The indications are that object association is closely related to other forms of ESP. In the following account from a session in 1844 with a French sensitive, Alexis Didier, an apparent case of CLAIRVOYANCE seemed to develop into a demonstration of object association. The session took place at a house in London and is described in a letter by the Reverend G. Sandby to the *Medical Times*, dated 8 July 1844.

Colonel Llewellyn, who was, I believe, rather sceptical, produced a morocco case, something like a surgical instrument case. Alexis took it, placed it to his stomach, and said, 'The object is a hard substance, not white, enclosed in something more white than itself; it is a bone taken from a greater body; a human bone – yours. It has been separated, and cut so as to leave a flat side.' Alexis opened the case, took out a piece of bone wrapped in silver paper, and said, 'The ball struck here; it was an extraordinary ball in effect; you received three separate injuries at the same moment; the bone was broken in three pieces; you were wounded early in the day whilst engaged in charging the enemy.' He also described the dress of the soldiers, and was right in all these particulars. This excited the astonishment of all the bystanders, especially the gallant Colonel. This account is drawn up, not only from my own notes, but from Colonel Llewellyn's statement made after the séance, and from a written account given me by a lady who was sitting close by.

The belief that events or traces of events persist in physical objects is an old one. Professor E. R. Dodds, formerly Regius Professor of Greek at Oxford University and President of the Society for Psychical Research 1961–3, informs us that the Greek philosopher Democritus, who lived in the late fifth and early fourth centuries B.C., believed that dreams result from 'the penetration through the pores of the dreamer's body of the "images" which are continually emitted by objects of all sorts and especially by living persons; . . . the images carry representations of the mental activities, the thoughts, characters, and emotions of the persons who originated them, "and thus charged, they have the effect of living agents: by their impact they communicate and transmit to the recipients the opinions, thoughts, and impulses of their senders, when they reach their goal with the images intact and undistorted".' The degree of distortion which the images suffer in transit depends partly on the weather, partly on the frequency of emission and on their initial velocity: "those which leap out from persons in an excited and inflamed condition yield, owing to their high frequency and rapid transit, especially vivid and significant representations".' As Dodds points out, modern observations confirm that many ESP impressions concern physical or mental crises (*124*).

Object Association and Sorcery

As with other types of psi phenomena, belief in object association is common in tribal societies. In practices involving the supposed psychical associations of objects, the purpose is usually not to obtain ESP information about the owner of an object but to exert a physical influence on him, usually for purposes of healing or harming him. Sir James Frazer referred to this practice in *The Golden Bough* as 'contagious magic'. It is the belief 'that things which have once been in contact with each other continue to act on each other at a distance after the physical contact has been severed'. Margaret Mead reports of the plains-dwelling Arapesh in New Guinea: 'It is important to the Plainsmen that they should be able to walk safely through the mountain country to obtain [the giant clam-shells] . . . They walk through haughtily, arrogantly, without fear, because of sorcery. With a bit of a victim's exuviae, a piece of half-eaten food, a strip of worn bark-cloth, or best of all a little sexual secretion, the Plains sorcerer is believed to be able to cause his victim to sicken and die. Once a mountain man or a beach man has lost his temper with a neighbour, stolen a piece of his "dirt", and delivered it into the hands of a sorcerer, the victim is for ever after in the sorcerer's power. The quarrel that caused the theft of the dirt may be healed, but the dirt remains in the hands of the sorcerer. On the strength of holding the lives of many mountain peoples in his hands, the sorcerer walks unafraid among them, and so do his brothers and his cousins and his sons' (*322a*).

It is interesting that the kinds of associated objects used by the sorcerers and witch-doctors in tribal societies are often the same as those preferred by psychics and mediums in the West. For instance, the sensitives studied by Dr Eugène Osty (1874–1938), a French physician and psychical researcher, liked to use 'some actual organic part of the distant person – hair, nail parings, a tooth, blood, or a fragment from an amputation' (*358a*). Similarly, in RADIESTHESIA and other methods of unorthodox healing a patient may be 'treated' by using a sample of his blood or sputum. The belief that a religious relic has a beneficial effect because it has belonged to a saint (or was a part of his body, such as a bone) also represents a belief in object association.

Mediums and Object Association

Object association is perhaps most familiar in the form in which it is practised by mediums and sensitives. As a rule, the associated object is a personal belonging or some other small item which the sensitive can handle. In a mediumistic 'reading', the

Dr S. G. Soal

medium often asks to hold the watch, ring or some other object which has been associated for a long time with the person for whom the reading is given. The reading will then proceed while the medium holds this object. If the inquirer wishes to obtain information about somebody other than himself, for instance, about a missing or deceased person, the medium may request an object which has belonged to that individual.

Dr S. G. Soal, formerly Lecturer in Mathematics at the University of London, conducted object association tests with a medium, Mrs Blanche Cooper. He was convinced that a physical link between a medium and the target situation the medium is trying to focus on is necessary (*429a*). The physical link can be either a person or an inanimate object. Soal was later to become known mainly for his ESP card experiments. He was President of the Society for Psychical Research 1950–1.

Another medium who relied extensively on object association was Mrs PIPER (see also MEDIUMS). One of those who investigated her was Mrs Eleanor Sidgwick (1845–1936), Principal of Newnham College, Cambridge, and President of the Society for Psychical Research, 1908–9. In an analysis of Mrs Piper's mediumship, Mrs Sidgwick quoted some statements by Mrs Piper when she was in trance about associated objects. Mrs Piper said, speaking as one of the spirit CONTROLS who appeared to communicate through her, that 'objects carry with them a light as distinct to us as the light is to you. The instant you hand us an object, that instant we get an impression of its owner, whether present or the past owner and often both'; and later, 'the object to us appears like a person or its light conveys to us an impression of its owner' (*425a*). Speaking as another control, she said that when a person

wears or handles an object this seems to infuse it with something similar to magnetic power, which from then on surrounds the object and enables a medium to obtain information about the person.

Dr W. H. C. Tenhaeff, Professor of Parapsychology at the University of Utrecht, Holland, has conducted investigations of object association with many Dutch sensitives including Peter HURKOS and Gerard CROISET. In several cases Tenhaeff and Croiset have helped the police and others in finding lost persons, using objects belonging to these persons as 'inductors'.

In the town Y., Mr. Z. was found to be missing at the end of 1947. Mr. Z. was a civil servant of the Municipal gasworks. After having finished his daily work he had not returned home. Some days later an acquaintance of the missing man came to Mr. Croiset and handed him Mr. Z.'s cap as an inductor [only saying that it concerned a loss]. 'This person,' said Mr. Croiset, 'is in a very nervous state of mind. I get the impression that he has got something to do with coal. Has this man been smuggling? I have the idea that he has swindled. I see him jump on a bicycle. He is wearing working trousers with a blue jacket. He cycles towards B. [This was incorrect. The person cycled in another direction], along a road with white piles. On his left is a pinewood. This man is no longer alive. He has hanged himself on a tree.' The dead body of Mr. Z., hanging on a tree, was found two days later. He was guilty of some fraudulent acts. When he became aware that his underhand dealings might be discovered, he had in despair committed suicide by hanging himself on a tree. The autopsy proved that he was already dead at the time of the consultation (*451a*).

As this example suggests, object association is not restricted to information about past events. Once the sensitive has established contact with a person by means of a personal belonging, the sensitive can apparently go backward or forward in this person's life beyond the time when the person last had the object.

Pagenstecher's Contribution

One of the pioneers in object association work was Dr Gustav Pagenstecher (1855–1942), a German physician practising in Mexico. Pagenstecher was the first to use the term 'associated objects' and he explored which of the many associations of an object are most likely to lead to an ESP impression in the mind of the sensitive. He worked with one person, Mrs Maria Zierold, whose psy-

chical abilities emerged during hypnotic treatments for insomnia.

Pagenstecher's material and other studies of object association show a resemblance between this and the association of ideas. Tests in object association are similar in some ways to word association tests. In both a physical stimulus is used and in both the investigator is interested in discovering the associations of this stimulus. In one case he is interested in the object's parapsychological associations, in the other he is interested in the psychological ones it arouses in the subject's mind. The similarity between the association of objects and of ideas have resulted in a theory for object association. This has been outlined by W. G. Roll in an analysis of Pagenstecher's material (*404a*):

The psychological laws of association are divided into the 'primary' and 'secondary' laws of association, the former being the laws of contiguity and similarity and the latter the laws of primacy, recency, frequency, and vividness. . . . The law of contiguity states that when two experiences have occurred together in time or place, the occurrence of one of them in perception or thought tends to bring the other to mind. 'The burnt child dreads the fire,' as the proverb has it. The phenomenon of object association suggests a parapsychological equivalent to this law. According to what we might call the 'parapsychological law of contiguity,' two objects or events that have occurred together in time or place remain parapsychologically associated though they may later be separated, so that if one of the objects is presented to a person, the other comes to his mind. Pagenstecher's experiments all conform to this law. For instance, in Experiment 62 . . . the experimental object was a string on which the identification plate belonging to a German ex-sergeant had been attached. It had been worn by him during World War I. When Mrs. Zierold held the string, she had a vision of a fire bomb exploding among a group of soldiers. The sergeant recognized this event as the one that had impressed him most during the war. . . . (*362a*).

The objects used in Pagenstecher's experiments had many events associated with them in addition to those described by Mrs Zierold. For instance, in the experiment with the identification string, the question arises why she described the bomb explosion rather than something else. Similarly, in the case of the association of ideas, one word or image often has several others connected with it. The word 'table' may be associated with 'chair', 'lamp', 'typewriter', 'ashtray', and the names of other objects which have been observed in the proximity of tables. If the investigator is interested in which of these related words are likely to come to mind first, he will refer to the secondary laws of association: the laws of primacy, recency, frequency, and vividness. Thus, if the subject in the past has more frequently experienced the combination 'table–chair' than the combination 'table-lamp', he is more likely to say chair than lamp in response to the stimulus word 'table', assuming that other factors, such as recency, are about the same for the two combinations.

In object association, the question which of the events associated with the experimental object are likely to be cognized by an ESP subject is answered by the parapsychological equivalents of the secondary laws of association. We may express these as follows: According to the law of primacy, all other things being equal, the first events in the history of an object are more likely to be cognized by ESP than others. The law of recency states that, all other things being equal, recent events in the history of an object are more likely to be cognized by ESP than others. The law of frequency says that, all other things being equal, frequent events in the history of an object are more likely to be cognized by ESP than others. And finally, according to the law of vividness, all other things being equal, events that were emotionally vivid or intense to a person connected with the history of an object are more likely to be cognized by ESP than others. . . . Mrs. Zierold's responses, in many cases . . . appear to follow the secondary laws of association, particularly the laws of primacy and vividness.

It was Pagenstecher's experience that vivid impressions took precedence over primary ones. This is illustrated in the following case where three pieces of paper were used as objects. One piece gave rise to impressions of a highly charged emotional event while other pieces apparently resulted in impressions of the paper mill.

The experimental objects were three pieces of paper from a pad belonging to a colleague of Pagenstecher's who had suffered a stroke. On the first piece of paper presented to Mrs. Zierold the doctor had written a call for medical help with his left hand since he had lost the use of his right hand and also could not speak. The second piece of paper presented was written shortly before, at the onset of the stroke, with the right hand, while he could still use it. Finally, the third piece was taken from the bottom of the pad and had presumably

not been touched by the doctor. Mrs. Zierold had the following impressions when she held the first piece of paper: 'I am in an office, sitting on a desk, in front of a man whose face has a bluish tint, whose eyes are languid and whose mouth is slightly distorted. He tries to write something with his left hand which apparently contains an order, as an elderly lady who is at his side with two other . . . women, leaves the room hurriedly and comes back with another woman. In the meantime a young man of about thirty-five years of age, has unfastened the collar of the sick man and gives him some water to drink. At his side stands a young girl of about sixteen or eighteen years who pets him and kisses him very affectionately. After some time a man of vigorous constitution enters the room and receives from the left hand of the sick man a small instrument which had been extracted by him from a pocket instrument case [a small lancet for bleeding]. Aided by the newcomer [the doctor called for] the young man already mentioned lifts up the invalid and carries him out of the room into an adjoining room . . .'

These impressions were correct. The doctor had suddenly been taken ill with a stroke, and the other events were also as described by Mrs. Zierold. In response to the second sheet of paper, she said, 'I do not understand what I see. It seems to me that there are *two conflicting visions*, superposed one on top of the other and blending together.' Her first impression was: 'I see in a large room, small boys with caps on their heads who push wheel carts filled with scraps of paper of different colors and also with old rags. I see women who separate the different colors with long forks. The scraps and pieces of rags are thrown into a large boiler.'

Mrs. Zierold continued and described her second impression: 'I see a very sick man, with bluish face, who tries to speak without results as I see only the movement of his lips and do not hear a word. He takes a pencil with his right hand and writes something on a blank paper. . . .' Finally, the third piece of paper (taken from the bottom of the pad) produced only images from the paper factory.

Pagenstecher once did a test to study the effect of frequency.

[He] placed a piece of broken pottery in the case of a wall clock and left it there for fifteen days. The clock struck the hours and half hours. He then gave the pottery to Mrs. Zierold, who said: 'I hear a *rhythmic noise*, very far off, like drops of rain

falling upon glass at equal intervals; besides, I hear, now and then, a *melodious noise* as if the wind were sighing through the woods.' A similar piece of pottery which had not been in the clock did not elicit any impressions of sounds. Pagenstecher then replaced the first piece in the clock and left it there for an additional seven days. This seemed to result in increased clarity of the impressions: '*I hear the rhythmic steps* of soldiers marching, and besides I perceive now and then the *sound of a musical band* playing far away.' Finally, the fragment was put in the clock an additional twenty-one days: 'I hear distinctly the *tick-tock of a clock* and the *harmonious striking of the clock bell* – one, one, two, three, four . . .'

The importance of frequency has been stressed by other investigators. Osty (*358a*) said that an experiment is most likely to succeed if the object has often been touched by the person about whom information is desired and touched little by anyone else. In an experiment with Richard Hodgson (1855–1905), Mrs Piper made a similar observation and in an experiment with someone else, also described by Hodgson, she said that 'it often causes confusion' if the objects have been 'handled often and by a great many persons'. Hodgson was one of the most active workers both in the English and American Societies for Psychical Research. In discussing the role of associated objects in tests with Mrs Piper, he concluded that any object can be used, if it 'has been handled or worn almost exclusively by specific persons' (*223a*). Similarly, H. F. Saltmarsh (1881–1943) noted that an English medium, Mrs Warren Elliott, objected to 'any article which has often been washed or handled by a great many people' (*411a*). Saltmarsh, a member of the Council of the Society for Psychical Research, made important contributions to the assessment of mediumistic responses.

In most cases of object association, the object used is a small personal belonging. There is no reason why larger objects could not serve equally well. Several parapsychologists have suggested that the (veridical) hallucinations of 'apparitions', 'footsteps', and so forth, which give some homes a reputation of being 'haunted' may be cases of object association and are not due to 'spirits'. In such cases parts of the house would be the associated objects. W. G. R.

(Further reading: see references in the article.)

Obsession See POSSESSION.

Occult Cosmology See COSMOLOGY.

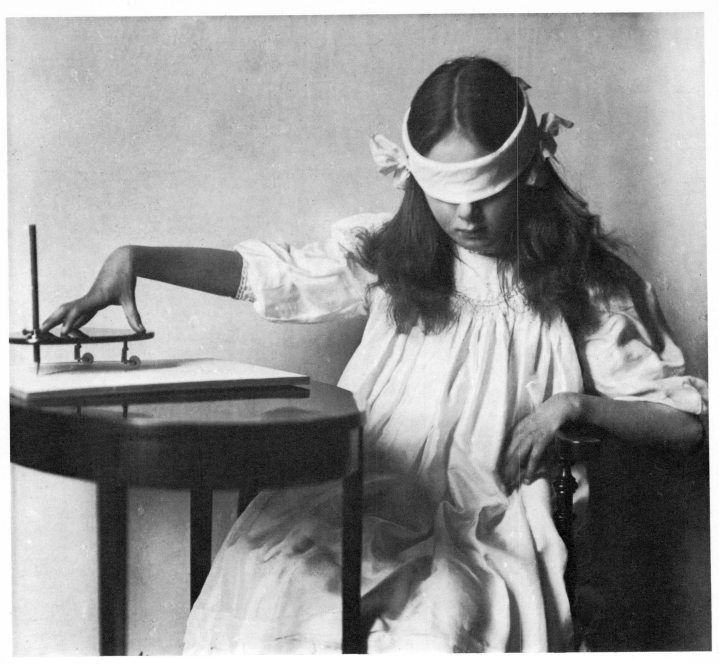

Using a planchette

Od, Odic Force, Odyle See HYPNOSIS; REICHENBACH; RITUAL MAGIC.

Henry Steel Olcott (1832-1907)

One of the founders of the Theosophical Society. Born in Orange, New Jersey, he became an expert on agricultural chemistry and a lawyer, in partnership with W. Q. JUDGE. He achieved the rank of Colonel in a non-combatant capacity in the Civil War. In 1874 he published articles on SPIRITUALISM in the New York *Daily Graphic* and in connection with these met Madame BLAVATSKY. He became her right-hand man and President of the T.S. on its foundation in 1875. He accompanied Madame Blavatsky to India in 1878

and subsequently became converted to Buddhism, writing *A Buddhist Catechism*. In 1882, in Ceylon, he succeeded in curing by suggestion a man who was partially paralysed and crowds of people came flocking to him for treatment. 'The colonel believed; the sufferers believed; and cures were effected by the dozen' (*510*). Olcott edited the Theosophical Society's journal, *The Theosophist*, till his death, and wrote *Theosophy, Religion and Occult Languages*, 1885, and a three-volume history of the movement, *Old Diary Leaves*, 1895–1904; see THEOSOPHICAL SOCIETY.

Om See AUM.

Oom the Omnipotent

The pseudonym of Pierre Bernard, the first

person to introduce the public teaching of tantric sex-magical techniques (see TANTRISM) in the West. Earlier groups, such as the O.T.O. and Aleister CROWLEY and his disciples, had practised sexual magic, but in secrecy. Bernard began his occult career in 1909 as a teacher of Hatha YOGA, but closed the institution he founded (the New York Sanskrit College) some two years later, after two young girls accused him, probably falsely, of indecent assault. He then moved to New Jersey and married a vaudeville dancer, Mlle de Bries, and with her help evolved a 'tantric health system', which combined Hatha Yoga, dancing, and certain elements derived from right-hand, or symbolic, Bengali Tantrism.

The Bernards acquired some extremely

wealthy followers, including two members of the Vanderbilt family, and opened the Brae Burn Club, a luxuriously appointed country club and occult college at Nyack, N.J., which was the headquarters of Bernard's Sacred Order of Tantriks. Here were celebrated peculiar rites devised by Oom himself: on one occasion a wedding banquet was eaten off coffins, and on another the Master himself ceremonially danced with a baby elephant. Despite these publicity methods, Bernard and his wife seem to have been sincere believers in their system, teaching a genuine if modified version of right-handed Tantrism. It is probable that an inner group at Nyack engaged in left-hand Tantrism, which involves actual, rather than merely symbolic, sexual intercourse. F. K.

(Further reading: *122, 263, 423.*)

Order of Bards, Ovates and Druids
See DRUIDS.

Order of the Cubic Stone
See CUBIC STONE; RITUAL MAGIC.

Order of Elect Cohens
See MARTINISM.

Order of the Golden Dawn
See GOLDEN DAWN.

Order of the Morning Star
See STELLA MATUTINA.

Order of New Templars
See GERMAN OCCULT GROUPS; LANZ VON LIEBENFELS.

Order of the Rose of Ruby and Cross of Gold
See GOLDEN DAWN.

Order of the Silver Star
See A∴A∴.

Order of the Star in the East
See THEOSOPHICAL SOCIETY.

Order of the Temple (or Templars) of the Orient
See O.T.O.

Ordre Kabbalistique de la Rose-Croix
See ROSICRUCIANS.

Orgone Energy
See REICH; TRANCE.

Oscilloclast
A radionic machine, also known as the Black Box, invented by Dr Albert Abrams: see RADIESTHESIA.

O.T.O.
The *Ordo Templi Orientis*, Order of the Temple of the Orient, or Order of Oriental Templars, an occult society much concerned with sex magic; founded in Germany in 1906

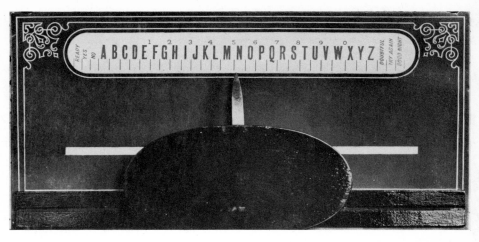

A ouija board

by Theodor Reuss, it is still in existence today, with branches in Germany and abroad: see GERMAN OCCULT GROUPS; see also CROWLEY; GNOSTICISM; ROSICRUCIANS.

Ouija Board, Planchette
Automatic writing devices. Their simplest form is a circle of letters on a table with an upturned glass in the centre, on which one or more participants rest the tips of their fingers. The glass moves from letter to letter, frequently spelling out gibberish but sometimes words and sentences. A ouija board ('ouija' combines the French and German words for 'yes') is a flat piece of polished wood with the letters of the alphabet written in a crescent along one side. On top of this is a small heart-shaped board mounted on casters which slides about when the participants put their finger-tips on it and again may spell out words and sentences. A planchette has a pencil attached to the heart-shaped pointer which writes on a sheet of paper placed on the larger board underneath. In the 19th century it was often assumed that the 'messages' communicated through these devices must come from the dead, and much of the agitation against the use of ouija boards in recent years seems to stem from a deep-rooted fear that they put the performers into perilous touch with either the dead or evil forces. Certainly, the devices do sometimes produce material that is frightening, startling, embarrassing or obscene – wherever it may come from – but the tendency now is to look to the subconscious minds of the performers themselves as the source of the material (that is, in cases where no one has been deliberately pushing the glass or pointer). This does not mean that the devices only produce material which has been forgotten or repressed: they lend themselves to ESP, and Rosalind Heywood has remarked that 'there are hints which cannot be ignored that the material which emerges by means of

this type of device does not always originate in the subconscious of any of the performers; occasionally it seems to be due to some unknown kind of contact with distant events or the thoughts of distant persons' (*303*): see AUTOMATISMS; CONSCIOUSNESS.

Peter Demianovitch Ouspensky (1878-1947)
The most influential disciple of Gurdjieff and expounder of his theories; he broke away from Gurdjieff in 1924 and continued his work independently; author of *Tertium Organum, A New Model of the Universe, In Search of the Miraculous, The Psychology of Man's Possible Evolution, The Fourth Way*: see GURDJIEFF. (*359, 360, 361*)

Out-of-the-Body Experiences (or Ecsomatic Experiences)
Cases in which people have the experience of quitting their physical bodies and observing them from some vantage-point outside. This seems particularly likely to happen in situations of stress, for example, when someone is knocked down by a car, hit by a bullet or undergoing surgery, but can also happen in quite ordinary circumstances. An example is one of the cases collected by Celia Green, of a person who was sitting peacefully on a double-decker bus: 'I was sitting at the rear of the bus looking out through the window when without warning I found myself looking at myself from the stairs of the bus. All my senses, sight, feelings and so on, seemed to be on the stairs, only my actual body remained at the seat.' The experience can also occur when the subject is asleep or apparently unconscious under anaesthetics. Miss Green distinguishes between *parasomatic* experiences, in which the subject finds himself 'in an alternative body, more or less closely resembling his physical one', and the more common *asomatic* experiences, in which 'the subject, at his new point of view, is not associated with any spatial entity at all': see also ASTRAL BODY; PHYSICAL POWERS. (*195*)

P

Padre Pio da Pietralcini

The name in religion of Francesco Forgione (1887–1968), an Italian Capuchin friar who reputedly received the STIGMATA in 1915. He was also credited with remarkable powers of CLAIRVOYANCE and PRECOGNITION, and pilgrims flocked to visit him, despite the reserved attitude of the Roman Catholic Church. (*81*)

Eusapia Palladino (1854-1918)

A celebrated Italian medium who was well known to resort to trickery whenever she thought she could get away with it, but who also produced what appeared to be genuine phenomena. Her phenomena were those frequently reported of physical mediums – materializations of heads and hands, and more rarely of complete forms, raps and knocks, mysterious lights, noises and scents, movements of objects, including the LEVITATION and tilting of tables, the smashing of crockery and billowing of curtains. Hereward Carrington, the American psychical researcher, was once hurled bodily out of her cabinet by some unknown force, together with a small table, after he had satisfied himself that there was nothing except the table inside the cabinet. Eusapia, who was claimed by one of her CONTROLS, John KING, to be his reincarnated daughter, was investigated by the Society for Psychical Research under very rigorous conditions in 1908: the investigators, who reported their conclusions in the S.P.R. *Proceedings*, 1909, felt 'compelled to ascribe Eusapia's phenomena to some supernormal cause': see MEDIUMS. (*119, 148a, 176, 303*)

Palmistry

Palmistry suffers a little from the simplifications implicit in its popular name. The practice does not start and stop with the palm of the hand, but concerns itself with everything about the hand from fingertips to wrists, and even sometimes with fingernails, though practitioners of 'onychomancy', if there still are any, would consider this a trespass. More accurate are the words growing out of the Greek root word for the hand, *cheir*. Generalized terms like 'chirosophy' or 'chirology' have been used fairly often, but usually the specialists speak of 'chirognomy', reading character in the hand, and 'chiromancy', reading the future in the hand.

This ever-popular form of divination has a long past, even if its apologists have never found proof of their belief that it goes back to dimmest primeval prehistory. Certainly it can be found mentioned in the Vedic writings of ancient India, 3,000 years ago; and Chinese texts, as old or older, contain allusions to it. In Western history, which takes little note of Asian origins, Aristotle is usually cited as the earliest writer of antiquity to refer to it, though something may be made of chirognomy in Biblical times from the vague assertion in Job that God 'sealeth up the hand of every man; that all men may know his work'. As for Aristotle, there was a legend that the philosopher found out about palmistry through his discovery in Egypt of a treatise written in gold and left upon an altar of Hermes, and that he sent the treatise (which was in a Semitic language) to Alexander the Great, who was financing Aristotle's knowledge-finding tour through the Near East. It is, however, perfectly possible that in some rather more prosaic way the art and science of palmistry did filter westwards from Asia to Greece and from there, with most other forms of human knowledge, to the rest of Europe – its dissemination stimulated by a nod from the learned Roman Pliny and a sneer from the satirist Juvenal.

So it often crops up in medieval manuscripts written by sages who gave it what attention they could spare from ALCHEMY, theology and such more usual preoccupations of learning. Naturally, palmistry was inevitably linked with that more established form of divination, ASTROLOGY. It was also often treated as a mere subdivision of physiognomy, then in its heyday as a refined and over-systematized form of character reading. In later centuries many scholars known for their work in other mystic or occult fields contributed to the literature of chiromancy – among them Paracelsus and Robert Fludd. Textbooks and handbooks flooded the market in the 16th and 17th centuries, and in the process the systematized 'rules' and parameters of hand-reading began to be firmly fixed, in spite of the continuing and more fluid oral tradition disseminated by the gypsies of Europe (who, incidentally, did not bring palmistry to England, as an old notion has it, but found it there when they arrived). The physiognomical links had not yet been severed, nor had the astrological: and the latter still remain integrally connected with palmistry, perhaps to inject something ethereal into what is after all a very flesh-oriented subject.

But by the 19th century the importance of physiognomy was waning, in spite of a comparatively short-lived flurry of interest in a new branch, PHRENOLOGY. And from its ruin only palmistry was to be salvaged on any broad level of popular interest. More and more books were now being written trying to make 'chirology' respectable, among them the American William G. Benham's *Laws of Scientific Hand Reading*, 1900, prying the subject loose from its gypsy-fraud connotations and giving it a reassuringly 'rational' colouration. Also contributing to this improved repute, but more especially contributing to the spread of its popularity, were the writings of Count Louis Hamon, who called himself 'Cheiro'.

Cheiro seems to have been a plausible charlatan who found a good thing (of which he always showed a very imperfect knowledge, historically and theoretically) and made a fortune from it. Yet according to the accounts of hordes of his clients, who in the 1890s and after included rich, famous, respectable and unimpeachably honest persons from many countries, the accuracy of his predictions was astonishing. The list of events that he apparently foresaw is nearly endless, and includes the exact dates of the deaths of Queen Victoria, Edward VII and Lord Kitchener. He remains an enigma and a controversial subject still; a confidence man who may have found to his surprise that he actually possessed the talent he claimed to have: but certainly still a dominant figure, through repeated editions of his books, in popular palmistry.

The advantage of hand-reading, of course, on a popular level, is its apparent simplicity. No extra paraphernalia are required, like crystal balls or ephemerides or TAROT cards, since the material from which the reading is taken is always, so to speak, at hand. And, once a few basic concepts are memorized (that finger shapes reveal this and palm lines refer to that) you can get right on with 'parlour palmistry' with your friends, and let the complexities and refinements of readings develop later, in their own good time, if at all. No wonder, then, that palmistry seems to rank even higher than tea-cup reading among do-it-yourself diviners. On less amateur levels, however, the subtleties of reading and interpreting hands far outclass those of peering at random shapes of tea-leaves.

Types of Hand

The reader of hands begins with the broad view and progressively narrows his focus. It seems to be generally agreed that the left

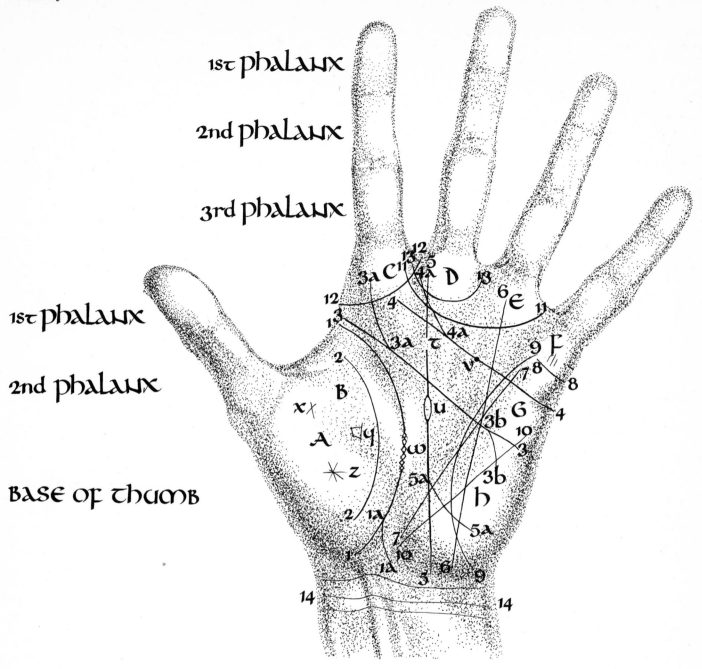

1st phalanx

2nd phalanx

3rd phalanx

1st phalanx

2nd phalanx

BASE OF THUMB

A Mount of Venus	**τ** break	**1** Line of Life	**4a** branch from Line of Heart to between 1st and 2nd fingers	**9** Line of Intuition
B Mount of Mars Positive	**u** island	**1a** branch from Line of Life, producing fork		**10** Via Lasciva
C Mount of Jupiter	**v** spot	**2** Line of Mars	**5** Line of Fate	**11** Girdle of Venus
D Mount of Saturn	**ω** chain	**3** Line of Head	**5a** line running up into the Line of Fate from the Mount of the Moon	**12** Ring of Solomon
E Mount of Apollo or the Sun	**x** cross	**3a** branch from Line of Head to Mount of Jupiter		**13** Ring of Saturn
F Mount of Mercury	**y** square	**3b** branch from Line of Head, producing fork	**6** Line of Fortune or the Sun	**14** Bracelets
G Mount of Mars Negative	**z** star	**4** Line of Heart	**7** Line of Health	
h Mount of the Moon			**8** Line of Marriage	

hand reveals the subject's inherited predispositions of character, while the right hand shows his individuality and its potential. (These are usually said to be reversed in left-handed people.) And of course no serious chirognomist would read one without the other. Again, reading from a distance as it were, the palmist can tell a certain amount about the subject from his or her use of the hands, though many of these 'gesture readings' are fairly obvious. Most of us will accept the idea that someone given to abrupt or violent gestures will be of a fairly nervous and perhaps aggressive temperament; or that languid gestures, extravagant gestures, graceful gestures, similarly mirror the maker's personality, as indeed does the habit of keeping the hands hidden or withdrawn, in pockets or with crossed arms.

More important, though, are the size and shape of the hand. And here the old human urge to classify people, by whatever criteria, comes into flower, creating the many systems of hand typing in chirognomy. Among the most common is the division into seven basic types, established by the 19th-century French palmist Casimir D'Arpentigny. The seven begin with the 'elemental' hand, primitive, thick, broad and powerful. Its owner, obviously, will be said to be slow, solid, earthy, probably a manual worker. The 'spatulate' hand is spade-shaped, flat with fairly straight fingers, and denotes a person of energy, shrewdness and ambition. The 'square' hand naturally indicates a practical, orderly, sensible sort of person. The 'philosophical' hand is broad-palmed with fairly knobbly joints, and indicates a rational and logical temperament. The 'artistic' hand is often long, or seems to be, and may be extremely flexible; it denotes not only artistic inclinations but intellectualism and perhaps a tendency to a sybaritic way of life. The 'conical' or 'idealistic' hand is delicate and beautiful, the hand of an impractical aesthete. And finally the 'mixed' hand complicates the whole system by revealing a combination of some of the previous categories.

Another 19th-century authority on palmistry, the German Carl Gustav Carus, found that he was perfectly content with only four pigeon-holes for hand types – a broader classification, then, but therefore rather more accommodating than D'Arpentigny's attempt at finer distinctions. Carus also began with an 'elementary' hand – that same crude, thick shape ascribed to the manual worker, on the level of Eugene O'Neill's 'Hairy Ape' or Edwin Markham's 'Man With a Hoe'. Slightly less brutalized is the 'motoric' hand, which Carus seems to have

The parts of the hand in palmistry

found among skilled craftsmen, technicians and businessmen, and which is strong, flexible, fairly large, and revealing of an outgoing, practical, lively nature. The 'sensitive' hand is not large and is usually flexible; it reveals qualities of energy, emotionalism, perhaps impracticality or changeability. And, fourth, the 'psychic' hand is slim, tapering, soft and attractive, denoting a vague, intuitive, sensitive personality with none too strong a hold on reality.

If a good deal of the human personality seems to be left out of this system, it is covered more adequately by another four-fold grouping devised by a modern chirognomist, Fred Gettings. He relates palm size and finger length to arrive at his four types, and he also connects them with the old four elements of earth, fire, air and water. His first is the 'practical' hand, square palm and short fingers, the earthy hand of reliable, solid, 'down-to-earth' people. Next is the 'intuitive' type, long palm and short fingers, related to fire and indicative of an active, changeable, ambitious, individualist nature. The 'sensitive' type of hand has a long palm and long fingers, is linked with water, and may show introversion, instability, emotionality, a tendency to fantasy. The fourth is the 'intellectual' hand, square palm and long fingers, linked with air, revealing an orderly, communicative, quick-witted, perceptive character.

Of course, Gettings offers interpretations of these types rich in qualifications, extensions, modifications and overlappings. Justice has not been done in these encapsulations to his apparently practicable system. But at least some picture will have emerged of the type of general interpretation that a palmist might make from the first glance at the shape of the subject's hands. He can also tell much from the flexibility or stiffness of a hand (reflecting comparable personality traits), from skin texture (revealing sensitivity or its lack), from perspiration (we all know what a damp and clammy palm is supposed to indicate), even from hairiness, general colour, and any random markings on the skin, all of which have come in for extensive analysis and imposition of 'rote' meanings (hairiness is said to reveal sexiness) over the centuries. But once all these overall studies of the hand are complete, the palmist moves in closer to look at the hand's different parts – analysis of which he must finally synthesize for his full interpretation. He can begin anywhere, but may choose to begin with the fingers.

'Murderer's Thumb'

A few of the standard 'meanings' of finger shapes, beloved by amateurs, may be mentioned. Some of them, indeed, find their way

into everyday folklore about temperament: in popular belief, as in divination, long fingers are supposed to denote sensitivity and short fingers the opposite. Also, it is said, pointed finger tips indicate imaginative ability, squared tips mean rationality, spatulate tips reveal an active person. Less commonplace are the traditional notions that pronounced joints on fingers indicate a logical and methodical person; smooth fingers speak of intuition, thick puffy fingers suggest sensuality, large fingers may mean a plodding temperament, crooked fingers indicate malice, widely separated fingers speak of independence. A large thumb reveals a strong personality, a thumb bent inwards indicates introversion and outwards its opposite, and an old wives' tale says that a special bulbousness of the first (the nail-bearing) joint is the shape called the 'murderer's thumb'.

As the palmist approaches the fingers individually, he keeps one eye carefully on the zodiac, for here is one of the points at which palmistry is correlated with astrology. Each finger is named after a Greco-Roman god, and shares the characteristics of that god; three of the fingers are named after gods who are also planets. The index finger, being dominant of the four, corresponds to the dominant, kingly god-planet, Jupiter. This finger reveals the subject's potential achievement in the *outer* life. So a short index finger, shorter than the third, may indicate insecurity, inability to cope; but a strong finger of Jupiter, especially when matched with a powerful thumb, means success, and indeed sometimes an overbearing dominance.

The second or middle finger is related to cold and dour old Saturn, and extreme length may reveal a comparable coldness. Sometimes a very long middle finger is said to reveal mental imbalance, even suicidal tendencies; but a short finger of Saturn indicates an intuitive and perhaps creative person.

The third finger belongs to Apollo, a complex god, concerned with such matters as the arts, medicine and oracles, but also with the Sun, which restores an astrological reference. Traditionally this finger is said to indicate the emotional quality of the subject: a well-shaped finger may mean emotional instability, a long one may indicate deep introversion. There is an old folk belief that a vein or artery runs directly from the left-hand third finger to the heart, hence the love symbolism of placing the betrothal or wedding ring on that finger. Palmistry reflects this belief, as when a crooked third finger is said to mean a predisposition to heart disease.

The little finger is related to Mercury, and is traditionally the finger of one's human relationships: if the finger is set apart from the others it means a difficulty in these relationships. If the finger pushes forward when at rest, the difficulty may be sexual. A long little finger indicates an intellectual, academic bent; an excessively short one has been said to indicate mental deficiency.

Now the focus can narrow further, when the palmist looks at separate parts of the fingers. Each segment or phalanx of the fingers and thumb has its special connections: so that a thin second phalanx of the thumb may show an impulsive tendency; a heavy first joint means abundant energy but little staying power; an inward bend of the first segment of the finger of Saturn points to emotional difficulties. Palmists also read much into the tips of the fingers (and so were delighted when modern forensic science accepted the use of fingerprinting): if a certain kind of specially sensitive pad of flesh occurs on the tip, it indicates the presence of high creative talent. The fingernails also tell the palmist much; square ones are said to mean practicality (square shapes usually do), short round ones indicate covetousness, excessively short nails may mean fanaticism.

Mounts and Lines

After this gathering of finger information, the palmist will usually turn to the closely related fleshy areas of the hand around the central palm. These are called the 'mounts', and are explicitly astrological in their references. The flesh at the base of the thumb forms the mount of Venus, sharing the associations of the planet: a large mount denotes abundant physical energy and a strong sexuality. On the other side of the hand is the mount of the Moon, which if well developed speaks of imagination and creativity, perhaps at extremes slipping into irrationality and even 'lunacy'. But an underdeveloped mount of the Moon hints at instability (the changeable moon) and a liking for interfering in the lives of others.

The other mounts lie at the bases of the fingers, and take their names from them. A large mount of Jupiter (index finger) hints at high ambition; a large mount of Saturn (middle) means seriousness tending towards gloominess; a large mount of Apollo or the Sun (third) indicates extraversion; a large mount of Mercury (little finger) means a critical personality. Of course each mount cannot really be considered in isolation: for instance, an apparent blending of the mounts of Jupiter and Saturn indicates a tendency to sharp practice and ruthlessness.

With all this information marshalled and interrelated, the chirognomist now turns his attention to those features of the hand that loom largest in the popular idea of palmistry:

the lines of the palm. These markings have standard names that signify the areas of the subject's existence to which they supposedly correspond. First and presumably most important is the life line, curving down towards the wrist.

Sensible modern palmists do *not* claim that the length of life can be read in the length of this line. They prefer to say that the length of the line indicates how much physical *vitality* the subject possesses, underlining the fact that a limited vitality or energy does not necessarily mean an early demise. But most palmists will look for breaks in the line, or crossings by lesser lines, as indications of ill health of varying severity. At the same time an apparent break might really be merely a severe bend or unevenness, which may have nothing to do with health but with a drastic alteration in the direction or the quality of life.

The beginnings of lines are crucial: a life line arising like a tributary from well along the head line may mean a cold, calculating personality (head- rather than body-dominated). If the life line arises below the head line, it denotes a lively, uninhibited personality.

The head line slashes across the centre of the palm, and refers to the subject's mental tendencies and abilities. A long line hints at a breadth of understanding, coupled with imaginative power if the line curves towards the mount of the Moon. And imagination is more and more dominant, even to an unbalanced degree, the more pronounced the wristward curve. If the line resembles a chain pattern, it speaks of intellectual activity occurring in bursts, because of a limited concentration span.

The heart line needs little elaboration. Amateur palmists like to dwell on this line, looking for breaks that indicate shifts of affection, fickleness and so on, or looking for a strong, long line that reveals emotional depth, fidelity and a healthy sexuality (as well as comparative safety from cardiac disorder, for the real as well as the metaphorical heart is traditionally linked with this line). A good chirognomist will read the heart line in connection with the head line, to see how mind and emotions correlate or balance, if at all, and also to watch for the so-called 'simian' line, when the two lines run together, with ominous indications to be outlined later.

The fate line runs vertically on the palm towards the finger of Saturn, and supposedly is central to divinatory palmistry. Appropriately, its shape can vary considerably. A strong line is said to indicate a strong personality and an ability to adapt oneself to circumstances. Interestingly, this line may

show more changes in early life than any other, perhaps because more choices are being made, and potentials being realized, that help to 'fix' the person's destiny.

Lesser lines include the girdle of Venus, which curves below the fingers of Saturn and Apollo, and indicates a highly emotional nature if it is pronounced. The line of Apollo runs up towards the third finger, and denotes the level of creativity and, some say, of intuitive ability; many small lines instead of one definite line indicate an abundance (perhaps an over-abundance) of areas of interest.

The line of Mercury (sometimes called the line of intuition) should rise from the fate line, or near it, and end on the mount of Mercury; if well defined it reveals a high psychic ability. Some palmists watch for the 'hepatic line' or line of health running diagonally from near the life line to near the mount of Mercury, and supposedly revealing the subject's potential health: breaks mean digestive trouble, chaining means headaches. And the lines around the wrist at the base of the hand, called the 'rascettes' or bracelets, have their own meanings: three clear rascettes spell out forthcoming health and wealth, but a chain pattern means that the subject must exert himself to avoid failure. If a line runs from the rascettes in the direction of the mount of Jupiter, a good marriage is foretold.

Finally, there are even more minor features that palmists may consider – small spottings, or little shapes like stars, crosses, squares, triangles and others. For example, the usual do-it-yourself textbook meanings are that a star (on a mount) may mean fame, spots may mean illness, a cross on a line means a trauma, a square means stability, an island means an obstacle to be overcome.

Modern Developments

By this time the reader may have been peering at his or her own hand, perhaps with some puzzlement, wondering indeed whether any sense at all can be made out of all the creases and wrinkles that can be seen. A chirognomist would suggest that, as with any other skill, a failure to master it immediately does not necessarily prove its worthlessness. But this leads to the crucial question, for the ordinary person who is neither avid believer nor rabid sceptic: can any worth, any validity, be found in the palmist's art?

To begin with, many people seem inclined to believe in palmistry, or at least to suspend disbelief, because it seems somehow more likely that some kind of account of our personalities and potentials should be discernible on our own flesh, rather than in the movements of immeasurably distant stars, in the random fall of tea-leaves, in the shuffling of bits of decorated card. And indeed, as has

A palmist at work

searchers into a fairly new discipline tentatively called 'dermatoglyphics' have been finding and verifying correlations between abnormal palm prints and inborn physical disorders. Prominent among the disorders are chromosome complications, heart defects and the like. And among the abnormalities of the palm looked for are a broad Y-shape – with the stem running up from the wrist and the arms fanning out towards the little and index fingers – and, even more importantly, the abnormality called the 'simian line', where the heart and head line run as one.

This line is so called because it occurs frequently in the larger apes; when it occurs in man, it is, in palmistry's traditions, a sign of 'degeneracy', as the older texts have it – meaning either insanity, criminality or mental subnormality. To us now it may seem tasteless to link these three conditions as if they were somehow comparable. But certainly the most modern research (such as that conducted by a team of doctors in New York in 1966) has proved that the simian line occurs in conjunction with mental retardation such as mongolism, or the mental or physical defects that can result from the pregnant mother's contracting German measles. In other words, the presence of the simian line, the Y-shape and one or two other more subtle abnormalities in the hand of a baby ought to cause doctors to look carefully for possible defects. In themselves these markings are not conclusive; but they can offer a valuable hint.

Whether or not these areas of scientific verification on the peripheries of palmistry can be taken as vindication of the whole art will depend upon the individual's willingness or unwillingness to be convinced. If any reader is convinced, and is about to buy an expensive text on 'Palmistry at Home for Fun and Profit', with which to read the fortunes of his friends and neighbours, this may be the place to echo and stress a common warning issued by professionals. Julius Spier, in his Jungian way, asserts that the human soul 'is in a state of continuous flux'. So then, presumably, are its outer manifestations. Fred Gettings mentions that a subject's hand markings can change to reflect some inner change: a pattern might reveal, say, a neurosis one year, but apparently another year, after a little therapy, that pattern might disappear entirely. This reservation is an unusual assertion of free will over the determinism that usually goes hand in hand with prophecy.

Gettings and others insist that it is unwise and dangerous for a palmist ever to predict serious illness, and especially death, from a hand. The palmist, being human, can err; or developments within the subject can alter his

been mentioned, no psychologist would deny that the individual's use of his hands, in gesture and in manual activity, reveals much. Further, no forensic scientist would disagree that patterns on the skin are wholly individualized, allowing identification by fingerprint; and of course individualized skin patterns on the hand are the starting point of palmistry.

But it is still a long way from give-away gestures or fingerprint differences to reading the state of one's health in the life line, or sexual potency in the mount of Venus. One must look elsewhere to find more concrete verification of chirognomy, if it is to be found. Many palmists think it can be found in some measure in the researches of a German psychologist, Julius Spier, who spent much of his life gathering prints of hands, studying and classifying them, towards the development of what he called 'psycho-chirology'. The hands he chose were those of children, whose 'true dispositions', as he put it, were still to be realized, so that any potential psychological problems could be perceived in the hands and then forestalled – in his terms again, psycho-chirology as prophylaxis rather than therapy.

Most of Spier's book, *The Hands of Children* – his only book, because of his assiduousness in spending years in gathering his material, leaving little time for writing before his death – reflects his variations on traditional hand-reading interpretations. No chirognomist could presumably be without Spier's psychological interpretations, but many psychologists seem to be able to get along without his chirology. Nonetheless, the presence of a reasonably respectable Jungian (C. G. Jung wrote a preface to his book) in the field of palmistry may confer on it some respectability (or may give further ammunition to those who scorn Jung for his interest in alchemy, astrology and allied matters).

Spier was not alone: other psychologists have turned to chirology, including Herta R. Levi, who edited and expanded Spier's book. More recently, we are told, a pediatrician in Los Angeles has built up a massive file of footprints of newborn babies, from which he has felt able to predict with reasonable accuracy what illnesses the owners of the feet would suffer in later life. It is interesting to recall that the ancient Chinese read with care the lines on the feet as well as on the hands, an art that – until now, at least – has been forgotten.

In the last decade or two, American re-

health, his likely future, and his palm. Whereas if the notion has been planted in his mind that he may die at such and such a time, it may at least create an anxiety state; at worst, it is said, the subject might be caused subconsciously to make the prediction come true. In other words, the palmists are saying – and who should know it better than they – that there is no telling how suggestible some people are. D. H.

(Further reading: *178, 220, 280, 383, 436.*)

Palm Sunday Case See MEDIUMS; MRS WILLETT.

Papus

The pseudonym of Gérard Encausse (1865–1916), a French doctor and a leading popularizer of occultism, author of *Traité élémentaire de science occulte*, 1888, *Le Tarot de Bohémiens*, 1889, *Traité méthodique de science occulte*, 1891. He was one of the Council of Twelve of the Ordre Kabbalistique de Rose-Croix (see ROSICRUCIANS) and in about 1891 took over the leadership of the Martinist Order (see MARTINISM), which later became closely connected with the German O.T.O. (*303*)

Parapsychology

Parapsychology is the science of 'psychic' abilities. Parapsychologists, the people who study these abilities, prefer the Greek letter *psi* to the popular word 'psychic', but the two terms have the same meaning. People in different countries also have different names for this branch of study. The term 'psychical research' originated in England. The word 'parapsychology' comes from *Parapsychologie* in German. In France the term *métapsychique* is used. 'Parapsychical' as an adjective goes better with parapsychology than do 'supernormal' and 'paranormal', which imply a wrong assumption of 'normality'. But psi has for the present taken over this adjectival usage.

Whatever name is applied to this relatively new branch of study, the abilities themselves can be clearly described. They enable a person to make contact with the world around him without the aid of his senses and muscles. On the receiving side, he obtains knowledge by extrasensory means, which is called extrasensory perception (ESP). On the outgoing side, the ability is known as 'mind over matter', or psychokinesis (PK). PK ability allows a person to influence his physical environment without the use of the motor system of his body, his muscles and glands.

The two main types of psi interaction, ESP and PK, make up the entire field covered by parapsychology thus far. The two-way communication may be called 'extrasensorimotor' to distinguish it from the sensorimotor interaction on which we mainly rely. To distinguish the varieties of psi phenomena that occur, each of the main types of psi is subdivided into three more specific groups, as follows.

Clairvoyance, Precognition, Telepathy

Extrasensory perception has been found to consist of three kinds of phenomena – clairvoyance, precognition, and telepathy. Clairvoyance is the awareness of things or objective events that is acquired without sensory means. The individual who has such an experience may know of the presence of a hidden object that he could not perceive in any sensorial way and that could not be identified by reasoning, or he may be aware of a physical process or action, such as the distant sinking of a ship.

In a precognitive experience the person knows of something that is going to happen at some future time. Of course no sensory ability can tell him that, and no way is known to predict a specific chance event by purely rational means. This is what is meant by prophecy – foreknowledge of an occurrence such as cannot reliably be inferred from present knowledge (as, of course, a great deal can be).

Telepathy is still more distinctive. The general idea is that one person makes direct mental contact with another without the sensorimotor mediation of language, code, clue, or other physical signalling. In other words, the communication is assumed to occur as a pure transfer of a mental message; hence the descriptive synonym 'thought-transference'.

These three inclusive categories of possible

A device for testing PK ability to make lamps glow in a designated order

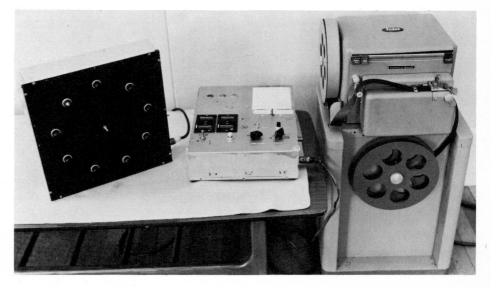

extrasensory exchange, although extremely different in the kinds of knowledge they convey, all have a common feature in addition to being extrasensory: the knowledge they bring shows intelligent purpose, often of great importance. For example, the message may concern a crisis occurring to a friend far enough away to exclude any possible sensory cues. Or ESP may occur to a person who falls asleep with an anxious concern over a lost object; he may dream of its location and find on waking that his clairvoyant awareness has solved the problem in his sleep. The experience of spontaneous precognition is probably familiar to most people. With this subtype, too, the dream is a frequent conveyor of information. The dreamer may see a vivid picture of an accident that is actually experienced days afterwards, and perhaps hundreds of miles away. He may visit in his dreams a new scene at which, days later, he unexpectedly finds himself (see also DREAMS).

Telepathy seems to be the most familiar kind of psi experience for most people, and sometimes seems almost to be a dependable method of exchange between two persons accustomed to close contact with each other. When it involves the sharing of a completely accidental experience occurring to one of the pair when the two are separated, it is most impressive; for example, a mother may feel much the same discomfort as her daughter while the latter (at an unexpected time) is giving birth to a child.

It is well to remember that in all such cases as these other explanations are possible, and it is best to be slow in reaching conclusions as to the psi interpretation. Although the science of parapsychology begins with cases like these because they suggest a possibility that calls for investigation, the more definite conclusions must be left for the more careful examination that is possible in experiments.

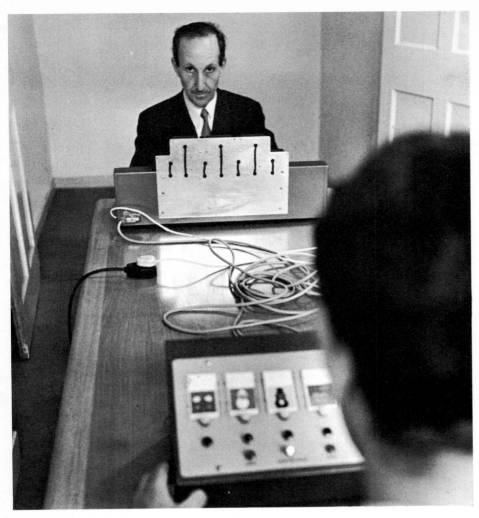

ESP testing apparatus, shown with the screen removed

Psychokinesis

Psychokinesis, too, falls into three subdivisions and, as with ESP, natural branches. Because PK is the direct influence of mind on matter, it is classified according to the three states of matter on which it can take effect. These are not, however, the three categories of solid, liquid, and gaseous known to every beginning student of physics, nor are they those of animal, vegetable, or mineral from the old guessing game. Rather, for the PK student, the material world is divided into moving, living, and static matter.

These three divisions are obviously loose classifications of matter, but they are particularly suited to the testing of PK. For example, many more individuals have thought they could mentally influence rolling dice or an arrow in flight than have believed they could make a stationary body move. This tendency to believe in the ability to exert PK on a moving target object made it easier to get subjects to try to demonstrate the suspected ability. In the form of dice-throwing, it became a gamelike test of PK, just as the

guessing of cards has made ESP tests essentially a kind of contest with chance.

As yet there is no name in parapsychology for the demonstration of PK on moving targets because it is still too new, but it is commonly referred to by the abbreviation PK–MT. This, of course, draws attention by contrast to the PK of static targets, which is called PK–ST. As will be seen later, our knowledge of this subtype from careful research still lags behind, but a growing number of persons believe they have observed stationary objects spontaneously moved by human agency without direct or indirect muscular effort. In other words, they have been convinced that they have witnessed PK–ST.

Regardless of how the physicist may classify matter for his own purposes, there is a distinctly different category which he usually omits, namely, living matter. This type of matter is, as everyone knows, different from inanimate substances, whether static or moving. Yet some people believe they have mentally influenced living matter in both plants and animals, in its special functions of growth, healing, and the like. This would be PK–LT. Fortunately, this is a phenomenon

that can be studied by means of controlled experiments; therefore, it is not necessary to try to decide whether these reports of personal experience provide acceptable evidence in themselves.

It should be remembered that it is not necessary to make up one's mind conclusively about the occurrence of each subtype or to try to decide whether each kind of psi phenomenon is independent of the other subtypes. More final decisions can be made at a later stage, at least in most cases, and one can study the evidence for certain aspects while making only tentative judgments as to its firmness and finality. It will be seen later that as a result of the more controlled experimental studies, clairvoyance and precognition are the more conclusively established subtypes of ESP; telepathy is still inconclusive (in its mind-to-mind interpretation). With regard to mind over matter, the PK of moving targets is very well established, but the PK of living targets is only moderately well established. The case for the PK of static targets should still be considered to belong in the inconclusive stage, even more so than telepathy, although it may not remain so for very long. In this way we can keep the question open and continue investigation. Although it is not as hazardous to accept a claim prematurely as to reject it, it is still a dangerous decision because it tends to stop the investigation.

While we suspend judgment about the acceptability of telepathy and of PK–ST, we can tentatively consider them possible and keep them in the tentative chart of the territory claimed by the science of parapsychology. The following outline of this territory will help to keep these subtypes in mind:

Psi ('Psychic') or Parapsychical Ability

Extrasensory Perception
Clairvoyance (conclusive)
Precognition (conclusive)
Telepathy (inconclusive)

Psychokinesis
PK–MT (conclusive)
PK–LT (marginal)
PK–ST (inconclusive)

In summing up this section of terms, definitions, and an outline of the field, it is important to remember that parapsychology is a progressive branch of study. It now seems that the types of phenomenon that belong to this field have a kind of unity and that psi ability may even be a single system, of which the subtypes are just the phenomena or effects that are produced as psi functions within the integrated individual. Therefore, in the sections that follow, this working view of the unified field will be evident; it will be especially interesting to see that general properties emerge that seem to apply to all the types as though they were a unit. Moreover, these properties of the various kinds of ESP and PK are, in some cases at least, unique to them and do not apply to other kinds of human behaviour. Such properties help to identify the field of parapsychology as a branch of study and to give it its importance.

At this point the reader may want to turn at once to the pages which explain what the most careful experimental science can teach him about this area of strange happenings – to the hard facts about what can be and has been firmly proved about them. But he may wish first to catch a glimpse of the importance that these unusual abilities have already had for mankind, and of how this great significance could have been, at least for a time, completely ruled out and set aside by the advances of science in other fields. This is the historical setting of this branch of inquiry, the story of its origins in brief review.

Spontaneous Psi Experiences

Not everyone has had a 'psychic' experience, or at least not everyone knows that he has. If, to choose a fairly clear-cut actual case, a woman has a nightmare in which she sees her brother shoot himself, in the haymow of his barn, and on arrival after travelling through the night to check on her dream, she actually finds him there, where she had thought she saw him fall, there is little doubt that this person has had an experience identifiable as clairvoyant extrasensory perception. If one can be sure that the story is true, and that the woman did not have information which suggested that this tragic outcome was a probable one, the case then becomes very impressive.

ESP may function intuitively without a person knowing how he got his information in an experience of spontaneous clairvoyance. He may have had what he called a hunch – for instance, a mere impulse to take a certain unaccustomed route home. Later he may discover that this enabled him to do something very important to him that he would otherwise have missed completely, and something of which he could have had no previous knowledge. His intuition may have come to him before the event could have begun to happen, and so would probably have been a precognition. But, supposing he can think of some possible rational reason for his decision to go out of his way on this particular occasion, then, if he is wise, he will not accept the case as an indication of his ESP capacity. One can see, however, how easy it would be for a rather flimsy conscious argument to

have been used if he had an *unconscious* urge to go on the strength of his assumed precognition that something serious would happen. Fortunately, no one needs to draw a conclusion in the many doubtful cases that are reported. But at least a question is raised as to whether some unknown ability or influence may have caused the experience.

What is of the greatest importance is that some of these spontaneous experiences, and naturally the strongest cases, have since ancient times impressed people so strongly that eventually in all major cultures they began to require some sort of theory. (These various types of occurrence and the form of the experiences have been described by Louisa E. Rhine in her *Hidden Channels of the Mind*.) Some individuals have had dreams that came true; others have had hunches or intuitions of approaching danger. Still others have had the gift of locating lost or hidden objects, by using methods developed in the particular culture. The various practices of magic or DIVINATION built up around the types of psi ability are as numerous as are the subcultural groups of mankind.

The Essential Role of Psi in Religion

We would have to speculate freely today to try to conceive how mankind's earliest experiences of these psychic abilities took hold and became seriously considered. But we can tell something about this from the use made of these assumed psychic powers in various cultures, especially in their religions and their practice of magic. The religions best illustrate this, and in a way, the part that psi plays in religion (and any supernatural religion can be used to illustrate this) represents the greatest use it has yet been given in human affairs. The entire element of the supernatural or miraculous in a religion is almost identical with the supposition of unlimited psi ability on the divine level. The assumption that deities had omniscience and omnipotence was the equivalent of attributing to them supreme powers of ESP and PK ability. There would have been no need to develop a theology that limited its deities to the sensorimotor range of man himself, because it must be supposed that in every culture there was ample awareness of the extrasensory and extramotor experiences that were probably always common enough among all men. These psi experiences would have seemed then, as they do now, to have so far transcended the reach of eye and hand as to be apparently divine. These phenomena were transcendent and gradually as religions developed a rationale, the natural powers of psi became the supernatural.

Thus it can be said that it is belief in the powers of psi that has given the founders of

the religions of mankind their ideas as to the forms of communication between the human and the divine. There is, of course, a great deal more to religion than these modes of interaction, but it is significant that what have come to be called the subtypes of psi in parapsychology match closely such terms of religious communication as prayer, revelation, prophecy, and the various types of physical miracles.

It is a good question whether, without this application of their belief in psi ability, men could have developed powerful systems of belief that gave to morality the authority of divine command. Without the concept of some kind of extraphysical or spiritual principle to interact with the material system of the body, it seems doubtful whether a sense of moral control over the physical functions of life could ever have been achieved. At any rate it seems fairly certain that these religious and moral aspects owed much indeed to the powers of psi.

Naturalization of the Supernatural

It follows that a serious situation was created when, with the advancement of science, scepticism grew as to whether these theological systems were true. Who could accept the physical miracles after becoming acquainted with the limitations of physical energies and after seeing how the miracles conflicted with the physical theory of nature? Progressively through the 18th, 19th and 20th centuries this scepticism has undermined the supernaturalism of religion, leaving it to such modifications as can subsist on the barren support of the physical sciences and behaviouristic psychology.

To the student of parapsychology it is clear, however, that psi principles are vitally important to religion, as emphasized by reliance on miracles and supernatural signs and demonstrations. Conversely, the first attempts at naturalistic theories of the universe had to account for the miraculous powers too. However, the first wild speculations did not last long in the critical light of science. For example, by the late 18th century the emergence of the science of physics had produced theories of universal fluids and interplanetary forces. Franz Anton MESMER developed a theory of a universal magnetic fluid, as universal as Newton's gravitation theory. Among its many other applications it explained telepathy, clairvoyance, and communication with the spirit world, at least for some of the mesmerists. Interest in spirit communication had, of course, always been part of the official or unofficial doctrines of religion. The great Swedish scientist Emanuel Swedenborg had practised such communication, and his influence as a religious leader had helped to spread the idea of such exchange. The practice of mesmerism likewise popularized the TRANCE state and encouraged the idea of psychical ability being favoured by such a susceptible condition.

The 19th-century concept of a universal ether and of wave-like communication in this medium favoured the search for a naturalistic explanation of what had been hitherto regarded as completely miraculous. It brought the claim of survival after death within the bounds of the more venturesome speculation of the day. Spirits could be ethereal bodies, and communication with the dead could be the transference of thought by means of ether waves (see ETHERIC BODY).

Generalizations followed each other like bubbles until pricked by some challenge of scientific thought. Mesmerism, although impressive, could not be well enough confirmed. The phenomenon worked too erratically, and the theory failed in scientific examination although HYPNOSIS emerged and survived. The search for spirit communication shifted to the religious cult of SPIRITUALISM, and the CHRISTIAN SCIENCE movement centred attention on the efficacy of mind (spirit) in healing. This looked like PK–LT (living targets).

With all the zigs and zags of these struggles with ideas that the Western world experienced in the 19th century, there was emerging a strong impulse to bridge the gap between religion and science, which were increasingly at war. Attention became particularly directed to the problem of whether

Professor J. B. and Dr Louisa E. Rhine

the existence of a superphysical soul, mind, or spirit, as assumed by religion, could be verified after the manner of science. Spiritualist claims that it could were taken seriously by a number of scholarly people in the West in the late 19th century; it was at least worth investigation. Enough evidence had accumulated from MEDIUMS to lead to the formation in Britain of the Society for Psychical Research (see PSYCHICAL RESEARCH SOCIETIES) to investigate mesmerist, psychical and Spiritualist claims, and the example was followed by similar societies in many other countries. This movement was especially well led in Britain and made considerable progress in bringing the problems connected with mediumship into better focus, but it did not succeed in bringing the major issue, that of spirit communication, to a scientific conclusion. Rather, there was a growing realization over the next forty years that the problem was much more difficult than the Spiritualist demonstrations had suggested. Nevertheless, the scientific residue that emerged from the overspecialized study of mediumship was the interest generated in the claim of thought-transference. It was obvious from the start that a medium would need to be gifted with telepathy to intermediate between two worlds. Some saw in telepathy a possible explanation of communication with the world of discarnate beings, which had long played an important role in most religions.

However, it came to be realized that the same gift of telepathy might enable mediums to obtain the information contained in their messages from living sources rather than discarnate ones. Either way, the question of

telepathy was evidently important and experimental work was conducted under the sponsorship of the Society for Psychical Research and also, during the first quarter of the century, in university departments of psychology, particularly in America. At the Universities of Harvard and Stanford in the United States and the University of Groningen in Holland important experimental efforts were made to investigate telepathy. These experiments at the three universities, judged by the standards of that day, fully justified continuance of the effort, and yet in no case was it continued. Telepathy turned out to be much more difficult to work with than most of the other mental abilities being tested. Ease of demonstration had much to do with the eligibility of a subject for a university program. Psychology itself was a new subject that was struggling for recognition. Psychical research could add nothing to its respectability, and it was not a suitable field for a young scientist to choose as a career. The time had not yet come.

However, even if the first quarter of the present century served only to stir up a few psychology departments and further aggravate the already old controversy between psychology and psychical research, there was an unexpected outcome. It did not come from any of these older and better established universities but from a new American university in North Carolina. It was the result of a fortunate culmination of circumstances that provided the sort of haven sought by the few researchers of the time.

Duke University and William McDougall

The period of parapsychological study at Duke University began in 1927, and the main reason for its beginning was the arrival there of the distinguished British psychologist William McDougall from Harvard. More than a year previously he had appealed in a lecture at Clark University for the inclusion of psychical research as a university study. He himself had made a thorough study of that subject, along with psychology and a number of other sciences; beyond doubt he was the best qualified to lead parapsychology in its accommodation to the natural sciences of the day. McDougall's view of man was dualistic; he considered the mind as real and distinctive although interactive with the brain.

He had taken a strong interest in the claims of mediumship and had actively investigated mediums. On his arrival at Duke in September 1927 he found two young biologists, J. B. and Louisa E. Rhine, awaiting him with the hope of working with him on a scientific study of mediumship. He promptly accepted and encouraged them. Like McDougall himself, they were not convinced of anything but the importance of the problem and the need to bring it to scientific solution if possible.

In the work jointly undertaken at Duke under Professor McDougall the question of survival of death was paramount, but because the importance of telepathy was also recognized, some research was carried out on that and related claims at the University while the major issue of survival was pursued.

The question was, however, whether there was a possibility of bringing the survival problem to a definite solution. Eight years later a tentative conclusion was reached that the mediumistic approach to the problem of survival could not bring a solution. The medium tested in the Duke Laboratory obtained reliable information pertinent to the appropriate sitter in the adjoining room, and the evaluation of the results was done under what are called double-blind conditions, but the question as to where the medium obtained her ESP information could not be answered. The method could not be considered conclusive because of the possibility that the medium could have obtained her information from the same source as the researchers did in checking the accuracy of her 'communications'. The problem had to be left at the time, and in the thirty-seven years that have followed no one has discovered a better way to deal with it.

Telepathy, of course, was part of the alternative explanation of the medium's success. If the medium had the telepathic ability required for contact with the assumed spirit communicator, this ability could be used to acquire information from the living as well. In fact, the general idea of mediumship takes ESP more or less implicitly for granted. Accordingly, as the survival question had lost ground ESP had received more attention, and by 1933 and 1934 it was clearly in the ascendancy. In 1934 the Duke Laboratory issued its first report, a monograph by J. B. Rhine entitled *Extrasensory Perception*, published obscurely by the Boston Society for Psychic Research.

Psi Phenomena Verified

The impact of the small monograph *Extrasensory Perception* was entirely unexpected both by the author and the publisher, and only a small printing had been made. Although it was given a scholarly introduction by Dr Walter Franklin Prince and a preface by Professor McDougall, this report of several years of ESP tests, with its pages heavily sprinkled with tables and graphs, was not expected to have popular appeal.

Fortunately for the book, however, the publisher had furnished the science editor of the *New York Times*, Waldemar Kaempffert, with a review copy, and he had given it a favourable and lengthy review. After that, other science writers followed suit and there was a great deal of writing about the subject in the form of books and articles over succeeding years. It was a turning point for parapsychology.

Before picking up the thread of the development of the ESP research, which is of course the main story, it may be worth while to look at the setting from which a stream of studies of various types of psi emerged in the decades that followed.

Fruitful contributions had been made earlier but they had not continued as the later efforts at Duke had the opportunity to do. When, nearly fifty years earlier, the distinguished French physiologist Charles Richet had what he considered good evidence of clairvoyant card guessing by his hypnotized subject, Leonie, his subject's ability failed her when the attempt was made to demonstrate her powers to a scientific group at Cambridge University. At the University of Groningen the Brugman tests of what was called telepathy were abandoned, even though they were strikingly successful and sponsored by the eminent Professor G. Heymans. The Harvard experiments on 'telepathy' by G. H. Estabrooks had been sponsored by the equally eminent Professor McDougall and had yielded highly significant results under test conditions that met the highest standards of the psychology laboratories of the day, but were not continued because later efforts gave much less significant results. Yet these and some other less impressive researches had contributed something to the fragmentary knowledge of how to go about the testing of ESP. They did something to encourage the efforts by others later.

At Duke, in the period of the beginning of the ESP researches, the Department of Psychology under McDougall was probably more strongly oriented toward psychical research than any department had ever been. McDougall himself acknowledged psychical research to be one of the two major scientific interests of his life. The founding president of Duke, Dr William Preston Few, gave forthright support to the investigation. Up to the point of the first publication there had been no internal disharmony in the department or in the university at large. Instead, there had been a broad sharing of interest and cooperation. The primary interest in the survival question already discussed gave the ESP experiments special significance. Undoubtedly the most interesting ESP tests carried out were those on the well-known medium, Eileen GARRETT, who was under investigation at Duke at different periods in the early 1930s. All these favourable conditions helped to provide an atmosphere which had much to do with the unusual persistence of the work started.

First Finding, Clairvoyant ESP

The ESP investigations at Duke were not uniformly successful. As we have seen, the effort to find out whether spirit communication was possible was a failure, or at least ended in an impasse. The problem of telepathy, which was the most interesting of all the claims of psychical research that remained, caused similar frustration. In fact, it hit a serious snag almost at the outset.

It was found on making a survey of all the past telepathy experiments that none had ever been carried out so as to permit a proper conclusion. The trouble was that the sender had always been given an object such as a card or a drawing on which to concentrate his attention while the receiver or percipient attempted to identify it in an extrasensory way. Thus there was always the possibility that any success could be attributed to the percipient's clairvoyance of the card itself. The sender's concentration on the target object need not have been involved. The main thing this showed was that those who were testing for telepathy considered they had no evidence of clairvoyance worth taking seriously and that there was no need to bar that possibility. Some of these experiments were conducted in the best of the psychology laboratories of the day; obviously the scraps of evidence of clairvoyance such as that obtained by Richet were too little known and unimpressive to be considered.

At Duke, however, there was a practical reason for preferring clairvoyance as a starting point in the exploration of claims of 'psychic' abilities. It is the simplest of the subtypes from the point of view of method and controls. In the first place, there is only one subject to have to deal with and keep under adequate observation. In controlling the conditions only the sense of sight need be involved. The target object has only to be hidden and this makes the testing very simple. Richet had already used the guessing of hidden playing cards, as had a number of other investigators.

Another fortunate decision was made at this time in following the practice of earlier researchers in the use of playing cards. Long experience in the use of these in games of chance gives good psychological reasons for considering them suitable to a test of an unknown ability. The test can be modelled almost in the form of a game. The mathematics of the casino provided the basis of chance expectation and permitted the easy evaluation of above-chance success. (Later it was discovered to be equally advantageous in measuring the extent of losing, or below-chance rates of success.)

The Duke experimenters wanted five suits or target symbols and especially wanted these to be as easily distinguished from each other as possible to avoid errors, whether by ESP or sensory perception. They adopted a pack of twenty-five cards with the symbols star, circle, square, cross, waves, and this pack has become a standard test device.

By the time (1933) when J. B. Rhine's monograph *Extrasensory Perception* was being written, the experiments with clairvoyance had been conducted with the subjects under such conditions as to allow the conclusion that extrasensory perception of the clair-voyant type had been demonstrated. The subject had been sent to a building 100 yards away from that in which the experimenter handled the target cards. These were isolated one at a time at one-minute intervals, and the card order was not recorded until after the run of twenty-five trials. The cards were kept face down throughout the run, and the subject in the other building recorded his guesses as he made them. Duplicate records of both the cards and the calls made double independent checking possible. With the completion of a planned series of 300 guesses under these conditions over a six-day period the results were so highly and uniformly successful that there was no doubt the results could not be due to chance. In 300 guesses 60 hits were expected on the basis of pure chance, but with 119 hits the odds were 1,000,000 to 1 against such results occurring by chance alone.

At this point it was arranged for a two-experimenter control to be introduced, to insure increased vigilance against error or deception. The experimenter had been J. B. Rhine, and the second observer, who actually handled the cards, was his assistant, J. G. Pratt, then a graduate student and now a well-known parapsychologist. In his reports Rhine called this experiment the Pearce–Pratt series.

Further steps were then taken to test other possible alternatives to the interpretation of extrasensory perception. As a matter of fact, this particular research was climactic, occurring as it did at the time of the publication of the book just mentioned, although only the first series of 300 guesses was completed in time for inclusion there. Because it was a sort of challenge to psychology it obtained a great deal of attention, both pro and con. But although the series was at the time a decisive experiment and led to new lines of investigation, it was soon superseded by a more advanced phase of ESP testing in which the same subject, H. P., took part. This was the work with precognition, which will be introduced later.

The Controversy over ESP

The reaction to the ESP work at Duke was at first comparatively friendly. There was practically no immediate hostility. Many psychologists and others undertook to repeat the Duke experiments, and in a fair number of instances they were successful in doing so. Some of these who did succeed did not want to publish their findings; they were not ready to be identified with the new field and its claims. Some of those who obtained only chance results, however, were strongly disposed to publicize their failures (as if they refuted the positive conclusions of others), and as these became better known through newspapers and other media there was increased and more outspoken criticism of ESP research. Because the press and radio gave this research an unusual amount of attention, and because it was suspected that the ESP researchers themselves were responsible for this, a noticeable strain developed over the ESP work.

Had it been easy for everyone to get significant evidence of ESP repeatedly and at will there would probably have been little criticism. If ESP had been as consciously controllable a capacity as those with which the psychologists were already familiar, unreserved acceptance probably would have followed. However, because a number of failures were reported and only a few of the successes reached publication, there was eventual disappointment with the new claims. Certain scientific groups, mainly the psychologists, held critical symposia (heresy trials, as some of the ESP workers called them), but the ESP proponents did not fare so badly as to be discouraged by these encounters in the late 1930s. The methods of the better experiments met the highest standards of the sciences of the day, but it took much time and discussion to make this clear.

By 1940 it was considered advisable to publish a book to round up the criticism and answer it. This volume, entitled *Extrasensory Perception after Sixty Years*, contained the statements of the seven leading (psychologist) critics who had been asked to read the text and reply. Following that publication both the quantity and quality of criticism declined. The main thing it showed was that parapsychology was able to furnish its own criticism, as, of course, any research science should. An inspection of the scientific periodicals of parapsychology (listed at the end of this article) indicates that this is still the case.

However, certain practices have been developed in psi research that, to an extent unusual in scientific work, insure against error. One of these is the appointment of one or more statistical editors to the *Journal of Parapsychology* staff. Unusually high standards of judging statistical significance have been maintained from the beginning. Certain procedures have been used to help workers to avoid hasty conclusions; one such procedure is the requirement of a confirmatory repetition of a research before publication. Others involve supplementary tests of consistency to buttress a finding that in other sciences would be accepted forthwith. Psi research, because of its frontier character, needs all the devices of scientific method to reinforce the inquiry at every point, and it especially needs deliberate judgment in reaching conclusions.

A special warning is needed about the critics of parapsychology themselves. Many people, including editors and administrators, have thought that the safest way to judge parapsychology was to consult those opposed to it, on the assumption that an antagonistic mind is a better critic than a neutral or favourable one. Experience has shown that if the critics of parapsychology were alien to the field to begin with, it did little good to answer their criticisms, even by conducting new and satisfactory experiments. On the other hand, if the critics were themselves within the field (as were Dr Robert H. Thouless and Dr S. G. Soal, to cite two leading critics of the Duke work), they joined eventually in the research itself with their own developments of method, and became important contributors to parapsychology.

Dr R. H. Thouless

The Advance into Precognition

Although progress in the ESP research at the Duke Laboratory was impeded by the stir aroused by the publication of the ESP monograph, the slender thread of research continued through the years after 1934, and the next subtype to be investigated was precognition. In December 1933, when H. P. had triumphantly finished the series at distances of 100 and 250 yards in clairvoyance tests, he was asked to try to predict the order of the pack of cards as it would be after it was shuffled.

In addition to the ancient beliefs in this capacity of prophecy there had been many spontaneous experiences to suggest the hypothesis of extrasensory perception of future events. The tests already carried out did not indicate a decline of success with increased distance of subject from the target. If space did not influence ESP performance there was no reason to expect time to limit success. There was no suggestion as to how precognition could occur, but then there was none for clairvoyance either. It was simply a question of whether time could bar anything that was going on in the ESP process, which distance had not been found to do.

Intellectually the step was not a big one to take following the advances made in the research by 1933. The subject, H. P., was already disposed to believe in prophecy; he was a theology student. He had believed his mother possessed this gift and he was more

Precognition tested by guessing the random order in which lights will appear

than willing to try it himself. The test itself was simple to devise and conduct. H. P. was asked to call down through a pack of 25 cards, one at a time, as the cards lay in the box. This was a sort of control based on his clairvoyant ability. Next he was asked to call down through another pack of the same type, guessing what the order would be after the pack was shuffled by a specified routine; this part would be the test for precognition. H. P. obtained approximately the same rate of scoring on the precognition test as he had on the clairvoyance tests. The time discrepancy did not make a significant difference in the scoring rates of the two conditions; ESP functioned both ways.

This method gave good enough results to justify reconsideration of the adequacy of the shuffling method. For instance, it was possible that the psi factor might have entered into the shuffling, even though this was considerably varied. At any rate, the randomization of the card order was further extended. It was, for example, decided by the research staff that hand shuffling of the cards could be guided by ESP itself and that this 'psychic shuffle' would have to be ruled out by changing the procedure. The method was shifted to the use of a mechanical shuffling device thereafter, and various kinds of mechanical shufflers were tried. However, the success of the precognition tests continued as if the mode of shuffling made no difference.

By that time no one in the laboratory thought it likely that the various ways of shuffling the cards had contributed to the continuing significance of the results in the

precognition experiments. Nevertheless, in each case the older method had to yield to a new substitute, and of course the final conclusion regarding the occurrence of precognition had to be delayed still further. No matter how much work had already been done, the possibility of an alternative interpretation threw the question back where it had been at the start. Therefore, mechanical shuffling of the target cards was abandoned, and although the test results from that method were still evidence of psi of some type, they were not proof of precognition.

During the years since 1933 a wide variety of methods of randomizing targets for precognition tests have been tried. Usually there has been some logical improvement added, some increased assurance of a chance distribution. The finding regarding precognition is still the same; no way has yet been found to prepare a random target order that has been beyond the reach of precognitive ESP. These developments of precautionary methods have now reached into the sophisticated technology of electronic devices based on radioactive decay.

The Conquest of PK

The testing of precognition at Duke had not gone far beyond its beginning in December 1933, when an incident occurred that opened up the problem of mind over matter for the field of parapsychology. In the early months of 1934, while the excitement over the early results in the prediction of target orders was still high, a young gambler, a student from another college, visited J. B. Rhine at Duke to discuss the still unpublished ESP test results. The young man, W. B., after comparing notes on the conditions of success in ESP testing, which he found in some agreement with his ideas of the conditions that favour success in gambling, affirmed his belief in the mind over matter effect in dice-throwing games. His proposal to demonstrate this was met with strong encouragement, and the ensuing demonstration of throwing dice for designated face combinations was sufficiently successful to initiate a research program of many years' duration.

The PK branch of psi research in the Psychology Department at Duke went through many phases, each of which introduced additional safeguards; only at the beginning were the conditions allowed to be free and easy. Special throwing cups were designed to insure against possible skills that would influence the fall of the dice. Next the dice were released, at first by manual devices and later by electrical methods, and allowed to fall by gravity. Still later, electrically driven rotating cages were used, as was automatic photography of the dice.

Professor Rhine testing PK with dice

The dice were thrown for designated targets of a single face or a combination of faces, such as sevens, high dice, or low dice. In course of progress the design of the selection of targets called for an even representation of each face of the die so as to obtain a balance against any quality that favoured or disfavoured one or another face. With this control against imperfection of the die and the avoidance of any influence of skilled throwing, the most common requirements for reliable testing were provided, but others were added as the research advanced.

In principle, however, the test consisted of asking the subjects to will the dice to fall with the target faces showing. A number of throws would be made in succession for this particular target before another target was selected. The expectation of hits could be computed quite as easily as it could be for the results of the card-guessing tests of ESP. A die thrown for the 'one' face would be expected to come up with that face on the average once every six throws and the same for each of the other faces, counting a throw as that of a single die. The number of hits above chance (or below, when psi-missing was being considered) could be evaluated in the same manner as the ESP results. These methods, which were standard practice for the statistician, depended on the mathematics of probability, which had had its origins more than a century earlier in the casinos of Western Europe, drawn from the frequencies of the fall of dice and the matching of cards. (For details see Chapter II of

Extrasensory Perception after Sixty Years and Chapter IX of *Parapsychology: Frontier Science of the Mind.*)

It was nearly ten years after the beginning of the PK research before it was thought advisable to begin publication. In some respects the PK tests with dice produced more difficulties of control over test methods than did, for example, precognition. In the latter a subject records his predictions, the record sheet is duplicated, and when the target sheets are prepared and duplicated a two-experimenter exchange provides what is effectively a perfect double-blind experiment. In the dice-throwing experiment this could only be approximated by having a double record maintained by two observers, and although this sometimes was done, it was not always convenient or possible.

A discovery was made, however, about eight years after the PK work started, that made it possible to convert the PK results, old and new, into almost equally tight evidence. The discovery was the diagonal decline of hits in the quarter distribution (QD) of the record sheet. These QDs were produced by dividing the record sheet into four equal parts, by drawing a vertical median line and a horizontal line. It was generally found that the upper left quarter gave the highest rate of success and the lower right gave the lowest; the other two were usually in-between. This was the picture for the large majority of the various series that had been carried out by 1942. The differences between the upper left and lower right quarters in their scoring rates were consistent enough to give odds of millions to one against a chance

occurrence of that order. Moreover, there were various other breakdowns into smaller units that showed the same tendency, even on a smaller scale, in the blocks of data on the record sheets.

Since any skills of throwing, inequalities of the dice, or intention to deceive could not have anticipated this discovery in the experimental data that had been accumulated, there seemed nothing to contradict the conclusion that this was crucial evidence of the operation of PK. The only thing in common throughout this extensive QD analysis was the fact that the tests had involved dice-throwing for the purpose of influencing the dice, and that the record sheets were such that they could be divided evenly into four quarters. The result indicated that the persistence of the diagonal decline must indeed be a rather strong characteristic of the PK principle.

But the diagonal decline in PK tests was not a single spontaneous discovery. It was a combination of declines that had been observed first of all in the early ESP tests at the Duke Laboratory. A falling-off of scoring rate in a column of trials had been frequently observed and declines had also been observed in some instances from the left-hand side of the record page to the right. It was the checking of the distribution on the page with both dimensions in view that brought out this position effect, the most remarkable that had yet emerged in the psi-testing program: that is, a more striking persistent tendency came out of looking for this diagonal direction of decline because it appeared to combine the two trends, downward and rightward.

What caused these declines? A partial answer at least can be given. It is noticeable that the declines are more clear-cut and significant when the subject is writing responses on the record sheet or watching the experimenter record. It is a psychological effect of the record sheet structure; it tends to be greater if the recording is done in smaller blocks (let us say four or eight to the page) than the entire page. The individual block shows a diagonal decline as great as or greater than the page as a whole. It is, then, a true position effect; that is, the position of the trial affects the scoring rate. It is not, however, fatigue, because the same structure appears in block after block filled out consecutively in a session. It is therefore evidently something that occurs in the mind of the subject as he goes, perhaps an accumulation of interference effects that grows as he proceeds down the column and from column to column across the record page. It shows what is for parapsychology a beautiful impression of orderly process. Psi is an orderly function as it responds to these test conditions, which encourages the thought that this orderliness will in time yield to still better understanding and in some manner and degree to eventual control.

The QD evidence for PK has been cited here as part of the historical development. It was the climax in the establishment of the occurrence of PK, making so strong a case that, coming as it did at the height of critical attack, it offered a challenge that was extended to any qualified committee of appraisal that the scientists of the day might wish to appoint to give this new science a fair examination. No one accepted; but the Parapsychology Laboratory, for its own assurance, invited an independent examiner to recheck the QD results completely. No errors of any consequence were found.

Trouble with Telepathy

The success with PK, following upon that with clairvoyance and precognition, however, had taken precedence over telepathy; by 1945, when the climax in the conclusiveness of the QD evidence of PK had been reached, a new wave of interest arose in the still inconclusive phenomenon of thought-transference. The evidence for the two other kinds of ESP had been strong even then, and with the strong support for PK now on the record and much of it already published, there was greater readiness to face the experimental complications of telepathy.

As mentioned already, the Duke workers had been unable to find any previous research on telepathy that had not failed to exclude the possibility of clairvoyance and precognition. Now that these phenomena were much better established, there was no question about the necessity of excluding them if there was to be a serious conclusion reached about results. Some steps had already been taken, and reported in *Extrasensory Perception*, to see if evidence suggestive of telepathy could be obtained when the sender did not have the object of which he was thinking before him at the time of the tests. There were series of tests in which the sender chose his target in one way or another (for example, by using a deck of number cards, coded to represent the ESP Zener card symbols of star, circle, square, cross, and waves), with the target recorded only after it was certain that the receiving subject had recorded his response. This was considered to rule out clairvoyance but not precognitive clairvoyance, and thus was not up to the standards of the Laboratory; these required double-blind and independent checking for any major finding of the research.

With great ingenuity, Dr Elizabeth McMahan and her co-workers designed and

The Zener card symbols

completed an experimental series that met the requirements and produced significant results. Her method was to share a secret code by having the sender think of a target symbol with another trained and trusted experimenter, and transfer the code by a complex system of association by implication, based on the common memories of the two persons. They could tell each other in this way what could not be recorded, and the targets could be picked up by the receiver only by telepathy; they chose a number to correspond to star, another for square, a third for cross, and so on. In this way they got around the counter-hypothesis of other forms of ESP and established the case for telepathy as far as the method permits. This work was later confirmed independently in England by Dr S. G. Soal with an essentially similar, though somewhat different, design.

Is this now a conclusive case for telepathy? It does not seem definitely so to some cautious workers in the field. The sender may have reflected in her vocal apparatus some objective basis of the symbol she was thinking of at the time; or even the brain record of the sender's memory could conceivably serve as a clairvoyant target. Until psychology discovers more definitely how to distinguish between mind and brain, it is difficult to be confident that there is not some alternative to the pure mind-to-mind contact that the concept of telepathy assumes.

This problem is similar to that of survival, already mentioned. The possibility of the medium making contact with living persons or existing records offers an alternative to direct contact with the supposed spirit world. Similarly, in a number of other problem areas of parapsychology this kind of impasse

confronts us. For example, it rules out a conclusive test design for retrocognition (extrasensory perception of the past), because the records against which the clarification would have to be checked are accessible to the same psi ability that could conceivably reach into the past (or is there any *existing* past in the universe?). Similarly, the popular and familiar concept of OUT-OF-THE-BODY EXPERIENCES raises the same question as telepathy, of getting past a difficult alternative interpretation. The individual who has such an experience reports that he travelled to some distant location in some sort of mental projection (unacceptably called astral). Sometimes he impressively relates information he could only have got by an extrasensory kind of contact with the distant place, and even claims to have made some physical disturbance on the spot. While these fascinating stories have their interest, they provide no scientific support for the idea that the mind as an entity has done this actual travelling, any more than the subject would have done if he had been asked to take part in a clairvoyance test to get the information at the distant location, or a distance PK test to see if he could influence an object at that distance. But if telepathy has to be left on the shelf for the present, like these and still other interesting problems of parapsychology, it is a shelf to which the venturesome explorer should turn from time to time to see whether a fresh consideration of the problem may give a better prospect of success. Perhaps telepathy will remain the most tempting of all these hypotheses waiting on the shelf of apparently insoluble problems, because it would be so important to the understanding of man's nature if it could be clearly demonstrated to be a subtype of the psi process.

The Unity of Psi

Although with the passing years the distinctions between the subtypes of psi ability showed up clearly, at least in some cases (clairvoyance, precognition, psychokinesis of the PK–MT type, and even telepathy, as far as it could be carried), the distinctions were only relative. Curiously, the more they were studied and separated, the more these subtypes revealed a basic common character. Actually there was no conflict between these findings. What were distinct were the effects of the appearance of the different subtypes. What was called clairvoyance had to do with existing targets and what was called precognition had to do with future events, but the basic function seemed increasingly to be the same. Many psi researchers began to think of ESP operating sometimes with distant targets in mind, and sometimes with future ones. Sometimes the targets would be objective, but at other times they would seem to be, as far as could be determined, subjective, although this has been hard to prove.

Even when it came to working with PK, and there seemed to be much more objectivity about the types of effect and the conditions producing them, the actual communication seemed to be basically similar. Louisa E. Rhine pointed out in her articles in the *Journal of Parapsychology* and in her book, *Hidden Channels of the Mind*, that in a spontaneous physical happening (for example, the falling of a picture of a family member who at the time was dying or undergoing a serious crisis) the message was much the same as if the experience had been a subjective one, such as an apparition of the individual (see APPARITIONS). In other words, the cognitive part of the psi process was involved, and the physical effect was a sort of phenomenal or surface aspect. Perhaps it might be called the instrumentation, the way of bringing the message to the attention of the subject responsible for it.

Even in the experiments with PK there was a recognizable element of intelligent guidance necessary for whatever the force of the PK process was. If no ESP work had been done before PK came on the scene, parapsychologists would have had to invent ESP

as a hypothesis to make sense of the way PK works, that is, to account for the intelligent direction and knowledge which is evident in the results.

What we see here is the slow but steady growth of theory in the advancement of this new field of science. The first step was to distinguish the boundaries, determining just what, if anything, could be called a parapsychological phenomenon. Clairvoyance served this purpose best. Next, the separate territories or special areas, as far as they could be separated, had to be marked off, and with all the distinctions that applied, the contiguity or overall common character of these subdivisions of the psi field has had to be surveyed and mapped.

As indicated earlier, some of the subdivisions are still being more carefully surveyed and outlined. Two types of PK are in an inconclusive position, as well as telepathy, and, furthermore, no one would want to say that the whole of parapsychology has been discovered or that this is the way it will remain, in terms of subdivisions. However, these cautious remarks would equally apply to any science known as yet. The history of each branch shows the same lack of finality in its outlines. Those of parapsychology are probably good enough for the present. A little later this aspect will be reconsidered in the larger relationship of parapsychology to the system of man and his universe.

Parapsychology as a Science

What makes parapsychology a science, as it is regarded now by those who have become most thoroughly acquainted with it? First, there are growing indications that the methods and standards used in its more advanced study are at least equal to those of comparable fields, for example, the other branches of behavioural science. Because of the extraordinary difficulties of working with psi phenomena this judgment has been accepted slowly, but well enough at least for certain criteria of recognition to be given. One of these signs was the acceptance in 1969 of the Parapsychological Association as an affiliated branch of the American Association for the Advancement of Science.

A large enough body of confirmatory evidence has now been contributed from independent research centres widely spread over the globe to make parapsychologists possibly impatient about the rate of full acceptance and recognition, but they cannot seriously doubt that it will only be a matter of time. The most severe of the critics have been silent, even if still unregenerate. The best indication that parapsychology is a science, however, is the emergence of generalization that shows an orderly system arising slowly

from the scattered researches, findings such as those noted in the previous section on the unification of the subtypes of psi. These general properties or principles, as they might be termed, deserve a section to themselves, because they are the larger units of relation that enter into the building of a theoretical picture of the psi process as part of the order of nature. At least a few of these general properties can be outlined briefly.

General Characteristics of Psi

The most distinctive common property of all psi phenomena is closely related to the principle that psi is extra-sensorimotor. This added common characteristic is that all types of psi operate without the physical basis on which the entire sensorimotor system depends, without the reaction to stimuli which is the function of the sense organs, and without the physical contact on which the motor functions depend for their response.

The first step in the broader exploration of psi followed immediately on the conclusion that a case had been made for clairvoyant ESP. The first question was whether the ability was affected by distance. Preliminary tests suggested that it was not; therefore, the next question concerned its relation to time, and that too confirmed the impressions gained from spontaneous experiences that space-time was not an effective limitation of psi. The various other tests that were made involved many other physical comparisons, one of the more spectacular being that of Professor L. L. Vasiliev in his tests of ESP with a subject in a room that excluded electromagnetic radiation. All these comparative tests ruled out the known physical principles of communication as a medium of exchange in the functioning of psi. Small traces of distance effects are claimed by Dr Karlis Osis, but nothing conclusive has yet been produced to indicate any physical basis for psi (Osis's results could be psychological effects). In no experiments centred on clairvoyant precognition or PK have known physical principles been found applicable.

Yet it is not advisable or necessary to stretch the generalization beyond its actual coverage. Our present terms and concepts may be inadequate. Definitely something new must be added to the description of nature to account for these results. Since psi effects are exchanges or communications that normally would have been expected to be physical and since we find no physical principle applicable, the logical step to follow is to suppose that an unknown energetic factor, a mental one, is operating. But it has to be interactive with the physical order to produce psi phenomena. It must also be part of the living system in some way not yet identified.

Parapsychology

These are frontier problems for parapsychology.

Another common property of psi seems to be its universality among living organisms, at least of the animal world. Such a remark, however, needs to be a guarded one. Obviously, only a small section of the human race has been tested, but it has led some observers to the working hypothesis that probably all human beings have a native endowment of psi capacity, even though a person is normally likely to go through life without any easily recognized manifestation of psi. It is difficult to obtain evidence of it when the experimenters deliberately try. It is difficult for the person who shows it to continue to show it under conditions that can permit its measurement. Yet the data accumulated from different cultures and with different age levels, sex, and other biological distinctions, strongly suggest that the ability exists in all persons, and the difficulty is in encouraging it to manifest or register. It seems possible that by working with children one could, with patience and encouragement, get everyone to show his share of psi capacity. This might best be considered a working hypothesis.

In the early 1950s when the Duke Laboratory began looking into the question of psi in animals, there was a great wealth of case material available in the past and current collections. This led to experimental testing of more promising species. Dogs, cats and pigeons were tried, with some success with the first two kinds of animal. More recent studies with rodents, first in France but with follow-up confirmations in the United States and Holland, have provided a very firm case for the existence of psi in animals. In fact, this strongly confirmed work with exceptionally well-controlled conditions and almost complete automation of the test program, puts all of parapsychology into a stronger position with regard to its scientific status.

One may well be cautious in generalizing about the animal world from these limited beginnings, but there would be no great risk in saying that it would now be justifiable to look as far as possible for psi capacity throughout the entire animal kingdom. The appropriate methods are developing to make this possible.

Until recent years ESP had been the exclusive type of psi in animals investigated at the Foundation for Research on the Nature of Man. This continues the work of the Duke Laboratory, which had begun testing animals around 1950. In 1970, however, the first evidence of PK exerted by an animal was obtained in the form of subtle physical effects exerted on the environment in the order of magnitude of single quantum effects. This work of Dr Helmut Schmidt, confirmed by Walter J. Levy Jr, opens up a new area of psi research. It should of course be viewed as complementary to the rather well-established case for ESP in animals. In a word, if psi is a unitary process, then the animals should be expected to show PK ability since they have ESP. Nevertheless, it is a major step forward to get the actual independent evidence to complete the picture, at least to an extent that now warrants continued research.

Difficult as it is to explore the range of psi ability in this vast territory of the biologist, it is harder yet to get the idea of psi across to the biologists, who have been, as a profession, rather strongly inclined to look only for physical explanations of all of life's processes. This only means that psi will be that much more revolutionary when the idea is accepted.

Let it be repeated that this generalization of psi capacity (of both types) throughout the animal kingdom is a working hypothesis. It will be interesting to see whether there are limitations or pockets to which it will not apply; it seems doubtful now.

Psi Is Unconscious

Psychologically, the most significant common property of the psi process is its unconsciousness. This does not mean that one has to be unconscious to experience psi, or even that it helps to be in an unconscious or subconscious state. What is meant is that the basic function of psi experience is unconscious. The individual does not know as a rule when a psi experience is taking place and cannot consciously direct it so as to apply it reliably to his aims and purposes. Many of the spontaneous psi happenings occur when the individual is asleep, and during his waking state he may get his psi information by intuition, in which case he does not know how he got it. Even if he does sometimes have a strong conviction that his hunch is a valid one, or that the dream he had the night before is going to come true, this conviction is not a necessary part of the psi experience. It often seems to be a secondary effect, as if perhaps the individual has a tip-off from his own unconscious that encourages him to accept with confidence the message that comes.

Many features of these experiences are individual, with respect to the degree of consciousness, and cannot be generalized, but the one almost universal psychological property of psi is that it hides itself very effectively from the conscious volitional control of the individual.

This, of course, is what makes experimenting with psi so difficult. No experimenter knows when he starts his experiment whether his subjects are going to be able to do well – that is, successfully demonstrate psi ability. This is what upsets beginners in parapsychology, especially those from general psychology. Much of what is learned in that field about the design of experiments is a hindrance in working with psi, since no matter how good an experimental plan may appear, it is bound to fail if the experimenter cannot get the ability to function.

Another effect that unconsciousness has on the subjects is the tendency (mentioned previously) for scores sometimes to go below chance when the subject is trying to score above. Thus the same ability used under somewhat strained conditions with too much anxiety about performance reverses the function in some way and the subject avoids the targets as accurately as normally he would be hitting them (psi-missing). Fortunately, after learning about the curious effects of unconsciousness in the psi process, researchers have been able to understand and have been able sometimes to avoid or control these shifts of scoring level. They have thus turned the results to good account, and these experimental psi researches into the unconscious level of man's mental life have uncovered some curious workings of the unconscious that should be of use throughout the behavioural sciences; these latter also have their own problems with the unconscious.

Another effect of this unconsciousness can now be identified. It will be recalled that the diagonal decline gave the most important evidence of PK when the distribution of hits on the record sheets was examined in the quarter distribution on the page. These declines and all the position effects in general seem to be a consequence of the unconsciousness of psi. In fact, the most important findings about the psychology of psi are mainly centred in this general common property of the unconsciousness of the way in which ESP and PK work.

These three general properties of psi (its non-physical nature, its probable universality in the species, and its unconsciousness) illustrate the type of findings which make parapsychology a science. But naturally a much stronger and more meaningful science develops as these generalizations are found to relate closely to the larger background of natural science and especially the nature of man. It will be of interest, therefore, to see to what extent psi connects with and relates to the other branches of science. On the degree of this interrelation, as it becomes known, will largely depend the amount of scientific acceptance of parapsychology.

Parapsychology and the Other Sciences

No branch of science is independent of all the

rest. Distinctive as parapsychology is, it is closely related to the other divisions of science. In fact, it takes most of its larger meaning from these interrelations. For convenience, let us divide the sciences into physics, biology, and psychology, but by each is meant a general division of the total area of science.

It is logical to ask first about the physical characteristics of new phenomena. It is the most objective and feasible thing to do, especially because physical characteristics are so obvious. Accordingly, the first step taken in research on the properties of psi was to test the effect of distance on the efficiency of psi; this was followed by a test of whether ESP could transcend the barrier of time. From the results of these experiments psi workers came to regard psi as extraphysical, meaning that it was not limited by the principal physical conditions known to science. However, that did not entirely remove the process from relevance and interest to physics. The very act of demonstrating that an unknown type of influence is represented in psi exchange is dependent on the physical system involved in the tests and in the operation of the subject himself. This means that whatever psi is, it interoperates in some way with the natural physical order; it necessarily implies the existence of a more general common principle as a basis of interoperation.

It is necessary in such a situation to infer another kind of influence or energy, to account for the effects observable in the physical system of nature as a consequence of the operation of psi. The logic of natural science leads to the inference that a non-physical influence is present that produces energetic effects. Since we do not know much as yet about the hypothetical psi energy, it is a very modest step to make this assumption. However, the concept will naturally become more realistic as more is learned about what the psi function does and how it relates to the rest of the natural order.

What this newly discovered relationship between parapsychology and physics will produce in the way of new problems, researches, and discoveries will depend on physicists as well as parapsychologists. Unfortunately, the heightened specialization of branches of modern science tends to deter workers from sharing interest in common boundaries. Whereas parapsychology in its earlier years was greatly helped by the interest of eminent physicists, no one today can be expected to achieve equal expertise in the two fields as they are now advancing, and no one has. So for the present, only very general statements can be made. A courageous attempt at pulling the two fields together, such as that made by Arthur Koestler in his

The Roots of Coincidence (*268*), draws some attention to the few earlier attempts that have been made.

However, the physicists will eventually have to consider this psi function seriously (as the term is used in parapsychology – a different usage from that which the physicists give it). The fact is that psi can be detected *only* through conversion to directly registerable readings of another energetic form. It is *only* as some observable physical process that the PK type of psi function can be manifested and measured. This transfer is now experimentally manageable and it opens a new frontier to the research physicist. He can, for instance, do something that has been hitherto considered impossible. He can react experimentally to a future event and can interact directly as from one mind to another (no matter as yet what a mind is) without going entirely out of his own field. Physics is not merely a study of inanimate bodies as an older academic viewpoint may have had it. In a modified way, it is biophysics, psychophysics and, of course, psiphysics. For most physicists this is too radical a step as yet. For them, as it was fifty years ago, energetics is still a subheading in their category of physics. In the revolutionary shift parapsychology is introducing into modern science, energetics becomes the generic term, with the physical energies just part of the energetic system of nature. This follows logically enough from the discovery that psi shows results that are beyond physical exploration. It opens up a larger view of nature itself, one that can accommodate capacities of mind that remain baffling to existing categories of the sciences.

The biological sciences are enormously complex, broad and mysterious. Here we are most concerned with the animal kingdom and more especially, though not completely, with man; we must deal with biology because psi communication is known only in connection with living beings. Even if parapsychology had found evidence of post-mortem survival by way of spirit communication (and it cannot be claimed to have done so), this would also have been part of the domain of biology. It would indeed have been an incomparably significant biological finding, establishing indirectly that the living organism had something indestructible by death, but something too for which no evidence thus far had been contributed from the study of living organisms.

The establishment of the widespread occurrence of psi ability in the human species and in several others has done more to the science of parapsychology, potentially at least, than can be indicated here. In fact, it does so much to change the general view of the organism that, by many of the conserva-

tive biologists, it is regarded as something of a threat. In their zeal to make biology as scientifically respectable as the physical sciences, biologists have tended to think that the great phenomena of living systems can be reduced eventually to physical principles. They fear the implications of any hypothesis that calls for a special vital factor or force. Many of them are still fighting the unscientific belief required by theological theories of creation.

Psi is a boon to both sides of this issue. It neatly puts the whole matter on the scales of reliable judgment by turning to those phenomena of living organisms that can provide a clear-cut decision as to whether there is anything non-physical to be demonstrated in animal or human behaviour. It is no longer a question of theology, metaphysics, or other speculative judgments. The answer is, as we have seen, that physics is most certainly not entitled to this entire territory. Biology is not just a specialized subdivision of physics. When the biologist recognizes the psi findings, he discovers that life is a bigger and more intricate system than it had earlier seemed, and that it has principles uniquely its own, whether one calls them vitalistic or simply, for the present, a new research area for biology.

It is time to turn then to see, as a few biologists are beginning to do, what this means and how far it goes to account for the greater problem-areas of life. The French biologists Duval and Montredon have broken new ground with their automated studies of precognition in mice, and their results have been independently confirmed, as has been stated, both in the United States and Holland. It looks as though parapsychology has been given its 'guinea pig'. Selective breeding has begun. Comparison of species has also been initiated, both on ESP and PK lines of research.

Need we ask whether biology will be seriously influenced by the developments in parapsychology? No one would think for a moment that these psi capacities were evolved in the organism just for laboratory purposes, such as card-guessing and dice-throwing. It will take time to discover the full significance of psi to biology; but its extent is beyond all conjecture. The psi principle that can act both on living and inanimate matter with intelligent purpose would seem likely to have some close relation to the nature of life itself. How far down the scale of life does this psi factor go? To the single cell perhaps, or beyond. What else in the system of nature does psi 'need' for its operation, what properties, conditions, energy sources?

But with selective breeding and the cooperation of biological laboratories for new approaches, parapsychology can make its own studies of physiological correlates with psi efficiency, and can draw upon comparative anatomy and a dozen other strategic areas of research.

For the present, it seems likely that the easiest advance will be into medical biology, perhaps over the pathway already tentatively laid down by the study of the effect of PK on healing. Medicine has accommodated itself considerably to the little understood area of psychosomatic medicine. Large numbers of experienced physicians have abandoned the academic dogma that there is nothing in the healing process that does not reduce to the mechanics and chemistry of body physiology. Results in parapsychology from PK tests with various types of living tissue (PK–LT) open up a larger question than the mere practical benefits. What kind of relation could it be that could influence the functions of life? Is this not perhaps a still unopened window on the nature of the healing function, or more broadly, on the nature of life itself? The main attraction, however, is not in any immediate conclusion, for this would be premature and uncalled for. Rather, it is in the new methods and exciting problems now in plain view (at least to parapsychologists) on this frontier with biology.

Psi and Psychology

Most workers in parapsychology (though not so many in psychology) would agree that at some future time parapsychology will have to be regarded as an important branch of the larger field of psychology. The word 'important' is added advisedly because it will require a great deal of adaptation to include it. While it is not desirable to push the matter, because general psychology is not yet ready to accept psi research and ought not to be embarrassed with having to deal with it prematurely, parapsychology rather clearly promises to be the most basic of the subdivisions of the behavioural sciences.

This is not, however, anything that has to be or could well be decided now. But a few questions may be disposed of. What is psychology in broad terms? The 'study of behaviour', as it is commonly put? Behaviour of what? And how does behaviour differ from the rest of the operations of nature? It seems obvious that the definitions of psychology have had to be evasive. The question of what a person really is has been avoided; yet the person is about as close to the unit of study in psychology as we can get. We think first of physics. Very well, then, what is the person with respect to the physical world? The possibilities are that he is totally physical, partly physical, or not at all physical. Psychology has been straining hard for over a

half century to adhere to the totally physical concept of man. More and more, in spite of the great progress of psychology along many lines, the concept is proving to be too limiting and ineffectual for an increasing number of psychologists. Yet they have found no way out of their confusing and confining definition.

The trouble is that no other branch of psychology has a way of proving or disproving any of the three possibilities on this basic territorial question of psychology. Parapsychology alone provides the answer. By the very nature of its phenomena it challenges the existing belief among psychologists – the physicalistic doctrine. By its evidence that a person can and demonstrably does behave in such a way that the physicalist theory breaks down, the question is answered. It is answered too by a quality of evidence and an amount of it that no other once-debatable issue in psychology has received.

What parapsychology has done, in other words, is to answer the question of the distinctive existence of mind. Psychology may now claim the reality of psychical or mental process as having actual influence in behaviour. Psychology is given a distinctive territory of its own, and as this is understood and its principles and properties further outlined, the field will cease to be logically a mere subdivision of its neighbouring territories of physics and physiology. Because of the basic change in the organization of psychology that will be required, it is highly important not to press the challenge of parapsychology inconsiderately upon the existing academic institutions. It is this branch that establishes the scientific case for the existence of a mental division of natural science. It can and wisely should proceed as an independent (although cooperative) study indefinitely, until it is time for eventual unity.

By far the most profitable approach to the interrelationship of parapsychology with general psychology lies in the search for common principles. This is likely to be in the area of unconscious mental functions. Parapsychology has learned much about quantitative experimentation with unconscious functions that can be shared across the whole field of the behavioural sciences, especially in the problems of subliminal sensory perception, cognitive malfunctioning, and other subnormalities. In general, future opportunities to collaborate may be greatest on the frontier of medical psychology, but all the organized professional disciplines that depend on a concept of man's nature are certain to present common problems with psi research.

It should not be surprising that we find that parapsychology is most pertinent to the

needs of religions, although this need has not been very strongly realized. This relevance is not surprising because, as has already been indicated, the religions generally assume and use a common popular knowledge of psychic abilities and a recognition of their reality. With the decline of the type of religious authority that depended on supernatural theology, it was pointed out that religion stood to gain support from psychical research. It is now apparent that the subtypes of psi capacity and the conditions under which they operate compare well with the system of communication assumed in, let us say, the Christian religion. Note the similarity of the types of communication believed to take place between the human and the divine orders and the ESP and PK methods of exchange and their subtypes. This is quite obviously a basis for the beginning of scientific re-examination of the entire discipline of the religions. It is comparable to the intrusion upon medicine of the beginnings of microbiology to give a natural explanation of functions hitherto considered only in a religious frame of reference. The psi discoveries should do for religion what the germ theory did for pathology.

The relation of parapsychology to medicine has been mentioned previously, and again it should be said that because of the progress of science in medicine, parapsychology is likely to find its relation to that discipline more quickly appreciated than its relation to religion. There are already many semi-scientific, or perhaps semi-cultist, practices that claim to use psi ability in diagnosis or treatment. While this may be, and in most cases probably is, premature, it is not premature to consider scientific research for the development of what is known about parapsychology that bears directly on medicine. One of the most urgent needs for this type of research is to furnish standards and methods of assessment for the guidance of those who are over-eager about application and, on the other hand, those who are apprehensive about the dangers of these cultist healing practices.

Another field on which parapsychology has a significant bearing is education. There is, of course, still a considerable mystery about the essential function of educational change. The researches in schools, which show the effect of the teacher-pupil relation on performance in psi tests, and the relation of this performance to learning achievement, indicate that this is another research area in which parapsychology can be useful. In the attention now being given to the needs of

Testing a child for clairvoyant ESP, and *below* checking the test

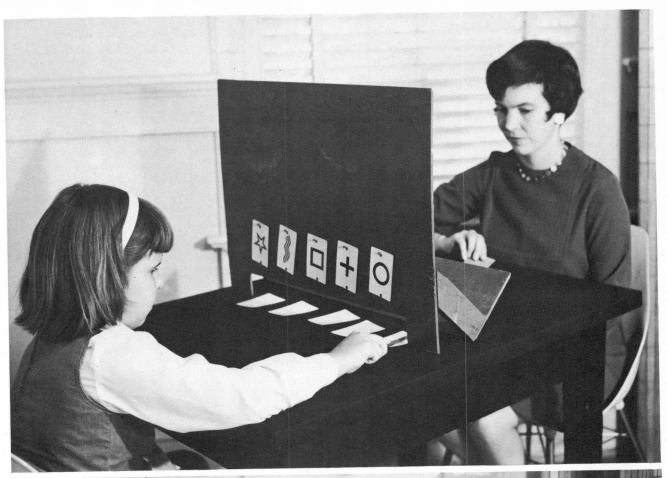

special groups, especially those individuals with limited potential, it seems likely that parapsychology will contribute a sensitive means of studying the essential educational exchange, and especially in getting an improved concept of the student as a person. The whole basic philosophy of education depends on what the school system assumes a person to be; this assumption is just as important to teachers as it is to psychiatrists or theologians.

Ultimately, it is man in all his aspects who is the centre of concern to which parapsychology has been trying to draw more insightful attention. What is going on in this creature, behind his sensorimotor system and behind all the mounds of data about him that are piling up? There is something there more subtle than his memories, though somewhat like them; more penetrating than his reasoning, though again with something in common; and more far ranging in its reach into the world about him than all his senses, muscles and instruments. One begins to suspect after looking over it all, as the facts of parapsychology have pictured it, that this may be the hidden essence of the human person that from the earliest ages has overawed the wisest of mankind and made man a little submissive, a little more ready to ask for help, and somewhat more appreciative of his own smallness against the greatness of a world he can only dimly understand. Parapsychology, along with other sciences, is contributing something to an improved understanding of what a man is. J. B. R.

(See also AUTOMATISMS; CONSCIOUSNESS; FAITH HEALING.) (Further reading: for general reviews of the subject, see *341, 393, 396a, 397, 456*; for technical books, see *384, 394*; for reviews of criticisms, see *316, 395, 418*; for spontaneous experiences, see *396*; see also *134, 253, 254, 255*.)

Parasomatic Experiences See OUT-OF-THE-BODY EXPERIENCES.

Paroptic Vision

One of numerous terms, including dermo-optical perception, eyeless sight and skin vision, for the often-repeated claim that a person can sometimes see with his skin. The capacity is usually located in the finger-tips or in the skin over the cheek bones. The claim is generally associated with some other current practice. In the 1840s it was related to mesmerism (as described in *369*): mesmerized subjects were said to 'see' with their finger-tips. About a century later, the alleged ability came to public attention again in connection with the book *Eyeless Vision* by Dr Louis Farigoule, whose pen-name is Jules Romains. He reported that this skin vision on

Phrenology: measuring the skull in 1907

the subject's cheek was produced in what he called the 'delta-state' (something like HYPNOSIS). An upsurge of interest occurred in the U.S.S.R. in the 1960s, with the opening up of discussion of PARAPSYCHOLOGY in books by Professor L. L. Vasiliev and others. This was followed by a number of experimental studies in that country and in the United States. In the United States a psychologist, Richard P. Youtz of Columbia University, and a parapsychologist, C. B. Nash of St Joseph College, Philadelphia, conducted tests of finger-tip vision of two-colour differences; both obtained results that convinced them that a delicate temperature sense was indicated (for example, black was warmer). This

would not, of course, be vision, nor would it apply to claims of skin vision that did not involve discrimination between colours. The whole area needs more thorough investigation before any conclusion is drawn. (*347a, 516b*)

Joséphin Péladan (1858-1918)

A leading and engagingly eccentric figure in the 'Rosicrucian' occult and aesthetic movement in France in the late 19th century: see ROSICRUCIANS.

Pendulums (in Divination) See DOWSING; RADIESTHESIA; see also DIVINATION.

Phantasms of the Living See APPARITIONS.

Philosopher's Stone See ALCHEMY.

Phrenology

The divination of character from the shape of the skull, a minor and relatively modern occult art which became popular for a time in the 19th century; some German groups in this century, the GERMANEN ORDER for example, were interested in it as a way of measuring 'racial purity': for 'phreno-magnetism', see HYPNOSIS. (303)

Physical Powers

The mythologies of the world are full of legends about the extraordinary powers possessed by the heroes of old who, with or without cloaks of invisibility, seven-league boots and magic swords, performed feats that defy the laws of nature and flout common sense. Where folklore and fairy-tale have left off, today's science fiction takes up the old threads, spinning out for an adult and sophisticated audience adventures that outstrip all the fantasies of the ancient storytellers.

Man's appetite for wonders is insatiable. The Christian world has a similar tradition in the hagiographies, which tell the stories of the saints and the many miracles associated with their lives. Those who find it difficult to accept them are usually prepared to give a little more credence to the present-day accounts brought back by tourists, travellers and anthropologists of the powers of the 'blackfellows' of Australia, the medicine-men of Africa, the shamans of Siberia, the sufis of Persia and Arabia, the yogis of India, and all the other hierophants and wonder-workers, some of whose feats have been described in detail by eyewitnesses, photographed in all their phases and discussed in learned journals. There is hardly a single marvel in remote legend without its corresponding analogue in modern times.

Everyone feels pain, yet analgesia or insensibility to pain, and immunity to wounding and poisoning have been observed in various circumstances. The rise of the French religious sect known as the Convulsionaries, from about 1727, was accompanied by great religious enthusiasm, during which certain inexplicable powers were manifested. Jeanne Maulet, a twenty-year-old girl, used to be beaten with a 20-pound hammer without injury. Gabrielle Moler, aged seventeen, had stout metal spikes pushed against her neck and breast with the full strength of three or four men behind them without it doing her any harm. Scores of similar 'miraculous' phenomena were witnessed and attested to in writing. The sceptical philosopher David Hume could find no argument to controvert the truth of the evidence of what took place.

Nearer our own time, an Egyptian fakir named Rahman Bey in about 1925 jabbed long stilettos into his cheeks and breast, and cut his body with a sharp knife without bleeding, and made the resultant wounds close up and heal in a matter of minutes. Henskes Arnold (d. 1947), a Dutchman, claimed complete invulnerability, and under medical supervision in Zurich was stabbed from the back with a long knife whose point reappeared at the front of his body; with the knife still inside him, he went to the X-ray department for examination. Neither the front nor the back wound showed any signs of bleeding. He later gave similar performances, from time to time. In 1934 in the presence of a Nobel Prize-winner, Sir C. V. Raman, and other distinguished scientists at Calcutta University, a yogi drank several doses of sulphuric acid, nitric acid and carbolic acid, and ate broken glass. After the demonstration he threw himself into a TRANCE to neutralize the effects of his lethal diet. He came out unharmed.

There are fire-walkers who seem to become temporarily immune to the effects of heat, and calmly walk over red-hot coals and white-hot stones which burn leaves and handkerchiefs to a cinder in a second. VOODOO practitioners in trance stir boiling water with their bare hands and juggle with burning hot iron balls. At one stage in his career Daniel Dunglas HOME, the famous medium, used to put his face over a blazing fire and move it in the flames as if washing in water. Even his eyebrows were not singed.

Related to this faculty is immunity to cold. Patagonians go about bare-bodied in winter where Europeans in the same place have to wear heavy woollen underwear and thick overcoats. A scientific team investigating the immunity to cold of desert aborigines in Central Australia found that even when the temperature dropped to freezing point, they did not feel the cold at all. A class of Tibetan yogis called *respas* live in caves throughout the coldest winter clad only in a single cotton garment. The test for a new initiate into their ranks is to sit naked on the shores of a lake in midwinter and in the course of a single night dry out several sheets that have been dipped into the icy waters and wrapped around his body.

We normally suppose that everyone needs sleep, but in fact there are some people who appear never to sleep. Of the dozens of fully authenticated cases two must suffice. Al Herpin (d. 1940) of Trenton, New Jersey, never slept throughout his infancy, childhood, boyhood or manhood. He was watched by observers in relays for several months but was never caught asleep. Yet his health remained normal and he lived to be ninety.

Valentine Medina (d. 1951), a Spanish farm labourer, had not slept for fifty years, and his physician thought it would be a good idea if he presented his case to specialists in Madrid. Medina walked from his village to the capital, a distance of 140 miles, in four days and nights, pausing only to give his feet a rest, and told the unbelieving physicians his story. They first put him through a rigorous test, which entirely confirmed his statement, and then found that they were unable to put him to sleep either. Confessing themselves utterly baffled, they paid his train-fare back home.

Similarly, we suppose that everyone must eat in order to stay alive. Yet some people have lived without eating for considerable periods. Inedia, as it is called, has a long-standing record in Christian annals, from the 'woman of Norwich', mentioned by Roger Bacon (1214–94), who ate nothing for twenty years, without detriment to her health, to Teresa NEUMANN (d. 1962), who apparently did without solid or liquid nourishment for several months at a stretch. The adepts of certain secret societies are said to subsist for weeks without taking a morsel of food.

Bilocation and Dematerialization

Other adepts reputedly have the power of disappearing and then reappearing in another place. Some are believed to be able to make themselves actually invisible. Indeed, so strongly was this idea ingrained in the magical tradition that more than a hundred 'recipes' for invisibility are to be found in medieval grimoires. Even this does not transcend the bounds of possibility when we consider that seance-room phenomena include what is known as APPORTATION, which is the appearance of an object out of nowhere. Mediums themselves have reputedly been apported to and from distant places. Stage conjurers, we know, do their disappearing tricks with the aid of mirrors, just as they perform other acts of 'magic' by sleight-of-hand. But the question whether conjuring in its higher reaches is not itself a form of magic is to be taken into account in considering the matter. Originally a conjurer was not a stage illusionist but a real magician who summoned demons by means of spells. Some of the most famous stage magicians were masters of 'glamour', and were able to give people the illusion of things by means of mass hypnotism.

The world's greatest escape artist, Harry HOUDINI (1874–1926), performed apparent miracles. Some of his feats were so extraordinary that they could not by duplicated by others, even with the aid of assistants. Those who made and sealed the boxes in which he was locked up, and who secured the ropes that held him, were not amateurs haphazardly chosen from the audience, but experts in their field. He was locked in cells, handcuffed, placed in chests, and thrown into rivers in stout boxes bound with rope, and yet in a matter of an hour or two was able to free himself. One expert craftsman in Birmingham worked for three years to perfect a set of manacles with intricate tumblers in each of its locks. Houdini extricated himself from them in ninety minutes.

Many of his feats were considered 'impossible', a paradox that was given a curious explanation by Sir Arthur Conan Doyle, who was a friend of Houdini. Doyle believed that Houdini was a genuine natural medium and that his feats could only be explained by his 'dematerializing', and then 'rematerializing' in another place, outside his handcuffs, or cell, or box. And Doyle was not the only person who believed in some such supernatural explanation. It is of interest to note

Harry Houdini

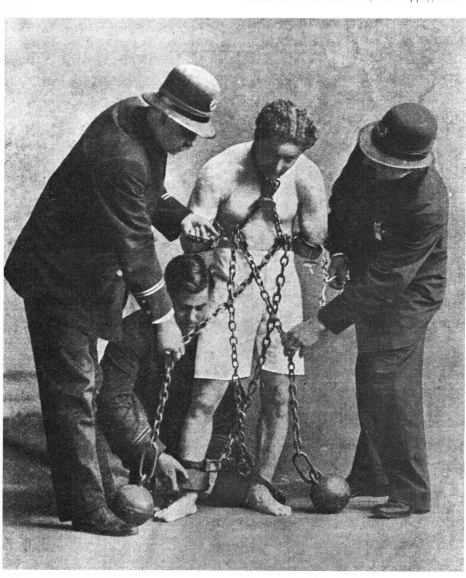

that Houdini was deeply and seriously interested in SPIRITUALISM and took a delight in exposing sham mediums.

Related to dematerialization are various other phenomena: in one, a person in one place is present in another place in his astral form, which sometimes assumes physical solidity; in such BILOCATION he appears to be physically in two places at the same time; in astral clairvoyance he witnesses events in other places while in the ASTRAL BODY. It is recorded that in 1774 Alphonse de Liguori (1696–1787), founder of a Christian monastic order and later canonized, while fasting in his monastery at Arezzo fell into a deep trance and remained immobile in his cell. He returned to consciousness to say that he had been present at the deathbed of Pope Clement XIV, four days' journey away. It was later confirmed by those who had attended the Pope in his last hours that the monk had indeed been present and had spoken to them and assisted at the last rites. In 1756 Emanuel SWEDENBORG (1688–1772), while

at Gothenburg, saw the fire which devastated Stockholm, although he was 300 miles away at the time. The astral body of a person may even appear to himself, as well as to others, and is commonly called a wraith. There are numerous records of wraiths. Ben Jonson (1572–1637), the dramatist, was visited by his son dying of the plague some distance away. John Donne (1573–1631), the poet, while in Paris saw the wraith of his wife who lived in London; she was carrying the body of a dead child at the very hour her infant son was born dead. Autophanic experiences, in which a person sees his own double, are recorded of Abraham Lincoln, Goethe, Shelley and others.

Flying and Levitation

Volition or flying through the air frequently occurs in legend. From ancient China comes the story of the two daughters of the Emperor Yao who taught the art of flying to Shun, and who both married him when Yao died. From Greece there is the legend of Daedalus, who escaped from confinement along with his son Icarus by making wings of feathers and wax and flying to freedom; Icarus flew too high, the heat of the sun melted the wax and he plunged to his death. During their rituals shamans are alleged sometimes to fly about like birds. In Christian legend Simon Magus was able to sail through the air, and was brought down by the prayers of St Peter. One of the greatest Tibetan lamas, Milarepa (1038–1120), was seen flying across the sky on a number of occasions. In Europe, the ability of witches to fly to the sabbath was widely believed in not only by the populace but by eminent ecclesiastics as well.

The persistence of this idea needs to be examined. Most instances, of course, can be dismissed as fantasy. A few may be reminiscences of OUT-OF-THE-BODY EXPERIENCES. Psychologists tend to attribute such legends to the mythifying of the wish to fly. But apart from these attempts to explain the phenomenon out of existence, it would appear that it is possible for the law of gravitation to be suspended, as in the case of LEVITATION, where a person is seen to rise in the air and float above the level of the ground.

Accounts of levitation are a commonplace in religious literature the world over, and are also recorded in psychical research. Of all the miracles attributed to the saints, perhaps none has been so persistent as that of their rising into the air as though gravitational force had temporarily abated for their benefit. The case of St Joseph of Copertino (d. 1663) is the best authenticated in Christian literature. Like many others to whom extraordinary powers suddenly descended, he

Sir Arthur Conan Doyle

lived a life of rigid austerity, eating food which he first used to sprinkle with a bitter powder in order to render it unpalatable, so much so that when a brother monk once tasted it he was ill for three days. He scourged himself with a barbed whip till the blood flowed down his back. One day while he was praying, his body left the ground and remained floating in the air. From then on his levitations increased. Once, when moved to ecstasy, he rose to the high altar and then to the pulpit ledge fifteen feet above the ground. If restrained, he would bear the others up with him. In the open air he would float to the level of the tree-tops, and if he alighted on one of the thinner branches at the top, it did not even bend under his weight. His levitations were witnessed by a host of eminent persons, kings, prelates and professors, including the philosopher Leibniz. The Protestant Duke of Brunswick was so overwhelmed by the miracle he witnessed that he became a convert to Roman Catholicism.

Certain Tibetan monastic schools have evolved a method by which a form of levitation or lightness of body could be acquired, enabling movement over long distances with great ease. Known as *lung-gom* or trance-walking, it once formed part of the training of a special class of cross-country messenger-runners. Lung-gom combines mental concentration with breathing exercises and has to be practised in seclusion for a period of about two or three years. Proof of proficiency is to sit with legs crossed on the meditation seat, and then jerk the body and lift it into the air clear off the seat. A European observer

who witnessed the feat said that it was 'so uncanny that I actually felt a cold sweat start from my pores'.

Burial Alive

Eastern yogis and fakirs are often trained to control the autonomic nervous system, that part of the nervous apparatus that is not normally under the control of the will, and that regulates such physiological activities as the heartbeat, body temperature, blood pressure, size of the pupils, respiration. Thus, by an act of will the pulse beats can be made to differ, so that the pulse on the right wrist differs from that of the left. Tahra Bey (*c.* 1925), an Egyptian, could by willing raise his pulse-rate to 140 beats a minute, or slow it down to 40, and in some instances stop it altogether. Hamid Bey, another Egyptian wonder-worker, examined by three physicians, could make his pulse-rate at the wrist differ from the rate of the heart-beat. On one occasion, the left recorded 102, the right 84, the heart 96, instead of all being uniformly near 72.

The most spectacular product of this discipline is suspended animation, in which the physiological activities of the entire body are apparently brought to a standstill and a person exhibits all the symptoms of death, with complete absence of heartbeat and respiration. Sometimes this occurs spontaneously. A man may be taken for dead and after a trance lasting hours, or sometimes as long as two or three days, will suddenly come back to life. Medical annals are filled with the records of such occurrences. But the same conditions can be induced by will. Indians, and Egyptians like Rahman Bey, have specialized in this form of wonder-working, and there is more than one record in the last century in India of yogis suspending their breathing or decreasing it till it was imperceptible, and allowing themselves to be buried alive for several days. In recent years, however, there have been so many casualties among holy men attempting this feat after inadequate training that the Indian authorities have put a stop to it.

A number of occult disciplines are practiced in many parts of the world that enable a person to acquire powers over himself, over others, over animals, or over natural phenomena. But there is invariably a specialization of such powers, and no one possesses an all-embracing power over things. The man who controls sharks in Ceylon cannot summon the porpoises in Polynesia. The snake-charmer has no hold over elephants. In Europe a similar specialization is found in healing. The cunning-man who can dismiss a wart in a week is helpless against scrofula.

The pursuit of 'powers' is one of the chief aims of much occultism, and most people who undertake occult training do so in order to obtain some extraordinary faculty or other. But such preoccupations are regarded as inimical to the proper goal of esoteric studies, which in essence concern knowledge and understanding. The Hindu philosopher Patanjali, of the 2nd century A.D., condemned the eagerness for such powers as an 'impediment to the attainment of the highest truth'.

Eight gifts or *siddhis* were traditionally promised in YOGA, namely: the power to become infinitely small, infinitely large, infinitely heavy, weightless, to be instantaneously transported to any part of the universe, to obtain all one's desires, to control all creatures, to have lordship over all things. These rather puerile objectives are worth noting for the striking similarity they bear to the visions induced by certain psychedelic DRUGS. LSD subjects have imagined themselves reduced to sub-atomic particles, or expanded to the proportions of a galaxy; have felt as immovable as the Himalayas, or floating like a cloud; have visited distant places, and have been convinced of their ability to control natural phenomena.

Hermann von Helmholtz, a German physicist of the 19th century, said, 'I would not accept any abnormal phenomena on the mere testimony of my eyes.' But for some time now the testimony of the senses has been reinforced by cameras, tape-recorders, X-rays and foolproof scientific equipment, and the actual occurrence of certain 'miracles' hardly admits of any doubt. What is in dispute is the nature of the explanation. Interpretation rather than observation is the crux of the matter today. Phenomena become significant when no dummy hands are found to be manipulating a moving table; when ECTOPLASM is found not to be cheese-cloth; when materializations are not done with mirrors; when stones fly about in the absence of earth tremors and subterranean water-currents; when a skewer in the abdomen is discovered not to be a trick gadget.

Charles Hoy Fort (1874–1932), an unorthodox American investigator of curious happenings, compared science to a car speeding along a modern highway built through a dense jungle, the driver quite unconcerned about the fascinating countryside stretching out on either side of him. T. H. Huxley (1825–95), speaking of certain psychic occurrences that had been brought to his notice, remarked, 'Supposing the phenomena to be genuine, they do not interest me.' But since his day science has become increasingly interested, and physics and metaphysics, fact and fiction, have touched at several points. There is surely much more to

Burial alive: the Egyptian Rahman Bey

be learned about the powers of that almost science-fiction entity, the human being. B. W.

(See also MEDIUMS; PARAPSYCHOLOGY.) (Further reading: *47, 90a, 187, 202a, 267, 502.*)

James Albert Pike (1913-69)

The Episcopal Bishop of California, well known for his unorthodox theological views, who wrote *The Other Side*, 1968. In 1966 his son, Jim, killed himself after experimenting with drugs. POLTERGEIST phenomena then began to occur and Bishop Pike felt that his son might be trying to communicate with him. In seances with a London medium, Mrs Ena Twigg, and with other mediums in America, including Arthur Ford (d. 1971) and George Daisley, he received messages which he believed did in fact come from his son. He died in the Israeli desert in 1969.

Three days before his body was discovered, he communicated with Mrs Twigg, telling her what had happened and where his body would be found: his wife was convinced that this communication did come from him. (*367*)

Leonora E. Piper (1857-1950)

A remarkable American trance medium, of Boston, Massachusetts. She was investigated under stringent conditions between 1887 and 1897 by the American S.P.R., in England in 1889–90 by the Society for Psychical Research, and later again by the American S.P.R. Her control was 'Phinuit', purportedly the spirit of a French doctor. Mrs Piper would go into deep trance and speak in the gruff male voice of Phinuit, 'in a curious mixture of Frenchisms, negro patois and Yankee slang, sometimes swearing vulgarly' (*176*). He would blatantly fish for information from the sitters and then try to pass it off as his own, but was also capable, unprompted, of relaying messages from the dead which turned out to be accurate to the tiniest detail. He was gradually replaced as control by 'George Pelham', when automatic writing became a more common feature of Mrs Piper's mediumship, and he in turn gave way to 'Imperator' and other spirits, who claimed to be the same group which had communicated through W. S. MOSES. Mrs Piper produced some of the scripts which form part of the CROSS-CORRESPONDENCES. That she was entirely honest was accepted by almost everyone who dealt with her, but whether her communications came from the dead or through ESP is disputed: see MEDIUMS. (*176, 213, 410*)

PK The abbreviation for PSYCHOKINESIS.

Planchette See OUIJA BOARD.

Planes (Occult) See ASTRAL BODY; CABALA.

Polish Messianism

Various Polish nationalists, revolutionaries and occultists of the 19th and 20th centuries, including LUTOSLAWSKI and TOWIANSKI, linked the Polish nation with both Christ and the sufferings of the Jews, comparing the numerous partitions and obliterations of Poland with the history of the Chosen People, persecuted and denied the right to exist as a nation. 'Poland was the Christ among peoples. Just as Christ's suffering had redeemed the human race, so Poland, by hers, would redeem all nations' (*493*).

Poltergeists

The word 'poltergeist' is German and means noisy or rattling (*poltern*) spirit (*Geist*). Some of the earliest recorded cases are in fact German. For instance, in 858, near the town of Bingen on the Rhine, falls of stones were reported and loud noises and knockings. The phenomena were believed to be caused by spirits. Whatever the cause, it was impervious to exorcism. We have another case in 1184 at the home of a William Nott in Wales when spirits were again thought to be on the rampage, tossing lumps of dirt and tearing up clothing. In 1682, Richard Chamberlain, Secretary of what was then the Province of New Hampshire, made a study of a series of unexplained falls of stones attributed to a 'stone-throwing devil' (*362*).

Poltergeist disturbances usually take place in the vicinity of a particular person, often a boy or girl at the age of puberty or in adolescence. As a rule the phenomena are distinguished from another group of unexplained disturbances, so-called hauntings. The word haunt comes ultimately from the same root as 'home' and implies the belief that a spirit of a deceased person has remained at or returned to his earthly habitat. As a rule, hauntings do not seem to depend upon any particular living person but are related to a special locality such as a 'haunted house'. There are other differences. Physical disturbances predominate in poltergeist incidents while hallucinatory experiences are common in hauntings. These experiences, which may include seeing 'ghosts' and hearing footsteps, are hallucinatory insofar as they are generally experienced only by some persons and not by others. Hallucinations in a haunted house differ from those of a mentally disturbed person because they resemble those that others have had independently in the same house or because they correspond to some event in the past. If there is such a correspondence with actual events they are called veridical hallucinations, that is, they are instances of ESP. Attempts to make scientific studies of hauntings have sometimes involved the collaboration of mediums and sensitives in the hope that they might be able by means of their ESP ability to respond to the 'ghosts' (see also MEDIUMS; OBJECT READING).

In poltergeist cases there are often daily movements and breakages of plates, knick-knacks, furniture and other movable household effects, whereas such incidents are more rare and more spread out in time in the typical haunting case, if they occur at all. However, hauntings tend to last longer. It is not unusual to hear of a house which has been haunted for several years. Poltergeist disturbances, on the other hand, are usually of a fairly short duration, rarely lasting more than a couple of months and often less.

Because poltergeist incidents usually occur in close proximity to a living person, parapsychologists tend to regard them as instances of PSYCHOKINESIS, or PK. Since poltergeist incidents are recurrent and arise unexpectedly and spontaneously, they are commonly referred to as instances of 'recurrent, spontaneous psychokinesis' or RSPK. They appear to be unconscious cases of PK since the person who seems to bring them about is usually unaware of his involvement. Some persons remain convinced that RSPK phenomena are due to the agency of an incorporeal entity, such as the spirit of a deceased person or a 'demon' which has attached itself to some living person and which causes the incidents by PK. However, since there is no evidence for such spirits apart from the phenomena themselves, most parapsychologists are of the opinion that poltergeist phenomena are examples of unconscious PK exercised by the person around whom they occur.

It is common nowadays to regard some of the miracles told in the Bible as possible cases of PK. It usually comes as more of a surprise that PK in the form of a poltergeist also has a place in the later history of Christianity, or at least in one branch of it, Methodism. For two months, in December and January 1716–17, the Parsonage at Epworth, the birthplace of John Wesley (1703–91), was the scene of violent poltergeist knockings. John was in his teens at the time of the outbreak but probably played no role in the phenomena since he was away from home. Mrs Wesley writes that beginning in early December the strange knocking noises were heard mostly in the attic or the nursery, usually in series of three. The phenomena nearly always consisted of sounds but there were a few physical events. For instance, the latch of the bedroom door of Samuel Wesley (John's father) was often lifted off when he was in bed, and, he said, 'I have been thrice pushed by an invisible power, once against the corner of my desk in the study, a second against the door of the matted chamber, a third time against the right side of the frame of my study door as I was going in.' The events seemed to be connected with Hetty, John's nineteen-year-old sister. Emily, another sister, stated, 'It never followed me as it did my sister Hetty. I have been with her when it has knocked under her, and when she has removed has followed; and still kept just under her feet' (368).

RSPK disturbances are in many respects similar to the phenomena produced by 'physical mediums'. A poltergeist agent can be regarded as a temporary physical medium. It is interesting that some physical mediums began their career as the centre of poltergeist disturbances. Undoubtedly the most remarkable of these was D. D. HOME (1833–86), who could apparently cause the levitation of furniture, and of himself, in full light. He began his career as a physical medium when he was the centre of poltergeist raps and movements of objects.

Poltergeist phenomena were among the unexplained occurrences which stimulated serious scientists and scholars to become interested in the scientific study of psychical phenomena. But because the phenomena happened spontaneously at some location, usually a private home, away from the experimental laboratory, there has always been a great deal of uncertainty as to whether the phenomena were genuine. When, in the 1940s, evidence was reported from the Parapsychology Laboratory at Duke University that experimental subjects could influence the fall of dice without any direct contact, and thus showed evidence for a 'mind over matter' ability, poltergeists were taken more seriously than they had been before. This interest became all the stronger when a PK effect could be demonstrated on moving objects, such as falling dice, but not on stationary ones. Obviously, if the reports from poltergeist homes could be trusted, stationary objects were indeed being moved. Perhaps therefore the poltergeist could tell parapsychologists something new about PK. The argument from the PK tests was supported by many older studies of poltergeist disturbances, particularly those conducted by members of the Society for Psychical Research (S.P.R.) in London, whose seemingly careful investigators were sometimes unable to explain the incidents away in terms of trickery, imagination and other normal causes.

British Investigations

One of the most active explorers of the poltergeist was Sir William Barrett (1844–1925), an eminent physicist and one of the founders of the Society for Psychical Research. In 1877 a series of disturbances plagued a farm in Derrygonnelly, Ireland, occupied by a widower and his five children. The phenomena, mostly consisting of knocking sounds and movements of objects, were centred upon Maggie, a twenty-year-old daughter. Once she and the children were lying quietly in bed, watched by Barrett, when loud knocks and raps were heard and a large pebble landed on the bed. The invisible entity or energy would knock to order. 'I mentally asked it, no word being spoken, to knock a certain number of times and it did so. To avoid any error or delusion on my part, I put my hands in the side pockets of my overcoat and asked it to knock the number of fingers I had open. It correctly did so. Then, with a different number of fingers open each time, the experiment was repeated four times in succession, and four times I obtained absolutely the correct number of raps' (20).

In most cases the poltergeist incidents had ceased by the time the S.P.R. heard of them, or a personal study was not possible for other reasons. However, there were often testimonials by seemingly reliable witnesses. In February and March 1883 there were strange breakages in the kitchen of the house of Joseph White in Worksop, Nottinghamshire. The destruction was worst in the presence of a feeble-minded girl who was visiting the family. Police Constable William Higgs was called in and in the presence of him and a physician who was on a visit to one of the children 'a basin was seen to rise slowly from the bin – no person being near it except Dr. Lloyd and Higgs. It touched the ceiling, and then fell suddenly to the floor, and was smashed' (370). Immediately afterwards, the two men examined some of the objects which had moved, but found no clue to the phenomena.

Mrs Best, her daughter and two orphan girls were living in Durweston, near Blandford, in December 1894 when knocks, scraping sounds and, later, movements of objects began to bother them. A neighbour, Mr Newman, was called in because a boot had struck the back door. While he was present it flew again and Mrs Best threw it out into the garden. Newman reported, '[I] went out and put my foot on it, and said, "I defy anything to move this boot." Just as I stepped off, it rose up behind me and knocked my hat off: there was no one behind me. The boot and the hat fell down together' (370).

Between November 1917 and December 1918, R. P. Jacques was building a bomb shelter at his home in Folkestone, Kent. It was never tested against German bombs but became a target for a poltergeist. One day Jacques inspected the shelter after the builder and his apprentice had gone and the shelter was empty. When he had finished, he closed the door but, he stated, 'Before taking my hand from the latch a stone came violently into contact with the inside of the door and immediately afterwards three others in quick succession'. Several more followed and Jacques went back in, finding the stones by the door, and again made sure that no one was present (21).

In August and September 1952, there were unexpected disturbances in the home of Sam Jones, a widower, in Runcorn, Cheshire. The events took place in a room occupied by Jones's grandson and a friend. The Reverend W. H. Stevens was present one evening and put out some objects including two books and a jigsaw puzzle on a table which had been particularly active. The lights were turned off and, while Stevens was near the table, the objects began to 'hurl themselves across the room. Eventually, I heard the two books fly across, then the rattle of the jigsaw in the box. That was what I was waiting for and straight-way I shone my torch. The jigsaw was travelling across the room rising about seven feet in the air. The two boys were well covered in their clothes in the exact position as they had been when the light was switched off' (*121*).

An investigation was made by A. R. G. Owen, lecturer in mathematics and genetics at Cambridge University, of poltergeist activities which had taken place in November and December 1960 in the Scottish village of Sauchie. Several movements of furniture and bedding were observed around Virginia Campbell, an eleven-year-old girl, by the family physician and the minister of Sauchie. Poltergeist disturbances rarely follow the person away from home but the Sauchie poltergeist went with Virginia to school. Several times her teacher, Miss Margaret Stewart, watched as the lid of Virginia's desk moved slowly up and down while Virginia had her hands on it, palms down, as if trying to keep the lid down. The girl had her feet on the ground so she could not be lifting the lid with her knees. Another time, while Miss Stewart was watching, an unoccupied desk behind Virginia slowly moved, settling down slightly out of line with the other desks. And once while the girl stood next to Miss Stewart's desk, her hands clasped behind her back, Miss Stewart suddenly saw the blackboard pointer, which was lying on her desk, start to vibrate and move until it reached the edge, when it fell to the floor. The desk itself then began to rotate in a counter-clockwise direction. Miss Stewart looked at her pupil, who was crying and saying, 'Please, Miss, I'm not trying it' (*362*).

Some German Poltergeists

One of the most important centres for the study of the poltergeist is located at Freiburg University, West Germany, and the main investigator is Hans Bender, a professor of psychology. In 1952 the Department of Public Health in the town of Neudorf in Baden asked Bender's help in dealing with an unusual situation that had developed in the home of the Mayor. When he came, Bender was told that the day before, the Mayor, his son and daughter-in-law had seen a collection of nails mysteriously appear about eight inches below the ceiling of a bedroom and then fall to the floor. Another son, the thirteen-year-old Bernard, was lying on the bed next to his mother. The nails came from

a locked cupboard in the kitchen. Another time the Mayor had seen a clothes-peg climb up a door to the top and then fly off at a right angle. Others had seen objects come out of a wall, moving at great speed. When they were picked up, they felt warm. The incidents only happened when Bernard was present, and ceased when he went away on vacation. To try to get to the root of the phenomena, the Freiburg team gave the boy psychological tests. There was a great deal of tension of the type connected with puberty and signs of frustration and aggression. Bender suspected that these tensions were connected with the phenomena (*34*).

The 'Bremen Boy' case began in June 1965, in a china shop in Bremen where glasses and dishes inexplicably tumbled from shelves and broke on the floor. The police and others who investigated the case could find no explanation for the occurrences. The turmoil seemed to revolve around a fifteen-year-old apprentice, Heiner, and the events ceased when he was dismissed. Bender and other members of the Freiburg team observed a phenomenon in March 1966. At that time, the breakages had been replaced by the spontaneous loosening of screws which the boy was installing with his new employer, an electrician. One of these occurrences was witnessed by the Freiburg team. The events finally ceased in July 1967 (*34*).

From November 1967, until January 1968, a series of disturbances took place in the office of Mr Adam, a lawyer in the town of Rosenheim. Movements of wall pictures and ceiling lamps, explosions of lamp bulbs, and other incidents took place in the neighbourhood of a nineteen-year-old female employee. The maintenance department of the town's electricity company, headed by Assistant Director P. Brunner, investigated the events, expecting to find a normal explanation. Deflections up to 50 amps were recorded on a voltage amplifier when some of the disturbances occurred. However, the house fuses, which should have blown as a result of such strong current, remained intact. Two physicists, F. Karger and G. Zicha, were then called in by Bender. They installed instruments to measure the current in the office main as well as other electrical effects. Marked deflections were again obtained. However, irregularities in the house current were not responsible since the mains voltage remained constant. Other known means to produce deflections were also excluded, such as electrostatic charges, faulty equipment, and fraud. The disturbances took place only when the young lady was present. Psychological studies of her and also of Heiner, the Bremen boy, showed that both had unstable personality structures with little ability to

tolerate frustration. Tensions due to aggression, accumulating quickly and having no overt release, apparently were discharged through the poltergeist occurrences (*34*).

Beginning in November 1968, and lasting for four months, the home of a labourer in Nickelheim was the scene of knocks on windows and doors, flying objects and, strangest of all, stones and other objects moving into or out of closed rooms. On one occasion when a priest was blessing the house, a stone fell from the ceiling though all doors and windows were closed. When he picked it up, it felt warm.

Mr Adam, the lawyer from Rosenheim, had become interested in poltergeist phenomena and went to see the Nickelheim family. They told him that objects which disappeared from the home would later be seen falling to the ground outside. Adam placed some bottles on the kitchen table and asked the family to go outside. Having closed all windows and doors, he too left. Shortly afterwards, the bottles appeared in the air at roof level and fell down in a zigzag manner.

One of the objects 'tele-apported' was Bender's own coat. It had been hung in a closet next to the kitchen and apparently moved outside, where it was found in the snow, while Bender was talking to the family.

Bender's group installed a container in which they placed some objects that had been disturbed previously, hoping they would again become targets for the poltergeist. Photoelectric switches were set to trigger three cameras and a red light, if any of the objects moved or left the box or if anybody tried to interfere with the box. On one occasion, when the Freiburg team was outside with the family, they noticed that the lights connected with the camera went on. They found that a Beatle figurine had fallen over. When the photographs and film were developed, they showed nothing suspicious and gave no clues to how this event took place.

The incidents centred around Brigitte, a thirteen-year-old daughter. As in other poltergeist cases which seemed to include genuine effects, when these began to wane, the focal person, in this case Brigitte, was discovered to cheat. Bender found the girl's fingerprints on a dish which she claimed the poltergeist had thrown out the window (*34*).

Bender has been particularly interested in the reports of objects coming through walls and other obstructions without leaving any openings. Such penetrations of matter by matter may be the greatest challenge the poltergeist has come up with to the theories of physics. Bender suggests that we may have to postulate the existence of 'higher space'. This would allow 'four-fold freedom of movement' and account for the apparent penetration of matter by matter (*34*).

Recent American Poltergeists

In recent years several poltergeist cases have been reported in the United States. The centre for studying them, since 1961, has been the Psychical Research Foundation in Durham, North Carolina, headed by W. G. Roll. The first case was the Seaford disturbances in Long Island which were investigated jointly by J. G. Pratt and Roll when they were at the Parapsychology Laboratory at Duke University. This Laboratory, directed by J. B. Rhine, has now become the Foundation for Research on the Nature of Man. The two foundations continue to collaborate in poltergeist and other studies. Pratt, who is President of the Psychical Research Foundation, is now a member of the Division of Parapsychology at the University of Virginia.

Beginning in early February 1958 and lasting for five weeks, the Seaford home of Mr and Mrs James Herrmann and their two children, James and Lucille, aged twelve and thirteen, was the scene of a series of strange disturbances. The unknown entity or energy made a wide sweep of the contents of the house, causing plates and figurines to fly and pieces of furniture to turn over. Many of the incidents involved bottles. These would lose their caps with loud explosive sounds, tip over and spill their contents. The bottles all had screw caps and contained such ordinary things as liquid starch, bleach and medicine. Mrs Herrmann put out bottles with holy water to ward off the invisible intruder but they too were affected. One of the 'bottle poppings' took place when J. G. Pratt and W. G. Roll were in the house. While they were with the family upstairs, they heard a loud explosive sound and a bottle of starch in the basement was found tipped over in its box, the screw cap lying some distance away. Nobody was in the basement at the time and the two parapsychologists were unable to explain the incident normally. Thinking that the bottles might contain a gas that forced the caps to come off, the investigators tried to cause caps to come off bottles in this way. If a gas built up enough, this would cause the bottle to explode or, alternatively, the pressure would be released around the threads of the cap; in no instance did this become unscrewed on its own. The family had called in the police at an early stage in the hope that they might solve the mystery and the police had examined the bottles for foreign substances. None were found. At one time when a police officer was with the family in the living-room and when nobody else was in the house, there was a bottle popping in the bathroom. There were also movements of objects. When a visiting relative was in the living-room with the two children she saw a porcelain figure on an end table next to the couch begin to 'wiggle' and then fly two feet into the room, landing on the rug with a loud crashing sound but without breaking. At the same time she had James in view, who was seated quietly on the middle of the couch with his arms folded (*374*).

It soon became clear that James was the centre of the disturbances. By measuring the distances at which objects flew in relation to his position, it was found that there was a regular decline in the number of incidents the further in space the objects were from the boy. This feature was repeated in later poltergeist cases. However strange these occurrences are, they seem to be governed by the same kinds of laws which affect known forms of energy: the further away from the source of energy, the weaker it usually is (*404*).

On 6 May 1961, the birthday of Ernest Rivers, disturbances began in the apartment which this thirteen-year-old boy shared with his grandmother in Newark, New Jersey. Among the sixty incidents which happened that month and the next, the most interesting took place when Charles D. Wrege, an assistant professor at the Department of Management at Rutgers, was making an investigation. One evening, when he was alone with the boy in the kitchen, there was a loud crash from the adjoining living-room. A large crockery lamp was found shattered on the floor about three feet from its table. When this happened, Wrege was making a phone call, holding the phone in one hand with his other arm around Ernest. Consequently he had full control over the boy. There was no one in the rest of the apartment and no evidence of strings or other mechanical devices by which the event could have been staged. Things also happened when other visitors were present and had the boy under observation.

In the hope that the incidents would stop if the boy was sent away, he went to stay with an uncle and everything quietened down. In September when W. G. Roll was present, Ernest came back and dishes and other objects again took off. The grandmother wanted to send Ernest out of the apartment, but Roll hoped to observe some of the disturbances under good conditions and asked that the boy might stay. Nobody had been hit by the objects while Roll was present and he pointed this out to the grandmother. 'It doesn't hit people,' he said, and at that instant a small bottle from an end table next to a couch hit Roll squarely on the head.

Ernest was sitting next to the table and Roll could not be certain that the boy had not thrown the bottle. Later on the boy was actually seen to throw some objects, though he denied this. When he was asked during hypnosis and during a polygraph ('lie-detection') test, he still denied. Interestingly enough, the polygraph record did not indicate the emotional reaction one expects to be associated with telling a lie. Apparently the boy was as unconscious of the throwing as he had been of the apparently genuine phenomena. In other poltergeist cases in which there seemed to be genuine phenomena these were later substituted by fraudulent imitations. The psychological and psychiatric studies of Ernest suggested the reason for this. Like other poltergeist persons, Ernest had strong feelings of anger which he was unable to express normally. These were particularly directed toward the grandmother. When the boy no longer possessed any genuine PK ability, he continued producing the phenomena normally, since this caused a separation between himself and his grandmother. With the cooperation of the child welfare authorities in Newark, it was arranged for Ernest to stay temporarily in a foster home and as a result the poltergeist phenomena, normal and possibly genuine ones alike, ceased (*404*).

One of the most unusual poltergeist eruptions recorded in recent times took place in Indianapolis, Indiana, during March and April 1962. Not only were there movements and breakages of objects, but the family was attacked by strange bites or woundings on different parts of the body. There were three persons in the house, a thirteen-year-old daughter and her mother and grandmother. In that case, however, it was not the daughter but the mother who seemed to be at the centre of the disturbances. It was usually the grandmother who received the bites. The case was investigated by W. G. Roll. On several occasions when he was present, the grandmother cried out and showed fresh puncture wounds on her arm, chest and other parts of her body. Sometimes the blood was flowing. Roll examined for insects and foreign objects but found nothing. Altogether she was wounded on fourteen occasions, her daughter on one, the number of individual punctures ranging from one to eight. It seemed impossible that an animal, whether an insect or a larger one, could have caused the woundings without being discovered, but the possibility could not be ruled out that they were self-inflicted. When the woundings stopped, strange knocking noises started close to the elderly lady. When Roll and a visiting psychologist, who was helping in the investigation, were present in the house, and while the psychologist was holding the hand of the grandmother, to prevent her from knocking on the wall, the same sounds were heard close by. Roll, with the mother, could see into the grand-daughter's room. None of them could have made the knocks in any normal way. Altogether there were twenty-five series of knockings which greatly frightened and disturbed the family and particularly the grandmother. There were also seventy-six movements recorded during this period. On one occasion, when the grandmother and grand-daughter were in their rooms and the mother was in the hallway outside these rooms, a large bathroom brush moved from the bathroom across the hall and on to the stairs while Roll was watching the mother and had the doors to the rooms of the others in view (*404*).

Among the most thoroughly investigated poltergeists was one that was on the rampage in what must be a favourite haunt for a poltergeist, a warehouse full of glasses, ashtrays, plates, and other breakables. The disturbances, which involved more than 200 individual incidents, took place in January 1967, in a wholesale novelty store in Miami, Florida. Police officers, a magician and others were unable to explain the incidents. The case was investigated by J. G. Pratt and W. G. Roll. It soon became clear that the incidents were concentrated in the vicinity of one of the employees, Julio, a nineteen-year-old shipping clerk. Certain areas of the large warehouse room where the disturbances took place were more frequently affected than others and these became the focus of the investigation. The investigators designated certain parts as target areas and placed objects in them hoping that the objects would be affected while Julio and the other employees were under observation. In several cases, target objects placed in these areas did move to the floor while Julio and the other employees were under observation (*405*). In the effort to discover physiological or psychological factors which might be connected with the phenomena, Julio came to Durham for testing and observation. No abnormal physical conditions were found and his EEG (brain wave) patterns were normal. As in other such cases, the psychological tests revealed strong feelings of hostility, especially towards parental figures, which Julio could not express openly and from which he felt personally detached. It appeared that he regarded the owners of the business in Miami as such figures and that the disturbances were a means to express aggression which could find no other outlet.

While in Durham, the young man was tested on several of the PK machines available at the Foundation for Research on the Nature of Man at the invitation of J. B. Rhine. Suggestive results of PK were produced on a mechanical dice-release machine. In addition there was an apparent RSPK disturbance of a vase in the hallway while Julio was standing with the parapsychologists several feet away (*404*).

In November 1968 a poltergeist almost took over the small home of an elderly couple in the village of Olive Hill in the Cumberland Mountains of Kentucky. Nearly all their breakable belongings finished up in pieces on the floor. The old couple moved, but this was no help, for the disturbances soon started up in the new home. In December an investigation was made by W. G. Roll and J. P. Stump. Once when Stump was in the living-room and facing the television set, a bowl and cloth doily suddenly fell behind the set, followed in slow motion by the plastic flowers which had been in the bowl. At the same time, a clock which had also stood on the set flew four feet from the set in the opposite direction, landing close to the feet of Stump. When he went to look for the other objects he found the bowl on the doily and the flowers in the bowl just as they had been when they had been on top of the set. The grandson of the elderly couple, Roger, a twelve-year-old boy, was in front of the TV set with his back to it and in full view of the investigator. He was usually close to the incidents, but on one occasion a perfume bottle moved about four feet from a bedroom dresser to the floor while Roll was facing the dresser and was the person closest to it, Roger being in another room. Another time, when Roll had followed the boy into the kitchen, the heavy kitchen table jumped up in the air, rotated about 45 degrees and settled on the backs of the chairs which were standing around it. Roll was looking at the boy, who stood next to the table, and saw no way in which he could have caused the incident normally. Nobody else was in the kitchen.

Altogether there were 179 incidents, most of these occurring when the boy was present. The case was particularly interesting from an evidential point of view because several of the incidents were directly observed by the visiting investigators. As in other poltergeist cases, there was a marked decrease in the number of incidents with increased distance from the boy, again suggesting that the energy in certain ways followed a known law (*404*). W. G. R.

(Further reading: see references in the text; see also *397*.)

Possession

In many societies all over the world madness, epilepsy, religious ecstasy, prophecy, poetic and artistic inspiration, drunken or sexual frenzy, states of TRANCE and other mental and physical states classified as peculiar and out of the ordinary, have been explained in terms of the invasion of the personality by a superhuman power, a god or spirit or demon which takes possession of a human being, moves his limbs as if he were a puppet, speaks through his mouth, writes with his hand, looks out through his eyes and thinks with his brain.

There are still legacies of this attitude to the unusual in everyday speech, when we say of someone who is behaving abnormally that he is 'not himself' or that we cannot understand 'what has got into him'. Sophisticated people do not usually mean literally that the person is temporarily someone or something else, but the implication is there and is accepted in many primitive societies and by a surprisingly large number of people even in the materialist modern West. The mentally disturbed and disturbing sensation of not being fully in control of yourself, of being dominated and impelled by an alien force, can induce a conviction that some personality from outside has entered you. People in severely disturbed states of mind may, for example, believe themselves to be controlled by an evil power which is driving them to commit murder or suicide against their will. On a milder level, all sorts of compulsive thoughts and actions – a compulsion never to pass a tree without touching it, for instance, or to count the spoons ten times a day – have the appearance of being dictated to a person in defiance of his reason and contrary to his will, and may create uneasy suspicions about a possessing or obsessing entity. The usual distinction drawn is that a possessing entity is one believed to be in control of a human being from the inside, while an obsessing entity is one which harasses him from the outside, persistently attempting to sway his thoughts and influence his actions.

These entities are not invariably thought to be evil. On the contrary, the guardian angel of hallowed tradition is a benevolent obsessing entity, and temporary total possession by the divine is one of the supreme goals of mysticism, Christian and other. Mystical experience of a great ultimate reality lying behind and transcending all surface appearances is frequently described as the sudden acquisition of sure knowledge of this reality, or as a clear vision of it, but is also sometimes described as an experience of union with it. 'God establishes himself in the interior of this soul in such a way', said St Teresa, 'that when she returns to herself, it is wholly

Exorcism by St Anthony of Padua

impossible for her to doubt that she has been in God, and God in her' (247). And St John of the Cross said that in the rapture of union with the divine, 'the soul seems to be God himself . . . The soul seems to be God rather than itself, and indeed it is God by participation' (435).

On the first day of Pentecost, soon after the death and resurrection of Jesus, his followers experienced possession by the Holy Spirit, which showed itself outwardly in inspired utterance or 'speaking in tongues' (Acts ii, 4). This sign of the divine presence, the use of languages with which the speakers were not familiar in a normal state of mind or of totally unknown languages which could only be interpreted with the aid of divine inspiration, was a major feature of early Christian worship. The entry of the Spirit into the believers also manifested itself in the gift of healing and the other 'gifts of the Spirit' listed by St Paul (I Corinthians xii, 4–11), which probably played an extremely important role in impressing unbelievers and making converts to the new religion. St Paul himself was no stranger to ecstatic experiences and felt the sense of being possessed by the divine which enabled him to say that 'it is no longer I who live, but Christ who lives in me' (Galatians ii, 20).

In this century, possession by the Holy Spirit, with the accompanying gift of tongues, has been brought back to the centre of Christian experience, for thousands of believers at least, largely by the Pentecostalist movement, founded when the Spirit descended to a group at Bethel College, Topeka, Kansas, on the first day of the new century. The largest of the Pentecostal groups, established first in the United States and subsequently spreading abroad, is the Assemblies of God, which counts its members in the hundreds of thousands and runs its own university. There are also numerous smaller groups which look for and experience the entry of the Spirit into the believer and the gift of tongues, including some within the Roman Catholic Church and the major Protestant Churches (see 509).

Streaming In Like Light

Feelings of possession can be stimulated by DRUGS on occasion. The great American psychologist William James concluded on the basis of his own experience with nitrous oxide that 'our normal waking consciousness, rational consciousness as we call it, is but one special type of consciousness, whilst all about it, parted from it by the flimsiest of screens, there lie potential forms of consciousness entirely different. We may go through life without suspecting their existence; but apply the requisite stimulus, and at a touch

they are there in all their completeness, definite types of mentality which probably somewhere have their field of application and adaptation.' He quotes John Addington Symonds, the Victorian critic and historian, who had an experience of this sort under chloroform in which he felt possessed by God. 'I thought that I was near death; when, suddenly, my soul became aware of God, who was manifestly dealing with me, handling me, so to speak, in an intense personal present reality. I felt him streaming in like light upon me . . . I cannot describe the ecstasy I felt.' Symonds was afterwards unhappily uncertain whether he had really felt the presence of God or whether he had been tricked by the abnormal excitement of his brain under the drug (247).

In many primitive communities, now and in the past, drugs, over-breathing, drumming and dancing, or the hypnotic repetition of a MANTRA, have been employed by a priest, shaman or medicine-man, to put himself into a state of trance or semi-trance in which he believes himself, and is believed by the faithful, to be possessed by a god or by the spirit of a deceased human being, which may then speak through his mouth to the worshippers. In the same societies, sufferers from diseases, especially mental illnesses, are thought to be possessed by spirits and it is the duty of the healer either to expel the possessing entity altogether or to reconcile it with its human host so that they can coexist together in reasonable amity. Methods of cure frequently involve putting the patient into a trance in which the possessing spirit speaks through his mouth and its nature and identity are discovered. The VOODOO religion of Haiti is centred on possession of worshippers by spirits, and Maya Deren, in her book on Voodoo, has given vivid descriptions of the experience of being possessed (116a).

In SPIRITUALISM it is the spirits of the dead who are believed to take possession of mediums and who are responsible for the production of automatic writing and art, and for spiritual healing and other mediumistic phenomena (see AUTOMATISMS; FAITH HEALING; MEDIUMS). A Spiritualist author has defined the term 'obsession' as follows: 'The state of a mind besieged. Medically, it refers to a fixed idea which threatens the mental balance. In Spiritualism it refers to the invasion of the living by a discarnate spirit or spirits, tending to complete possession for the purpose of selfish gratification. Trance mediumship operates on the same principle but is the result of co-operation between an intelligent spirit and the medium . . . The obsessing spirits are usually ignorant or earth-bound, not necessarily evil – any

harm they cause may be unintentional' (48).

In modern Western magic the trance-possession states of primitive priest-magicians have their counterpart in techniques for inducing possession by 'gods' or 'god-forms' (see RITUAL MAGIC; SPIRITS AND FORCES), though an operation of this sort is as much one of the magician taking possession of and using a superhuman force as of its taking possession of him. Drugs are sometimes used as an aid, so are mantras and sometimes sex, but the essential ingredients are imagination and concentration. The god which is invoked is a force or entity or reality of some sort, upon which the magician concentrates until he has a vividly imagined mental picture of it – a painting or image of it may be used to help him to visualize it. By focusing upon it all his mental and emotional energies, all the force of his will and longing, he summons it to take possession of him and feels that he has become it. He may sense it as a gigantic form towering over and dwarfing him. When it takes control, according to one modern magician, 'the adept will feel an exquisite giddiness somewhere at the base of his skull and quickly convulsing the whole of his body. As this happens, and while the power is surging into him, he forces himself to visualise the thing he wants his magic to accomplish, and wills its success. He must put all he has into this and . . . whip himself into a veritable frenzy. It is at this point that the force evoked will be expelled to realise the ritual intention' (96).

It is significant that 'possessing' is a common term for sexual intercourse. Sexual desire and orgasm do create a sense of being caught in the grip of some overwhelming power from outside oneself, which lies behind the personification of desire as a powerful deity in the past, and mutual orgasm can induce feelings of mutual possession of each partner by the other. Sex is employed in magical possession rituals because it contributes to the magician's 'veritable frenzy' and to his sense of possessing and being possessed by the force he has summoned up. Tantric sects in India have long used sex to induce union of the worshippers with supernatural beings (see TANTRISM) and in the last hundred years or so tantric techniques have been adopted by some Western occultists. The initiates of the German O.T.O. are an example: 'To invoke the powers of a god into themselves they mentally concentrated on the god throughout their sexual intercourse, building up the form of the deity in their imaginations and attempting to imbue it with life. At the moment of orgasm they identified themselves with the imagined form, mentally seeing their own bodies and that of the god blending into one' (263).

The descent of the Holy Spirit, symbolized by a dove, at Pentecost

A Mind Besieged

Sex, or frustrated sex, appears to have played an important role in the epidemics of 'demonic possession' in French convents in the 16th and 17th centuries, when devils screamed out torrents of blasphemy and obscenity through the mouths of nuns who reviled all things Christian, writhed in acrobatic and extraordinary contortions, sometimes appearing to be in orgasm, and in response to leading questions from their exorcists supplied detailed and horrific accounts of worshipping Satan at witches' sabbaths, engaging in orgies with demons and other witches, and devouring the bodies of children.

The parallel with the behaviour of some patients in the early days of hypnosis was noted by the official Commission which investigated Mesmer's cures in the late 18th century (see HYPNOSIS). In both cases the majority of the patients were women, their hysterical excitement was contagious and rapidly spread to others, they experienced or appeared to experience orgasm, and they were highly suggestible, readily responding to the slightest hint or spur provided by the exorcist or hypnotist.

In his classic work on *Possession*, first published in Germany in 1921, T. K. Oesterreich drew attention to what he regarded as the basic identity between possession phenomena reported from the ancient world and primitive societies, the behaviour of people believed to be possessed by demons in medieval and modern Europe, and certain phenomena of hypnosis and mediumship, all of which he treated as examples of abnormal human psychology. He thought that in cases of supposed possession or obsession by evil spirits, 'there develops in the psyche a sort of secondary system of personality which directs the person's life against his will. The subject loses control over a considerable number of his states, and it is this part of his personality which plays the obsessive role of a demon.'

A leading British psychiatrist, Dr William Sargant, has emphasized the important part played by spirit-possession all over the world, including mystical or revivalist possession by God or the Holy Spirit, in inculcating and confirming convinced faith in a great variety of gods, spirits, demons and other supernatural beings. He sees the same basic physiological and psychological processes at work behind the phenomena of possession and exorcism; brainwashing techniques which convert people to religious, political or other doctrines, often totally at variance with their previous beliefs and outlook; the effects of powerful revivalist preaching; mob-oratory and other methods of crowd persuasion; and the effects of abreactive methods of treatment in modern psychiatry, which depend essentially on inducing extreme fear or anger in a patient and working him up into a state of intense excitement. This may lead to a temporary collapse, followed by a recovery and a sense of release from the 'possessing' agency, whether it be a demon or some traumatic memory. Dr Sargant traces the whole process to the behaviour of the brain under stress, with the development of greatly heightened suggestibility, and finds no reason to suppose that any external spiritual or supernatural agency is at work. Others, however, continue to believe that in at least some cases of possession or obsession spiritual

Possession

beings and powers, good or evil, invade and control the human mind.

Exorcism

The Christian method of expelling a demon from a possessed person appears to have remained essentially the same since the time of Christ, and is paralleled in other traditions. The exorcist speaks to the demon and commands it in the name of God to come out of its victim, threatening it with pains and penalties if it does not. The demon will very often reply abusively and at length, and may quarrel violently with the exorcist, attempting to maintain itself against severe psychological pressure. This pressure, reinforced in more primitive methods by beating and ill-treating the patient, is exerted through the use of holy symbols, commanding language, and the concentrated and confident will and personality of the exorcist. The demon is often ordered to state his name and give some account of himself: in effect, when the nature of the disturbance is expressed in words, this seems to help in getting rid of it. The exorcist's commands and threats create intense anger and fear in the demon, and if this is worked up to a high enough pitch the demon may leave the patient, often in collapse or convulsion.

Oesterreich quotes a typical case from Germany in 1714, reported by a pastor who attempted to exorcise a woman possessed by Satan. He had the woman brought into church and read passages of the Bible to her. 'Satan who was in the possessed cried to me from below the pulpit: "Won't you soon have done?" After I had replied, "When it is enough for God it will be enough for thee, demon!" Satan broke into complaints against me: "How dost thou oppress, how dost thou torment me!..." When at last I addressed to him the most violent exhortations in the name of Jesus, he cried out: "Oh, I burn, I burn! Oh, what torture! What torture!" or loaded me with furious invectives: "What ails thee to jabber in this fashion?" During all these prayers, clamourings and disputes, Satan tortured the poor creature horribly, howled through her mouth in a frightful manner and threw her to the ground so rigid, so insensible that she became as cold as ice and lay as if dead, at which time we could not perceive the slightest breath until at last with God's help she came to herself...' But the demon returned to her later.

The Roman Catholic ritual of exorcism is contained in the *Rituale Romanum* of 1614, which prescribes that great care should be taken to distinguish genuine possession from certain forms of disease. The exorcisms themselves, which are interspersed with prayers, psalms and readings from the Bible, are couched in superbly impressive Latin. 'Exorciso te, imundissime spiritus, omnis incursio adversarii, omne phantasma, omnis legio, in nomine Domini nostri Jesu Christi; eradicare et effugare ab hoc plasmata Dei. Ipse tibi imperat, qui te de supernis coelorum in inferiora terrae demergi praecipit. Ipse tibi imperat, qui mari, ventis et tempestatibus imperavit. Audi ergo et time satana, inimice fidei, hostis generis humani, mortis adductor, vitae raptor, iustitiae declinator, malorum radix, fomes vitiorum, seductor hominum, proditor gentium, incitator invidiae, origo avaritiae, causa discordiae, excitator dolorum...' ('I exorcise thee, most unclean spirit, every incursion of the enemy, every spectre, every legion, in the name of our Lord Jesus Christ; be thou rooted out and put to flight from this creature of God. He commands thee, who has bid thee be cast down from the highest heavens into the depths of the earth. He commands thee, who rules the sea, the winds and the tempests. Hear, therefore, and fear, Satan, injurer of the faith, enemy of the human race, procurer of death, destroyer of life, perverter of justice, root of evils, fomentor of vices, seducer of men, betrayer of nations, inciter of envy, fount of greed, cause of discord, instigator of griefs...')

And again: 'Adiuro te serpens antique, per Judicem vivorum et mortuorum, per factorem tuum, per factorem mundi, per eum qui habet potestatem mittendi te in gehennam, ut ab hoc famulo Dei, qui ad Ecclesiae sinum recurrit, cum metu et exercitu furoris tui festinus discedas...' ('I adjure thee, thou old serpent, by the Judge of the living and the dead, by thy maker, by the maker of the world, by him who hath power to send thee to hell, that from this servant of God, who returns to the bosom of the Church, with thy fear and the torment of thy terror thou swiftly depart...') (*442*)

Several authorities have suggested that an important factor in successful exorcism is the faith of the exorcist and his conviction that the victim is genuinely possessed. 'If the prayer and conjuration are not carried out with the most complete faith that there is a real demon incarnate (and not poison from a scratch, etc.) no cure follows' (*355*). Certainly among some modern practitioners the immense mental and physical effort required and the strain imposed on the exorcist are very evident. One experienced exorcist, the Reverend J. C. Neil-Smith, has said that successful exorcism depends more on the exorcist's own gifts than on the ritual.

There has been a revival of exorcism in recent years. Either there are many more people who believe themselves to be possessed or obsessed by evil spirits and malignant ghosts, or there are many more who are prepared to say so. Christian clergymen who practise exorcism report themselves overwhelmed by the number of those who come to them for help. Many of these patients may not be genuinely possessed but may respond to the exorcist's treatment all the same. A

The 'ghost-hunter' Harry Price

Roman Catholic exorcist, Father de Tonqué-dec, who acted for the archdiocese of Paris for twenty years up to 1939, thought that more than 90 per cent of the cases he observed did not involve genuine possession, but that a small minority of cases did. R. C.

(Further reading: *198, 238, 288, 355, 416, 417.*)

Pranayama See YOGA.

Precognition

Knowledge of the future which cannot reliably be inferred from present knowledge; a type of extrasensory perception: see PARAPSYCHOLOGY; see also DIVINATION; DREAMS.

Premonition

A hunch or intuition of what is going to happen in the future, frequently but not always a sense of some impending tragedy or disaster; if not inferred from present knowledge, it is a type of PRECOGNITION: see PARAPSYCHOLOGY.

Harry Price (1881-1948)

The British psychical researcher and 'ghost-hunter', founder of the National Library of Psychical Research, who exposed various fraudulent mediums but whose own reputation has come under serious attack in connection with his investigations at Borley Rectory, on the borders of Essex and Suffolk, famous as the 'most haunted house in England'; author of *Fifty Years of Psychical Research*, 1939, *The Most Haunted House in England*, 1940, *The End of Borley Rectory*, 1945, *Poltergeist over England*, 1945. (*120, 204, 375, 376*)

Proxy Sitting

A sitting with a medium at which the inquirer is represented by someone else, a proxy, who knows nothing about the dead person from whom a communication is desired: see MEDIUMS; SPIRITUALISM.

Psi

The parapsychological term for 'psychic' abilities which 'enable a person to make contact with the world around him without the aid of his senses and muscles', and the phenomena related to these abilities (extrasensory perception, psychokinesis, etc.): 'psi-missing' means the exercise of psi ability in a way that avoids the target which the subject is trying to hit (not the same as a lack of psi ability): see PARAPSYCHOLOGY.

Psychical Research See PARAPSYCHOLOGY and related articles; see also MEDIUMS; SPIRITUALISM.

Psychical Research Societies

The Society for Psychical Research (S.P.R.), which has its headquarters in London, was founded in 1882. Its purpose is, in the Society's own words, 'to examine without prejudice or prepossession and in a scientific spirit those faculties of man, real or supposed, which appear to be inexplicable on any generally recognised hypothesis. The Society does not hold or express corporate views.' Among the founding and early members of the S.P.R. were F. W. H. Myers (1843–1901), Edmund Gurney (1847–88), Sir William Barrett (1844–1925), Professor of Physics at University College, Dublin, Henry Sidgwick (1838–1900), Professor of Moral Philosophy at Cambridge and the first president of the S.P.R., his wife, Eleanor Sidgwick (1845–1936), Principal of Newnham College, Cambridge, and Sir Oliver Lodge (1831–1940), the physicist. The Society's presidents have included William James, Andrew Lang, Henri Bergson, Gilbert Murray, Lord Rayleigh, William McDougall, C. D. Broad, H. H. Price, E. R. Dodds, Sir Alister Hardy, and other distinguished scholars. The American Society for Psychical Research (A.S.P.R.) was originally founded in 1885. Its first president was an astronomer, Professor Simon Newcomb, and William James was a leading figure in its early history. Richard Hodgson (1855-1905), an Australian, took over the management of the A.S.P.R. in 1887 and played a prominent role in investigating Mrs PIPER and other mediums. Experimental research under laboratory conditions was pioneered at Duke University, North Carolina, from 1927 onwards, under the leadership of J. B. Rhine, and the Duke Parapsychology Laboratory eventually became the Foundation for Research on the Nature of Man: see PARAPSYCHOLOGY. (*176, 253, 254, 255, 378*).

Psychokinesis

'Mind over matter', the parapsychical ability to influence an object or event by mind alone: see PARAPSYCHOLOGY; see also POLTERGEISTS; TELEKINESIS.

Psychometry

An alternative term for OBJECT READING.

Marquis de Puységur (1751-1825)

A pupil of Mesmer and a pioneer of experiment in HYPNOSIS. He distrusted the hysterical convulsions which were an essential element of Mesmer's cures and put his patients into a 'somnabulic' or sleeplike state in which he found they could be cured just as effectively. His patients in hypnotic TRANCE were highly suggestible and often appeared to have clairvoyant powers.

Qabalah See CABALA.

Quest Society

A group founded by G. R. S. MEAD in 1909: see THEOSOPHICAL SOCIETY.

Phineas Parkhurst Quimby (1802-66)

An American healer and forerunner of CHRISTIAN SCIENCE and the NEW THOUGHT movement. Born in Lebanon, New Hampshire, he spent most of his life in Belfast, Maine. He became interested in mesmerism in 1838 and practised successfully as a mesmeric healer, but he eventually came to the conclusion that physical diseases were the outcome of wrong-headed ideas and attitudes, and that patients could be cured by changing their beliefs, or 'mental healing': see HYPNOSIS. (*129*)

P. P. Quimby

R

Radiesthesia, Radionics

There is considerable confusion about the correct use of the term radiesthesia. For the purposes of this article it is defined as (a) the body of theory and practice, including the use of radionic 'machines' and eccentric therapeutics, that have grown up around DOWSING, and (b) map dowsing by means of pendulums.

Curiously enough, the origins of radiesthesia lie not in dowsing itself but in a 19th-century Spiritualistic practice ultimately derived from a medieval magical technique known as 'the ring and the disc'. This involved suspending a gold or silver ring on a silken thread over a parchment disc on which were written the words 'yes' and 'no'. The magician first invoked the spirit he wished to consult, by means of prayer, and then, holding the silken thread between his thumb and forefinger, asked questions of it, the gyrations of the ring over the disc supposedly indicating the spirit's replies.

French Spiritualists of the 1850s simplified this method by replacing the ring with a simple pendulum or bob which was suspended over a wine glass, the taps of the bob against the rim of the glass being interpreted according to a simple code, one tap for *oui*, two taps for *non*. Among those who interpreted this modified system in operation was a certain M. Chevreul, director of the French Museum of Natural History, who embarked on a series of experiments. He soon satisfied himself that muscular force was being imparted to the pendulum by the person holding it and that no mysterious energy, drawn from the world of spirits, was involved. On the other hand, Chevreul was satisfied that no deliberate fraud was involved, that no movement was *consciously* imparted to the pendulum. He found that the bob was capable of following its holder's imagination but not his will-power; thus, however powerfully he willed it to move from, say, right to left, the pendulum remained motionless, but as soon as he shut his eyes and *imagined* it swinging in the desired direction an uncon-

scious exertion of muscular force took place and the pendulum began to move.

Chevreul's experiments interested several French practitioners of dowsing, among whom were some Roman Catholic priests, who began to substitute the pendulum for the dowser's traditional forked twig, on the grounds that the pendulum was more 'sensitive'. This belief was entirely justified: the amount of muscular energy required to impart motion to a pendulum is so small that many would-be dowsers have achieved results with it although they have been completely unsuccessful when experimenting with more traditional implements.

At first the French dowsers used their pendulums in exactly the same way as they had used their divining rods, going out into the fields and walking over the ground they were investigating. Soon, however, some of them reached the conclusion that the dowsing faculty was of a psychic nature, that it was only necessary to sit at home dangling one's pendulum over a map and the phenomenon of 'resonance' would do the rest. This 19th-century theory of resonance is still adhered to by many practitioners of radiesthesia. For example, John Wilcox has written: 'What occurs when a dowser obtains a reaction from his dowsing rod . . . is evidently in some way associated with the phenomenon of *resonance* . . . his projected *thought-form* unites in some way with the water radiations present . . . If there is no water, his thought-form finds, as it were, no target, and there is no response from his instrument' (*503*). A remarkable example of map dowsing was the establishment of a Pendulum Institute at Berlin during the Second World War, where attempts were made to locate British and American shipping at sea by dangling pendulums over maps of the oceans (see DIVINATION).

Pendulums and Disease

Medical radiesthesia seems to have originated with a female dowser, Mlle Chantereine, who claimed to be able to ascertain the exact nature of any sample of polluted water by holding a pendulum in one hand and, one by one, samples of various bacterial cultures in the other. When the bacterial culture corresponded to the nature of the pollutant, the pendulum began to gyrate.

Unorthodox medical practitioners, particularly homoeopaths, took up this idea with enthusiasm. Soon they extended it not only to diagnosis but to deciding on an appropriate course of treatment. The methods evolved – and still used today – varied from one practitioner to another. Some used large cards, rather like enormous OUIJA BOARDS, on which were written the names of all

human diseases, and the pendulum was used to show which disease was present. Diagnosis having been completed, the appropriate remedy was selected by a similar process.

Other practitioners believed that they had established, by trial and error, varying rates of pendulum vibration for each illness and each drug. A spot of the patient's blood, frequently placed on a piece of blotting paper, was used to establish the diagnosis, and then the remedy was selected by a method similar to that used by Mlle Chantereine in establishing the exact nature of water-pollution. This system is still popular today, though it is now often employed in a modified form in which the patient does not actually take the prescribed drug. Instead, a quantity of the drug is placed on the bloodspot and, by some process of sympathetic magic, a rapport is established between the patient and the drug. It is not necessary for the physician to examine the patient, to see what progress is being made; it is enough for the bloodspot to be examined each day – by pendulum, of course.

This method of therapy undeniably has certain disadvantages. One of its contemporary practitioners has recorded with dismay, and with commendable honesty, his acute surprise when, shortly after the pendulum had recorded a remarkable improvement in the health of a female patient, a messenger arrived to inform him that she was dead. Though puzzled, this physician did not for one moment consider that his whole system might be based on self-deception, and he cast about for an explanation. He soon found one: the pendulum, he decided, did not actually deal with the physical body but with the ETHERIC BODY, with which, according to THEOSOPHICAL theory, the former is so closely connected during life that for all practical purposes they are one and the same. At death, however, the two 'vehicles' are separated and, as the etheric body will feel better when parted from its sickly physical shell, the pendulum will accordingly record a marked improvement in health.

Radionics

In recent years, many medical radiesthesists have become fascinated by a new development of their art, the pseudo-science of radionics, which deals with the construction and use of quasi-machines employed in radiesthesia. The real originator of radionics was a San Francisco physician named Albert Abrams. Abrams was no quack, or not at first. He had a perfectly good medical degree from Heidelberg, carried out postgraduate studies at London, Vienna and Berlin, and by 1910, when he was forty-seven, he was chief of the medical clinic at Cooper Medical

College and seemed to be on his way to becoming a neurologist of some eminence. In that same year he blasted his reputation by publishing a book called *Spondylotherapy*, in which he advocated a new form of manual therapeutics of that name. Spondylotherapy, described by the California Medical Society as a 'hybrid of upstage osteopathy and chiropractic', did not find favour with the medical profession but attracted a large lay following. A Spondylotherapic Association was established in 1912 and Abrams toured the country giving courses in the new 'science' at $200 a time.

Four years later, Abrams published *New Concepts of Diagnosis and Treatment*, in which he announced that all disease was a 'disharmony of electronic oscillation', that diagnosis must be based on measurement of this disharmony, and that therapeutics should consist of 'restoring a harmonious electronic oscillation'. Shortly afterwards, Abrams began to manufacture and sell a machine, variously known as the Black Box, the E.R.A., or the Oscilloclast, designed to achieve these admirable aims. The machines consisted of a number of variable rheostats in a sealed box, a thin sheet of rubber stretched over a metal plate, and an imposing number of dials, and were leased out at the astonishingly high rental of $300 a year. The American Medical Association described how they worked: 'All that was needed was a drop of blood from the patient . . . The drop of blood on a piece of white blotting paper . . . was put into the diagnostic machine which in turn was connected by means of a wire to a piece of metal connected to the forehead of a healthy individual while Abrams . . . tapped on the abdomen of the individual who . . . had to stand facing west in a dim light. According to various "areas of dullness" that were found by tapping upon the healthy subject's abdomen there was determined the disease from which the patient . . . was suffering and also the location of the diseased area.'

It was perhaps inevitable that this versatile machine was subjected to abuse by cynical physicians who dispatched the blood of healthy animals for diagnosis. A chicken was diagnosed by Abrams as suffering from syphilis and a sheep as 'suffering from acute motor-neurotic tensions with a pre-clinical neoplasm caused by the strains of modern life'.

Abrams died in 1924, in which year the British Medical Association set up a committee under Sir Thomas Horder to investigate the Black Box and, by implication, its British users – mostly osteopaths and dowsers. Its conclusions were most unexpected: it stated that its tests had convinced it of the existence of a mysterious, hitherto unknown

force and that 'no more convincing exposition of the reality of the phenomena could possibly be desired'. In spite of this favourable verdict and the fact that two of the committee's members seem to have been highly suggestible (Horder and another member felt their muscles subjected to a mysterious tension when they attempted to operate the Black Box), the committee was unable to regard the use of the Abrams machine as ethically justified, because of the mysterious nature of the force employed.

After Abrams's death his theories continued to attract devoted disciples but for some time there was no real development of them. In the last quarter of a century, however, there has been a revival of interest in radionics, especially in connection with elaborate devices developed by the late Dr Ruth Drown in the U.S.A. and by the late George de la Warr in England. These two seem to have been working along similar lines: both devised modified Abrams boxes and mysterious cameras designed to produce 'etheric photographs' from bloodspots.

In 1950 a test of the diagnostic abilities of the Drown black box at Chicago University produced such disappointing results that Dr Drown withdrew from the investigation. The Drown camera was an even worse fiasco, the investigating committee coming to the conclusion that the photographs it took were valueless.

Ten years later, the de la Warr box was in the news when a woman who had bought one of them sued the de la Warr laboratories for the return of her money on the ground that she was unable to obtain satisfactory results from it – she said that some of her patients were recorded by the box as changing sex from day to day. She lost her case on the grounds that, whether or not the box was effective, de la Warr honestly believed in it and had no fraudulent intentions. All the same, the judge's comments on the de la Warr camera were scathing. 'The totality of the evidence', he said, 'suggested that the camera was completely bogus and that the photographs were fakes.'

In spite of the unsatisfactory nature of the evidence, however, it is possible that radionic devices do 'work' for some practitioners. This is not because of the boxes themselves, the circuits of which simply do not make sense from the point of view of electronics, but because a belief in their efficacy may enable a gifted individual to achieve a temporary dissociation of consciousness and bring the mysterious dowsing faculty into action. F. K.

(See also AUTOMATISMS; FAITH HEALING.)
(Further reading: *224, 242, 324, 499, 503*.)

Radionics See RADIESTHESIA.

Pascal Beverly Randolph (1825-71)

The American founder of numerous occult groups, including a Hermetic Brotherhood of Light in France; he was one of the first Western occultists to interest himself in the consciousness-expanding properties of DRUGS, including ether and hashish: see ROSICRUCIANS.

Raphael

The pseudonym of a succession of British astrologers, the first of whom was Robert Cross Smith (1795–1832), who wrote *The Prophetic Messenger*, a predictive almanac first published in 1826 and still in existence under the title of *Raphael's Almanac, Predictive Messenger and Weather Guide*. Smith also wrote *The Manual of Astrology*, 1828, *The Royal Book of Fate*, 1829, *The Royal Book of Dreams*, 1830, etc. One of his successors was Robert T. Cross (1850–1923), author of *Guide to Astrology*, 1877–79. (*234*)

Raudive Experiments See VOICE PHENOMENA.

Francis Israel Regardie (b.1907)

The author of a number of exceptionally illuminating books on magic; born in England, he has spent most of his life in the United States. In 1928 he became secretary and companion to Aleister CROWLEY, from whom he later broke away. He joined the STELLA MATUTINA in 1934. He published the rituals of the Order of the GOLDEN DAWN, to much outcry from those associated with it, in 1937–40. More recently he has become a Reichian therapist (see REICH). His other books include *My Rosicrucian Adventure*, *The Tree of Life*, *The Garden of Pomegranates*, *The Eye in the Triangle*, *Roll Away the Stone*, *The Art of True Healing*. (*387* to *391* inclusive.) (See also *262*.)

Wilhelm Reich (1897-1957)

Wilhelm Reich, whose personality and writings are now the centre of a large and growing cult, was born in Austro-Hungary of semi-assimilated and agnostic Jewish parents. He graduated from a technical high school in 1915 with 'excellent' in all subjects and immediately enlisted in the Austrian army, fighting on the Italian front and rising to the rank of lieutenant. With the end of the war and demobilization he became a medical student at Vienna University, working under great pressure, for ex-soldiers were allowed to cram into four years the medical training that normally extended over six.

Early in 1919 a number of Reich's fellow students decided that sexology was unduly neglected by the University's medical faculty and set up an unofficial sexological seminar.

Reich was a member of this, but was repelled by the sexual attitudes of the other participants; he felt a similar aversion for the point of view displayed by a Freudian psychoanalyst whose lectures he attended. It is probable that Reich's aversions sprang from a refusal to recognize certain elements in his own sexual make-up – to the end of his life he seems to have retained a deep dislike of certain forms of sexual expression, notably male homosexuality – but, nevertheless, he came to the conclusion that sexuality was the 'centre around which revolves the whole of social life as well as the inner life of the individual'.

Reich qualified as a physician in the summer of 1922 and spent the next two years doing postgraduate neurological work under the famous Professor Wagner-Jauregg. As Reich was now practising Freudian analysis and was a full member of the Vienna Psychoanalytic Society, he found Wagner-Jauregg and his University Neurological Clinic difficult to cope with. For the former missed no opportunity of poking fun at psycho-analysis while at the latter neurotics were treated with bromides and suggestion. According to Reich, Wagner-Jauregg's claim that 90 per cent of neurotics were successfully cured by these methods was quite untrue; either, said Reich, there was a spontaneous remission of symptoms or a 'cure' was claimed simply because some individual symptom had disappeared. The 10 per cent of the inmates whom even Wagner-Jauregg could not regard as cured were simply sent off to the Steinhof, a vast psychiatric institution in which something approaching 20,000 patient-prisoners were incarcerated.

Nevertheless, Reich's two years at the clinic were of great importance to his intellectual development, for his experiences there led him to formulate two of his most characteristic theoretical concepts, that of 'physiological armouring' and that of schizophrenia as a 'bottling up' of energy in the autonomic nervous system.

Reich arrived at the first of these ideas – that physical symptoms without any neurological cause were the result of the body adopting a posture, gesture or appearance designed to communicate an inner, psychological happening – as the result of examining a young girl patient whose arms had been paralysed since she raised them protectively against a man who was trying to clasp her in his arms. He developed the second of these concepts after seeing a normally immobilized catatonic burst into frenzied – and clearly pleasurable – activity; this convinced Reich that 'psychic *content* of the catatonic fantasy could not be the *cause* of the somatic process'.

Wilhelm Reich

In the later 1920s Reich became a member of the KPD, the German Communist Party. He was never an orthodox Marxist, however, and while he accepted the materialist interpretation of history he denied that the working class could be economically emancipated until it had first achieved sexual emancipation. There is no doubt that, in spite of the denials made by Reich's later disciples, Marxist thought was a major influence in Reich's own intellectual development. Reich's concept of muscular armouring, for example, owes much to Marxist dialectic. Reich's idea was that psychic disturbances cause muscular tension, that this tension (armouring) reinforces the original psychic upheaval and that, by a dialectical interaction between mind and muscle, a self-

perpetuating process of progressive physical and psychological degeneration is established. Reich believed that this process could only be reversed by a therapy designed to treat both mind and body. The first was to be tackled by fairly orthodox psycho-analytic treatment, the second by deep massage and physical manipulations designed to break up muscular armouring. Reich called the latter process *vegetotherapy* because he believed that the energy prevented from being released by armouring was stored up in the autonomic (or vegetative) nervous system. It must be emphasized that Reich was not so physiologically illiterate (as some Freudians have suggested) as to believe that the muscles are part of the autonomic system!

Orgone Energy

Even when still a student Reich had been

fascinated by the idea of psychic processes as a by-product of biological activity; he had found the idea of the 'life-force' an intriguing one and some of his fellow students had gone so far as to regard him as a disciple of Bergson, the French philosopher of the life-force who had been a brother-in-law of the English magician S. L. MacGregor MATHERS. For a time, preoccupied with Marxist and Freudian theory, he put such ideas behind him but by the early 1930s he returned to them. He felt that there must be a physical, biological process behind the profound organic changes that often accompany psychiatric illness and he began a course of experiments designed to prove that such a process existed. At first these experiments were designed only to ascertain whether sexual excitement, tumescence, etc., were associated with an increase of the bio-electric potential of the genitals. He found that they were, and on this basis formulated an ambitious theory which, he believed, resolved the conflict between the vitalist and mechanist schools of biology.

In 1936 he began a more ambitious series of experiments, the results of which show either that Reich had made a series of discoveries of world-shaking importance (as his disciples believe) or that (as his opponents believe) he had become totally insane. He announced that he had discovered 'bions', artificially produced blue energy-vesicles halfway between dead and living matter and capable of developing into protozoa, cancer cells, etc. Reich believed that he had produced these bions from such substances as sterilized coal and soot, but his findings were not accepted by his fellow scientists, who argued that the alleged bions were small particles of matter and that their movements were simply the result of the Brownian phenomenon well known to all physicists.

Undeterred by these criticisms, which he attributed to a combination of professional jealousy and psychiatric sickness, Reich continued with his experiments, concentrating on a particular type of 'radiating bion' which he believed he had derived from sea-sand. He came to believe that the radiation given off by these SAPA ('Sand-packet') bions was a new form of energy, orgone, the basic life-stuff of the universe, and devoted the rest of his life to its study.

In spite of his voluminous writings on the subject it is difficult to understand exactly what Reich believed orgone energy to be. From some of his references it seems possible that at times he regarded it as more or less identical with static electricity – thus in *Ether, God or Devil* he made the extraordinary statement that all radio interference was produced by orgone energy – but at other times he regarded almost everything, from the blueness of the sky to an Atlantic hurricane, as being a particular manifestation of orgone energy.

Reich believed that orgone energy could be extracted from the atmosphere, by means of an 'orgone energy accumulator', and used in the treatment of every variety of physical and mental illness. These accumulators, large upright boxes, big enough for a man to sit in and rather resembling an old-fashioned outdoor privy in appearance, were made of alternate layers of metal and some substance of organic origin, usually wood. The more wood-metal layers, the more powerful the accumulator (or, to use Reich's own words, 'the higher the orgonotic potential'); one with three wood-metal layers was referred to as a '3X accumulator', one with five as a '5X accumulator'.

By this time Reich had settled in the United States, and he soon became engaged in the sale of his books and orgone devices through the mails. This attracted the attention of the U.S. Food and Drug Administration, which decided that orgone energy did not exist and that Reich's accumulators were fraudulent devices; and, in 1950, obtained an injunction forbidding their distribution. Reich disregarded this injunction – he did not believe that any court had the right to adjudicate on a matter of scientific theory. He was sent to prison for contempt of court, and died there in November 1957. Before this, however, he had announced many more discoveries. He had learned, for example, how to disperse clouds with orgone energy, and the real nature of 'flying saucers'. Earth, he announced, was the centre of an inter-galactic war; some flying saucers were hostile, engaged in stealing orgone energy from Earth's atmosphere, others were friendly, engaged in replacing it.

For some years after Reich's death it appeared that he would soon be forgotten. His followers split into competing groups of varying degrees of eccentricity – one of them devoted itself to sitting in semi-darkness, clad in blue robes, communicating with the Master through a ouija-board. In the last few years, however, there has been a great revival of interest in Reich among both hippies and occultists. The former see him as a champion of sexual freedom, the latter as an 'unconscious magician' whose orgone energy is really the 'astral light' of Paracelsus, Eliphas LÉVI and Aleister CROWLEY.   F. K.

(Further reading: *263, 391a to e*.)

Karl von Reichenbach (1788-1869)
The author of *Physico-Physiological Researches on the Dynamics of Magnetism*, 1850, and *Letters on Od and Magnetism*, 1852. He claimed to have discovered a radiation emitted by human beings, animals, plants, magnets, metals and crystals which could be seen and felt in the dark by sensitives (see AURA) and for which he coined the terms od, odic force and odyle. Od was a supposed force, resembling magnetism or electricity, which permeated all the phenomena of the universe, and which explains TELEPATHY, the phenomena of mesmerism (see HYPNOSIS) and many of the phenomena of SPIRITUALISM. Some Spiritualists in the 19th century thought that the spirits used the Ødic force in a medium's body to speak, write, move objects or make knocks and rappings: see also RITUAL MAGIC. (*176, 392*)

Reincarnation
The doctrine of reincarnation rests on the belief that each individual possesses an element, independent of his physical being, which after his death can be reborn into another body. Though this idea has been most fully developed in Eastern religions, it has appeared at various times all over the world and is at present attracting increasing interest in the West, where for many people it evidently has a stronger appeal than the orthodox Christian view that a soul after death passes into heaven, hell or purgatory. If the Christian doctrine is true, then a human being has only one life in which to determine the fate of his soul, but the theory of reincarnation postulates that a human being's lives are like rungs on a ladder; each time he is reborn he either falls back or mounts upward, depending on how well he has lived in the previous life. One of the theory's attractions is that it accounts for the existence of suffering and the apparent unfairness of fate in giving some people happy lives and others misfortune.

The idea of reincarnation is probably as old as religion itself, for it crops up in the beliefs of primitive peoples all over the world as well as in many of the more highly developed religions. It has a particularly important position in Hinduism. The ancient Hindu sacred writings known as the Upanishads state that if the soul enters a heaven or a hell after death, it is only for a temporary sojourn before returning to earth. Hinduism developed, in association with this idea, the doctrine of KARMA, that a man is born with a balance sheet of assets and liabilities carried over from his previous existence. The Brihad Aranyaka Upanishad says of a man's soul: 'According as were his works and walks in [another] life, so he becomes. He that does righteously becomes righteous. He that does evil becomes evil. He becomes holy through holy works and evil through evil.'

The Bhagavad Gita, probably the most

widely known of Indian religious writings, also affirms the doctrine of reincarnation:

> Worn-out garments
> Are shed by the body:
> Worn-out bodies
> Are shed by the dweller
> Within the body;
> New bodies are donned
> By the dweller, like garments
> (*430*).

The Hindu theory of reincarnation allows for regression to animal forms or to lower castes; and one of the less desirable side-effects of the reincarnation theory was that it helped to reinforce the caste system.

Reincarnation was one of the Hindu concepts that passed into Buddhism, together with the doctrine of *karma*. The name Buddhism itself indirectly implies reincarnation since the term 'Buddha' refers not to an individual but to a type. The word is a Sanskrit one meaning somebody who is 'fully enlightened'. The man who has become known as the historical Buddha, Siddartha Gautama, who lived in northern India about 500 B.C., was, according to Buddhist theory, only one of a succession of Buddhas, each of whom prepared over many lives for his reincarnation as a supremely enlightened teacher and each of whom, before becoming a Buddha, had to pass through the intermediate stage of being a Bodhisattva. Siddartha Gautama, it is said, began his preparation for Buddhahood under the previous Buddha, Dipankara, countless aeons ago. In the distant future another Buddha, Maitreya, is due to appear.

To the Buddhist, rebirth into the world, unless you are destined for Buddhahood, is not something to be desired, and the ultimate aim of existence is to reach a state of such perfect enlightenment that reincarnation is no longer necessary. The Tibetan Book of the Dead describes how, after death, the consciousness, 'having no object on which to rest, will be tossed about by the wind, riding on the horse of breath. At about that time the fierce wind of karma, terrific and hard to bear, will drive you onwards, from behind, in dreadful gusts. And after a while the thought will occur to you, "O what would I not give to possess a body." ' After a time the soul will be enticed with visions of humans and animals copulating and will feel a compulsion to take the place of one of the parties. 'Do not try to take the place of one of them!' the Book of the Dead counsels. 'The feeling which you would then experience would make you faint away, just at the moment when egg and sperm are about to unite. And afterwards you will find that you have been conceived as a human being or as an animal' (*62*).

The Vast Sea of Life

In the West the doctrine of reincarnation has had a more difficult passage. It appears in Plato and in the Graeco-Egyptian esoteric writings of the period immediately before and after the birth of Christ, known as the HERMETICA. In one fragment, translated by G. R. S. Mead in his *Thrice-Greatest Hermes*, we read:

> From one Soul of the universe are all Souls derived . . . Of these Souls there are many changes, some into a more fortunate estate, and some quite contrary. And they which are of creeping things are changed into those of watery things, and those of things living in the water to those of things living on the land; and airy ones into men. Human souls that lay hold of immortality are changed into holy powers. And so they go into the sphere of the Gods . . . And this is the most perfect glory of the soul . . .

> Not all human souls but only the pious ones are divine. Once separated from the body and after the struggle to acquire piety, which consists in knowing God and injuring none, such a soul becomes all intelligence. The impious soul, however, punishes itself by seeking a human body to enter into, for no other body can receive a human soul; it cannot enter the body of an animal devoid of reason. Divine law preserves the human soul from such infamy (*321*).

This passage, incidentally, contradicts the Hindu and Buddhist belief in regression to an animal state.

The early Church Fathers were influenced by the Hermetic writings, and many of them accepted reincarnation. Origen, one of the most influential of the Fathers, taught a form of the reincarnation theory. He asserted that souls had existed in previous worlds and that they would be reborn into future worlds. He may also have believed that they are reborn into this present world, though there is some doubt about his views on this point. Origen's teachings were later condemned by the Church, and the reincarnation theory was anathematized by the Second Council of Constantinople in A.D. 553. It survived, however, in the various Gnostic movements that continued underground and broke out occasionally in open defiance of the Church, including the Catharist sects of the Middle Ages, such as the Albigenses and the Balkan Bogomils. The Albigenses, who taught reincarnation, flourished for a time in southern France but were savagely suppressed at the instigation of the Church, and after they had been crushed in the 13th century the doctrine of reincarnation became a heresy.

For many centuries the theory played little

part in Western thought, though individual thinkers toyed with it and hints of it are to be found among the writings of Renaissance Hermetists, Rosicrucians, Cabalists and other esoteric schools of thought. Partly under the influence of these schools, it gradually came out into the open again along with many other forgotten or forbidden ideas, and in the 18th and 19th centuries more and more thinkers began to turn to it with interest. The great wave of enthusiasm for Eastern and mystical thought towards the end of the 19th century caused yet more interest in reincarnation, and today it has become popular with people holding a wide variety of religious beliefs.

For philosophers, writers and poets, the theory has always held an appeal, even at times when it was unfashionable. Schopenhauer, Goethe, Heine and Thoreau, to name only a few, were attracted by it. One of the most remarkable 20th-century literary presentations of reincarnation is to be found in Clifford Bax's long narrative poem, *The Traveller's Tale* (*24*). It tells the story of a soul that is incarnated successively as a Stone Age savage, a Babylonian, a Greek scribe, a Roman soldier, a medieval bishop, a modern English vicar and lastly a spiritual teacher. At each stage it learns a different lesson and, having achieved enlightenment, is finally released from the bonds of earthly life. When the teacher is murdered by a jealous cynic his soul has a vision of all his previous lives and then suddenly feels itself free.

> The brilliant crystal bursts;
> A crash of thunder booms along my
>   brain,
> And the vast sea of life laps me no more.
> . . . .
> The universe without and I within
> Burn into one sole diamond-point of light,
> Not great nor small but measureless and
>   the sum
> Of whatever shall be, is or was.

One of the problems in finding evidence for reincarnation is that very few people are able, under normal circumstances, to remember their previous lives. This is understandable, for if reincarnation is a fact it would clearly present problems if one's life were flooded with memories of one's previous existences. Recently, however, attempts have been made to remove this amnesia. One method used is hypnotism, and some startling evidence has been brought to light by this means. There was, for example, the phenomenon of Edgar CAYCE, a comparatively uneducated photographer's assistant from Kentucky, who discovered that in trance he could not only diagnose and prescribe cures for illnesses but could also apparently describe people's previous lives. In one case he told a man that he had been a Confederate soldier during the Civil War; he also told him his former name and address. These details were later checked, and the records showed that there had indeed been such a man, who had enlisted in Lee's army in 1862.

The Bridey Murphy Case

More recently, a stir was caused by the revelations of Morey Bernstein in his book *The Search for Bridey Murphy (37)*. Bernstein, a Colorado businessman and amateur hypnotist, became interested in the theory of reincarnation in spite of initial scepticism, and began to experiment with hypnotic regression – taking the hypnotized person back in time. His main subject was a young Colorado housewife whom he called by the pseudonym of Ruth Simmons. Under hypnosis she began to talk about her life as a woman called Bridey MURPHY, who had lived in Ireland in the early part of the 19th century. She spoke with an Irish accent and supplied details of obscure place names and Irish words, many of which were subsequently checked and verified. She was also able, under post-hypnotic suggestion, to dance a special kind of Irish jig after coming out of the trance. What made the case particularly convincing on the face of it was the undramatic, even prosaic, nature of Bridey's character and life. However, many critics have maintained that the accurate information given by Ruth Simmons was really drawn from buried memories of accounts she had heard and stories she had read in her childhood.

Attempts have also been made to use hypnotic regression in the treatment of psychological disorders, by bringing to light the cause of the trouble from a previous existence. This application is expounded in a book called *Many Lifetimes*, by Joan Grant and Denys Kelsey (*188*), a husband and wife who practise this form of therapy. Before meeting Kelsey, Joan Grant was already well-known as the author of a number of books describing some of her own previous incarnations. In one of them, *Winged Pharaoh*, she gave an account of her life as an Egyptian priestess in about 3000 B.C. Denys Kelsey is a psychiatrist who came to reincarnation via hypnotism. He had been practising age regression with his patients for some time when a young female patient relived, under hypnosis, the circumstances, not only of her life in the womb, but of her conception. This implied the existence of a non-physical component in man, but it was not until Kelsey read Joan Grant's *Winged Pharaoh* that he became convinced of the reality of reincarnation. He sought out the author, and they agreed to work together. One of the

cases they treated was that of a young man who was obsessed by the idea that his father had developed arthritis because as a boy he (the patient) had once wiped a wet cloth over the sheets of his parents' bed. Kelsey had previously failed to effect a cure by ordinary psychiatric means, so this time the young man was regressed, under hypnosis, to a previous life as a young Edwardian woman who had tried to kill a hated aunt by dampening her sheets. The fury of the aunt on discovering the attempt had led to a stroke, which kept her bed-ridden for many years, nursed by the girl who now dared not leave her for fear that her attempt at murder would be exposed. The patient accepted this event as the cause of his obsession and afterwards had no recurrence of his trouble.

Another hypnotist, Peter Blythe, though more sceptical about the theory of reincarnation, believes that it can be a useful hypothesis in certain cases. In his book *Hypnotism, its Power and Practice (49)*, he writes: ' . . . my scepticism about hypnotic reincarnation-regression does not mean that it cannot be used by hypno-analysts to bring into consciousness attitudes which the patient is forced to repress'. He suggests a procedure by which a recalcitrant patient could be told of the theory that a traumatic incident can be passed down through the ages as a kind of ancestral memory. The hypno-analyst would say to the patient: 'This may or may not be correct. I don't know, but if you would like to explore this further I am prepared to help. Do you think it is worth while?' If the answer is Yes, then the hypno-analyst can proceed to try to identify the memory concerned.

An ancestral memory is not, of course, the same thing as a memory of one's own previous existence. Yet, assuming that far memory is possible, one phenomenon could easily be mistaken for the other. There are other theories also which account for apparent memories of former lives. If, for example, as some people believe, everything that happens leaves its imprint on the 'ether', then a person with the right sensitivity should be able to give an account of any past event by tuning in to the appropriate etheric channel (see AKASHIC RECORD). The Colorado housewife who thought she had been Bridey Murphy would on this hypothesis have been watching a kind of etheric television programme of Bridey Murphy's life. But this, of course, does not account for the psychological problems which are said to be caused by some memories of previous incarnations. Nor does it provide for the idea of progression, which is one of the most appealing features of the theory of reincarnation. Whatever the arguments for and against the theory, it is certain that many people will

continue to believe, as W. B. Yeats put it in one of his poems, *Under Ben Bulben*: 'Many times man lives and dies, between his two eternities.' C. M.

(See also HYPNOSIS.) (Further reading: *37, 188, 197, 208, 209*.)

Retrocognition

The extrasensory perception of the past.

Theodor Reuss (d. 1924)

The founder of the O.T.O.: see GERMAN OCCULT GROUPS; ROSICRUCIANS.

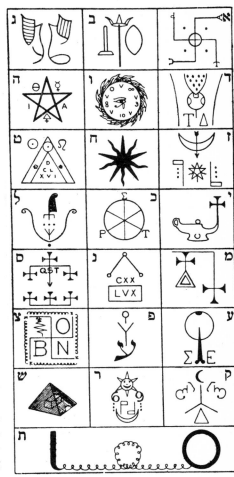

Magic diagrams used by Aleister Crowley

Ritual Magic

The use of ceremonial to obtain power, both material and spiritual, to get into touch with the world of spirits, to gain love, friends, wealth, and almost anything else that a human being could possibly desire – even to 'hindering a sportsman from catching game' – is currently enjoying a remarkable revival. There are do-it-yourself books on the theory and practice of ritual magic, there are business firms whose only function is the supply of consecrated candles, incenses, herbs and other materials used in magic, and there is at least one craftsman in London, England, who makes his living by manufacturing and selling swords, daggers and other instruments and accessories constructed in accordance with the directions given in such textbooks of magic as the *Key of Solomon* (*314*) and the *Book of True Black Magic*.

The general public has only recently become vaguely aware of this renaissance of ritual magic, but the revival itself started with the publication in 1801 of Francis Barrett's *The Magus, or Celestial Intelligencer* (*19*). During the 18th century ritual magic seemed dead: it was true that the peasantry kept a sort of folk-magic alive but, no doubt, with the advance of the Age of Reason these primitive survivals would die a natural death. No one seriously considered the possibility of a revival of the highly contrived and intellectual magical systems which had enthralled such 16th-century figures as Paracelsus or John Dee. Nevertheless, such a revival did occur, and Barrett's book played an important part in it, despite the almost insufferable tedium of the author's style and the ossified form in which he presented the traditions of ceremonial magic.

Lévi's Laws of Magic

Barrett's *Magus* was studied by small groups, but a far greater influence was exerted by the writing of Eliphas LÉVI, a flamboyant French romantic with a flair for publicity and an astonishing ability to make ceremonial magic interesting to a 19th-century audience. In his *Dogma and Ritual of High Magic*, 1856 (*284*), Lévi put forward a theory of how magic works, or supposedly works, which in a modified form still dominates the thinking of magicians today. Lévi believed that there were three fundamental 'laws' of magic. The first was the law of human will-power, which in Lévi's view was not some abstract concept but a material force, 'as real', to use his own expression, 'as steam or the galvanic current'. This doctrine did not originate with Lévi. Many of the mesmerists (see HYPNOSIS) believed in something very like it, and Edgar Allan Poe, in one of his most terrifying stories, *The Case of M. Valdemar*, summarized it in an invented quotation which he put in the mouth of the 17th-century theologian Joseph Glanvill: 'And the will therein lieth, which dieth not. Who knoweth the mysteries of the Will with its vigour? For God is but a great Will pervading all things by nature of its intentness. Man doth not yield himself to the angels nor to death utterly, save only through the weakness of his feeble will.'

What was new in Lévi was his application of this mesmeric theory to ritual magic. For him all the materials of the art – incense, geometrical figures, lights, and the rest – were mere aids, designed to assist the magi-

cian to concentrate his will.

Lévi's second law was that of the astral light, a supposed imponderable medium permeating all space, through the existence of which the magician was able to exert action-at-a-distance (see also ASTRAL BODY). Lévi held that it was through the extrusion of astral light, in the form of a semi-material arm and hand, that Spiritualist mediums were able to move tables, write on locked slates and produce all the other astonishing phenomena associated with the physical mediumship of Lévi's own time (see MEDIUMS; SPIRITUALISM). Again, Lévi was not the originator of this idea. The astral light bears some resemblance to the ether of pre-Einsteinian physics, and more to the 'odic force' of Baron von REICHENBACH and other mesmerists of the 19th century.

Lévi's third law, which was later extended and codified by such British magicians as MacGregor MATHERS and Aleister CROWLEY, was that of correspondence. This was an updated version of the medieval doctrine of the macrocosm (the great world) and the microcosm (the little world), according to which every factor in the macrocosm – the universe – had a corresponding factor in the microcosm – the individual human being. For example, the stars making up the constellation Capricorn were thought to correspond to the knees, and those of Scorpio to the genitals. Lévi regarded the correspondences as real, but as less crudely physical. It was not so much the body as the soul of man that was held to be a 'magical mirror of the universe' – to use a phrase still popular with contemporary practitioners of ritual magic. According to Lévi, any factor present in the universe was also present in the soul of man: thus the force personified as Diana corresponded to physical sexuality, and that personified as Hermes to human wisdom. Ritual magicians believe that a knowledge of the correspondences involved enables them to 'call down' (invoke) into themselves any cosmic force they wish to draw upon, or alternatively to 'call up' (evoke) the same force from their own souls and project it into a magic triangle where, if a 'material basis' such as incense or blood has been provided, there is a physical manifestation of the evoked force.

The Golden Dawn

Though he wrote extensively on magic and for the last twenty years of his life made his living by teaching it, Lévi was not really a practising ritual magician, and on only three occasions in his life was he actually present at a magical ceremony. Even on these occasion, no notable effects were achieved except for a 'peculiar numbness of the body and fainting spells' – almost certainly the symp-

toms of a mild attack of carbon monoxide poisoning caused by burning charcoal in a confined space. Lévi's English disciples, the chiefs of the Hermetic Order of the GOLDEN DAWN, were more adventurous. Not only did they amplify their master's teachings, but they practised the magic he had preached.

Their major addition to Lévi's doctrines was to add a fourth law to his three. They claimed that he had deliberately omitted, probably on the instructions of mysterious unknown superiors, the law of imagination. Will-power, they said, was almost totally ineffective unless directed by the trained imagination – and vice versa. 'To practise magic,' wrote a leading member of the Order, Very Honoured Frater Resurgam (in private life, a Dr Edward Berridge), 'both the Imagination and the Will must be called into action, they are co-equal in the work. Nay more, the Imagination must precede the Will in order to produce the greatest possible effect. The Will unaided can send forth a current, and that current cannot be wholly inoperative; yet its effect is vague and indefinite, because the Will unaided sends forth nothing but the current or force. The Imagination unaided can create an image and this image must have an existence of varying duration; yet it can do nothing of importance, unless vitalised and directed by the Will. When, however, the two are conjoined – when the Imagination creates an image – and the Will directs and uses that image, marvellous magical effects may be obtained' (*264*).

The same magician described exactly how the imagination was to be used in his account of how he dealt with a vampire. The vampire in question was not the traditional Dracula-like creature, making its home in an ornate tomb and living on a diet of fresh blood, but a 'prosy, fidgety old gentleman', whom Berridge had decided was a vampire on no better evidence than the fact that he found 'protracted interviews' with him exhausting. Berridge decided that the old gentleman was an 'intentional vampire', however, 'for he acknowledged that he was about to marry a young wife in order, if possible, to recuperate his exhausted system'. When Berridge was next visited by the alleged vampire, he imagined that he had formed himself a 'complete investiture of odic fluid' (i.e. astral light), surrounding himself on all sides and 'impenetrable to any hostile currents'.

Lévi's law of correspondence was expanded by the Golden Dawn into one of the most elaborate and coherent systems of ritual magic ever devised. Every Egyptian, Greek and Roman god, every spirit named in the *Key of Solomon* and other medieval magical textbooks, every name in the Jewish and

Christian angelologies, was attributed to one or other of the sefiroth and twenty-two paths of the cabalistic Tree of Life (see CABALA; TAROT). To each of them were also attributed colours, animals, precious stones, scents, magical formulae, and so on. The ritual magician who wished to evoke the force appropriate to a particular god simply looked up the table corresponding to that deity and devised his ceremony accordingly. If he wanted to evoke the spirit of Mercury, he looked up his tables of correspondences and found that Taphthartharath, the spirit

Used in ritual magic, the alchemical symbol of a crucified snake

in question, corresponded to the number eight, the colour orange, white wine, the snake, the fish, and many other things. The rubric of an evocation of Taphthartharath in this system (still widely used by magicians) has survived and shows how the law of correspondence is applied in practice.

This evocation was conducted by Charles Rosher, one-time court physician to the Sultan of Morocco and inventor of an 'improved' water-closet with such a violent flush that at least one user mistook it for a shower-bath; Frederick Leigh Gardner, a London stockbroker with a passion for ALCHEMY and a remarkable flair for making disastrous investments; Florence Farr, an actress whose

hobbies were bicycling and travelling on the astral plane; and Alan BENNETT, an asthmatic electrical engineer who was to end his life as a Buddhist monk. The four magicians stood inside an octagonal figure drawn on the floor in orange-yellow chalk. At each of its angles a lamp burned olive oil impregnated with snake fat. Outside the figure, on its south-west side, was drawn the triangle in which the spirit was expected to appear: the south-west was chosen because the planet Mercury was in that quarter of the heavens at the time. At each angle of the triangle stood a censer in which smouldered the incense of mercury: the mercurial spirit was supposed to construct a 'body' for himself from its smoke. At the centre of the octagon stood a brass cauldron, heated by a lamp which was fuelled by alcohol in which a snake had been preserved. This cauldron contained the 'hell-broth', a compound of allegedly mercurial substances, the destruction of which by fire was one of the high points of the ritual.

'Accept of us', intoned Florence Farr, 'these magical sacrifices, prepared to give Thee body and form . . . For the sweet scent of the mace is that which shall purify Thee . . . And the heat of the magical fire is my will . . . enabling Thee to manifest Thyself in pleasing form before us . . . And the flesh of the serpent is the symbol of Thy body . . . And the blood of the serpent is the symbol of the Magic of the Word Messiah . . . And the all-binding Milk is the magical water of Thy purification . . .' As each substance was named, Alan Bennett cast it into the hell-broth, after which Florence Farr invoked the spirit by the great magic word StiBeTTChe-PhMeFShihSS; successfully, it seems, for among Bennett's papers survives a talisman drawn on parchment and allegedly consecrated by 'being placed on the spirit's head after he had materialised'. There is evidence that at least one, and possibly all, of the participants in the rite had supplemented the 'great Magic word' with DRUGS, which may explain the appearance of the spirit.

The Cubic Stone

The Golden Dawn system of correspondences can be applied to any type of magical ritual, and is not confined to invocation and evocation: there are instructions for applying it to astral projection, spiritual development, alchemy, and even the achievement of invisibility. But the system is so complicated and difficult – snake blood, for instance, is not a readily available commodity – that while it is still used by the majority of magicians in Britain and the United States, it has been considerably simplified. For example, the invocations and magical workings included in the do-it-yourself book by David Edwards

(*137*), a young magician from the English Midlands, are based on the Golden Dawn system but so simplified that they could be carried out in a small bed-sitting-room. They are also much shorter: few of them could take more than half an hour to perform, whereas Florence Farr's invocation must have occupied at least three hours. I have no reason to believe, however, that these simplified rites are any less effective – or ineffective – than their long-winded predecessors.

David Edwards was at one time a chief of the Order of the Cubic Stone, a small magical fraternity which describes its teachings as deriving 'from the Golden Dawn and other similar sources' and whose members seem fairly typical of the rising generation of ritual magicians. The Order's magazine, *The Monolith*, contains many details of the beliefs and practices of its members. They 'cast the runes', a form of ritual divination, they study the ENOCHIAN MAGIC of the Elizabethan occultists Dee and Kelley, and they engage in lengthy rituals of self-initiation, such as that recorded in an article on 'The Magical Ladder of Frater L.Z.I.' If this record is to be believed, the magicians of the Cubic Stone produce many astonishing phenomena in their temple. On one occasion the temple lit up with a rose-coloured glow, on another the room took on a 'deep golden glow' caused by Frater L.Z.I.'s cutting a cross on his own breast. On a third occasion, perhaps the most momentous of all, a mysterious Arab head appeared and uttered the single word WAZROM.

Abramelin Magic

A more individualist type of ceremonial magic, the system of 'Abramelin the Mage', now enjoys increasing popularity in Europe and the United States. The textbook of this system, *The Book of the Sacred Magic of Abra-Melin the Mage* (*311*; see ABRAMELIN MAGIC), was first made available to English-speaking occultists in 1898, in a translation by Mac-Gregor Mathers from a French MS.: it allegedly dates from 1458 but is almost certainly of 18th-century origin.

Abramelin magic is curiously unlike any other European ritual system: its approach verges on the quietistic and is more reminiscent of Jansenism than of the flamboyance of the grimoires or the Golden Dawn and its successors. The Abramelin magician does not even use the traditional magic circle. Instead, he selects and purifies a 'holy place' – either an altar constructed in an isolated wood and surrounded by shrubs and flowers, or a consecrated room leading on to a terrace – and in this he conducts the activities intended to lead to the 'attainment of the Knowledge

and Conversation of the Holy Guardian Angel'.

For six months the devotee leads a yogi-like existence. He 'enflames himself with prayer', burns perfumes, invokes the angels and reads 'holy books' for at least two hours each day. Then a young child – a favourite source of mediumistic power with occultists of all ages – is introduced into the proceedings. Together the magician and the child kneel before the altar, on which has been set a silver plate. The Holy Guardian Angel then supposedly manifests himself to the child, who sees the supernatural figure write a message (meaningful only to the magician himself) on the plate.

There follows a week of extraordinary phenoma. The Holy Guardian Angel appears to the magician and teaches him how to control both good and evil spirits. Only when this has occurred should the magician proceed to use the so-called 'Abramelin talismans' – mysteriously gnomic squares designed to produce such wonders as an ever-full purse, overwhelming sexual attraction and even invisible armies of phantom soldiers.

Though the Abramelin system is currently popular and thought effective – perhaps largely as a result of Aleister Crowley's enthusiasm for it – some modern magicians regard it as extremely dangerous. The use of the talismans without having carried out the full six months of preparatory work successfully is considered particularly foolhardy. The following account, originally published in the *Occult Review*, is frequently quoted by opponents of the system:

> I resorted to the System of Abramelin, and to this end prepared a copy of the necessary Talisman . . . my ritual was imperfect and I only rendered the Talisman useless without in any way impairing the activities of the entity invoked . . . I . . . saw the entity which was rapidly obsessing me . . . The eyes were closed and it was bearded with long flowing hair. It seemed a blind force slowly waking to activity . . . I have had nightmares before, but no nightmare that I have ever had could hold my mind in its grip for minutes at a time as this thing did . . . About midnight I was suddenly awakened by a voice . . . and at once I became aware of a red serpent coiling and uncoiling itself under my bed . . . After this there was peace until . . . the real climax came . . . I was awakened by a violent noise . . . caused by a great red obelisk which crashed through the west wall of my room . . . smashing both that and the window to pieces.

All these phenomena were, of course,

entirely subjective. All the same, the magician who experienced them found no peace until she received help from another practitioner, a 'good friend . . . who knew much of these things'.

Modern Sex Magic

Modified Golden Dawn systems and Abramelin magic have had the field almost to themselves in recent years, but there are signs that they are being challenged by a peculiar synthesis of ritual magic and that Westernized TANTRISM which was the basis of Aleister Crowley's sexual magic. Crowley himself was trained in the ceremonial magic of the Golden Dawn, but he ultimately abandoned it for the altogether simpler sexo-magical techniques of the *Ordo Templi Orientis*. Before this, however, there was an intermediate stage in Crowley's occult development, during which he combined sex and ritual, as in the 'Paris Working' of 1914, a series of invocations of the gods Jupiter and Hermes in which rituals culminated in homosexual activity.

As early as 1945, some of Crowley's American disciples, gathered together in the Agape Lodge of California, had attempted a revival of sexo-magical ritual work. The most prominent figure in this group was Jack Parsons, a brilliant physical chemist who had a burning desire to be a great master magician and complete faith in Thelema, Crowley's new religion of 'force and fire'. Parsons had recently lost his mistress, who had transferred her affections to a new member of the Agape Lodge. He had earlier lost his wife to yet another magician so, feeling disillusioned with human beings, decided that his next sexual partner would be an ELEMENTAL, who would naturally need to be incarnated in an ordinary woman's body.

The Crowleyan technique of controlling elementals involves calling them 'by the Keys of Enoch . . . and let there be after the Calls an evocation by the Wand and let the Marrow of the Wand be preserved within the pyramids . . .' The 'Keys of Enoch' are the strange invocations of the magical system of John Dee and Edward Kelley; the 'Wand' is the penis of the magician; the 'pyramids' were talismans drawn on parchment in the shape of truncated pyramids; the 'Marrow of the Wand' means the male sexual secretions. Parsons managed to transform these fairly simple operations into an elaborate ceremony, repeated on eleven consecutive nights and culminating in autosexual activity. After an appropriate period of gestation, the elemental duly appeared in the shape of a green-eyed, red-haired New York poetess, who soon became Parsons's mistress and magical partner. Together they celebrated

Crowley's 'Gnostic Mass'; together they conducted an elaborate sexual rite designed to incarnate Babalon – the Crowleyan female principle – in the elemental's womb; together they feasted to honour Parsons's change of name, by deed-poll, to Belarion Armiluss Al Dajjal Antichrist. Not until 1952, when Parsons blew himself up with mercuric fulminate, was their partnership dissolved.

After Parsons's death this type of magic almost disappeared as well, but with the growing interest in Crowley in the 1960s came a revival, and it is practised today by individuals and groups in several countries, notably in the United States. For obvious reasons, it is difficult to give any detailed report of these activities.

Whether those who practise any form of ritual magic actually achieve objective physical results seems comparatively unimportant. What seems certain is that these magicians find that their activities satisfy an emotional and intellectual need, and therefore that the magical renaissance is likely to endure. F. K.

(See also SATANISM; TRANCE.) (Further reading: 70, 85, 189, 235, 262, 264, 314, 389, 391.)

Root Races

According to Madame BLAVATSKY, these are seven successive races living on the earth: the Polarian (or Adamic), the Hyperborean, the Lemurian, the Atlantean, the Aryan, and two which are still to come. 'The first root race lived near the North Pole and they were invisible, being made of fire-mist; the second, living in northern Asia, were just visible – they invented sexual intercourse; the third root race were the ape-like giants of Lemuria, who communicated telepathically and could not reason in our sense; the fourth were the Atlanteans, who were destroyed through black magic; we are the fifth . . .; the sixth root race will evolve from the present human race and will live on Lemuria (in the Pacific) again; after the seventh root race, life will leave our earth and start up on Mercury' (510): see also LEMURIA.

Rosicrucians

Between the years 1614 and 1616 the Rosicrucian Brotherhood announced itself to the world in a series of pamphlets published in Germany. At a time when the upheavals of Renaissance and Reformation seemed to have put all certainties in question, the appearance of a mysterious fraternity claiming or implying a claim to possess spiritual secrets could not fail to make an appeal to the European mind. Society was so disordered in its views on the ultimate verities that there were witch-burnings right and left while

The Rosicrucian ideal in allegory

members of Catholic and reformed religions met more often on the battlefield than worshipping a mutually accepted God. At the same time, the Renaissance had seen the rise of the figure of the Magus: Giordano Bruno, Paracelsus or Dr Dee, whose strivings after truth in the natural world were paralleled by a search for supernatural truth which made use of the techniques of heretical philosophies and knew little of modern distinctions between magic and science. In an age when the occult appeared to many as a possible avenue to both knowledge and salvation, the enigmatic Rosicrucians were a lodestone for the wise.

It has frequently been doubted whether the Brotherhood ever really existed. Seekers for truth liked to imply that they were privy to the secrets of the Rosicrucians and it was equally fashionable to apply the epithet 'Rosicrucian' to wise men past or present. The original pamphlets embody a symbolism of spiritual rebirth like the teaching of ALCHEMY and can be seen as part of a general current of mystical speculation throughout the centuries. If the society which so attracted the 17th century never existed it would make little difference to modern organizations claiming to be Rosicrucian; for despite their often elaborate pedigrees the modern Rosicrucian groups have only a

continuity of aspiration with the brotherhood whose name they bear.

There is one rather doubtful link between the 17th-century Rosicrucians and their descendants. This is the growth among the 18th-century orders of speculative Freemasons of 'Rose Cross' degrees. It has been argued that such degrees indicate a real link with the original Rosicrucians, and it is certainly true that the modern Rosicrucians spring from the fringes of Masonry. The alternative explanation is that occultists who admired the tone of the Rosicrucian pamphlets, and sympathized with what they imagined was their philosophy, instituted degrees of their own invention. This is certainly what happened in other cases during the 18th century, and indeed the quest of those denied spiritual certainty in the Age of Reason was responsible for the incorporation of Freemasonry into occult mythology altogether. Just as the aspiring magus of the Renaissance made inquiries after the Rosicrucian Brotherhood, so his 18th-century successor pounced upon Masonry. As far as is known, Freemasonry was at that time the remains of the medieval masons' craft-guilds, which once had made a rule of secrecy to protect the secrets of the trade but later preserved the tradition as a matter of form. To some this secret society seemed possibly to contain the relics of the classical MYSTERY RELIGIONS; and William Stukeley, for example, who is responsible for much later nonsense about DRUIDS and stone circles, joined the Masons with this idea in mind. Ever higher degrees were introduced, based on esoteric symbolism; and Masonry became more and more occult under the pressure of occultists.

The Artist as Priest and Magician

In 1866 the English Societas Rosicruciana in Anglia was founded by Robert Wentworth Little on the basis of ancient rituals he was supposed to have discovered. This body counted among its members Kenneth MAC-KENZIE, the author of the *Royal Masonic Cyclopaedia*, and was much influenced by Hargrave JENNINGS's book *The Rosicrucians,*

A Rosicrucian certificate

Their Rites and Mysteries, 1870. Jennings argued that the basis of all religion was phallicism, and anticipated caricatures of Freud by discovering sexual associations at every turn. His book has been obscurely important in the development of modern Rosicrucianism.

Three of the founder-members of the magical order most usually known as the GOLDEN DAWN were members of the Societas Rosicruciana in Anglia, and one – Dr Wynn WESTCOTT, a London coroner – had been its Supreme Magus. Together with the eccentric S. L. MacGregor MATHERS, Westcott and his colleagues established in 1888 the first temple of the Golden Dawn. The basis was a series of cipher manuscripts purporting to give the outline of Rosicrucian rituals associated with one Anna Sprengel of Nurem-

burg. The legend goes that Mathers and Westcott began a correspondence with the mysterious Fräulein Sprengel and were authorized to set up their temple in London. However, Anna Sprengel and her Rosicrucian associations may well have been a figment of Westcott's imagination. The Golden Dawn rapidly developed its own synthesis of theurgic techniques, incorporating elements from many sources; although its Rosicrucian associations were maintained in the traditions and ceremony of the Order.

Towards the end of the last century there was a similar upsurge of interest in the Rosicrucians among the Symbolist poets and artists of Paris. The leading figures in the world of French Rosicrucianism were the Marquis Stanislas de GUAITA (1860–98) and Joséphin Péladan (1858–1918). De Guaita was attracted to Péladan by the publication in 1884 of the latter's novel entitled *Le vice supreme.* The Marquis had been writing verse in the approved fashion of the *poète maudit,* and Péladan had made a name for himself the year before by his uncompromising condemnation of the Salon of 1883 with its slogan: 'I believe in the Ideal, Tradition and Hierarchy.' For a short period the two lived together, although the impossible temperament of Péladan made this arrangement only temporary.

In 1885 Péladan declared himself Grand Master of the Rose-Croix on the death of his brother Adrien, who had been initiated into a group of Rosicrucian Masons. Three years later he and de Guaita 'revived' – in fact created – the Ordre Kabbalistique de la Rose-Croix, which consisted of three degrees – 'Biology', 'Theory' and 'Practice' – and was said to be directed by a Council of Twelve, of whom six remained unknown to carry on the Order if it were broken up. In 1890 de Guaita claimed over a hundred adherents. It is very unlikely that this figure was ever reached, and the six 'hidden' members of the Council of Twelve never existed. Besides the founders, the chief Rosicrucians were PAPUS (Gérard Encausse), the leading popularizer of occultism in France, the novelist Paul Adam, and two older occultists known as Barlet (Alfred Faucheux) and Alta (Charles Melinge). The Order was an important factor in the underworld of poets and magicians which made up the Symbolist movement.

In 1890 a schism took place, caused chiefly by the incurable self-importance of Péladan, who combined a real sense of his artistic mission with an outrageousness which surpassed Oscar Wilde's. Péladan's hair and beard were thick and untamed: his dress varied between the cloaks and wide-brimmed hats expected of an artist, and medieval

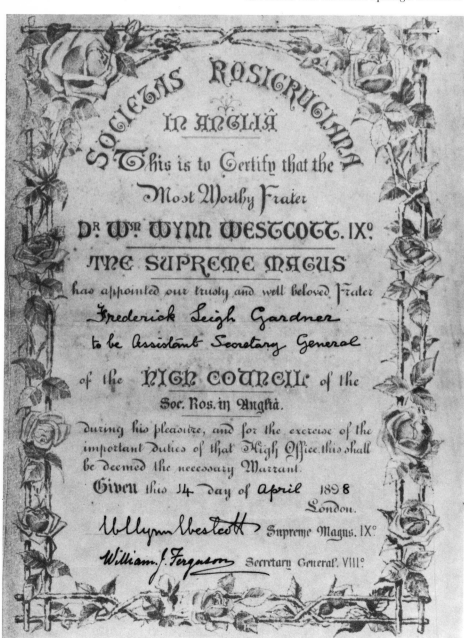

garb. He adopted the title of 'Sar', or King in Assyrian, and took the name Merodack from the leading character in his own novel. These eccentricities were tolerated by his fellow Rosicrucians until Sar Merodack issued a series of proclamations. The first called on all artists to submit to Péladan's direction in aesthetic matters, the second complained to the Cardinal Archbishop of Paris about the introduction of bullfighting into the city, and the third issued a stinging condemnation of a woman member of the Rothschild family, who was proposing to demolish a building of which the Sar was particularly fond. De Guaita and his friends attempted to restrain Péladan's extravagance, but Sar Merodack countered with a repudiation of various beliefs current among the Rose-Croix, reminded the Order that he had been concerned with occultism longer than any of them, and signed himself 'Sar Merodack Péladan, Roman Catholic Legate'. He then announced the formation of a new Order, the Rose-Croix Catholique.

The Rose-Croix of Péladan was concerned above all with the arts. The Sar's chief colleagues were Albert Jounet, Elémir Bourges, Count Léonce de Larmandie and Count Antoine de la Rochefoucauld. Jounet had been a member of de Guaita's Order, but gradually drifted away from Péladan. Bourges emulated the dandyism of the Sar, while de Larmandie wrote esoteric novels and married off his niece to the head of the Rose-Croix Catholique. De la Rochefoucauld was a painter of talent, and it was largely through his influence that Péladan was able to stage the first of his Salons de la Rose-Croix, although during the exhibition the two quarrelled over aesthetics and de la Rochefoucauld withdrew.

Péladan announced that the object of his aesthetic Rose-Croix was to 'restore the cult of the IDEAL' through the representation of Beauty on the basis of Tradition. Catholic subjects were preferred above all others; but anything remotely 'spiritual' – like allegories and Eastern religious subjects – was accepted. Architecture was deemed dead since 1789; and Péladan admitted only restoration projects or fantasies to consideration. The aesthetic of the Salons de la Rose-Croix bears comparison with that of the English Pre-Raphaelites, and stands in the mainstream of the French Catholic Reaction. At the first of the five Salons the presiding spirits were Gustave Moreau, Puvis de Chavannes and Félicien Rops. Khnopff and Rouault also exhibited. But during the later manifestations, the number of famous supporters declined, and Péladan himself was pushed further towards the realms of eccentricity.

Péladan's proclamation that the artist embodied in himself the functions of king, priest and magician represents the extreme form of a belief which dominated much of the creative activity of the day: that of the divine function of art. Through Beauty, the Artist came to God. Péladan did not confine himself to pronouncements on painting, and he instituted concerts of music by his hero Wagner, while appointing Erik Satie official composer to his Order. His prodigious output of novels and esoteric philosophy produced less and less effect, and the leonine Sar subsided at length into misunderstanding and a tamed old age.

Magical Combat

From Péladan's artistic activities, de Guaita and his group dissociated themselves, declaring the Sar a schismatic and an apostate. At the time of the first Salon, the members of the Rose-Croix Kabbalistique were engaged in a series of magical conflicts with the novelist J.-K. Huysmans and the Abbé BOULLAN. Boullan was a Catholic priest with a bent for the most sensational aspects of religion who had first attracted the attention of the ecclesiastical authorities in the 1860s, when he was thought to have been practising magical cures of an obscene sort on nuns of a community with which he was involved. He had also fairly certainly murdered a child; but despite an investigation at Rome he was reinstated, and was not defrocked until 1875. This year was that of the death of a Norman prophet, Pierre VINTRAS, whose apocalyptic cult had spread throughout the Calvados to the accompaniment of apparitions of the Virgin and miraculously bleeding hosts. Boullan had been in correspondence with Vintras, discovered that his personal heresies agreed remarkably with those of the Norman prophet, and after being defrocked established himself as the head of a sect of Vintrasians in Lyon. In 1891 Huysmans, who was gathering material for his novel *Là-bas*, went to stay with Boullan, whom he discovered directing magical rites against de Guaita and Péladan in Paris.

The Paris occultists had made contact with Boullan in two ways. About 1886, Stanislas de Guaita went to stay with the Abbé, and left hurriedly with the manuscript of one of Boullan's magical rituals. Boullan soon afterwards suffered a series of heart-attacks, which he attributed to the sorceries of de Guaita. Another Rosicrucian, de Guaita's secretary Oswald Wirth, had previously made overtures to Boullan under a pretence of friendship. Wirth discovered that Boullan practised an unpleasing form of sexual mysticism, and laid his findings before de Guaita's Order. While Huysmans was staying at

Lyons, there arrived for Boullan a letter from de Guaita condemning the Abbé to 'death by the fluids'. The novelist believed that he himself was also the victim of sorcerous attacks, and after his return to Paris accused de Guaita of Boullan's magical murder.

The result of this accusation was a challenge by de Guaita to a duel. Huysmans retracted his charges and published an apology. However, a journalist called Jules Bois renewed his attacks, and a complicated wrangle ensued which resulted in Bois having to fight both de Guaita and his Rosicrucian colleague Papus. In the duel with the Marquis, Bois claimed that his pistol bullet had failed to fire; while on his way to the encounter with Papus the journalist was twice halted when the horses pulling his carriage fell between the shafts. By the conclusion of the affair Bois was more convinced than ever of the reality of magic.

De Guaita himself died young and blind, after producing a series of lengthy tomes on the sorcerer's art. His life was decadent and sinister: he rarely emerged from his scarlet-hung apartments except to search for books on occultism. His magical experiments entailed the heavy use of drugs, particularly hashish, morphine and cocaine; and the magus was responsible for converting to his morphine addiction the poet and friend of Huysmans, Edouard Dubus. The death of Dubus and the death of de Guaita were largely the results of their drug-taking. If Péladan represented the part of the Artist's soul that aspired to reach God through Beauty, de Guaita stood for the temperament which sought – like Baudelaire – to achieve divinity by passage through the fire.

There were other claimants to the style of 'Rosicrucian' in Germany and Austro-Hungary. The Prague Lodge of the Blue Star, to which belonged the novelist Gustav Meyrink, became affiliated to a mystical group surrounding an elderly weaver who had been initiated, so the story ran, by a 'genuine Rosicrucian'. Possibly some of the Viennese Theosophists also belonged to this circle: another recruit was the Theosophist Franz HARTMANN, who himself published a translation of a supposedly Rosicrucian work known as the *Geheime Figuren*, besides a romance dealing with adventures in a mysterious Rosicrucian monastery. Hartmann was also a member of an organization called the Order of the Temple of the Orient, which gave birth to another brand of modern Rosicrucianism. The O.T.O. originated in a charter given by an English hawker of masonic orders and diplomas, John Yarker, to a band of German occultists of whom the most important were Hartmann and Theodor REUSS: the Order practised some form of sexual occultism. It is all the more extraordinary that this organization was the source of some of the inspiration of Rudolf STEINER, founder of Anthroposophy.

In 1906 Steiner was installed as head of an irregular Masonic lodge called the Mysteria Mystica Aeterna (see GERMAN OCCULT GROUPS). He claimed that this move was directed on his part by a desire to obtain the 'formal authorisation, in historic succession, to direct a symbolic-cultural activity'. In other words, he wanted a form of 'apostolic succession' to give authority to certain ideas of his own. For Steiner had his personal conception of Rosicrucianism, an interest which undoubtedly originated from his early preoccupation with the esoteric theories of Goethe. Whereas the English Rosicrucians were primarily occultists, the French to a large extent artists and literary men, those German-speaking Rosicrucians who followed Steiner stood in the tradition of German scholarship and criticism which has found the 16th-century Brotherhood an object of perpetual fascination.

Steiner's Rosicrucianism holds that Christian Rosenkreuz, the legendary founder of the Rosicrucians, originally presided over a brotherhood of the 15th century; but the knowledge which he guarded was only allowed to flow out of this small community in the 18th century. Goethe was the supreme example of a man influenced by this wisdom. However, the connection with the Rosicrucians begins and ends with Steiner's use of the name. The doctrine he advances as 'Rosicrucian' is his own early brand of Germanized THEOSOPHY. Steiner placed emphasis on his theory that CLAIRVOYANCE was the only pathway to higher knowledge, and enumerated the seven stages of the development of this vision. Most modern Rosicrucians he condemned as charlatans, and in his mind the equation seems to have formed itself: Anthroposophy is the truth – Rosicrucianism is said to have been the truth – therefore Anthroposophy is also Rosicrucianism. His acceptance of a charter from the O.T.O. may well have been to quiet a restive conscience.

American Groups

Generally speaking, American Rosicrucians derive from one or other of the European groups already named. Max Grashof, alias Max Heindel, the founder of the Rosicrucian Fellowship of California, obtained most of the material he published as 'Letters of Instruction' from lectures by Rudolf Steiner which he had attended in Berlin in the early 1900s. After Heindel's death in 1919 his succession was continued by Manly Palmer HALL. The ideas he had taken from Steiner

were reimported into Germany about the time of Heindel's death by a charlatan called Hugo Vollrath, whom Steiner had already expelled from his society.

Another American group derives from the O.T.O. Theodor Reuss, about 1915 or 1916, chartered Harvey Spencer Lewis to run a lodge of his organization. Lewis founded the Ancient and Mystic Order Rosae Crucis (AMORC), whose advertisements are still prominent today. It seems that, after numerous attempts, Lewis's Order was properly established in Florida only in 1925; two years later AMORC moved its headquarters to California and acquired a printing plant and a radio transmitter. The group was attacked by its former Grand Treasurer, Leon Batchelor, who disclosed that the 'Supreme Council' consisted of Lewis himself, his wife, his son and daughter-in-law. From the end of 1933 to 1935, Lewis was involved in a running dispute about the authenticity of the word 'Rosicrucian' with Reuben Swinburne Clymer, who claimed that the tradition to which he belonged was alone entitled to the term.

According to Clymer, the effectual founder of the Rosicrucian movements in America was Paschal Beverley RANDOLPH, a social reformer and popular writer on the War of Independence. Randolph was a talented, eccentric and interesting man, who would repay further investigation. Whether his affiliations with European Rosicrucians were as direct as those recorded by Swinburne Clymer is another matter. According to Clymer, Randolph met and was influenced by Bulwer Lytton, Eliphas LÉVI, Kenneth Mackenzie and Hargrave Jennings: all this in the service of a world-wide 'Rosicrucian Brotherhood'. Though Randolph had undoubtedly read the literature of Rosicrucianism and made many occult contacts, the doctrine he preached originated in his own researches. He had encountered great difficulty because it was supposed that he had Negro blood. 'So I called myself The Rosicrucian and gave my thought to the world as Rosicrucian thought; and lo! the world greeted with loud applause what it supposed had its origin and birth elsewhere than in the soul of P. B. Randolph.' Randolph's teachings once more embodied sexual doctrine. Until he resigned, proclaimed Randolph, he had been the Grand Master of the only Rosicrucian temple on the face of the earth.

This explicit confession hampered Clymer not a whit. In 1922 he had succeeded to the supremacy of all the organizations begun by Randolph and spent a vast amount of time and effort constructing pedigrees, charters and affiliations for his groups that encompassed every notable in the occult canon. In 1933 Spencer Lewis challenged him to a

public debate on the relative justice of their claims, and Clymer issued a counter-proposal to submit to investigation all the documents he possessed. Eventually, Clymer applied to the State of Pennsylvania for registration of almost any title embodying the idea of the 'Rosicrucian Brotherhood'. In 1935 the authorities allowed him to register the names on the basis of his elaborate files. Not content with this victory over Lewis, Clymer proceeded to Europe, where at a meeting in 1939 at the Hotel Georges V in Paris he inaugurated the Universal Federation of Orders, Societies and Fraternities of Initiates, in concert with C. M. Chevillon. Chevillon had inherited the Rose-Croix Kabbalistique of de Guaita by way of its succession through Papus, and had contrived to gather most of the surviving French occult orders under his wing. He was shot by the Gestapo in 1944.

The tale of modern Rosicrucians is complicated and obscure. Many different strands have gone into the weave. Of the surviving groups which claim some relationship to these strands of 'Rosicrucianism', the most flourishing are certain of the successors to the Golden Dawn of Mathers and Westcott, although their practice probably bears no relation to that of the original Rose Cross (for modern interpretation of the sign, see plate, page 237). In the end, those who have tried to investigate the mysterious Rosicrucians of the 17th century and to divine their purpose have often concluded that such purposes do not require orders or ceremonial at all. Psychologists like Herbert Silberer and JUNG, or mystics like A. E. WAITE can provide more meat for the mind to chew on than the caperings – however diverting – of countless Grand Masters.   J.W.

(Further reading: *93, 262, 263, 439b, 480, 493, 516*.)

Rosicrucian Society in England See
SOC. ROS.

Runes

The letters used in northern Europe in the early centuries A.D., which were believed to contain magical power; it was to win mastery of them that the god Odin hung nine days and nights on the World Tree. They became a preoccupation of various German nationalists and occultists in this century who saw in them emblems of the Aryan master race and credited them with mysterious powers. Guido von LIST wrote a book on the runes in 1908, the chiefs of the GERMANEN ORDER signed their names in runes, and the ASSOCIATION OF INVISIBLE ARYANS was much preoccupied with rune occultism: see GERMAN OCCULT GROUPS. (303)

S

Sabbat, Sabbath

The old term for a meeting of witches, probably originally applied to them through hostile association with the Jews, as 'synagogue' was another common name for a gathering of witches or heretics. Margaret MURRAY drew a distinction between the 'esbat' or minor routine meeting, and the 'sabbat', a major festival, and this has been adopted by modern witches, who celebrate eight sabbats each year: see WITCHCRAFT.

Sacred Order of Tantriks See OOM.

Sahasrara

The Lotus of the Thousand Petals in Hindu occult physiology: see CHAKRAS.

Samadhi

Mystical ecstasy, the final stage of Hatha Yoga: see YOGA; see also MEDITATION.

Sasquatch (or Bigfoot)

The North American version of the ABOMINABLE SNOWMAN of the Himalayas. Sasquatch is an Indian word meaning 'hairy man' and the creature is said to stand eight feet tall or more, with long arms, an ape-like face with a flat nose, and a pelt of thick hair. It inhabits mountain caves in British Columbia and the Pacific Northwest. There have been numerous reports of sightings of the creature or its footprints – more than 1,000 of them since 1955 – but expeditions searching for it have so far been unsuccessful (347a).

Satanism

Despite the impression given to the casual reader by sensational novels, authentic Satanism – the conscious worship of the powers of evil – is, and always has been, extremely uncommon. It is also of comparatively recent origin and, while it would be going too far to deny that individual Satanists existed in the Middle Ages, it is almost certain that organized Satanic groups of any size did not come into existence until the 17th century. It is true, of course, that in the medieval period

there existed underground dualistic groups, notably the Bogomils and the Cathars, both spiritually descended from the Manichees of the later Roman Empire, and that these groups were condemned by the Church as Satanists. But in reality these groups were ultra-puritanical in their morality and the stories of cannibalism, incest and other horrors which were told about them, especially by Dominican heresy-hunters, can safely be relegated to the realms of fantasy.

It seems likely that Satanism, far from being of Cathar origin, actually had its roots in the bad theology of a minority of Roman Catholic priests. Exactly what the doctrines of the early Church were concerning the Mass – the sacramental consumption of bread and wine – is uncertain, but by A.D. 700 a belief in the Real Presence of Christ in the sacramental elements, approximating to the later scholastic doctrine of transubstantiation, was widespread in western Europe. Once it was accepted that any priest, however ignorant, however unworthy, had the power to transform bread and wine into the Body and Blood of Christ by the words of institution, it was only a step to believing that both the priest and the Mass were possessed of inherent magical powers. Theologians,

Witches flying to a sabbat

naturally, did not share this belief, and saw a vast gulf between the sacramental gifts of the Holy Ghost and any form of magic, but the distinction went unperceived by many ordinary people and many of the frequently illiterate secular clergy. As a result, some priests were prepared to turn their supposed magical powers to evil ends: as early as the 7th century, the Council of Toledo prohibited the performance of Requiem Masses sung, not for souls in purgatory, but for living men with the intention of killing them. Belief in the effectiveness of such practices survived among simple Catholics into the 19th century and Frazer recorded it in *The Golden Bough* as current Breton folklore, under the name of 'the Mass of St Sécaire'. The evocative term 'Black Mass' probably originated with this practice, for until comparatively recently Black Mass was an unusual but perfectly respectable alternative term for a Requiem Mass. Thus Hadrian VII, the hero of F. W. Rolfe's novel recently turned into a play by Peter Luke, remarked that after ordination his first act would be the celebration of a Black Mass.

It was not only for death that priests were believed to be able to say special Masses. Just as a Mass could be sung for some pious special intention, such as going on a pilgrimage, so it could be sung for sexual or financial success. Once priests, or some priests, had come to believe these things, an underground literature came into existence, designed to give instruction in the practical techniques involved. Typical of these manuals was the *Grimoire of Honorius*, first printed in the 17th century but probably circulated in manuscript several centuries earlier, which was clearly aimed at a clerical market, since almost all of its magical ceremonies required the saying of at least one Mass. To obtain a demon servitor, for example, the magician is instructed to begin by saying a Mass of the Holy Ghost. After this he must tear out the eyes of a live cockerel, recite a long evocation and throw a mouse to the materialized demon. The Anglo-Catholic writer Charles Williams remarked in his book on *Witchcraft* (*506*) that any priest who could follow a Mass with such blasphemous cruelty was quite likely to imagine that he saw a demon, and with the *Grimoire of Honorius* one leaves the domain of bad theology and unworthy priesthood and enters that of Satanism itself, the giving of tribute, even if only a mouse, to the powers of evil.

The Montespan Affair

It is difficult to know how widespread such Satanist activities were among the non-monastic clergy of the Middle Ages, but they seem to have become common in the 16th and 17th centuries. Exactly how common, no one knows, but if the rest of Catholic Europe was anything like the ecclesiastical underworld of Paris at that time, then they were very common indeed. For in France Satanism had attained the status of big business, its practitioners forming a kind of occult Mafia, a noisome octopus with tentacles which reached into almost every segment of Parisian society and which was uncovered by Nicolas de la Reynie, the Police Commissioner of Paris.

La Reynie had suspected the existence of Satanism on a large scale since November 1678, when he had arrested Louis de Vanens, who openly boasted of being a Satanist, for forgery. For over a year he was unable to obtain any definite evidence, but with the arrest, for poisoning, of a fortune-teller named Catherine Deshayes, better known as La Voisin, he began to accumulate significant information. At La Voisin's home he found not only such poisons as arsenic, henbane and cantharides but ingredients like dried toad, semen, blood and graveyard dust, all used in the manufacture of philtres designed to bring love or death.

Under interrogation La Voisin admitted not only to selling poisons to young wives anxious to rid themselves of elderly husbands but to being the leading Parisian abortionist – it seems that the ashes of over 2,000 infants and embryos were found buried in her garden – and to organizing the performance of magical Masses intended to murder or to provoke love. Several priests were her accomplices, the most notorious of them being the Abbé Guibourg, described by La Reynie as: 'A priest 67 years of age . . . A libertine who has travelled a good deal . . . and who is at present attached to the church of Saint Marcel. For twenty years he has engaged in the practice of poison, sacrilege and every evil business. He has cut the throats and sacrificed uncounted numbers of children on his evil altar . . . A man who at times seems a raving lunatic . . . It is no ordinary man who thinks it a natural thing to sacrifice infants by slitting their throats and to say Mass upon the bodies of naked women.'

According to the evidence of La Voisin's daughter and of Guibourg himself, some of these Black Masses were celebrated at the request of Madame de Montespan, mistress of Louis XIV, a woman prepared to go to any lengths to retain the king's favour and destroy the chances of her numerous rivals. The earlier Masses – the first was said in 1667 – were of a comparatively mild nature and did not involve child sacrifice: the most diabolic of them being the third of the series, at which two doves, symbols of Venus, were consecrated to the king and Madame de

Madame de Montespan

Montespan, were kept on the altar throughout the rite and were finally sacrificed. These ceremonies were supplemented by the use of love philtres – Madame de Montespan secretly added 'Spanish fly', dried cockerels' testicles and other ingredients to her lover's food – and were evidently found adequate enough until 1673, when the first real Black Mass of the series was celebrated upon the body of a naked woman. At the moment of consecration a child's throat was cut and its blood was poured into the chalice, prayers were said to Asmodeus and Ashtaroth, two leading demons of the Judaeo-Christian tradition, and the consecrated host was subjected to various unpleasant sexual manipulations. Finally blood, wine and the entrails of the murdered child were taken away to be secretly administered to Louis in his food.

Another series of Masses was performed in 1678 but by 1679 it was clear that Madame de Montespan was passing out of favour. Love turned to hate and either de Montespan herself or one of her associates decided to murder the King by means of a Black Mass. The ceremony, which was not successful, involved even more disgusting rites than the amatory Masses, but before any further attempts could be made La Reynie had begun his series of arrests.

La Reynie arrested 360 persons in all, of whom only 110 were tried, for once it became clear that individuals close to the King were involved all further publicity was avoided by the use of *lettres de cachet*. Those surviving prisoners who were not released were simply imprisoned for life, the last of them dying more than forty years afterwards. Madame de Montespan was spared. For ten years Louis simulated a continuing friendship for her and she was then sent into retirement into the country, where she spent her last years in good works, prayer and, perhaps, repentance.

The Temple of Satan
If Satanism survived in the 18th century, it has left no traces. In England, it is true, there was the Hell-Fire Club of Francis Dashwood and John Wilkes, together with other similar sodalities (such as the Brimstone Boys and the Mohocks) but, sensational journalism to the contrary, these groups were not Satanist in any true sense of the term but drunken assemblies of debauchees whose members liked to combine a little adolescent blasphemy with their orgies.

An undoubted Satanist of the 19th century was the notorious Abbé BOULLAN. Born in 1824, Boullan had been a pious youth – as Guibourg had been before him – and was ordained priest at the age of twenty-five. Subsequently, about 1854, he became the confessor of a nun named Adèle Chevalier, who became his mistress and bore him two, or possibly more, children. Boullan and Chevalier, simulating great piety, founded the Society for the Reparation of Souls, which specialized in exorcism of a peculiarly scatological type: supposedly demon-possessed nuns were cured by the administration of consecrated hosts mixed with human excrement. All this, eccentric as it was, was a front for Satanist activities resembling those of Guibourg and there is good evidence that in January 1860 the pair conducted a Black mass during which they sacrificed one of their own children.

In 1875 Boullan became the head of a small splinter-group, which was an offshoot of a minor neo-Gnostic body calling itself the Church of the Carmel. Boullan led his tiny 'Church' until his death eighteen years later and, while he assumed a mask of piety which deceived some people, notably the novelist J.-K. Huysmans, there is little doubt that Boullan's Church was a Satanist group. This was established by two eccentric ROSICRUCIANS, Stanislas de GUAITA and Oswald Wirth who, posing as disciples, penetrated Boullan's group, learned its secrets and published them in an exposé entitled *The Temple of Satan*. In spite of its lurid title and its even more lurid language – Boullan was described as a 'pontiff of infamy, a base idol of the mystical Sodom . . . an evil sorcerer' – there is independent evidence that the book's revelations were accurate and that Boullan engaged in Satanic rites involving sexual and scatological perversions and the evocation of incubi and succubi, the unclean sexual demons of medieval theology.

Other Satanist groups may also have been

J.-K. Huysmans

operating in Paris in the late 19th century. In his novel *Là-bas*, Huysmans described a Black Mass at which he claimed to have been present: the words of the Mass were chanted backwards, the crucifix was upside down, the acolytes were painted, simpering male prostitutes, the host was obscenely defiled and the whole proceeding culminated in a sexual orgy. Clearly, much subsequent occult fiction, including A. E. W. Mason's *Prisoner in the Opal*, owed its inspiration to Huysmans. Though Huysmans was not altogether a reliable reporter of occult matters, as witness his odd belief that his pet cat was attacked by demons, it seems probable that he was present at some such ceremony as he described, though whether it was a genuine Satanist rite or merely a sexual orgy to which blasphemy was added for further excitement is uncertain.

A Crucified Toad
In this century two openly 'Satanist' groups have gained some publicity. The smaller of the two has its headquarters in Manchester, England, where its activities have caused some surprise but no great alarm. The Mancunian Satanists do call their god Satan, but as they attribute all the Christian virtues to this deity and preach love and charity, they are certainly not Satanists in the true sense of the term. The second group is the Church of Satan, based in San Francisco, whose claims to diabolist orthodoxy are equally tenuous. The Church does preach a non-Christian ethic of material success and physical pleasure, but there is nothing peculiarly Satanic about this, the standard wisdom of the stock exchange and the racetrack. On the whole, one gets the impression that the Devil could safely leave the members of the Church of Satan to the World and the Flesh.

Aleister CROWLEY is popularly regarded as a 20th-century Satanist, a view denied not only by Crowley's followers but by most of those who have studied his writings. However, it is possible to make a strong case for describing Crowley as a practising Satanist, in the sense that he devised and performed ceremonies which were not only anti-Christian but were deliberately intended to destroy Jesus Christ in the same way that Guibourg or Boullan believed that they destroyed Christ when they desecrated the host. In 1916, for example, Crowley carried out a lengthy magical operation in which he baptized a toad as Jesus of Nazareth and then crucified it: the rubric of this ritual has been published in John Symonds's *The Great Beast* (*446*). Even more significant is the as yet unpublished VI Degree ritual of Crowley's O.T.O. This involves a parody of the crucifixion – in which scourging, a crown of thorns, and a sponge of vinegar all play a part – and an ultra-Satanic denunciation of Christianity. Finally, perhaps conclusively, there are Crowley's own words: 'Satan is not the enemy of Man . . . He is . . . Life . . . Love . . . Light.' Real Satanism, as distinct from play-acting by exhibitionists, has hitherto been rare: if Crowley was a Satanist, it may well become more common, for Crowley dead has more disciples than Crowley alive. F. K.

(Further reading: *12, 85, 263, 275, 276, 337, 399, 401.*)

Saturn-Gnosis See FRATERNITAS SATURNI.

Rudi Schneider (1908-57)
An Austrian, said to have been 'one of the most exhaustively investigated and carefully controlled physical mediums of all time' (*303*). His elder brother, Willi, was also a medium, whose CONTROL was named Olga. Olga transferred herself to Rudi when the latter was only eleven. His phenomena included mysterious movements of objects, LEVITATION and visible spirit-forms. He was tested in Paris in 1930–1 by Dr Eugène Osty, who set up an infra-red alarm system which would automatically sound bells and take photographs if an arm or a device of any sort approached the table on which the objects to be moved were placed. The alarm was set off several times, at moments when Olga announced that she was 'going into the ray', but by no discernible agency, the photographs showing that the infra-red rays

had been interrupted by, apparently, nothing. The same thing happened the following year in London. There were fierce disputes about Rudi's genuineness, in which Harry PRICE seems to have played a disingenuous role. After this the medium's powers slowly faded away: see MEDIUMS. (*195a*)

Scrying

The word 'scrying' comes from the archaic English word 'descry', meaning to see. It now has the restricted sense of seeing paranormal visions, usually of the future, by looking at an object with a polished or shiny surface. Mirrors and crystals are the objects most commonly used, but a wide variety of other materials can serve for scrying purposes, from water to fingernails. The art has been practised in various forms all over the world from remote antiquity, and a number of curious similarities crop up in the rules for scrying as observed by different communities. Often, for example, the fortune-teller did not look into the mirror or crystal himself, but employed a virgin boy or girl for the purpose.

In ancient Greece there were a number of springs used for scrying. Pausanius, in his *Description of Greece*, records that at one spring, at Patrae, 'they tie a mirror to a fine cord, and let it down so far that it shall not plunge into the spring, but merely graze the surface of the water with its rim. Then, after praying to the goddess and burning incense, they look into the mirror, and it shows them the sick person either living or dead. So truthful is this water.' Another spring, at Taenarum, ceased to be effective for scrying after a woman had washed her laundry in it.

The Romans, surprisingly enough, used scrying very little, but during the Middle Ages the practice was widespread and often incurred condemnation. In the 12th century, for example, John of Salisbury inveighed against those who divine in 'objects which are polished and shining, like a kettle of good brass, glasses, cups and different kinds of mirrors'. In 1398 the Faculty of Theology in Paris condemned scrying as being of Satanic origin.

The fulminations of the Church were, however, unavailing, and the practice continued to be popular, though the scryers often fell foul of authority. One who got into trouble was William Byg, who in 1467 was tried at Wombwell in Yorkshire on a charge of heresy. He was found guilty and, as a punishment, had to walk round the Cathedral Church of York with a lighted torch in his right hand and his books depending from a stick in his left; he also had to wear placards describing him as *sortilegus* (soothsayer) and *invocator spiritum* (invoker of spirits). He was

Reading coffee-grounds

required to make a full recantation and to burn his books.

The practice of scrying has left its mark in a number of folk customs. At North Kelsey, in Lincolnshire, there existed, and perhaps still exists, a custom by which a girl who wanted to know who her sweetheart would be went to the Maiden's Well. She approached backwards, walked around the well three times in the same direction, and then looked into the water, in which the face of her lover would then supposedly appear. Another tradition exists in many parts of the United States, where it is said that if on Hallowe'en a girl goes down the cellar stairs backwards looking into a mirror she will see the face of her future husband.

One of the most fanatical of English scryers was John Dee (1527–1608), philosopher, magus and fortune-teller to Queen Elizabeth I, who used a crystal that he claimed had been given to him by angels (see also ENOCHIAN MAGIC). His associate, Edward Kelley, looked into the stone, and Dee recorded the visions. His diary of the experiments runs to several bulky volumes.

Scrying was particularly widespread in the Islamic world. Leo Africanus, writing of the scryers of Fez, describes how they peered into vessels of water and saw swarms of demons who responded to their questions by gestures. In certain parts of the Arab world looking into mirrors or containers of water was thought to cure illness. Examining fingernails and gazing at the blade of a sword were among the variations practised by the Arabs.

It was a 14th-century Arabic writer, 'Abd al-Rahman ibn Muhammad ibn Khaldun, who gave one of the most sensible accounts of divination by scrying. He wrote:

Those who gaze at diaphanous bodies, such as mirrors, basins filled with water, and liquids . . . belong to the category of diviners. But, because of the radical imperfection of their nature, they occupy an inferior grade in that category. To remove the veil of the senses, the genuine diviner does not employ great efforts; as for the others they try to achieve their ends in seeking to concentrate in a single sense all their perceptions. As sight is the noblest sense, they give it preference, and fixing their gaze on an object with a level surface, they regard it with attention until they perceive the thing that they wish to announce. Some people believe that the image so perceived appears on the surface of the mirror, but they are mistaken. The diviner looks fixedly at the surface until it disappears and a fog-like curtain interposes itself between his eyes and the mirror. On this curtain the shapes that he desires to see form themselves . . .

'Wonders of Clairvoyance'

Crystal-gazing, along with other forms of divination, revived in the 19th century. The Victorian novelist and occultist Edward Bulwer, Lord Lytton, owned a crystal ball which is still preserved among his personal possessions on display at Knebworth House, his ancestral home in Hertfordshire. This revival has continued into the present century, and books on the subject are numerous.

One of the most detailed manuals is John Melville's *Crystal-Gazing and the Wonders of Clairvoyance (323)*, published in 1920, which sets out an elaborate method involving the use of cabalistic formulae.

The crystal [says Melville] should be about 1½ inch in *diameter*, or at least the size of a small orange. It should be enclosed in a frame of ivory, ebony, or box-wood, highly polished, or stood upon a glass or crystal pedestal.

When following strictly the ancient methods described herein, the Crystal is to be stood upon the Lamen or table, but if simply *held in the hand*, its top end should be held so that no reflections or shadows appear therein. If stood upon a table, the folds of a black silk handkerchief may be arranged about the crystal so as to shut out reflections.

The mystic names to be engraved in raised letters of gold round about the frame, according to some authorities, are:

    On the N.   Tetragrammaton
    „   „   E.   Emmanuel
    „   „   S.   Agla
    „   „   W.   Adonay

The pedestal which supports the frame should bear the mystical name

    SADAY;

while on the pedestals of the two candle-sticks [part of the ritual equipment]

    ELOHIM and
    ELOHE

must be respectively embossed . . .

No crystal or mirror should be handled by other than the owner, because such handling mixes the magnetisms, and tends to destroy their sensitiveness. Others may *look* into them, but should not touch them, except the person who may be consulting the gazer, as already mentioned. If the surface becomes dirty or soiled, it may be cleaned with fine soapsuds, rinsed well, washed with alcohol or vinegar and water, and then polished with soft velvet or a chamois leather.

The crystal or mirror should be frequently magnetised by passes made with the *right hand*, for about five minutes at a time. This *aids* to give it *strength* and *power*. Similar passes with the *left hand* add to the *sensitiveness* of the crystal.

The back of the mirror or crystal should be held *toward* the *light*, but its face never.

The *Magnetism* with which the surface of the mirror or crystal becomes charged, *collects there from the eyes of the gazer*, and from the universal ether, the Brain being as it were switched on to the Universe, the crystal being the medium.

Melville sets out the following guide giving

A crystal-gazer in London's West End

the significance of different appearances in the crystal:

White Clouds indicate
    Good, the affirmative; favour.
Black Clouds indicate
    Bad; inauspicious.
Violet, Green, Blue indicate
    Coming joy; excellent.
Red, Crimson, Orange, Yellow indicate
    Danger, trouble, sickness; 'beware'; deception, grief, betrayal, slander, loss; surprises of a disagreeable nature.
Ascending Clouds indicate
    Affirmative replies to questions asked. Yes! If the query is a silent one it makes no difference.
Descending Clouds indicate
    The negation of all questions. No!

Melville advises the person learning crystal-gazing to select a quiet room free from mirrors, ornaments, pictures and glaring colours. Several sittings are often necessary, he says, before any results are obtained. On the first occasion the would-be seer should 'commence by sitting comfortably with the eyes fixed upon the crystal, not by a fierce stare, but with a steady calm gaze, for ten minutes only'. Later the periods can be extended. 'When you find the crystal begins to look dull or cloudy, with small pin points of light glittering therein, like tiny stars, you may know that you are *commencing* to obtain that for which you seek – viz., crystalline vision.'

In scrying, as in other forms of divination, the method used acts as a catalyst to activate the clairvoyant's perceptions. But with more complex systems such as the TAROT, the I CHING and ASTROLOGY, the symbols used constitute a model of the cosmos and are credited with a value far beyond their divinatory function. Scrying is therefore generally regarded as more direct, but less exalted, than these other methods. C. M.

(Further reading: *39, 280, 323.*)

Rudolf, Freiherr von Sebottendorf

The style adopted by Adam Glauer (1875–1945), the German adventurer who became a leading member of the GERMANEN ORDER. He founded the Thule Society, a right-wing anti-Semitic group, wrote prolifically on astrology, including a history of the subject which he published in 1923, and was also much concerned with pendulum DOWSING and the SUFIS. He spent much of his life in Turkey, and died there, by drowning, in 1945. (*234*)

Secret Chiefs See MASTERS.

Sensitive

A person who has psychic gifts: see MEDIUMS.

Sensory Automatisms See CONSCIOUSNESS.

Sepharial

The pseudonym of Walter Gorn Old (1864–1929), British astrologer. As a young man he joined the THEOSOPHICAL SOCIETY and became an intimate of Madame BLAVATSKY, who called him 'the astral tramp' because of his habit of 'roaming about in his astral body at night'. He wrote numerous books, including *Kabbalistic Astrology* and a *Book of Charms and Talismans*, and specialized in selling astrological systems for predicting the winners of horse races. (*234*)

Ted Serios

Ted Serios

An American medium who was apparently able to cause photographs to appear on a film by concentrating on the camera; these included photographs of objects which, ostensibly, were not there at the time they were photographed. (*140*)

Sex Magic See ALCHEMY; GERMAN OCCULT GROUPS; POSSESSION; RITUAL MAGIC; TANTRISM; WITCHCRAFT.

Siddhis

In Hinduism, mysterious powers, either naturally inherent in an individual or acquired through asceticism, drugs, meditation or mystical and magical practices; eight major siddhis are believed to be acquirable through YOGA: see PHYSICAL POWERS.

Sidereal Zodiac

This should be distinguished from the 'tropical' zodiac, used in traditional ASTROLOGY, which is out of step with the constellations in the sky, as a result of the precession of the equinoxes, so that when a traditional astrologer says, for example, that the Sun is 'in' Aries it is actually 'in' the preceding constellation Pisces (and, quite soon, it will be in the constellation before that, Aquarius: see AQUARIAN AGE). To meet this difficulty, MacGregor MATHERS used the 'sidereal' zodiac, corresponding to the visible positions of the constellations, and a small number of astrologers have followed suit, with confusing consequences for those accustomed to the tropical zodiac. (*182*)

Skin Vision See PAROPTIC VISION.

Sleep See DREAMS.

Hélène Smith

The pseudonym of Catherine Elise Müller (1861–1929), a Swiss medium famous for her accounts of life on Mars. Various historical characters appeared to control her at seances, including Cagliostro and Marie Antoinette, and her voice and expression changed dramatically with each new personality. As Cagliostro, for instance, she spoke slowly in a bass voice with an Italian accent, her eyelids drooped and her throat swelled into a double chin. She had the experience of feeling that she had left her body and visited Mars, and she also received communications from spirits of dead human beings who had supposedly been reincarnated there. In a long series of seances she gave descriptions of Mars and the Martians, and delivered by automatic writing a complete Martian language. Her case was described by a Swiss psychologist, Théodore Flournoy, in his book *Des Indes à la Planète Mars*, 1900. He traced her phenomena entirely to her own subconscious mental processes. (*155*)

Society for Psychical Research (S.P.R.) See PSYCHICAL RESEARCH SOCIETIES.

Soc. Ros.

The *Societas Rosicruciana in Anglia*, Rosicrucian Society in England; founded in 1866 by Robert Wentworth Little, a clerk at Freemasons' Hall in London. The society used the grade names of the Gold and Rosy Cross, a German order of the late 18th century (see GERMAN OCCULT GROUPS). Several members played important roles in the GOLDEN DAWN: see ROSICRUCIANS. (*235, 480*)

Austin Osman Spare (1886-1956)

Austin Spare was born at Snowhill, London, the son of a City of London policeman. When he left school, at the age of thirteen, he worked in a stained-glass factory, and in the evenings attended the Lambeth School of Art, where he obtained a scholarship to the Royal College of Art, Kensington. At this period, Spare's father surreptitiously sent one of Austin's drawings to the Royal Academy. It was accepted and exhibited, and the painter John Singer Sargent hailed him as a genius. Not long afterwards, G. F. Watts declared that Spare had 'already done enough to justify his fame'.

But although the way to conventional success seemed clear and assured, Spare's future had already been determined otherwise. As a child he had not got on well with his mother, and at an early age he formed a close friendship with a strange old lady who claimed to be a witch. Spare knew her simply as Mrs Paterson, and he described her as his 'second mother' or, more appositely, as his witch-mother. Her attraction for the young and imaginative Austin lay in her otherness, her total remoteness from all the things that constituted his prosaic surroundings. She claimed to be descended from a line of Salem witches that Cotton Mather had failed to extirpate.

The witch-mother taught Spare not only how to visualize and reify dream imagery, but also how to evoke SPIRITS and ELEMENTALS to visible appearance. Combined with his mastery of graphic art the amalgam produced the weird creations with which Spare's name is associated. Although he could, and often did, produce straightforward works of art 'as fine as any by Dürer or Rembrandt', as his friend Hannen Swaffer once observed, Spare preferred to depict the denizens of unseen worlds, the elementals and familiar spirits that constantly haunted him.

Spare evolved a highly individualistic system of sorcery based on the teaching of his witch-mother. In 1913 he published *The Book of Pleasure (Self-love)*, subtitled *The Psychology of Ecstasy*, in which he concentrated in his own peculiar dream-like style the substance of his occult researches. His sorcery is based on the hypothesis that superhuman powers may be invoked from vastly ancient strata of the subconscious mind. He developed a technique which he called the

Formula of Atavistic Resurgence (see plate, page 238), and at the request of two inquisitive people he once reified an ATAVISM from these deep layers of consciousness, so appalling that one of the witnesses committed suicide shortly afterwards, and the other went mad.

Austin Spare

Mrs Paterson initiated Spare into the mysteries of the witches' SABBATH, which he claimed to have attended with her on several occasions. It took place, he said, not on this earth but in extra-spatial dimensions of consciousness. He frequently spoke of 'spaces outside space', into which he was suddenly and abruptly precipitated. On his return to earth, despite his aptitude for graphic ex-

pression, he found himself completely unable to depict his experiences. He supposed he had seen the 'geometry of the future', fantastic cities constructed of lines and angles that bore no semblance to anything earthly.

Spare co-edited two quarterly reviews of the Arts, the magazines *Form*, 1916, and *The Golden Hind*, 1921. Both magazines contain some of his finest work. In 1921 he published

The Focus of Life, in which he developed the magical philosophy he had originally formulated in *The Book of Pleasure*. From 1927 until his death, in 1956, Spare lived as a semi-recluse in the decaying back streets of South London. Although he held several exhibitions in local public bars and galleries, and fascinated all who met him, he remained an essentially solitary man although he greatly enjoyed the companionship of cats. K. G.

(Further reading: *189, 189b*.)

Speaking in Tongues See AUTOMATISMS; POSSESSION.

Spirit Healing, Spiritual Healing

Healing through MEDIUMS, which in Spiritualist theory may be due either to divine power or to the work of doctors in the spirit-world; Spiritualists draw a distinction between spiritual healing and FAITH HEALING, on the ground that the former does not necessarily involve faith on the patient's part; on the contrary, in some cases of ABSENT HEALING, the patient does not even know that healing is being attempted.

Spirits and Forces (in Occult Theory)

Belief in spirits and supernatural beings, variously conceived, has been common to men in all ages and all over the world: this article is concerned with these entities or forces in terms of modern occult theory. Among those universally recognized, and most dreaded, are the spirits of the dead, and some occultists believe that the first awareness of a world of spirits occurred when primitive man, who was a natural sensitive, observed the apparitions or doubles of the dead. These were feared and propitiated because they haunted the earth in search of renewed life. Being intangible, they required subtle forms of sustenance, such as the emanations from freshly spilt blood, in which the vital element still lingered. This led to an early mental association between the ideas of spirits, death, blood-lust and vampirism.

The spirits of the dead were therefore propitiated with blood sacrifices and the smoke of burnt offerings. That blood is the source of life, or spirit, is an extremely old and widespread belief. It may lie behind the name given to the first man in Genesis, for Adam can be literally interpreted to mean 'the red earth', or in effect, congealed blood, or flesh. Also according to Jewish tradition, when King Solomon, the prototypal magician, banished the spirits he had summoned, they fled to the Red Sea and were drowned in it, which is a way of saying that they were absorbed back into their source.

Elemental spirits drawn by Austin Spare

In ancient Egypt the basis of life was represented by the *ankh*, which has the form of a loop, knot, or tie, and has been conjectured to have been based on the knotted strip of fabric that formed the first garment necessitated by the onset of puberty in the female. It was the feminine nature that gave rise to the ankh sign, when spirit was equated with and based upon the life-giving blood of the mother. The sign still survives in stylized form as the astrological symbol of Venus, goddess of love and manifestation.

A different, and later, concept attributed spirit to air, or breath. In Genesis, for example, God breathes into Adam to give him life, and there are parallels in many other traditions. The transition from blood to breath or, symbolically speaking, from water to air as the source of life and the vehicle of spirit, underlies the change from blood sacrifice to the burning of incense. In China, to this day, the smoke of incense is known as the fragrant repast of spirits.

Propitiation of the spirits of the dead developed inevitably into ancestor worship. Offerings were laid in the tomb, rites were performed, and the ancestral spirits were consulted before important activities were undertaken. This cult of the dead attained its apotheosis in the religion of ancient Egypt, where the 'dead' were considered to be infinitely more alive than the beings who peopled the earth. The mummy, far from being an image of ultimate inertia, was a symbol of eternal consciousness, of the spirit that dwelt in Amenta, the underworld or 'earth of eternity'. In Amenta it purged itself of all desire to haunt the upper earth and its pleasures, before ascending to heaven as a glorified spirit in the presence of the never-setting stars in the 'sky of eternity'.

These and certain other stars were typified on earth by birds, beasts and reptiles which were believed to possess superhuman powers. It was these powers, not the animals, that were deified and identified with particular celestial bodies. Certain creatures which 'see in the dark' – for example the jackal, the cat, the owl – were assimilated to particular stars and planets, which were then conceived as focusing the influence represented by the animal, and the animal was considered to be the 'god-form' or vehicle of this influence. One of the god-forms of Anubis, who guided the souls in the darkness of the underworld, was the jackal or desert-dog. His constellation was the complex of stars now known as Ursa Minor and his planetary vehicle was Mercury.

The god-form of Sekhet, the goddess of sexual pleasure and intoxicating liquor, was the lioness, typical of solar heat in its feminine phase, which, as the maneless lion, she re-presented. Sekhet can therefore be interpreted as the power of the sun in its fermenting and oestrus aspect, with its gentler aspect formulated as the goddess Bâst, whose god-form was the cat, celestially imaged by the moon. In respect of their fierce and mild aspects, Sekhet and Bâst bore much the same relationship to each other in Egypt as did Kali and Bhavani in India.

The Assumption of God-forms

Prayers, or magical invocations, were not addressed to the animal but to the deity, the specific power, which the creature represented. Egyptian priest-magicians sought to acquire such power, if only temporarily, by simulating the form of the beast that possessed it. This they did by assuming its god-form astrally, and wearing the horns, pelt, or skin of the animal physically. The process is known to initiates as the Formula of the Divine Ape, because the mimicking, or aping, of the god has a profound effect upon the psychology of the magician, in awaking dormant powers sealed up in the pre-human strata of consciousness (see also POSSESSION).

Man evolved from the beasts, and he therefore naturally, if unknowingly, embodies such powers. One of the god-forms of Thoth, the Egyptian deity of magic or transformation, is the ape, because the ape is the link between man and beast. Among other things it represents the Word of Magical Power, on the theory that the first forms of human utterance were based upon its primitive articulations.

The cow was a god-form of Hathor, the Egyptian earth-goddess whose star, Sothis, heralded the annual inundation of the river Nile which brought fertility to Egypt. The sky-goddess, Nuit, was depicted as a multitude of stars, themselves regarded as elemental symbols of human spirits which had attained beatitude. Hathor and Nuit were depicted on the inner casings of the coffins which contained the dead. Hathor, on the floor or ground of the coffin welcomed the spirit of the deceased to Amenta. Nuit, arching over the corpse in the lid of the coffin, welcomed it at last to the ultimate paradise imaged by the circumpolar stars that never set, or died. The mummy, laid out horizontally, represented the shade or ghost in Amenta, still attached by desires to mundane existence. When the mummy was turned up on end, during the sacred rites, it represented the risen or resurrected spirit, exalted to the heavens.

Guardian Spirits

Two subtle components of the human organism, recognized in occultism (see ASTRAL BODY), are represented by the prostrate mummy and the upright mummy respectively: the astral shade and the spiritual intelligence. These same components appear again in the old concept of the seducing demon and the guardian angel which accompany each human being through life. The latter is the spirit of light; the former, its shadow and twin, is the spirit of the dark. The dark shade haunted the primitive imagination and engendered legends of the ghoul, the vampire and the evil genius. The bright spirit gave birth to beliefs in angels, guardian angels, the good genii that guide humanity and inspire its most exalted creations.

The guardian angel was a concept common to all the major cults of antiquity. The Egyptians referred to it as Asar-Un-Nefer, the Self Made Perfect; the Chinese called it the Great Person; the Hindus know it as the Ishva-devata or Chosen God; the Cabalists call it Jechidah, the Higher Self; the Buddhists designate it Adi-Buddha, the root of light or enlightenment; the Gnostics referred to it as the Logos; the Greek mystics knew it as the Augoeides, the Luminous Self. More recently, the Theosophists have popularized the idea of the guardian angel as the Silent Watcher or the Great Master (see MASTERS).

The cult of the guardian spirit achieved its apotheosis in magical literature in the 'book of the sacred magic which God gave to Moses, Aaron, David, Solomon, and other Holy Patriarchs and Prophets'. This grimoire, or magical textbook, purportedly written down by Abraham the Jew and delivered by him to his son, Lamech, in 1458, inspired Bulwer Lytton, Eliphas LÉVI and Aleister CROWLEY among others. Crowley described it as the 'best and most dangerous book ever written', and added 'It is by far the most convincing mediaeval magical document in existence.' It was translated into English as *The Book of the Sacred Magic of Abramelin the Mage* (see ABRAMELIN) by S. MacGregor MATHERS, an adept of the GOLDEN DAWN.

Dion FORTUNE, who shared Crowley's view of the book, described Abramelin's system of magic as the 'most potent and complete that we possess. The operator after a prolonged period of purification and preparation, evokes not only the angelic forces, but also the demonic ones.' She goes on to say that many people have burned their fingers while using it.

The magic squares, included in the third part of the book, contain the words of power and the names of dark spirits such as Kobha, who appears in the form of an ape; Alampis, who renders one invisible; Catan, who arranges adulteries; Qaqah, who destroys towns. The squares themselves, quite apart from their use by the operator, are said to be instinct with a demonic life which works through them automatically. According to Crowley, the Abramelin talismans are 'as easy to explode as iodide of nitrogen and a sight more dangerous'. He cites the case of his friend, Captain J. F. C. FULLER. 'Fuller once marked his place in the book with his butcher's bill. A couple of days later the butcher was at work; his knife slipped, pierced his thigh, and killed him. As Fuller observed at the time: "It may be only coincidence, but it's just as bad for the butcher!"'

Philip Heseltine, the musical composer better known as Peter Warlock, once evoked an Abramelin demon in order to induce his wife to return to him. This he did by tracing the appropriate magical square on his arm. It was only too effective; his wife came back and he committed suicide shortly afterwards.

Abramelin's system may only be used with impunity by an adept who has successfully completed the preliminary course of spiritual purification that results in the 'attainment of the Knowledge and Conversation of the Holy Guardian Angel'. In other words, the astral double, the dark shade, must have been transformed and exalted to the status of a spiritual entity.

Shells and Elementals

The ability to function consciously in the spirit world is the fruit of concentrated mystical culture, and genuine spiritualism originated in the activities of the glorified dead, which demonstrated immortality by appearing to kindred spirits on earth. But the term spiritualism is not always used in its proper sense, and there is nothing very spiritual about most spectral visitants. The genuine science of spirits should therefore be distinguished from commerce with the mere shells of the dead. The latter are included in cabalistic lore among a class of entities known as the *qliphoth*; their appearances are deceptive and their utterances false; they are related directly to demonic spirits which, ghoul-like, feed upon the waning vital substance which lingers on in the newly dead. Because the shades of the recently deceased are decomposing, they attract the larval denizens of the *qliphoth*; it is therefore unwise to arouse such shades from the torpor into which the process of their corruption immerses them.

Functioning consciously in the shade, or astral body, is one of the most ancient of all magical practices and the earliest mediums were those who were able to control and project the subtle body. Such persons were (and in some primitive societies still are) greatly revered for their ability to communicate with spirits and with elementals, or non-human spirits.

Elementals in occult theory are of several kinds, of which three are particularly important. First there are the spirits or subtle essences of the elements of water, air, earth, and fire. These spirits have been classified as undines (water), sylphs (air), gnomes (earth), and salamanders (fire). Secondly, there are elemental spirits of trees and woods (dryads); lakes and pools (naiads); mountains and caves (chthonians), and other natural features. The third class, and perhaps the most important from the point of view of practical magic, are the energies of the subconscious mind that assume a sensible form when properly evoked (see frontispiece, and plate, page 255). They represent the powers possessed by consciousness in times preceding its embodiment in human form. They are, therefore, in the nature of ATAVISMS, and are conjured by adepts wishing to perform superhuman activities; they are then known as servitors, *famuli*, or familiar spirits.

Elementals should not be confused with elementaries, which Madame Blavatsky described as the 'disembodied souls of the depraved; these souls having at some time prior to death separated from themselves their divine spirits, and so lost their chance of immortality'. Elementaries represent the dark shade divorced from its light or angelic counterpart.

Thought-forms

The suppression of natural instinct imposed by ascetic tendencies in medieval Europe gave rise to a lurid complex of ideas about astral monstrosities. Incubi and succubi, or sexually insatiable demons generated by nocturnal emissions, haunted the inmates of religious communities and attacked sexually unsatisfied devotees. Paracelsus mentions several classes of such demons, one of which consists of elementaries, or the shades of dead persons who have carnal intercourse with amorously disposed men or women. Paracelsus claimed that sorcerers and witches could generate incubi and succubi, or project out of themselves the organisms necessary for the conscious enjoyment of sexual pleasure with sleeping human beings of either sex. The latter kind of demon, which he calls an *aquastor*, is created by an imaginative manipulation of astral substance into various magical forms: an elemental for superhuman contacts, an incubus or succubus for sexual pleasure, a vampire for the satisfaction of blood-lust, and so on. According to Franz HARTMANN, in his *Life of Paracelsus*, 'such imaginary but nevertheless real forms may obtain life from the person by whose imagination they are created, and under certain circumstances they may even become visible and tangible'.

The human will allied to a controlled and

vivid imagination, or image-making faculty, can engender various kinds of thought-forms. Some occultists claim that every thought possesses a characteristic form of its own. But although it requires very little mental effort to suggest ideas or thoughts to other people, without the use of a physical medium, it does require great concentrative ability to transfer an actual thought-form to the mind of another person.

Annie BESANT and C. W. LEADBEATER, two indefatigable Theosophists, collaborated on a book entitled *Thought Forms* (1901), in which they maintained that every kind of thought possesses its own distinctive colour and lineal pattern, depending upon the vibration-rate of the vitality that informs it. Lustful, angry, loving, ambitious, avaricious, idealistic thoughts have each their own vehicle or thought-form. The problem of the magician is how to animate these thought-forms and project them into the minds of others in order to bring about desired results. The answer no doubt lies in the same direction as the animation of god-forms practised by the ancient Egyptians.

One of the more curious types of occult force is the phenomenon known as the POLTERGEIST, a German word meaning a noisy ghost. The poltergeist is held responsible for violent disturbances such as the throwing about of furniture, the sudden and unaccountable falling of mirrors, breaking of windows, smashing of crockery; all without any evident agency or purpose. In many of the cases so far documented, the afflicted household includes an adolescent, which suggests that the poltergeist is a dynamic reflex of superfluous sexual energy.

These invisible forces sometimes manifest themselves in the form of ECTOPLASM extruded from the human body. This is usually emitted from peculiarly constituted individuals while in a state of trance or other abnormal condition. Ectoplasm is a substance resembling gelatinous vapour, repellent to sight and touch. Spirits are alleged to use it as a basis for materialization, and no doubt sometimes do so, and the results have been photographed. Such photographs have been submitted as proof of the existence of disembodied spirits, but the image impressed on the plasm being human in form may merely imply the existence of the astral double, if not of some projected and substantiated thought-form of the medium, or one of her clients.

On the other hand, subhuman forces occasionally project their emanations into the ambience of humanity by means of ectoplasm, in which case the substance throws off an odour of badly smelling drains. Arthur Machen, who had profound insight into the darker phases of occultism, describes in his horror story *The Novel of the Black Seal* the intrusion into everyday life of hideous occult forces that manifest through the ectoplasmic emissions of an idiot.

Demons

This is a very different matter from actual POSSESSION, examples of which occur in VOODOO and in primitive societies in other parts of the world. In medieval Europe mental disorders were usually attributed to possession by demons, and a service of exorcism was the cure. Belief in demons and witches was widespread, and the fate reserved for those convicted of witchcraft or trafficking with demons was burning at the stake, as in the case of Joan of Arc, who refused to admit that her spiritual contacts were demonic. At the same time, the mysteries of demonology were explored, its territories mapped out and its denizens explicitly identified.

The word 'demon' has come to mean a malevolent entity, bent upon the destruction, or at least the harassment, of humanity (see illustration, page 18), But the word comes from the Greek *daimon*, which meant any spirit, good or bad, and some of the celebrated manuals of demonology treat of both good and evil spirits.

Many of the grimoires, or magical textbooks, contain extensive lists of spirits, which are allotted to distinct hierarchies of kings, dukes, princes, prelates, marquises, and so on. The *Lemegeton*, or *Lesser Key of Solomon*,

Eva C. producing ectoplasm

lists the names, functions and visible appearance of the seventy-two spirits which King Solomon sealed up in a brass vessel because of their inordinate pride. According to one tradition, he deposited the vessel in a deep lake in ancient Babylon, and soon afterwards the Babylonians, thinking to discover great treasure, retrieved the vessel and broke open the seal. Out flew the spirits, with their legions following them. They were all restored to their original abodes in the spirit world with the exception of Belial, who entered a certain image and uttered oracles whenever sacrifices were offered to it.

It was soon discovered that demons conform to laws as definite as those which govern human actions. Magicians claimed to understand these laws and proceeded to evolve rites accordingly. In a sense, the initiated medieval magician was a scientist: his laboratory was the magic circle; his appliances were the magical instruments which he had fashioned according to rules based on a precise canon derived from constant intercourse with denizens of transmundane spheres.

No demon could be evoked with impunity unless it was confined to the 'triangle of art', which was traced outside the magic circle that protected the magician. He stepped out of it at his peril. If through vanity or the promised satisfaction of earthly desires he was persuaded to quit his circle, obsession or sudden death would be the consequence. No sooner had the demon's blandishments proved successful than the alluring shape would dislimn, and in its place, mocking the magician, would appear the outward form of the weakness that had caused his undoing.

This belief that the demon objectivized some inner quality of the operator makes it possible to recognize this type of magic for what it really was – a system for the control of consciousness. Modern research has shown that the brain is divided into specific regions which govern specialized forms of activity. The stimulation of a particular zone produces specific experiences and sensations. When the magical formulae of the grimoires are understood in this light, there emerges a logical method for evoking latent powers of consciousness that are transmitted through obscure regions of the brain. By a skilful use of odours, sounds, colours, and other sensory stimulants, magicians were able to tap these regions. The symbols, seals and personal monograms of the demons, which the grimoires supply, are not mere decorative designs but vectors of occult force potent to animate the entities which they represent. K. G.

(See also RITUAL MAGIC; TRANCE.) (Further reading: *64, 85, 102, 161, 189, 273, 307, 311, 421.*)

From left Margaretta, Leah and Kate Fox, the originators of modern Spiritualism

Spiritualism

The belief that it may, under certain circumstances, be possible to communicate with the surviving personalities of deceased human beings has been held or at least entertained in most of the societies of which we have records. In some societies such communication has been put upon a systematic footing, usually through the agency of shamans, seers, or other peculiarly gifted persons, and has come to play a prominent part in religious belief and medical practice (see *143, 270*). The modern Spiritualist movement, which dates from 1848, has thus many parallels and many predecessors. (On the history of modern Spiritualism, see *59, 221, 368*; for contemporary Spiritualism, see *16, 17, 277, 350*.)

What distinguishes modern Spiritualism from its analogues is perhaps most of all the directness of its appeal to *evidence*. The spirits of the departed, manifesting through persons whose unusual capabilities make them 'mediums' of communication between this world and the next, are required first of all to prove their identities by giving correct information about their earthly lives and concerns. Their credentials being thus established by satisfactory evidence, it is held that their statements about their present (post-mortem) situations and prospects, and about religious matters in general, can be accorded a corresponding weight. In short, Spiritualists take evidence that the 'communicators' are the persons they purport to be as grounds justifying acceptance of the teachings delivered by these same communicators. It is for this reason that Spiritualists so often claim that theirs is a religion based on science. Moreover scientific (or, as detractors would

say, pseudo-scientific) statements concerning the process of communication, the nature of the next world and the composition of the human psyche frequently occur in the communications themselves.

It is customary to divide the ways in which spirits, purportedly, communicate through mediums into two broad classes, 'physical' and 'mental' (see also MEDIUMS). This classification is not altogether satisfactory, but for present purposes it will serve. The phenomena of physical mediumship, or at least some of them, are closely similar to certain occurrences reported in POLTERGEIST cases, and it was out of what appeared at first sight to be just another poltergeist case that the modern Spiritualist movement arose. Towards the close of 1847, a Methodist farmer named J. D. Fox moved with his wife and daughters Margaretta (aged fourteen) and Catherine or Kate (aged twelve) into a small wooden house in Hydesville, New York State. For several months the Foxes' new home was disturbed, particularly at night, by inexplicable noises, mostly raps and bangs, which often kept the whole family awake. At the end of March 1848, the noises became especially troublesome, and the family concluded that the house was haunted. One night little Kate, listening to the raps, suddenly exclaimed (or so her mother's testimony avers), 'Do as I do', and began to clap her hands. The raps imitated the pattern of the handclaps. Mrs Fox then began to question the unseen rapper by means of a primitive code. 'He' replied that he had been murdered in the house and was buried in the cellar. The Foxes called in various of their neighbours. The noises continued and the rapper inti-

mated that he had been murdered for his money by a previous occupant of the cottage. Mr Fox subsequently stated that in the summer of 1848 he did in fact unearth some human remains from the cellar.

The noises went on for several months. Margaretta Fox then went to stay with a married sister in Rochester, New York State, and Kate went to friends at Auburn, not far from Rochester. Rappings broke out at both these places, and large numbers of people came to hear them. The rappings gave messages supposedly from deceased friends and relations of persons present, and claimed that a new revelation was at hand. Furthermore they spread by a kind of contagion. Persons who came to witness the phenomena would find similar phenomena breaking out in their own homes. The Fox sisters and other mediums began to give public demonstrations, and sometimes to charge fees. The phenomena received a good deal of attention in the press, and within two or three years were to be found over much of the United States. Soon they were exported to Britain and Europe in the demonstrations of itinerant mediums.

Spirit Materializations

At the same time there appeared other varieties of mediumship, and by about the mid-1850s Spiritualism had assumed very much the form it still retains. Among the commonest physical phenomena were instances of TELEKINESIS – the paranormal movement of objects and items of furniture in the vicinity of the medium. The most extraordinary telekinetic effects ever reported are perhaps those which occurred in the presence of the famous medium D. D. HOME. Home often produced phenomena in fair light, and raps and object-movements were instrumentally recorded by the celebrated chemist Sir William Crookes (1832–1919), who took a keen interest in Spiritualism.

Object-movements, though sometimes spectacular, did not constitute an efficient means of communication; but fresh means of communication developed out of them in a somewhat indirect manner. One of the oddest features of the telekinetic phenomena which occurred in Home's seances was that supernumerary hands were sometimes observed carrying them out:

All our fourteen hands [wrote one witness] were on the table, when a hand, delicate and shadowy yet defined, appeared, dancing slowly just to the other side of the table and gradually creeping up higher until, above the elbow, it terminated in a mist. The hand slowly came nearer to Mrs. — at the right side of the table, and seemed to pat her face. 'Could it take a fan?' cried her husband. Three raps responded 'Yes,' and the lady put her fan near it, which it seemed to be trying to take. 'Give it the handle,' said her husband. The wife obeyed, and it commenced fanning her with much grace. 'Could it fan the rest of the company?' someone exclaimed, when three raps signified assent, and the hand, passing round, fanned each of the company and then slowly was lost to view (59).

Now, if spirits can, in favourable circumstances, 'materialize' hands which can produce physical effects, why should they not, under optimum conditions, materialize vocal organs with which to speak, or indeed complete corporeal anatomies? Both these developments are alleged to have taken place quite early in the history of the Spiritualist movement, and a body of received tradition has subsequently grown up concerning the mechanism by which such phenomena are brought about. It is commonly alleged that physical mediums are persons whose organisms contain abundant supplies of a fluidic substance known as ECTOPLASM. Under certain circumstances ectoplasm is supposedly extruded through the orifices of the body. It can then produce telekinetic effects, and can be moulded by the spirits to form the surrogate vocal organs, hands, limbs and bodies which are utilized at DIRECT VOICE and materialization seances. In many direct-voice seances spirits speak with the ectoplasmic vocal organs into speaking trumpets provided for the purpose by medium or sitters. These trumpets serve both to 'concentrate' the ectoplasm and to magnify the voices. They move round the room from sitter to sitter, the spirits allegedly manipulating them by means of ectoplasmic rods.

The idea that ectoplasm or 'power' may become concentrated in enclosed dark spaces is widespread, and in sittings for 'full-form' materializations it is customary for the medium to sit either inside or else immediately in front of a small curtained-off recess called a 'cabinet'. Indeed, direct-voice and materialization mediums commonly work in darkness or very dim light, it being widely claimed that light, especially short wavelength light from the blue end of the spectrum, damages the delicate ectoplasmic structures. This circumstance has often led critics to allege that all the phenomena of these classes are fraudulently produced. Spiritualists would probably reply that while there have undoubtedly been many instances of barefaced fraud, not all the reported phenomena of direct voice and materialization can be so explained. For example, the physicist Sir William Barrett (1845–1925), one of the founders of the Society for Psychical Research, thus describes part of a sitting with Mrs Etta Wriedt, an American direct-voice medium:

. . . one of the electric lights over our head was left on to illuminate the room. We sat on chairs adjoining each other; I sat next to Mrs. Wriedt and held her hand. Miss Ramsden sat on my left. We asked Mrs. Wriedt to let us try in the light first, and at her suggestion Miss R[amsden] held the small end of a large aluminium trumpet to her ear; the larger end I supported with my left hand. My body therefore came between the trumpet and the medium. I had previously looked into the trumpet, which was perfectly bare and smooth. Presently Miss Ramsden said she heard a voice speaking to her, and entered into conversation with the voice. I only heard a faint whispering sound, but no articulate words. To avoid the possibility of Mrs. Wriedt being the source of the whispering, I engaged her in talk, and while she was speaking Miss Ramsden still heard the faint voice in the trumpet, but begged us to stop speaking, as it prevented her hearing distinctly what the voice said. Miss Ramsden assured me afterwards that there could be no doubt whatever that the voice in the trumpet was independent of Mrs. Wriedt, and I can testify that I watched the medium and saw nothing suspicious in the movement of her lips. She did not move from her place, and no accomplice or concealed arrangement could possibly have produced the voice (334).

Miss Ramsden added a note detailing the

Sir William Crookes

(evidential) message which she received. J. Arthur Findlay (1883–1964) gives the following account of his first sitting with John Sloan (1870–1951), a non-professional direct-voice medium:

. . . suddenly right in front of my face a strong voice spoke to me. 'Yes, who are you?' I enquired, to receive the answer:

'Your father, Robert Downie Findlay.'

The voice continued speaking . . . 'I am very sorry I did not take you into my business. I would have liked to do so but Kidston opposed it. If you had been with me it would have greatly eased my life, as I found business a great strain on me. David Kidston is standing beside me and would also like to talk to you about this matter.'

Then a voice claiming to be that of David Kidston spoke, saying:

'I am David Kidston. I was wrong opposing your coming into our office. I am sorry I did it but now you need have no regrets. I am glad to get that off my chest at last.'

That was all true, but only my father, myself and Kidston knew about it . . . (154)

Findlay was so struck by this message that he had a further thirty-nine sittings with Sloan in the next five years. He satisfied himself that Sloan was not responsible for the voices which were heard, sometimes two or three simultaneously, at the sittings. Voices continued to come from the trumpets whilst Findlay had his ear to Sloan's mouth. Findlay subsequently became one of Spiritualism's best-known proponents.

In recent years physical mediums of all kinds have become very scarce.

A materialization

Clairvoyant and Trance Mediums

By the early 1850s various kinds of 'mental' mediumship had become an established part of the Spiritualist scene. This development represented a grafting on to the nascent Spiritualist movement of factors and phenomena which had already attained some prominence in the 'mesmeric' movement of the preceding half-century (see HYPNOSIS). Many mesmerists claimed to have found subjects who, when in the 'mesmeric trance', would exhibit 'clairvoyance' and other paranormal powers. These subjects might, for instance, allegedly read the contents of sealed packages, correctly visualize distant scenes, and even seem to themselves to be present at those distant scenes ('travelling clairvoyance'). Some mesmerists were prone to explain these phenomena on the supposition that during the mesmeric trance the soul is partially freed from the body, and when thus unencumbered by the flesh may exercise 'higher' faculties not ordinarily within its reach.

Now if the soul can indeed be detached from the body and in that condition exercise clairvoyant faculties, two questions naturally arise. (a) Can souls thus partly emancipated become aware of, and perhaps communicate with, other and more fully emancipated souls, namely those who by death have freed themselves from the body for ever? (b) If, during the mesmeric trance, a mesmeric subject's soul is partly freed from his body, might it be possible for the soul of some other person, especially a deceased person, to assume control of that body and thus communicate with those still on earth? A number of mesmerists believed themselves to have observed phenomena of class (a) and a few believed themselves to have observed phenomena approximating to class (b). The early Spiritualist movement to a large extent took over the theoretical framework and the repertoire of phenomena of this part of the mesmeric movement. The theoretical framework has been much modified since that time, but the phenomena of 'mental' mediumship may conveniently be considered under headings corresponding to (a) and (b) above.

(a) Much the commonest form of mediumship in contemporary Spiritualism is that of the 'clairvoyant' who believes himself or herself to have supernormal awareness of deceased persons. A demonstration of 'platform clairvoyance' is the centrepiece of most Spiritualist meetings and church services. The clairvoyant (unlike the original mesmeric clairvoyants) is usually not entranced, or at least only partly so. He claims to be able to 'see' (CLAIRVOYANCE) and 'hear' (clairaudience) deceased friends and relations of members of the audience. He gives descriptions of them and relays messages from them. In favourable instances both may be exceedingly accurate. Something of the flavour of

The Rev. Stainton Moses

such demonstrations may be obtained from the following verbatim transcript:

Medium . . . See, a boy comes in your surroundings. He looks to me to be about 17 or 18, and I think there will have been a good deal of sorrow over the passing away of this boy. A lady brings this boy, and she wants the parents to know about him. Whether he passed away in weakness or not, I don't know. He is a very beautiful boy; she is telling me that it is Herbert Ernest. There is somebody belonging to him called Seth. I cannot get along with it. Do you know anybody called Seth and Mary that had a boy called Herbert Ernest Hobson?

Answer You are right, friend.

Medium They want you to know.

Right in the corner there [pointing]. I don't know what to make of this at all. It is a youth, I should take him to be about 18. There is a gentleman with this youth; and I have a very curious feeling. I rather think this youth will have been killed from shock. Now he comes and shows me. He is without jacket, and his clothes are covered with colour. He is holding out his hands and there is a reddish dye on them. He may have worked in a dye works. I feel I would fall over. He may have met with his death in a dye works. It is Mrs. Miller's boy, William Henry Miller; lived in Valley Place, and I think he would be killed in a dye works. Not more than four or five years ago, as far as I can see in the surroundings. This gentleman comes with him. He is Henry Mitchell, and he used to belong to Yeadon. He is helping the boy forward.

(*All correct, except that Henry Mitchell is unrecognised. Mr. Holden, my informant, knew William Henry Miller. Leg hurt at dye works, blood poisoning, died about 1911. Valley Dye Works.*)

Answer I know this man (*221*).

(b) The most spectacular forms of mental mediumship are those in which the medium's body, or part of it, is purportedly 'controlled' by a discarnate person and used for the purpose of communication. When part of the body is controlled we have such phenomena as automatic writing and automatic speaking; when the whole body is controlled we have what on the face of it is total POSSESSION by a spirit. Automatic writing has been a vehicle by which spirits have not just ostensibly communicated, giving correct information about their earthly lives, but have transmitted detailed and often lengthy accounts of the next world and its occupants, together with ethical and theological teachings. The most famous of such writings are perhaps those of the Reverend W. Stainton MOSES (1839–92), a British clergyman whose *Spirit Teachings* (1883) has been many times reprinted and is often referred to as the 'Bible' of Spiritualism. Another considerable class of automatic writings is that of historical romances written ostensibly under the influence of some deceased person possessing special knowledge of the events concerned. *The Scripts of Cleophas* (1928), *Paul in Athens* (1930), and *When Nero was Dictator* (1939), produced by Miss Geraldine CUMMINS, are celebrated examples (see also AUTOMATISMS).

Mental mediums whose normal personality is liable to be displaced completely by that of the purported controlling spirit are commonly referred to as 'trance' mediums, though in point of fact trance may be a feature of almost any kind of mediumship. The term is, however, appropriate in that such mediums commonly pass into a trance before the controlling spirit 'takes over', and also very commonly have afterwards no memory of what took place during the period of control. It is impossible here to enter into the many fascinating problems raised by this form of mediumship, or to give an account of its many famous practitioners. A brief resumé of the career of one of the most celebrated, and also one of the most carefully investigated trance mediums, Mrs Gladys Osborne LEONARD, who died in 1968, will serve as an illustration.

Mrs Leonard's childhood, according to the account in her autobiography *My Life in Two Worlds*, 1931, was marked by various visionary experiences which she kept from her parents. She discovered her mediumship in her early twenties when she passed into a trance whilst engaged in 'table-tipping' with some friends. Her principal 'control' and so-called 'guide' was a self-styled Indian girl named Feda, who spoke at almost every sitting. Feda would relay messages from deceased friends and relations of sitters. The friends and relations might also speak themselves. Feda took a keen interest in the various scientific investigations of Mrs Leonard's mediumship, and tried in several ways to demonstrate that she and the other communicators were not just secondary personalities of Mrs Leonard's built up with the aid of information obtained telepathically from the sitters. To this end she cooperated in various 'book tests' – attempts, often strikingly successful, to read designated pages and lines in books not ordinarily accessible to the medium – and in a considerable number of 'proxy' sittings: sittings, that is, in which the sitter tries to obtain messages for an absent third party of whose concerns he knows little. Here is a summary of three proxy sittings

had with Mrs Leonard by Mrs Lydia W. Allison of the American Society for Psychical Research on behalf of a fellow American, 'Mr Blair'. Mrs Allison gave Mrs Leonard (as was customary) a small article belonging to the late Mrs Blair to hold.

A curious feature of Mrs Leonard's mediumship was that although she did not sit in darkness, a 'direct voice' (or rather whisper) would sometimes join in the conversation at a sitting, frequently prompting Feda in an appropriate fashion. The whispers appeared

Summary of Sittings

Feda	*Annotations by Mr. Blair*
This lady (Mrs. B.?) died in the prime of life.	She was 37 years of age.
She was not fussy or shouted much.	She was a woman of strong but restrained character. Correct as stated.
She had an exhausted feeling at death. It happened within 5 days. Until the illness came she had a strong constitution.	She had been well for the greater part of her life.
Before she died he (Mr. B.?) tried to do something on a Monday. He did not succeed. He tried to see important people but failed. H. and M. are the letters connected with them.	I returned home on the Monday before Mrs. Blair died. I found her seriously ill. We went to a specialist that day and a minor operation was performed without beneficial results. Later I called in Dr. M. and wanted to get a Dr. H., but didn't. We have three daughters.
Her thoughts go to a man and her daughter. She is anxious to get in touch with F.B.	My initials.
This man (F.B.) has something to do with an office.	I am a lawyer and of course have an office.
This lady's ancestors were not ordinary people.	The Lorens – my wife's folks – were definitely not ordinary people. She had some outstanding ancestors.
She speaks of a Charlie.	Her brother.
He (F.B.) is closely linked with a big institution.	I am Director of Works in my State.
He's been doing something special lately, signing his name, something big.	The oath of office of Director of Public Works is signed in a large book in the Comptroller's office. I signed it.
He is at the top of this institute, a leader.	See previous remarks.
He was photographed much and didn't like it.	The press took pictures of my being sworn in by the new Comptroller and I didn't like it.
He's had special unusual clothes lately.	I think this refers to my honorary degree. I dressed up in an academic cap and gown.
He has lots of people before him. They listen to him like the Day of Judgment. They want his opinion.	See previous remarks.
He has something to seal.	Seals are relevant to a lawyer's business.
Is he fond of music?	Doubtful.
He has at last realized what we both talked over together so often.	Correct.
He has got more money lately but is careless about it.	There has been a more or less favourable turn in some of my investments. I do not think about money – probably not as much as I should.
He was doing something big connected with a platform.	The honorary degree was conferred on a platform.
Was he connected with invalids or cripples in some big way?	I am a Trustee for a hospital for crippled children (*10*).

Spiritualism

to come from the air in front of the medium. They were heard by a number of competent investigators.

Both Mrs Leonard and an equally celebrated earlier trance medium, Mrs Leonora E. PIPER (1857–1950) of Boston, Massachusetts, would, upon awakening from their trances, sometimes ostensibly recall having been in the other world and having spoken with its inhabitants. On some occasions information was obtained about deceased persons which apparently could not have been known to the mediums by ordinary means.

The Teachings of the Spirits

So much by way of a brief account of the types of phenomena which, Spiritualists hold, justify us in accepting the alleged communicators at face value, and in according a corresponding weight to their moral, theological and cosmological teachings. What of the teachings themselves? Critics of Spiritualism often allege that the teachings given through different mediums diverge so widely that it is not possible to extract any coherent picture from them, but this is an exaggeration. There is a detectable 'main stream' of thinking in Anglo-American Spiritualism and within it the particular differences between the doctrines propounded through different mediums are outweighed by the generic similarities. French Spiritualism, following the tradition of 'Allan KARDEC', differs from Anglo-American Spiritualism primarily in its espousal of reincarnationist doctrines, and this form of Spiritualism has become established in South America: Brazil is reputed to have a higher percentage of Spiritualists in its population than any other country. However, in recent years Anglo-American Spiritualism has shown some signs of making concessions to reincarnationism, by admitting, for instance, that reincarnation may take place in some cases.

The 'main stream' of Anglo-American Spiritualist belief, as represented by Stainton Moses's *Spirit Teachings* or the extremely influential books of J. Arthur Findlay (*151* to *154*), embraces a cosmological picture whose main outlines can be traced back at least to the writings of SWEDENBORG and, according to some, to the doctrines of the Neo-Platonists. A distinction is commonly made between body, soul and spirit. The soul is a duplicate body, made of rarefied matter or, as is often said, matter at a higher rate of 'vibration' than the matter known to physical science. The soul is the lodging-house of the spirit, or animating intelligent principle, and soul and spirit together survive the death of the earthly body. Thus upon 'passing over', you find yourself still possessed of a substantial

A 'home circle' seance in London

body. You also find yourself amid scenery similar to, though generally more beautiful than, that which you knew on earth. The next world contains houses, hills, books, flowers, waterfalls, food, and every other kind of material object. Like the soul, these surroundings are composed of matter at a high rate of vibration, and they can actually be moulded by your thoughts and wishes. It is, however, incorrect to talk of *the* next world. There are said to be a number of such worlds, arranged as it were in a series, and the keynote of the teachings is that one *progresses* from the lower to the higher 'spheres' as one advances in knowledge and in moral qualities. The spheres were originally thought of as encircling the earth one above the other like the successive layers of an onion; but nowadays they are more commonly supposed to interpenetrate each other but to exist at different rates of vibration. The occupants of the spirit spheres are generally pictured as engaged in worthy tasks – study, discussion, assisting the newly arrived 'dead', guiding persons still on earth – or in tranquil but enjoyable recreations. There is no 'judgment of the dead', but persons who have led evil lives will find themselves drawn into squalid and degrading regions where others like them dwell and from which they may need to be rescued by 'higher' spirits dedicated to missionary work.

These 'cosmological' teachings are com-

monly presented together with moral teachings of a liberal and progressive but hardly novel kind. God is frequently referred to and his beneficence is much dwelt upon; but he is rather a background to the teachings than a part of the cosmological scene. Christ is often held to be human rather than divine, an exemplar rather than a redeemer. Spirits have sometimes expressed political views of an advanced kind, and in the 19th century Spiritualism was often linked with socialism. Several short-lived Socialist-Spiritualist communities were set up.

Organized Spiritualism

It seems likely that at the present day interest in Spiritualism, as in so many other unorthodox religions, is growing. However, figures quoted by G. K. Nelson (*350*) rather suggest that membership of Spiritualist organizations is declining. Thus a leading British Spiritualist organization, the Spiritualists' National Union, had 19,003 Church members in 1950, but the number had sunk to 14,662 in 1964. Nation-wide Spiritualist organizations, to which a large number of Spiritualist Churches affiliate themselves, have by and large had only a limited amount of success. G. K. Nelson suggests that this is because 'Spiritualism is dependent upon mediumship and shamanship and consequently takes the form of a movement rather than an organization, a movement dependent upon the renewal of charismatic leadership, which would be stifled by the growth of routinization.' There are a good many local Spiritualist churches, and informal Spiritualist groups, which are not affiliated to any national organization, and derive most of their inspiration from some outstanding medium or other leader.

The S.N.U. recognizes seven principles to which all members must subscribe. These are as follows:

1 The fatherhood of God
2 The brotherhood of Man
3 The communion of spirits and the ministry of angels
4 The continuous existence of the human soul
5 Personal responsibility
6 Compensation and retribution hereafter for all the good and evil deeds done on earth
7 Eternal progress open to every human soul

Somewhat similar, but rather lengthier, principles are adhered to by the National Spiritualist Association of America, while the Greater World Christian Spiritualist League requires its members to affirm their belief in principles referring to the 'leadership' and 'redemptive power' of Jesus Christ.

The largest unitary Spiritualist organization in the world is said to be the Spiritualist Association of Great Britain, which has its headquarters in Belgrave Square, London. It has a membership of about 7,000. There are no branches. Members are not required to subscribe to any creed, and the Association concentrates upon providing seances, demonstrations, lectures and a wide selection of Spiritualist literature.

In concluding this brief survey, one comment may be in order. Critics often make out their case by concentrating on the seamy or absurd side of Spiritualism – on instances of proven fraud or on the reams of rubbish purportedly emanating from the spirits of Shakespeare, Benjamin Franklin and other deceased notables. But this procedure is quite futile, for the problems raised by the more strikingly 'evidential' cases remain as intractable as ever. On the other hand, the best cases cannot be properly assessed in isolation. There is a continuum between the best cases and the worst, and the intervening region is filled with communications in which striking hits may be combined with palpable absurdities. Spiritualists are apt to accept the hits while explaining away the absurdities. Contrariwise, more moderate critics seem to feel that the absence of any discontinuity between almost completely convincing cases and much less convincing ones suggests that whatever explanations in the way of TELEPATHY between

medium and sitters, unconscious dramatization by the medium, and so on and so forth, are applicable to the latter must also be applicable to the former, and must accordingly vitiate the claims of even the most plausible communicators. Each party is able to interpret the phenomena in the terms it favours, and it is not easy to see any way of deciding who is right. A. G.

(See also APPARITIONS; PARAPSYCHOLOGY; TRANCE.) (Further reading: see references in the text; on the problem of survival, see also *25, 130, 206, 346.*)

Spontaneous Psi Experiences

The general category of experiences in which the mind obtains information through means other than the known senses, or produces effects without the use of the muscles, not satisfactorily explainable in terms of imagination, fantasy or delusion, and occurring naturally and unplanned (as distinct from,

for example, experiences under experimental conditions or at seances); they include the seeing or sensing of a ghost or apparition, premonitions and hunches, sudden and mysterious 'awarenesses', true DREAMS, and apparently uncaused movements of objects: see APPARITIONS; PARAPSYCHOLOGY.

S.P.R.

The Society for Psychical Research: see PSYCHICAL RESEARCH SOCIETIES.

Sri Yantra See YANTRA.

Ely Star

The pseudonym of Eugène Jacob (1847–1942), French astrologer, quack doctor and seller of magical amulets; author of *Les mystères de l'horoscope*, 1887; he was a member of MATHERS's Ahathoor Temple in Paris.

Rudolf Steiner (1861-1925)

Rudolf Steiner, the founder of the Anthroposophical Society, was born at Kraljevic,

Rudolf Steiner

Rudolf Steiner

Steiner

which was then in Austro-Hungary and is now in Yugoslavia. Steiner's father was a railway employee, and the family spent Steiner's childhood moving up and down the Austrian railway system until finally settling near Vienna so that the son could go to the Technische Hochschule in 1879. Soon after this move Steiner met a rustic herbalist named Felix Kogutski, whom he greatly admired as a possessor of traditional wisdom. In Vienna, Steiner met the influential Theosophist Friedrich Ekstein and through him was introduced to the circle of Viennese idealism which was presided over by Marie Lang and whose young lions used to surround Eckstein, the politician Victor Adler and the writer Hermann Bahr in the Cafe Griensteidl on the Michaelerplatz. Through Eckstein and his friends, Steiner was introduced to mysticism and the textbooks of Theosophy; but at the same time he became friends with the feminist Rosa Mayreder and concerned in progressive social thought. He also fell heavily under the spell of Goethe, and in 1883 was invited to edit Goethe's scientific writings for the standard edition. In 1890 the young academic left Vienna to work at the Goethe Archive at Weimar, bearing with him not only the academic training which was to earn him a Ph.D. next year at Rostock but a mass of general knowledge accumulated during the days in Vienna when he had taken tutoring jobs to pay his way.

In Weimar he continued his work on Goethe and published several books of philosophy. In 1897 he moved to Berlin and became editor of the *Magazin für Literatur*. Steiner rapidly became a figure of note in the intellectual and socially-concerned world of the capital. He lectured at the Berlin Worker's School and was concerned with the Free Literary Society. He formed a friendship with John Henry Mackay, a half-Scots, half-German anarchist of some notoriety, who had admired Steiner's book *The Philosophy of Freedom*. When Steiner married the widow Anna Eunicke – with whom he had lodged at Weimar – in October 1899, Mackay was the witness. This first marriage of Steiner has given rise to all sorts of accusations and counter-accusations, but what is certain is that it was not a success, and that Steiner's wife left him in 1906. When she died in 1911 the lunatic fringe of the occult press spread rumours that Steiner had 'strangled her astrally'.

About the time of his marriage to Frau Eunicke, Steiner's interests returned to the mystical preoccupations which had formed part of his education in Vienna. Such occult interests were the rule rather than the exception in the idealistic and reforming circles in which Steiner lived, and the movement of the Herr Doktor from Rostock towards the THEOSOPHICAL SOCIETY should cause little surprise. Steiner's case is very like that of Annie BESANT, and his conversion from Goethe-specialist to prophet of esotericism was complete by the time his first wife left him. The transitional period 1900–6 was marked by the increasing ascendency over Steiner of Marie von Sivers (1867–1948), a Baltic Russian and frustrated actress, who was present as a keen Theosophist at the second lecture-series Steiner gave under the auspices of her society.

This took place in the house of Count and Countess Brockdorff, the leaders of the Berlin Theosophists. In 1899 Steiner had taken his first step into esotericism by expounding the occult significance of a story by Goethe. In 1900 he lectured on 'Christianity as a Mystical Fact'. Two years later Steiner and Marie von Sivers travelled to London to the conference of the Theosophical Society, and about this time Steiner was induced by the Brockdorff group to apply for a charter for a new German section of Theosophists. He also delivered a lecture on 'Monism and Theosophy' to a group organized to study the theories of the biologist Ernst Haeckel: this he was later to regard as the basic lecture of his emerging 'spiritual science'.

Anthroposophy: 'Man-Wisdom'

It is obvious that Steiner brought into the Theosophical Society, which derived its teachings from a mixture of Hinduism, Buddhism and European occultism, a mind completely at variance with much of what the Society stood for. Although his acquaintanceship with Theosophy in Vienna and his knowledge of the esoteric sources of Goethe had prepared him for Theosophical doctrines proper, he was out of sympathy with much of what passed for 'occultism' in those regions. Steiner himself claimed that he had entered the Theosophical Society because it was the only group at the time 'in which there was present a real spiritual life'. He cannot wholly be acquitted of the charge of joining the Theosophists in order to take them over. In any case there was bound to be friction between Steiner's supporters and the old guard of German Theosophists, who had allowed their original impetus to decline but resented the intrusion of the new man. One determined opponent of Steiner was Franz HARTMANN, a Theosophist of unsavoury reputation. The old guard and the Steinerites contrived to live and let live until 1912, when two causes contributed to a split. Steiner expelled from the German Theosophical Society an occult adventurer and charlatan called Hugo Vollrath, who

was a disciple of Franz Hartmann; and at the same time became disillusioned with the growing power of Annie Besant's grotesque Order of the Star in the East, the organization which was founded to propagate the cult of the coming Messiah, Jiddu Krishnamurti. In 1913 most of the German Theosophists broke away and followed Steiner into his new Anthroposophical Society.

Between 1902 and 1913 much had happened in the development of Steiner's thought. He steadily built up a personal following and really established himself with a lecture-series delivered in Paris in 1906. This series was given at the same time as the Theosophical conference and attracted more attention than the official events. It had originally been intended to give the cycle in Russia, but because of the revolution of 1905, most of the support obtained by Marie von Sivers for Steiner's ideas was found among the exiles. At the 1906 series were present such literary figures as Dmitri Merezhkovsky and Zenaida Hippius, and the influence exercised by Steiner over the Russian intelligentsia dates from this event.

In the same year Steiner accepted a charter from an occult organization of doubtful provenance, the O.T.O., or Order of the Temple of the Orient. This licensed him to work a lodge of the Order with the name of the Mysteria Mystica Aeterna. Steiner claimed that his motive was to achieve some sort of 'apostolic succession' and that he never intended to 'work in the spirit of such a society'. The O.T.O. practised sexual magic, and Steiner's numerous opponents later used this incident to attack the Anthroposophists. It is very unlikely that Steiner adopted the O.T.O.'s sex practices, but it is probable that he nursed the ambition of creating a large occult federation, based on the structure of the 'Rosicrucian' societies allied to the O.T.O. At the same time, these studies probably gave him the impulse to construct his own form of Rosicrucianism which embodied meditational exercises of an unspecified sort (see ROSICRUCIANS).

Steiner's 'Rosicrucianism' was, like his 'Theosophy', a personal creation. He took over from the Theosophists the notions of KARMA and REINCARNATION, mingled them with elements of European occultism, and added much of Goethe and a new Christianity of his own invention. The resulting Anthroposophy – 'man-wisdom' as opposed to the 'God-wisdom' of Theosophy – provided the solution to artistic, political and social problems.

The sign of the Rosicrucians: an interpretation by Steffi Grant (see page 218, and compare plate, page 120)

236

FORMULA OF · · ZOS · VEL · THANATOS

The source of all these revelations lay in Steiner's 'spiritual perception'. He claimed to have developed his clairvoyant faculties early in his Vienna period, but later connected the technique with Goethe's method of immersing himself in the essence of things. As a man developed his 'spiritual eyes', the beings of higher worlds would make themselves known and he would advance in knowledge. Steiner also seems to have used his clairvoyant faculties in the manner of a medium, to give comfort to possible supporters. Not only could he clairvoyantly obtain perceptions of truth to guide his flock, but he was able to use his supernatural senses to scan the past and write the history of ATLANTIS and LEMURIA. This was very much in the tradition of H. P. BLAVATSKY, with the difference that Steiner saw man as evolving, not forwards but *back* towards a lost divine condition. The ascent towards perfection was impeded by two powers to which Steiner gave the names of Lucifer and Ahriman. Lucifer is pride and self-sufficiency, while Ahriman is the material world. This conception probably stems from Gnostic and Zoroastrian sources, on which Steiner is said to have worked about 1906.

Gradually the figure of Christ assumed a central place in Steiner's world view. He thought the coming of Christ to be the equivalent on a cosmic scale to the effect produced on the individual by initiation into the MYSTERY RELIGIONS: to return man to a consciousness of his divine origins. He envisaged a complex process occurring in the universe which he called the 'etherization of the blood'. In the individual human being this affected the bloodstream around the region of the heart, turning it into 'etherized blood'. When the individual had obtained a correct understanding of Christ, this etherized blood mingled with that of Christ, present in the Cosmos. From Steiner's Christology sprang a sub-group of the Anthroposophical Society called the Christian Community. In 1921 several of Steiner's disciples approached him with the request that he construct a rite for those of his followers who were Christians. The result was 'The Act of the Consecration of Man' and the group was placed under the direction of the Protestant pastor Friedrich Rittelmeyer. The Christian Community has recently had close ties with the Iona Community.

The Anthroposophists soon had branches all over the German-speaking countries, and after the First World War established themselves in Britain. Almost until his death, Steiner continued to pour forth a torrent of

Austin Spare's Formula of Atavistic Resurgence (see page 225)

words in exposition of his ideas. It is not entirely because so many of his published works represent unedited lecture-notes that they give the impression of lacking content. Steiner could not stop talking: his revelations are couched in such an excess of language that it is difficult to escape the conclusion that he was a prophet by inner compulsion. There were Anthroposophical precepts for medicine, farming and physical culture. Today the Society runs clinics and a mental hospital, and has marketed a cancer-cure. Medicine is based on magical ideas: syphilis is seen as a punishment for lack of affection. Anthroposophical farming has been highly successful, and is now in vogue, as it is based on 'bio-dynamic' principles which forbid chemical fertilizers and recommend planting crops according to the phases of the moon. Through Marie von Sivers – whom he married secretly in 1914 – Steiner developed a system of 'eurhythmy' which has had considerable influence in schools.

Education and Art
The field in which Anthroposophical doctrines have been most successfully applied, in fact, is that of education. As a private tutor and later as a lecturer, Steiner had great experience in this field, and although his principles were based on his occult theories, these were not allowed to obscure the realities with which he was familiar. 'We can awaken what is in the child,' he wrote, 'but we cannot implant a content in him.' And: 'We must know on what part of the human being we have especially to work at a certain age, and how we can work upon it in the proper way.' Such principles – whether occult or not – made Steiner a notable figure among progressive educators just after the First World War, and in 1962 there were over seventy schools run on Anthroposophical lines throughout the world.

Steiner's theories of colour and proportion, derived from Goethe and a long line of metaphysical speculation, had an influence on several artists and architects of the day. Kandinsky and Jawlensky attended his lectures, and Mondrian treasured his writings. Steiner's principles of architecture were embodied in the two Goetheanum buildings which his society erected at Dornach in Switzerland. The Anthroposophists were refused permission to build in Munich, and moved across the border. The first Goetheanum was designed by Steiner and built of the same combination of woods that is used in making a violin. It consisted of two domed structures, the larger slightly bigger than the dome of St Peter's, and was highly inflammable. On New Year's Eve 1922–3, an arsonist set the nearly completed building on

fire, to the great delight of Steiner's local opponents. The second Goetheanum, almost as remarkable, is constructed of concrete.

The Threefold Commonwealth
The viciousness of the campaign against Steiner was not only that of bigotry and intolerance. It was to a large extent the outcome of the conspiracy-theories which dominated German politics after the defeat of the First World War. The legend of the 'stab in the back' which gained currency was combined with the fear-engendered vision of a Jewish–Bolshevik conspiracy. For various reasons, occultists and secret societies were implicated in the conspiracy myth from the start. Rivalries and fears complicated the issue, and eventually most occult groups were regarded as part of the plot against society. Steiner was said to have mesmerized his supporter General von Moltke during a visit he paid to him in 1914, and rendered him militarily incompetent. The burning of the Goetheanum and the ferocious opposition to Steiner in Germany after 1918 were in part connected with anti-Semitic phobia.

Steiner did not improve matters by himself making a bid to enter politics. In the confusion of 1919 he produced a theory of society, which he called the 'Threefold Commonwealth' and which was derived from the 19th-century French occultist Saint-Yves d'Alveydre. He and his supporters formed organizations and founded newspapers to publicize the idea; and the book embodying the theory sold in massive quantities. Anthroposophists approached political figures about an alliance with Steiner. But this was trespassing on the ground of certain irrationalist politicians who were hoping to capitalize on the confusion on their own account, and merely intensified the campaign against the Anthroposophists.

Steiner died in 1925. At the very least an interesting thinker, and certainly an influential one, he may easily be overestimated in a brief analysis. Summarized, his thought and his achievement seem more cogent than they really are. Rambling and diffuse, Steiner's writings are largely disappointing. The very fact that something can be extracted from them will continue to persuade some people to make the effort, and although Anthroposophy will probably never regain its earlier popularity, the work of Rudolf Steiner has produced tangible results. It is more than can be said of most occultists. J. W.

(See also GERMAN OCCULT GROUPS.) (Further reading: numerous books by Steiner are published by the Rudolf Steiner Press, including *Occult Science: an Outline, The Course of My Life, Christianity as Mystical Fact, The Threefold Commonwealth, The Philosophy of*

The first Goetheanum, destroyed by fire, and *right* the one that replaced it

Spiritual Activity, Knowledge of the Higher Worlds and Its Attainment; see also *439*.)

Stella Matutina

The Order of the Morning Star, an offshoot of the GOLDEN DAWN. Dion FORTUNE, Israel REGARDIE and W. B. YEATS were members, as was E. Nesbit, the writer of children's stories. It became dormant in the mid-1930s: for its connections with Rudolf STEINER, see GERMAN OCCULT GROUPS. (*235*)

Stigmata

Wounds or marks on the body corresponding to the wounds suffered by Christ on the cross, in the hands, feet and side; stigmatics may also bear the bruise on the shoulder caused by carrying the cross, rope-marks on the wrists and ankles, the marks of scourging and those of the crown of thorns on the forehead. St Francis of Assisi and some 300 other persons of sanctity are alleged to have received the stigmata, but the Roman Catholic Church, from whose ranks practically all stigmatics have come, has long adopted an extremely cautious attitude to the phenomenon. The general modern tendency is to attribute the stigmata and other curious physical phenomena of mysticism to auto-suggestion. The most famous stigmatics of this century have been Teresa NEUMANN and PADRE PIO. (*303, 443, 457*)

Stonehenge (in Modern Occult Theory) See DRUIDS; GLASTONBURY ZODIAC.

Subtle Body See ASTRAL BODY; ETHERIC BODY; YOGA.

Subud

The movement founded on the teaching of Mohammad Subuh Sumohadiwidjojo, known as Bapak (Indonesian for 'Father'). His mission began in 1925 when, as a clerk in the municipal treasurer's office in Semarang, Java, he underwent a transforming experience. He was walking home one evening when a ball of light descended from the sky and entered his body through the top of his head. Afterwards he felt purified and in possession of a new power. He decided to transmit his newly acquired force to others, and a brotherhood was formed. After the war it was brought to England and adopted enthusiastically by a group of GURDJIEFF's

A stigmatized hand, and stigmatic tears of blood on Teresa Neumann

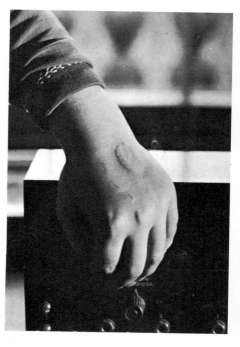

followers. Since then it has gained a following all over the world.

Initiation takes place through a process known as 'opening', during which the 'contact' is transmitted to the initiate by one or more members of Subud who are specially authorized. The operation consists of the candidate simply standing for about half an hour with his 'openers' and allowing the 'Life Force' to enter him. Subsequently he attends regular half-hourly sessions of what is known as the latihan (Indonesian for 'exercise'), which are intended to increase the force. A practitioner of Subud, J. P. Barter, describes the process as follows (*22*): 'The force flows to the different parts of the body-mind, purging them of the effects of past error and past evil. The process can be felt and observed. As with other forms of purging, the purifying action is not always pleasant. After the latihan the body and the mind feel healthier and more calm. A sort of resurrection has taken place. At the same time, gradually or not according to the person attending the latihan, a new being or self is born.' C. M.

(See also LATIHAN.) (Further reading: *22, 349, 403, 472*.)

Sufis

The mystics of Islam; see MEDITATION. Small groups devoted to Sufism in the West have recently been formed. 'Sufism Re-oriented' is an organization of followers of MEHER BABA. (*349*)

Summerland

The name coined by Andrew Jackson DAVIS for part of the spirit world, a 'blissful land of rest and harmony, partly a creation of the

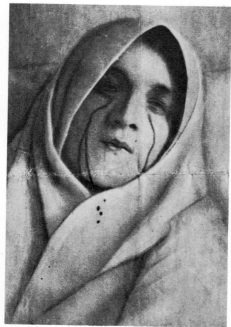

Emanuel Swedenborg

inhabitant's own desires, but to what extent we cannot determine' (*48*).

Montague Summers (1880-1948)

The author of numerous books on witchcraft, demonology and allied subjects; he also edited translations of many of the classic works in his field, including the *Malleus Maleficarum* and books by Boguet, Guazzo, Remy and Richard Bovet. His firm, almost medieval, belief in the reality and powers of the evil forces about which he wrote – he publicly advocated the reintroduction of the death penalty for witchcraft – makes his books unfashionably credulous, but they are valuable collections of source material. He was also an authority on the history of the stage. (*50, 52a, 195b, 302, 392b, 441 to 443b* inclusive)

Superstitions See LUCK.

Survival of Death See APPARITIONS;
MEDIUMS; PARAPSYCHOLOGY; SPIRITUAL-ISM.

Emanuel Swedenborg (1688-1772)

The Swedish philosopher, scientist, mystic, prophet and visionary, an important influence on modern occultism, SPIRITUALISM and, by way of JUNG, on psychology, through his claim to have been in touch with the dead and with higher planes of being. He saw mysterious flashes of light, heard otherworldly conversations and dreamed strange dreams, and eventually in visions 'heaven was opened to him', as he said, and he conversed with angels and spirits, recording his observations in several weighty books. He appears to have had clairvoyant powers (see PHYSICAL POWERS). The Church of the New Jerusalem, or Swedenborgian Church, was founded after his death. Andrew Jackson DAVIS, the leading theorist of Spiritualism in its early days, claimed that during a trance in 1844 the secrets of the universe were revealed to him by three spirits, one of whom was Swedenborg. (For his influence, see *493*.)

Synchronicity

Synchronicity is an 'acausal connecting principle', in the words of C. G. JUNG, who devised the term. That is to say that the idea of synchronicity can be used to link a series of events which seem to be connected, but about which there is not sufficient evidence to place them in a relationship of cause and effect. For example, if two people discovered that they had a series of chance encounters in the street – different streets, but always outside a house with a green front door – there would be no possible way in which evidence could link with certainty the greenness of the front doors and the nature of the meetings. All that could be said is that there seemed to be an inexplicable connection and that it appeared unlikely that the green front doors actually *caused* the encounters. It could then be said that here was a case of synchronicity. The word means 'occurring at the same time'; and one way of explaining the process is to imagine that the series of chance encounters and the appearance of green front doors take place as the result of some much larger process – even of a cosmic order – which cannot be apprehended. Put symbolically, it is as if a large cosmic hand fitted itself into a glove composed of the elements of the physical world and waggled its fingers. The action of the thumb produces the meetings in the street, while the little finger somehow associates these with a by-product of its own activity – an incidence of green front doors.

Jung published his own exposition of synchronicity in 1952, basing his argument on material derived from ASTROLOGY. He used a batch of 180 horoscopes of married couples which had been collected some years previously for astrological purposes. Jung knew that attempts by astrologers to show significant statistical proof of their methods had not been successful, but allowed that it was 'just conceivable' that astrology might rest on a causal basis. But from his study of the horoscopes he was convinced that there was a definite connection between the traditional astrological correlations and the lives of his subjects. The chances against this were huge: as Jung wrote, 'You take matchboxes, put 1,000 black ants in the first, 10,000 in the second and 50 in the third, together with one white ant in each, shut the boxes and bore a hole in each of them, small enough to allow only one ant to crawl through at a time. The first ant to come out of the boxes is always the white one.'

To account for this remarkable result, Jung developed the idea of synchronicity, of which he found traces in magical and esoteric writers. The connecting principle must lie in the '*equal significance* of parallel events'. Synchronicity might extend its workings to the inner world of man. 'One and the same (transcendental) meaning might manifest itself simultaneously in the human psyche and in the arrangement of an external and independent event.' J. W.

(See also I. CHING.) (Further reading: *256e, 258.*)

T

Talisman An object charged with occult power: see LUCK; RITUAL MAGIC.

Tantrism

Tantrism is claimed by its exponents as the oldest of Indian religions, long antecedent to all the others in the subcontinent, and also unequalled in the beauty and sublimity of its teachings. The claim to priority can be disputed, but there can be no doubt that it is one of the most unusual cults ever conceived. Though its underlying philosophy has a large element that is indistinguishable from orthodox Hinduism and Buddhism, the greater part of its doctrines and practices are anathema to the devout.

The sources of Tantrism are obscure. In one tradition it originated outside India, in a region somewhere in the north-west, near Afghanistan, or further north in a place known by different names, such as Urgyan, Uddiyana, Shambhala and Agharta, around which fabulous legends have grown. Some of the distinguishing features of Tantrism are also found in Chinese Taoism, and existed in China long before the Buddhist conversion of that country, so that some hypothetical area between India and China might be accepted for the present as the original location of the cult. A hoary tradition survives in India about this mysterious region of Uddiyana, which produced its own semi-mythical rulers and its beautiful princesses, and the extraordinary rites of sex mysticism to which they were devoted. One of Tibet's greatest adepts, Padma Sambhava (fl. A.D. 750) was a native of this land who came to India, taught at a Tantrik university in Bihar, and then journeyed to Tibet to found a famous school of philosophy based on Tantrik principles.

Historically, the first reliable evidence of Tantrism as we know it today is traceable to the 8th century A.D., by which time the identification of the cult as a 'Chinese-way' was already well established. Many aspects of Tantrism have Chinese affinities. In India it was first taught and practised in certain border districts, in areas along the foothills of

the Himalayas, and in Bengal and Assam, and teachers like Padma Sambhava carried its doctrines to Tibet, Nepal, Bhutan and Sikkim. In the middle of the last century a handful of English savants studied the Tantrik cult and published some of its scriptures. Ignored by more conservative scholars, the new discovery was exploited to the full by esoteric organizations. In Western occultism the Tantrik religion as such, with its Hindu background and the Tantrik gods, has been largely discarded, but its rites and practices have been adapted to suit the Western milieu. Tantrism as found in the occult schools of Europe and America today consists of a medley of Middle Eastern, Central Asian and Chinese elements added to its essential Indian core, and may be further garbed in the various forms adopted by the ROSICRUCIANS, the HERMETICA, Freemasonry and the CABALA.

Warp and Woof

The chief deity in Tantrism is the female principle, personified as the goddess Shakti. Her name means 'Power', and she stands for the primal energy underlying the cosmos. She has many forms, some of benign aspect, such as Parvati, goddess of beauty; and others fierce, like the goddess Kali, who is depicted with a garland of skulls around her neck, a bloodstained sword in her hand, and her lips red from drinking the gore of her many human victims. The consort of Shakti is Shiva, and these two, Shakti and Shiva, together form the cosmos: he representing the constituent elements, she the dynamic principle that causes these elements to function. But the dominant one of the two is always Shakti, for she alone charges the universe with all the potencies inherent in it. A Tantrik saying goes, 'Shiva without Shakti is a corpse.'

The writings in which the doctrines of this cult are embodied are known as the Tantras, a name derived from a word meaning 'loom', suggestive of the two principles, male and female, that comprise the warp and woof from which the fabric of the universe is woven. They are often set in the form of a dialogue between Shakti and Shiva, in the course of which the teachings are expounded. Much of the teaching is concealed in a secret 'twilight' language, ostensibly meaning one thing, while actually signifying another. Tantrik texts are open to evaluation at more than one level. The truths are never clearly written down, but hidden under an almost impenetrable veil. Secrecy enhances the beauty of Tantrism, which is meant only for the true devotees of the doctrine. Other religions, they say, which expound their lessons without symbolism are like harlots who

expose their persons to all and sundry, whereas Tantrism is like a virtuous wife who reveals her beauty only to her lawful husband.

According to Tantriks, each age has its specific scripture, and while the orthodox Hindu scriptures, the Vedas, were appropriate for the earlier ages, they are quite irrelevant to the present age. Historic time can be measured in recurrent phases of four aeons, or *yugas*, which succeed one another in endless rotation, with a world-wide cataclysm bringing the cycle to an end, after which it starts again. The first is a Golden Age, when men are long-lived, beautiful to look at, and without envy, malice, guile, pride, hatred, cruelty and lust. The next three ages, ending with the Kali Yuga or Black Age, see a successive decline in the vitality and moral qualities of mankind. At present we are living in the Kali Yuga, the fourth and terminal phase, which began five thousand years ago and is now nearing its climax. It is a time of violence and strife, of degeneration and moral decay. It is a time when youth no longer respects its elders, and when elders are no longer worthy of respect; when no value is placed on marriage vows, social contracts, personal obligations and duties, and there is a universal preoccupation with sensual indulgence and material gain. Homosexuality and perversion are rife, and men and women of high moral calibre are rare, and when found are mocked. Man has become like the *pashu*, or animal.

For this age, the older Vedic scriptures are obviously of no use. Material desires must be met; physical appetites must be appeased; sexual urges must be satisfied. But there is a correct method of providing for these wants. Man's activity in this direction must be ritualized, and sensual passion and sexual gratification elevated and transformed into an act of worship. The gross satisfactions of the flesh are appropriate for the pashu herd, but the Tantrik must offer the tokens of his senses to the divinity as a sacrament.

The Rite of Maithuna

The rites involved in Tantrism include magic circles (MANDALAS), spells (MANTRAS), gestures (mudras), breath control (pranayama), internal alchemy (rasavada), physical culture, heliotherapy or obtaining vigour through worship of the sun, the activation of the CHAKRAS or subtle centres of the body, and the use of bells, incense, and the other paraphernalia of the occultist's craft. All this is interwoven with antinomian practices, for the Tantrik places himself above the conventional law. What others condemn, he assumes as a badge of nobility. What poisons others, nourishes him. What sends the herd to hell, ensures his salvation. Hence prohibited acts are used as the rungs of the ladder by which he ascends to the heights: alcoholic liquor must be drunk; meats like beef, taboo to the Hindu, must be eaten; forbidden sexuality like incest and adultery must be practised.

One rite in particular covers all these requirements, for here all the social prohibitions are contravened. Called *chakra-puja*, 'circle-worship', it is usually performed in a special ritual chamber. As the participants enter the chamber, each woman takes off her bodice and deposits it in a box which is kept in the custody of the guru. At the end of the preliminary ceremonies each man picks a bodice from the box, and the woman to whom it belongs becomes his *shakti* or partner for the rest of the rite, even if that woman is his sister or his mother. The men and women squat in a circle on the floor, each man's partner seated on his left. The circle forms a living mandala in which the divine energy of the goddess becomes manifest, and it is from this circle that the rite gets its name. In the centre of the circle sit the guru and his shakti, in some cases a nude girl, representing the goddess. Alternatively, a drawing of the *yoni* or female sex organ is made in the middle of the floor, again designed to represent the goddess, since she is the presiding deity of all Tantrik rites, and her symbol, either a living representative or a symbolical drawing, must be present.

The participants now join in a sacramental meal consisting of wine, red meat, fish and dry cereal cake, followed by *maithuna* or sexual intercourse, each with his allotted partner. In Sanskrit the terms for these five elements all begin with the letter *m*, and the partaking of these 'five *ms*' constitutes the Tantrik sacrament. The rite of maithuna has a sublime significance in Tantrik philosophy, and in Buddhist Tantrik paintings and sculptures the gods and goddesses of the pantheon were sometimes depicted in a variety of sexual postures symbolizing the divine union.

The pre-eminence of the female is everywhere stressed in Tantrism. One of the reasons for the Tantrik claim to superiority, in fact, is this higher status assigned to women in their cult, as compared with the inferior rating of women in Hinduism and Buddhism. Every man's female partner in religious rites is a representative of the goddess, and therefore referred to as a shakti, for man is incomplete in himself and needs the female to assist in his physical and psychic integration. Women are the way to salvation. One Tantrik text states, 'Women are the deities; women are life; women are ornaments. Be ever among women in thought.'

During the ritual act of maithuna, according to the Tantriks, a woman gives off a certain vital element. Taoists also recognized this in their concept of YIN as embodied in the female, which they called *khuai*. When

A practitioner of Tantrism

sexually excited, women are thought to send forth tumultuous tides of energy, but this is normally dissipated and is of no use to the man unless it can be channelled and utilized. The virtues given off during the period of female sexual desire are greatly intensified during her orgasm, when there is a sudden release of this energy, both physical and magical. But here again it is of little value to the man unless he knows how to make use of it. The powerful current can also prove detrimental to him, for a woman during the process of invagination magnetically receives the male organ, his seed and his psychic power at the same time. Women are natural psychic sponges who drain a man of his energy whenever he has intercourse with them.

Tantrik Techniques

Many Tantrik sex techniques have therefore been evolved to prevent this loss, and are concerned with the conservation of the sex fluids and their utilization for magical ends, and the attainment of spiritual enlightenment by this means. There are many variations: a special method of *coitus reservatus* in which the man does not ejaculate, but takes in the energy from the woman each time she has an orgasm; intercourse in which the man intrajaculates – that is, directs the ejaculation into himself, at first by perineal pressure and then by will power; normal ejaculation followed by drawing up the seed, along with the female secretions, into himself, and in all cases sending the seed upward, for it is believed that whoever gives an upward flow to the stream becomes immortal.

The techniques involve certain seemingly improbable methods known collectively as the *oli* techniques, such as vajroli, sahajoli, and amaroli, all variant modes of absorbing the seminal essence after ejaculation. Proficiency in this is acquired by long and difficult exercises for muscularizing the urethral passage and training it in upward peristalsis. These are combined with breathing exercises, and the ejaculated sperm is drawn up again and absorbed into the system. The Chinese Taoist practitioner of similar methods used them at group orgies, having intercourse with a number of women and 'inhaling' with his penis their expended orgasmic 'breaths'.

The proper performance of the rite of maithuna is in Tantrism one of the chief aims of life, and can be a means of spiritual emancipation. Because of the natural antagonism which it might evoke in those ignorant of its true meaning, and the dangers inherent in its indiscriminate practice, maithuna was taught with great secrecy. To the Tantrik, ignorance is not intellectual stupidity but spiritual obtuseness, and true knowledge lies in the realization of the sacred truths of his religion. Man is placed in a physical environment so that he may make use of it and benefit by the opportunities for advancement that it provides. He is given sensual appetites for the furtherance of his spiritual needs. The soul can only be saved through the body; that is why the soul has been provided with a physical vehicle in which its emancipation may be achieved. In reality, there is no antagonism between spirit and body, and for those who know how, the body can be made to serve the spirit.

The ancient precepts of renunciation have been completely misunderstood by orthodox ascetics, so the Tantriks maintain. The principle underlying abnegation was valid only insofar as it implied a restraint on the expenditure of the male fluid. A Tantrik text says, 'The seed must not fall. The falling of the seed leads to death. The keeping of the seed is life.' The loss of semen is considered detrimental to all bodily, mental and spiritual powers, for semen contains the life force; it is the source of energy from which the spirit receives its sustenance. Semen stored in the body and properly utilized enhances all one's faculties and gives one great power.

In other words, it is not the sexual climax but ejaculation that devitalizes the body and attenuates the soul. There are practices that produce prolonged orgasm without ejaculation, which are among the secrets of Tantrism and which are likened to ecstatic states of spiritual exaltation. True asceticism merely implies the building up of sexual tension, and then directing the built-up energy into an internal circuit. Sexual desire is progressively heightened in Tantrik rites and thus, empowered by restraint, becomes a perennial fount of energy.

An important and indeed essential element in all Tantrik practice is the guru or preceptor, without whom, it is believed, the teachings cannot be acquired. His guidance is necessary during the training in physical exercises and sex techniques. Even with the most precise written directions the pupil can proceed only so far, as it is virtually impossible for him to know whether he is carrying out the exercises as required. Many of the exercises are not only difficult but physically hazardous. Any undue haste, a wrong interpretation of the instructions (which in any case are set down in coded form), the absence of a guide at critical moments, can lead to psychic disaster and might mean the difference between sanity and insanity, or even life and death. One student practising pranayama, breath control, lost the natural rhythm of his respiration. His reflexes went out of control and he gasped like an asthmatic, struggling for breath till he nearly suffocated. His guru was hastily summoned and helped him, but it still took several weeks for him to return completely to normal. Apart from physical training, there is the communication to the initiate of the secret cult mantra, or spell. The vibrations of this mantra, it is said, penetrate the meshing of the physical body and reverberate in the ASTRAL BODY, and can only be communicated by the living voice of the guru. B. W.

(Further reading: *41, 110, 263, 385a, 426, 485, 486.*)

Tarot

The Tarot pack is probably the ancestor of our modern packs of playing cards and, like them, can be used for games and for fortune-telling (see CARDS). Occultists, however, see in the Tarot, and especially in the twenty-two cards known as the 'major trumps', something far more important than a mere set of emblems for diversion or divination. The Tarot is thought to embody a complete symbolic system which is a key to the mysteries, which holds the secret of the true nature of man, the universe and God. All sorts of influences – Cabalistic, Hermetic, Gnostic, Neo-Platonic, Cathar and Waldensian – have been discerned behind the cards, and it has been suggested that they originated in China or India, were brought into Europe by the gypsies, or were devised by a conference of cabalistic adepts in the year 1200. Many occultists like to believe that the Tarot is a compendium of the arcane wisdom of ancient Egypt, a notion which derives from Antoine Court de Gébelin (1725–84), a French scholar and Freemason who investigated the pack at a time when fascination with all things Egyptian was very much in the air.

The fact is that the early history of playing cards is impenetrably shrouded in obscurity, and nobody really knows when, where, how or why the Tarot came into existence. Some magnificent Tarot cards believed to have belonged to a pack made for the mad King Charles VI of France in the late 14th century are still preserved, and there are several 15th-century examples of packs of cards designed to instruct and elevate as well as to amuse. An Italian pack attributed to Andrea Mantegna, for instance, has fifty cards, representing ten conditions of man, Apollo and the nine Muses, the ten sciences, the three cosmic principles and the seven virtues, the seven planets and the three spheres of the fixed stars, the Prime Mover and the First Cause. You were apparently intended to play a real game with these cards but they were also an educational device, showing the order and construction of the universe. Correctly arranged, they formed a 'symbolic ladder leading from Heaven to earth', but every ladder runs two ways and, reading from bottom to top, the cards showed that 'man may gradually raise himself in the spiritual order' (*425*).

The same thing may be true, and is certainly accepted by occultists as true, of the early Tarot itself, though its emblems, unlike those of the 'Mantegna' pack, do not fit readily into any simple or orthodox scheme. There are, in fact, several varieties of Tarot pack, with different designs and different names for the suits and trumps. What is now accepted as the standard pack has seventy-eight cards. The minor cards, or 'lesser arcana', consist of four suits of fourteen cards each – king, queen, knight, page, and the ten down to the ace. The suits are Swords (the Spades of an ordinary pack), Cups (Hearts), Wands or Staffs (Clubs) and Coins or Pentacles (Diamonds). It has been suggested that these suits represent four sacred objects of the Grail legends – respectively the sword, cup, lance and dish. Much more attention, however, has been paid to the twenty-two extra cards, the major trumps or 'greater arcana'. Their correct order is disputed but they are usually listed as:

0   The Fool
1   The Juggler
2   The Female Pope
3   The Empress
4   The Emperor
5   The Pope
6   The Lovers
7   The Chariot
8   Justice
9   The Hermit
10   The Wheel of Fortune
11   Strength
12   The Hanged Man
13   Death
14   Temperance
15   The Devil
16   The Falling Tower
17   The Star
18   The Moon
19   The Sun
20   The Day of Judgment
21   The World

Modern adepts, including A. E. WAITE and Aleister CROWLEY, have produced Tarot packs of their own, altering the older designs in the interests of what they took to be the 'correct' symbolism. Probably the best-known pack, which is unfortunately singularly ugly, is the one designed by Pamela Colman Smith under the direction of A. E. Waite.

The Major Trumps

There are many different systems of interpreting the cards – Christian, gypsy, Jungian, Theosophical, Hermetic or Cabalist. Their richness of symbolism and suggestion is such that no two observers are likely to gain exactly the same impressions from them,

and most students of the cards might agree that 'it may be that the deepest occult wisdom of the Tarot cannot be put into words at all ... in the end, the seeker is told only what he cannot find for himself' (*192*). Certainly the cards have a powerful fascination, a sense of some hidden and ultimately unfathomable mystery, an ability to open 'magic casements' in the mind.

The fact that there are twenty-two trumps has been a major factor in riveting attention on them, for in cabalistic numerology twenty-two is the number of 'all things', the entire universe, and the trumps are assigned to the twenty-two letters of the Hebrew alphabet and to the Twenty-Two Paths, which are lines drawn on the Tree of Life of the CABALA, connecting the sefiroth together. In this form the trumps, paths and letters provide a plan of the construction of the universe and display both the emanation of

From a Swiss pack: 'The Juggler'

the universe from God and, in reverse order, climbing the Tree, the mystical road to union with the divine or the magical route to supreme power, the ascent by which man makes himself God.

Complicated systems of CORRESPONDENCES have been worked out, which link the trumps and paths with planets and zodiac signs, pagan deities, animals, plants, colours, precious stones, magical weapons, perfumes, geometric figures, and images, all of which are intended to express and illuminate the meanings of the cards themselves (an extensive system of this sort will be found in

Crowley's *Magick* and *777*). Modern cabalistic interpretations also bristle with erotic symbolism. What follows is necessarily a very brief and rough indication of some of the principal ideas connected with the Tarot trumps in various systems of interpretation.

An early French version of 'The Fool'

0 The Fool. The placing of this card is one of the chief problems of the Tarot, but if put at the head of the trumps it can be related to the hidden godhead of the Cabala, the ultimate source of all existence, the nothing from which everything proceeds: it is also man carried to the highest power, and the Fool's folly is a divine madness.

1 The Juggler (or Magician, Magus). The creative will of both God and man, the First Cause, the erect phallus: the infinite: unity and activity, the union of opposites: the Logos or divine Word, the life-giving Spirit of God hovering above the waters of chaos at the outset of creation.

2 The Female Pope (or Pope Joan, High Priestess). Woman, duality, the balance of opposites, the gateway of the Temple, the threshold of the Mysteries: the divine Thought, the spiritual Mother and Bride, the goddess Isis, the Virgin Mary: the *gnosis* or 'knowledge' of the divine: the unconscious mind: the soul; the Jungian archetype of the *anima*.

3 *The Empress.* The divine evolving from infinite to finite in the creation of the universe: the fecundity and teeming life of nature, the Mother Goddess, the fruitful Earth impregnated by the Spirit: Venus, beauty, desire, pleasure, the earthly paradise.

4 *The Emperor.* The male principle corresponding to the Empress: God or man imposing form and order upon chaos: virile energy, intelligence and authority: the guardian of the Grail: reason, intellect: temporal power, leadership, government.

5 *The Pope* (or High Priest, Hierophant). Spiritual authority and power: traditional teaching, orthodox religion on its 'outer' side, the Church: the channel of divine grace, the bridge between God and man, the revealer of sacred things: the keys of heaven and hell, the knowledge of good and evil: inspiration.

6 *The Lovers* (or Marriage). Adam and Eve, the gulf between God and man crossed through the creation of humanity in God's image, and conversely the crossing of the abyss between man and God: the union of opposites, love bringing unity, the two sexes transcended: innocence, free will, temptation: the choice between good and evil.

7 *The Chariot.* Triumph, mastery: 'he is conquest on all planes – in the mind, in science, in progress, in certain trials of initiation . . . He is above all things triumph in the mind' (*483*): the vision of the Chariot in Ezekiel, Chapter 1: the dominance of animal passions, or dominance through the animal passions: the union of the sexes, the balance of opposites: God or man as master of the lower world: Plato in the *Phaedrus* pictured the soul as a charioteer (reason), driving two horses (the bodily passions and higher emotions).

8 *Strength.* Both Waite and Crowley transpose this card with Justice: force, occult power: ecstasy: self-confidence, the confidence of those whose strength is in God: the higher nature taming the passions: Crowley's formula of 'the Beast conjoined with the Woman'.

9 *The Hermit.* Wisdom, prudence, the Sage, the Adept: the attainment of the truth within oneself: isolation, self-reliance, uninvolvement with the world outside: the man who finds his way by the divine light in his own soul, and who is also a beacon to others: austerity, silence, conservation of spiritual energy.

10 *The Wheel of Fortune.* The cosmic rhythms of life and death, growth and decay, in their ceaseless ebb and flow: time, fate, KARMA, actions have consequences, 'as a man sows, so shall he reap': movement and stability: reincarnation, and liberation from it.

'The Wheel of Fortune' from an Italian pack

11 *Justice.* Balance, equilibrium, the cancelling out of warring opposites: purgatory: a new beginning, a state of passivity in which the true self is conceived: divine justice, the weighing of the heart in the ancient Egyptian judgement of the dead.

12 *The Hanged Man* (or Judas). The most famous and enticingly mysterious of the trumps: sacrifice, martyrdom: in terms of erotic symbolism, the 'death' of orgasm, through which new life is created: the death of the outer self preceding the emergence of the true self: 'after the sacred Mystery of Death there is a glorious Mystery of Resurrection' (*483*): the Messiah: the dying and rising god: the 'vivification of nature by an exterior, spiritual agency' (*290*): water, the depths of the mind: the Norse god Odin hanging in agony on the World Tree.

13 *Death.* Change, transformation, passage from one spiritual condition to another: death and new life: connected with 'raising the dead to life' in terms of phallic symbolism: the death of the old self, the 'old Adam', leading to rebirth in the Spirit: destruction and creation as part of one process: the manifestation of the divine on the physical plane: renewal of life, reincarnation: the dark night of the soul.

An Italian card representing 'Death'

14 *Temperance.* Inspiration flowing from above: the descent of the Spirit into matter and conversely the soul mounting from a lower plane to a higher: the combination of active and passive forces, the union of positive and negative, male and female, spiritual and material: spiritual healing, the flow of vital force from the healer: 'if attention is directed to the unconscious the unconscious will yield up its contents, and these in turn will fructify the conscious like a fountain of living water' (*256c*).

15 *The Devil.* Lust: pride, ambition: unbridled passions: mastery in this world: power misused, nature red in tooth and claw, the god Pan: the animal nature of man: evil, black magic, the choice of the wrong path: the goat of the witches' sabbath, the Baphomet of the Templars: Lucifer as both fallen angel and light-bringer: temptation: the 'dweller on the threshold', a personification of the evil in oneself.

16 *The Falling Tower* (or Tower Struck by Lightning, Tower of Babel, House of God). Confusion, ruin, the fall of man, the expulsion from paradise: the destruction of false doctrines and mistaken attitudes: discipline, cruelty, pain: sexually, a symbol of ejaculation.

17 The Star (or Sirius, Dog-Star, Star of the Magi). Hope: the water of life, new life: expectation, the shining possibilities of the future, what is potential rather than actual: intuition: the gifts of the Spirit: youth and beauty: truth in the soul.

18 The Moon. Danger: terrors, illusions and abominations in the fluid depths of the mind: dreams, fantasies, the imagination: light penetrating darkness in the mind, the dissolution of accepted ideas and accustomed habits of thought: initiation, the forming of the solid from the nebulous, the child in the womb: fear of the path into the unknown.

19 The Sun. Enlightenment, freeing the mind from conventional wisdom, orthodox ideas, petty concerns and worries: the magician begins to soar towards the sun: identification with the One Life of the universe: man as a little child, in the sense of innocence and simplicity – 'a little child shall lead them'.

20 The Day of Judgment. Renewal: desire, spiritual or sexual, and the 'lower' nature rising in response to it: yearning, aspiration, longing for betterment: death and resurrection, life gained through the transformation of man's earthly nature: 'we can rise from the grave of our old dead self even now . . . if our ears are not deaf to the trumpet call from on high' (*290*).

21 The World. Joy: release, the entry into the world of the spirit: the ASTRAL PLANE: conversely, as the last of the trumps, the world as it is, earthly existence, the flesh and the senses.

A card designed by Aleister Crowley

The Tarot in Divination

Besides being used as objects of meditation and guideposts to the mystical and magical paths, the Tarot cards are also employed in fortune-telling. The same rules and methods apply as in divination with ordinary playing cards. The following is a brief list of meanings frequently attached to the cards, varying according to whether the card falls the right way up or 'reversed', upside down.

Suit of Cups

King An influential man of good character, responsible, helpful; a business or professional man. (Reversed: a dishonest man; injustice; loss.)

Queen A good wife and mother. (Reversed: an untrustworthy woman; vice; a rich marriage.)

Knight A romantic young man; a visitor or a message. (Reversed: a rogue; cunning, trickery.)

Page A handsome boy or pretty girl; news. (Reversed: seduction; deceit.)

Ten Happy marriage and family life; friendship. (Reversed: quarrels.)

Nine Contentment, satisfaction. (Reversed: loyalty.)

Eight Modesty, good temper. (Reversed: happiness.)

Seven Fantasies. (Reversed: desire; determination.)

Six Fond memories. (Reversed: an inheritance.)

Five A disappointing inheritance. (Reversed: a reunion.)

Four Sadness. (Reversed: a new relationship.)

Three Abundance. (Reversed: an achievement; excess, an orgy.)

Two Love, romance, friendship. (Reversed: passion.)

Ace Love and joy. (Reversed: change, instability.)

Suit of Wands

King A prosperous, honest man; a countryman; a good marriage; good news. (Reversed: good advice.)

Queen An affectionate, honourable woman; business success. (Reversed: deception, trickery.)

Knight An impetuous young man; separation; a departure. (Reversed: quarrels, a parting.)

Page A faithful lover or reliable messenger. (Reversed: bad news, indecision.)

Ten Burdens to carry, oppression, difficulties. (Reversed: difficulties.)

Nine Strength, resilience. (Reversed: ill luck, adversity.)

Eight Falling in love; a journey. (Reversed: jealousy.)

Seven Success. (Reversed: anxiety, indecision.)

Six Good news. (Reversed: fear, a betrayal.)

Five Struggle. (Reversed: disputes, legal actions.)

Four Rest, peace and quiet. (Reversed: prosperity and happiness.)

Three Efficient help. (Reversed: troubles at an end.)

Two Wealth. (Reversed: a surprise.)

Ace A birth, a beginning. (Reversed: a false start; things going wrong, disappointments.)

Suit of Swords

King A powerful, authoritative man; a lawyer or doctor. (Reversed: an enemy; treachery, cruelty.)

Queen A widow; mourning; sterility. (Reversed: an evil woman; hostility; deceit.)

Knight A handsome young man, chivalrous, brave, a very perfect gentle knight; a gallant soldier. (Reversed: rivalry; extravagance.)

Page A lively boy or 'tomboy' girl; watchfulness, spying. (Reversed: prying eyes, surprising news, illness.)

Ten Pain, trouble, sorrow, an ill-omened card. (Reversed: temporary success.)

Nine Death, failure, sorrow, an extremely ill-omened card. (Reversed: fear, doubt; prison.)

Eight A crisis; bad news; scandal; uncertainty; illness. (Reversed: difficulties; an accident, something unexpected.)

Seven Hope; a wish; possibility of failure. (Reversed: good advice.)

Six A journey by water. (Reversed: an announcement; a declaration of love.)

Five Pride and a fall; loss. (Reversed: a funeral, mourning.)

Four A coffin; a will; a retreat. (Reversed: economy, foresight, precautions.)

Three Antagonism, division, separation. (Reversed: confusion, loss.)

Two Trickery. (Reversed: disloyalty, deceit.)

Ace A death. (Reversed: defeat, a broken marriage or engagement.)

Suit of Pentacles

King A successful man; profit in business; courage and intelligence. (Reversed: an old, wicked man; danger, corruption, vice.)

Queen A clever, perceptive, sensuous woman; wealth, security. (Reversed: evil; suspicion; ill health.)

Knight A responsible, proper, perhaps rather heavy-going young man. (Reversed: stagnation, unemployment.)

Page A dreamer; a scholar; a messenger. (Reversed: extravagance; bad news.)

Ten Money, profit; a house. (Reversed: robbery, loss.)

Nine Security, foresight, success. (Reversed: disappointed hopes.)

Eight Profitable work. (Reversed: greed; cunning.)

Seven Money, business, a loan. (Reversed: anxiety about money; impatience.)

Six A gift. (Reversed: greed, jealousy.)

Five Poverty; deception. (Reversed: ruin, waste; troubles in love.)

Four A gift or legacy. (Reversed: uncertainty, delay.)

Three Fame; skill. (Reversed: obscurity; unsatisfactory performance.)

Two A social occasion, cheerfulness, harmony; messages. (Reversed: surface harmony, pretended enjoyment; letters.)

Ace Riches; happiness; the most fortunate of the cards. (Reversed: wealth which corrupts.)

Trumps

0 The Fool. Folly, extravagance, madness. (Reversed: turning away from life, apathy, carelessness.)

1 The Juggler. A man; a choice, a gamble; skill, subtlety. (Reversed: a doctor; failure, confusion; cheating; uneasiness.)

2 The Female Pope. A woman; secrets; wisdom. (Reversed: passion; illicit sex.)

3 The Empress. Creativity, fruitfulness; action, initiative. (Reversed: disagreement, argument; bad health; danger of insanity.)

4 The Emperor. Success, stability, authority; help, protection. (Reversed: obstruction, sorrow; death in battle; serious injury.)

5 The Pope. Assistance; inspiration; religious interests. (Reversed: danger, persecution; weakness.)

6 The Lovers. Love, sex; marriage; a choice, uncertainty. (Reversed: quarrels, divorce; failure; indecision.)

7 The Chariot. Victory, success, fame; travel, exploration. (Reversed: misfortune, bad news; accidents, sudden defeat.)

8 Justice. Balance, harmony; a test. (Reversed: unfairness; legal complications, miscarriage of justice.)

9 The Hermit. Prudence, caution; diplomacy, dissimulation; a guide; old age. (Reversed: secrecy; lies; fear.)

10 The Wheel of Fortune. Good luck, success, wealth; destiny. (Reversed: bad luck, change for the worse; instability.)

11 Strength. Health, strength, courage, dominance; a good woman's influence. (Reversed: tyranny, ill temper; illness, weakness; a bad woman's influence.)

12 The Hanged Man. Sacrifice, suffering; tests; an early death; patience, submission; unconventional behaviour. (Reversed: crime and punishment; pain; selfishness.)

13 Death. Death, destruction; force; change, transformation. (Reversed: a birth; long life; sleep, laziness.)

14 Temperance. Good management; good health. (Reversed: trouble, disputes; poverty; drunkenness; matters connected with priests and churches.)

15 The Devil. Sex; the arts; fate. (Reversed: evil fate; spite; weakness.)

16 The Falling Tower. Ruin, unforeseen disaster, an accident; sweeping change. (Reversed: change for the better; risks.)

17. The Star. Hope, good prospects. (Reversed: failure, bad luck.)

18 The Moon. Fear, darkness, danger; concealed enemies; illicit love. (Reversed: deception; blame.)

19 The Sun. Achievement, prosperity, happiness; a fortunate marriage. (Reversed: obscurity; trouble; a broken marriage or engagement.)

20 The Day of Judgment. Change, a fresh start; a reunion. (Reversed: mistakes, disillusion, suffering, loss.)

21 The World. Assured success; travel. (Reversed: failure, stagnation, despair.)

A preponderance of Cups in the layout is said to mean happiness and good news; of Wands change; of Swords bad luck; and of Pentacles wealth. The cards are often dealt out in the pattern of the Tree of Life (see CABALA), with ten piles of seven cards each. The cards left over are put aside but can be read after all the others if further clarification is needed. The ten piles are taken to refer to: (1) the divine, intelligence, idealism; (2) creative ability, wisdom, matters of fatherhood; (3) knowledge, matters of motherhood; (4) mercy, kindliness, good qualities, virtues; (5) severity, conquest, physical or intellectual strength; (6) sacrifice, health; (7) love and sex; (8) the arts and crafts, children; (9) the imagination; (10) wordly matters, house and home, the body.

A simpler method can be used to give the consulter the answer to a question or advice about a problem. After removing the consulter's card from the pack and the usual shuffling and cutting, the reader turns up the first ten cards. The first indicates the general atmosphere surrounding the question or problem; the second, the forces opposing the consulter; the third, the basis of the present situation; the fourth, an influence that has just passed away or is now passing; the fifth, an influence which may be coming into operation; the sixth, an influence which will come into play soon; the seventh, the consulter's own fears, doubts and negative attitudes; the eighth, the influence of the consulter's family and friends; the ninth, the consulter's ambitions, hopes and positive attitudes; the tenth, the final outcome. R. C.

(Further reading: *82, 85, 99, 192, 290, 338, 382, 383, 483.*)

Telekinesis

Parapsychical movements of objects, frequently associated with MEDIUMS. Tables which tilt, sway about and rap out messages with their feet are familiar examples and there are many reports of the independent movement and even the LEVITATION of tables and other objects, including some extraordinary cases connected with D. D. HOME (see SPIRITUALISM). In Spiritualist theory, the objects are moved by spirits, but PSYCHOKINESIS seems to supply the best explanation of genuine cases.

Telepathy

Direct contact between one mind and another; the ability to sense another person's thoughts and mental states, or to convey your own to other people, without the use of speech, gesture or other physical signalling: see PARAPSYCHOLOGY; TWINS; for its bearing on apparitions and the question of survival of death, see APPARITIONS.

Teleportation

The mysterious transportation of people and things from one location to another; sometimes reported in connection with 'flying saucers' (see SPACE): see APPORTATION.

Theosophical Society

The Theosophical Society was founded in New York on 13 September 1875 by Helena Petrovna BLAVATSKY, Colonel Henry Steel OLCOTT and William Quan JUDGE. It was the successor to an earlier attempt to found an occult group, which Madame Blavatsky had called 'the Miracle Club', and the earliest Theosophists represented various strands of the occultism of the day. There was the spirit medium Emma HARDINGE-BRITTEN, Dr Seth Pancoast of Philadelphia, who was learned in the Cabala and an exponent of colour-therapy, a Portuguese Jew called de Lara, who was probably also acquainted with the traditions of European occultism, and a collection of minor characters. The opening lecture of the new society

Colonel H. S. Olcott

'progressive' circles of Europe and America almost as a universal palliative; for it embodied in one magnificently undefined whole the idealistic aspirations of a large section of the educated or semi-educated classes. These were a hazy desire for a better world, an urgent need to find some substitute for the God whom materialist science was rapidly pushing beyond his physical creation, and a hankering for the realms of magic and mystery which the age of the machine seemed to have abolished altogether. The crisis which present and past changes in society had brought about reached a peak of hysteria some ten years after Madame Blavatsky founded her society in New York. It was the achievement of that remarkable lady to tailor her occultism to the needs of her contemporaries.

Madame Blavatsky

H. P. Blavatsky was born Helena von Hahn in 1831 at Ekaterinoslav in the Ukraine. Her early life has been the subject of constant debate. According to her distant cousin, Count Witte, Helena married Nikifor Blavatsky, the Vice-Governor of the province of Erivan, at the age of eighteen, but left him soon afterwards. She then attached herself to the captain of an English steamer and travelled with him to Constantinople, where she may have worked in a circus until she was picked up by the Hungarian tenor Agardi Mitrovitch. Her activities become increasingly shadowy: she is reported in Paris as the assistant of the spirit medium Daniel Dunglas HOME, and also directed the Serbian Royal Choir. It seems that her well-known hatred of Christianity was deeply founded, for on her own admission she turned up at one of the frequent battles in divided Italy 'to kill Papishes'. With Mitrovitch she lived for a time in Kiev, but was forced to leave after publicly lampooning the Governor-General. On the way to Cairo the ship in which she and Mitrovitch were travelling sank; her protector was drowned, and Madame Blavatsky was marooned in Egypt.

In Cairo, H.P.B. – as her devoted following were to call her – ran faked seances and made experiments with hashish. Her further movements are unclear, until she appears in America at the Vermont home of the two spirit mediums, the Eddys, where she met Colonel Olcott. Olcott was a seeker after occult truth and had arrived at the Vermont farmhouse to report on the Eddys for a newspaper. He was quickly captivated by Madame Blavatsky, whose own occult powers, it appeared, were superior to those of the mediums he had come to investigate. The pair made a study of Spiritualism and established a joint apartment in New York.

was given by an engineer, George Felt, on 'The Lost Canon of Proportion of the Egyptians, Greeks and Romans'.

This eclectic assemblage of occult elements was even further complicated through the addition of Eastern and Spiritualist ideas by Colonel Olcott and H. P. Blavatsky. The society which they founded was to be the chief agent in diffusing occult theory during the last twenty years of the 19th century, and in its origins can be seen clearly how it was to develop. Many small occult bodies originated in the large cities of Europe and America in the same period, for it was the time when the early miracles of SPIRITUALISM and the mesmeric movement (see HYPNOSIS) were giving place to a more ambitious probing of

things unseen. But none of these bodies possessed the remarkable person of H. P. Blavatsky, without whom the unspecific concern of the early Theosophical Society with miracles and mysticism of all sorts would have made no mark at all on the world.

As it was, the world was waiting for just such an occult teaching as Madame Blavatsky was able to provide. The strength of the Theosophical Society always lay in the broadness of its appeal. Its objects gradually altered until the formation of the 'nucleus of a universal brotherhood of humanity' took pride of place over the 'investigation of powers latent in man'. The quarrels which beset the movement were always the result of specific claims on the part of the proponents, and there was never much conflict of principle. Theosophy was welcomed into the

The well-known Spiritualist technique of the APPORT soon brought the Colonel a letter from a mysterious being signing himself 'Tuitit Bey' of the 'Brotherhood of Luxor', a body with which H.P.B. seemed to have a close connection. Olcott plunged into occult study and from this association arose the Miracle Club and the Theosophical Society, whose third most prominent member was the lawyer W. Q. Judge.

Madame Blavatsky set out to make a compilation of occult doctrine. The word 'theosophy' has a lengthy pedigree and means literally 'God-knowledge'; but since the founding of the Theosophical Society, the term has come to be associated with the approach to the occult made by H. P. Blavatsky and her successors. The foundress's first book, *Isis Unveiled*, is a 1,300-page compilation of mysticism, tall stories and archaeology, which hints at a lost knowledge that had been familiar to the initiates of antiquity. Colonel Olcott's description of his flat-mate's method of verifying her references has become notorious: H.P.B. would suddenly pause in her writing and seem to focus her eyes on the air in front of her. She was reading 'from the astral light' (see AKASHIC RECORD) and in this way was able to complete her book with a reference library of just over a hundred books. Modern scholars have suggested that H.P.B. did in fact draw much of her inspiration from the novels of Bulwer Lytton, and there may be some truth in this; or she could have followed up Lytton's own sources in European occultism. The result was both vitriolic and garbled, but *Isis Unveiled* was to provide endless scope for interpretation.

Olcott and H.P.B. decided to carry their quest to India, the land of marvels. Through an Indian friend, the Colonel came to hear of the Hindu revivalist movement known as the Arya Samaj. This seemed to him to be a sort of Indian Theosophical Society; and he wrote to the leader of the Arya Samaj suggesting an affiliation. Some form of association took place, and the Theosophical Society for a time added the phrase 'of the Arya Samaj' to its title. There were probably strong practical reasons for leaving America as well as the pursuance of the mystical search. Olcott seems to have completely abandoned his wife, and another Theosophist travelling with the party had a lawsuit pending. The first port of call of Olcott and Blavatsky was London, where some interest in the new Society was shown. When the travellers reached India they established themselves at Adyar, near Madras. The property they acquired grew with their influence, and at the headquarters at Adyar were soon to be found eager European occul-

tists vying for esoteric favours with Indian disciples.

From their interest in the revived Hinduism of the Arya Samaj, Olcott and H.P.B. turned to Buddhism, and in 1880 became Buddhists on a visit to Ceylon. Among Indians the Theosophical Society gained converts and made a considerable reputation as almost the first body of Western opinion to accept Eastern doctrines on their own merits. To the elements of Eastern doctrine which Theosophy incorporated into its synthesis Madame Blavatsky added features which derived from her own prodigal imagination. It gradually emerged that the Theosophical Society had been chosen to bring a new message to the new age. Those who had chosen it were known as MASTERS and lived chiefly in Tibet. They were perfected men, whose task it was to watch over humanity and guide it on the path of evolution. The two most concerned with the Theosophical Society were called Morya and KOOT HOOMI.

Apart from the fact that Madame Blavatsky imposed her own definitions on the Orient, the creed which began to emerge as peculiarly Theosophical had particular attractions for Westerners in search of a religion. To the convenient father-figures of the Masters in Tibet, H.P.B. added miracles of the sort beloved of Spiritualism. Everywhere she went, the atmosphere resounded with 'spirit rappings' and 'astral bells'. The most famous of her miracles took place during a picnic and resulted in the conversion of A. P. Sinnett, then editor of an influential Anglo-Indian paper, *The Pioneer*. It was discovered that a teacup and saucer were missing. Madame Blavatsky directed one of the picnic party to dig in the ground, and the cup and saucer were found buried in the earth. Similar 'phenomena' were recorded by Sinnett in his books *Esoteric Buddhism* and *The Occult World*, which introduced Theosophy to Europe. The interest aroused by Sinnett's accounts in a Europe hungry for marvels led to the return of Olcott and Madame Blavatsky in 1884, when they established the nucleus of what soon became a large movement in Britain and no fewer than three Theosophical Societies in Paris.

Unfortunately for H.P.B., while she and the Colonel were away, a certain Madame Coulomb, whom she had known in Cairo and now employed at Adyar, showed some damaging letters to the editor of a Madras Christian magazine. Urged on by the missionaries, Madame Coulomb published two articles purporting to show that she and her husband had been employed to fake 'phenomena'. In London the Society for Psychical Research had examined Sinnett, Olcott and others, and decided that there was a *prima*

facie case for the examination of Theosophical phenomena. Before the leaders of the Theosophical Society could return from their triumphant evangelism, the S.P.R. had sent out Richard Hodgson to report from Adyar. The results were disastrous. Hodgson discovered conjuror's apparatus – like the so-called 'shrine' in which messages from the Masters were supposed to appear and which had a false back; he cast doubt on almost all the 'phenomena' reported, and accused Madame Blavatsky of hiring people to impersonate the Masters. For good measure Hodgson decided that she was probably a Russian spy.

The result of the report published by the S.P.R. was a chaos in which Madame Blavatsky confessed, retracted, bemoaned her foolishness in thinking that 'phenomena' would attract attention to her real work, and accused the Coulombs of plotting to destroy her. The Hodgson report proved the assertion that no publicity is bad publicity; for despite the natural disillusionment of some supporters, the S.P.R. verdict did little to stop the rapid growth of the Society. The days of phenomena were over, and Madame Blavatsky left the Colonel to his educational work in India. She retired to Europe, tried to consolidate the ground won, and wrote another enormous book before her death in 1891.

The Secret Doctrine contains the developed occultism of H.P.B. It is slightly less intractable than *Isis Unveiled*, largely because its authoress had capable assistance from Bertram Keightley, Richard Harte and G. R. S. MEAD. Apart from the always controversial question of the Masters, the book contains all the doctrine that can be said to be distinctively Theosophical. In essence it was a development of the idea of evolution on a spiritual plane. Darwin appeared to have removed the divine pedigree of man and left nothing in its place: now H.P.B. admitted the fact of evolution and turned the tables on the materialists by asserting that if man had not been created in the image of God his task was to use the evolutionary process itself to attain that image. The rules of personal evolution were determined by REINCARNATION and KARMA. Karma in H.P.B.'s interpretation means the sum of accumulated debts from past lives, an inherited burden of merit or demerit which decides a person's fate in the present. The goal of personal evolution is to advance to the state of human perfection attained by the Masters themselves, but the *Secret Doctrine* sets the process of individual evolution within a vastly complex and obscure cosmology in which the evolution of whole races of life on earth assume more significance. H.P.B. thought that life was evolving towards a new 'root-race', a new species of psychically-equipped humanity.

A notable convert to Theosophy, acquired after publication of *The Secret Doctrine* in 1888, was Annie BESANT, who was already a celebrity through her agitation for social reform and birth control. It was largely owing to her energy and enthusiasm that Theosophy entered the area of 'progressive' thought in which it was to become so pervasive. *The Secret Doctrine* was translated into various languages and Theosophy spread throughout Europe and America. There arose an implicit split in the movement that was to come into prominence after the death of Madame Blavatsky, which permitted a clash of personalities to take place. On the one hand there was the occult aspect of the society, represented by H.P.B. herself, and on the other the work of Colonel Olcott, concerned with education and the translation of Eastern texts. Annie Besant combined both enthusiasms, becoming joint leader in H.P.B.'s 'Esoteric Section' with William Quan Judge, while maintaining interests in social reform which were to cement her alliance with Colonel Olcott.

The Disputed Succession

The death of Madame Blavatsky removed the flamboyant, outrageous and attractive personality who for all her failings had proved the mainstay of the Theosophical cause. Immediately every mystic, 'psychic' and occultist with delusions of grandeur began to claim that he had supernatural intelligence, that he was the appointed successor of H.P.B. In 1892 both Judge and Mrs Besant claimed to have received letters from the Masters and there ensued a complex wrangle which lasted for three years. As joint heads of Madame Blavatsky's Esoteric Section there had been a certain friendship between Annie Besant and Judge, but in 1893 when Mrs Besant visited Chicago for the World's Parliament of Religions she came under the influence of Professor G. N. Chakravarti, the Brahminical spokesman at the Parliament. Chakravarti's influence helped to draw Mrs Besant away from H.P.B.'s type of occultism, and her ties with Judge lessened as those with Olcott increased. The rival sets of Mahatma letters began to become an embarrassment, and in 1894 a 'Judicial Committee' appointed by Olcott on the inducement of Annie Besant met in London to inquire into Judge's letters from the Masters. The Committee wisely decided that it had no jurisdiction over the case – for then Colonel Olcott's and Mrs Besant's letters might come in question. However, two events of the same year ensured that Judge and his

supporters would find further cause for complaint. The astrologer Walter Gorn Old (see SEPHARIAL) became offended with Annie Besant and revealed the secrets of the Esoteric Section in the press. Judge immediately suspected Annie Besant of breaking her pledges of secrecy and declared her expelled from the Esoteric Section. In retaliation the Theosophical Convention held at Adyar at Christmas 1894 revived the charges against Judge that he had forged his Master letters.

In April 1895 Judge led the majority of the American Theosophists into secession from the Besant–Olcott Society and the group styled itself the 'Theosophical Society in America'. However, scarcely a year had elapsed when Judge himself died and the schismatic body was itself faced with schism. Immediately after Judge's death, his close associate E. T. Hargrove called the New York eminences of the Theosophical Society to sign a document declaring that Judge had left papers designating a successor. It was announced that the Masters had imposed one condition: the successor was to remain unknown for the period of a year. In Theosophical publications the new head of the society was referred to in veiled terms, as 'Promise', the 'Light of the Lodge' and the 'Purple Mother'. A month after the death of Judge, Hargrove was elected President of the Theosophical Society in America, and it was only a month later than he announced that the Purple Mother was Katherine Tingley, a spirit medium with an interest in welfare work.

The Purple Mother

Katherine Tingley (1847–1929) had only recently emerged from a life of complete obscurity. She had had three husbands, but apart from the Theosophical claims that she had experienced religious visions in childhood little of note is known about her life until the age of forty, when she came into prominence as a spirit medium and administered the Do-Good Mission on the East Side of New York. Through the mission she met Judge and became involved in Theosophical circles. By her own account, the impression made by Judge was strong; 'I was face to face with a new type of human nature,' she wrote, 'with something akin to that which my inner consciousness had told me a perfect human being might be.'

Immediately her identity as Judge's successor had been revealed, the Purple Mother set out on a 'Crusade' around the world. During this expedition she claimed to have met H.P.B.'s Master near Darjeeling – he had advocated early rising – and on her return to the United States laid the foundation stone of the 'School for the Revival of the

Lost Mysteries of Antiquity' at Point Loma in California. Point Loma became the American equivalent of Adyar, with a Greek Theatre and a school, called the 'Raja-Yoga School'. But just as the original schism had arisen between Judge and Mrs Besant partly over the conflict of esotericism and social work, Katherine Tingley discovered that her interest in social reform conflicted with the demands of esotericism. In 1898 she put to the Convention of the Theosophical Society in America the constitution of a body to be known as the Universal Brotherhood which was to absorb the society as constituted. In the upshot it absorbed about 90 per cent, while Hargrove and his following withdrew. Further dissensions took place, and one body of Theosophists drifted into a Spiritualistic 'Temple of the People', while some survivors from the early Judge days founded yet another Theosophical Society.

Katherine Tingley's own work concerned itself chiefly with social service. She founded schools and orphanages; during the Spanish–American War she set up a military hospital. She received Government aid to establish hospitals in Cuba and in 1925 was awarded the Medal of Honour of the German Red Cross. Wealthy supporters gave funds to enlarge Point Loma, but Katherine Tingley was sometimes forced to contest their gifts at law. Finally, in 1925 came a suit brought by a Mrs Irene Mohn, who accused the Theosophical Society of alienating the affections of her husband. The lower courts fined Mrs Tingley $100,000, and although the verdict was reversed on appeal, the Purple Mother afterwards lived mainly in Europe, where she met her death in 1929 as the result of a car accident. She was succeeded by Dr Gottfried de Purucker.

The Star in the East

Meanwhile, the Theosophical Society of Mrs Besant and Colonel Olcott had undergone many changes. There was a revival of controversy over an alleged appearance of the Masters in 1907 at the death-bed of Colonel Olcott, but that death-bed left Mrs Besant in sole control of the Indian and most of the European Theosophists. Another cause of dissension had arisen, which involved the man who was to be Annie Besant's right hand in running the Theosophical Society from that time on: Charles Webster LEADBEATER.

Leadbeater was a Church of England clergyman who had been won over by Madame Blavatsky, although he always claimed that his first contact with Theosophy had been at the school of Pythagoras on Samos in 540 B.C. He was an incurable romantic and romancer, and his reputation in Theosophical circles was made as a clairvoyant. He and Mrs Besant undertook clairvoyant investigations of THOUGHT-FORMS – the shapes assumed by emotions and thoughts – and 'occult chemistry', which was an examination of the nature of matter carried out clairvoyantly. To these activities Leadbeater added homosexual tastes, and as early as 1906 charges of misconduct with boys at Theosophical Headquarters forced his resignation. After two years, which Leadbeater spent investigating occult chemistry in self-imposed exile on the Continent, Annie Besant managed to manoeuvre him back into the Society; and once she was released from all higher authority by Olcott's death, A.B. and C.W.L. became in effect the joint directors of the society's activities.

Under the supervision of the two clairvoyants the nature of Theosophy began to change. The direct 'phenomena' and physical visitations by Masters which had characterized Theosophical occultism in the days of Madame Blavatsky no longer found a place. There had in fact been one notable tragedy, when an over-enthusiastic pupil set off to the Himalayas in search of his guru and was frozen to death. Matters were much easier for later Theosophists, who travelled to meet their Masters in their ASTRAL BODIES while asleep. But as the only reporters of such meetings were the clairvoyant leaders, it was natural that hero-worship of Leadbeater and Mrs Besant would supplant exclusive veneration for the Masters. So might things have continued had not yet another innovation diverted the course of the Theosophical Society.

This new development was really Leadbeater's responsibility. His clairvoyant investigations had extended themselves to the previous lives of members of the Society. One day he discovered on the seashore near Adyar a boy who was the son of one of the servants at the Theosophical Headquarters, and decided to include his previous lives in his researches. He was astonished at what he found, and wrote to Mrs Besant that 'the boy was surely not here by accident'. Gradually it became common knowledge that the body of the boy Krishnamurti was to become the vehicle for the coming World Teacher of the new age, the new race of humanity prophesied by Madame Blavatsky. This Teacher was to be the Master who had inhabited the body of Jesus in ancient Palestine and would take possession of the body of Krishnamurti in the same fashion. In 1911 was founded the Order of the Star in the East, an organization to support the coming Teacher, and on 28 December Krishnamurti ceremonially blessed the membership certifi-

Jiddu Krishnamurti

cates of the Order amidst scenes of intense emotion. A certain Star member flung himself at the feet of the Christ-to-be and there followed an outburst of tears and prostrations which was brought to a climax by Krishnamurti's brother, who came from his position behind Krishnamurti to join in the communal fervour.

Before the movement could get fully started a development took place which nearly wrecked the plans of the tutors of the Messiah. Krishnamurti's father demanded the return of his son, and alleged that Leadbeater was a corrupting influence. There is little doubt that Mrs Besant's opponents instigated the legal proceedings which followed, and that the fees of the prosecuting counsel were paid by a newspaper, *The Hindu*. There is also little doubt that Leadbeater had been up to his tricks again, but in court at Madras the argument turned on another issue. Krishnamurti's father claimed that he had made his sons Mrs Besant's wards in order to secure them a good education. But what sort of an education was it which had as its object the creation of a Messiah? The decision of the judge was to make Krishnamurti and his brother wards of court. No further steps were taken against the Theosophical Society, which must certainly have disappointed the instigators of the prosecution, and Mrs Besant took the case to

the Privy Council, where the verdict was reversed.

Further dissension racked the Society, and Leadbeater's conduct provided ample reason for dissidents to claim that Mrs Besant was protecting her friend. In 1909 G. R. S. MEAD, who had at one time been Madame Blavatsky's secretary, broke away and founded his Quest Society which continued to meet in London until the 1930s. The Quest Society, with its magazine of the same name, concentrated on comparative religion and numbered some distinguished names among its supporters: John Masefield and Ezra Pound read papers, and other contributors to the magazine were Jessie L. Weston and G. Wilson Knight. Another intellectual group of Theosophists detached itself the same year in America and established itself in Los Angeles under the name of the United Lodge of Theosophists and the leadership of Robert Crosbie. The United Lodge also attracted distinguished support and, particularly after the defection to them in 1922 of B. P. Wadia – from the 'orthodox' Besant persuasion – made an appeal to the Theosophically-inclined among the intellectuals. Starting in the 1930s the United Lodge published from India a magazine called *The Aryan Path* which had close links with the circle around A. R. Orage and J. D. Beresford, both of whom contributed frequently to the early volumes.

The most serious defection was that of Dr

Rudolf STEINER, the head of the German Section of the Theosophical Society. For this there were two main reasons. The first was the expulsion by Steiner of a rogue called Hugo Vollrath from his Section, and Vollrath's reinstatement by Annie Besant. The second was the growing emphasis placed in the Theosophical Society generally on the Order of the Star in the East. Just as the Masters had earlier caused dissent, now the cult of the coming World Teacher provided the subject of contention. Finally, Steiner found himself unable to stomach the grotesqueries of the Order of the Star, and seceded in 1913 to found his own Anthroposophical Society, a very different matter from Theosophical Societies of any kind.

The Order of the Star prospered and grew, with badges, newspapers and a whole heraldry to propagate the faith. Krishnamurti travelled the world, speaking to camps at centres in India, California and Ommen in the Netherlands, where the Order had its headquarters in a castle given by a noble supporter. Eventually, on 28 December 1925, the World Teacher appeared. Mary Lutyens has described how Krishnamurti indicated the Teacher's arrival:

> He [Krishnamurti] had been saying, 'He comes to lead us. He comes only to those who have understood, who have suffered, who are unhappy, who are enlightened. He comes only to those who want, who desire, who long.' And then the voice changed and rang out, 'And I come for those who want sympathy, who want happiness in all things. I come to reform, not to tear down. I come not to destroy, but to build.'

But the Order of the Star lasted only four years longer. In 1929 it was dissolved by Krishnamurti himself, who renounced all claims to be other than himself, and repudiated all religious sects and organizations. Truth, he maintained, was a 'pathless land' and help came only from within; the whole structure which had been built up for him came to nothing. From that date Krishnamurti has taught his personal philosophy, which is certainly unlike any creed professed by the Theosophical Society. The Society itself declined rapidly. The millennarian enthusiasm of the high period of the Order of the Star burst like a pricked balloon, and by 1932 the Theosophical Society had shrunk to 33,000 members; next year Mrs Besant died, and at about this time Krishnamurti lost all memory of events before 1929.

C. W. Leadbeater had bowed out of the action quite early. He had surrendered his tutorship of Krishnamurti to George Arun-

Mrs Besant beside Krishnamurti at a Star of the East assembly

dale, a former schoolmaster, and retired to Australia, where he headed a flourishing Australian section, and made his headquarters in a house known as 'The Manor', in which his own room was lined with copper for occult purposes. His clairvoyant investigations continued, as did his homosexual activities. Gradually his interest in Krishnamurti waned and he became alarmed at the excessive zeal shown by Mrs Besant in the propagation of her Order of the Star. 'I hope she will not wreck the Society,' he confided to his secretary.

The World Teacher had been supplanted in Leadbeater's affections by the Bishopric he had received in the Liberal Catholic Church. This was a small body owing its succession to the Utrecht Dissenters or Old Catholics, and until 1915 was under the control of Arnold MATHEW, one of the WANDERING BISHOPS who flourished – and still flourish – on the borderlands of occultism. In 1913 Mathew had consecrated James Wedgwood, the General Secretary of the Theosophical Society in England, and in so doing lost control of his tiny Church, which Wedgwood infected most thoroughly with Theosophy. In 1915 Mathew denounced the doctrines of the Order of the Star in the East, dissolved his episcopal chapter and submitted himself to Rome. The next year

Wedgwood, by this time a Bishop, set sail for Sidney, where he consecrated Leadbeater and Arundale. Leadbeater originally saw the Liberal Catholic Church as a weapon in the hands of the coming World Teacher, but in time the Church itself became more important to him than the cause of Krishnamurti. As a Bishop he devoted himself to the clairvoyant investigation of the thought forms generated by church services, and the elaboration of Theosophical church ritual came to absorb most of his time.

The Quest

The occult or esoteric aspects of the Theosophical Society suffered a decline in the period which followed. From 1914 Annie Besant's concern with Indian politics had involved the Society in the movement for Indian nationalism, and in many ways the Society's influence lost much of its Theosophical character. The organization was used to encourage the good works which had always formed part of its programme. The Theosophists were particularly prominent in education. In the United States Katherine Tingley had set up schools, and the Raja-Yoga School at Point Loma was run on progressive lines. The foundation of progressive education in England was laid by a Theosophical experiment in coeducation at Letchworth, and it was on a Theosophical basis that the New Educational Fellowship evolved to prominence in the 1920s.

With the renunciation of Krishnamurti there came to an end the last claim of the Theosophical Society to provide a revelation of its own. These attempts had always ended in disaster. The reality or otherwise of the Masters caused many of the early quarrels; while many of the later secessions were rooted in dissatisfaction with the Order of the Star in the East. While the Society confined itself to its more general objects it could count on a wide appeal, but – although H.P.B.'s 'phenomena' and Mrs Besant's Messiah temporarily increased recruiting – when its leaders produced any tangible result of their occult quest, it was ten to one that dissension would break out. It was the general principle of seeking, the general myth of the occult quest, which held attractions for the 'people of advanced ideas' who were drawn to Theosophy. The Society was always prevented from imposing dogmas on its membership. The belief in Masters could never be made compulsory. But insofar as there was an approach to occultism which was distinctively Theosophical, it is provided by *The Secret Doctrine* and other products of H. P. Blavatsky's prolific and confusing mind. This accounts for a perpetual cry of 'back to Blavatsky' which is heard in sections of the Theosophical Society almost throughout its history after the Old Lady's death.

Once again – although there are still groups who try to tease sense out of every syllable she wrote – it is less the system of cosmology and anthropology worked out by H.P.B. which has left a lasting impression than the general principle of search, the idea that from certain elements of Eastern and Western traditions there may be deduced a system of knowledge which will provide the key to the universe. Since H. P. Blavatsky set the example, there have been numberless attempts at occult syntheses. All have been different, and many more comprehensible. Many have accepted one idea which H.P.B. embodied in *The Secret Doctrine,* and which has become something of an occult orthodoxy: that humanity is evolving towards a new form of being. In different ways this theory was broached by Nietzsche, Bergson and Teilhard de Chardin. But Blavatsky was the first – because the nearest to Darwin in point of time – and it is in her more occult version that the idea survives most strongly even today.

It can scarcely be stressed sufficiently that the Theosophical Society was the most active agent in the diffusion of the various elements which made up the late-19th-century occult revival. Because no particular doctrine was binding on its members, other than a common humanitarianism and transcendentalism, the most varied theories were adopted, passed on, or transformed in the bowels of the Society. For example, the 'esoteric Christianity' of Anna KINGSFORD and Edward Maitland was incorporated into the Society's semi-orthodoxy. In a similar way, after the Society itself failed to provide food for thought or marvels to contemplate its members moved on, filled with the spirit of search, to other things. In this way many who had been touched by the Theosophical wand passed to GURDJIEFF and OUSPENSKY, or turned to the study of Zen. Perhaps one of the greatest services performed by this remarkably influential group of people was to direct the attention of Western man to Eastern traditions in a way which involved getting under the skin of Oriental civilization. The Theosophical approach may have had stars in its eyes, but it provided a way for those to whom the austere approach of the scholar or the deliberate proselytizing of the convert to an Eastern faith did not appeal.

Nowadays the Theosophical Society is relatively quiescent. There may still be travail and turmoil in the lodges, but those interested in the occult now use other terminologies, other approaches to the eternal problems. The Society was founded as a response to an age of crisis, and its great success reflected the crisis of the age. A Society which counted among its adherents at one time or another W. B. YEATS, George Russell (Æ), Gustav Meyrink and George Lansbury cannot be entirely negligible. If Theosophy with a capital letter is dead, with a small letter it is far from being so. Perhaps it is the measure of a not inconsiderable achievement that a group which has often appeared ridiculous has had a large part in bringing this about. J. W.

(Further reading: *43, 44, 351, 352, 445, 493.*)

Theurgy
Neo-Platonist system of achieving direct contact with the divine; it was banned in the 6th century A.D. One of its methods was to induce the temporary presence of a god in a human being, a medium, through whom the deity could communicate with the worshippers. The phenomena reported by the theurgists have interesting parallels in modern mediumship (see *123, 124*).

Third Eye
A mysterious organ of occult vision and centre of inner illumination, one of the CHAKRAS of Hinduism and YOGA, situated in the middle of the forehead just above the point between the eyebrows; attempts have been made to connect it with the pineal gland, which in adepts is said to move forward from the mid-brain at the end of an invisible stalk, so that it can be seen on the forehead by sensitives.

Thompson-Gifford Case
A celebrated American case of automatic painting. In 1905 a man named Frederick Thompson experienced an overwhelming impulse to paint; he also had hallucinations of landscapes and painted some of them. A year later, he visited an exhibition of paintings by a deceased artist, Robert Swain Gifford, and heard a voice saying, 'Can you not take up and finish my work?' Thompson continued to paint, depicting scenes which had been well known to Gifford in life, but which Thompson himself had apparently never seen: see AUTOMATISMS.

Thought-forms
The shapes assumed by thoughts and emotions; in occult theory, all thoughts, ideas, desires and imaginings have visible and sensible form on the ASTRAL PLANE: see SPIRITS AND FORCES; see also RADIESTHESIA.

Thought-transference See TELEPATHY.

Thule Society See GERMAN OCCULT GROUPS.

The Tibetan See Alice BAILEY.

Katherine Tingley (1847-1929)
The medium who, as the 'Purple Mother', became head of the American Theosophical Society: see THEOSOPHICAL SOCIETY.

Andrei Towianski
Towianski was the leading representative of the school of thought known as POLISH MESSIANISM, which was brought into France by the Polish emigration of 1830-1 and was influential in the growth of modern occultism. He was born in Lithuania, and studied at the University of Wilno. Early in life he became involved in Polish mystical circles, and in 1832 abandoned his profession of the law to travel to Russia. Here he sat at the feet of the Martinist painter Joseph Olesciewicz and returned through Poland on his way to France. En route to Paris he made a pilgrimage to the field of Waterloo, and his musings on the defeat of Napoleon formed the first text of his cult, in which the figure of a Napoleon-Messiah plays a great part. In the French capital Towianski secured the permanent allegiance of the Polish national poet, Adam Mickiewicz, and was introduced by him to the Polish emigrés assembled in Nôtre Dame. Towianski's preaching was

Spirit forces: elementals drawn symbolically by Steffi Grant (see page 228)

thought so inflammatory that the Archbishop of Paris organized his expulsion in 1842.

Towianski had already formed the circle of the 'Work of God', which he directed through Mickiewicz from Switzerland. This group formed an alliance with the heretical church of the Norman prophet VINTRAS, and created a stir by organized demonstrations of its support for the mission of Towianski during Adam Mickiewicz's tenure of the chair of Slavonic Literature at the Collège de France. Towianski re-entered France only once more, during the revolution of 1848, and was sentenced to be deported to Cayenne.

The influence of Mickiewicz saved him; but after the poet's lectures had made him the laughing-stock of Paris, the 'Work of God' faded from sight. Its influence continued to be felt in the underground of mysticism and idealistic Socialism inhabited by the magician Eliphas LÉVI and the Abbé Lammenais, which found continuing inspiration in the idea of social Messianism which the Poles had first adopted.   J. W.

(Further reading: 493.)

Trance

The forms of trance – an abnormal state of mind characterized by some degree of DISSOCIATION of consciousness – are many. Those most familiar to the layman are hypnotic and mediumistic trance, but in addition to these there are types of trance induced by physical debility, by DRUGS, by music and dance, and by, quite literally, hundreds of other things. At root, however, all types of trance are identical. The differences are of degree, ranging from the 'light trance' of a person who can remember everything that happened during the abnormal state to the ecstatic possession of a VOODOO devotee who has no memory of what occurred while he or she was 'ridden' by a deity. There are also differences of cultural behaviour patterns, but in spite of the apparently wide gulf between, say, the actions of a frenzied, dancing UMBANDA priest in Brazil and the dignified bearing and solemn statements of a Tibetan oracle, both are undergoing the same experience, a dissociation of consciousness and a tapping of the subliminal layers of the mind.

No doubt the earliest men discovered trance accidentally, for concussion induced by a blow on the head is often associated with a state indistinguishable from trance – a condition in which the person has part of his mind 'split off' from the rest of it. He may continue to talk and move about, or he may

Archbishop Harold Percival Nicholson (see page 271)

lie half-comatose, he may act in a way entirely compatible with his usual pattern of behaviour or widely at variance with it, but in most cases he will not have complete memory of what happened during the period of dissociation. It was this phenomenon, not fully understood today and totally mysterious to early man, which probably lay behind the theory that during trance the soul had left the body, which had then been temporarily occupied by another tenant – god, demon or ghost (see POSSESSION).

Once the trance state had been accepted as desirable, as a way of putting human beings into direct touch with superhuman forces, it was inevitable that men would begin to seek methods of deliberately inducing it. Possibly the trepanning – the drilling of holes in the skulls of living men – practised skilfully by men in the Stone Age, was one such trance-induction technique but, if so, drugs, physical privation and breathing exercises replaced it.

The common belief that there is something peculiarly modern about the use of psychotropic drugs – those which produce alterations in consciousness – is mistaken. On the contrary, the use of such substances to achieve dissociation is extremely old. The Delphic oracle chewed the 'herbs of Apollo', the shamans of Siberia took fly agaric (the 'sacred mushroom' of modern theories), and the semi-divine heroes of ancient India drank the mysterious soma, which was possibly an infusion of fly agaric, or possibly alcohol – a psychotrope for those who lack genetic semi-immunity to its effects. Today, the Tantric magicians of Bengal (see TANTRISM) still smoke hashish as a preliminary to trance-inducing rituals, and the mediums of the semi-Spiritualist, semi-Voodoo cults of Brazil drink large quantities of cane spirit both before and throughout the duration of their trance states.

The exact physiological mechanism by which trance is induced is uncertain, but it seems likely that any gross, prolonged stress inflicted upon the brain, by way of either the body or the mind, is ultimately capable of producing trance. Drugs, for example, in the main produce their effects by initiating a partial oxygen starvation of the brain: breathing exercises, on the other hand, which almost always involve some degree of hyper-ventilation, flood the body with oxygen and deprive the brain of sugar. This is the easiest way of inducing trance and sufficiently prolonged, deep, very rapid breathing will produce trance in almost anyone. The practice can be extremely dangerous and should in no circumstances be attempted without prior medical examination and approval.

The Cave of Trophonius

Trance resulting from physical deprivation is particularly associated with cathartic religion and with modern totalitarian political movements. In classical antiquity the oracular priests of Trophonius appear to have induced trance in those who consulted the oracle through a combination of fasting, physical ill-treatment and, perhaps, drugs. The consultation of the oracle, the 'descent into the Cave of Trophonius', was preceded by a stay in a temple sacred to Good Fortune during which the inquirer was subjected to a strict dietary regime, purges and emetics and, one suspects, the secret administration of one or more hallucinogenic drugs. The actual visit to the oracle's cave, which appears to have lasted for something like thirty-six hours, began with the inquirer's lying on the ground with his feet dangling over a narrow cleft. Then, quite suddenly, he was dragged into the cleft, 'just as a man might be caught and dragged down by the swirl of a mighty and rapid river'. What happened then was described by Plutarch (in *The Daemon of Socrates*): he derived his account from that of a young student of philosophy named Timarchus. 'As soon as he entered, a thick darkness surrounded him; then, after he had prayed, he lay a long while upon the ground, but was not certain whether awake or in a dream, only he imagined that a smart stroke fell upon his head, and . . . his soul flew out . . .'

This feeling that the soul has 'flown out' is typical of many types of trance. The subsequent experiences of Timarchus seem compounded of hallucination and erroneous interpretation of things actually experienced: 'he saw no earth, but certain islands shining with a gentle fire, which interchanged colours according to the different variation of the light, innumerable and very large, unequal but all round . . .' This eerie experience may perhaps have been caused by a primitive equivalent of the modern 'light show', a device often used in association with 'pop' music and productive of a state approximating to trance in many of those subjected to it. Contemporary light shows are sometimes accompanied by electronically derived random noise, and something of this sort seems to have been used by the priests of Trophonius as part of their trance-induction technique: ' . . . a thousand howlings and bellowings of beasts, cries of children, groans of men and women, and all sorts of terrible noises reached his ears; but faintly and far off and rising through the vast hollow; and this terrified him exceedingly'.

After this, a mysterious voice gave Trophonius much esoteric teaching. Finally he turned his head to discover who had spoken, 'but a violent pain . . . seized his head so that he lost all sense and understanding; but in a little while recovering, he found himself in the entrance to the cave where he first lay down'.

By the use of very similar methods the secret policemen of modern totalitarian regimes, both Fascist and Communist, have succeeded in extracting untruthful 'confessions' from their victims. The technique is to induce a trance state in the prisoner by means of sensory deprivation, starvation, lack of sleep and, above all, physical violence: at the Twentieth Congress of the Communist Party of the Soviet Union, Nikita Khruschev described the methods of the secret police as 'beat, beat and beat again'. Anyone who is in a state of trance is highly suggestible. The possessed Voodoo worshipper will behave in the way that his fellow-worshippers expect the deity possessing him to behave; the Spiritualist medium will deliver the type of message from 'beyond the grave' that the sitters expect to hear; and the political prisoner will confess to the crimes which his captors expect him to admit.

These methods can be used not only for breaking down the enemies of a regime but for building up the enthusiasm of its supporters. At the Nuremberg rallies of the Nazi Party hysterical enthusiasm indistinguishable from trance was deliberately induced by the use of rhythmic drumming, marching, coloured banners, flaring torches, strategically placed spotlights and, most important of all, the long monotonous chanting of the phrase *Sieg Heil*. Such methods undoubtedly achieve their aims. As Aldous Huxley said: 'No man . . . can listen for very long to African drumming or Indian chanting . . . and retain intact his critical and self-conscious personality. It would be interesting to take a group of the most eminent philosophers, shut them up in a hot room with Moroccan dervishes or Haitian Voodooists and measure . . . the strength of their psychological resistance to the effects of rhythmic sound . . . all we can safely predict is that, if exposed long enough to the tomtoms and the singing, every one of our philosophers would end by capering and howling with the savages' (*238*).

The Method of Z2

These methods which Huxley predicted would cause the philosophers to caper and howl, and which Hitler and his colleagues used to whip up the emotional blood-lust of their brown-shirted battalions, are basically identical with those employed by such magicians as MacGregor MATHERS and Aleister CROWLEY to achieve ecstatic union with the gods.

Mathers's system, still widely used by Western practitioners of RITUAL MAGIC, is described in a GOLDEN DAWN manuscript known as Z2. The idea is to surround yourself with coloured geometrical figures and other objects which supposedly have a correspondence with the god invoked. Whether these CORRESPONDENCES have any objective link with the god or force invoked is neither here nor there. As long as the magician is, in his subconscious, absolutely convinced that the correspondences are real, a condition of extreme suggestibility, or in other words of light, auto-hypnotic trance, can easily be achieved. Then the magician, his 'temple' already full of the fumes of incense, some types of which are authentically hallucinogenic, begins to chant his invocation in as sonorous and rhythmic a fashion as he can. This, the correct way of 'magical vibration', is held to be one of the essential keys to the successful practice of ritual magic. The climax of the ritual is the frenzied utterance of the 'barbarous words of evocation', polysyllabic and weird-sounding names of great antiquity, the real meaning of most of which has long been forgotten. This is continued until 'breakthrough', the point at which dissociation of consciousness occurs and the magician is possessed by the god, which is presumably a split-off part of his own mind.

Suns of Green and Red

Simpler but equally potent methods of achieving trance are used by initiates of the modern witch-cult (see WITCHCRAFT). Here is a hitherto unpublished account by a third-degree witch of how he first entered trance and what it felt like.

After we had finished performing the written ritual, which I felt to be a bit sentimental and 'literary', the real festival began. We had been lucky in that X—— was a cousin of the owner of —— Wood (which is completely fenced off and private) who lent it to us for the night. We were in a largeish empty space, now planted with conifers, about half a mile away from the A4 [trunk road]. Our fire was set to the side of where we had had the circle and it was in any case a warm night. The only distraction was the noise of heavy lorries changing gear which the wind carried from the road. X—— played his recorder, not my favourite instrument, and after a while hit upon a folksong, modal but in peculiar 3/4 time, which seemed to fit our mood. He repeated it again and again and we began a snake dance, Diana leading us and playing upon the bongoes which she had slung round her neck by her cord. After a while Diana

started leading us to jump over the fire, which was dying down a bit, on every third circuit. Once in a while somebody would drop out and take a glass of witch punch which I had prepared earlier in the 'cauldron' (actually a cleaned-up brass coal scuttle). It was fairly strong stuff, red wine, brandy and various herbs I had added in honour of the Goddess, but somehow all the exertion and the general mood made one drink a lot and we were all a bit affected by it.

X—— abandoned his recorder and joined the dance, but Diana continued drumming and speeded up the rhythm. We continued to dance and I suddenly began to get that otherworldly feeling one sometimes gets on long drives. I was conscious of everything I was doing and yet at the same time I felt curiously detached from my body. I was still *in it*, of course, I hadn't astrally projected or something, but only as an impartial observer, just along for the ride, emotionally unattached. A moment later G——, who was third in the snake, threw herself out of the dance and upon the ground, writhing convulsively and trying to speak but just gabbling. For half a second we faltered but Diana, still drumming, called out to us, 'It's the Goddess. Keep dancing.' On the following circle I jumped short as we came to the fire and landed in the red embers which stuck to the soles of my feet. I noted with surprise but no interest that there was no longer any sensation in my feet, no feeling of contact with the ground, no burning from the fire. The only things that mattered were the drumming and the dance, somehow my body was one with them both.

Time became distorted, stretched. Each step of the dance lasted an age, each leap over the fire left me suspended, levitated over the fire for an eternity, and all the time the lack of sensation that had begun in the feet crept upwards through the body to thighs, belly and breast. I knew it must reach my head and it did so. I saw stars, quite literally, great flaming suns of green and red, all turning inside me. It all blacked out and the next thing I knew I was lying on the ground shivering under a blanket with my feet hurting like hell. For almost half an hour my body had been used by the god.

Aleister Crowley employed very similar methods of trance induction, although they were more sophisticated and had a heavier

An entranced Lapp, drum on back, about to prophesy

259

sexual orientation. He asked, 'How can ecstasy be obtained?' and gave the answer, 'By the invocation of Bacchus, Aphrodite and Apollo' – in other words, wine, woman and song. Crowley pondered deeply on this subject and recorded his conclusions in an essay on 'Energised Enthusiasm' which he published in an issue of his own magazine, *The Equinox*. He decided that the most effective music was that provided by the tom-tom (as Aldous Huxley also thought) and that the most effective drink was the 'loving cup' which he had introduced from Mexico, an infusion of the hallucinogenic drug mescalin in alcohol. The obscenity laws of the time prevented him from recording his opinion as to how Aphrodite should be invoked, perhaps fortunately, for when he put his theories into practice in a series of magical rites collectively known as the 'Paris Working', the sexual components of the ceremonies were exclusively homosexual. The Paris Working seems to have been most successful: both Crowley and his disciple Victor NEUBURG were possessed on various occasions, or thought they were possessed, by the gods they invoked. Unfortunately, however, most of the information and teaching which the gods conveyed through the mouths of the possessed magicians turned out to be respectively untrue or unhelpful.

Another means of obtaining dissociation used by Crowley and his followers strongly resembles the technique of the 'Method' school of acting. The magicians act parts in a type of mystery play and strongly identify themselves with their parts. A magician playing the role of John the Baptist, for example, does his best to forget that he is merely acting and to *be* John, with all the latter's thoughts, emotions and beliefs. Crowley wrote a series of mystery plays, *The Rites of Eleusis*, designed to be used in this way. On one occasion they were performed at a private house in Dorset and Neuburg, taking the part of Mars, became entranced and, supposedly, possessed by that warlike deity. According to Crowley, the god – that is, the entranced Neuburg – successfully predicted not only the Balkan War of 1912 but also the World War of 1914–18.

Mediumistic Trance

With the magical revival now at full flood, many Western occultists are achieving trance in such ways as those described above. But magicians and witches normally carry on their activities in tightly-knit, secret circles and the type of trance most easily observed by the general public is that associated with Spiritualist mediumship which, while less spectacular, is in many ways even more interesting.

Mediumistic trance is sometimes simulated, of course. There have always been, and no doubt always will be, fraudulent mediums ready to prey on the bereaved. Fraud has been particularly prevalent in the field of physical mediumship and some contemporary 'transfiguration mediums', whose faces are allegedly transformed into those of discarnate communicators, must be regarded with grave suspicion. All the same, the existence of forged money does not disprove the existence of the genuine article, and there is no need to suspect the *bona fides* of most mediums. This is not to say that one must accept the Spiritualist hypotheses, of communication with the dead, and so on, that have been built up to explain the phenomena of trance mediumship.

Genuine mediums appear to be individuals who can voluntarily achieve dissociation of consciousness without going through the stresses which magicians and witches have to impose on themselves. Many mediums describe their entry into the trance state as going through 'layers of trance': in other words, a progressive dissociation starting with something very like the day-dreaming which everyone has experienced and going on to a stage in which communicators are 'seen' (CLAIRVOYANCE) or 'heard' (clairaudience). In some, but not all, cases the process continues until the state of deep trance is reached. At first this resembles restless sleep and the medium tends to breathe heavily, and even to snort in an almost porcine fashion, but then she awakes, not as herself, but as her CONTROL. This is theoretically a discarnate entity, a celestial telephone operator, as it were, whose function is to connect the medium's body with the spirits of the dead, but in reality is almost certainly a secondary personality of the medium herself. The control usually keeps the other communicating entities at a distance, reporting their observations and messages, but on occasion it will allow one or more of them to take over the medium's body. The results can be spectacular: the medium's speech-patterns and even her physical appearance are markedly changed and sitters report that they are talking to a dead relative or friend. Even so, it is difficult to accept the Spiritualist hypothesis, though it cannot be entirely ruled out, and most serious investigators believe that the communicators are not discarnate beings but split-off segments of the medium's unconscious mind.

Psychologists of all schools of thought have taken much interest in trance in recent years and have given their various explanations of it. The disciples of Wilhelm REICH have explained trance as the mind's reaction to the physical effects produced by the mysterious

'orgone energy': this has not prevented some members of the American Orgonomic Association from attempting to use it to get in touch with their dead master. Some Jungians look on trance as a 'descent into the collective unconscious': though, even if the collective unconscious exists, this phrase is a description rather than a definition. Perhaps the most satisfactory approach to trance is the one favoured by the behaviourists. These latter-day Pavlovians regard trance as an aspect of what they call trans-marginal inhibition, the protective mechanism through which the brain, under stress, can radically alter the way in which it responds to external stimuli. Mediums are people who need comparatively little stress exerted on them before they reach this state and their inhibition has become a conditioned pattern of brain activity. In one sense, at least, the explanations are unimportant. The person who experiences trance is usually uninterested in its mechanism, physiological or psychological: for him it is the experience itself which matters. F. K.

(See also CONSCIOUSNESS; FAITH HEALING; HYPNOSIS; MEDIUMS; SPIRITUALISM.)
(Further reading: *416, 417, 492.*)

Transcendental Meditation (T.M.) See MEDITATION.

Transcendental Movement

The New England Transcendentalists were a group of writers and thinkers who flourished in and around Boston, Massachusetts, in the 1830s and '40s and included the poet and essayist Ralph Waldo Emerson (1803–82), the writer Henry Thoreau (1817–62) and the educationist Amos Bronson Alcott (1799–1888), father of Louisa M. Alcott. They shared a common attitude of mind which encompassed religion, philosophy and literature, and also inspired a number of practical experiments in living.

The movement had its roots in Unitarianism, which was imported from Europe during the 18th century. Unitarianism, with its denial of the Trinity, its egalitarian approach to society and its tolerant attitude towards other religions, found ready support among thoughtful Americans looking for a more rational form of worship than they had found in other Christian sects. Emerson was the son of a Unitarian minister and for a time followed his father's profession, though he later left the ministry.

It was on this ground that there fell, in the early 19th century, the seeds of certain European works of philosophy and literature – particularly German – which took root and produced their own special flowering. Specially influential were the works of Immanuel

Kant, who argued that certain ideas are acquired by intuition rather than by experience. He called these ideas 'transcendental'. This was a doctrine that greatly appealed to Emerson and his circle because it accorded with their leanings towards individual mystical experience. A number of European romantic writers and poets also influenced the Emersonian group. An intense interest in nature, as expressed in the poems of Wordsworth, went hand-in-hand with Kant's doctrines.

The result was the development of a school of thought holding that God dwelt in all things and that by communion with nature the individual could directly glimpse the divine. Insight, instinct and intuition were the faculties admired by the group. Along with these ideas went a respect for non-Christian religions which was remarkable for its time.

The Transcendentalists were only loosely gathered under the same banner, but they were aware of being part of a movement. Their conscious identity as a group can possibly be dated from the year 1836 when regular gatherings began to take place in Boston at the house of George Ripley, a Unitarian minister. To the outside world the group who attended these gatherings came to be known as the 'Transcendental Club'.

In due course the leaders of the movement felt that they ought to have a literary organ, and in 1840 a journal called the *Dial* appeared, with Margaret Fuller as editor and George Ripley as assistant editor. Margaret Fuller ran it for two years, and Emerson took over for a further two, after which it ceased publication. Though the journal was never a financial success it was a lively and influential organ, covering theology, philosophy, art, music and literature. One of its most important services was to publish a series of extracts from Eastern scriptures. These began in the issue of July 1842, together with an introduction by Emerson which expresses a highly enlightened attitude towards non-Christian faiths: 'Each nation has its bible more or less pure; none has yet been willing or able in a wise and devout spirit to collate its own with those of other nations, and sinking the civil-historical and ritual portions to bring together the grand expressions of moral sentiment in different ages and races, the rules for the guidance of life, the bursts of piety and of abandonment to the Invisible and Eternal.'

One of the issues contained selections by Henry Thoreau from the Hindu book the *Ordinances of Menu* (the now accepted transliteration is Manu), which set out the Indian system of religious and civil duties and which had recently appeared in an English translation. Thoreau's own enthusiastic views on the

book are recorded in his journal: 'Everywhere the speech of Menu demands the widest apprehension and proceeds from the loftiest plateau of the soul.'

Thoreau carried the Transcendentalist philosophy into his practical life by retreating in 1845 to a small cabin he had built for himself on the shore of Walden Pond, where he lived as simply as possible, supporting himself by surveying work, odd jobs and the tillage of a few acres of land. He remained there for two years, communing with nature and recording his observations in voluminous diaries. His book *Walden*, published in 1854, was the record of these two years. Thoreau was attracted by the ascetic aspects of oriental religion, and in one passage of his writings describes himself as being an occasional practitioner of YOGA.

Emerson was also drawn towards Eastern thought and expressed Indian mystical ideas in some of his poems, notably *Brahma*, which so mystified his publishers that they implored him, without success, to leave it out of his selected poems, published in 1876. Part of the poem reads:

If the red slayer thinks he slays,
Or if the slain thinks he is slain,
They know not well the subtle ways
I keep, and pass, and turn again.

Far or forgot to me is near;
Shadow and sunlight are the same;
The vanished gods to me appear;
And one to me are shame and fame.

They reckon ill who leave me out;
When me they fly, I am the wings;
I am the doubter and the doubt,
And I the hymn the Brahmin sings.

This drew upon itself the following parody, published in the *Atlantic Monthly*:

If the gray tom-cat thinks he sings,
Or if the song think it be sung,
He little knows who boot-jacks flings
How many bricks at him I've flung.

This was typical of the kind of mockery that the Transcendentalists aroused among certain sections of the public. They also provoked some more violent reactions. For example, the orthodox Presbyterian *Princeton Review* said: 'We feel it to be our solemn duty to warn our readers, and in our measure, the public, against this German atheism, which the spirit of darkness is employing ministers of the gospel to smuggle in among us under false pretences.'

The quarrel with orthodox Unitarianism led to George Ripley's resignation of his Unitarian ministry, and in 1841 he and his wife started a community at Brook Farm, near the village of West Roxbury, based on

Transcendentalist ideas. The purpose behind Brook Farm is set out in an article by Elizabeth Peabody in the *Dial*, of January 1842: 'A few individuals . . . aiming at the same object, – of being wholly true to their natures as men and women – have been made acquainted with one another, and have determined to become the Faculty of the Embryo University.' Agriculture was to be the basis of their life as being most simple and direct in relation to nature. The Brook Farm experiment lasted until 1857.

Henry Thoreau

The Transcendental movement was at its height during the years 1835–45. The winding up of the *Dial* signalled the beginning of its decline, and after the collapse of Brook Farm it gradually petered out, though the attitudes it engendered persisted in the minds of individual thinkers. In its religious eclecticism it was ahead of its time, and later eclectic movements such as THEOSOPHY were, consciously or unconsciously, following paths already mapped out by the Transcendentalists. C. M.

(Further reading: *91*.)

Transfiguration Medium

A medium whose face, purportedly, takes on the likeness of a deceased communicator; Hélène SMITH is an example: see TRANCE.

Tree of Life See CABALA; see also ASTRAL BODY; TAROT.

Twins and Their Psychic Powers

Twins, and multiple births in general, are among the most interesting of biological oddities in the human species. It is, of course, the one-egg (monozygotic) twins, with their striking similarities in appearance and behaviour, that attract the most attention. Among their most notable aspects are the curious biology of multiple births, their vital statistics, and the illuminating comparisons of identical with fraternal twins. Twin studies have also thrown light on the inheritance of factors in mental health, intelligence, criminal tendencies, and the like. In these and other areas the value of twins to scientific study has been very great.

This article, however, is concerned with what is known about the 'psychic powers' of twins. Are they specially gifted in telepathic exchange or in any of the unusual (psi or parapsychical) capacities that have been investigated in PARAPSYCHOLOGY? Certainly there is a ready popular interest in this question and even a widespread belief that identical twins do have an uncommon amount of telepathic ability.

One other fact to be remembered at the outset is that any event happening to a pair of twins is more newsworthy than the same story would be if no twins were involved. When, for example, in November 1970 in a village in Finland, twin girls of twenty-three both died within a few minutes of each other, with no cause whatsoever indicated, the news went pretty well around the world. Moreover, this complicated event will probably continue to be discussed by scientists for a long time to come, even though (or is it because?) the case is still a pure unadulterated mystery. One of the firm facts about it, however, is that it indicates that the medical sciences have much yet to discover about the nature of life and death, and that two individuals can live and die almost as one.

The case of the Finnish girls has a better-documented parallel in the simultaneous deaths of the Eller twins, which occurred in the state mental hospital in Morganton, North Carolina, in April 1962. These young women (thirty-two years of age) had been diagnosed as suffering from schizophrenia, and hospitalized. Then, because of difficulty over medication, the twins were separated, in spite of their strong protests. It was during the first night after they were moved to different wards that they were both found to have died. The deaths had occurred at nearly the same time. Both bodies were found in a similar foetal position. No cause of death was revealed by the autopsy. There had been stories of apparent telepathic awareness between these two women, but these simultaneous deaths in different wards of the hospital, in which they could have had no sensory communication, suggested a very strong telepathic bond between them. This suggests at least some power of mind over matter, or PSYCHOKINESIS, by which they may have willed themselves to end their lives.

Physicians can draw no conclusion in

The original 'Siamese twins'

cases of this type, and for this reason they have not always been reported; however, they offer a challenge to investigate that science cannot properly longer ignore. It takes only a few cases to raise a question, even though it may take much work to answer it. The question is: do identical twins have any special means of coordinating their activities that others do not?

The answer seems to be of the yes-and-no type. On the negative side is the fact that types of unusual psi or psychic experience studied in parapsychology have not shown an inordinate number of cases coming from identical twins. Statistics are not available, but this is the view taken by Dr Louisa E. Rhine in her book, *Hidden Channels of the Mind* (*396*). The frequency of birth of identical twins is generally known (although it varies with different countries, and other circumstances) but the general frequency of identical twins among those who report unusual psi experiences is not disproportionately high. In any case, an estimate of this kind could only be suggestive; but such as it is, it has not encouraged experienced research workers in parapsychology to search out identical twins for their experimental subjects.

Only a few exploratory studies have been made to compare identical twins with other people in their psychic (or psi) ability. None has given results allowing a conclusion that they are superior in this capacity. No one of

these comparative studies has revealed anything warranting a review here. The most recent study (and the only one conducted by experienced workers in parapsychology) is a preliminary type of test series comparing the clairvoyant card-guessing ability of identical and fraternal twins. The test is known as GESP, meaning general extrasensory perception (see PARAPSYCHOLOGY). The identical twins did somewhat better, but not significantly so, so no conclusion can be drawn. Since the entire group showed evidence of the ability, all that can be said is that identical twins seem to be as good as fraternal, and that is the indication from all the other sources. Another public impression has been discounted.

What, then, is the reason for the great public interest in the idea of telepathy in twins, and how can these outstanding cases of twins who died simultaneously be harmonized with the lack of any unusual frequency of exceptional ESP in twins?

First, the newsworthiness of any event involving a pair of identical twins is something to reckon with. This alone could account for the fact that the public probably knows more about the 3.5 cases of identical twins out of 1,000 human births than about any other subdivision of the 1,000. Second, there is the more significant idea that when something in the personality of a pair of twins happens to lead to a strong reliance of one upon the other (usually it is a one-way relation; one is the more dominant), such a situation may, in extreme cases, do something to strengthen the telepathic type of psychic bond between them. It is suspected that such a relationship may equally develop between a mother and child, or between other non-twin couples, and may even become abnormal in its intensity. The illusion grows that one mind is serving two bodies. But if such a couple are not twins they are not likely to attract international attention.

For the study of parapsychology twins are, even in these few unusual cases, raising questions that are extremely important. The further study of a much larger number of twins should greatly assist in making it possible to give better explanations. At the same time, because of the potential significance of these rare examples, it can be conceded that the public interest is justified, and this interest does help to bring such cases to scientific attention. In fact, there is enough mystery awaiting exploration to justify collecting all the data needed to understand how such a bond as that of the Eller twins could be so binding through health and disease, right up to the threshold of death.   J. B. R.

(Further reading: *66, 169.*)

Umbanda (or Macumba)

A Brazilian religion which combines features of Afro-Christian CANDOMBLÉ and KARDEK spiritism. Its world of spirits is organized into seven different 'lines' or armies, each subdivided into divisions and battalions. It worships West African gods, originally imported into Brazil by black slaves, who are identified with Jesus Christ, the Virgin Mary and Christian saints. These mixed deities preside over the seven lines of spirits. Ceremonies involve drumming, dancing and the POSSESSION of worshippers by the deities. Healing by prayer and by the laying on of hands is also practised. Umbanda appears to have been organized in the 1920s, largely by a white Brazilian Catholic named Zélio de Moraes, who was possessed by the spirits of dead Indians. *(437)*

Unidentified Flying Objects

On 24 June 1947, private pilot Kenneth Arnold took off from Chehalis, Washington, to help in the search for an aeroplane which had crashed among the Cascade Mountains. Alerted by a flash in the sky, he suddenly observed nine bright 'flying' objects, disc-shaped and metallic in appearance. They passed in two files between the peaks of Mount Rainier and Mount Adams in an undulating flight path. A quick calculation of their speed, based on their time of passage over the known distance, showed it to be about twice that of sound – a velocity attained in those days only by rockets. When asked to describe the objects, Arnold, little knowing how his phrase would be taken up, likened their movement to that of 'saucers when skipped over water'. A news reporter spotted the opportunity for a snap headline, and the age of the 'flying saucer' had dawned.

There were many other reports of flying saucers that summer, largely from the western United States. Interest spread rapidly, and there was much puzzlement over the nature of these strange 'machines' which were reported to perform, at speed, abrupt and seemingly controlled manoeuvres which

would have involved 'g'-forces sufficient to kill any human occupant.

We were living on the threshold of the Space Age in 1947, and it is not surprising that the questions on many lips were: 'Are these objects vehicles of extraterrestrial origin, and do they carry pilots from other planets?' Scientists considered such a possibility to be negligible, and this, with the silly name, the plague of hoaxes and the cheap commercial exploitation which followed the first burst of public interest, quickly frightened away those who might otherwise have made a serious study of the reports. Flying saucers as visiting craft from space soon lost credibility and respectability.

So, from the earliest days of flying-saucer publicity, it was left to the haphazard efforts of private individuals and groups rather than organized science to collect and evaluate the information. As public interest was maintained, the United States Air Force established an investigatory project – Project Sign – which was renamed Grudge, and finally Blue Book: explanations in conventional terms were attempted in respect of all reports submitted to them. The project earned a bad name due to the improbability of some of its explanations, and it was known to some as the 'Society for the Explanation of the Uninvestigated'.

UFO Sightings

Over the years UFO reports continued to be made, regardless of the U.S. Air Force attitude, and it was later observed that they came in distinct 'waves'. These peaks of activity were seen in 1947, 1948, 1950 and, very important, 1952. Reports were made by people of all occupations, and particularly by pilots of aircraft. One report typical of this period was made by Captain Clarence S. Chiles and his co-pilot, John B. Whitted, of an Eastern Airlines DC-3 (Dakota).

At 2.45 a.m. on 23 July 1948, a cloudless night with bright moonlight, Chiles saw a projectile-like object heading for his airliner on a south-westerly course. They were 20 miles west of Montgomery, Alabama. He swung the DC-3 into a left turn, and the UFO passed them at a distance of about 200 yards. Whitted then saw that the object was cigar-shaped, of metallic appearance and wingless, and that it had 'portholes' from which came an uncanny light. A 15-yard flame belched from the 'tail'. At the moment of drawing level with the DC-3 the object *stopped dead*, then shot upwards at great speed. The DC-3 wobbled as though caught in a blast. Chiles went aft and found one passenger awake, and very much concerned about the great streak of light he had seen outside the plane.

In 1952 many spectacular UFO events occurred, but none more so than one on the night of 20 July when seven UFOs invaded the sacrosanct airspace over the White House and the Capitol in Washington D.C. The objects were tracked by radar at three different airfields, and were observed visually from the ground as they performed remarkable gyrations. An interceptor was scrambled and vectored on to one of the UFOs. The fighter closed with the luminous object and the pilot was heard to cry out with surprise as the UFO then broke away at incredible speed and vanished: at the same time it *faded out* on the radar screens.

The importance of 1952, however, was that this was the year when the full global nature of the phenomenon was realized, when it was generally accepted that this was not just another American gimmick.

Some of the most interesting European sightings occurred in France, where a small ovoidal object was seen to land on, and take off from, Marignane airfield at Marseille; where scores of people watched great cloud-like cigar-shaped objects over Oloron, and then Gaillac, on two separate days in October. These eerie monsters were accompanied by twenty or thirty wheeling and circling luminous discs. Were these giants the carriers of smaller craft? Some later sightings seemed to confirm this. For instance there were the small discs which were seen to drop one by one from the lower end of a vertical and motionless cigar which then faded and vanished (Vernon, on the River Seine, August 1954). Then there was the giant shape-changing UFO accompanied by six smaller objects which were seen by the captain, crew and passengers of a B.O.A.C. transatlantic airliner; smaller objects which, on the approach of a fighter plane, *joined* the larger object which then faded and vanished (off Labrador, 29 June 1954).

In January 1953 there came a dampening of the excitement: a small panel of scientists – the Robertson Committee – spent four days in official deliberations, studying some twenty case histories. Summarized, their publicized findings were that UFOs posed no threat to the security of the United States, that they were not artifacts of a hostile foreign power, and that people should be trained in the recognition of natural phenomena. The full report of the Committee, however, was put on the secret list. Twelve years later it was routinely declassified. The late Dr James E. McDonald, atmospheric physicist and professor at the University of Arizona, visited Blue Book, where he was permitted to look at the report. On 22 April 1967, at a Washington lecture, he told the American Society of Newspaper Editors that he had found in

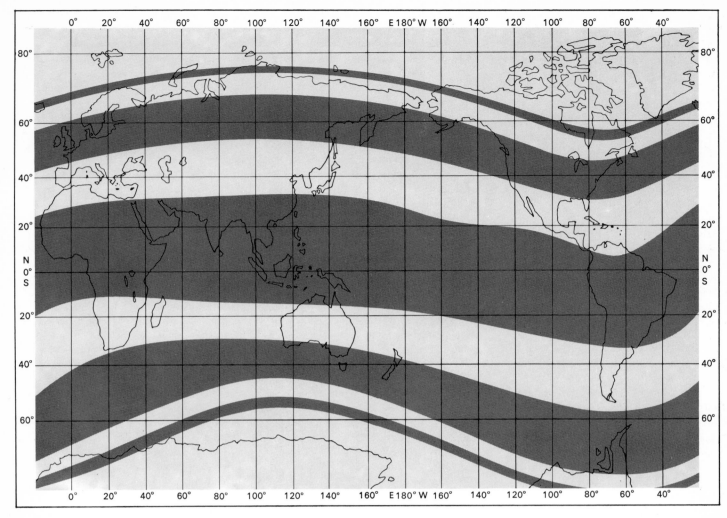

UFO sightings shown as dark bands

the Robertson Report a CIA recommendation that service personnel should debunk flying saucers at every opportunity. After he had made this discovery, the report was re-classified.

Civilian airline crews everywhere were ordered to make UFO reports only to their respective Defence Agencies. Airline UFO incidents made news only when the passengers also saw what happened.

Not unexpectedly, the phenomenon continued, and people all over the globe reported what they saw. The wave incidence was particularly strong in 1954 and 1965, when reports reached enormous numbers, and to only slightly lesser effect in 1957, 1958 and 1964. The year 1966 was quite busy in the United States, and interest in reports of the phenomenon was so widespread, and indignation at the unlikely Blue Book explanations was so great, that the U.S. Air Force allocated $500,000 for a scientific investigation of UFOs. A committee of scientists was assembled at Colorado University under Dr Edward U. Condon; their study occupied two years. A report – known unofficially as

the Condon Report – was published in January 1969. Condon's conclusions were, broadly speaking, that nothing of value to science had come from the study of UFO reports, and that further study could not be justified in the expectation that science would be advanced thereby.

The Condon conclusion was arrived at despite the fact that about one in three of the eighty-seven case histories investigated by the team remained unexplained in the report. The U.S. Air Force thereafter shed its responsibility for the evaluation of UFO reports and Project Blue Book was disbanded in December 1969.

One of the events left completely unidentified by the Condon team occurred over Britain in 1956. The episode began at the R.A.F. station at Bentwaters in Suffolk – leased to the U.S.A.F. – at 9.30 p.m. on 13 August. GCA (Ground Control Approach) radar followed a target which moved off scope at 5,000 m.p.h. Then a group of slow-moving objects were tracked out to sea, where they linked up to form one large, solitary radar echo before moving go-stop-go off scope. Another high-speed radar target was plotted at 10.00 p.m. Then, at 10.55 p.m.,

another object was tracked coming from the east at more than 2,000 m.p.h. Observers outside the GCA were alerted, and they saw a blurred light pass overhead: there was no sonic boom. It happened that a C-47 aircraft was flying over Bentwaters at 4,000 feet at that moment, and its crew reported seeing the UFO passing *below* them.

The GCA crew at Lakenheath R.A.F. station in Norfolk were warned of the approaching UFO, and it was seen, both visually and by radar, to approach, stop, and then move away to the east. More targets were tracked on both the GCA and RATCC search radars at Lakenheath, and R.A.F. Waterbeach was asked to scramble fighters to investigate. A Venom interceptor with nose radar was vectored on to two UFOs in succession. Closing with the second, the pilot achieved gun-radar lock-on, and he also watched the glowing object. Then, without warning, the UFO flipped over and stationed itself on the tail of the Venom, a manoeuvre that was watched on the ground radars. The pilot tried to shake the UFO off his tail by using every aerobatic twist and turn he knew, but in vain. Finally he set off back to Waterbeach with the UFO trailing him for part of the way. He reported that it was the clearest radar target he had ever had.

This summary is condensed from a paper given by Professor James E. McDonald to the American Association for the Advancement of Science in December 1969, subsequently published in *Flying Saucer Review* in March 1970, and later in *Astronautics and Aeronautics*, the journal of the American Institute of Astronautics and Aeronautics.

Visitors from Space?

Events of this kind indicated some form of possible intelligent surveillance. A French science journalist and parapsychologist, Aimé Michel, studied reports of the huge UFO wave of 1954 over Europe, particularly France, in detail. He made a discovery that seemed to confirm this surveillance theory. When the locations of reliable reports were plotted on the map on a day-by-day basis, several of the points could be linked in multi-point straight lines. The first day that he studied was 24 September 1954. Six reliable reports – and others, thought to be not so reliable – were found to lie on a straight line that ran between (and beyond) the towns of Bayonne and Vichy, a line that has become known to researchers as BAVIC. The straight-line theory was named 'Orthoteny'. The discovery was published in *Flying Saucers and the Straight Line Mystery* (the American title for his book, later published in France as *Mysterieux Objets Célestes*).

Visitors from space? Astronomers and others, including the space agencies, have insisted that UFOs have never been seen *entering* the atmosphere, but the extraterrestrial hypothesis has remained the most popular among amateur researchers, who defend the idea of 'nuts and bolts' craft visiting Earth. Yet these are the people who most vigorously deny the evidence from some sources which would seem to support their theory, namely the 'contactees'. The contactee cases should not be confused with the close contact landing and humanoid cases which will be discussed later. The 'contactee' is one who claims to have been met by spacemen from a landed flying saucer, taken for a ride (to the Moon, or Venus, and back) and given messages of love, brotherhood, and ban-the-bomb, addressed to man for his salvation. These beings invariably claim that they are from Mars, or Venus, or some unknown planet, and enthusiastic cults spring up around the 'contactee'.

If not extraterrestrial, then what? It is possible that a clue might be found in the thousands of close-encounter, landing and humanoid reports of the non-contactee kind.

Scores of the reported landings have left a residue of marks and damage: holes, flat-tened crops, swirled reeds, broken tree limbs. There have been accounts of human witnesses harmed, even killed by too close an encounter with a UFO, and there are occasional UFO-related reports of TELEPORTATIONS, and some total abductions. Significantly, animals and birds may also be affected. The journal *Flying Saucer Review* (FSR) has serialized a catalogue of more than 200 known cases of animal reactions. UFOs have also stopped cars, doused headlights, and affected TV sets.

UFOs seem also to be related to unusual light effects: beams of light, some of which stop short of the ground; beams of light that *advance slowly*, horizontally, from landed objects; beams of light that are cool to touch, yet generate great heat at their targets (as at Trancas, Argentina).

Quite common are UFOs which 'land' on water, or *emerge* from the sea; less common, but on record, are objects that pass through walls. There are others that change size and shape before the witnesses' eyes – one has been photographed doing just that over Streatham in south-west London.

Readers will recognize many effects also reported in psychical research. Harold Chibbett, a veteran investigator of paranormal phenomena, recognized the possible overlap of the phenomena as long ago as 1947, and conducted experiments with a medium, under hypnosis, who came into alarming contact with flying-saucer 'entities'.

Flying-Saucer 'Men'

There remain the two most fascinating classes of report in the close encounter category. These are the miraculous healings, and the ever-growing list of reported occupants, both inside and outside the 'craft'; seldom the friendly message-touting 'Venusians' of the contactees, but at best creatures that wave, frequently creatures that 'do not want to know', at worst characters that are very unpleasant. In most instances the activities of these creatures, which are reported by a wide cross-section of respectable, responsible citizens – who do not write books or engage in lecture tours after their experiences – seem quite pointless. For instance, at the height of the UFO wave in, of all places, remote, undeveloped New Guinea, a large circular object with legs hovered silently near Boianai Mission. It was watched by the missionary, Fr William Gill, and thirty-six of his congregation. Moving occupants were observed on a top 'deck', and the assembled witnesses shouted and waved, and were delighted to see one occupant wave back.

A preliminary study of landings and occupants reports was made by FSR in 1966. Published under the title *The Humanoids*, it appeared again in an augmented version in 1969 (53): patterns of similarities in reports were observed, and one theory put forward was that the creatures are 'projections' into the minds of percipients from a solid, visiting craft, be it from an extraterrestrial source, or from some hidden, parallel universe. For instance, some reports speak of humanoids which appear from the UFO in only a partially solid state, with, say, the legs transparent. Again, some witnesses have been found to be clairvoyant: perhaps it is psychic people who are affected by UFOs. Ivan T. Sanderson asked later if they are 'reflections' from a hidden world.

On 1 July 1965, Monsieur M. Masse, a lavender farmer of Valensole in the Basses Alpes of France, saw a landed, egg-shaped object the size of a car, with six legs and a central pivot. Near it two 'boys' were bending over lavender plants. Masse approached stealthily through a vineyard. As he stepped from cover to apprehend the culprits, they faced him. For once they were reported without headgear: Masse saw small 'men' with large craniums, long slanting eyes, high puffy cheeks, slits for mouths and very pointed chins. Similar characteristics were seen by A. V. Boas in Brazil (53) and by Betty and Barney Hill (166). A 'stick' was pointed at Masse, and he was immobilized. The creatures watched him awhile, and then 'bubbled' up a beam of light into the craft. The legs whirled, the pivot 'thumped' and the object floated away for 20 metres, then disappeared. The pivot left a muddy hole in otherwise bone-dry ground, and the legs left four marks. Close to the site all lavender plants died, and new plants would not grow.

Aimé Michel has published a study of a case of 'miraculous' healing. A French doctor, partly paralysed by a wound received in Algeria in 1958, and with a bad leg wound from a gardening accident on 29 October 1968, was awakened in the small hours of 2 November 1968 by his baby son. He hobbled to the kitchen to get a drink for the child, and saw flashing lights outside. Puzzled, he went on to the terrace and saw two UFOs approach. Opposite him they *merged into one*, came lower, and shone a beam of light on him, then vanished like a TV picture going off. He went back to his bedroom to tell his wife, and she realized he was *running*: his leg wound was healed. Next day the paralysis too had gone for good – a cure which many doctors and months in hospital had failed to achieve. Since the encounter both the doctor and the boy have had recurring appearances of a triangular 'rash' around their navels.

Visitors from space, outer or inner? Dr Jacques Vallée, a computer language expert long associated with Aimé Michel and Dr J.

Allen Hynek, has made a fascinating study of UFO-related humanoids, comparing them with reports of ELEMENTALS in his *Passport to Magonia* (*470*); Magonia being a mythical land from which aerial visitors, reportedly captured in the Middle Ages, said they had come. The entities responsible for the UFO phenomenon could have been here on (or in) Earth for a long time. It has been suggested that they have hoodwinked men into thinking they were space visitors, just before our Space Age dawned; that they were aerial visitors in 1897 covering the United States in a primitive 'airship', six years before the Wrights flew powered machines. This is all pure speculation, but interesting. Just as speculative are those who see an unexpected revelation of evidence of 'space visitors' in every archaeological discovery, when every

A glowing UFO with its trail

ancient representation of a sun god becomes a helmeted spaceman. Nevertheless *some* discoveries from the past are impressive, like some modern interpretations of Biblical stories. What of the 'pillar of cloud by day and of fire by night'? What of Elijah's UFO departure, witnessed by Elisha? What of Ezekiel's description of a 'UFO' and space-suited entities (how else could he describe such a sight)?

So it is possible that UFO events have plagued men for countless centuries. Strange signs among the famous cave paintings in France and Spain have puzzled the savants. Artists' signatures, or traffic signs, or phallic symbolism? Aimé Michel has suggested that they are the same shapes that Dr Condon said, in 1969, do not exist: many display remarkable movement, while some even have landing legs and occupants. In his study *Palaeolithic UFO-shapes* (FSR) he shows that

one hunted creature has a pointed chin and slant eyes. Furthermore, the only caves with the UFO shapes lie along, or near to, the BAVIC line. C. B.

(See also AETHERIUS SOCIETY.) (Further reading: *53*, *86*, *166*, *241*, *259*, *327*, *328*, *414*, *415*, *452*, *461*, *468*, *469*, *470*, *477*; see also *Flying Saucer Review*.)

Urantia

The real name of the earth, according to *The Urantia Bible*, a work produced at the turn of the century. 'We are part of the local universe of Nebadon which in turn is part of a super-universe called Orvonton from whose capital, Uversa, came the committee that dictated the book. Seven superuniverses circle the eternal center universe of Havona which contains the stationary isle of Paradise, where God dwells at the geographic center of infinity' (*163*).

Vedanta

One of the major systems of Hindu philosophy, exported to the West in the 19th century by Swami Vivekananda (1863–1902), who attended the Parliament of Religions in Chicago in 1893 as the representative of Hinduism and who later founded the Vedanta Society in San Francisco. Vedanta claims to expound the inner truths of the Vedas, the ancient Hindu scriptures. In Vedanta, 'the whole phenomenal world around us, of nature and of man, has merely a phantom existence' and is a 'veil concealing from our vision the nature of the True Reality'. This reality is Brahma, the ultimate One, and the goal of Vedanta is the realization 'that Brahma is all, and that we too are Brahma' (485).

Vegetotherapy See REICH.

Immanuel Velikovsky

The Russian–Jewish doctor who wrote *Worlds in Collision*, 1950, in which he argued that various catastrophes and extraordinary events of the past, recorded in legends, were caused by close approaches of comets to the earth. These events included the parting of the waters of the Red Sea, which allowed Moses and the Israelites to cross, the collapse of the walls of Jericho and the standing still of the sun at Joshua's command, and the fall of ATLANTIS. (*116, 473, 474, 475*)

Versailles Adventure

The curious experience of two English ladies, Miss Moberley and Miss Jourdain, who in 1901 visited the Petit Trianon at Versailles, where Marie Antoinette had lived before the French Revolution, and appear to have been carried back in time to the year 1770, seeing features and people in the costume of that period: they published their account in *An Adventure*, 1911. (*144, 180, 243, 297*)

Vibrations See ASTROLOGY; NUMEROLOGY; RADIESTHESIA; SPIRITUALISM; TRANCE.

Joseph René Vilatte (d. 1929) See WANDERING BISHOPS.

Pierre-Michel Vintras (1807-75)

The 'Prophet of Tilly', born Eugène Vintras, a prophet and wonder-worker whose movement, the Work of Compassion (*Oeuvre de la Miséricorde*) was for a time very popular in Normandy. In 1851 he adopted the title of Strathaniel, 'herald of God'. He saw visions of Christ, the Virgin Mary and the Archangel Michael, and received heavenly warnings of impending doom and frightful catastrophes about to be visited upon the earth. He was famous for the apparently miraculous appearance of bleeding hosts on his altar. There was a close connection between his movement and the *Oeuvre de Dieu*, a Polish movement organized by Andrei TOWIANSKI. After the death of Vintras, the Abbé BOULLAN seized the leadership of part of his sect. (*493*)

Voice Phenomena

In 1959 the Swedish film producer Friedrich Jürgenson discovered voice manifestations on tape recordings which on further examination were found to be sentences, purporting to have been spoken by persons known to be dead. Dr Konstantin Raudive, a Latvian psychologist, joined Mr Jürgenson in 1964 and, together with leading scientists, they conducted hundreds of experiments designed to reproduce the voice phenomena. By 1969 Dr Raudive had collected about 100,000 voice samples on tape. Professor Dr H. Bender of the University of Freiburg, Germany, and Dr F. Karger of the Max Planck Institute, Munich, carried out a series of tests, including experiments with a voice printer at the Central Office for Telegraphic Technology, Berlin. Scientific papers were published by Professor Bender in Germany which stated: 'An extensive examination with better technical equipment in May 1970 made the paranormal hypothesis of the origin of the Voice Phenomena highly probable.'

Dr Raudive published his extensive research under the title *BREAKTHROUGH – An Amazing Experiment in Electronic Communication with the Dead*. Before allowing publication in the English language, Sir Robert Mayer, chairman of the publishing house, insisted that further experiments should be carried out in Britain and that the findings should be verified by independent scientists and electronic engineers. Mr Peter Bander, a senior lecturer and trained psychologist, was asked by the publishers to coordinate a series of controlled tests.

Sponsored by a national newspaper, one of the controlled experiments was carried out by two chief engineers of Pye Ltd in the presence of other scientists. Over 200 voices manifested themselves during a twenty-minute recording, of which 27 were clear enough to be played back over a loudspeaker. Among the material were four sentences purporting to come from the late Artur Schnabel (a life-long friend of Sir Robert Mayer, who was also present) and various voices directed at experimenters. A further test was carried out by A. Peter Hale, Britain's leading expert in electronic screen suppression, in a laboratory at Belling & Lee Ltd. Afterwards, Mr Hale issued the statement: 'From the results obtained . . . something is happening which I can't explain in normal physical terms.'

Subsequent experiments, especially those designed to break the mystery of the voices, failed to disprove Raudive's theory that the originators of the voices were, in fact, people who had died. Telefis Eireann (Irish Television) devoted two programmes to the phenomenon; representatives of the Catholic Church were present as well as electronic experts, psychologists and scientists. The subsequent publicity in the press and on radio and television caused further experiments to be carried out, and statements were made by leading churchmen explaining the position of the Catholic and Anglican Churches: while unable to comment on the electronic aspects of the phenomenon, neither Church felt that the experiments or the results obtained contradicted their teachings, and the theory that these are the voices of the dead would simply confirm the theological belief in a life after death.

Two alternative theories were put forward: Professor Bender developed the *animistic* theory; he suggested that electronic impulses are sent out by the subconscious mind and register as human speech on the tape. The other theory was that these voices might be transmitted by an unknown method from perhaps another planet or an intelligent source somewhere in the universe.

During the year after Dr Raudive's publication, Peter Bander collected the facts, test results and opinions of the scientists involved in the experiments. He dismisses Professor Bender's theory on the ground that the mathematical chance of electronic impulses from the subconscious converting themselves into human language is too remote to consider, especially as languages recorded were often not spoken or understood by the experimenters. For the theory of transmissions from other planets Mr Bander has found no evidence at all; he concentrates on the claim that these voices might come from discarnate entities who appear to communicate on an electro-magnetic tape.

Although very critical of some aspects of Raudive's research, Bander and his collaborators give their full backing to the theory that, until proven otherwise, Raudive's claims are valid in principle. Friedrich Jürgenson, the discoverer of the voice phenomena, has always maintained that electronic communication with the dead is possible. He was recently created a Commander of the Order of St Gregory the Great by Pope Paul VI. Although there has never been an official attitude by the Catholic Church to the voices, it appears from the number of theologians who have cooperated with Jüfgenson, Bander and Raudive, that the voice phenomena are taken very seriously.

Technical Data and Methods of Recording

Although the controlled experiments have been carried out with extremely sophisticated instruments, equally good results have been obtained with ordinary domestic tape recorders. No particular commercial brand has given better results than others, but it appears that the more sophisticated tape recorders secure a clearer play-back. On the other hand, some excellent recordings were made by Telefis Eireann's senior researcher, Mrs Pan Collins, on a small cassette recorder.

Three methods of recording electronic voices appear to be favoured: the Microphone Method; the Diode Recording; and the Inter-frequency Recording.

In the first method, the tape recorder is set on 'record' with the microphone connected in the usual way. The volume is set on maximum. This method often produces

Dr Raudive at a voice recording

resonant or whispering voices. However, the drawback is that the microphone will register all noises in the room, and unless the experimenter can be absolutely certain that none of the 'voices' or noises recorded have a natural and explainable origin, there is a danger of interpreting even the ticking of a clock as rhythmic speech. Peter Bander feels that this method is scientifically too unreliable for use in controlled experiments.

Alternatively, a diode is substituted for the microphone; this is probably the most reliable method of recording the phenomenon. The quality of the voices obtained varies according to conditions. Both Raudive and Bander have used a variety of diodes successfully; in fact, all controlled experiments in Britain were carried out by this method. Two engineers, Rudolph (Telefunken, Germany) and Seidl (Austria) have developed more sophisticated diodes, the Goniometer and the Psychofon. Raudive has successfully used both but the results do not differ from those obtained with an ordinary diode.

Thirdly, the Interfrequency Method employs a radio which is set on a true interfrequency. Although used by Raudive, it is probably the most difficult method and, according to Bander, the most suspect. Because of overcrowding of the wave bands, it is almost impossible to obtain a true interfrequency which is not being used by some broadcasting station.

The human elements of error, auto-suggestion and impatience appear to have been the downfall of some enthusiastic amateurs. Dr Raudive's meticulous collection of research material indicates that a great deal of time must be spent on play-back of individual recordings; his results (voices) are usually in more than one language and polyglot. Ban-

der's book, which deals mainly with tests carried out by English-speaking experimenters, contradicts Raudive's conclusions in many respects: he explains that the 'messages' appear to have been in one language at a time, though different sentences had sometimes been in more than one language when Dr Raudive was present.

In 1970 and 1971 Trinity College, Cambridge, awarded postgraduate studentships for the investigation of the voice phenomena. However, much more research will have to be carried out before a person who wishes to communicate with the dead can 'dial M for Mother'. J. van D.

(Further reading: *15, 385.*)

Voodoo

The native religion of Haiti, stemming from West African cults and with parallels in other parts of the West Indies and in Brazil (see CANDOMBLÉ; UMBANDA). It is centred on ceremonies in which the worshippers are 'ridden' or taken POSSESSION of by gods and spirits. It has influenced magical practices and minor cults among American Negroes. (*116a, 240, 325, 417, 507*)

Vril

The name coined by Bulwer Lytton, the novelist, for a mysterious wonder-working current of power, of which he wrote: 'I did not mean Vril for mesmerism, but for electricity, developed into uses as yet only dimly guessed, and including whatever there may be genuine in mesmerism . . .' In the early 1930s there was a Vril Society, or Luminous Lodge, in Berlin, which concentrated on developing the Vril power in the human body through exercises similar to those of YOGA. (*303*)

Arthur Edward Waite (1857-c.1940)

Mystic, occultist and prolific author, Waite was born in Brooklyn, New York, though he spent most of his life in England. He joined the THEOSOPHICAL SOCIETY but was unable to believe in the MASTERS. He became a member of the GOLDEN DAWN, published an occult magazine, *The Unknown World*, and in 1903 took control of the G.D.'s Isis-Urania temple in London, rewriting all the rituals in a Christian spirit. Among the members of his version of the G.D. were Evelyn Underhill, the writer on mysticism, and Charles Williams, the esoteric novelist. Waite wrote an autobiography, *Shadows of Life and Thought*, 1938, and in a series of massive and ponderous tomes attempted to trace the history of a 'secret tradition' which he discerned beneath the surface of Christianity, the CABALA, ALCHEMY, Freemasonry and the Grail legends. His books include *The Brotherhood of the Rosy Cross*, *The Real History of the Rosicrucians*, *The Holy Kabbalah*, *The Book of Black Magic and of Pacts*, later revised as *The Book of*

A. E. Waite

Ceremonial Magic, *The Holy Grail*, *The Secret Tradition in Alchemy*, *Lives of Alchemistical Philosophers*, *The Secret Tradition in Freemasonry*, *The Pictorial Key to the Tarot*. He also translated Eliphas LÉVI's *Dogme et Rituel de la haute magie* into English (*284*) and presided over the design of a set of deplorably ugly TAROT cards, which are now the best-known version of the pack. He was caricatured in Aleister CROWLEY's novel *Moonchild* (*103*) as the character Arthwait, 'a dull and inaccurate pedant without imagination or real magical perception', who 'tippled habitually' and was 'comically ignorant of the languages in which he boasted scholarship'. Other, less prejudiced writers have also criticized Waite's scholarship, though it is worth noticing that the leading scholarly authority on the Cabala describes his treatment of that subject as showing a 'real insight into the world of Kabbalism' (*420*). (*235, 262, 479 to 484* inclusive)

Wandering Bishops

The meaning of this title differs greatly in usage and application from its medieval origin. Today it is the description given to founders and leaders of some strange religious movements within a fringe, or underworld, of the Christian Church. In almost every known case Wandering Bishops have been obsessed with the desire to obtain valid episcopal consecration from sources which are usually remote and questionable.

Broadly speaking, these religious movements are of a 'Catholic' type, but with personal interpretations of a doctrine. High-sounding titles, elaborate rituals and ceremonies, and the unreality of the ecclesiastical dreamworld of the majority of Wandering Bishops, have nevertheless profoundly influenced the lives of a large number of ordinary people, often leading to financial disasters for individuals. Although there have been many court cases involving Wandering Bishops, lack of evidence has made it an impossible task to condemn or exonerate their status. Three months before his death in 1968, the late Archbishop Harold P. Nicholson sold his entire archives to a publisher and for the first time the intricate workings and operations of some of the Wandering Bishops became documented. This will, in due course, lead to an entirely new assessment of their role in society. The first court cases against Wandering Bishops, based on this evidence, have recently started in the U.S.A. and the findings of the U.S. Federal Courts will have repercussions on future legal disputes of this kind all over the world.

Seen in the context of their activities, Wandering Bishops of the 20th century are certainly wrongly named. Unlike their histo-

rical predecessors, they no longer 'wander'; they usually operate from an obscure address in the suburbs of cities. Among them are undoubtedly a few who believe that they have a true vocation to the ministry of one of the historic Churches; their rejection by such Churches on grounds of unsuitability may have led them into the ever-open arms of some Wandering Bishop who, without hesitation and usually for a fee, has conferred upon them episcopal orders and thus continued the never-ending chain of more Wandering Bishops.

Historical Development

Wandering Bishops can be traced back to the Middle Ages; if a Bishop had been deprived of his office because of heresy or misconduct, or if a person had been consecrated to a see and his intended flock refused to elect him to the position afterwards, such a Bishop was compelled to 'wander' and seek another place where he might earn his living. In the 17th and 18th centuries, many Missionary Bishops from Ireland wandered on the Continent and in America. Councils and Synods legislated against them, not because their consecration was in doubt, but because of the disruption they caused in the administration of the Church. It was only in the 19th century that the episcopal status of many Wandering Bishops was questioned. During the last seventy years, hundreds of autocephalous Churches (independent bodies without any connection with the historical Churches) have been founded. All these Churches claim to be 'Apostolic', 'Catholic' or 'Orthodox' and most of them claim an 'Eastern' origin.

The claim to be a valid Bishop is based on the apostolic succession, an unbroken line of consecration going back to one of the Apostles, some 1,950 years ago. The decision whether a Bishop is valid or not is complicated by two contrasting views which have been held within the historical Churches: the Augustinian and the Cyprianic theories, named after St Augustine and St Cyprian. The Cyprianic theory states: 'Once a Bishop, always a Bishop.' The interpreters of St Augustine carried this one step further, saying: 'Once possessing the powers of a Bishop, always possessing the powers of a Bishop.' According to St Cyprian, a Bishop can only carry out his function, especially that of consecrating other Bishops, if and when he acts with the authority of the true Catholic Church. This viewpoint is today held by both the Roman Catholic Church and the traditional Orthodox Churches. St Augustine's theory, on the other hand, appears to be cited by those who consider validity regardless of a Bishop's allegiance to a Church and even outside the broadest Christian concept.

Wandering Bishops

The established and traditional Churches require exoteric evidence and authenticity before judging a Bishop to be valid.

A second factor in deciding whether a Bishop is validly consecrated or not, is less tangible and therefore more difficult to prove or disprove; it concerns the esoteric evidence of 'intention'. For a consecration to be valid, the Holy Ghost has to be present and both parties, the consecrator and the consecrated Bishop, must have the 'intention' to pass on and receive the Holy Spirit and his powers. It is because of the esoteric evidence or lack of it that no court has so far been able to pronounce on the validity of Wandering Bishops and give a definite ruling; neither plaintiffs nor defendants in any actions which have been heard were able to produce the Holy Spirit to testify in court. There is little doubt that some of the Wandering Bishops are validly ordained in the esoteric sense; this applies particularly to those whose apostolic successions go back to a valid Roman Catholic Bishop who, for some reason, was excommunicated from his Church. But what

A congress of 'wandering bishops'

constitutes a 'valid Bishop' in the legal sense can only be gauged by exoteric evidence; approval and authorization by a *bona fide* Church. Because of the confusion which has arisen over the last few decades, especially as most of the Wandering Bishops ordain each other *sub conditione*, the established Churches refer to Wandering Bishops as 'irregular' rather than 'invalid'.

Sub conditione, 'on condition', refers to a second ordination or consecration which is given in case the first one was invalid. For example, a number of Church of England clergymen who doubted the validity of their own orders, because they had been ordained in a period when the laying on of hands during ordination was not practised, had themselves ordained *sub conditione* by Wandering Bishops. This has caused great embarrassment in the Anglican Church. Ordination and consecration *sub conditione* has become a routine practice among Wandering Bishops through which they confer upon each other apostolic lines of succession: thus Mr de Willmott Newman (see below) claims to have been received into no fewer than twenty-three of such different lines, having

had himself consecrated time after time.

Lines of Succession

The three main lines of apostolic succession are named after those men who constitute in the eyes of the Wandering Bishops the link between the traditional Churches and their own autocephalous organizations. *The Ferrette Succession* is claimed by the following Churches and all the Wandering Bishops and their organizations who, in turn, base their origin on them:

Ancient British Church
English Orthodox Church
English Episcopal Church
Evangelical Church of England
Free Protestant Episcopal Church of
  England
Western Orthodox Catholic Church
Indian Orthodox Church
Free Catholic Church, Apostolic
  Catholic Church
United Armenian Catholic Church
South African Episcopal Church

Jules Ferrette (d. 1904), a convert to the Roman Catholic Church, became a priest in

1855, but left within one year of ordination. In 1866, he claimed to have been consecrated Bishop of Iona by the Jacobite Patriarch of Antioch, who also allegedly created him an independent Patriarch. No convincing evidence has ever been produced to substantiate the claim of the ex-priest Jules Ferrette, though photographs of alleged documents, proving the 'irrefutable validity' of Jules Ferrette, have been circulated by Wandering Bishops for the past 100 years.

The Vilatte Succession is claimed by:

Old Catholic Christian Church
Catholic Christian Church
Orthodox Catholic Church in England
Autonomous African Universal Church
Orthodox-Keltic Church of the British
   Commonwealth of Nations
Autonomous British Eastern Church
   (Orthodox-Catholic Province of our
   Lady of England, Devon and
   Cornwall)
Jesuene or Free Orthodox Catholic
   Church
Holy Orthodox-Catholic Church of
   Great Britain

American Catholic Church
American Catholic Church (Western
   Orthodox)
American Episcopal Church
American Catholic Church (Syro-
   Antiochean)
American Holy Orthodox Catholic
   Apostolic Eastern Church, affiliated
   with the Holy Orthodox Catholic
   Patriachate of America

Eglise Catholique Française
Eglise Orthodoxe Gallicane Autocéphale
Eglise Primitive Catholique et
   Apostolique
Eglise Catholique Apostolique Primitive
   d'Antioche Orthodoxe et de
   Tradition Syro-Byzantine
Sainte Eglise Apostolique et Gallicane
Sainte Eglise Celtique en Bretagne
Sainte Eglise Apostolique
Communion Evangelica Catholica
   Eucharistica
Hochkirche in Österreich
Indian National Church

African Orthodox Church
African Orthodox Church of New York
   and Massachusetts
Afro-American Catholic Church
African Greek Orthodox Church

Joseph René Vilatte (d. 1929), like Jules Ferrette, a lapsed Catholic, changed allegiance to various Churches during his lifetime. In 1892 Vilatte was consecrated by a Goan priest who had been a Brahmin,

Antonio Alvarez, now styled Mar Julius I, Metropolitan of the Independent Catholic Church of Ceylon. Most American Churches issued statements declaring Vilatte's consecration null and void.

The Mathew Succession is claimed by the following Churches:

Old Roman Catholic Church (Pro-
   Uniate Rite)
Old Roman Catholic Church (English
   Rite)
Old Roman Catholic Church in North
   America (Two Groups)
Old Catholic Church in Ireland
Old Catholic Orthodox Church
Old Catholic Evangelical Church of God
Old Holy Catholic Church (Church of
   the One Life)
English (Old Roman Catholic) Rite
North American Old Roman Catholic
   Church
Mexican Old Roman Catholic Church
Diocese-Vicariate of Niagara Falls
Old Catholic Church in America
Catholic Church of North America
Independent Episcopal Church of the
   United States and Canada
Liberal Catholic Church (three different
   Churches)
Eglise Catholique Evangélique
Canonical Old Roman Catholic Church
   in Communion with the Primatial
   See of Caer-Glow
Free Anglo-Catholic Church and Order
   of Llanthony Brothers

During his forty-three years of religious activity and the twelve years of his episcopate, Arnold Harris MATHEW (1852–1919) changed his religious opinions and allegiances quite frequently. All his life he was torn between Rome and Canterbury. He trained for the Anglican Ministry, changed to Rome and was ordained a priest in 1877. In 1889 he left the Roman Catholic Church and became a Unitarian. Although he was never officially received into the Anglican Church, he had the Bishop of London's permission to officiate. In 1894 Mathew laid claim to the title of Earl of Llandaff. In 1908 he was consecrated by the Bishops of the Old Catholic Church – the well-established, though comparatively small, communion which is today mainly confined to the Netherlands – and the historic validity of his apostolic succession cannot be questioned. In view of the fact that the Old Catholic community in England was practically non-existent, Bishop Mathew became, in the true sense, a Wandering Bishop.

The Catholicate of the West

Probably the best-known, certainly the

most ambitious, of all the Wandering Bishops is His Sacred Beatitude Mar Georgius I (Hugh George de Willmott Newman), Patriarch of Glastonbury, holder of innumerable academic degrees, Prince de Mardin, Prince of Saxe-Noricum, etc., etc. Once a Secretary of the National Association of Cycle Traders, he soon rose to incredible heights in the world of nobility and later in 'ecclesiastical circles'. In Archbishop Nicholson's archives are well-documented references to the Prince of Saxe-Noricum (Mr de Willmott Newman), who in 1935 made the newspaper headlines during an appearance in court. By 1938 he appears to have had a calling to the priesthood and was ordained by Bishop James McFall. In 1941 the Bishop of the Old Orthodox Catholic Church in England appointed him an Abbot and in 1943 he obtained episcopal consecration as Archbishop of Glastonbury. In 1944 he founded the Western Orthodox Catholic Church and constituted the Catholicate of the West. He has looked upon it as his foremost duty to establish and secure a 'legitimate and validly ordained ministry' in the Catholic sense. In the course of the following years he collected a great number of episcopal consecrations (*sub conditione*) and claims today to hold at least twenty-three lines of apostolic succession. He is the founder or chancellor of various Universities, one of which, the University of St John, was sold in 1962 for £50 to Archbishop Wolsey of America and Canada; the latter established a flourishing trade in degrees in the United States. The Patriarch of Glastonbury's most successful 'creation' was the Archbishop of Karim (His Grace Mar Joannes The Most Reverend Harold Percival Nicholson, D.D., Ph.D., M.A., etc., etc.) who, in turn, founded the British Ancient Catholic Church.

Harold Percival Nicholson (see plate, page 256), former head waiter at the St James Hotel in London, has been by far the most successful Wandering Bishop on record. His adviser and close collaborator has been, with brief temporary breaks, the Patriarch of Glastonbury. Between 1949 and 1952, Nicholson's annual income, always provided by women, is estimated in the region of £100,000. One woman friend, the late Mrs Mary Tucker Smith, bought him a cathedral in Chelsea, London, and records show that she alone spent in the region of £1m. on Archbishop Nicholson during the last few years of her life. A power of attorney, witnessed by the Patriarch of Glastonbury, gave Archbishop Nicholson full charge of the financial fortunes of another wealthy old lady, who after Nicholson's death found herself penniless in the geriatric ward of a London hospital.

Between 1951 and 1952 Nicholson spent

£33,000 on robes, jewelry and other ecclesiastical paraphernalia. After the death of Mrs Tucker Smith, his fortune declined until, in 1968, he died a pauper. During his heyday in London, he lived in great style, undertook many world cruises and even paid 'State Visits' to other countries where he was received by cabinet ministers and civil authorities, on many of whom he bestowed Knighthoods and Orders of Chivalry.

Since 1945 Mar Georgius (Newman) and Mar Joannes (Nicholson) have dominated the ecclesiastical fringe world. Together with the Prince Patriarch Joannes Maria van Assendelft, whom they had consecrated Archbishop of France, they restored the old Roman Empire when van Assendelft, claiming to be the 147th successor of St Peter, crowned a young man on the 18 November 1956 as the 269th Roman Emperor. His Imperial Majesty Marziano II, in turn, bestowed high titles of nobility upon the Spiritual Fathers who, at the same ceremony, also made the coronation of the Dowager Empress Olga possible.

One of the great mysteries has always been the *bona fide* passports, issued by H.M. Government to some of the Wandering Bishops, which gave them their full ecclesiastical titles. The passport of Mr Nicholson was made out to His Grace the Most Reverend Dr H. P. Nicholson, and his designation was given as Titular Archbishop of Karim and Primate of the A.C.C. Many of their successes abroad have been entirely due to entering foreign countries with a passport issued by the British Government, testifying to their credentials. Recent investigations have shown that such passports have been obtained legitimately, but by cunningly devised means of presenting authenticated evidence for their claims to such titles. With unlimited financial funds at his disposal, Nicholson employed a Commissioner of Oaths to be present during the ceremonies of consecration. This gentleman afterwards witnessed, under his signature and seal, that a ceremony had taken place during which various Bishops (all given with their full names and titles) had validly consecrated a certain person and that these Bishops had placed their signature upon the document. Typewritten copies of such documents were then sent to the same Commissioner of Oaths and declared to be true copies of the original. These copies were then stamped and registered with Somerset House and submitted to the Foreign Office. Because there has never been any reason to doubt the good faith of the Commissioner of Oaths or the documents he had testified to, passports have been issued to applicants, giving them their full episcopal status under the seal of the Foreign Office.

Archbishop Nicholson receiving communion

Bearing in mind the great number of Bishops created by Nicholson, usually assisted by Newman, the revenue from such consecrations has been very substantial. Records show that the fees charged varied from £259 to £700, which usually included a doctorate granted by one of Newman's 'Universities' and often a title of nobility granted by the 'International College of Arms and Noblesse', also founded by Newman.

Allegations that all Wandering Bishops are associated with black magic or similar rites, have never been proven. There is a strong element of THEOSOPHY and in some cases of Masonry in most of their Churches, but it is impossible to define the beliefs or philosophies of the Wandering Bishops clearly. As to the number of adherents, members of the various Churches, ordained priests, deacons, deaconesses, and so on, no reliable figures are available. Those issued by the Wandering Bishops themselves are usually exaggerated. In many cases the Bishops and priests greatly outnumber the laity. The world of the Wandering Bishops is a dream world, full of fantasies and imagination. Men like Mar Georgius and Archbishop Nicholson are exceptions to the rule. J. VAN D.

(Further reading: *6, 55, 471*.)

Warlock

A romantic term for a male witch, seldom if ever used by witches themselves.

Water Divining, Water Witching See DOWSING.

William Wynn Westcott (1848-1925)

One of the founders of the GOLDEN DAWN; he was also a leading member of the SOC. ROS. and an associate of Madame BLAVATSKY and Anna KINGSFORD. His magical mottoes in the G.D. were *Sapere Aude* ('Dare To Be Wise') and *Non Omnis Moriar* ('I Shall Not Wholly Die'). He translated the *Sefer Yetsirah* (Book of Formation, see CABALA) and the *Chaldean Oracles of Zoroaster* into English. (*235, 262*)

West London Zodiac See GLASTONBURY ZODIAC.

Wicca

The term used by modern witches for their craft: see WITCHCRAFT.

Burning witches in the 16th century

Mrs Willett

The pseudonym of Mrs Charles Coombe Tennant (1874–1956), British medium. Two of the founders of the S.P.R., F. W. H. Myers and Edmund Gurney, purportedly communicated through her by automatic writing and trance-speech, and insisted that she should give sittings in the presence of Sir Oliver Lodge and Gerald Balfour. She played an important part in the CROSS-CORRESPONDENCES. She also produced between 1912 and 1918 a series of scripts and utterances in trance which referred to the private life of A. J. Balfour (1848–1930), the Conservative politician and Prime Minister; this episode being known as the 'Palm Sunday case'. In 1910 she wrote a note about a script which she had obtained: 'I came downstairs from resting and suddenly felt I was getting very dazed and light-headed with a hot sort of feeling on the back of my neck – I was looking at the *Times* newspaper – I did not think of script until I felt my hands being as it were drawn together – I could not seem to keep them apart and the feeling got worse – and with a sort of *rush* I felt compelled to get writing materials and sit

down though [people] were in the room . . .' The script which she then produced began: 'You felt the call it I it is I who write Myers. I need urgently you say this tell Lodge this word Myers Myers . . .' (S.P.R. *Proceedings*, June 1911). After her own death, Mrs Willett purportedly communicated through Geraldine CUMMINS to write *Swan on a Black Sea*: see MEDIUMS. (*13, 14, 108, 213, 303*)

Witchcraft (Modern)

Twenty years ago, only a few eccentrics claimed to be practising traditional witchcraft; today devotees of the rapidly expanding witch-cult are to be found in every important urban centre in both Great Britain and the United States. The number of active witches in Britain is conservatively estimated at between five and ten thousand; in the U.S.A. there are possibly twice that number.

In spite of frequent claims to the contrary made by cultists who claim to be able to trace their 'witch ancestry' back for 400 or 500 years, it is most improbable that the origins of present-day witchcraft go back any further than the publication of Margaret MURRAY's *The Witch-Cult in Western Europe*,

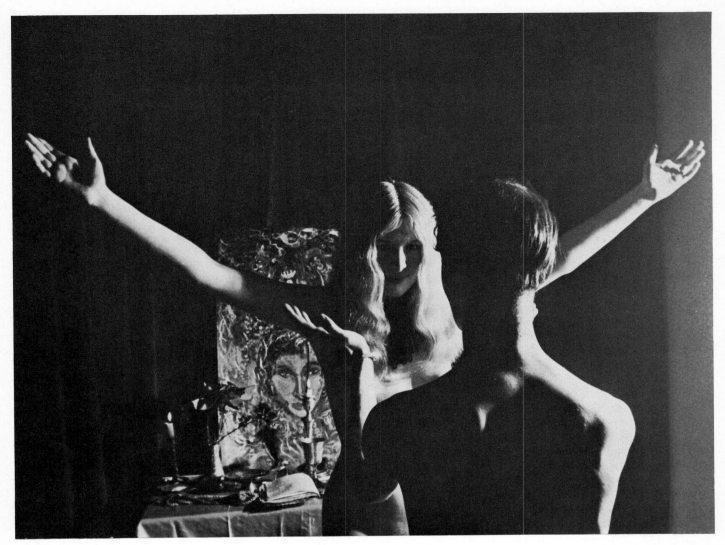

A modern priestess of the craft, and *opposite* a 16th-century invocation

1921 (*343*; see also *344, 345*). Dr Murray's basic theses were:

1   That the late-medieval and Renaissance witch trials were no mere intellectual aberrations, but the outcome of a conflict between Christianity and an organized counter-religion.

2   That this counter-religion of witchcraft, which Dr Murray preferred to call the 'Dianic Cult', could be traced back to the pre-classical cults of the fertile Great Mother and the Divine King, the incarnate god ritually slain to ensure the good of his people and the fertility of their crops.

3   That as late as the 17th century this Dianic cult retained its own religious hierarchy, its own festivals, its own holy places and its own peculiar structure – the witches being supposedly organized in cells, usually of thirteen members, known as covens.

4   That some of the kings of England had been high-ranking members of the cult and that at least one of them – William Rufus – had been a divine king, an incarnate deity joyfully willing his own death in accordance with his Dianic faith.

An overwhelming majority of scholars regard the 'Murray theory' as historically and anthropologically untenable. Nevertheless, it has unquestionably exerted, and still does exert, a considerable influence upon occultists. It is perhaps significant that Dr Murray derived a great deal of her material from the 19th-century 'Rosicrucian' writer, Hargrave JENNINGS: curiously enough she seems to have made no acknowledgment of his influence in spite of the fact that some passages in her writings are little more than abbreviated quotations from Jennings's odd book *The Rosicrucians, Their Rites and Mysteries.*

Gerald Gardner

Though the contemporary witch-cult prob-

ably originated about 1921, it has been alleged that even this late date is too early by something like thirty years and that the entire witchcraft revival sprang from the sexual and occult fantasies of an elderly Englishman named Gerald GARDNER. This is probably an overstatement, for there is reason to believe that in the early 1940s Gardner was in touch with groups of self-styled witches in both the New Forest and the English town of St Albans. There is no doubt, however, that it was Gardner, a superb publicist, who was largely responsible for the rapid growth of the cult.

Gardner, a retired customs official who dabbled in Spiritualism, anthropology and folklore, was possessed of both unorthodox sexual tastes and an inclination towards occultism. He seems to have felt that it would be pleasant to combine the two into a new 'Gardnerian' witch-cult, which would employ a set of rituals involving nudity, scourging and copulation. Gardner appears to have been a sado-masochist (as a boy he had enjoyed being beaten by his governess), an exhibitionist and a voyeur.

He must have felt that the literary task of composing such rituals was beyond him, for he approached Aleister Crowley (see CROWLEY), of whose *Ordo Templi Orientis* (O.T.O.) he was an initiate, and asked him to undertake the job. Crowley agreed to do so: apart from the fact that Gardner was willing to pay him a suitable fee, he had for many years been convinced of the need for a religion of fertility and fun that would present his own new faith of Thelema in popularized form. As long ago as 1915 he had written to his disciple C. S. JONES urging the creation of just such a cult as Gardner's projected witchcraft: 'The time is just ripe for a natural religion. People like rites and ceremonies, and they are tired of hypothetical gods. Insist on the real benefits of the Sun, the Mother-Force, the Father-Force and so on. . . In short be the founder of a new and greater Pagan cult in the beautiful land which you have made your home. . .'

For some time this new Gardnerian witchcraft, based on Crowley's literary compositions as revised by Gardner, remained semidormant, being practised only by Gardner and a few of his close associates. In 1954, however, Gardner published *Witchcraft Today* (*171*), a book in which he rehashed Margaret Murray's basic theses and claimed that witchcraft covens were still operating and that he was associated with them. Gardner immediately received a flood of letters and inquiries from would-be witches, both male and female, and many of these were eventually admitted to the cult. These newly-made witches in their turn initiated others, and within a few years there were groups ('covens') of witches in every major British city.

The Book of Shadows

The rituals and instructions for operative witchcraft produced by Crowley became collectively known as *The Book of Shadows* and this work is still the basic technical manual used by almost all covens of the cult. It is a curious blend of elements largely derived from Crowley's religion of Thelema, on the one hand, and the Gnostic survivals recorded by C. C. LELAND in his 19th-century studies of Italian folklore (*Aradia, or the Gospel of the Witches*) and Romany folklore (*Gypsy Sorcery*), on the other.

This mingling of seemingly incompatible elements into a homogeneous whole is well illustrated by the section of *The Book of Shadows* known as The Charge:

Listen to the words of the Great Mother who was of old called among men Artemis, Astarte, Diana, Melusine, Ceridwen, Arianrod, Baich and by many other names.

At mine altars the youths of Lacedaemon and Sparta made due sacrifice.

Whenever ye have need of anything, once in the month and better it be if the Moon is full then shall ye assemble in some secret place and adore Me who am Queen of all Witcheries. There shall ye assemble, ye who are fain to learn all sorcery. I shall teach ye things unknown and ye shall be free from all slavery. As a sign that ye be really free ye shall be naked in your rites and ye shall dance, sing, feast, make music, make love – all in Praise of Me. For Mine is the ecstasy of the spirit and Mine is joy on earth, for my Law is Love under Will.

Mine is the secret door of youth, Mine is the Cup of the Wine of Life, Mine is the Cauldron of Ceridwen, Mine is the Holy Grail.

I am the gracious Goddess who gives the gift of joy unto the heart of Man. Upon earth I give unimaginable joys; upon death I give peace, rest and ecstasy. Nor do I demand aught in sacrifice.

Hear ye the words of the Star Goddess, She whose feet crush the host of Heaven, She Whose body encircles the Universe:

I am the Beauty of the Green Earth and the Moon among the Stars, the Mystery of the Waters and the desire in the heart of Man. Arise and come unto Me! From Me all things proceed, unto Me all things return. Before my face ye shall be enfolded in the rapture of the Infinite.

Let my worship be within the heart that rejoiceth. For all acts of love and pleasure are my rituals . . .

Thou who thinkest to seek for Me, know that thy seeking and yearning shall avail thee not unless thou know the Mystery, that if that which thou seekest thou findest not within thee, thou shalt never find it without thee.

For, behold! I have been with thee from the beginning and I am that which is attained at the end of desire.

Most of this invocation comes from Leland's *Aradia*, but there are also elements drawn from Crowley's own writings. For example, the italicized paragraph is a slightly modified version of Chapter 1, Verse 58, of Crowley's *Book of the Law*.

Witchcraft Initiation Rituals

There are three grades or degrees in contemporary witchcraft. They are, in ascending order of importance: (a) Priest and Witch of the Great Goddess; (b) Witch Queen or, in the case of a male, Magus; and (c) High Priestess or High Priest.

In the first degree the candidate is led naked, blindfolded and with his hands tied

behind his back, into the 'Circle of Power'. After various occult mutterings from the leader of the coven (sometimes unkindly referred to as 'witchery-poo'), the postulant receives the five-fold kiss (on feet, knees, genitals, breast and lips) and forty strokes of the scourge, and takes an oath of secrecy: 'I, X. . . ., in the presence of the Mighty Ones do of my own free will and accord most solemnly swear that I will ever keep secret and never reveal the secrets of the Art except it be to a proper person, properly prepared, with a Circle such as this. And that I will never deny the secrets of the Art to such a person if he or she be vouched for by a Brother or Sister of the Art. All this I swear by my hopes of a future life mindful that my measure has been taken and may my magical weapons turn against me if I break this my solemn oath.'

It can safely be said that no oath has so often been broken as this one; for the 'secrets of the Art' have been recorded in books, shown on television and described in the popular Press.

Following the administration of the oath, the candidate is handed various implements, known as the 'working tools of the Art', and has their use explained to him. For example, he is given the athame, a black-hilted knife, the design of which Crowley and Gardner took from the old textbook of magic known as the *Key of Solomon* (*314*), and told that with it he can 'form all Magic Circles, dominate, enslave and punish all rebellious spirits and demons and persuade angels and good spirits'.

Finally, the candidate is informed that he is now 'Priest and Witch of the Great Goddess'.

The second degree again incorporates scourging; the aspirant is asked whether he is willing to 'suffer and be purified in order to learn', and after he has answered in the affirmative duly receives forty strokes of the scourge. The leader of the coven then states that 'in Witchcraft thou must ever give as thou receive, but triple', and the candidate is instructed to administer 120 strokes of the scourge to the initiator. These proceedings being concluded, the 'legend of the Goddess' is then either read out aloud or, in some covens, acted as a mystery play. This 'legend' is a variant on the classical myth of Persephone and concludes with the words: 'There are three great events in the life of Man; Love, Death and Resurrection in a new body. Magic rules them all. For to make Love perfect you must return at the same time and place as the loved one, remember the past and love again.'

At the end of the reading or play the aspirant is led around the Circle and it is

A witches' wedding

proclaimed to the 'Mighty Ones of the Elements' that a new Magus or Witch Queen has been consecrated.

The third degree is centred around ritual sexual intercourse in the Circle between the candidate and the initiator. The rite is of little interest except to voyeurs and in many covens it takes place in symbolic form only. When this latter course is followed, the magic knife (athame) is solemnly dipped into a chalice of wine and the onlookers are informed that 'as is the Woman to Man so is the Cup to the Athame'.

Festivals of the Cult

There are eight main festivals, or sabbaths, celebrated by modern witches. They are May Eve (30 April, the Walpurgis Night of medieval legend), Hallowe'en (31 October, the night before All Hallows or All Saints),

Candlemas (2 February), Lammas (2 August), the two equinoxes (21 March and 21 September) and the summer and winter solstices (21 June and 21 December).

The rituals vary considerably between one coven and another, but the following outline of the basic structure of the Candlemas festival can be taken as typical: 'Proceed to the site with a dance step, waving brooms and lighted torches; the High Priestess carries a broomstick shaped like an erect phallus. All, dancing, form the Magic Circle. The High Priest enters, in his right hand the consecrated Magic Sword, in his left hand a wooden image of an erect phallus. Priest and Priestess exchange the fivefold kiss; the Priestess then invokes the god into the Priest with the Invocation, "Dread Lord of Death and Resurrection, Lord of Life, Giver of Life, Thou Whose Name is Mystery of Mysteries, encourage our hearts! Let thy light crystallise in our Blood, bringing us to

Resurrection. For there is no part of us that is not of the gods! Descend, we pray Thee, upon thy servant and Priest!" Initiations are then to be held (if there are any) followed by the Cakes and Wine ceremony, the Great Rite if possible, a feast and a communal dance.'

The 'Great Rite' referred to here is ritual sexual intercourse between Priest and Priestess. The 'Cakes and Wine ceremony' bears some resemblance to the Christian Holy Communion. Both the wine – a sweet sherry is generally used – and the cakes are blessed by the High Priestess. The cakes, which are compounded of salt, honey, wine, meal, oil, and (in some covens) blood, are usually crescent-shaped (in honour of the Moon-goddess), but they seem to be more or less identical with the 'Cakes of Light' which Crowley's *Book of the Law* instructs should be eaten in honour of the god Horus.

These cakes are also used in a magical

ceremony which combines various unpleasantnesses inflicted on the Moon-goddess with a sexual orgy in her honour. The *Book of Shadows* describes how this should be done: 'Put the crescent cakes to bake, saying: "I do not bake the meal nor the salt, nor do I cook the honey and the oil with the wine. I bake the blood and the body and the soul of Great Aradia that she shall know neither rest nor peace and ever be in cruel suffering till she grant the fulfillment of my innermost desire. If the grace be granted, O Aradia, in honour of thee I will hold a feast. We will drain the goblet deep, we will wildly dance and leap. And if thou grantest the grace which I desire, then, when the dance is wildest, we shall extinguish the lamps and love freely, caring for neither age nor kin." Thus it shall be done. All shall sit down to the supper and, the feast ended, they shall dance and sing and make music and then shall they make love in the darkness, with all the lights extinguished – for it is Great Aradia who extinguishes them.'

Witchcraft since Gardner

After the death of Gardner in 1964 the witch-cult suffered a considerable fragmentation. Even while Gardner had been alive there had been a tendency for covens to go their own way, some of them abandoning the 'Great Rite' and the more sado-masochistic Gardnerian practices, others emphasizing the sexual aspects of 'the Craft' even more than their master had done, still others deciding that rival groups were not practising 'real' witchcraft. From 1965 these fissiparous tendencies became more pronounced and today the cult can be divided into three well-defined groups.

Probably the largest of these groups, and certainly the one that receives the most publicity, is led by a certain Alec Sanders (its members being known as Alexandrians) and is of comparatively recent origin. According to his own account, Sanders was initiated into witchcraft when he was only nine years old in a Manchester back kitchen by his aged grandmother; according to rival witches, he has never been formally initiated into the cult but attained his title of 'High Priest and Witch King' by the simple expedient of declaring himself to be such. The version he uses of the *Book of Shadows* is almost word for word identical with the Crowley–Gardner compilation used by Gardnerian covens, although the Alexandrians deny any connection with, and have the greatest contempt for, Gardnerian witchdraft.

Alexandrian witchcraft can be defined as Gardnerian witchcraft combined with elements drawn from other varieties of modern occultism. For example, it teaches the use of certain herbal extracts as 'fluid condensors' – preparations designed to enable evoked spirits to manifest themselves on the physical plane. Both the names and the recipes of these types of 'instant ectoplasm' seem to have been derived from the works of Franz Bardon, a German-speaking magician who was, until his recent death, a member of the *Ordo Templi Orientis*.

It is probably this synthesizing tendency that has accounted for the success of Alexandrian witchcraft. It has something for everybody – Gardnerian fun and games for some, the ceremonial magic of the GOLDEN DAWN (in modified form) for others, and even the intellectual austerities and the barbarous 'angelic language' of Dee's Enochian magic for a select few (see ENOCHIAN LANGUAGE). Alexandrian covens now exist not only in the British Isles but in France, Germany and the United States, where they are particularly strong, and there is an *Alexandrian Newsletter*, a quarterly publication through which the various covens keep in touch with each other's activities.

The second group, the Gardnerians, are themselves fragmented; the Sheffield coven, for example, has little sympathy with most of the covens operating in the Greater London area, which maintain that the Sheffield version of the *Book of Shadows* is incomplete. The largest and most orthodox section of the Gardnerians is that led by Mrs Monique Wilson. Mrs Wilson, known to her followers as 'the Lady Olwen', was the major beneficiary of Gardner's will, inheriting the copyrights of his books, his extraordinary collection of swords and daggers and, notably, the Witchcraft Museum (the Witches' Mill) at Castletown in the Isle of Man. From their home Mrs Wilson and her husband, 'Scotty', conduct a large correspondence with witches all over the world. The Wilsons have received a great deal of unfavourable publicity from sensational journalists; one story, for example, affirmed that Mr Wilson wore a sinister 'flying penis' in his buttonhole. Most of this criticism seems unjustified (when I examined the 'flying penis' I discovered it to be a perfectly ordinary R.A.F. badge – Mr Wilson is an ex-pilot), and while the Wilsons' religious beliefs and practices are no doubt eccentric by ordinary standards, there is no reason to believe that they are either sinister or dishonest.

On the whole, pure Gardnerian witchcraft is in a state of decline and its hard-core membership seems to be diminishing. Nevertheless, there is a continual influx of new initiates, whose membership is usually of short duration; Gardnerian witchcraft today resembles an army transit camp – a great many people go through it but very few join the permanent staff.

Finally, the so-called 'robed covens' have, as their name implies, abandoned nudity. Many of their members display an attitude of marked hostility to Gardnerian and Alexandrian witchcraft and claim to be hereditary witches. It is almost needless to say that no satisfactory proof of the latter assertion is ever produced, and lacking evidence to the contrary, one is forced to regard them as a Gardnerian 'heresy'. Some of the robed groups use heavily edited versions of the *Book of Shadows* but most of them have their own rituals, supposedly traditional but usually displaying the influence of such literary sources as Robert Graves's *White Goddess* and Israel Regardie's edition of the ritual and instructional material of the Hermetic Order of the Golden Dawn (*389*).

There is great diversity within the robed covens and it is difficult to make any generalizations about them. Some have abandoned magic altogether, concentrating their energies upon the worship of the old deities of pagan Britain; others have developed the magical aspects of witchcraft and show signs of eventually becoming occult fraternities similar to the ORDRE KABBALISTIQUE DE LA ROSE-CROIX or the STELLA MATUTINA.

Modern witchcraft is an evolving religion. In its Gardnerian form, probably, it is already on its way out, but it seems to have a real capacity for adaptation, and in one form or another it may well survive. F. K.

(See also TRANCE.) (Further reading: for modern witchcraft, see *148, 171, 172, 262, 263, 429*; for the earlier history of witchcraft, see *18, 50, 111, 145, 146, 195b, 225, 266, 278, 302, 392b, 401, 406, 409a, 441, 442, 458, 462, 506*.)

Alfred Witte (1878-1941) See HAMBURG SCHOOL.

Patience Worth

The 'spirit' of a woman who, purportedly, had lived in England in the 17th century and had emigrated to America, where she was killed by Indians, and who from 1913 onwards dictated a mass of material to Mrs John H. Curran of St Louis. Mrs Curran at first produced automatic scripts on a OUIJA BOARD and later automatic speech. She did not go into trance, remaining conscious but abstracted during the experience. Dictating at tremendous speed, Patience Worth produced novels, including *The Sorry Tale*, *Hope Trueblood* and *Telka*, and poetry, which she created almost instantly on any suggested theme: see AUTOMATISMS. (*213, 377*)

Wroński See HOENE-WROŃSKI.

Y

Yang See YIN AND YANG.

Yantra

'Instrument' or 'engine', the term in TAN-TRISM for a special type of MANDALA used in the worship of deities, each of whom has a special symbolic design. The most powerful of yantras, the Sri Yantra, is a diagram enclosing symbols of the male and female sex organs and 'sanctuaries' for certain deities within lotus petals. (*485*)

William Butler Yeats (1865-1939)

No one can fully comprehend the poetry of W. B. Yeats without taking account of his deep and lifelong preoccupation with occultism and mysticism. In one of his letters he wrote: 'The mystical life is the centre of all that I do and all that I think and all that I write.'

Yeats's mysticism passed through a number of phases. The first was his involvement with THEOSOPHY, to which he was introduced in Dublin at the age of seventeen or eighteen. In 1885 he met in Dublin the Indian Theosophist Mohini Chatterji, who had gone there to lecture, and was introduced by him to the Bhagavad Gita and the writings of the 8th-century Indian philosopher Samkara, who taught the supremacy of the individual self and the unreality of the external world. Yeats joined the Theosophical Society, but resigned in 1890.

He moved with his parents to London in 1887, and the date of his resignation from the Theosophical Society coincides roughly with his initiation into the Hermetic Order of the GOLDEN DAWN, a magical society run by MacGregor MATHERS, whose members included Aleister CROWLEY and the actress Florence Farr. Every member of the society took a magical motto, and Yeats's motto was *Daemon Est Deus Inversus* ('The Devil Is the Reverse of God'). Through the Golden Dawn Years became acquainted with the rich world of magical symbolism. The CABALA, ASTROLOGY, ROSICRUCIANISM – all played a part in his poetry. The Rosicrucian influence is seen

in his fondness for the rose as a poetical motif. He was also interested in the TAROT, and his own pack of Tarot cards, inscribed with remarks in his own hand, is still preserved. His involvement with the Golden Dawn ceased when it broke up into splinter groups in the early part of the century.

Later he was influenced by the Indian poet and mystic Rabindranath Tagore, and by another Indian teacher, Purohit Swami. A mystical kind of Irish patriotism also played a part in his thought. His wife, whom he married in 1917, shared his interest in the occult. He synthesized the various occult and mystical influences of his life into his own system which he set out in his work, *A Vision*, published in 1925. C. M.

(Further reading: *235*.)

W. B. Yeats

Yeti See ABOMINABLE SNOWMAN.

Yi King See I CHING.

Yin and Yang

The two great cosmic principles of Chinese belief; they play an important role in the philosophy and divinatory technique of the I CHING; see also TANTRISM.

Yoga

The term 'religion' is sometimes said to be derived from a Latin word meaning 'to bind', suggesting the uniting of the soul with God. The Sanskrit word *yoga* implies a similar union, being derived from a root word for 'yoke' or 'join'. In essence Yoga is a form of religion, and in spite of changes of connotation in the course of centuries, it is still basically a religious practice, a means of mystical ascent. But here the means is not left to chance. Yoga is a practical method of self-development, carefully planned, for achieving the union of the individual soul with the Universal Soul.

Yoga is the fourth of the six orthodox systems of Hindu philosophy, all of which have as their objective the release of the incarnated ego from the cycle of birth–death–rebirth. They are spoken of as orthodox because they are based on the Vedic canon. They comprise: Nyaya, concerned principally with logic or the laws governing the processes of reasoning and the stratagems of controversy; Vaisheshika, which is supplementary to Nyaya and takes in the nature of the physical world and deals with space, time, cause, substance, the elements, motion and relationships; Samkhya, dealing mainly with abstract philosophical categories; Yoga, concerned with practical techniques for developing mental and physical preparedness for union with the Absolute; Mimamsa, concerned largely with ritualistic practice; and the rigidly monistic VEDANTA, founded on the Upanishads and based on the principle that Brahma is the only reality, final and indivisible.

The development of Yoga from its presumed origin in Indus Valley India can only be tenuously traced. Some forms of it are attributable to the predecessors of the Aryans, and fragments of Yoga doctrine are also associated with ancient sages like Yajnavalkya, author of certain portions of the Vedic text. From traditions recorded of the itinerant philosophers who wandered about the country, like the Sophists of Greece, we hear of early practices that included breath control, long periods of trance-like MEDITATION, the intoning of MANTRAS or magical spells, and mystical exercises carried out for the purpose of attaining occult powers.

The Buddhists, Jains and other religious groups also practised meditation and interior exercises, but the underlying rationale and precise procedures remained amorphous until they were put together in succinct form by the philosopher Patanjali, who lived in the second century B.C. and whose codification became the nucleus of early Yoga philosophy. The proliferation of yogic methods was a post-Patanjali phenomenon, much of it the product of medieval schools, and the attempt to sort out the various threads that have contributed to the fabric that is today called Yoga has yet to be made.

The practical disciplines of Yoga are not, religiously speaking, Hindu, and men of all religious denominations have studied and practised it. Philosophically it is said to be a branch of the Samkhya system, and a 'theistic' development of it. To the list of categories or principles of Samkhya, Yoga adds its own, namely, God. But the deity of yogic texts is only one of several types of 'souls', although the highest of them all, and is not usually the object of contemplation in the Yoga exercises.

There are several kinds of Yoga, which in time were resolved into about half a dozen, and later branched out into numerous offshoots, the suffix '-yoga' being frequently employed as '-ism' or '-ology' would be in English. There is Mantra-yoga, dealing with spells; Kundalini-yoga, aimed at developing the 'sex-and-fire' force; Dharma-yoga concerned with the saving virtues of religious duties; Kriya-yoga with the value of everyday life and domestic ritual; Karma-yoga based on proper action; Bhakti-yoga centred on devotion. The precedence of KARMA as distinguished from *bhakti* was as bitterly debated among the medieval pandits as was St Paul's 'faith' and St James's 'works' by the theologians of the Reformation. Raja-yoga or 'King-yoga', a moral and mental discipline, sets forth the methods by which the highest qualities in man may be exercised.

By far the most popular of all yogas is Hatha-yoga, and its eight stages served as a prototype for many of the other forms. Highly developed and systematized, it is of comparatively recent development, and its growth continues. The earliest texts on Hatha-yoga only just precede the time of the Muslim invasion of India in the 7th century A.D. A substantial contribution to its variety was made by the schools of TANTRISM, with which Hatha-yoga was closely associated, and in India an overtone of 'magician' is still attached to the designation 'jogi', the colloquial term for yogi. Hatha-yoga is sometimes defined as the yoga of power, not only because it bestows personal power, but also because its methods make a bold assault on the psychic plane. The determined yogi, according to the texts, can 'get whatever he desires'.

Stages of Hatha-yoga

Before embarking on the practical side of Yoga the student must guard against the obstacles that might confront him and which he will have to overcome if he wishes to advance in his training. Among these obstacles is sickness, or the disturbance of physical equilibrium, for good health is an essential requirement. Where sickness is present, it must be treated and the balance restored by natural methods; certain yogic exercises will help in this direction. Other obstacles are laziness or the lack of mental discipline necessary for the task in hand; indecision or doubt about the value of what is undertaken and the path being pursued; attachment to passion and to things that please the senses is also a formidable hindrance to progress; false knowledge has to be guarded against, for such knowledge will lead one astray from the proper course. Mental instability follows false knowledge and leads one into the evils of wrath, violence, impatience, hatred and lust.

The first two stages of Hatha-yoga are *yama* and *niyama*, mainly ethical in purpose and concerned with the practice of specific virtues and the progressive adoption of a way of life obligatory for the more exacting disciplines to follow. The primary aims at this stage are calculated to adapt one's outlook for a course of rigorous training, which will exclude all frivolities that dissipate energy and divert attention from the attainment of the higher goal in view.

Yama and niyama develop the moral virtues of restraint. The desire for possessions must be inhibited by thoughts of non-acquisition, non-covetousness, non-stealing. Truthfulness comes by eschewing non-righteousness. Truth is imperative in all circumstances, even when one's life is at stake, for truth is a quality that has an absolute validity which must not be imperilled by expediency or survival. *Ahimsa* or non-violence, another basic tenet, was one of the leading principles of Gandhi's life. In its strictest form it implies a restraint from all activity that is likely to harm another living being. Finally comes *brahmacharya* or continence. In the case of the married householder only the essential need of procreation may be satisfied and no indulgence in sex by thought or deed is to be sought. At its most stringent level total asceticism constitutes an indispensable discipline to progress in Yoga.

The third stage, *asana* or posture, is an aspect of Yoga commonly associated in the Western mind with Hinduism in practice. Patanjali recommended a sitting position that was 'firm and agreeable', steady and comfortable. Attempts to meet this need have resulted in more than a thousand different postures, only three or four of which can really be said to fulfil the very modest requirements laid down. Many asanas are, as it were, plastic moulds assumed by the human body in the shape of some object, plant or animal, in the belief that the qualities that characterize that thing will imbue the yogi assuming it. There are asanas named after the lion, bull, camel, tortoise, swan, crane, locust, scorpion, tree, lotus, thunderbolt, bow, plough, and hundreds more. Each brings its own benefit and is intended to approximate by sympathetic vibratory resonance to the object or

The lotus seat in Yoga

animal concerned. Photographs of the contortions invented by practitioners reveal their extraordinary ingenuity in trying to fit the human body into preconceived moulds of these various prototypes.

The commonest asanas are those in the ordinary cross-legged position, with the hands resting loosely on the knees and the fingers arranged in one or other of the simple hand-positions, or *mudras*. Another simple asana is performed by standing on one foot, a posture that is believed to concentrate occult power. The Druid priests of ancient Britain stood on one leg and pointed one finger towards an offender when they pronounced their dreaded curses. One-legged asanas give direction to one's concentration and emphasize purpose. Yogis can maintain the one-legged stance for hours.

The headstand, a very old asana, was known to the Taoists of China and to the Cabiri of Asia Minor. It is practised in several variations and is believed to have therapeutic as well as mystical virtues. According to its advocates it flushes the brain, gives strength to the eyes, clears the sinuses, improves the hearing. Properly performed it can also be a means of enlightenment.

The Breath-way
The fourth stage, *pranayama*, is the most important of all the physical stages of Yoga. This is the 'breath-way', a method of occult advancement and illumination through breathing. Many supra-normal faculties are opened for those who have mastered the art of pranayama. The body glows, the eyes radiate magnetic force, the gestures of the hand assume kingly command. Breath is life and the proper techniques of drawing in breath, retaining it, absorbing its quintessence, and exhaling its residue are fundamental to yogic training. The breathing process is broken down into four stages: inhaling, retaining, exhaling, holding. Each of these performs a specific function, and a ratio has to be established for each kind of breathing. Thus, if one breathes in for the duration of two seconds, retains for three seconds, exhales for two seconds and then holds the breathing for four seconds, the ratio would be expressed as 2.3.2.4. This may be doubled to 4.6.4.8, or trebled to 6.9.6.12, but they all have the same effect, except that the longer periods would give more of the benefit in question.

More important is the ability to use breath, for the air breathed in contains a vital essence which can be made to course through both the physical frame and the 'pneumatic' or ETHERIC DOUBLE, and charge the whole

The solar plexus externally controlled

system with a surging dynamism. This vital essence is called *prana*, a term that is also synonymous with 'life' and 'soul'. When a breath is drawn into the lungs the body should divest it of its pranic content and send it through the arteries of the subtle body. Normally most of the pranic content in the body is dissipated with each exhalation, only a weak dilution being retained by the ordinary person. But by pranayama techniques this prana can be utilized to the full and the body transformed into a living TALISMAN.

Having disciplined the body, the cultivation of the mental powers is next in line. The fifth, sixth and seventh stages of Hatha-yoga are concerned with mental development, and they rise in progressive ranges from the simple to the more difficult, in preparation for the climactic supra-mental stage of *samadhi*.

Pratyahara, the fifth stage, is an outwardly passive, inwardly active technique of withdrawing the senses from the objects to which they are drawn by nature and habit. Yama and niyama, the first and second stages, have already conditioned the student to resist the urge of his physical organs for sensual pleasures, but now the process is carried further towards a total extinction of all sense experience. Things do not matter. The phenomenal world is an illusion and its evanescence must be recognized. The practice of excluding from one's attention all external matters that impinge on the senses must be carried on till perfection is attained.

A symbolical pose is sometimes assumed, as if to make the body a living configuration of resistance to the incoming impressions of sense. The yogi sits in a cross-legged pose and devotes some time to thinking out the preliminaries of his withdrawal. When he has reached a certain stage of indifference to the inrush of outside impressions, he makes the gesture that imprints this sign upon his higher self. He raises his hands to his face and shuts his ears with his thumbs, and thus shuts out the whole distracting world of sound, the siren lure of rhythm and music, the specious design of words and 'philosophies', the familiar voices of his everyday environment, the cacophany of crowds. He must rest within the inner stillness. With his index fingers he closes his eyes and excludes from his purview the insidious invitation of the world of fleshly joys, all beauty of form and colour. They fade out, presenting instead the same innocuous and neutral aspect of a blank wall. The middle fingers press on the nostrils and thus blot from his interest the world of smells, the scent of jasmine and sandalwood, the perfume of women, the heady incense that arises from domestic and temple worship, the spicy fragrance of the

kitchen. His little fingers press on the lower lips and the ring fingers on the upper, and thus symbolically prohibit the entry of tasty foods and sweet drinks, and silence the tongue which would otherwise weave its tissues of gossip, slander, lies, intrigues and self-glorification.

Concentration and Meditation
Concentration, called *dharana*, is the sixth stage. This is the keynote to all mental operations for without it the mental forces are diffused and dissipated, and no amount of physical culture can take its place. The mind, emptied by the preceding discipline, must now be drawn together, free from the distractions of the body or the perturbations of the intellect, and then slowly, determinedly, undeviatingly, rendered fixed and steady. The term dharana comes from a root word meaning 'hold', implying a firm and unshakeable grip that the mind retains on the subject of its concentration. Another favourite term is 'one-pointedness', suggesting the same convergence of the mental faculties upon a single idea, to the exclusion of everything else.

In one exercise the yogi sits about six feet from a wall, upon which a tiny black speck has been previously marked at eye level. The wall should preferably contain several distracting objects and colours. Others pick a distant object like the topmost branch of a tree, the window of a house, the summit of a hill. The mind is then focused on the object in question and, if the practice is successfully performed, all the surrounding things vanish, and one is conscious only of the tiny point one has chosen. At first one may be so taken up with the wonder of the phenomenon that the adjacent objects come flooding back into view, but the exercise must be continued without intermission, until the point is held without the intruding elements. It is as if one were in a long and dark tunnel with only a single bright light visible at the far end. One's concentration should be such that one is able to 'practice dharana on a battlefield'.

The penultimate stage of yoga is known as *dhyana*, which is meditation proper. The mind has now been emptied, the mental forces marshalled, but to what end? On what does the mind meditate? This is not a question of random selection. Not all meditative aids are useful to all men. People differ in their attitudes, capacities, inclinations, upbringing, in their family, social and religious background. In India the matter is simply decided: one may meditate on one's personal deity, or on one's guru or teacher; one may concentrate on certain parts of one's own body: the space between the eybrows, the tip of the nose, the navel. One may, in short, choose from a wide variety of aids.

But for a number of reasons such props are not universally acceptable. The atheist might be quite unable to give his attention to an object with religious associations; the Muslim might find the representation of a deity unacceptable to his religious beliefs; the Christian might find difficulty in adopting any of the Hindu devices. Hence the selection of suitable meditative aids becomes a matter of great importance. One can at such a time easily 'pick up' the vibrations with which a particular symbol has been impregnated through centuries of adoration, veneration and worship. Meditation on the Cross, for example, cannot but evoke the whole 'mythos' of Christianity, which will tincture the mind of the student and imbue him with its significance. If he is a Christian this is all to the good; if he is not he will unconsciously resist and reject it. In considering the symbolism of the meditative device, the various factors mentioned above have to be given serious consideration.

Dhyana is the last stage that can be attained by the practitioner's own efforts, being a condition still under the control of his will, and subject to the direction of his intellectual faculties. Yoga itself has been defined as the 'science of contemplation', and sometimes equated with a kind of self-induced hypnosis spoken of as *yoga-nidra* or 'yoga-sleep'. It is of interest to note that the word dhyana is the origin of the Japanese term Zen, the name of a school of Mahayana Buddhism based on contemplation and specialized methods of attaining enlightenment.

The ultimate aim of Yoga is to break the cycle of birth–death–rebirth through union with the Ultimate Principle, be that principle a pantheistic power diffused through the universe or a personal deity. Yoga, though starting with an impersonal god, later provided for both. Methods of attaining this union were precisely laid down, stage by stage. Yoga follows the path of ethical observance, physical culture and mental discipline to still the flux of thought and suspend all mental processes. Yoga is even described as the inhibition of mental activity, when not a single thought ripples the placid surface of the mind. This objective is achieved in the eighth and final stage of yoga, *samadhi*.

Samadhi is roughly defined as a 'trance state'. It lies beyond the range and reach of the intellect, and no amount of physical training, concentration and intellectual discipline can guarantee that a person will experience it. It comes when the time is ripe. People have attained samadhi at first sitting, so to speak, without any preparatory work.

Others have failed to experience it after a lifetime of preparation. But many do reach it through Yoga. In short, the predisposition to attain samadhi is gifted, although samadhi may sometimes be the reward of effort.

One is suddenly there. The state is reached, and is beyond description. It is the *nirvana* of the Buddhists, the ecstasy of the saints and sufis. It embraces many ranges of mystical experience. There is the samadhi in which the yogi retains his identity and experiences from his individual standpoint the vision of the divine presence, or he may melt into the vision and lose ego and identity and thus cease to have any awareness of self. The flame of self is extinguished.

The Subtle Body

Closely related to Hatha-yoga and sometimes regarded as a component part of it is Laya-yoga, devoted to the subtle body (see ASTRAL BODY). Though beyond the reach of sense perception, the subtle body is believed to exist, so much so that its descriptions fill pages and pages of texts on Yoga. Yoga is as much concerned with the subtle body as with the physical, and if the physical body is cultivated it is largely in order that it may serve the subtle body.

The physical and subtle bodies meet at certain points known as CHAKRAS, meaning 'wheels', figuratively called 'lotuses', and generally translated 'plexuses'. They represent psychic vortices or power-houses of occult force. Many chakras exist throughout the body, but all are controlled from seven major centres, which some modern exponents equate with the ductless glands.

The topmost plexus, known as the *sahasrara*, the lotus of a thousand petals, is situated in the head and regarded as the abode of the god Shiva. Its eminence in esoteric anatomy is manifest by the halo which can be seen to surround the heads of those who have attained beatitude. The lowest chakra lies in the perineum near the tailbone. Known as the *muladhara*, 'root foundation', it forms the other end of the chakra axis. Between these two chakras situated at the head and tail, five other chakras reside.

The five intermediate chakras are located roughly as follows: near the sex organs, near the navel, in the heart, behind the throat, and between the eyebrows. This latter is believed to be the site of the mysterious organ of occult vision called the THIRD EYE. Normally all the chakras are dormant, and their activation is one of the objectives of Laya-yoga. All the chakras are situated along the periphery of the spinal column, within which lies a major subtle artery called the *sushumna*. To the right and left of the sushumna lie two subsidiary subtle arteries.

Under normal conditions the central artery remains closed, and the two side arteries are open. The muladhara chakra at the base of the spine is the home of what is known as the *kundalini*, a subtle centre of 'sex-and-fire', regarded as the abode of Shiva's spouse Shakti. Figuratively the kundalini is compared to a tiny serpent lying coiled and asleep at the base of the spine. Unless one knows how, it is considered unwise to disturb it. Its almost imperceptible breathing sends a gentle pulsation through the chakras, but otherwise the whole chakra system is quiescent.

The energizing of the chakras is the specific goal of what is called Kundalini-yoga, and the incendiary point for the whole procedure is the muladhara. Learning the art of arousing the kundalini is a long and arduous process involving many exterior and interior exercises, including asanas (physical postures), mudras (hand gestures), pranayama (breath control), mandalas (mystical diagrams), and mantras (spells). The technique must be thoroughly mastered and the training takes several years.

The cultivation of two kinds of breath or 'winds' is a prerequisite to its success. One wind generates in the subtle body and one in the physical; ones moves downward and one upward along the spinal column. At a given moment the two breaths are impacted and the full force of the colliding energies is directed towards the kundalini. This results in the closing of the two side arteries in the spinal column and the opening of the sushumna or middle artery, whereupon a series of extraordinary events is precipitated. The kundalini, aroused, begins to tremble, uncoils itself, and starts its journey upwards, piercing each chakra through the middle and causing its petals to open. Each chakra as it opens contributes to the awakening of a particular occult faculty, and thus stage by stage the yogi becomes progressively enlightened.

It is generally believed that no progress beyond the eyebrow chakra is possible by the usual yogic methods. Thereafter, techniques of a higher esoteric order are required before the kundalini can ascend to the sahasrara. The meeting of kundalini and sahasrara is in fact the supreme moment, for then the god and goddess are united, and the yogi in whose person this mystical event takes place shares in the immortal bliss of the divine union. B. W.

(Further reading: *36, 97, 131, 142, 301, 400, 485, 513.*)

Yugas

In Hinduism and Tantrism, stages in the cycle of time: see TANTRISM.

Zadkiel

The pseudonym of Richard James Morrison (1795–1874), a British naval officer who became a professional astrologer and published *Zadkiel's Almanac*. He was the author of several books, including *An Introduction to Astrology*, *The Grammar of Astrology*, *Handbook of Astrology*, and *The Solar System as it is, and not as it is represented*, 1857, in which he main-

Zen: awaiting the timeless moment

tained that the earth remains stationary at the centre of the solar system. He was also interested in crystal-gazing. He was fiercely attacked in the Press, and became involved in a libel action which damaged his reputation – though he said it improved his sales – after he had predicted ill health for the Prince Consort during 1861 and Prince Albert died in December of that year. After Morrison's death the almanac was edited by Alfred James Pearce (1840–1923); it eventually ceased publication in 1931. (*234*)

Zain

The pseudonym of Elbert Benjamine, an astrologer who in 1918 founded the Church of Light, Los Angeles, which is still flourishing; it conducts classes in astrology and sells Zain's twenty-one books on the religion of the stars. Zain claimed that in 1909 he became a member of the controlling council of the Brotherhood of Light, a secret group of adepts originating in ancient Egypt. (*163*)

Zen

A Japanese form of Buddhism which for a

time became very popular and much discussed in the West; one of its most powerful attractions is its use of paradox in the form known as a *koan*: see MEDITATION. (*132, 211, 444, 491*)

Zodiac See ASTROLOGY; GLASTONBURY ZODIAC; SIDEREAL ZODIAC; for a spirit named Zodiac, see MOYES.

Karl Georg Zschaetzsch

A German Atlantis-theorist after the First World War who identified the people of Atlantis as the original Aryans. When Atlantis was destroyed, he thought, 'the only survivors of the sinking were Wotan, his daughter, and his pregnant sister, who took refuge in a cave among the roots of a giant tree beside a cold geyser. Wotan's sister died in childbirth and a she-wolf suckled her infant. The blood of these noble Nordics became mixed with that of the non-Aryans of the mainland, and their degenerate descendants resorted to meat-eating and to the loathsome practice of fermenting liquors . . .' (*115*): see ATLANTIS.

Bibliography

The following abbreviations are used in this bibliography:
- A.S.P.R.   American Society for Psychical Research
- S.P.R.   Society for Psychical Research
- T.P.H.   Theosophical Publishing House

1   ABBOT, A. E., *Encyclopaedia of Numbers*, Emerson Press, London

2   ADAMENKO, V., 'Electrodynamics of Living Systems', *Journal of Paraphysics*, Vol. 4, 1970

3   ADAMS, Evangeline, *Astrology For Everyone*, Dodd, Mead, New York, 1960 reprint

4   AMBROSE, G., and NEWBOLD, G., *A Handbook of Medical Hypnosis*, Ballière, Tindall & Cox, London, 3rd edn, 1968; Williams & Wilkins, Baltimore, 3rd edn, 1968

5   ANGUS, S., *The Mystery Religions and Christianity*, Murray, London, 1929

6   ANSON, P. F., *Bishops at Large*, Faber, London, 1964

7   ASH, M., *Health, Radiation and Healing*, Darton, Longman & Todd, London, 1962

8   BABA RAM DASS, *Be Here Now*, Lama Foundation, 1971

9   BAILEY, Alice, *Unfinished Autobiography*, Lucis, New York, 1951

10 BAIRD, A. T., *One Hundred Cases for Survival after Death*, Werner Laurie, London, 1943

11 BAKAN, D., *Sigmund Freud and the Jewish Mystical Tradition*, Schocken, New York, 1965, paperback

12 BALDICK, R., *The Life of J.-K. Huysmans*, Clarendon Press, Oxford, 1955; Oxford University Press, New York, 1955

13 BALFOUR, G., 'A Study of the Psychological Aspects of Mrs Willett's Mediumship', S.P.R. *Proceedings*, 1935

14 BALFOUR, J., 'The "Palm Sunday" Case', S.P.R. *Proceedings*, February 1960

15 BANDER, P., *Carry On Talking*, Colin Smythe, London, 1972

16 BARBANELL, Maurice, *This Is Spiritualism*, Jenkins, London, 1959

17 BARBANELL, Maurice, *Spiritualism Today*, Jenkins, London, 1969

18 BAROJA, J. C., *The World of the Witches*, Weidenfeld, London, 1964

19 BARRETT, F., *The Magus*, University Books, New York, 1967 reprint

20 BARRETT, W. F., 'Poltergeists Old and New', S.P.R. *Proceedings*, 1911

21 BARRETT, W. F., 'The Folkestone Poltergeists', S.P.R. *Journal*, Vol. 18, 1917–18

22 BARTER, J. P., *Towards Subud*, Gollancz, London, 1967

23 BASHAM, A. L., *The Wonder That Was India*, Sidgwick & Jackson, London, 1954; Grove Press, New York, 1959, paperback

24 BAX, C., *The Traveller's Tale*, Blackwell, Oxford, 1921

25 BEARD, P., *Survival of Death*, Hodder, London, 1966

26 BEASLEY, Norman, *The Cross and the Crown*, Allen & Unwin, London, 1953; Hawthorne, New York, 1952

27 BEASLEY, Norman, *Mary Baker Eddy*, Allen & Unwin, London, 1964

28 BELL, A. H., ed., *Practical Dowsing*, Bell, London, 1965

29 BELL, E. T., *The Magic of Numbers*, McGraw-Hill, New York, 1946

30 BELLAMY, H. S., *Moons, Myths and Man*, Faber, London, 1936

31 BELLAMY, H. S., *The Atlantis Myth*, Faber, London, 1948

32 BELLAMY, H. S., *A Life History of Our Earth*, Faber, London, 1951

33 BELOFF, J., *The Existence of Mind*, MacGibbon & Kee, London, 1962

34 BENDER, H., 'New Developments in Poltergeist Research', *Proceedings* of the Parapsychological Association, Vol. 6, 1969

35 BENNETT, J. G., *The Dramatic Universe*, Hodder, London, 1956

36 BERNARD, T., *Hatha Yoga*, Rider, London, 1950; Wehman, Hackensack, New Jersey

37 BERNSTEIN, Morey, *The Search for Bridey Murphy*, Hutchinson, London, 1956; Doubleday, Garden City, New York, 1965, revised edn

38 BESANT, Annie, and LEADBEATER, C. W., *Man: Whence, How and Whither*, T.P.H., 1967 reprint

39 BESTERMAN, T., *Crystal-Gazing*, Rider, London, 1924

40 *Bhagavad Gita*: see *The Song of God*

41 BHARATI, A., *The Tantric Tradition*, Rider, London, 1965; Hillary, New York, 1965, and Doubleday, Garden City, New York, 1970, paperback

42 BLACK, S., *Mind and Body*, Kimber, London, 1969

42a BLAU, J. L., *The Christian Interpretation of the Cabala in the Renaissance*, Columbia University Press and Kennikat Press, New York, 1944

43 BLAVATSKY, H. P., *Isis Unveiled*, T.P.H., numerous edns

44 BLAVATSKY, H. P., *The Secret Doctrine*, T.P.H., numerous edns

46 BLOFELD, J., *The Book of Change*, Allen & Unwin, London, 1968; Dutton, New York, paperback

47 BLOFELD, J., *The Way of Power*, Allen & Unwin,

London, 1970

48 BLUNSDON, N., *A Popular Dictionary of Spiritualism*, Arco, London, 1962; Fernhill, New York, 1961

49 BLYTHE, P., *Hypnotism, its Power and Practice*, Barker, London, 1971; Taplinger, New York, 1971

50 BOGUET, H., *An Examen of Witches*, Muller, London, 1971 reprint; Barnes & Noble, New York 1971 reprint of 1928 edn

51 BOSMAN, L., *The Meaning and Philosophy of Numbers*, Rider, London, 1932

52 BOUQUET, A. C., *Hinduism*, Hutchinson, London and New York, 1966 reprint

52a BOVET, R., *Pandaemonium*, Hand & Flower Press, Aldington, 1951

53 BOWEN, Charles, ed., *The Humanoids*, Spearman, London, 1969; Wehman, Hackensack, New Jersey

54 BRADEN, C. S., *Christian Science Today*, Allen & Unwin, London, 1959; Southern Methodist University Press, Dallas, Texas, 1958

55 BRANDRETH, H. R. T., *Episcopi Vagantes and the Anglican Church*, S.P.C.K., 1947

56 BROAD, C. D., *Lectures on Psychical Research*, Routledge, London, 1962; Humanities Press, New York, 1962

57 BROAD, C. D., 'The Phenomenology of Mrs Leonard's Trance', *A.S.P.R. Journal*, April 1955

58 BROWN, Rosemary, *Unfinished Symphonies*, Souvenir Press, London, 1971; Morrow, New York, 1971

59 BROWN, S., *The Heyday of Spiritualism*, Hawthorn, New York, 1970

60 BUBER, M., *Tales of the Hasidim*, Schocken, New York, 1947

61 BUCKE, R. M., *Cosmic Consciousness*, University Books, New York, 1961 reprint, and Dutton, New York, revised edn

62 *Buddhist Scriptures*, trans. E. Conze, Penguin, Harmondsworth and Baltimore, 1959

63 BUDGE, E. A. Wallis, *Amulets and Talismans*, University Books, New York, 1961 reprint, and P. F. Collier, New York, 1970, paperback

64 BUDGE, E. A. Wallis, *The Egyptian Book of the Dead*, Routledge, London, 1951; Peter Smith, Gloucester, Massachusetts

65 BUDGE, E. A. Wallis, *Egyptian Magic*, University Books, New York, reprint, and Dover, New York, 1971 paperback reprint of 1899 edn

66 BULMER, M. G., *The Biology of Twinning in Man*, Oxford University Press, England and New York, 1970

67 BURLAND, C. A., *The Arts of the Alchemists*, Weidenfeld, London, 1967

68 BURNET, J., *Early Greek Philosophy*, Black, London, 4th edn, 1930; Barnes & Noble, New York, 4th edn, 1968

68a BURTON, M., *The Elusive Monster*, Hart-Davis, London, 1961; *Elusive Monsters*, Dufour, Chester Springs, Pennsylvania, 1961

69 BUTLER, C., *Number Symbolism*, Routledge, London, 1970; Barnes & Noble, New York, 1970

70 BUTLER, W. E., *Magic: Its Ritual, Power and Purpose*, Aquarian Press, London, 1961; Weiser, New York

71 BUTLER, W. E., *The Magician: His Training and Work*, Aquarian Press, London, 1963; Weiser, New York

72 BUTLER, W. E., *Apprenticed to Magic*, Aquarian Press, London, 1965; Wehman, Hackensack, New Jersey, 1962

73 BUTLER, W. E., *Magic and the Qabalah*, Aquarian Press, London, 1968; Wehman, Hackensack, New Jersey, 1964

75 CALDWELL, W. W., *LSD Psychotherapy*, Grove Press, New York, 1968

76 CAMPBELL, F., *Your Days Are Numbered*, Gateway, New York, 1931

77 CAMPBELL, J., ed., *The Mysteries*, Eranos Yearbooks, Vol. 2, 1955

78 CARTER, C. E. O., *The Principles of Astrology*, T.P.H., 4th edn, 1952

79 CARTER, C. E. O., *Astrological Aspects*, T.P.H., revised edn 1951

80 CARTER, C. E. O., *An Encyclopedia of Psychological Astrology*, T.P.H., 4th edn, 1954

81 CARTY, C. M., *The Two Stigmatists: Padre Pio and Teresa Neumann*, Veritas, Dublin, 1956

82 CASE, P. F., *The Tarot*, Macoy, New York, 1947

83 CASTANEDA, C., *The Teachings of Don Juan*, University of California Press, 1968

84 CASTANEDA, C., *A Separate Reality*, Simon & Schuster, New York, 1971

85 CAVENDISH, Richard, *The Black Arts*, Routledge, London, 1967; Putnam, New York, 1967, and paperback 1968

86 CHAPMAN, R., *Unidentified Flying Objects*, Barker, London, 1969

87 CHEASLEY, C. W., *Numerology*, Rider, London, 1926

88 CHEETHAM, E., *The Prophecies of Nostradamus*, Putnam, New York, 1972

89 CHEIRO, *The Language of the Hand*, Corgi, London, 1968 reprint; Arc Books, New York, 1968 reprint

90 CHEIRO, *Cheiro's Book of Numbers*, Jenkins, London; Wehman, Hackensack, New Jersey

90a CHRISTOPHER, M., *Seers, Psychics and ESP*, Cassell, London, 1971; Thomas Y. Crowell, New York, 1970

91 CHRISTY, A., *The Orient in American Transcendentalism*, Columbia University Press, 1932, and Octagon Books, New York, 1963

91a CHURCHWARD, J., *The Lost Continent of Mu*, Washburn, New York, 1926, and Paperback Library, New York, 1968

91b CHURCHWARD, J., *The Children of Mu*, Washburn, New York, 1931, and Paperback Library, New York, 1968

91c CHURCHWARD, J., *The Sacred Symbols of Mu*,

Washburn, New York, 1933, and Paperback Library, New York, 1968

91d CHURCHWARD, J., *Cosmic Forces of Mu*, Washburn, New York, 1934, and reprints by Wehman, Hackensack, New Jersey, and Paperback Library, New York

92 CLAUS, E. P., and others, *Pharmacognosy*, Lea & Febiger, Philadelphia, 6th edn, 1970

93 CLYMER, R. S., *The Rosicrucian Fraternity in America*, Rosicrucian Foundation, Quakerstown, 1935

94 COCKREN, A., *Alchemy Rediscovered and Restored*, Rider, London, 1940.

95 COLLIN, R., *The Theory of Celestial Influence*, Stuart & J. M. Watkins, London, 1955

96 CONWAY, D., *Magic: An Occult Primer*, Cape, London, 1972

97 COSTER, G., *Yoga and Western Psychology*, Oxford University Press, 1950, and Lawrence Verry, Mystic, Connecticut

98 CROW, W. B., *Precious Stones*, Aquarian Press, London, 1968; Weiser, New York, 1968

99 CROWLEY, Aleister, *The Book of Thoth*, Shambalah, California, 1969 reprint, and Weiser, New York

100 CROWLEY, Aleister, *The Confessions of Aleister Crowley*, ed. John Symonds and Kenneth Grant, Cape, London, 1969; Hill & Wang, New York, 1970

101 CROWLEY, Aleister, *The Magical Record of the Beast 666*, ed. John Symonds and Kenneth Grant, Duckworth, London, 1972

102 CROWLEY, Aleister, *Magick*, ed. John Symonds and Kenneth Grant, Routledge, London, 1973; Wehman, Hackensack, New Jersey

103 CROWLEY, Aleister, *Moonchild*, Sphere, London, 1972, paperback; Llewellyn, St Paul, Minnesota

104 CROWLEY, Aleister, *777*, Weiser, New York, 1970 reprint

105a CULLING, L. T., *The Complete Magick Curriculum of the Secret Order G.B.G.*, Llewellyn, St Paul, Minnesota, 1969

105b CULLING, L. T., *A Manual of Sex Magick*, Llewellyn, St Paul, Minnesota, 1971

106 CUMMINS, Geraldine, *Unseen Adventures*, Rider, London, 1951

107 CUMMINS, Geraldine, *Mind in Life and Death*, Aquarian Press, London, 1956

108 CUMMINS, Geraldine, *Swan on a Black Sea*, Routledge, London, 1965; Weiser, New York

109 CUMONT, F., *Oriental Religions in Roman Paganism*, Dover, New York, 1956 reprint, and Peter Smith, Gloucester, Massachusetts

110 DASGUPTA, S. B., *An Introduction to Tantrik Buddhism*, Calcutta University Press, 1950

111 DAVIDSON, T., *Rowan Tree and Red Thread*, Oliver & Boyd, Edinburgh, 1949

112 DAY, L., and DE LA WARR, G., *New Worlds Beyond the Atom*, Stuart & J. M. Watkins, London, 1956

113 DEACON, R., *John Dee*, Muller, London, 1968; Transatlantic Arts, New York, 1971

114 DE BECKER, R., *The Meaning of Dreams*, Allen & Unwin, London, 1968

115 DE CAMP, L. Sprague, *Lost Continents*, Dover, New York, 1970, paperback

116 DE GRAZIA, A., ed., *The Velikovsky Affair*, Sidgwick & Jackson, London, 1966

116a DEREN, M., *Divine Horsemen: The Living Gods of Haiti*, Thames & Hudson, London, 1953; Vanguard, New York

117 DIAMOND, E., *The Science of Dreams*, Eyre & Spottiswoode, London, 1962

118 DINGWALL, E. J., *Some Human Oddities*, Home & Van Thal, London, 1947

119 DINGWALL, E. J., *Very Peculiar People*, Rider, London, 1951

120 DINGWALL, E. J., and others, *The Haunting of Borley Rectory*, Duckworth, London, 1956

121 DINGWALL, E. J., and HALL, Trevor H., *Four Modern Ghosts*, Duckworth, London, 1958

122 DOCKERILL, M., *My Life in a Love Cult*, Better Publishing, New Jersey, 1932

123 DODDS, E. R., *The Greeks and the Irrational*, University of California Press, Berkeley, California, 1951

124 DODDS, E. R., 'Supernormal Phenomena in Classical Antiquity', S.P.R. *Proceedings*, March 1971

125 DONNELLY, I., and SYKES, E., *Atlantis*, Sidgwick & Jackson, London, revised edn, 1970; Steiner, New York, paperback

126 DORESSE, J., *The Secret Books of the Egyptian Gnostics*, Hollis & Carter, London, 1960; AMS Press, New York

127 DOUGLAS, A., *The Tarot*, Gollancz, London, 1972

128 DOUGLAS, A., *The Oracle of Change*, Penguin, Harmondsworth, 1972; Putnam, New York, 1971

129 DRESSER, H. W., ed., *The Quimby Manuscripts*, Julian Press, New York, 1961 reprint

130 DUCASSE, C. J., *The Belief in a Life After Death*, Charles C Thomas, Springfield, Illinois, 1961

131 DUKES, Paul, *The Yoga of Health, Youth and Joy*, Cassell, London, 1960

132 DUMOULIN, H., *A History of Zen Buddhism*, Pantheon, New York, 1960

133 DUNNE, J. W., *An Experiment With Time*, Faber, London, 1939; Hillary, New York, 1958, paperback

134 EBON, M., *Test Your ESP*, World, New York, 1970; New American Library, New York, 1971, paperback

135 EDDY, Mary Baker, *Science and Health, with Key to the Scriptures*, Christian Science Publishing Society, numerous edns

136 EDMUNDS, S., *Spiritualism: A Critical Survey*, Aquarian Press, London, 1966; International Publications Service, New York, 1966

137 EDWARDS, D., *Dare to Make Magic*, Rigel, London, 1971

138 EDWARDS, Harry, *Spirit Healing*, Jenkins, London, 1960

139 EDWARDS, Harry, *The Power of Spiritual Healing*,

Jenkins, London, 1963

140 EISENBUD, J., *The World of Ted Serios*, Morrow, New York, 1967; Pocket Books (Simon & Schuster), New York, 1969, paperback

141 ELIADE, M., *The Forge and the Crucible*, Harper Torchbooks, New York, 1971, paperback

142 ELIADE, M., *Yoga, Immortality and Freedom*, Routledge, London, 1958; Princeton University Press, Bollingen Series No. 56, 1970, and paperback

143 ELIADE, M., *Shamanism*, Routledge, London, 1964

143a EMBODEN, W., *Narcotic Plants*, Macmillan, New York, 1972

144 EVANS, J., ed., *An Adventure*, Faber, London, 5th edn, 1955

145 EWEN, C. L'E., *Witchcraft and Demonianism*, Muller, London, 1970 reprint

146 EWEN, C. L'E., *Witch Hunting and Witch Trials*, Muller, London, 1970 reprint

147 EYSENCK, H. J., *Uses and Abuses of Psychology*, Penguin, Harmondsworth and Baltimore, 1953

148 FARRAR, S., *What Witches Do*, Peter Davies, London, 1971

148a FEILDING, E., *Sittings With Eusapia Palladino and Other Studies*, University Books, New York, 1963

149 FESTUGIÈRE, A. J., *La Révélation d'Hermès Trismégiste*, Paris, 1944–54

150 FESTUGIÈRE, A. J., *Hermétisme et mystique païenne*, Paris, 1967

151 FINDLAY, J. Arthur, *On the Edge of the Etheric*, Rider, London, 1931; Branden Press, Boston

152 FINDLAY, J. Arthur, *The Rock of Truth*, Rider, London, 1933; Branden Press, Boston

153 FINDLAY, J. Arthur, *The Way of Life*, Psychic Press, London, 1953; Branden Press, Boston

154 FINDLAY, J. Arthur, *Looking Back*, Psychic Press, London, 1955; Branden Press, Boston

155 FLOURNOY, T., *From India to the Planet Mars*, University Books, New York, reprint

156 FORTUNE, Dion, *Applied Magic*, Aquarian Press, London, 1962 reprint

157 FORTUNE, Dion, *Aspects of Occultism*, Aquarian Press, London, 1962 reprint; Wehman, Hackensack, New Jersey, 1962

158 FORTUNE, Dion, *The Cosmic Doctrine*, Helios, Toddington, 1966; Wehman, Hackensack, New Jersey, 1966

159 FORTUNE, Dion, *Moon Magic*, Aquarian Press, London, 1958 reprint

160 FORTUNE, Dion, *The Mystical Qabalah*, Benn, London, 1970 reprint; Weiser, New York

161 FORTUNE, Dion, *Psychic Self-Defence*, Aquarian Press, London, 1967 reprint; Wehman, Hackensack, New Jersey

162 FOX, O., *Astral Projection*, University Books, New York, 1962

163 FREEDLAND, N., *The Occult Explosion*, Michael Joseph, London, 1972; Putnam, New York, 1972

164 FREUD, Sigmund, *The Interpretation of Dreams*, Allen & Unwin, London, 1954 reprint; Modern Library, New York

165 FULLER, J. F. C., *The Star in the West*, Scott, New York, 1907

166 FULLER, J. G., *The Interrupted Journey*, Dial Press, New York, 1966

167 FULLER, J. O., *The Magical Dilemma of Victor Neuburg*, Allen, London, 1965

168 FURST, P. T., *The Flesh of the Gods*, Praeger, New York, 1972

169 GADDIS, V. and M., *The Curious World of Twins*, Hawthorn, New York, 1972

170 GALANOPOULOS, A. G., and BACON, E., *Atlantis*, Nelson, London, 1969; Bobbs-Merrill, Indianapolis, New York, 1969

171 GARDNER, G. B., *Witchcraft Today*, Rider, London, 1954

172 GARDNER, G. B., *The Meaning of Witchcraft*, Aquarian Press, London, 1959; Weiser, New York

173 GARDNER, M., *Fads and Fallacies in the Name of Science*, Macmillan, New York, and Dover, New York, 1957, paperback

174 GARRETT, Eileen J., *Many Voices: the Autobiography of a Medium*, Putnam, New York, 1968

175 GARRETT, Eileen J., *Adventures in the Supernormal*, Paperback Library, New York, 1968 reprint

176 GAULD, Alan, *The Founders of Psychical Research*, Routledge, London, 1968; Schocken, New York, 1968

177 GAULD, Alan, 'A Series of "Drop-In" Communicators', S.P.R. *Proceedings*, July 1971

178 GETTINGS, Fred, *The Book of the Hand*, Hamlyn, London, 1965

179 GHYKA, M., *The Geometry of Art and Life*, Sheed, New York, 1958

180 GIBBONS, A. O., ed., *The Trianon Adventure*, Museum Press, London, 1958

181 GINSBURG, C. D., *The Kabbalah*, Routledge, London, 1955 reprint; Weiser, New York, 1970 reprint

182 GLEADOW, Rupert, *Your Character in the Zodiac*, Phoenix House, London, 1968; Funk & Wagnalls, New York, 1969

183 GOLDSMITH, J., *The Art of Spiritual Healing*, Allen & Unwin, London, 1960; Harper & Row, New York, 1959

184 GOODMAN, L. S., and GILMAN, A., ed., *The Pharmacological Basis of Therapeutics*, Macmillan, New York, 4th edn, 1970

185 GOVINDA, A., 'Time and Space and the Problem of Free Will', *Main Currents*, Vol. 26, 1970

186 GOVINDA, A., 'The Conception of Space in Ancient Buddhist Thought', *Main Currents*, Vol. 26, 1970

187 GRAEF, H., *The Case of Therese Neumann*, Mercier, Cork, 1952

188 GRANT, Joan, and KELSEY, Denys, *Many Lifetimes*, Gollancz, London, 1969; Pocket Books, New York, 1969

189 GRANT, Kenneth, *The Magical Revival*, Muller,

London, 1972

189a GRANT, Kenneth, *Aleister Crowley and the Hidden God*, Muller, London, 1973

189b GRANT, Kenneth, *Images and Oracles of Austin Osman Spare*, forthcoming

190 GRANT, R. M., *Gnosticism, an Anthology*, Collins, London, 1961

191 GRANT, R. M., *Gnosticism and Early Christianity*, Columbia University Press, and Harper Torchbooks, New York, 1966

192 GRAY, E., *The Tarot Revealed*, Inspiration House, New York, 1960

193 GRAY, W., *Inner Traditions of Magic*, Aquarian Press, London, 1970; Weiser, New York

194 GREEN, C., *Lucid Dreams*, Faber, London, 1968

195 GREEN, C., *Out-of-the-Body Experiences*, Faber, London, 1968

195a GREGORY, A., 'The Physical Mediumship of Rudi Schneider', *Proceedings* of the Parapsychological Association, Vol. 5, 1968

195b GUAZZO, F. M., *Compendium Maleficarum*, Muller, London, 1970 reprint; Book Notes (Barnes & Noble), New York, 1970 reprint

196 GUIRDHAM, A., *The Nature of Healing*, Allen & Unwin, London, 1964; Fernhill, New York, 1964

197 GUIRDHAM, A., *The Cathars and Reincarnation*, Spearman, London, 1971

198 GUIRDHAM, A., *Obsession*, Spearman, London, 1972

199 GURDJIEFF, G. I., *All and Everything*. First series, *Beelzebub's Tales to His Grandson*, Routledge, London, 1950; Dutton, New York, 1964. Second series, *Meetings With Remarkable Men*, Routledge, London, 1963; Dutton, New York, 1969, and paperback

200 GURNEY, Edmund, with MYERS, F. W. H., and PODMORE, Frank, *Phantasms of the Living*, Trubner, London, 1886; Scholars' Facsimiles, Gainsville, Florida, 1970

201 HALL, C. S., *The Meaning of Dreams*, Dell, New York, 1959; McGraw-Hill, 1966, paperback

202a HALL, Manly Palmer, *Man: the Grand Symbol of the Mysteries*, Philosophical Research Society, Los Angeles, 1947

202b HALL, Manly Palmer, *The Philosophy of Astrology*, Philosophical Research Society, Los Angeles, 1943

203 HALL, Trevor H., *The Spiritualists*, Duckworth, London, 1962; Garrett-Helix, New York, 1963

204 HALL, Trevor H., *New Light on Old Ghosts*, Duckworth, London, 1965; Transatlantic Arts, New York, 1965

205 HARRIS, S., *The Incredible Father Divine*, Allen, London, 1954; Collier (Macmillan), New York, 1971, paperback

206 HART, H., *The Enigma of Survival*, Rider, London, 1959

207 HARTLEY, C., *The Western Mystery Tradition*, Aquarian Press, London, 1968

208 HEAD, J., and CRANSTON, S. L., *Reincarnation:*

An East–West Anthology, Julian Press, New York, 1961

209 HEAD, J., and CRANSTON, S. L., *Reincarnation in World Thought*, Julian Press, New York, 1967

210 HEINE, H. G., *The Vital Sense*, Cassell, London, 1960

211 HERRIGEL, E., *Zen in the Art of Archery*, Routledge, London, 1972 paperback; Random House, New York, 1971, paperback

212 HEUVELMANS, B., *On the Track of Unknown Animals*, Hart-Davis, London, 1958; Hill & Wang, New York, 1965, abridged

212a HEUVELMANS, B., *In the Wake of the Sea-Serpents*, Hart-Davis, London, 1968; Hill & Wang, New York, 1968

213 HEYWOOD, R., *The Sixth Sense*, Chatto, London, 1959

214 HEYWOOD, R., *The Infinite Hive*, Pan, London, 1966 paperback

215 HEYWOOD, R., 'Notes on the Mediumship of Geraldine Cummins', S.P.R. *Journal*, December 1970

216 HEYWOOD, R., 'Notes on Rosemary Brown', S.P.R. *Journal*, December 1971

217 HILL, Douglas, and WILLIAMS, P., *The Supernatural*, Aldus, London, 1965; Hawthorn, New York, 1966

218 HILL, Douglas, *Magic and Superstition*, Hamlyn, London, 1968

219 HILL, Douglas, *Return From the Dead*, Macdonald, London, 1970

220 HILL, Douglas, *Fortune Telling*, Hamlyn, London, 1972

221 HILL, J. A., *Spiritualism: its History, Phenomena and Doctrine*, Cassell, London, 1918

222 HILL, W. C. O., 'Abominable Snowman, the Present Position', *Oryx*, August 1961

223 HILU, V., ed., *Beloved Prophet*, Barrie & Jenkins, London, 1972

223a HODGSON, R., 'A Record of Observations of Certain Phenomena of Trance', S.P.R. *Proceedings*, 1892

224 HOLBROOK, S. H., *The Golden Age of Quackery*, Macmillan, New York, 1959

225 HOLE, C., *Witchcraft in England*, Scribner, New York, 1947, and Macmillan, New York, 1966, paperback

226 HOLE, C., ed., *Encyclopaedia of Superstitions*, Hutchinson, London, revised edn, 1961

227 HOLMYARD, E. J., *Alchemy*, Penguin, Harmondsworth, 1957; Penguin, Baltimore, 1968

228 HOLZER, H., *Psychic Photography*, Souvenir Press, London, 1970; McGraw-Hill, New York, 1969

229 HONE, Margaret E., *The Modern Text-Book of Astrology*, Fowler, London, 4th edn, 1968; Weiser, New York

230 HONORTON, C., and others, 'Feedback-augmented EEG Alpha', A.S.P.R. *Journal*, Vol. 65, 1971

231 HOOVER, E. L., 'Alpha, the First Step to a New Level of Reality', *Human Behaviour*, 1972

232 HOPKINS, A. J., *Alchemy Child of Greek Philosophy*, Columbia University Press, 1934, and AMS Press, New York, 1934

233 HOPPER, V. F., *Medieval Number Symbolism*, Columbia University Press, 1938, and Lansdowne Press, Philadelphia, 1971

234 HOWE, Ellic, *Urania's Children*, Kimber, London, 1967

235 HOWE, Ellic, *The Magicians of the Golden Dawn*, Routledge, London, 1972

236 HULL, C. L., *Hypnosis and Suggestibility*, Appleton-Century, New York, 1933

237 HURKOS, Peter, *Psychic*, Barker, London, 1961; Popular Library, New York, 1971, paperback

238 HUXLEY, Aldous, *The Devils of Loudon*, Harper & Row, New York, 1953, and 1971 paperback

239 HUXLEY, Aldous, *The Doors of Perception*, Chatto, London, 1954; Harper & Row, New York

240 HUXLEY, F., *The Invisibles*, Hart-Davis, London, 1966; McGraw-Hill, New York, 1969

241 HYNEK, J. A., *The UFO Experience*, Regnery, Chicago, 1972

242 INGLIS, Brian, *Fringe Medicine*, Faber, London, 1964; *The Case for Unorthodox Medicine*, Putnam, New York, 1965

243 IREMONGER, L., *The Ghosts of Versailles*, Faber, London, 1957

244 IZZARD, R., *The Abominable Snowman Adventure*, Hodder, London, 1955

245 JACOBI, J., *The Psychology of C. G. Jung*, Routledge, London, 6th edn, 1951; Yale University Press, New Haven, Connecticut, 1963

246 JAHODA, G., *The Psychology of Superstition*, Allen Lane, London, 1969; Penguin, Baltimore, 1971

247 JAMES, William, *The Varieties of Religious Experience*, Dolphin, New York, paperback reprint

247a JAMES, William, 'Report of the Committee on Mediumistic Phenomena', A.S.P.R..*Proceedings*, Vol. 1, 1886–9

247b JAMES, William, 'Report on Mrs Piper's Hodgson Control', S.P.R. *Proceedings*, 1909

248 JENNY, H., *Cymatics*, Basilius, Basel, 1966

249 JOHNSTON, J., *Mary Baker Eddy*, Christian Science Publishing Society, 1946

249a JOINES, W. T., and ARTLEY, J. L., 'Study of a Haunted House', *Theta*, Vol. 27, 1969

250 JONAS, H., *The Gnostic Religion*, Beacon, Boston, 2nd edn, 1963

251 JONES, C. S., *The Anatomy of the Body of God*, Weiser, New York, 1969 reprint

252 JONES, C. S., *QBL, or The Bride's Reception*, Weiser, New York, 1969 reprint

253 *Journal of the American Society for Psychical Research*, published by the A.S.P.R., New York

254 *Journal of Parapsychology*, published by the Parapsychology Press, Durham, North Carolina

255 *Journal of the Society for Psychical Research*, published by the S.P.R., London

256 JUNG, C. G., *Collected Works*, Routledge, London; Princeton University Press (various dates). Volumes include:

256a   *Archetypes and the Collective Unconscious*, 1959

256b   *The Interpretation of Nature and the Psyche*, 1955

256c   *Mysterium Coniunctionis*, 1963

256d   *Psychology and Alchemy*, 1953

256e   *The Structure and Dynamics of the Psyche*

257 JUNG, C. G., *Memories, Dreams, Reflections*, Fontana, London, 1972, paperback; Pantheon Books, New York, 1963

258 JUNG, C. G., *Synchronicity*, Routledge, London, 1972

259 KEEL, J. A., *Operation Trojan Horse*, Putnam, New York, 1970

260 KENNEDY-WINNER, A., *The Basic Ideas of Occult Wisdom*, T.P.H., 1970, paperback

261 KILNER, W. J., *The Human Atmosphere*, University Books, New York, reprint

262 KING, Francis, *Ritual Magic in England*, Spearman, London, 1970

263 KING, Francis, *Sexuality, Magic and Perversion*, Spearman, London, 1971

264 KING, Francis, ed., *Astral Projection, Magic and Alchemy*, Spearman, London, 1971

265 KIRK, G. S., and RAVEN, J. E., *The Pre-Socratic Philosophers*, Cambridge University Press, 1960

266 KITTREDGE, G. L., *Witchcraft in Old and New England*, Harvard University Press, Cambridge, Massachusetts, 1929

267 KNOX, Ronald A., *Enthusiasm*, Clarendon Press, Oxford, 1950; Oxford University Press, New York, 1961, paperback

268 KOESTLER, A., *The Roots of Coincidence*, Hutchinson, London, 1972

269 KUNZ, G. F., *The Magic Jewels and Charms*, Lippincott, Philadelphia, 1915

270 LANG, Andrew, *Cock Lane and Common Sense*, Longmans, London, 1894; AMS Press, New York, 1970

271 LANGDON-DAVIES, J., *Man: the Known and Unknown*, Secker & Warburg, London, 1960

272 LANGLEY, N., *Edgar Cayce on Reincarnation*, Paperback Library, New York, 1967, 1971

273 LANGTON, E., *Essentials of Demonology*, Epworth, London, 1949

274 LAVER, J., *Nostradamus, or the Future Foretold*, Penguin, Harmondsworth, 1952

275 LAVER, J., *The First Decadent*, Faber, London, 1954

276 LA VEY, Anton S., *The Satanic Bible*, Avon, New York, 1969, paperback

277 LAWTON, G., *The Drama of Life After Death*, Constable, London, 1933

278 LEA, H. C., *Materials Towards a History of Witchcraft*, Yoseloff, New York, 1957 reprint

279 LEADBEATER, C. W., *The Astral Plane*, T.P.H., 1968 reprint

280 LEEK, Sybil, *Book of Fortune-Telling*, Allen, London, 1970; Macmillan, New York, 1969

281 LEFF, G., *Heresy in the Later Middle Ages*, Manchester University Press, 1967; Book Notes (Barnes & Noble), New York, 1967

282 LELAND, C. G., *Gypsy Sorcery and Fortune-Telling*,

Dover, New York, 1971 reprint, paperback

283 LE SHAN, L., 'A "Spontaneous" Psychometry Experiment with Mrs Eileen Garrett', S.P.R. *Journal*, March 1967

283a LE SHAN, L., 'The Vanished Man', A.S.P.R. *Journal*, No. 62, 1968

284 LEVI, Eliphas, *Transcendental Magic: Its Doctrine and Ritual*, Rider, London, 1962 reprint; Wehman, Hackensack, New Jersey, and Weiser, New York, 1970, paperback

285 LEVI, Eliphas, *History of Magic*, Rider, London, 1968 reprint; Weiser, New York, 1969, paperback

286 LEVI, Eliphas, *The Key of the Mysteries*, Rider, London, 1968 reprint; Wehman, Hackensack, New Jersey, and Weiser, New York, 1970, paperback

287 LEWIS, H. S., *Rosicrucian Questions and Answers*, Rosicrucian Library, California, 1932

288 LHERMITTE, J., *Diabolical Possession, True and False*, Burns, Oates, London, 1963

289 LINCOLN, J. S., *The Dream in Primitive Cultures*, Cresset, London, 1935; Johnson Reprint Corpn (Academic Press), New York, 1970

290 LIND, F., *How to Understand the Tarot*, Aquarian Press, London, 1969; Llewellyn, St Paul, Minnesota

291 LINDSAY, J., *The Origins of Alchemy in Graeco-Roman Egypt*, Muller, London, 1970; Barnes & Noble, New York

292 LOBSANG RAMPA, *The Third Eye*, Secker & Warburg, London, 1956; Ballantine, New York, 1970, paperback

293 LONG, M. F., *The Secret Science Behind Miracles*, San Francisco, 1954; DeVorss, Santa Monica, California, 1948

294 LOPEZ, V., *Numerology*, Citadel, New York, 1961

295 LUCE, G. G., and SEGAL, J., *Sleep*, Heinemann, London, 1967; Coward, McCann, New York, 1966

296 LUCE, J. V., *The End of Atlantis*, Thames & Hudson, London, 1969

297 MACKENZIE, A., *The Unexplained: Some Strange Cases of Psychical Research*, Barker, London, 1966; Abelard-Schuman, New York, 1970

298 MACKENZIE, A., *Frontiers of the Unknown*, Barker, London, 1968

299 MACKENZIE, A., *Apparitions and Ghosts*, Barker, London, 1971

300 MACKENZIE, N., *Dreams and Dreaming*, Aldus, London, 1965; Vanguard, New York

301 MAJUMDAR, S. K., *Introduction to Yoga Principles and Practice*, Pelham, London, 1967

302 *Malleus Maleficarum*, Pushkin, London, 1951

303 *Man, Myth and Magic*, ed. Richard Cavendish, Purnell, London, 1970–2, 112 parts

304 MANN, F., *Acupuncture: the Ancient Chinese Art of Healing*, Heinemann, London, 1962

305 MAPLE, Eric, *Superstition and the Superstitious*, Allen, London, 1971; A. S. Barnes, Cranbury, New Jersey

306 MARTIN, K., *Telling Fortunes With Cards*, Collier (Macmillan), New York, 1971 paperback

307 MASSEY, G., *Ancient Egypt*, Stuart & J. M. Watkins, London, 1971; Weiser, New York

308 MASTERS, R. E. L., *Eros and Evil*, Julian Press, New York, 1962

309 MASTERS, R. E. L., and HOUSTON, J., *The Varieties of Psychedelic Experience*, Blond, London, 1967; Holt, Rinehart & Winston, New York, 1966

310 MATAS, F., and PANTAS, L., 'A PK Experiment Comparing Meditating Versus Non-meditating Subjects', *Proceedings* of the Parapsychological Association, Vol. 8, 1971

311 MATHERS, S. L. M., *The Book of the Sacred Magic of Abra-Melin, the Mage*, de Laurence, Chicago, 1948 reprint, and Wehman, Hackensack, New Jersey

312 MATHERS, S. L. M., *The Grimoire of Armadel*, Routledge, London, forthcoming

313 MATHERS, S. L. M., *The Kabbalah Unveiled*, Routledge, London, 1970 reprint; Weiser, New York, 1970

314 MATHERS, S. L. M., *The Key of Solomon*, Routledge, London, 1972 reprint; Wehman, Hackensack, New Jersey

315 MAYO, J., *Teach Yourself Astrology*, English Universities Press, London, 1964

316 McCONNELL, R. A., *ESP Curriculum Guide*, Simon & Schuster, New York, 1970, 1971

317 McINTOSH, Christopher, *The Astrologers and Their Creed*, Hutchinson, London, 1969; Praeger, New York, 1970

318 McINTOSH, Christopher, *Astrology*, Macdonald, London, 1970

319 McINTOSH, Christopher, *Eliphas Lévi and the French Occult Revival*, Rider, London, 1972

320 McKENZIE, J. H., *Spirit Intercourse*, Simpkin Marshall, London, 1916

321 MEAD, G. R. S., *Thrice-Greatest Hermes*, Stuart & J. M. Watkins, London, 1964 reprint

322 MEAD, G. R. S., *Fragments of a Faith Forgotten*, University Books, New York, 1960 reprint

322a MEAD, M., *Sex and Temperament in Three Primitive Societies*, Morrow, New York, 1935, and Peter Smith, Gloucester, Massachusetts

323 MELVILLE, J., *Crystal Gazing*, Weiser, New York, 1970 reprint

324 MERMET, A., *Principles and Practice of Radiesthesia*, Stuart, London, 1959

325 MÉTRAUX, A., *Voodoo in Haiti*, Deutsch, London, 1959

326 MIALL, A. M., *Complete Fortune Telling*, Greenberg, New York, 1950, and Wehman, Hackensack, New Jersey, 1962

327 MICHEL, A., *The Truth About Flying Saucers*, Hale, London, 1957

328 MICHEL, A., *Flying Saucers and the Straight Line Mystery*, Criterion, New York, 1958

330 MILLARD, J., *Edgar Cayce, Mystery Man of Miracles*, Fawcett, New York, 1967

331 MILLER, P., *Born to Heal*, Spiritualist Press, London,

1962

332 MONTGOMERY, R., *A Gift of Prophecy*, Bantam, New York, 1966

333 MONTROSE, *Numerology for Everybody*, Blue Ribbon, New York, 1940

334 MOORE, W. V., *The Voices*, Watts, London, 1913

335 MORRIS, R. L., and others, 'EEG Patterns and ESP Results in Forced-Choice Experiments', A.S.P.R. *Journal*, in press

336 MOSES, W. Stainton, *Spirit Teachings*, Spiritualist Press, London, 1962 reprint

337 MOSSIKER, F., *The Affair of the Poisons*, Gollancz, London, 1970; Knopf, New York, 1969

338 MOUNI SADHU, *The Tarot*, Allen & Unwin, London, 1962; Wehman, Hackensack, New Jersey, 1962

339 MÜHL, D., *Automatic Writing*, Steinkopf, Dresden, 1930

340 MULDOON, Sylvan, and CARRINGTON, Hereward, *The Projection of the Astral Body*, Rider, London, 1929; Weiser, New York, 1970

341 MURPHY, G., *The Challenge of Psychical Research*, Harper, New York, 1961

342 MURRAY, G., *Frontiers of Healing*, Parrish, London, 1958

343 MURRAY, Margaret A., *The Witch-Cult in Western Europe*, Clarendon Press, Oxford, 1962 paperback reprint; Oxford University Press, New York, paperback

344 MURRAY, Margaret A., *The God of the Witches*, Anchor, New York, 1960 paperback reprint; Oxford University Press, New York, 1970, paperback

345 MURRAY, Margaret A., *The Divine King in England*, Faber, London, 1954

346 MYERS, F. W. H., *Human Personality and Its Survival of Bodily Death*, University Books, New York, 1961 reprint

347 MYLONAS, G. E., *Eleusis and the Eleusinian Mysteries*, Routledge, London, 1962; Princeton University Press, Princeton, New Jersey, 1961

347a NAPIER, J., *Bigfoot*, Cape, London, 1972

347b NASH, C. B., 'Cutaneous Perception of Color with a Head Box', A.S.P.R. *Journal*, Vol. 65, 1971

348 NEAME, A., *The Happening at Lourdes*, Hodder, London, 1968; Simon & Schuster, New York, 1968

349 NEEDLEMAN, J., *The New Religions*, Doubleday, Garden City, New York, 1970

350 NELSON, G. K., *Spiritualism and Society*, Routledge, London, 1969; Schocken, New York, 1969

351 NETHERCOT, A. H., *The First Five Lives of Annie Besant*, Hart-Davis, London, 1961; University of Chicago Press, Chicago, Illinois

352 NETHERCOT, A. H., *The Last Four Lives of Annie Besant*, Hart-Davis, London, 1963; University of Chicago Press, Chicago, Illinois

353 NICHOLSON, R. A., *The Mystics of Islam*, Routledge, London, 1966; Dufour, Chester Springs, Pennsylvania

354 NOCK, A. D., *Early Gentile Christianity and Its Hellenistic Background*, Harper Torchbooks, New York, 1964

355 OESTERREICH, T. K., *Possession*, Routledge, London, 1930

356 OPIE, P. and I., *The Lore and Language of Schoolchildren*, Clarendon Press, Oxford, 1959; Oxford University Press, New York, 1959

357 OSIS, K., and BOKERT, E., 'ESP and Changed States of Consciousness Induced by Meditation', A.S.P.R. *Journal*, Vol. 65, 1971

358 OSTRANDER, S., and SCHROEDER, L., *Psychic Discoveries Behind the Iron Curtain*, Prentice Hall, New York, 1970

358a OSTY, E., *Supernormal Faculties in Man*, Methuen, London, 1923

359 OUSPENSKY, P. D., *In Search of the Miraculous*, Routledge, London, 1950; Harcourt Brace Jovanovich, New York, paperback

360 OUSPENSKY, P. D., *A New Model of the Universe*, Routledge, London, 1948; Harcourt Brace Jovanovich, New York

361 OUSPENSKY, P. D., *The Psychology of Man's Possible Evolution*, Hodder, London, 1951; Knopf, New York, 1954

362 OWEN, A. R. G., *Can We Explain the Poltergeist?*, Garrett-Helix, New York, 1964

362a PAGENSTECHER, G., 'A Notable Psychometric Test', A.S.P.R. *Journal*, No. 14, 1920

363 PARACELSUS, *Selected Writings*, Routledge, London, 1951; Princeton University Press, Princeton, New Jersey, 1958

364 PAYNE, Phoebe, and BENDIT, Laurence, *The Psychic Sense*, Faber, London, 1958; T.P.H., Wheaton, Illinois, 1967, paperback

365 PEEL, R., *Mary Baker Eddy*, Holt, Rinehart & Winston, New York, 1966

366 PHILIP, J. A., *Pythagoras and Early Pythagoreanism*, University of Toronto Press, 1966

366a PIDDINGTON, J. G., 'A Series of Concordant Automatisms', S.P.R. *Proceedings*, 1908

367 PIKE, J. A., *The Other Side*, W. H. Allen, London, 1969; Dell, New York, 1969, paperback

368 PODMORE, Frank, *Modern Spiritualism*, Methuen, London, 1902

369 PODMORE, Frank, *Mesmerism and Christian Science*, Methuen, London, 1909

370 PODMORE, Frank, 'Poltergeists', S.P.R. *Proceedings*, Vol. 12, 1896–7

371 POLLACK, J. H., *Croiset the Clairvoyant*, Doubleday, Garden City, New York, 1964

372 PORTA, G. Della, *Natural Magick*, Basic Books, New York, 1957

373 POWELL, A. E., *The Astral Body*, T.P.H., London, 1954 reprint; T.P.H., Wheaton, Illinois, 1956

374 PRATT, J. G., and ROLL, W. G., 'The Seaford Disturbances', *Journal of Parapsychology*, Vol. 22, 1958

375 PRICE, Harry, *The Most Haunted House in England*, Longmans, London, 1940

376 PRICE, Harry, *Fifty Years of Psychical Research*, Longmans, London, 1939

377 PRINCE, W. F., *The Case of Patience Worth*, Boston S.P.R., 1927

378 *Proceedings of the Society for Psychical Research*, published by the S.P.R., London

379 PUHARICH, A., *The Sacred Mushroom*, Doubleday, Garden City, New York, 1959

380 PUHARICH, A., *Beyond Telepathy*, Doubleday, Garden City, New York, 1962

381 RADHAKRISHNAN, S., *Indian Philosophy*, Allen & Unwin, London, 1948; Humanities Press, New York

382 RAKOCZI, B. I., *The Painted Caravan*, Brucher, The Hague, 1954; Wehman, Hackensack, New Jersey

383 RAKOCZI, B. I., *Fortune Telling*, Macdonald, London, 1970

384 RAO, K. R., *Experimental Parapsychology*, Charles C Thomas, Springfield, Illinois, 1966

385 RAUDIVE, Konstantin, *Breakthrough – An Amazing Experiment in Electronic Communication with the Dead*, Colin Smythe, London, 1971; Taplinger, New York, 1971

385a RAWSON, P., *The Art of Tantra*, Thomas & Hudson, London, 1973

386 READ, J., *Through Alchemy to Chemistry*, Bell, London, 1957

387 REGARDIE, Israel, *The Art of True Healing*, Helios, Toddington, 1964; Weiser, New York

388 REGARDIE, Israel, *The Eye in the Triangle*, Llewellyn, St Paul, Minnesota, 1970

389 REGARDIE, Israel, *The Golden Dawn*, Llewellyn, St Paul, Minnesota, 3rd edn, 1970

390 REGARDIE, Israel, *Roll Away the Stone*, Llewellyn, St Paul, Minnesota, 1968

391 REGARDIE, Israel, *The Tree of Life*, Weiser, New York, 2nd edn, 1969

391a REICH, Wilhelm, *Contact With Space*, Core Pilot, New York, 1957

391b REICH, Wilhelm, *Ether, God or Devil*, Orgone Institute, Maine, 1951

391c REICH, Wilhelm, *The Function of the Orgasm*, Panther, London, 1968 paperback; Farrar, Straus & Giroux, New York, 1961, and World Publishing, New York, paperback

391d REICH, Wilhelm, *The Sexual Revolution*, Vision Press, London, 1952; Farrar, Straus & Giroux, New York, 1963, paperback

391e REICH, Wilhelm, *Selected Writings*, Vision Press, London, 1958; Farrar, Straus & Giroux, New York, 1960

392 REICHENBACH, K. Von, *The Odic Force: Letters on Od and Magnetism*, University Books, New York, 1968 reprint

392a REJDAK, Z., 'Nina Kulagina's Mind Over Matter', *Psychic*, June 1971

392b REMY, N., *Demonolatry*, Muller, London, 1970 reprint; Barnes & Noble, New York, 1970

393 RHINE, J. B., *The Reach of the Mind*, Morrow, New York, 1947

393a RHINE, J. B., *New World of the Mind*, Sloane, New York, 1953

394 RHINE, J. B., and PRATT, J. G., *Parapsychology: Frontier Science of the Mind*, Charles C Thomas, Springfield, Illinois, 1957

395 RHINE, J. B., and others, *Extrasensory Perception After Sixty Years*, Humphries, Boston, 1966

396 RHINE, Louisa E., *Hidden Channels of the Mind*, Gollancz, London, 1962; Apollo Books, Woodbridge, Connecticut, 1966 paperback

396a RHINE, Louisa E., *ESP in Life and Lab*, Macmillan, New York, 1967

397 RHINE, Louisa E., *Mind Over Matter*, Macmillan, New York, 1970

398a RHINE, Louisa E., 'Subjective Forms of Spontaneous Psi Experiences', *Journal of Parapsychology*, Vol. 17, 1953

398b RHINE, Louisa E., 'The Relationship of Agent and Percipient in Spontaneous Telepathy', *Journal of Parapsychology*, Vol. 20, 1956

398c RHINE, Louisa E., 'Hallucinatory Psi Experiences', *Journal of Parapsychology*, Vol. 20, 1956, Vol. 21, 1957

398d RHINE, Louisa E., 'The Evaluation of Non-Recurrent Psi Experiences Bearing on Post-Mortem Survival', *Journal of Parapsychology*, Vol. 24, 1960

399 RHODES, H. T. F., *The Satanic Mass*, Jarrolds, Norwich, 1968, and Arrow Books, London, 1973, paperback; Citadel Press, New York, 1955

400 RICHMOND, S., *Common Sense About Yoga*, MacGibbon & Kee, London, 1971

401 ROBBINS, R. H., *The Encyclopaedia of Witchcraft and Demonology*, Crown, New York, 1959

402 ROBERTS, O., *Healing Through Faith*, Tulsa, 1958

403 ROFÉ, H., *The Path of Subud*, Rider, London, 1959

404 ROLL, W. G., *The Poltergeist*, Universe Books, New York, 1971

404a ROLL, W. G., 'Pagenstecher's Contribution to Parapsychology', A.S.P.R. *Journal*, No. 61, 1967

405 ROLL, W. G., and PRATT, J. G., 'The Miami Disturbances', A.S.P.R. *Journal*, Vol. 65, 1971

406 ROSE, E., *A Razor for a Goat*, University of Toronto Press, 1962

407 ROSE, L., *Faith Healing*, Gollancz, London, 1968; Penguin, Baltimore, 1971, paperback

408 RUDHYAR, D., *The Astrology of Personality*, Lucis, New York, 1936

409 RUNCIMAN, S., *The Mediaeval Manichee*, Cambridge University Press, England and New York, 1947

409a RUSSELL, J. B., *Witchcraft in the Middle Ages*, Cornell University Press, 1972

410 SALTER, W. H., *Zoar*, Sidgwick & Jackson, London, 1961

411 SALTMARSH, H. F., *Evidence of Personal Survival from Cross Correspondences*, Bell, London, 1938

411a SALTMARSH, H. F., 'Report on the Investigation of Some Sittings with Mrs. Warren Elliott', S.P.R.

Proceedings, No. 39, pp. 130–1

412 SANDERS, E., *The Family*, Dutton, New York, 1971

413 SANDERSON, I. T., *The Abominable Snowman*, Chelton, Philadelphia, 1961

414 SANDERSON, I. T., *Uninvited Visitors*, Spearman, London, 1967; Wehman, Hackensack, New Jersey

415 SANDERSON, I. T., *Invisible Residents*, World Publishing, New York, 1970

416 SARGANT, W., *Battle For the Mind*, Heinemann, London, 1957

417 SARGANT, W., *The Mind Possessed*, Heinemann, London, forthcoming

418 SCHMEIDLER, G., *Extrasensory Perception*, Atherton, New York, 1969

419 SCHMEIDLER, G., 'High ESP Scores After a Swami's Brief Instruction in Meditation and Breathing', A.S.P.R. *Journal*, Vol. 64, 1970

419a SCHMEIDLER, G., 'Quantitative Investigation of a Haunted House', A.S.P.R. *Journal*, Vol. 60, 1966

420 SCHOLEM, G. G., *Major Trends in Jewish Mysticism*, Thames & Hudson, London, 1955; Schocken, New York, 1961

421 SCHOLEM, G. G., *On the Kabbalah and Its Symbolism*, Routledge, London, 1965; Schocken, New York, 1965

421a SCHULTES, R.E., and HOFMANN, A., *The Botany and Chemistry of Hallucinogens*, Charles C Thomas, Springfield, Illinois, 1973

422 SCOTT-ELLIOT, W., *The Story of Atlantis and the Lost Lemuria*, T.P.H., London and Wheaton, Illinois, 1962 reprint

423 SEABROOK, W., *Witchcraft: Its Power in the World Today*, Harcourt Brace, New York, 1940, and Lancer Books, New York, paperback

424 SEN, K. M., *Hinduism*, Penguin, Harmondsworth, 1961, and Baltimore, 1962

425 SEZNEC, J., *The Survival of the Pagan Gods*, Harper Torchbooks, New York, 1961, paperback

425a SIDGWICK, Mrs. H., 'A Contribution to the Study of the Psychology of Mrs. Piper's Trance Phenomena', S.P.R. *Proceedings*, No. 28, 1915

426 SIERKSMA, F., *Tibet's Terrifying Deities*, Moulton, The Hague, 1966; C. E. Tuttle, Rutland, Vermont, 1966

427 SIVANANDA, S., *Japa Yoga: A Comprehensive Treatise on Mantrasastra*, Sivananda Ashram, Rishikesh, 1952

428 SIWEK, P., *The Riddle of Konnersreuth*, Browne & Nolan, Dublin, 1954

429 SMYTH, F., *Modern Witchcraft*, Macdonald, London, 1970

429a SOAL, S. G., 'A Report on Some Communications Received Through Mrs. Blanche Cooper', S.P.R. *Proceedings*, No. 35, 1926

430 *The Song of God: Bhagavad Gita*, Phoenix House, London, 1968

431 SPENCE, L., *The Problem of Atlantis*, Rider, London, 1924

432 SPENCE, L., *Atlantis in America*, Rider, London, 1925

433 SPENCE, L., *The History of Atlantis*, Rider, London, 1926

434 SPENCE, L., *Will Europe Follow Atlantis?*, Rider, London, 1942

435 SPENCER, S., *Mysticism in World Religion*, Penguin, Harmondsworth, 1963

436 SPIER, J., *The Hands of Children*, Routledge, London, 1955

437 St CLAIR, D., *Drum and Candle*, Macdonald, London, 1971

438 STEARN, J., *Edgar Cayce – The Sleeping Prophet*, Doubleday, Garden City, New York, 1967

439 STEINER, Rudolf: see the article

439a STEINER, Rudolf, *Atlantis and Lemuria*, Anthroposophical Publications, 1923

439b STEINER, Rudolf, *Theosophy of the Rosicrucians*, Steiner Press, London, 1953

440 'The Story of the Aetherius Society', Aetherius Society, Los Angeles

441 SUMMERS, Montague, *The Geography of Witchcraft*, Kegan Paul, London, 1927

442 SUMMERS, Montague, *The History of Witchcraft and Demonology*, Routledge, London, 1965 reprint; Barnes & Noble, New York, 1965

443 SUMMERS, Montague, *The Physical Phenomena of Mysticism*, Rider, London, 1950

443a SUMMERS, Montague, *The Vampire in Europe*, University Books, New York, reprint

443b SUMMERS, Montague, *The Werewolf*, University Books, New York, 1966, reprint

444 SUZUKI, D. T., *Zen Buddhism*, Anchor, New York, 1956 paperback

445 SYMONDS, John, *Madame Blavatsky, Medium and Magician*, Odhams, London, 1958

446 SYMONDS, John, *The Great Beast*, Macdonald, London, 1971

447 TART, C., ed., *Altered States of Consciousness*, Wiley, New York, 1969

448 TAYLOR, E. S., *History of Playing Cards*, Hotten, London, 1865

449 TAYLOR, F. S., *The Alchemists*, Schuman, New York, 1949

450 TCHERNINE, Odette, *The Snowman and Company*, Hale, London, 1961

451 TCHERNINE, Odette, *The Yeti*, Spearman, London, 1970

451a TENHAEFF, W. H. C., 'Psychoscopic Experiments on Behalf of the Police Conference Report No. 41', First International Conference of Parapsychological Studies, Utrecht, The Netherlands, 1953

451b THOMAS, C. D., *Some New Evidence for Human Survival*, Collins, London, 1922

452 THOMAS, P., *Flying Saucers Through the Ages*, Spearman, London, 1965; Wehman, Hackensack, New Jersey, 1965

453 THOMPSON, C. J. S., *Magic and Healing*, Rider, London, 1947

454 THORNDIKE, L., *A History of Magic and Experimental Science*, Columbia University Press, 1923–58

455 THOULESS, R. H., *Experimental Psychical Research*, Penguin, Harmondsworth, 1963; Gannon, Santa Fe, New Mexico, 1963

456 THOULESS, R. H., *From Anecdote to Experiment in Psychical Research*, Routledge, London, 1972

457 THURSTON, H., *The Physical Phenomena of Mysticism*, Burns, Oates, London, 1952

458 TINDALL, G., *A Handbook on Witches*, Barker, London, 1965; Atheneum, New York, 1966

459 TOMLINSON, H., *Medical Divination*, Health Science Press, London, 1966

460 TRACHTENBERG, J., *Jewish Magic and Superstition*, Meridian, New York, 1961, paperback

461 TRENCH, B. Le P., *The Flying Saucer Story*, Spearman, London, 1966; Wehman, Hackensack, New Jersey, 1966

462 TREVOR-ROPER, H. R., *The European Witch-Craze of the 16th and 17th Centuries*, Penguin, Harmondsworth, 1969; Harper & Row, New York, 1969, paperback

463 TUCCI, G., *The Theory and Practice of the Mandala*, Rider, London, 1961; Wehman, Hackensack, New Jersey, and Weiser, New York, paperback

464 TYRREL, G. N. M., *Apparitions*, Duckworth, London, 1943; Macmillan, New York, 1970

465 TYRREL, G. N. M., *The Personality of Man*, Penguin, Harmondsworth, 1948

466 TYRREL, G. N. M., *Science and Psychical Phenomena*, University Books, New York, 1961

467 ULLMAN, M., and KRIPPNER, S., *Dream Studies and Telepathy: An Experimental Approach*, Parapsychology Foundation, New York, 1970

468 VALLÉE, J., *Anatomy of a Phenomenon*, Spearman, London, 1965; Regnery, Chicago, 1965, and Ace Books, New York, paperback

469 VALLÉE, J., *Challenge to Science*, Spearman, London, 1966; Wehman, Hackensack, New Jersey

470 VALLÉE, J., *Passport to Magonia*, Spearman, London, 1970; Regnery, Chicago, 1969

471 VAN DUREN, Jan, *Crooks and Croziers*, Colin Smythe, London, forthcoming

472 VAN HIEN, G., *What is Subud?*, Rider, London, 1963

473 VELIKOVSKY, I., *Worlds in Collision*, Doubleday, Garden City, New York, 1950, and Dell, New York, paperback

474 VELIKOVSKY, I., *Ages in Chaos*, Doubleday, Garden City, New York, 1953

475 VELIKOVSKY, I., *Earth in Upheaval*, Doubleday, Garden City, New York, 1956; Dell, New York, 1968, paperback

476 VERMASEREN, M. J., *Mithras, the Secret God*, Chatto, London, 1959; Barnes & Noble, New York, 1963

477 VON DANIKEN, E., *Chariots of the Gods*, Souvenir Press, London, 1969; Putnam, New York, 1970

478 WACHSMUTH, G., *The Life and Work of Rudolf Steiner*, Anthroposophic Press, New York

479 WAITE, A. E., *The Book of Ceremonial Magic*, University Books, New York, 1961 reprint, and Citadel Press, New York, paperback

480 WAITE, A. E., *The Brotherhood of the Rosy Cross*, University Books, New York, reprint

481 WAITE, A. E., *The Holy Grail*, University Books, New York, reprint

482 WAITE, A. E., *The Holy Kabbalah*, University Books, New York, reprint

483 WAITE, A. E., *The Pictorial Key to the Tarot*, Rider, London, 1971 reprint

484 WAITE, A. E., *The Secret Tradition in Alchemy*, Stuart & J. M. Watkins, London, 1972 reprint; Weiser, New York, 1970

485 WALKER, Benjamin, *Hindu World*, Allen & Unwin, London, 1968; Praeger, New York, 1968

486 WALKER, Benjamin, *Sex and the Supernatural*, Macdonald, London, 1970

487 WALKER, K., *Life's Long Journey*, Gollancz, London, 1967

488 WALLACE, R. K., and BENSON, H., 'The Physiology of Meditation', *Scientific American*, No. 226, 1972

489 WASSON, R. G., *Soma: The Divine Mushroom*, Harcourt Brace Jovanovich, Italy

490 WATSON, T. T. B., *Radiesthesia and Some Associated Phenomena*, Markham House, London, 1957

491 WATTS, A. W., *The Way of Zen*, Pantheon, New York, 1957

492 WAVELL, S., *Trance*, Allen & Unwin, London, 1967

493 WEBB, James, *The Flight From Reason*, Macdonald, London, 1971; as *The Occult Revival*, Library Press, New York, 1973

494 WEBB, James, *The Occult Liberation*, Alcove Press, London, 1973; Library Press, New York, 1973

495 WEBB, James, *The Harmonious Circus*, Putnam, New York, forthcoming

496 WEST, D. J., *Eleven Lourdes Miracles*, London, 1951

497 WEST, D. J., *Psychical Research Today*, Duckworth, London, 1954; Hillary, New York, 1956

498 WEST, J. A., and TOONDER, J. G., *The Case For Astrology*, Macdonald, London, 1970

499 WETHERED, V. D., *Introduction to Medical Radiesthesia and Radionics*, Daniel, London, 1957

500 WHITE, R. A., 'A Comparison of Old and New Methods of Response to Targets in ESP Experiments', *A.S.P.R. Journal*, Vol. 58, 1964

501 WHITEMAN, J. H. M., *The Mystical Life*, Faber, London, 1961

502 WIESINGER, A., *Occult Phenomena in the Light of Theology*, Burns, Oates, London, 1957

503 WILCOX, J., *Radionics*, Jenkins, London, 1960

504 WILHELM, R., *I Ching*, Routledge, London, 1970

505 WILHELM, R., *The Secret of the Golden Flower*, Routledge, London, 1972 paperback; Wehman, Hackensack, New Jersey

506 WILLIAMS, C., *Witchcraft*, Meridian, New York,

1959 paperback

507 WILLIAMS, S., *Voodoo and the Art of Haiti*, Morland Lee, London, paperback

508 WILLIAMSON, Hugh Ross, *The Arrow and the Sword*, Faber, London, 1947; Fernhill, New York, 1955

509 WILSON, B. R., *Sects and Society*, Heinemann, London, 1961

510 WILSON, Colin, *The Occult*, Hodder, London, 1971; Random House, New York, 1971

511 WIND, E., *Pagan Mysteries in the Renaissance*, Peregrine, London, 1967 paperback; Barnes & Noble, New York, 1968 reprint

512 WOODS, B., *The Healing Ministry*, Rider, London, 1961

513 WOODS, J. H., ed., *The Yoga System of Patanjali*, Harvard Oriental Series, 1927

514 WOODS, R. L., *The World of Dreams*, Random House, New York, 1947

515 YATES, F. A., *Giordano Bruno and the Hermetic Tradition*, Routledge, London, 1964; University of Chicago Press, 1964, and Random House, New York, 1969, paperback

516 YATES, F. A., *The Rosicrucian Enlightenment*, Routledge, London, 1972

516a YOUTZ, R. P., 'The Case for Skin Sensitivity to Color', summary of a report to the Psychonomic Society, Niagara Falls, Ontario, 1964

517 YU, L. K., *The Secrets of Chinese Meditation*, Rider, London, 1969

518 ZAEHNER, R. C., *Hinduism*, Oxford University Press, England, 1962, and New York, 1966, paperback

519 ZAEHNER, R. C., *Mysticism Sacred and Profane*, Clarendon Press, Oxford, 1957; Oxford University Press, New York, 1961, paperback

520 ZAEHNER, R. C., *Drugs, Mysticism and Makebelieve*, Collins, London, 1972

521 ZORAB, G., 'Were D. D. Home's "Spirit Hands" Ever Fraudulently Produced?', S.P.R. *Journal*, December 1971

Notes on the Illustrations, and Acknowledgments

The producers of this book wish to express their thanks to all who are indicated by the list below: the governing bodies and staffs of the libraries and museums, or the individual owners, who have kindly given permission for items from their collections to be reproduced here, and also to the photographers who have taken pictures specially or have supplied them from their records.

Abbreviations used are:
FRNM   Foundation for Research on the Nature of Man, Durham, North Carolina.
Keystone   Keystone Press Agency, London.
Mary Evans   Mary Evans Picture Library, London.
Mansell   The Mansell Collection, London.
Phoebus   Phoebus Picture Library, London.
Radio Times Hulton   Radio Times Hulton Picture Library, London.

Jacket Design: Jonathan Gill-Skelton. Photo front: Christopher Ridley.
Frontispiece: Elemental spirits, by Steffi Grant. Photo: Derrick Witty.

161 Roman magic hand. British Museum. Photo: Michael Holford.

162-3 Mithras slaying the bull. Louvre. Photo: Michael Holford.

164 Tibetan wall-hanging. Victoria and Albert Museum. Photo: Michael Holford.

166 Pythagoras. Radio Times Hulton.

169 Dr S. G. Soal. Camera Press.

171 A planchette. Harry Price Library.

172 A ouija board. Psychic News.

174 Parts of the hand in palmistry. Artwork: Jim Gibson.

177 A palmist at work. Camera Press.

179 ESP testing apparatus. FRNM.

181 Prof. and Dr Rhine. FRNM.

183 Dr R. H. Thouless. Psychic News.

184 Testing precognition. FRNM.

185 Testing PK with dice. FRNM.

186 Zener card symbols. Camera Press. Photo: Don Last.

191 Testing for ESP. FRNM.

192 Measuring the skull. Radio Times Hulton.

194 Harry Houdini. Harry Price Library.

195 Sir Arthur Conan Doyle. Psychic News.

196 Rahman Bey buried alive. Harry Price Library.

201 Exorcism by St Anthony of Padua. Mansell.

203 Pentecost, from 'Office of the Virgin', Neapolitan, 15th century. Victoria and Albert Museum.

204 Harry Price. Psychic News.

205 P. P. Quimby. Culver Collection.

208 Wilhelm Reich. Still from Makaveyev's film 'WR – Mysteries of the Organism'. Photo: Connoisseur Films Ltd.

211 Magic diagram used by Crowley. Kenneth Grant. Photo: Derrick Witty.

213 Crucified snake, from *Livre des figures hiéroglifiques* by Abraham the Jew, 18th century. Bibliothèque Nationale.

215 Rosicrucian ideal in allegory. Phoebus.

216 Certificate of the English Rosicrucians. Kenneth Grant. Photo: Derrick Witty.

219 Witches flying to a sabbat. Mansell.

220 Madame de Montespan, by Pierre Mignard. Mansell.

221 J.-K. Huysmans. Radio Times Hulton.

222 Reading coffee-grounds. Radio Times Hulton.

223 A crystal-gazer. Radio Times Hulton.

224 Ted Serios. Psychic News.

225 Austin Spare. Radio Times Hulton.

227 Elemental spirits, by Austin Spare. Kenneth Grant. Photo: Derrick Witty.

229 Eva C. Harry Price Library.

230 The Fox sisters. Psychic News.

231 Sir William Crookes. Psychic News.

232 *Col. 1* A materialization. London Spiritualist Alliance. Psychic News. *Col. 2* The Rev. Stainton Moses. Psychic News.

234 A seance. Camera Press. Photo: Tom Smith.

235 Rudolf Steiner. Philosophisch Anthroposophisch Verlag, Dornach, Switzerland.

237 Rosicrucian sign. Kenneth Grant. Photo: Derrick Witty.

238 Formula of Atavistic Resurgence, by Austin Spare. Kenneth Grant. Photo: Derrick Witty.

240 *Cols. 1 and 2 top* The first Goetheanum and the one that replaced it. Philosophisch Anthroposophisch Verlag, Dornach, Switzerland. *Col. 2 bottom* A stigmatized hand. Harry Price Library. *Col. 3* Stigmatic tears. Harry Price Library.

241 Emanuel Swedenborg. Mansell.

243 Tantrism. Photo: John Freeman.

245 *Col. 2* Tarot card. Photo: Rainbird. *Col. 3* Tarot card. Phoebus.

246 *Col. 2* Tarot card. Phoebus. *Col. 3* Tarot card. Phoebus.

247 Tarot card designed by Crowley. Phoebus.

249 Colonel H. S. Olcott. Radio Times Hulton.

252 Krishnamurti, from *God is My Adventure* by Rom Landau. Photo: Edward Weston, 1934.

253 Mrs Besant and Krishnamurti. Radio Times Hulton.

255 Elementals, by Steffi Grant. Photo: Derrick Witty.

256 Archbishop Nicholson. Photo: Colin Smythe Ltd.

259 An entranced Lapp. Radio Times Hulton.

261 Henry Thoreau. Radio Times Hulton.

262 The original 'Siamese twins'. Radio Times Hulton.

264 Chart of UFO sitings. Artwork: Tom Stalker-Miller.

266 A glowing UFO. Charles H. Gibbs-Smith.

268 Dr Raudive. Photo: Colin Smythe Ltd.

269 A. E. Waite. Mansell.

270 Wandering bishops. Photo: Colin Smythe Ltd.

272 Archbishop Nicholson. Photo: Colin Smythe Ltd.

273 Burning witches, 16th century. Radio Times Hulton.

274 Witches' invocation, 16th-century engraving by Frans Francken. Victoria and Albert Museum. Radio Times Hulton.

275 A modern witch. Camera Press. Photo: John Drysdale.

277 A witches' wedding. Camera Press. Photo: John Moss.

279 W. B. Yeats. Radio Times Hulton.

281-2 A practitioner of Yoga. Camera Press. Photos: B. Bhensali.

285 Zen. Camera Press. Photo: William MacQuitty.

Index of Persons and Book Titles

Index of Persons and Book Titles